The New Social Studies

People, Projects, and Perspectives

A volume in
Studies in the History of Education

Series Editor:
Karen L. Riley, *Auburn University at Montgomery*

Studies in the History of Education

Karen L. Riley, Series Editor

The New Social Studies: People, Projects, and Perspectives (2010)
edited by Barbara Slater Stern

Educational Research, The National Agenda, and Educational Reform (2008)
edited by Erwin V. Johanningmeir and Theresa R. Richardson

Language of the Land: Policy, Politics, Identity (2007)
edited by Katherine Schuster and David Witkosky

This Happened in America:
Harold Rugg and the Censure of Social Studies (2007)
edited by Ronald W. Evans

Social Reconstruction: People, Politics, Perspectives (2006)
edited by Karen L. Riley

The New Social Studies

People, Projects, and Perspectives

edited by

Barbara Slater Stern
James Madison University

Information Age Publishing, Inc.
Charlotte, North Carolina • www.infoagepub.com

Library of Congress Cataloging-in-Publication Data

The new social studies : people, projects, and perspectives / edited by Barbara Slater Stern.
    p. cm. -- (Studies in the history of education)
 Includes bibliographical references.
 ISBN 978-1-60752-219-5 (pbk.) -- ISBN 978-1-60752-220-1 (hardcover) 1. Social sciences--Study and teaching. 2. Social science teachers--Training of. 3. Curriculm planning. 4. Curriculum change. 5. Educational evaluation. I. Stern, Barbara Slater, 1949-
 H62.N485 2009
 300.71--dc22

                                                                                    2009025613

CONTENTS

v

FOREWORD

At last! The long-awaited New Social Studies book, edited by Barbara Slater Stern, offers the reader a glimpse into the origins, visions, and failures of the storied rise and fall of one of the most ambitious curriculum initiatives of the twentieth century. Following in the wake of Sputnik, the New Social Studies movement promised to overhaul the entire field through projects in every area from sociology to geography, anthropology to civics, geography to history and beyond, lest students enrolled in schools throughout the United States fail to lead the postindustrialized world in academics. Visionary professors in their respective fields of social science set about the task of creating classroom materials and approaches to teaching destined for K–12 classrooms. However, one major obstacle to implementation existed—the nature of school culture.

The fact is and was, college classrooms are not eighth-grade classrooms and eighth grade teachers require a different set of classroom tools than college professors. That said, few could argue with the notion that discipline experts coupled with classroom teachers should have been able to design and implement dynamic curricula. Well, they did. As many of the authors in this text point out, the curriculum materials developed throughout the period of the New Social Studies were among the most innovative and creative that educators, parents, and students had access to in decades. This sweeping curriculum reform movement promised to change the way schools went about the business of teaching social science.

Unfortunately, the New Social Studies star, which burned brightly for a brief time, faded from view rather quickly. Stern's book on the New Social Studies chronicles both the lesser and the stellar lights of the movement, as well as the curriculum materials they developed. Included in this "glimpse of a movement" are several chapters that offer the reader a more articulated or nuanced view of the politics surrounding a number of projects that to this day remain controversial, for example, Man: A Course of Study (traditionally called MACOS). But perhaps of greater importance is that for the first time, Stern has assembled an extraordinary panel of writers determined to produce an academic piece of work that will excite not only those of us who are teacher educators, charged with introducing preservice teachers to the history of education, but also university students who heretofore have little to no knowledge about—to borrow the words of Murry Nelson—a "galaxy far far away" called the New Social Studies. Read on. Enjoy.

Karen L. Riley,
Series Editor

ACKNOWLEDGMENTS

As with any long term endeavor, there are several people to thank for assistance with the final product first, I want to thank Karen L. Riley, the series editor, for her faith in me by assigning me this project. Karen and I were doctoral students together during our first year of studies and our friendship, personal, and professional, has endured for over 15 years.

Both O. L. Davis, Jr., University of Texas at Austin and Jim Davis from the Social Science Education Consortium met with me to discuss the table of contents, the format of the book and to suggest potential authors for the individual chapters. Their assistance was invaluable in locating the right individuals to author the chapters. John Rossi also met with me at the very inception of the project to discuss his ideas about the New Social Studies from his perspective as both a teacher and a teacher educator. He deserves a thank you.

A thank you to all the contributing authors who provided me with chapters that are well researched, interesting, and timely. The authors adhered to the focus questions and willingly made revisions in a timely manner. Although the project, like most, took more time than originally anticipated, I believe the final project will demonstrate why the delays were worth it.

James Madison University deserves a thank you for support with both professional development leave and graduate student assistance. I was able to use the professional development semester to read in depth on the New Social Studies in general and on Hilda Taba in particular. Over the past 2 years Gregory Thompson, Christopher Mauthe, and Caitlin Lilley have worked with me as student assistants performing whatever duties were needed including proofreading, scanning documents, checking APA reference lists, and so forth. The support from my department chair and colleagues has also been appreciated.

Last, a thank you to my husband, Mark Stern, who is still my biggest cheerleader. He always believes that I can accomplish what I set out to do and he cheerfully navigates around the stacks of books and papers that I leave around our living room when I am immersed in a writing project.

INTRODUCTION

Barbara Slater Stern

When I was in the sixth grade, our teacher told us that we were going to try something new and we would be rotating classrooms for part of the day. We would have science with him, social studies with another teacher and mathematics with a third teacher. In the science class new materials appeared: microscopes, Petri dishes, slides, and so forth. In social studies we learned geography and prepared reports on what we now term "developing" nations. Students became involved in class instruction in a different way than we had for the first half of the year and it was exciting.

In the seventh grade we had "core" which consisted of two periods of English and one of social studies with the same teacher. In addition to the interdisciplinary nature of our assignments as the course content bridged both subjects, my teacher tried other experimental ideas including a unit on the urban renewal project that was just getting underway in a part of our village very few of us even knew existed. He taught us how this project would relocate people considered by the village council to be "undesirable" to temporary housing outside village limits. He predicted, correctly as it turned out, that this project would never be completed in the promised three years and that the residents from this area would never be able to return. Many of us went home and asked our parents about this social issue. I imagine that for most of us, this was our introduction to the idea of learning about controversial issues in the social studies class.

Thus, in 1993 at a meeting of the Association of Supervisors and Curriculum Developers (ASCD) when Charlotte Crabtree from the National Center for History in the Schools (NCHS) introduced a draft of the National History Standards and said "we learned in the 60's that post-holing doesn't work!", I was puzzled. One of the reasons I became a social studies teacher was those project experiences I had in those middle years of my education. And, while I did not love the science classes, and while the new math totally confused me, the new social studies (NSS) enthralled me. I could not wait to get to class each day to find out what was on the agenda that would increase my knowledge and deepen my understanding.

In my early years of teaching, materials developed during the NSS could still be found in storage closets in the social studies classroom wing of the school building. Within the pages of these unearthed books, I found great activities to use with my inner city, all African American students. A search for materials only made more intense by the fact that I had 30 textbooks for 150 students who did not easily relate to a course titled "European Culture Studies!" Thus, it is not surprising that beginning with my doctoral work and throughout my career in academe, I have been interested in the history of teaching history/social studies in general and the New Social Studies in particular.

This volume, *The New Social Studies: People, Projects and Perspectives* is not an attempt to be *the* comprehensive book on the era. Given the sheer number of projects, for example, listed in the table of contents in *The Social Studies Curriculum Materials Data Book* (Social Studies Education Consortium, 1971) were reports on 100 projects, 135 textbooks, 100 games and simulations, 100 sets of supplementary materials and 75 sets of teacher resource materials! Thus, as Hilda Taba used to explain, content sampling was the only feasible way to proceed (see Taba chapter, this volume). However, the current lack of knowledge about these programs, people, and projects of the NSS is unfortunate as it often appears that new scholars are reinventing the wheel due to their lack of knowledge about the history of the social studies field.

The goal of this book then, is to sample the projects and individuals involved with the New Social Studies (NSS) in an attempt to provide an understanding of what came before and to suggest guidance to those concerned with social studies reform in the future—especially in light of the standardization of curriculum and assessment currently underway in many states. The authors who contributed to this project were recruited with several goals in mind including a broad range of ages, interests and experiences with the NSS from participants during the NSS era through new, young scholars who had never heard much about the NSS. As many of the authors remind us in their chapters, much has been written of the failure of the NSS. However, in every chapter of this book, the authors also point out the remnants of the projects that remain. Further, when examining some of the "reform" suggestions circulating today, it is clear that the antecedents of the ideas stem from NSS era. This past week I had a conversation in which I explained that "backward design" is really not something completely new, it is just a reworking of what came before with different terminology. The assistant professor I was discussing this with appeared surprised to receive this information. This speaks to the need for these historical studies.

To promote understanding, the book is arranged as follows. First, Ronald Evans will set the historical context of the times with his chapter "National Security Trumps Social Progress: The Era of the New Social Studies in Retrospect." A respected historian of the social studies, Evans divides the NSS into what he terms the "new" and the "newer" social studies. His chapter focuses on the origins, development, successes, and general failure of the new and newer social studies. Evans reminds us in his chapter that education and politics are not separate entities. He also sets the stage for the two wings or approaches of the NSS: the inquiry and the structure-of-the disciplines approach and the interdisciplinary, social and/or controversial issues approach (see also Rossi, 1992).

The book is then divided into three sections: people, projects, and perspectives. Within these sections the basic approach has been chronological which raises some difficulties as many of these projects were developed simultaneously. This was due to the tremendous availability of federal funding following the launching of Sputnik by the former Soviet Union and the need for the United States to complete in all Cold War endeavors including education. Nonetheless, an attempt was made to give some chronological perspective to the chapters within each section.

The People section begins with "Hilda Taba: Social Studies Reform from the Bottom Up." Although Taba died in 1967 and was not formally a NSS adherent, the fact remains that her work is not only a good fit for NSS approaches but also, it predates the gap between the structures of the disciplines and interdisciplinary work before this split became so evident during the NSS period. Taba's approach demonstrates that both disciplinary and interdisciplinary learning can be achieved in an integrated fashion in a well executed curriculum. Further, Taba's work can be seen as a warning sign of one of the main failures of the NSS; Taba worked with teachers to develop curriculum from the "bottom up" based on their felt needs for themselves and their students. One of the largest criticisms of the NSS is that it was imposed on teachers who were not really respected as knowledgeable or as necessary participants in the curriculum development process. Last, Taba's focus on conceptual learning in conjunction with a spiraling curriculum is fully in keeping with the beliefs of the attendees at the 1959 Wood's Hole Conference chaired by Jerome Bruner.

Another early practitioner who is not always grouped with the NSS is Fannie Shaftel. Jane Bernard Powers, a scholar well versed in the NSS, traces Shaftel's work as part of a dominant thread of NSS which focused on discipline learning combined with innovative instructional strategies.

Shaftel's work on role-playing for social values is fully explained in this chapter as well as recognizing her contributions as a feminist social studies scholar. Since new instructional strategies, focusing on what we now term "active learning," were an integral part of the NSS, this chapter samples the relationship of instruction to NSS ideals.

Ted Fenton, often called the "father of the New Social Studies" contributed much to the teaching of the discipline of history. These contributions are explored by Michelle Cude in "Can You Still Catch Fish With New Social Studies Bait? Ted Fenton and the Carnegie-Mellon (Social Studies) Project." Fenton came on the scene early and was a huge presence throughout the era of the NSS. He is also one of the people who has written on why the movement failed. In her chapter, Cude, a new young scholar who did not experience the NSS, analyzes his beliefs and the voluminous materials Fenton created.

In "The Quest for Relevancy": Allan Kownslar and Historical Inquiry in the New Social Studies Movement," Elizabeth Yeager Washington and Robert L. Dahlgren enlighten us on the work in the field of history attributed to Allan Kownslar, one of the lesser known NSS practitioners. O. L. Davis, Jr. (personal communication) stated that this chapter and recognition for Kownslar's contributions are long overdue. The chapter continues the focus on the academic discipline of history by stressing the importance of asking the right questions in inquiry-based history instruction. As history is often listed as the centerpiece of social studies education, this chapter focuses on the "New History" advocated early on by Kownslar and then continues to trace his career as a method's professor at Trinity University where he stressed inquiry-oriented point and counterpoint approaches to teaching both American and Texas History.

As mentioned before, the NSS had an interdisciplinary as well as a disciplinary wing. The Harvard Social Studies Project with its "leader-writers" represents the interdisciplinary wing. Chara Haeussler Bohan and Joseph R. Feinberg present the work of Donald Oliver, Fred Newmann and James Shaver to the New Social Studies movement. Oliver, the Harvard professor and his then doctoral students, Shaver and Newmann, worked in a team with high school teachers as well as other doctoral students to create the *Public Issues Series*. The approach Bohan and Feinberg take is to examine each of these individuals separately and then to discuss their joint efforts on the *Public Issues Series,* an interdisciplinary set of pamphlets on controversial issues that could be used either *in toto* or as individual units in high school courses ranging from U.S. History, American Studies electives, to sociology, or special topics electives. The chapter closes with a discussion of the lasting legacy of the Harvard Social Studies Project and the teaching of controversial issues.

Another of Oliver's students is Harold Berlak. Carol Klages researched the Metropolitan St. Louis Social Studies Project. The focus in this chapter is citizenship education, local history and, unlike the Harvard Project, elementary social studies. Berlak has been a social studies educator for his entire career and his social studies center not only provided units for social studies teaching, but also served as a centrally located resource repository. Klages' chapter details the contributions of this approach and its legacy in her chapter. Although now retired, Berlak is still writing about social studies and schools today, especially in sources such as *Rethinking Schools* (2009) publications.

The Projects section of the book opens with "A Red Headed Stepchild of Social Reconstruction: Sociology and the New Social Studies" by Karen L. Riley. This chapter chronicles the rise and fall of the sociology project in general, and the fate of the *Sociological Resources for the Social Studies* (SRSS) in particular. It also offers a look at the important individuals involved with the development of SRSS along with the secondary course titled "Inquiries in Sociology." Riley contends that there were multiple factors involved with the failure of the sociology projects but that the lack of status accorded to the professoriate when they worked with the public schools was a large part of the problem. Thus, when the funding disappeared, so did the interest in the NSS by sociologists at the university level. Since sociology was never widely accepted as a school subject, the lack of involvement of teachers in designing the curriculum hastened its demise.

In "Geography and the New Social Studies: The High School Geography Project and the Georgia Geography Curriculum Project," Joseph P. Stoltman analyzes developments in the teaching of geography during the NSS by looking intensively at two curricula from the period. Stoltman explains that "the discipline of geography made a major change in its scholarly focus, from descriptive to analytical and spatial analysis of both the human and physical Earth systems, giving rise to the "New Geography." This important change in the substance of what students study in a course in geography is still controversial today. Coupled with the new technologies available to geographers, the curriculum in geography is currently in transition again making this chapter a "must read" for anyone involved in the field of geography. Stoltman's detailed analysis of geography includes the impact of the projects and their legacy beyond the borders of the United States.

In her chapter on "Economics Education," Beverly Armento provides a comprehensive discussion of the issues surrounding the discipline by looking at the work of Lawrence Senesh and William Rader. Armento states that

Teaching sophisticated economic concepts to young children was really unheard of at this time—but Senesh and Rader and their teams—persisted and developed creative materials.... Today, these ideas are reflected in the K–12 economic education focus taken by the Council on Economic Education, the inclusion of economic concepts in the National Council for the Social Studies Standards, as well as the inclusion of economic concepts in many state social studies standards for elementary schools, and in well-used elementary school textbooks.

In addition to the elementary materials discussed, Armento includes the secondary school level mentioning three major economics projects that usually are identified as part of the New Social Studies movement: (a) The Manpower and Economic Education Project, (b) the Carnegie-Mellon University Social Studies Curriculum Project, and (c) the San Jose State, ECON 12 or Economics in Society project. Last, she covers the Developmental Economic Education Program (DEEP) (supported by a U.S. Office of Education grant), an innovative idea developed by the Joint Council on Economic Education. As economics is again a "hot topic" with state legislatures focusing on adding more economics and personal finance to the curriculum, this chapter provides some evidence of well thought-out curriculum, ripe for resuscitation.

Another often neglected social science, at least at the K–12 level, is anthropology. Murry Nelson provides a glimpse into the subject in his chapter, "Anthropology and the Anthropology Projects, Long Ago in a Galaxy Far Away." Nelson states:

There was an excitement and a promise of greater cultural exploration and understanding that would lead to greater student appreciation of the cultural complexities of the world. Today, this seems cruelly idealistic and makes one's views border on cynicism, but the period and the goals need to be more fully contextualized in order to appreciate how such idealistic notions could have been so widely accepted.

Nelson's chapter, marked by his long experience in the field, is followed by the first of two chapters in this volume on MACOS or *Man: A Course of Study*, a fifth grade anthropology project. By far the most controversial of the NSS curricula, the MACOS chapter in this section is "Making Sense of It All: A Research Synthesis on the Impact of Man: A Course of Study" written by a young, new scholar Chrystal S. Johnson. Johnson readily explains that many people have written about the MACOS project but that most of the contemporary literature on MACOS catalogues its sociopolitical context and curricular flaws. Newer MACOS studies include discussions of how it left an indelible mark on the social studies field but "What is missing, though, is a cogent synthesis of actual research on

MACOS itself." Johnson performs this meta-analysis by examining MACOS' origin and then focusing on two questions: (a) What impact did MACOS have on teachers and learners? And (b) Did MACOS, as a curriculum, meet its overall goal?

In "American Political Behavior: The Project and the People," Carole L. Hahn moves the NSS forward chronologically by focusing on the government and civics projects that were not initiated until later on in the NSS time frame. Hahn was a graduate student at the inception of this project and worked on teacher training with the materials during the time period. She has spent a good portion of her career researching knowledge about government and civic knowledge both nationally and internationally. Her chapter integrates both her personal experiences and her research in detailing the NSS approaches to teaching government.

This section of the book is rounded out with John Hoge's chapter detailing several of the smaller NSS projects that were not covered in individual chapters. In "Small Projects of the New Social Studies (Bring Back the Best)" Hoge states:

> My purpose is to demonstrate that models of outstanding social studies instruction came from the NSS movement as it was manifested in schools and classrooms across the nation. My goal is that contemporary readers will be inspired by what they see here and recognize that what was advocated by the NSS is still worthwhile in today's classrooms.

This fascinating chapter examines a plethora of projects across grade levels and social science disciplines. Hoge details criteria by which one can judge successful social studies projects and curriculum. He rightly tells us that some of the impediments to successful implementation of these projects have been eliminated by today's available technology. In addition to the body of the chapter, the reader might be interested in searching the reference section of this chapter and resurrecting some of the curriculum projects listed.

The Perspectives section of this volume opens with a second look at MACOS. Larry Kraus examines political struggles over MACOS. Kraus relates that not only was the content of MACOS unusual and controversial, but also the manner in which it had been funded raised issues. Kraus states: "To understand MACOS and the attendant controversies, we must also understand the political and educational climate." Unlike the research synthesis in the earlier MACOS chapter, this chapter focuses firmly on the political aspects of creating, financing, and implementing such a controversial curricular project. The chapter stands as a warning to future curriculum developers of problems to be anticipated when attempting change.

MACOS was not the only controversial project of the NSS. Questions about methodology, not only content, were and to some extent still are, problematic. "The 'History Problem' in Curricular Reform: A Warning to Constructivists from the New Social Studies Movement" by Geoffrey Scheurman and Keith Reynolds revisits the problem of student centered history education. The entire "inquiry approach" to teaching history, or any of the social sciences, is the topic of this chapter. Scheurman and Reynolds are concerned that:

> While others have offered myriad reasons for the apparent failure of the New Social Studies (NSS) to reform teaching in explicit or permanent ways, few have considered how the movement failed to fully accommodate itself to the unique nature of history as both a scholarly pursuit and a curriculum domain.

This is a curriculum war that points both to teacher and student preparation as well as the question of whether history, as a school subject, should be taught from a constructivist viewpoint. Should students function as "young historians" or should they memorize and learn the facts that history teachers and textbooks deliver? This is a question that is applicable to all the social science projects that were part of the NSS.

What of the voices of the participants? In "We Won't Get Fooled Again; Will We? Teacher Perceptions of the New Social Studies," Mark A. Previte examines the role of the teachers in the creation and delivery of NSS projects. While other authors in their chapters have discussed the problem of the exclusion of teachers from the creation of the NSS projects, Previte focuses his entire chapter on the role of the teacher in creating and delivering any curriculum package. Can any curriculum ever be successful if the teachers do not believe in materials? It is not only the lack of training to use materials, but also the ownership of the curriculum that is part of the discussion in the chapter.

Then, in "The New Social Studies and the Ethos of Multiculturalism," Gloria Contreras looks at another often ignored aspect of participants in her examination of whether or not there were multiple perspectives explored in the NSS curricula being presented to students. Although the word multicultural wasn't used at the time, it is clear that the students on the receiving end of the curriculum were not all of one ethnic, racial or religious group. Given the Civil Rights Movement, the Vietnam War and other political events that serve as a backdrop for the development of the NSS materials, was anyone paying attention to multiple voices? Contreras addresses this issue in her chapter.

"Lies and History: Unmasking Academic Complacency" by David Warren Saxe takes a different tack. Saxe, currently known as a critic of the NSS and/or the type of social studies curriculum it espouses has worked in the past with author Ronald Evans on the *Handbook on Teaching Social Issues* (2007). Thus, Saxe is quite familiar with the approaches and underlying beliefs espoused by the NSS as he explains in his chapter opening. Here, Saxe undertakes a critical review of James Loewen's *Lies My Teacher Told Me* (2005). In an interesting turn of the tables, Saxe accuses the revisionist history of Loewen and his suggestions for teachers as violating the best principles of NSS curriculum, especially as it comes to the teaching and learning of the discipline of history. This chapter presents an alternative set of concerns representing the points of critics in the field who view social studies and the NSS in particular as lacking in rigor. Saxe believes a rigorous, disciplinary approach is part of what is lacking in Loewen's work.

The next two chapters are by authors who review the impact of the NSS on themselves as participants. Both Mary Haas and Jack Zevin experienced the NSS as beginning teachers who later became teacher educators and carried on the traditions of their participation into their current work in one form or another. In "The Wisdom of Experience and Practice" Mary E. Haas details her early experiences with the geography project. In "Inquiry Teaching and Learning: Is There, Was There, a Cutting Edge in Social Studies? Or, My Life as an 'Inquiry' Social Studies Teacher" Zack Zevin focuses on his early teaching with the anthropology materials. Both these authors detail how these projects influenced not only their high school classroom teaching practice, but also the rest of their careers, especially in their roles as teacher educators, researchers and social studies authors still active in the field. Thus, the chapters written by Haas and Zevin provide the reader with insights from individuals who can view the NSS as teacher participants, those individuals accused by many authors in this volume as not buying into the NSS curricula because of the way it was imposed upon them or developed without them. These two chapters serve to dispel this notion for at least some teachers.

The last chapter is by a new scholar who focuses on the integration of technology into social studies education. "Leveraging Technology for Student Inquiry: Technology in the New Social Studies and Today" by Meghan McGlinn Manfra addresses the role of technology in inquiry education. Her chapter follows the Zevin chapter in order to maintain a focus on inquiry as an instructional methodology that was the core of the NSS and continues to be the core of many suggested reforms today. Manfra's words: "for real sustained reform of the social studies curriculum to occur, educators must learn from the experience of the New Social Studies," will serve as a beacon for those of us who may use this volume to learn from the past to improve social studies education for the future.

It is that hope, the improvement of social studies education for all students, which motivated the curriculum developers and implementers of the New Social Studies projects. Thus, while this volume is not a complete look at every aspect of the NSS movement, it is an attempt to focus on many of the people and projects, disciplinary and interdisciplinary, and to point out possibilities for today's educators. It is with these possibilities in mind that I invite the reader to explore the legacy of the New Social Studies.

REFERENCES

Evans, R. W., & Saxe, D. W. (2007). *Handbook on Teaching Social Issues NCSS Bulletin No. 93*. Charlotte, NC: Information Age.

Loewen, J. W. (2005). *Lies my teacher told me* (10th anniversary ed.) New York: New Press.

Rethinking schools. (2009). Retrieved March 21, 2009, from www.rethinking schools.org

Rossi, J. (1992, January/February), Uniformity, diversity, and the "new social studies." *The Social Studies, 83,* 41–45.

Social Science Education Consortium. (1971) *Social studies curriculum materials data book.* Boulder, CO: Author.

CHAPTER 1

NATIONAL SECURITY TRUMPS SOCIAL PROGRESS

The Era of the New Social Studies in Retrospect

Ronald W. Evans

The purpose of this chapter is to provide an overview of the curriculum reform movements and projects from the era of the new and newer social studies during the 1960s and 1970s as a case study in curricular change and to place the era in historical context. The chapter includes discussion of the origins of the new and newer social studies; the theoretical foundations for the new reforms; the projects; the outcomes; critiques made at the time; the aftermath—academic freedom controversies; and, the limited impact of the reforms in schools. The chapter will focus mainly on trying to comprehend the origins, development, successes, and general failure of the new and newer social studies.[1]

The New Social Studies: People, Projects, and Perspectives, pp. 1–37
Copyright © 2010 by Information Age Publishing
All rights of reproduction in any form reserved.

1

ORIGINS

The new social studies came to fruition during the 1960s, but was, in most ways, a product of the 1950s and the Cold War struggle against Communism. It was born of Cold War manpower development concerns and as a carryover from developments in science and mathematics. Largely discipline-centered, the social studies projects of the era, which received unprecedented federal and private financial support, were a direct outgrowth of the criticism of progressive education and of progressive social studies that had been brewing for decades. In a very real sense, this was an extension of the war on social studies and a culmination of decades of criticism.

The War on Social Studies. In a recent book, I develop the argument that controversies and criticism over the social studies curriculum developed in a sequential pattern, with the controversy becoming broader and more damaging to progressive social studies as the years went on. Criticism of progressive social studies emerged and intensified in three major episodes which preceded the era of the new social studies, the Rugg textbook controversy which spanned 1939–1942, the controversy over American history, 1942–1944, and the controversy over progressive education, 1947–1958. As I have argued previously, these three controversies were instrumental in the eventual evolution of the era of the new social studies, and were a strong reflection of the historical context (Evans, 2004). The Rugg textbook controversy developed in the early years of the Second World War. Stirred in part by war related fears and the activism of conservative business and patriotic groups, attacks on the Rugg textbooks led to their elimination from schools, and to a broader questioning of progressive forms of social studies education, especially those which raised questions about the capitalist economic system. Attacks on Rugg and his textbook series embodied questions about content and interpretations that critics considered controversial, and concerns over the replacement of traditional discipline based, history and social science coursework with a broader form called social studies (Evans, 2007). That questioning of the "omnibus" social studies led to the controversy over American history initiated by a *New York Times Magazine* article written by Pulitzer Prize winning historian Allan Nevins which charged that the schools were no longer teaching American history. These wartime controversies combined to stir the passions of educational critics of various stripes, but especially those who wanted a stronger focus on the disciplines and a traditional view of the American way. In the postwar era, the controversy would spread to encompass all of progressive education.

The Cold War Critiques of Progressive Education. In the late 1940s and early 50s, a growing crescendo of criticisms of progressive education emerged—

with many of the most negative observations focused on social studies—
packaged and marketed under colorful titles such as: *Educational Wastelands*
(Bestor, 1953), *Quackery in the Public Schools* (Lynd, 1953), *Progressive Education is REDucation* (Jones & Olivier, 1956), and "Who Own's Your Child's
Mind?" (Flynn, 1951). Arthur Bestor, perhaps the most respected critic,
called social studies an anti-intellectual "social stew" (Bestor, 1953). Bestor
and others critiqued the "scrambling" of history, geography, and government into the social studies; they bemoaned the "anti-intellectualism" of
educators who they derisively called "educationists"; and, they frequently
linked progressive education to Communism, all critiques which had been
raised during the Rugg and Nevins controversies, only this time, the deluge of attacks was longer and more intense. Educators responded with articles and books countering the charges—though it was a relatively muted
response, reflecting the times.

The social mileu of the Cold War era is especially pertinent to a deeper
understanding of the origins of the new social studies. With the dropping
of atomic bombs on Japan, and the subsequent development of the
nuclear arms race, the world had entered the nuclear age, and the threat
of global holocaust was very real. Competition with the Soviet Union,
growing national security concerns, the development of McCarthyism,
and the deluge of intellectual and red-baiting attacks on progressive education were all conditioned by this context.

Manpower Concerns. The impetus for the broader curriculum reform
movement which gave rise to the new social studies also grew, in part, out
of Cold War manpower studies conducted by the Central Intelligence
Agency. Manpower concerns were raised beginning in the late 1940s and
early 1950s and were partly behind creation of the National Science Foundation (NSF) in 1950. The NSF, established by Congress in 1950 with the
aim of promoting basic research and education in the sciences, initially
had little to do with the lower schools, though it did begin to sponsor
science fairs and summer institutes for teachers in science and math.
Manpower concerns were heightened by a series of confidential CIA
reports on developments in the Soviet Union. The first of these reports
provided evidence that the Soviets were training scientists, engineers, and
technical manpower at a rapid rate, and employing the "Stakhanov"
movement, or "socialist competition" to spur productivity gains. They
were giving monetary awards for innovation and "Stalin Prizes" and
"Hero of Socialist Labor" awards. In short, the report showed that the
Soviet Union was an awakening industrial giant (National Intelligence
Survey [NIS], 1953). A later report confirmed the earlier findings and
indicated that the Soviets were devoting "large sums to education, especially in the fields of science and engineering," and that in many fields,
"Soviet technology equals or even exceeds that of the west" (NIS, 1958,

pp. 13, 15). By 1963, a "secret" report found that Soviet productivity was "second only to the U.S." and that the Soviets had made especially rapid progress in "development of engineering and other professional and technical manpower," with a 237% increase in engineers from 1939 to 1959 (NIS, 1963, pp. 1, 4).

Among U.S. policymakers, the CIA manpower reports were cause for alarm at the highest levels and led to a manpower report from the Office of Defense Mobilization (ODM) commissioned by President Dwight D. Eisenhower (Eisenhower, 1953). The ODM study reported on the "availability of manpower simultaneously to operate a military training program, to supply military personnel for active service, and to meet the needs of the civilian economy." In essence, civilian scientific and technical manpower was viewed as an adjunct to military power and as an essential part of national security (Fleming, 1954). The report stated that manpower resources, especially "our supply of highly trained and skilled workers" was not keeping abreast of the current and potential requirements of the rapidly expanding technology" on which the nation's "growth and security depend." The authors of the report cast manpower as a key ingredient for "success on the diplomatic front" (Committee on Manpower, 1953, p. 1). By the fall of 1954 national security and manpower concerns had become the subject of alarming media coverage. An interview with NSF Director Alan T. Waterman published in *Nation's Business* organ of the U.S. Chamber of Commerce, was titled, "Russian Science Threatens the West" (1954), and a *New York Times* article reported, "Russia is Overtaking U.S. in Training of Technicians" (Fine, 1954). Manpower concerns continued to loom large throughout the Cold War era and stood behind government and business led efforts to develop more scientific and technical personnel, and better trained citizens.

The curriculum reform movement which would eventually result in creation of the new social studies also had its seeds in two projects which began, almost unnoticed, at two universities in the 1950s. The University of Illinois Committee on School Mathematics was formed in 1951 out of concerns over the math deficiencies of entering freshmen at the University of Illinois. Based on similar concerns in science, Jerrold Zacharias at the Massachusetts Institute of Technology wrote a memo in 1956 to James Killian, MIT president, titled, "Movie Aids for Teaching Physics in High School," in which he proposed a project for the improvement of physics teaching by creating 90 films 20 minutes in length as the heart of the curriculum, each with a "real physicist" (Zacharias, 1956). Zacharias' memorandum led to the creation of what was called the Physical Science Study Committee (PSSC) which received NSF funding. In each case, the rationale for the development of the curriculum improvement projects was rooted in manpower concerns which surfaced earlier, and which continued to be aired, in one form or another, throughout the period.

These early curriculum development programs established initial patterns for the funding of national curriculum development projects that would largely continue for the next 15 to 20 years. One pattern, represented by the University of Illinois Committee, was initial funding by private foundations (often Carnegie or Ford) followed by support from the NSF or the U.S. Office of Education (USOE). A second pattern, represented by the MIT Committee, was long-term funding by the NSF or USOE from start-up to publication. By 1956, six national projects were established and funded in science and math, five of which aimed at curriculum reform. By this time, it was apparent that several broad assumptions or guidelines were shared by virtually all of these endeavors, and included: the need to change the content, materials, and methods of instruction; a focus on the textbook or learning materials; directors of projects drawn from the academic disciplines; a focus on courses for the academically talented and gifted because it was seen as more critical to the national interest; overriding concern about the integrity of the academic disciplines and their "structures;" learning by discovery and inquiry; and a focus on the cognitive over affective, personal, or social action dimensions (Haas, 1977). Another shared assumption, if the problem with schools was the shoddy stuff they taught, the solution was to bypass the teacher by creating new and innovative materials under the direction of some of the leading minds in each discipline.

Wartime Research Model. Virtually all of the later curriculum development projects involved an application of the same innovative model of research and development embodied in the initial projects. Reformers, most of whom had little previous experience with educational reform efforts, imported methods of research and development from military research programs to the field of education. In effect, the projects owed much of their form to the military-industrial research complex as it evolved during and after World War II. The reforms of the era were "designed and implemented by a small cadre of scientists," led by Jerrold Zacharias of MIT, who transferred techniques "almost seamlessly" from military weapons research and development programs of the postwar period to the field of education. Though the push for a more rigorous and academic education originated in critiques of progressivism and Cold War manpower concerns, the trend was enhanced and given its "fundamental operational characteristics," along with its conception of the essential "problem of education, and the means of its solution," by the newer research and development techniques drawn from wartime weapons research. The particular "intellectual skills and technical methods" involved had proven their worth during World War II (Rudolph, 2002, pp. 213–214).

In the eyes of scientists and policymakers during the Cold War era, there seemed no limit to the power of these techniques to solve virtually any problem. Partly due to its origins in wartime research and development, the reform strategy took little account of culture, history, mores, or social and economic context of the school. If its reform implementation strategies were flawed, an oversimplification that failed to understand the complexities of schools and teaching, few inside the growing reform juggernaut were aware of its limitations. Indeed, through the myopic vantage point of those most involved, the educational possibilities seemed limitless, even "revolutionary" (Bruner, 1983).

The ideological turn behind passage of the National Defense Education Act (NDEA) developed over many years of red-baiting and criticism of progressive education from academic critics. The stage was set, and the launching of Sputnik, the Soviet satellite, on October 4, 1957, affirmed the criticism and unleashed funds for educational reform. Sputnik served as a clarion call for education in science and math, and other studies that would strengthen U.S. brainpower for the Cold War. That call was answered by the NDEA, passed in early 1958, providing unprecedented categorical aid in the hundreds of millions of dollars for the improvement of mathematics, science, and foreign language instruction. The NDEA was supported by two main arguments: that national security required the "fullest development of the mental resources and technical skills of American youth, and that the national interest required federal" "assistance to education for programs which are important to our national defense" (Gutek, 1986).

Following Sputnik, national magazines and a new round of books stoked the fires of a renewed "crisis" in education. Critics such as Vice Admiral Hyman G. Rickover, father of the nuclear submarine, blamed the schools for our nation falling behind the Russians in science, math, and engineering, endangering national security. In his criticisms of American education, published in a book titled, *Education and Freedom* (1959), he called attention to Soviet successes and described the superiority of the Soviet and European educational systems. Another vociferous critic, E. Merrill Root, authored a critique of textbooks that exemplified the anti-Communist tenor of the times and contributed to the crisis mentality. In *Brainwashing in the High Schools* (1958), Root sought to demonstrate that the United States was losing the Cold War because of the unpatriotic textbooks filled with misleading propaganda for socialism and communism. Another book that appeared shortly after Sputnik seemed to sum up many of the criticisms of education spawned by Cold War fears and competition. *Second Rate Brains* contained a compendium of thought on Soviet schools and scientists, and offering critiques of the mediocrity in American schools (Lansner, 1958). The cumulative effect of these persistent and strident attacks on education supported new directions, and a renewed emphasis on discipline-based academic study.

A Broadened Agenda. Following Sputnik, and passage of the NDEA, the growth of research and development for curriculum improvement which began in the technical fields, in math and science, was gradually broadened to include the humanities and social sciences. Two important meetings took place in April, 1958, 6 months after the launch of Sputnik, and shortly after passage of the NDEA, which would have an important influence on the direction of curriculum reform. The first of these was a conference on Psychological Research in Education aimed at investigating better approaches to teaching science and math "than are now being utilized" (Proposed Conference, 1958). The second was a meeting held at the National Academy of Sciences at which virtually all of the major decision makers in funding the growing curriculum reform movement were present. At that meeting it was decided to broaden the PSSC curriculum reform model to other science areas. That decision would open the door to curriculum reform in social studies. At the same meeting, it was agreed that the PSSC would form a small corporation known as Educational Services Incorporated or ESI (Whaley, 1958).

The furor and flurry of interest in education that followed Sputnik provided an invaluable assist to those who wanted schools to raise academic standards and give more attention to gifted students. At the NSF, the "crisis" in education and the intense interest following Sputnik increased the Foundation's role in secondary school reform. Projects proliferated, made possible by increased funding from the NSF and the USOE following passage of the NDEA in 1958, and inspired by Sputnik. At the heart of the the curriculum reform movement was Jerrold Zacharias. As Jerome Bruner later recalled, "I think it was Zach, more that anybody else, who converted the Sputnik shock into the curriculum reform movement that it became rather than taking some other form" (Bruner, 1983, p. 180). Gradually, the directors of funded projects became the new "leadership" in American education. With the backing of the national government, these new reforms represented a sort of "official" direction for the creation and transmission of knowledge in the nation's schools, one that was built around the academic disciplines and the Cold War aim of manpower development, even if few of those involved seldom seemed to explicitly acknowledge it at the time.

EMERGENCE

The aim of the new social studies movement was to "transform ... students into junior historians and social scientists." The developments of the

1960s rested, in part, on a small, influential book, *The Process of Education*, written by Jerome Bruner, reporting on the proceedings of the Woods Hole Conference.

Woods Hole. The Woods Hole Conference, held in September, 1959, at Woods Hole, Massachusetts, at a large mansion owned by MIT, brought together leaders in the new reforms in science and math, and led to a concise and well crafted formulation of the principles of curriculum development shared in the new movement. Among the 35 participants were luminaries such as conference director Jerome Bruner, Richard Alpert, Lee Cronbach, Robert Gagne, Jerold Zacharias, and John Morton Blum. Key participants included the curriculum-makers, biologists, mathematicians, and physicists, along with a few psychologists, several educators, and a couple of historians and a classicist. The National Academy of Scientists, the institution behind putting the conference together, wanted to have a closer look at the curriculum reform movement, and infuse some new thinking from psychology. Other sponsors of the conference included the USOE Cooperative Research Program, the Rand Corporation, the Air Research and Development Command, and the NSF. From a larger perspective, the conference was fueled by the reaction to Sputnik and the complaints of critics such as Vice Admiral Rickover, and was funded by a range of federal agencies. In a sense, what was emerging was a manufactured consensus, paid for by stakeholders with an interest in education conducted on behalf of national security.

In *The Process of Education,* Bruner (1960) summarized his own "sense of the meeting" based on the reports of five working groups formed at the conference. The conference took the "structure of the disciplines" as its central theme and overriding assumption, and examined in some depth, "the role of structure in learning and how it may be made central in teaching." The conferees assumed the goal of "giving students an understanding of the fundamental structure of whatever subjects we choose to teach," and the "teaching and learning of structure" rather than simply the "mastery of facts and techniques" (pp. 2–3, 11–12).

The second theme of the conference had to do with readiness for learning and "the hypothesis that any subject can be taught effectively in some intellectually honest form to any child at any stage of development" (Bruner, 1960, p. 33). A third theme involved the nature of intuition and the training of hunches. "The shrewd guess, the fertile hypothesis," Bruner asserted, "is a much-neglected and essential feature of productive thinking." These three themes, Bruner wrote, were all premised on a central conviction, "that intellectual activity anywhere is the same, whether at the frontier of knowledge or in a third-grade classroom.... The difference is in degree, not in kind" (pp. 13–14). A fourth theme centered on how to stimulate student motivation through interest in the material. The essence of the reform centered on finding means that would help the learner get through the "surface clutter" of details "to the pure, unflawed idea behind it: the deep structure" (Bruner, 1983, p. 181). That meant, in the case of history, for example, "you don't just think *about* history, you think history." In other words, history was not just a description of the past, but a way of getting to that description, a process. As Bruner would frame it later, "knowing how something is put together ... allows you to go beyond it" (p. 183).

Not all of these ideas were new. The concept of inquiry or discovery oriented teaching had been around at least since the days of the scientific historians in the nineteenth century, and was increasingly championed by many progressive educators. Motivation through student interest was also an old song. Parts of the new curriculum movement were a recapitulation of common ideas in the rhetoric of education. The focus on the "structures" of the disciplines was a reformulation, though what it actually meant in terms of classroom practice remained somewhat unclear.

Though there was little explicit acknowledgement of the Cold War backdrop to which the conferees at Woods Hole owed their existence, Bruner, a Cold War liberal in politics, did refer somewhat obliquely to the social milieu. He wrote: "if all students are helped to the full utilization of their intellectual powers, we will have a better chance of surviving as a democracy in an age of enormous technological and social complexity" (1960, p. 10). A part of that "complexity" was no doubt entangled in the Cold War struggle with totalitarian Communism in the minds of Bruner and his colleagues.

In his role as director, during the conference Bruner wrote memos to each of five working groups on: the apparatus of teaching; the sequence of the curriculum; the motivation of learning; the role of intuition; and, cognitive processes. One of the most telling comments was contained in Bruner's memo to the work group on the apparatus of teaching. "Perhaps rather unfortunately," the memo began,

> we introduced this subject for discussion today by suggesting the analogy to a weapon system—proposing that the teacher, the book, the laboratory, the teaching machine, the film, and the organization of the craft might serve together to form a balanced teaching system. (Bruner, 1959)

It was a revealing comment. It alluded to the Cold War backdrop, through which the entire program of curriculum reform might be seen as both a weapons system and an outgrowth of national security concerns, and it made an implicit connection to the earlier involvement of Bruner and Zacharias in the development of weapons systems. Bruner's initial direct involvement with the wartime research model apparently came with his work on Project Troy, a highly classified summer study invited by the State Department and ostensibly created to find a way to overcome Soviet jamming of Radio Free Europe, but with the broader aim of getting "the truth behind the Iron Curtain" by bringing together some of the "best brains in the country" to work on the problem and to counter the Soviet propaganda program (Needell, 1998). Zacharias was also deeply involved in similar wartime government projects and had been for some time, with key leadership roles in the MIT radiation lab and the Manhattan Project, as a consultant on Project Troy, and notably, as director of Project Hartwell, focused initially on antisubmarine warfare and completed at MIT in 1950 with funding from the Office of Navy Research (Goldstein, 1992). These involvements provided a model and many of the personnel for what would become large-scale consultancies involving scientists, social scientists, the U.S. military, intelligence, and propaganda agencies. The model was later applied to social studies education as an arm of the propaganda effort, that is, improve manpower development on a broad scale, improve social science instruction, and win the Cold War, assuming, of course, that students gain strong inquiry skills and reach the proper conclusions. In the case of Bruner, participation in Project Troy was "a rather heady experience" and led to a regular monthly dinner meeting at the St. Botolph's Club in Boston the first Friday evening of each month for the next 15 years" which he later described as "the best club I ever belonged to" (Bruner, 1983, p. 210).

Following Woods Hole, other theorists added to the mix, creating building blocks for the new reform and fleshing out the rationale. The era of the new social studies was introduced most clearly when an article by Charles R. Keller, director of the John Hay Fellows Program, and a former college history teacher, appeared in the *Saturday Review*. Keller's article was titled, "Needed: Revolution in Social Studies," and appeared in 1961. His thesis was that social studies was "in the educational doldrums," partly traceable to the fact that "social studies" was a "federation of subjects, ... often merged in inexact and confusing ways" (Keller, 1961, p. 60). Social studies teachers too frequently "depend on textbooks," leading to "unimaginative, unenthusiastic, pedantic teaching." The remedy, according to Keller, was "a possible revolution in social studies," beginning with "eliminating the term 'social studies,' which is vague, murky, and too all-inclusive and substitute for it the term 'history and the social sciences,' which is exact and hence meaningful" (pp. 61–62). Keller then echoed many of Bruner's recommendations, a clarion call for a social studies reform movement along the lines already begun in other subject areas.

Prior to the appearance of Keller's article, social studies reformers were already engaged in pioneering work in a few isolated places. Lawrence

Senesh, a scholar in economics at Purdue University, was busily creating an economics program for elementary age students, drawing on the disciplines in creating a progressive oriented program and textbook series, "Our Working World." Edwin Fenton, a historian at Carnegie Institute of Technology in Pittsburgh who had been given responsibility for preservice teacher education in history, was bothered by the pat assertions found in high school history textbooks and by the boredom and loathing of his own students for many history and social science courses. In an attempt to bring history to life and rekindle student curiosity he introduced primary source documents as a means of stimulating students, asking them to experience the work of historians, and to make sense of raw data. Fenton's experiences with using primary source documents led to publication of a book titled *32 Problems in World History* and an eventual leadership role in the new social studies movement (Fenton, 1964).

Endicott House. During the period before and after the Woods Hole conference, a series of meetings took place with the general theme of broadening the curriculum reform projects to include other areas, such as English and social studies. Perhaps the single most interesting and relevant of these meeting occurred at Endicott House in Cambridge in June of 1962. The Endicott House meeting was the first comprehensive meeting to grow out of the reform movement to examine the need for curriculum reform in social studies in some depth. During the Kennedy administration, Jerrold Zacharias served as chair of the President's Science Advisory Committee and sponsored a number of meetings on a variety of topics aimed at further developing and broadening the educational reform movement. The Endicott House meeting was a more immediate and direct outgrowth of a January, 1962, meeting at which Zacharias recommended development of an ESI social studies program.

The Endicott House Conference was held in June of 1962 at a secluded estate ten miles from Harvard Square with 47 scholars and teachers representing a broad spectrum of disciplines in the social sciences and humanities, and a wide range of views. Controversy emerged almost immediately after Robert Feldmesser, a sociologist, blamed the poor condition of social studies teaching in the schools on historians, and the dominance of history in the curriculum. "We shall make no progress in transforming the social studies into social science," he said, "until we slaughter the sacred cow of history" (Dow, 1991, p. 42). Feldmesser proposed inclusion of more social science materials at all levels, and that children be introduced to the inquiry methods and conceptual structure of the social sciences so that they could develop a more critical attitude toward the social world. Most of the historians at the meeting were offended by Feldmesser's comments, and for a time the conference descended into a turf battle over whose content was most valuable. Edwin Fenton, a historian from Carnegie-Mellon, was one of the few historians at the meeting who agreed with Feldmesser that traditional history had dominated the curriculum for too long.

Gradually, however, as the 2-week session went on, and other voices were heard, a consensus began to develop around the notion that the problem in the schools had more to do with how history was typically taught, rather than with the subject matter itself. What emerged from the Endicott House meeting was a proposal for more in-depth study, later given the name "post-holing," that would engage students in source material and the process of inquiry and that would expose them to the uncertainty, speculation, and imagination that are part of scientific and historical investigation. As at Woods Hole, the latter part of the conference was devoted to presentations by working group that had been meeting regularly throughout the two weeks to develop concrete suggestions for curriculum reform. In the end, the meeting produced a few suggestions about where the emerging reform of social studies might head, but did not create a blueprint for reform (Dow, 1991). Following the conference, Zacharias's new ESI social studies group began meeting regularly to develop a refined and concrete proposal to submit to the Ford Foundation, eventually evolving into the MACOS curriculum.

THE PROJECTS

In the October, 1962, issue of *Social Education*, the same month as the Cuban missile crisis, a small, two paragraph, "Announcement for Project Social Studies," appeared on the bottom half of one page. The announcement read, in part, "The United States Office of Education has announced the initiation of Project Social Studies, which is designed to improve research, instruction, teacher education, and the dissemination of information in this field." The announcement also stated that funds were available for research projects, curriculum study centers, and conferences and seminars (Announcement, 1962). The fact that the announcement coincided with the height of Cold War tension is not lost in hindsight, though at the time the de-politicization of education made it appear a rather innocuous research and development notice, with exciting possibilities for scholars and teachers.

The earliest social science projects had begun to receive funding prior to the announcement of Project Social Studies, and received support from the NSF as well as private foundations such as Ford or Carnegie. Senesh and Fenton had already begun work on their projects in the 1950s, and had received at least some private funding for their efforts. A similar endeavor, the Amherst history project, had its beginnings in the 1959–1960 school year under the leadership of Van Halsey (1963).

Three additional projects were launched in 1961, all emanating from professional associations. All three eventually received funding from the NSF. These included the High School Geography Project, Sociological Resources for the Secondary Schools, and the Anthropology Curriculum Study Project.

Following up on the announcement of Project Social Studies, in July, 1963, USOE reported that 7 curriculum centers, 11 research projects, and 2 developmental activities had been approved for funding (Smith, 1963). These included Fenton's project in American history, and Donald Oliver's project at Harvard focused on analysis of public issues. Four additional new projects were funded in 1964. By 1965 there were some two-dozen projects that made up the new social studies movement, funded by the NSF, the USOE, or private foundations. Most notable among the new additions was the Harvard Educational Development Center's Man: A Course of Study (MACOS), for which Jerome Bruner served as the intellectual architect. The vast majority of the projects fit the general theme of the "structures of the disciplines," but there was some diversity in orientation. Perhaps the least compatible with the discipline-based focus was the Harvard Project, with its focus on public issues as the heart of citizenship education.

Clearly, a revolution of sorts was brewing, but what was its nature? In April, 1965, *Social Education* devoted virtually the entire issue to a "Report on Project Social Studies," with an overview provided by Edwin Fenton and John Good. Their report began with a bold and confident statement:

> The curriculum revolution which began in mathematics, the natural sciences, and modern foreign languages about a decade ago has at last reached the social studies. More than 40 curriculum development projects of national significance promise to revolutionize teaching about man and society. (Fenton & Good, 1965, p. 206)

Calling the sum of the projects "the new social studies," in what appears to be the first use of this term, Fenton and Good (1965) provide a succinct summary of some of the general themes of the activities supported by Project Social Studies and other funding sources including the emphasis on structure, inductive teaching, the disciplines, sequential learning, new types of materials, new subjects, and emphases on evaluation. Though the article gave a concise overview of the new reform the authors demonstrated little awareness of the contextual origins of the movement.

After 1965 another wave of projects was christened. By 1967 more than 50 national projects were in progress, though curricular materials were slow to appear and were not issued in significant amounts until 1967. The projects created after 1967 all claimed loyalty to the principles of the new social studies, but in actuality, "moved off in all imaginable directions" (Haas, 1977, p. 58). Though there were many variations and permutations of the general themes of the new social studies, the general parameter of discipline-based inquiry appears to have held fairly constant as a working guideline for the vast majority of projects.

From a distance, it appears that the new social studies movement reached its zenith in 1967. In this year, the total number of funded projects appears to have peaked, and new social studies topics and concerns dominated both *Social Education* and the NCSS annual conference. Moreover, for many of the initial projects, funding periods were at or near their end. The years after 1967 would be spent dealing with publication, dissemination, and diffusion of materials.

A second wave of projects received initial funding from 1968 to 1972. Several of the newly funded projects added selected use of contemporary social problems as topics for study and as criteria for selection of social science content. Adding to the general ferment, nonproject social studies curriculum workers, teachers, and teacher educators labored in the field, often providing conferences and workshops and receiving funds from the USOE, state departments of education, and local school districts.

If 1967 was the zenith of enthusiasm for the new movement, the years following, through the early to mid-1970s, represented a continuing presence with activity at a lower level of intensity. As we shall see, events in the society, many of which impinged directly on schools, may have diluted teacher enthusiasm for the new social studies and its general focus on inquiry based in the disciplines, a step removed from the conflicts and dilemmas of the social world.

In retrospect, the materials produced in the era of the new social studies were among the most innovative and influential commodities ever produced for use in social studies classrooms. Despite the historical context out of which they were born, and perhaps partly because of it, projects funded by millions of grant dollars from the NSF, the USOE, and other sources contributed to creation of a rich and multifaceted explosion of curriculum development the likes of which may never be seen again. The projects and materials set a tone for an era of innovation and inquiry that spread to other curriculum materials, textbooks, and curriculum guides. Yet, as in each of the previous attempts to reform social studies, this one too had its problems.

CONCERNS AND CRITIQUES

The profession was far from united behind the new reform movement. In fact, there were many contemporary critiques of what came to be called the new social studies, and they originated from several different quarters. Perhaps the earliest published critique of the new social studies came from Donald Robinson in an article which appeared in 1963, shortly after the launch of Project Social Studies, which cautioned that "everyone has a different notion of what the social studies should attempt," and concluded that social studies curricular practice would continue to be fashioned by "a combination of national tradition, suggestive state programs, locally prescribed curricula, the considerable influence of textbooks, universities, and professional organizations" (Robinson, 1963, pp. 360, 362).

Another similar caution came from James Becker (1965) who observed, in 1965, that there was a new consensus emerging on the need for reform in social studies. Yet, ironically, he noted, "never before in our history has there been less general agreement about precisely what needs changing" and described a "nearly total confusion" on goals. Becker cautioned that prospects were slim for any kind of radical change (p. 20).

Also among the earliest critiques were those voiced in a group of letters published in *Social Education*. Fred M. Newmann wrote that "we must be cautious to avoid seduction by the fashionable emphasis on 'inductive thinking' or 'discovery method' when the major objectives of most of the projects centered on "communication of the structure of one discipline," and too frequently aimed at guiding students to predetermined generalizations. Byron G. Massialas charged that the projects "concentrate on the empirical and cognitive dimensions of learning" neglecting the normative and affective components," and assumed, "what is good for the social scientist acting as a researcher is good for the child." Richard E. Gross suggested that the projects suffered from a failure to clearly delineate purposes, a tendency to concentrate on average and above average students, and development of "teacher-proof" materials which could reduce the teacher's role to that of technician ("Reactions to the Reports," 1965).

Another critique by Mark M. Krug (1966) charged that the new reforms had conceptual flaws, that there was no logical structure of ideas in the social sciences, and asked why all children should explore "the kinds of questions that interest historians, political scientists (and) economists?" Krug charged that Bruner slighted this need, and urged a restoration of traditional history (pp. 401–402). James P. Shaver lamented the new social studies projects' "general failure ... to examine the basic rationale for social studies instruction" and labeled them "scholacentric" (Shaver, 1967, pp. 592, 596).

Somewhat surprisingly, another contemporary critique of the new curriculum movement was written by one of its founders, Jerome Bruner. Bruner (1971) wrote that the rational structuralism of the *Process of Education,* "was based on a formula of faith: that learning was what students wanted to do, that they wanted to achieve an expertise in some particular subject matter. Their motivation was taken for granted" (p. 19).

THE NEWER SOCIAL STUDIES

The projects of the new social studies ran into problems almost immediately partly because their vocabulary and conceptual level were high, but also because they too frequently failed to address the pressing concerns of the 1960s: civil rights, the war in Vietnam, campus unrest. The events of 1968 seemed the culmination of the building turmoil of the decade. The assassinations of the Reverand Martin Luther King, Jr., and inspiring presidential candidate Robert F. Kennedy, rioting in cities, student strikes, antiwar demonstrators confronting police, and rising militancy by minorities contributed to a crisis atmosphere in the nation and calls for massive social change. The social studies response to this turmoil took shape in the code-word, "relevance," and piqued interest in social problems. Perhaps the most significant effect of this new trend was its impact on course offerings, contributing to a short-term flurry of expansion in which high schools suddenly offered minicourses on a cornucopia of topics: Black history, Native American history, and women's history, among others. Though the minicourse revolution was short lived, it had a significant impact on the curriculum.

The turmoil in the streets was accompanied by drastic changes in the journal *Social Education* in both content and style. Though a reflection of the times, the shift in the pages of social education was a reflection of a change of editors, from Lewis Paul Todd to Daniel Roselle. There was a crescendo toward change form the early 1960s and before. In the newer movement, the student as little league social scientist was replaced by the student as social activist. The newer social studies had an issues-centered focus, largely presentist in orientation. Following the initial explosion, a new wave of topical interest evolved including a focus on urbanization, environmentalism, population, futurism, women's studies, and area studies, especially a focus on Africa and Asia. Concurrent with the topical focus on issues was a growing emphasis on newer methods and techniques including simulation and values clarification. Most of the curricular innovations of the time employed new social studies terminology of inquiry, valuing, and decision making, and were facilitated by the increased availability of a new and diverse array of classroom materials in a variety of mediums.

During the late 1960s and early 1970s the rhetoric of social redemption through schooling experienced a brief revival. The new focus on the present dilemmas of American society had an implicit social reconstructionist orientation. The social reconstructionist camp had been largely moribund for some time, though a few scholars had kept the tradition alive. By the late 1960s there was something of a revivial of social reconstructionism in social studies. In an article titled, "The Year of the Non-Curriculum: A Proposal," Gerald Leinwand (1968) proposed a poststructuralist focus on social issues, an idea which appeared prophetic for a time. Deriding both the new social studies and traditional practice, Leinwand blamed the lack of improvement in classrooms on "the fact that there is such a thing as a social studies curriculum," and charged that

> students learn a distorted, rather euphoric lesson in national and world events and emerge ill-equipped to wrestle with the evils that do exist and with which the revolutions of our day are involved ... the social studies ... remain detached and aloof, perhaps even alienated, from the throbbing events of our time as the curriculum bulletin decrees one thing but events show something quite different. (pp. 542–543)

Leinwand (1968) then listed and discussed 11 problem-topics as the focus of the meeting including many of the most pressing issues of the late 1960s: air and water pollution, traffic and transit, urban and rural slums, adult crime and juvenile delinquency, civil rights and civil liberties, the Negro in the city, urban and rural poverty, Black Power, protest—violent and nonviolent, the draft, and war and peace. He later developed and edited a paperback anthology series titled, *Problems of American Society*, which seemed ubiquitous for a time and contributed to the ferment for teaching social issues (Leinwand, 1968–1969).

The development which I am labeling the newer social studies coincided with an explosion of interest in education. A veritable slew of books drew attention to the problems of the schools and proposed reform, revolution, or exit through creation of alternatives. Among the new wave were books critical of educational practice in general, and of "ghetto-school" education in particular, including Nat Hentoff's *Our Children Are Dying* (1966), James Herndon's *The Way It Spozed To Be* (1968), John Holt's *How Children Fail* (1964) and *How Children Learn* (1967), and Jonathan Kozol's *Death at an Early Age* (1967). Each of these authors, with the exception of Hentoff, were writing about their own experiences as teachers. They suggested greater concern with the affective aspects of schooling than with academic excellence, and called for humanizing teaching and the school bureaucracy, as well as a return to some of the best aspects of progressivism. The new wave literature was critical of a system which too often stifled creative teaching, a curriculum which was frequently outmoded and dysfunctional, and testing which was often counterproductive. It was also critical of many teachers who behaved in an ignorant if not destructive manner toward children (Sobel, 1968).

This new wave was accompanied by a host of additional titles in a similar though more radical vein, sharing, but frequently going beyond the new wave critique. These included John Goodman's *Compulsory Miseducation* (1966), Everett Reimer's *School is Dead* (1971), and Postman and Weingartner's *Teaching as a Subversive Activity* (1969). At least two influential books, published earlier, became popular again, notably Paul Goodman's *Growing Up Absurd* (1960), and A. S. Neill's *Summerhill* (1960), the classic seminal work on open education which proved a forerunner of the new wave. Charles Silberman's *Crisis in the Classroom* (1970) attempted to capture the new impulse toward open education. A later addition was Ivan Illich's *Deschooling Society* (1971). These works shared the new wave disdain for traditional schooling and bore some resemblance, in many cases, to child-centered progressivism and its Rousseauan orientation. They mirrored the social trends and critiques of the time and were written partly in response to the inadequacies of American schooling for children of color, the atmosphere of racial unrest, student rebellion, and the antiwar movement.

The critique of the schools generated by the new radical literature was devastating. According to the critics, schools were institutions of conformity that destroyed the souls of children, coerced them to sit through hours of boring classes, and neglected the needs of individuals while oppressing the culture and history of students of color. The schools were attached to a boring, irrelevant curriculum and antiquated teaching methods that destroyed student curiosity. It seemed there was no alternative but to transform the schools or abandon them (Barrow, 1978; Gross, 1971; Sobel, 1968). The new radical perspectives on schooling and the movement to create open and alternative schools exemplified the tone of the late 1960s and early 1970s, and set an intellectual context for the newer social studies.

Then there were the issues. Never before in American history had a confluence of issues exploded upon the scene the way they did in the 1960s. Perhaps most prominent were the multicultural issues of race, class, and gender, with the antiwar movement equally if not more powerful in generating a growing opposition to mainstream culture. Though social studies journals and literature had given occasional though often superficial attention to racial issues, in the late 1960s, there was a burst of activity. An article by James A. Banks in 1969 recommended that, "Inquiries into black power, poverty, racism, the black revolt, and historical reactions to oppression should characterize social studies for black pupils" (p. 11). The April 1969 issue of *Social Education* was devoted, in its entirety to "Black Americans and Social Studies" and "minority groups in American society." Other special issues and articles followed, devoted to American Indians, and women in history. There were articles on "Women and the Language of Inequality," and "Clarifying Sexist Values." Later, there was a special section on "Eliminating Sexism From the Schools."

The 1971 NCSS Curriculum Guidelines embodied the tenor of the times, proposing an issues-centered approach to social studies. The guidelines, developed by an NCSS Task Force composed of Gary Manson, Gerald Marker, Anna Ochoa, and Jan Tucker suggested that students of social studies "should apply their knowledge, abilities, and commitments toward the improvement of the human condition." The guidelines included recommendations that social studies should be "directly related to concerns of students, focus on the real social world, draw from the social sciences, provide clear objectives and engaging and active learning experiences," .... "Deal with the Real Social World," and should emphasize social issues, controversial problems, study of race and cultural groups, and participation in the real world. They suggested that, "Schools ought to encourage minicourses, independent study, small group interest sections, specially planned days or weeks focused on social problems, alternative courses of study proposed by students, or other innovative plans for unfreezing the frigid school year" (NCSS, 1971).

What has been called the minicourse explosion may also be some indication of the possible impact of the guidelines, though there were no doubt many other influences contributing to this trend of the 1970s. In the April 1973 issue of the *The Clearing House* (Guenther & Ridgeway, 1973) a proposal was presented for the restructuring of traditional-length courses into a series of minicourses that are more accommodating of student interests and needs. Accompanying the proposal was a survey of minicourse offerings in schools, an indication that the trend was well underway by that time. A survey conducted in the mid-1970s indicated that 31% of the public high schools in Kansas had developed minicourse programs in social studies, most commonly in American history and government. The most frequently offered minicourses in American history were courses on the Civil War, recent American history, the American West, and the Colonies. The most frequently offered government courses were State and Local Government, the Presidency, The Constitution, and Youth and the Law (Guenther & Hansen, 1977; Guenther & Ridgeway, 1973).

A listing of social studies course offerings from Tamalpais High School in Marin, County, California, 1976–1977, provides a good example of a minicourse curriculum. The school offered 44 social studies courses, grouped under American Studies, World Studies, and General Studies, with 1 year of study required in each area. Most were one-semester in length, though a few were quarter-length courses. The list included many interesting sounding topical courses such as "Bread and Roses," "Minorities in American History," "Revolutionary Movements," "Is War

Necessary?" and "Human Sexuality," as well as the more traditional survey courses (Branson, 1977). This kind of rich array of alternatives to the usual social studies curriculum persisted in some school districts into the early 1980s.

The burst of issues oriented materials and concerns, reflecting 1960s issues in the society, had been building for some time. The origins of the newer social studies may be found in the burning issues of the times, and in a culmination of much of the educational thought and criticism of the 1960s. There were several influences at work behind the explosion. The tradition of issues-centered education was strong in the educational rhetoric of the times and may have had some influence on the thinking in journals and schools. The approach was a natural fit with 1960s social issues and the emerging alternative educational culture, and for a time it caught the attention and imagination of both teachers and the public. Its strong appeal and meteoric rise reflected the concerns of a time when the counter-culture and social criticism were in vogue, a time when American society was coming apart at the seams.

Unfortunately this burst of energy was short lived. The long-term trends in curriculum of the time were discipline-based, and by the mid-1970s, toward a back-to-basics approach. The war in Vietnam ended. Optimism was replaced by cynicism, spurred by Watergate, the perceived American failure overseas, and the continuing specter of nuclear holocaust. All denied the possibility of social improvement. During the 1970s both the new and newer social studies suffered due to attacks on teachers, textbooks, and curricular programs. Those attacks, especially when combined with a trend toward more traditional forms of schooling, marked the beginning of the end for a remarkable era.

AFTERMATH

In the late 1960s and early 1970s there were growing concerns over academic freedom which coincided with the growth of issues-oriented approaches in the newer social studies. A number of academic freedom cases signaled potential problems with public reactions to the new and newer curricular approaches, and likely had a chilling effect on attempts at reform. Textbook controversies recurred, stirred by conservative activists.

Academic Freedom Cases. There were several academic freedom cases involving individual teachers during the period. In one case an English teacher named Luke Callaway was dismissed from his position at a suburban Atlanta high school after implementing an open-ended curriculum. Another case involved history teacher Bennie G. Thompson, a young

African American teacher in Madison, Mississippi, and centered on the charge that Thompson presented for discussion and written assignments issues that were not popular with the County School Board and other members of the white power structure in Mississippi (National Education Association [NEA], 1970).

Another case involved Keith Sterzing, a high school political science and economics teacher in Sugarland, Texas, who frequently stressed current issues and debate, and often played a devil's advocate role in his classes. Following a 7½ year fight in federal court, Sterzing was awarded a $40,000 out-of-court settlement. The case was hailed as "precedential" in giving teachers wider latitude in dealing with controversial issues, though Sterzing never returned to teaching and was effectively silenced (Hartshorn, 1972; Matthews, 1975).

Another interesting case involved Francis Ahern who taught for 10 years at a Grand Island, Nebraska high school prior to attending an NDEA summer institute. Following the institute, she used student participation in planning her classes. While Ahern was attending a follow-up conference a student in her third period consumer politics class was struck by the substitute teacher, who followed a traditional method of instruction and classroom management. Subsequently, Ms. Ahern was ordered by the school principal to change her philosophy, not to discuss the incident with students, and to return to more traditional teaching methods. "Her philosophy does not fit in this school," he stated. She was later dismissed, her contract for the following school year rescinded (Judge Denies, 1970; NEA, 1970).

Another academic freedom case involving a Gay Liberation speaker left teachers feeling, "a bit gun-shy ... in the direction of censorship" (Kochheiser, 1975). Another case involved an English teacher, John Fogarty, who planned to use Ken Kesey's *One Flew Over the Cuckoo's Nest* with his students. Parents complained about "objectionable language," and the school principal ordered removal of the novel (Siegel, 1978).

There were also textbook controversies in a number of locations during the 1970s. Perhaps the most well known was the battle over adoption of more that 300 separate books from several publishers for use in language arts classes in Kanawha County, West Virginia, in 1973–1974. The battle was perhaps the most violent of any textbook controversy in the history of the nation, involving stormy meetings and several individual acts of violence and intimidation including dynamite used against school property and bullets shot at student-less school buses, spurred by citizens who wanted a school program "that emphasizes basic skills and patriotic indoctrination" (Clark, 1975).

A textbook controversy also occurred in Georgia over a series of new social studies textbooks on American history by Edwin Fenton. The State

Board of Education ruled out inclusion of the Fenton texts on a motion by one member, Kenneth Kilpatrick, who charged that the book tends "to create disruption and dissension in our society. In many respects it's a biased book" (Cutts, 1972; Linthicum, 1971).

Censorship pressures came from a number of sources, played a role in each of these cases, and certainly contributed to the national climate (Carp, 1968). One study reported a "probable decrease in educator's optimism about the climate for innovation in the nation" (Morrissett, 1975). Censorship pressures and academic freedom cases suggest a climate of growing restraint on teacher freedom. While a number of the contestants in the cases related above received support from the NEA's DuShane Fund, the NCSS Defense Fund, the ACLU or other sympathetic groups, the damage done by the charges and the interruption of teachers lives sent a message across the land that freedom had its limits.

The MACOS Controversy. The academic freedom battles of the 1970s climaxed in the MACOS controversy, which signaled the virtual end of the funding period for new social studies projects. Many conservatives and traditionalists who wanted the schools to transmit the "American way" perceived MACOS as a threat. MACOS, or Man: A Course of Study, drew from anthropological sources and focused on the middle Grades (4–6) and on the question, "What is human about human beings?" Dramatic and graphic scenes of Netsilik Eskimo life were included, among them a film depicting senilicide and other taboos of mainstream U.S. society (Dow, 1991).

In the fall of 1970 a parent and fundamentalist minister in Florida denounced MACOS as "hippie-jippie philosophy" and linked it to "humanism, socialism, gun control, and evolution." An avalanche of hostile criticism was unleashed. Critics included the John Birch Society, the Heritage Foundation, conservative columnist James J. Kilpatrick, and the Council for Basic Education, which was, ironically, an early supporter of new social studies reform (Goetz, 1995).

The federal funding behind MACOS inflamed the situation and led to assaults on the materials in Congress led by Congressman John B. Conlan of Arizona. The congressman charged that, "Thousands of parents across America view MACOS as a dangerous assault on cherished values and attitudes concerning morals, social behavior, religion, and our unique American economic and political lifestyle." Conlan quoted Dow's statement that MACOS is "designed to raise questions, not to answer them," but alleged that the materials give "the implicit view that man not only evolved from lower animals, but also derived his social behavior from them." He then charged that children are:

exposed for a full semester to the alien Netsilik Eskimo subculture, in which the following practices are rationalized and approvingly examined in free-wheeling classroom discussions:

- Killing the elderly and female infants
- Wife-swapping and trial marriage
- Communal living
- Witchcraft and the occult
- Cannibalism.

Conlan called the program a "brainwash" and heralded the congressional call for the end of federal funding for the "promotion and marketing" of classroom materials (Conlan, 1975; Dow, 1975). Subsequently, MACOS took a public relations beating. Sales of the program took a "precipitous fall" and never recovered (NCSS, 1975; Wiley, 1976). Despite internal disagreement within the NSF over how to handle the controversy, Director H. Guyford Stever caved under the pressure and cut funding to MACOS in order to salvage funds for other education programs (Paige, 1975, pp. 24–26). Following Stever's decision, funding for social studies curriculum reform was gutted, and the era of the new social studies was all but over.

In response to the MACOS controversy, in May, 1976, NCSS held a conference on "Freedom and Responsibility in the Selection and Use of Educational Materials and Learning Strategies in the Social Studies," at the Wingspread Conference Center in Wisconsin, receiving financial support from the Johnson Foundation. Congressman Conlan, invited to speak, sent his legislative assistant, George H. Archibald, whose remarks were revealing, offering a cultural conservative's critique of the new social studies. Archibald (1976) stated that since the efforts to stop federal funding to promote and market MACOS:

> We have found that hundreds of thousands of parents throughout the country view the academic-bureaucracy complex—comprised of the nation's colleges of education, the NEA and its state affiliates, in league with the Federal government with its vast power and resources—as the principal national threat to their values, families, spiritual, social, economic, and political freedoms, and our national heritage itself ... MACOS is an obvious example of global education—now called "world order education. (pp. 1, 17)

This was, in essence, the 1970s version of the "interlocking directorate" allegation against progressive education. Archibald went on to relate a partially factual history of an episode where the New Social Studies "got its start," at the Wingspread Conference in June, 1968, when "40 educationists met for a week's discussion about the need to radically revamp social studies." According to Archibald, the conference theme of "survival" recommended a curricular focus on the "arms buildup," and the gulf between rich and poor in the United States, along with "alleged social and economic injustice," pollution and natural resources "threatened" by "corporations and government," and the population explosion. "The Wingspread Report declared," Archibald continued, "that traditional practices and approaches were no longer adequate," and called for a new, interdisciplinary social studies centered around "Socratic dialogue, role playing, debate..." with more time devoted "to inquiry, analysis, and decision, less to the acquisition of facts."

Archibald (1976) called the 1968 Wingspread Conference,

> a classic example of an unrepresentative minority of educationists ... (seeking) ... to radically alter American education for the purpose of socio-economic and political change, without the approval of the people. This call for a new nationwide social studies curriculum centered around global studies and de-emphasizing American history and our American heritage, completely disregards the wishes of local citizens and taxpayers. (pp. 18–20, 25)

Archibald then made a strong case for traditional history and a return to the basics, a return "to perpetuating in their schools each community's social, religious, political, and economic way of life" (pp. 18–20, 25).

He closed his speech with the following warning:

> If you educators and the National Council for the Social Studies choose to press this ideological approach to public education, there will be a collision of major proportions between yourselves and the general public in every community throughout America.... Make no mistake about it: taxpayers and parents are ready to marshall every resource at their disposal to ensure that they win. And win they will. (p. 24)

Archibald's statement on behalf of Congressman Conlan sounded the ominous tone of a renewal of the war on social studies that had been going on for decades. Defenders and eloquent statements in support of academic freedom notwithstanding, the bottom line in the aftermath of the MACOS controversy was that there were profound limits on both teacher freedom and government support for curriculum materials development. Archibald gave voice to social studies reformers' worst fears.[2]

Earlier, controversies regarding academic freedom had contributed to the decline of progressive education. In this case, the impact of conservative critics was especially ironic because the new social studies was a discipline-based response to progressive education's excesses and seemed to match conservative preferences. The controversy over MACOS and other new social studies materials proved that even the disciplines and the new inquiry models, with students as junior social scientists, could be controversial because they asked students to develop their own conclusions. Educational conservatives and many members of the public, it seemed, wanted a more traditionally "American" and authoritative perspective fed to students.

The overall pattern of the era of the new and newer social studies seemed largely a replay of what had occurred during the progressive era, experimentation and development followed by attacks on teacher freedom and defensive statements from NCSS and various social studies spokespersons. Boom and bust, innovation and reaction had become a now familiar cycle to many in the social studies profession. To veteran teachers, the impact of all this must have seemed somewhat bewildering, if they were paying attention.

REFLECTIONS

To what extent had social studies as a field changed as a result of the reform movements and the millions of dollars devoted to support them? Course enrollment figures indicate some changes in social studies course offerings and enrollments during the era of the new social studies. While enrollments in history remained fairly steady, social science electives such as sociology and psychology grew dramatically, reflecting a new emphasis on the "other" social sciences. During the mid-to-late 1970s, reports on the status of social studies proliferated, a result of unprecedented federal funding for such research. Several surveys, based primarily on the NSF funded studies of science, math, and social studies came to somewhat similar and disappointing conclusions on the status of classroom practice in social studies, suggesting that recent reform efforts had made little difference. An interpretation of the NSF data, written by Shaver, Davis, and Helburn (1979) did a good job of summarizing the general findings. With the caveat that many exceptions can be found, their study revealed a pattern of constancy with traditional school and classroom practices, and little that was new. They found that materials from the new social studies were not used widely, and explained their lack of influence with the fact that "inquiry methods and suggestions for student participation education fly in the face" of teachers content orientation and need to maintain order (Shaver, 1979, p. 3).

A similar depiction of the status of social studies classroom practice was expressed by a number of other writers and researchers summarizing the NSF data and other sources (Morrissett and Project Span Staff, 1982; Ponder, 1979;Superka, Hawke, & Morrissett, 1980; Weiss, 1978; Wiley & Race, 1977). Two additional sources from the period provided historical and anthropological perspectives on the constancy of classroom teaching in social studies and other subjects. The first of these was an article by Hoetker and Ahlbrand (1969) titled, "The Persistence of the Recitation." The article concluded, based on a review of historical studies, that recitation, a question and answer pattern of instruction dominated by teacher talk, was a remarkably stable and dominant form of classroom verbal behavior over the past half century or longer. More recently, Larry Cuban argued much the same thing, that during the past 60 years, the social studies classroom has been dominated by teacher-centered instruction that includes lecture, the textbook as the solitary source of information, discussion, texts, and seatwork (Cuban, 1991).

Another important study of the 1970s with serious implications for social studies was Alan Peshkin's (1978) *Growing Up American* which provided strong evidence of a virulent socialization process with little or no counter-socialization and described an educational system clearly in-step with community desires for conformity and social control, and a social studies curriculum which inculcated allegiance to "God and Country" through a fairly traditional pattern of content and instruction.

At least one work on the status of social studies drew a more optimistic conclusion, finding that there is "a large unrealized potential for learning among youth and that it is possible for our school systems to move toward greater realization of that potential." The authors argued that "we know a great deal about learning and teaching" and about educational change and intervention, but that knowledge has been "insufficiently applied" Moreover, they suggested, the educational reform efforts of the 1960s and 1970s,

> while viewed by many as a source of chaos and frustration, supply many building blocks that can be used fruitfully in new efforts to improve the social studies ... (including) knowledge of new approaches to content and method, a large array of social problem areas from which to choose, a greatly expanded data base ... and an expanded corps of interested and experienced persons concerned with social studies improvement. (Superka, Hawke, & Morrissett, 1980, pp. 368–369)

While there was some truth to this positive spin, James Becker had predicted in 1965 that social studies was largely unchangeable. As it turned out, he was more or less correct. Institutional obstacles and external reactions suggested, once again, that reformers face a difficult task in any effort to change social studies.

In reflecting on the legacy of the new social studies, it seems that curricular change in social studies is possible but difficult to sustain and spread beyond a relatively small group of adherents. The ultimate failure of the new social studies reform movement was due to a complex set of conditions that make most any effort at educational reform difficult. As to the extent of adoption of new social studies materials, terminology, and practices, there is little evidence that the adoption of materials got very far. Analysts of the NSF case studies reported that fewer that 20% of teachers heard of or used the materials. John Haas, who authored the most complete previous history of the new social studies, suggested that it had an influence on, at most, 5% of teachers. Nonetheless, a number of studies found that teachers reported using the approaches associated with the new social studies movement, particularly inquiry, concepts, and simulation games. Moreover, respondents to one survey agreed that teaching styles were materially influenced by the new social studies projects, though the projects themselves had only minimal influence on textbook selection and materials adoption. However, they reported very limited use of the new projects in schools. Yet, a number of projects did wield influence, among them the High School Geography Project, the Carnegie-Mellon History Project, Sociological Resources for the Social Studies, American Political Behavior, and the Public Issues Series of the Harvard Project. At the elementary level, among the most influential were MACOS, the TABA Social Studies Program, and Senesh's Our Working World (Gross, 1971). Evidence from other sources suggests that the terminology of the movement had a wider, though more superficial impact. So, it is clear that the new social studies movement was not a complete debacle. Nonetheless, it largely disappointed the lofty expectations of its proponents, project directors, and staunch advocates. Reasons for its failure to have the expected influence relate to the sociopolitical context of the 1960s and early 1970s, the nature of the reforms proposed, and attributes of the school as an institution as well as elements of the culture in which teaching and learning are embedded.

The social, political, and cultural context of schooling profoundly influenced creation of the new social studies and largely precipitated its decline. As we have seen the new social studies projects were a stepchild of Sputnik. They had their origins in the curriculum politics of the Cold War, and their orientation was, in part, a legacy of manpower studies conducted by the CIA, and of the general climate of the times favoring the academic disciplines, and taking a critical stance toward progressivism and its meliorist focus aimed at social progress. It was, in the final analysis, a curriculum reform movement born of national security concerns. From 1968 on, the social studies was confronted by a new context created by protests against the Vietnam war, the Civil Rights Movement, a youth rebellion, a new focus on the problems of the disadvantaged both in school and out, the widespread alienation of youth, and the paradox created by the distance between purported national values and social realities. As a consequence, the society, and curriculum reform projects, were subject to a more critical assessment. Instead of being seen as a smoothly functioning institution operating for the benefit of all, schools were increasingly viewed as problematic.

Another major factor in the failure of the new social studies was related to the nature of the reforms proposed. The reforms were largely aimed at replacing the existing social studies curriculum, a revolutionary rather than evolutionary intent. Yet, taken as a program, the new social studies projects and materials did not offer a coherent alternative to what had become the standard scope and sequence and the traditional approach to teaching relying on textbooks, lecture, seatwork, discussion, and tests. There was no overall plan or scope and sequence alternative proposed as part of the reform. In addition, many of the reform projects and the materials generated lacked a strong rationale or a clear purpose, an element that is crucial for any reform's success (Nachtigal, 1972). Though almost all of the materials which resulted from the projects were of high quality, their interest generating power was "misperceived" by many teachers who adopted the materials. As it turned out, their use frequently required a thoughtful and committed teacher preparation and did not result in a magical and automatic increase in student interest (Marker, 1980). Many of the projects created materials especially for the same slot in the school program, senior year social science electives, thus limiting their influence in the total school program (Fenton, 1985). Moreover, many of the materials created were not highly readable for the majority of students. Average and below-average students were generally not well served by the materials.

The projects and materials also made unarticulated and mistaken assumptions about the culture of schooling. They assumed that the project materials and their conceptualization would be compatible with the prevailing culture of the schools. Unfortunately, this turned out not to be the case. The philosophy and materials produced were largely incompatible with the prevailing culture of schools. In fact, one analyst suggests that the new social studies movement "proceeded in the absence of any well-developed or explicit theory or conception of the sociology of schools and schooling." The architects of the new social studies assumed that old content could be extracted and replaced with new content; that if social studies teachers could be taught to think seriously about their work, they would adopt the new reforms; and, that schooling as an institution served functions of social equality, individual development, and social integration.

Unfortunately, on the whole, these assumptions were faulty. The integrative function was predominant, with schools serving to socialize students to a society characterized by extensive social stratification. Schools served as selection and certification agencies, measuring, sorting, and labeling students. Thus, instructional materials, teaching practices, and the content itself became mechanisms for the process of socialization and were functional in the school environment as they contributed to the process of sorting and labeling. Reforms in social studies were valued, at least in part, for the degree to which they were compatible with this function. Many features of the new social studies were at odds with this basic sociocultural function of schooling (Anderson, 1982).

From a critical perspective, the discipline-centered curricula created by the majority of new social studies projects served to draw a veil between students and more immediate concerns in the community. The projects generally focused upon forms of knowledge that moved students away from the particular and the local. The scientific and structural nature of the knowledge encapsulated in the reform served the latent function of socializing students into a way of thinking that too frequently discouraged students from making connections with everyday realities. Detachment from social relationships can make those relationships less amenable to individual control and gives greater power and legitimacy to experts who interpret reality. Thus, the new social studies could be seen as a curriculum driven by secondary abstractions which move students away from face-to-face confrontation with value dilemmas and conflict situations (Popkewitz, 1975). Moreover, creation of teacher-proof materials treated teachers as mere technicians. By and large, the new social studies projects did not ask teachers to arrive at their own philosophical rationale for social studies and to develop their own congruent approaches to teaching. Instead, teachers were often offered the opportunity to implement materials created by university researchers, an opportunity proffered from above. Hence, this was an approach to reform that was in many instances, undemocratic.

The reform plan under which these new social studies programs were implemented was equally flawed. According to many postmortem evaluations, the new social studies movement and other curriculum reform efforts of the time made serious strategic errors. It was a top-down, hierarchical approach to reform designed by university researchers who had little experience in schools. Teachers and professors of education were seldom involved in the design of the materials. A Rand study of the process of educational change suggested that district-level support and commitment were crucial, and that projects designed by "outside experts," or which utilized commercially prepared materials, generally failed to gather the necessary support (Greenwood, Mann, & McLaughlin, 1975). Another evaluation study implied that reformers sought to influence too many schools, that objectives and techniques were not sharply defined, that many projects failed to reach clear agreement on their specific purpose, nature, and limitations. Those projects which were most successful had a clear operating design and a charismatic, hard-working, and omnipresent director (Nachtigal, 1972).

Critical aspects of the school as an institution also created obstacles to the success of the reform movement, and made it likely that teachers would stick with the more traditional teaching approaches, or return to them after a period of experimentation. The reformers generally seemed to hold naïve conceptions on the perspectives of teachers and students and the inertia and persistence of traditional teaching practices. Most teachers were severely constrained by the conditions under which they worked: 5 classes a day, 30 or 40 students per class, 2 or 3 preparations per night, and additional nonteaching duties. Hard to change institutional factors, which Tyack and Cuban have called the grammar of schooling, made it hard for teachers to adopt new ways, even when they wanted to (Fenton, 1991; Tyack & Cuban, 1995). Moreover, students, other teachers, and most administrators expected traditional forms of teaching. By the 1970s, many of the teachers who used new social studies materials had come to view the programs as "a parade of fads" (Nelson & Drake, 1994).

The newer social studies which emerged in the late 1960s was in many respects a revitalized, reconstructionist oriented progressive education. With the new social studies it shared an inquiry orientation, but there the similarities ended. The newer social studies were driven by the very societal change and turmoil which had upset the new social studies. Where the earlier program focused on the structure-of-the-disciplines, the newer trend championed valuing, relevance, and social activism. In the context of civil rights marches, antiwar protests, student sit-ins, and the sex and drug revolts, the new social studies seemed archaic. The newer movement did, however, share a similar fate to the new social studies. Its impact on the field was similarly limited.

Several aspects of the era have continuing implications for us today. First, money and power, from the government, foundations, and other sources, seem to readily influence the direction of rhetoric on social studies, and may have some influence on curricular content, though they have less influence on pedagogy and entrenched patterns of classroom and school practice. The "grammar of schooling" seems largely resistant to reform (Tyack & Cuban, 1995). Second, manpower concerns have played a critical role in the rhetoric and influence of educational reform since the mid-twentieth century and earlier. The perceived need to develop technical manpower to win the Cold War in the form of developing more scientists and engineers, and then social scientists and students who could emulate the social scientist mode of thought and research, was a mainstay of the curriculum reform movement. In more recent years, reformers have continued to push for schooling to develop other forms of human capital, with a continued focus on improving performance in math and science. In each case, the direction of reform created a skewed and limited vision of education which largely ignored important value questions and social issues.

A third implication may be found by considering the top-down, scientific model for reform embodied in the new social studies projects, and the science and math reforms which preceded them, which had origins in wartime weapons research. The current reform movement, built around accountability via the imposition of standards and high stakes testing, also employs a top-down, scientific model for reform, though with more significant influence from a business orientation and mentality. In both cases, a link to national security and economic progress is a central component.

Fourth, the inquiry and structure-of-the-disciplines approach common to the era of the new social studies, and the social reconstructionist, issues-oriented approach of the newer social studies have their counterparts today in the current literature of school reform. The recent interest in authentic pedagogy and constructivism has many similarities to the Brunerian reforms of the new social studies era. The banner of the issues-oriented newer social studies maintains a strong presence in the literature of the field. All of these similarities suggest the cyclical nature of efforts at school reform, and reflect the general resistance of educational institutions and practices to reform, regardless of its origins or direction.

NOTES

1. Substantial portions of the text of this manuscript are drawn from the author's recent book on the history of social studies. Additional materials from the original draft manuscript, cut from the book due to length considerations, are also included here. The book's thesis is that what began as a struggle over the curriculum among competing camps evolved into a war on social studies that has changed the curriculum. The book's framework is focused on the struggle among camps which are multiple, overlapping, and not always distinct. These include: traditional history, social science, education for social efficiency, meliorist or progressive, critical/social reconstructionist, consensus/eclectic and more. See Ronald W. Evans, *The Social Studies Wars: What Should We Teach the Children?* (New York: Teachers College, 2004).

    The manuscript is also drawn from an extensive review of primary and secondary sources including literature pertaining to the teaching of history and the social sciences, that is, books, journals, bulletins, and so forth, from the time under study, primary source materials from several archives including the archives of the National Council for the Social Studies, the National Archives Civilian Record Unit, and the National Academy of Sciences. The chapter also draws on previously published works on the history of social studies and curriculum, and numerous doctoral dissertations.

Finally, the manuscript draws on portions of the author's draft (in preparation) of a book-length volume on the era of the new social studies tentatively titled, *The Tragedy of American School Reform: How Big Science, Big Government, and Big Business Have Diverted Us from Democracy.*

2. In 2003 the National Film Board of Canada produced a documentary on the MACOS controversy. "Through These Eyes." 2003. Fifty-five minutes. Color. Charles Laird (Dir.). Distributed by Documentary Educational Resources, Watertown, MA. See Jay Ruby. (2005). Anthropology as a subversive art: A review of Through These Eyes. *American Anthropologist, 107*(4), pp. 684–693.

REFERENCES

Anderson, L. F. (1982). Barriers to change in social studies. In I. R. Morrissett, C. Hawk, & D. Superka (Eds.), *The current state of social studies: A report of project SPAN* (pp. 265–313). Boulder, CO: Social Science Education Consortium.

Announcement for project social studies. (1962). *Social Education, 26,* 300.

Archibald, G. H. (1976, May 16). George Archibald speech at the NCSS Wingspread Conference. Wingspread Conference Center, Racine, Wisconsin. "Wingspread Conference" folder box 2, Accession #850625, NCSS Archives, Gottesman Library, Teachers College, Columbia University.

Banks, J. A. (1969, January). Relevant social studies for Black pupils. *Social Education, 33,* 66–68.

Barrow, R. (1978). *Radical education: A critique of freeschooling and deschooling.* New York: Wiley.

Becker, J. M. (1965). Prospect for change in the social studies. *Social Education, 29,* 20–22.

Bestor, A. (1953). *Educational wastelands: The retreat from learning in our public schools.* Urbana: University of Illinois Press.

Branson, M. S. (1977). The status of social studies: Marin County. *Social Education, 41,* 591-594.

Bruner, J. (1959). Memorandum to the work group on the apparatus of teaching, "General" folder, Woods Hole Papers, National Academy of Sciences Archive, Washington, DC.

Bruner, J. (1960). *The process of education.* Cambridge, MA: Harvard University Press.

Bruner, J. (1971). The process of education revisited. *Phi Delta Kappan, 53,* 18–21.

Bruner, J. (1983). *In search of mind: Essays in autobiography.* New York: Harper & Row.

Carp, R. A. (1968). Censorship pressure on social studies teachers. *Social Education, 32,* 487–488, 492.

Clark, T. (1975). The West Virginia textbook controversy: A personal account. *Social Education, 39,* 216–119.

Committee on Manpower Resources for National Security. (1953). Manpower resources for national security: A report to the director of the Office of Defense Mobilization, "Committee on Manpower Resources for National Security" folder, subject file "M," box 11, 1951–1956, RG 307, Alan T. Waterman Papers, National Science Foundation Director's Office Files, National Archives II, College Park, Maryland.

Conlon, J. B. (1975). MACOS: The push for a uniform national curriculum. *Social Education, 39,* 388–392.

Cuban, L. (1991). History of teaching in social studies. In J. P. Shaver. (Ed.), *Handbook of research on social studies teaching and learning* (pp. 197–209). New York: Macmillan.

Cutts, B. (1972, May 19). Educators won't finance textbook: But 'Americans' is not Banned. *The Atlanta Constitution,* p. 6-A.

Dow, P. B. (1975). MACOS revisited: A commentary on the most frequently asked questions about Man: A Course of Study. *Social Education, 39,* 388, 393–398

Dow, P. B. (1991). *Schoolhouse politics: Lessons from the Sputnik era.* Cambridge, MA: Harvard University Press.

Eisenhower, D. D. (1953). Dwight D. Eisenhower to Arthur S. Fleming, August 1, 1953, "Subject files, M," Box 11, RG 307, National Science Foundation Director's Office Files, National Archives II, College Park, Maryland.

Evans, R. W. (2004). *The social studies wars: What should we teach the children?* New York: Teachers College Press.

Evans, R. W. (2007). *This happened in America: Harold Rugg and the censure of social studies.* Charlotte, NC: Information Age.

Fenton, E. P. (1964). *32 problems in world history.* Glenview, IL: Scott, Foresman.

Fenton, E. P. (1985, November). *Reflections on the "new social studies."* Paper presented at the annual meeting of the National Council for the Social Studies, Chicago.

Fenton, E. P. (1991). Reflections on the "new social studies." *The Social Studies, 82,* 84–90.

Fenton, E. P., & Good, J. M. (1965). Project social studies: A progress report. *Social Education, 29,* 206–208.

Fine, B. (1954). Russia is overtaking U. S. in training of technicians, November 7, 1954, *New York Times,* November 7, 1954, "Scientists and Engineers File," box 71, Record Group 12, United States Office of Education Commissioner's Office Files, 1939-1980, National Archives II, College Park, Maryland.

Fleming, A. S. (1954). Arthur S. Fleming, Director, Office of Defense Mobilization, to Dwight D. Eisenhower, January 6, 1954, "Subject files, M," Box 11, RG 307, National Science Foundation Director's Office Files, National Archives II, College Park, Maryland.

Flynn, J. T. (1951, October). Who owns your child's mind? *The Reader's Digest,* pp. 23–28.

Goetz, W. W. (1995). The rise and fall of MACOS: A blip on the historical screen? *Theory and Research in Social Education, 23,* 515–522.

Goldstein, J. S. (1992). *A different sort of time: The life of Jerrold Zacharias.* Cambridge, MA: MIT Press.

Greenwood, P. W., Mann, D., & McLaughlin, M. W. (1975). *Federal programs supporting educational change: The process of change* (Vol. III). Santa Monica, CA: Rand.

Gross, R. (1971). From innovations to alternatives: A decade of change in education. *Phi Delta Kappan, 70*, 22–24.

Guenther, J., & Hansen, P. (1977). Organizational change in the social studies: Mini-course subject options. *Educational Leadership, 34*, 64–68.

Guenther, J., & Ridgeway, R. (1973). Mini-courses: Promising alternative to the social studies. *The Clearing House, 47*, 486–489.

Haas, J. D. (1977). *The era of the new social studies.* Boulder, CO: Social Science Education Consortium.

Halsey, V. R., Jr. (1963). American history: A new high school course. *Social Education, 27*, 249–252.

Hartshorn, M. (1972, May 1). Memo from Merrill Hartshorn to NCSS Legal Defense Fund. File: Sterzing Case Correspondence and Clippings, Box 44, Series 4D, NCSS Archive.

Herndon, J. (1968). *The way it spozed to be.* New York: Simon & Shuster.

Hoetker, J., & Ahlbrand, W. P. (1969). The persistence of the recitation. *American Educational Research Journal, 6*(2), 145–167.

Holt, J. (1964). *How children fail.* New York: Pittman.

Holt, J. (1967). *How children learn.* New York: Pittman.

Goldstein, J. S. (1992). *A different sort of time: The life of Jerrold R. Zacharias; scientist, engineer, educator.* Cambridge, MA: Massachusetts Institute of Technology.

Goodman, P. (1960). *Growing up absurd: Problems of youth in the organized system.* New York: Random House.

Goodman, P. (1966). *Compulsory mis-education, and the community of scholars.* New York: Vintage Books.

Gutek, G. (1986). *Education in the United States: An historical perspective.* Englewood Cliffs, NJ: Prentice-Hall.

Illich, I. (1971). *Deschooling society.* New York: Harper & Row.

Jones, K., & Olivier, R. (1956). *Progressive education is REDucation.* Boston: Meador.

Judge denies dismissal plea. (1970, February 11). *Grand Island Independent.*

Keller, C. R. (1961, September 16). Needed: Revolution in the social studies. *Saturday Review*, 60–62.

Kochheiser, C. (1975). What happened when a speaker for gay liberation addressed high school students. *Social Education, 39*, 219–221.

Kozol, J. (1967). *Death at an early age.* Boston: Houghton Mifflin.

Krug, M. M. (1966). Bruner's new social studies: A critique. *Social Education, 30*, 400-406.

Lansner, K. (Ed.). (1958). *Second rate brains.* New York: Doubleday News Books.

Leinwand, G. (1968). The year of the non-curriculum: A proposal. *Social Education, 32*, 542–545, 549.

Leinwand, G. (Ed.). (1968–1969). *Problems of American society* (series). New York: Washington Square Press.

Linthicum, T. (1971, December). School bars 10 texts by Fenton. *The Atlanta Constitution*, 17.

Lynd, A. (1953). *Quackery in the public schools.* Boston: Little, Brown.

Marker, G. W. (1980). Why schools abandon the "new social studies" materials. *Theory and Research in Social Education, 7*(4), 35–57.

Matthews, J. (1975, June 10). Fired teacher settles for $40,000. *Washington Star,* A-2.

Morrissett, I. R. (1975). Curriculum information network, fourth report: Controversies in the classroom. *Social Education, 29,* 246–252.

Morrissett, I. R., & Project Span Staff. (1982). *The current state of social studies: A Report of Project SPAN.* Boulder, CO: Social Science Education Consortium.

Nachtigal, P. (1972). *A foundation goes to school: The Ford Foundation Comprehensive School Improvement Program, 1960–1970.* New York: Ford Foundation.

National Council for the Social Studies. (1975, June 20). The MACOS question: Views of 'Man: A course of study,' and the roles of the National Science Foundation and the federal government in curriculum development and implementation. Box 1, Executive Director Office Files, 1974-1980, Accession # 820912, NCSS Archive.

National Council for the Social Studies Task Force on Curriculum Guidelines. (1971). Social studies curriculum guidelines. *Social Education, 35,* 853–867.

National Education Association. (1970). Callaway and Thompson cases. NCSS Archive, "Academic Freedom" folder, box 1, series 10, Special Projects, 1933-1973, NCSS Archive, Gottesman Libraries, Teachers College, Columbia University.

National Intelligence Survey. (1953). "National Intelligence Survey, U.S.S.R., Section 44, Manpower," February 1, 1953, Record Group 263, National Intelligence Surveys, 1948-1965, Box 125, National Archives II, College Park, Maryland.

National Intelligence Survey. (1958). "National Intelligence Survey, U.S.S.R., Section 44, Manpower," January 01, 1958, Record Group 263, National Intelligence Surveys, 1948-1965, Box 125, National Archives II, College Park, Maryland.

National Intelligence Survey. (1963). "National Intelligence Survey, U.S.S.R., Section 44, Manpower," March 1, 1963, Record Group 263, National Intelligence Surveys, 1948-1965, Box 125, National Archives II, College Park, Maryland.

Needell, A. A. (1998). Project Troy and the Cold War annexation of the social sciences. In C. Simpson (Ed.), *Universities and empire: Money and politics in the social sciences during the Cold War* (pp. 3–38). New York: The New Press.

Neill, A. S. (1960). *Summerhill: A radical approach to child rearing.* New York: Hart.

Nelson, L. R., & Drake, F. R. (1994). Secondary teachers' reactions to the new social studies. *Theory and Research in Social Education, 22,* 44–73.

Paige, L. J. (1975). J. M. England interview with Dr. Lowell J. Paige, Assistant Director for Education, "Interview Lowell J. Paige, August 20, 1975" folder, Box 44, Record Group 304, National Archives II, College Park, Maryland.

Peshkin, A. (1978). *Growing up American: Schooling and the survival of community.* Chicago: University of Chicago Press.

Ponder, G. (1979, April). The more things change … : The status of social studies. *Educational Leadership,* 515–518.

Popkewitz, T. (1975, November). *Latent values in discipline-centered curriculum.* Paper presented at the annual meeting of the national council for the social studies, Atlanta, Georgia.

Postman, N., & Weingartner, C. (1969). *Teaching as a subversive activity.* New York: Delacorte.

Proposed Conference (1958). Memo from Advisory Board on Education, to Lanier et al., March 5, 1958. Enclosure, "Proposed Conference on Psychological Research in Education," "Proposed conf." folder, Advisory Board on Education, National Academy of the Sciences Archives, Washington, DC.

Reactions to the Reports on Project Social Studies. (1965). *Social Education, 29,* 356–360.

Reimer, E. (1971). *School is dead: Alternatives in education.* Garden City, NJ: Doubleday.

Rickover, H. G. (1959). *Education and freedom.* New York: E. P. Dutton.

Robinson, D. W. (1963). Ferment in the social studies. *Social Education, 27,* 360–364, 410.

Root, E. M. (1958). *Brainwashing in the high schools.* New York: Devin-Adair.

Rudolph, J. L. (2002). From world war to Woods Hole: The use of wartime reasearch models for curriculum reform. *Teachers College Record, 104*(2), 212–241.

Russian science threatens the west. (1954, September). *Nation's Business,* 42–54, in "Scientists and Engineers" folder, Box 71, Scientists, Record Group 12, U. S. Office of Education, Commissioner's Office Files, 1939–1980, National Archives II, College Park, Maryland.

Shaver, J. P. (1967). Social studies: The need for redefinition. *Social Education, 31,* 588–592, 596.

Shaver, J. P. (1979). Status in social studies and educational innovation: Implications of the NSF and the RAND reports for the ABA Youth Education for Citizenship Education Committee, A Summary of Comments by James P. Shaver at the October 6, 1979 meeting of the YEFC Committee, from the personal fliles of James P. Shaver.

Shaver, J. P., Davis, O. L. Jr., & Helburn, S. W. (1979). The status of social studies education: Impressions from Three NSF Studies. *Social Education, 42,* 150–153.

Siegel, B. (1978, March 12). Cuckoo drops a bomb on private world. *Los Angeles Times,* Part IV, pp. 1, 16–19.

Silberman, C. (1970). *Crisis in the classroom: The remaking of American education.* New York: Random House.

Smith, G. R. (1963). Project social studies—a report. *Social Education, 27,* 357–359, 409.

Sobel, H. W. (1968). The new wave of educational literature. *Phi Delta Kappan, 50,* 109–111.

Superka, D. P., Hawke, S., & Morrissett, I. R. (1980). The current and future status of social studies. *Social Education, 44*(5), 362–369.

Tyack, D., & Cuban, L. (1995). *Tinkering toward utopia: A century of public school reform.* Cambridge, MA: Harvard University Press.

Weiss, I. R. (1978). *Report of the 1977 national survey of science, mathematics, and social studies education: Final report* (Report No. RT 1/1266/06-01 F). Research Triangle Park, NC: Center for Educational Research and Evaluation.

Whaley, R. M. (1958). R. M. Whaley Notes, National Academy of Sciences—National Research Council Governing Board, Advisory Board on Education, Meeting re: PSSC, April 22, 1958, "Coordination with MIT PSSC/Formation of ESI" folder, Governing Board, Advisory Board on Education, 1958, National Academy of Sciences Archives, Washington, DC.

Wiley, K. B. (1976). *The NSF science education controversy: Issues, events, decisions.* Boulder, CO: ERIC Clearinghouse for Social Studies/Social Science Education and Social Science Education Consortium.

Wiley, K. B., & Race, J. (1977). *The status of pre-college science, mathematics, and social science education: 1955–1975. Volume III: Social science education.* Washington, DC: National Science Foundation.

Zacharias, J. R. (1956). Jerrold Zacharias to James Killian, March, 1956, "Movie Aids for Teaching Physics in High School." In J. S. Goldstein (Ed.), *A different sort of time: The life of Jerrold R. Zacharias* (p. 152). Cambridge, MA: MIT Press.

SECTION I

PEOPLE

CHAPTER 2

HILDA TABA

Social Studies Reform From the Bottom Up

Barbara Slater Stern

INTRODUCTION

Causality, conflict, cooperation, cultural change, differences, interdependence, modification, power, societal control, tradition and values.
—Taba, Durkin, Fraenkel, & NcNaughton (1971, pp. 24–26)

These 11 key concepts form the core of the Contra Costa K–8 social studies curriculum program developed by Hilda Taba, her research team and most importantly, the teachers who would be teaching this curriculum. The development of that curriculum encompassed the last 16 years of Taba's life from 1951–1967 and is the culmination of her life's work in teacher education and curriculum development. And, while it is technically somewhat early for the label "the New Social Studies," the case can easily be made that when analyzing the final product, the resultant curriculum marks a definitive break from traditional social studies practice and

The New Social Studies: People, Projects, and Perspectives, pp. 41–61
Copyright © 2010 by Information Age Publishing

aligns itself clearly with the foundational beliefs and goals of the New Social Studies movement. This chapter examines the Taba social studies program as a beacon of hope for meaningful social studies teaching and learning in an age of standardization and high stakes testing. Taba is particularly instructive in this arena as her curriculum development model, based on the "traditional" Tyler Rationale, included evaluation of learning as a major component of all curriculum planning, not as an afterthought. Further, according to Jack Fraenkel (personal communication, February 12, 2007), the concepts, once extrapolated, can form the basis of a national or state curriculum while still allowing for the factual content to remain locally decided. This idea suggests a compromise that could please the major stakeholders advocating various social studies curricula today.

In order to understand the relevance of Taba's ideas today, this chapter first will briefly examine Taba's beliefs about teaching and learning, the curriculum development process and the needs of modern society. Then, the Contra Costa program will be explained and sampled. The chapter will continue with a discussion of the links between the Taba social studies program and the "New Social Studies" to demonstrate the synchronicity of her ideas with the goals and objectives of that movement. Last, the relevance of these ideas today will be presented in a discussion of a short lived, modern curriculum, Florida *Connections, Challenges, and Choices* by analyzing the difficulties facing educators wishing to implement meaningful reform.

Background: Curriculum, Teaching, and Learning

Hilda Taba was born in Kooraste, a small town in southeast Estonia in December, 1902. She came from a large family that valued education as her father was a teacher. After graduating from the Viru High School for Girls and, according to Krull, a professor at Taba's alma mater the University of Tartu, she decided to become an elementary teacher and passed her qualifying exam for certification at the Didactic Seminar of Tartu. However, she but changed her mind and instead matriculated at the university where under the tutelage of the faculty of philosophy she received her AB degree in history and education in 1926 (Krull, 2003). It was during this time that she was first exposed to progressive education and the ideas of John Dewey. Upon her graduation, Taba received a fellowship to continue her studies in the United States and after only 1 year of coursework, she received her master's degree from Bryn Mawr College in 1927 where she had continued exploring ideas central to progressive education philosophy. Taba then moved to New York City to complete doctoral work at Teachers College, Columbia University graduating in 1931 and publishing her dissertation, *The Dynamics of Education*, in 1932.

According to the *Education Encyclopedia* (2007b), Taba's dissertation established a foundation for much of her later work by focusing on three key ideas. First, she argued that learning and the study of learning should be modeled after dynamic models derived from contemporary physics. As opposed to a transmission model of education and evaluation, educators should see learning as a dynamic, interactive phenomena informed by the field of cognitive psychology. Second, in keeping with the ideas of John Dewey and the progressives, she argued that education for democracy was a critical component of contemporary schooling and curricula, and that it needed to be experiential, that is, children learn to solve problems and resolve conflicts together. This thinking in democratic education foreshadowed constructivist curricula and the workshop approach to curriculum development. Third, she argued that educators had to provide conceptually sound curriculum that was organized and taught effectively, and that student understanding had to be evaluated using appropriate tools and processes.

Unable to find a suitable position back home in Estonia, Taba retuned to the United States and accepted a position with a progressive private school in New York, The Dalton School (Education Encyclopedia, 2007a). Taba worked with teachers in her role as curriculum director. The Dalton school plan was to develop curriculum that would "revolve around a central theme that reflected recurrent and perennial problems in human life and thought (Isham, 1984). Specific subject areas and content would be chosen by three criteria: the relevance of a problem to understanding civilization including the significance and persistence of the problem; the extent to which any given academic content sheds lights on or assists with the understandings and concepts necessary for the intelligent mind; and the level of understanding and interest of the material chosen to the students. According to Isham, these first two criteria related to selection of themes and academic content and the third criterion related to the needs and interests of the learners (p. 87). Important considerations behind this curriculum included an emphasis on the needs of the students rather than on the subject matter, a reduction of the scope and number of problems to reduce traditional coverage and replace it with depth, experiential learning, encouragement of student initiative, integration of subject matter and the creation of a unified curriculum that was continuous over years to provide continuity emphasizing those topics that would lead to understanding contemporary society (p. 93).

When the Dalton School's decided to participate in the "Eight Year Study"—an evaluation of progressive school programs to assess how students from progressive schools would perform in college—Taba met

Ralph Tyler, director of the study. In 1935 Taba accepted an invitation from Tyler to join the Eight Year Study evaluation team working out of the Ohio State University. Taba was put in charge of the team evaluating social sensitivity, a topic related to the goal of preparing students for effective democratic participation. "Social sensitivity" focuses on attitudes about class, race and ethnicity generally seen in students' social lives rather than in their academic preparation. In developing instruments that would accomplish the task, Taba became one of the major consultants to social studies teachers (Isham, 1984, p. 106). Taba's approach was to work "bottom up" starting with the teachers, meeting to identify problems, formulate objectives, clarify the meaning of the objectives and then design, develop and field test evaluation instruments.

The important factor is the understanding that for Taba the process centered on the team and their work with the teachers was to define, clarify, restate, and insure that everyone involved in education was working with the same definitions and criteria. This was amplified by Taba's learning, through these meetings, the difficulty the teachers had in "working with, identifying, and selecting significant ideas" (Isham, 1984, p. 116). Thus, a crucial part of any Taba curriculum plan became staff development—working intensively, often in workshops, with teachers to assist them in understanding the concepts, ideas, and pedagogy necessary to implement the curriculum. This approach involved the teachers struggling over a significant time period with what was important and, only once that step was achieved, with how to teach that material effectively. Significantly, the very first step was for the teachers to identify problems they were having in their classsrooms with the curriculum and/or student learning. Everything flowed from the felt problems of the teachers with curriculum changes coming afterwards as part of the solution to the teachers' problems. Another basic understanding of Taba's was that until teachers truly understood their curriculum—what they were doing and why they were doing it, no significantly effective learning could take place in their classrooms. In other words, deep teacher understanding promotes student learning.

Upon completion of the Eight Year Study, Taba taught curriculum courses at the University of Chicago until, in 1944, she was asked to head the Intergroup Education in Cooperating Schools project sponsored by the American Council on Education and Funded by the National Conference of Christians and Jews (Middaugh & Perlstein, 2005). This was not only a natural outgrowth of her work on social sensitivity but also a response to the changes in demographics of America's cities in the wake of World War II and the problems created by these changes that were the impetus behind this project. As project director, Taba called for educators to: "develop students' empathy toward the perspectives of different cultures, and appreciation of their richness." Taba's approach was consistent with her prior work; thus she began by asking the teachers gathered in the Integroup workshops to diagnose their students' situations and needs. This diagnosis, typical of the progressive philosophy of education, would shape the curricular choices of the teachers. While the units of study would vary according to the needs of the students, the overall objective of prejudice reduction would remain constant for all participating schools. The important idea here is that the while specific academic content may change for a given locality, the overarching conceptual framework reflects what is currently referred to as the "big ideas" or the "essential questions" (see for example: Newmann & Associates, 1996; or Wiggins & McTighe, 2005).

Isham (1984) summarized Taba's experience with the Intergroup Education Project by demonstrating how her use of action research projects focused teachers on their own concerns and values while the use of consultants (Taba's team) as facilitators assisted teachers in interpreting data about student needs and translating that data into "workable, meaningful curriculum experience (p. 183). Further, he credits the ideas about the sequence of curriculum development and learning experiences to this project summarizing the steps as a rational process beginning with teachers understanding the needs and demands of learners and society, and then brainstorming instructional objectives from those needs and demands. These objectives would be tentative and serve as guides for materials and instructional strategies. Continual evaluation would be needed as the curriculum was assessed in effectiveness and objectives were continually refined. It is these background experiences that Taba drew upon when she moved to California as a professor of education at San Francisco State College starting in 1951 and began her work as a consultant with the social studies teachers in Contra Costa, California.

The Contra Costa Social Studies Program

As she embarked on her final curriculum development project, Taba remained consistent with the general beliefs and process for creating meaningful curriculum described above. Middaugh and Perlstein (2005) illustrate stating:

> Taba remained committed to deepening students' understandings of themselves and their world; to teaching them to think independently, abstractly and rationally; and to fostering the social and academic knowledge and skills necessary for participating effectively and humanely in a rapidly changing world…. The regular social studies program needed to be grounded in a synthesis of social science and the "core values" of a democratic society…. Instead of preparing students to solve the as yet unforeseen problems they

would confront as adults, social studies classes imposed an "obsolescent" curriculum. "Teaching for coverage of descriptive, factual knowledge," Taba charged, "burden[ed] the memory without training the mind." The Taba curriculum, on the other hand, focused on "durable knowledge, such as powerful generalizations, significant ideas and concepts." The ultimate goal was "continuous development of an increasingly complex mental organization ... with which to view the world and to solve problems of a diverse and pluralistic democratic society. (pp. 249–250)

The creation of this curriculum involved intensive work with the social studies teachers, her research team and the curriculum consultants for the school district. The development of the curriculum spanned 16 years and it is likely, that had Taba's untimely death not occurred, it would have continued indefinitely in keeping with the dynamic view of teaching, learning and curriculum that Taba reflected. The curriculum was published posthumously in 1971 by Addison-Wesley listing Taba (deceased), Mary Durkin, Jack Fraenkel, and Anthony McNaughton as the authors.

Chapter 1 of *The Teacher's Handbook to Elementary Social Studies* (Taba, Durkin, Fraenkel, & NcNaughton, 1971) delineates five steps necessary to curriculum development. The decisions that need to be made are: (1) the overall goals and specific objectives to be attained; (2) the content from the social sciences and related disciplines that would be included; (3) the selection and organization of the learning activities; (4) the selection and organization of the instructional strategies to be employed; and (5) the selection and development of the evaluation instruments to be used (p. 8). Now these steps are not necessarily a departure from the traditional curriculum development process unless one takes into account the emphases placed on the individual steps and, more importantly, their interrelationships. Thus, the case is put forth that the Taba curriculum presented in the *Handbook* differs from a traditional curriculum development process in eight ways:

1. It contains multiple objectives: thinking, knowing, valuing, and skills; and provides for the implementation of each.
2. It emphasizes the acquisition, understanding and use of ideas and concepts.
3. It defines carefully the outcomes or "terminal behaviors" expected from students.
4. It includes instructional strategies tailored to encourage the development of specified intellectual skills, for example, inductive models like concept attainment and concept development.

5. It contained supplementary procedures for adapting materials to the circumstances in particular classroom situations (diverse student populations).

6. It encourages student examination of attitudes and values held by themselves and others.

7. It consists of sequentially designed learning activities to encourage cumulative learning (spiral curriculum).

8. It provides for a continuous evaluation of student progress by both teachers and students (pp. 6–7).

Of course, when reading this list, it is striking how common this list appears to today's curriculum developer. However, when one considers that the teachers were part of the development team and that the instructional strategies were considered to be an integral part of the curriculum and not simply the means by which the curriculum would be implemented, it is easy to see how divergent Taba's et al. (1971) process really was for its time. That is especially true when examining the first element above, the call for multiple objectives.

The four categories of objectives are reminiscent of the four wings of the social studies that are considered part of the Essentials of the Social Studies (National Council for the Social Studies [NCSS], 1980) which include critical thinking, content knowledge, social studies skills and civic action. With the exception of the "action" wing which Taba et al. (1971) did not seem to emphasize beyond the classroom—other than the qualities that students might develop in their daily behavior—the idea that social studies curriculum must master the intellectual skills of critical thinking and social science, the academic content and the attitudes and values of democratic citizens are all present.

In terms of critical thinking objectives, it is important to state that Taba et al. (1971) believed that *all* students were capable of thinking abstractly. Her call was for diverse or heterogenous classrooms at a time when tracking was becoming the rule of the day. Further, rather than stressing large amounts of factual knowledge (see for example, E. D. Hirsch's (1987) concept of cultural literacy) Taba believed, based on research she cited from cognitive psychology, that thinking is learned developmentally and that thinking skills can and *should* be systematically taught. Although ability levels would differ within classrooms, the Taba instructional strategies allows for differentiated teaching with heterogenous groups of students. Three instructional strategies developed by Taba to assist teachers in attaining the thinking outcomes required by the social studies curriculum are: developing concepts, inferring and generalizing, and applying generalizations (p. 11). Note that Taba was not advocating the teaching of thinking divorced from academic subject matter but rather intentional focus on developing thinking skills by *all* students as part of their acquisition of subject matter. She absolutely did not believe that critical thinking belonged only to the advanced or gifted students and sought to move all students to the highest levels of Bloom's taxonomy, something she was aware of at its inception.

Knowledge objectives were subdivided into multiple levels: key concepts; main, organizing and contributing ideas; and specific factual samples. The *key concepts* are very abstract ideas and are represented by the eleven words at the opening of this chapter. Interestingly, these concepts bridge multiple academic disciplines and can thus serve as themes uniting not only a social studies program but an entire school curriculum. Each concept can serve as a unit or recommended topic of study and these concepts can be revisited (spiraled) at ever more complex levels throughout the course of study over a K–12 curriculum. *Main, organizing, or contributing ideas* are formulated as sentences that assist students in understanding the more abstract key concept. These ideas increase in complexity vertically across the grade levels. *Content samples* represent the specific factual data that will illustrate, explain or develop the ideas (sentences or generalizations). Content sampling enables students the time to explore an idea in full. Over a period of years, the increasing complexity and total number of the content samples will cement the understanding of the key concepts. Content samples for any given unit or grade level are chosen using the specific criteria of validity, significance, relevance (both to today's world and to student interests), relationship to student needs and development, depth (richness), breadth (of applicability) and their ability to reinforce the other curricular objectives (Taba et al., p. 13).

Attitudes, feelings and values objectives assist students in developing their own beliefs and learning to analyze and understand the beliefs of others. The goal is to enable students to participate as citizens in a diverse society locally, nationally and globally. The subgoals to be encouraged in this category include: empathy, open-mindedness, self-security, expectance of change, and "a tolerance for uncertainty and ambiguity with minimal anxiety" (Taba et al., p. 13). The concurrent teaching strategies that are suggested are exploring feelings, interpersonal problem solving and values analysis. Much of this work certainly came out of the social sensitivity study and the Intergroup project. Also, on a personal level as an immigrant who struggled with language difficulties throughout her career, understanding self and others was of prime importance from Taba's point of view.

The last category of objectives, academic, and social skills include the traditional social studies skills such as reading and interpreting maps, charts, graphs, and timelines; ability to take notes, outline, perform basic research tasks such as collection and analysis of data, ask questions, develop and test hypotheses. Additionally social skills focused on group process, nowadays often grouped with cooperative learning skills, are listed. These skills foster democratic classrooms and provide students with the opportunity to practice valued citizenship skills.

Each of these four categories of objectives need to work together although it is obvious that different objectives will take differing amounts of time and that differing instructional strategies are necessary to achieve desired student outcomes. Thus, the design of all learning activities must be organized and sequenced very carefully to take into account the incremental learning that needs to occur if students are to build ever more competence and understanding across their school careers. The instructional or teaching strategies were "patterns and combinations of teaching acts." Taba envisioned teaching strategies to be, first, "consciously formulated plans" and second, [as] the translation of those plans "into activities and conditions of learning, arranged into sequences according to both the logical requirements of the learning tasks and the psychological requirements of the learner' " (Isham, 1982, p. 116). In other words, the instructional strategies were designed to foster attainment of learning objectives and could not be divorced from the curriculum document.

How did all this really operate? Key concepts were chosen for their ability to organize and synthesize large amounts of information. To begin it is best to look at a simple geography example. Figure 2.1 (Taba et al., 1971, p. 33) illustrates the difference between a Taba approach and the traditional approach—in Taba's curriculum instead of studying a series of individual countries in Latin America and amassing a large number of facts about each nation, the new approach is to study a concept, in this case

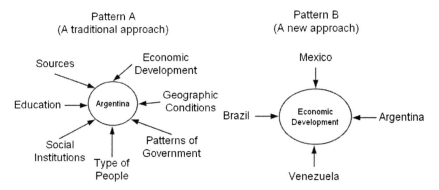

Figure 2.1.   The difference between a Taba approach and the traditional approach.

economic development, and to examine that concept in as many countries as necessary to obtain understanding of the concept—the goal here is not the factual material about each nation, but the deep understanding of the concept—the facts are simply part of the case study or content sampling—of any concept. The goal has moved from the acquisition of factual knowledge to the understanding of the key concepts about the society and world we inhabit.

Further, once those fundamental concepts are decided upon, they need to be taught at higher and higher levels of abstraction across the years of schooling. The best demonstration of this spiral curriculum is outline of the curriculum developed by the teachers in Contra Costa, California. Each concept could be acquired and utilized on multiple levels of abstraction, complexity, and generality.

Thus, the Contra Costa K–8 social studies teachers, working with the Taba team over an extended period of time, considered their students needs, the social sciences, world affairs, and so forth, and decided on the following concepts: causality, conflict, cooperation, cultural change, differences, interdependence, modification, power, societal control, tradition, and values. These 11 concepts would be taught in a spiral by revisiting the concepts at higher levels of abstraction with each succeeding school year. As Figure 2.2 (Taba et al., 1971, p. 20) illustrates by reading from the bottom to the top of the chart.

It is important to note that the sequence that assumes the understanding at each higher level is based on acquisition of the earlier understanding. The specific content for study grows increasingly more complex and abstract as the curriculum develops, This is important not only vertically in a spiral curriculum but horizontally in terms of differentiation within a grade level or particular classroom. At each grade level, the relationships can be taught to a variety of student ability levels without compromising the basic understanding of the concept.

8th level between the governments of nations
7th level between nations with different ideas
6th level between nations with different physical resources
5th level between industries and governments
4th level between industries and specialized workers
3rd level between communities with different economic bases
2nd level between community workers
1st level between family members

Figure 2.2.   Interdependence in people-to-people relationships.

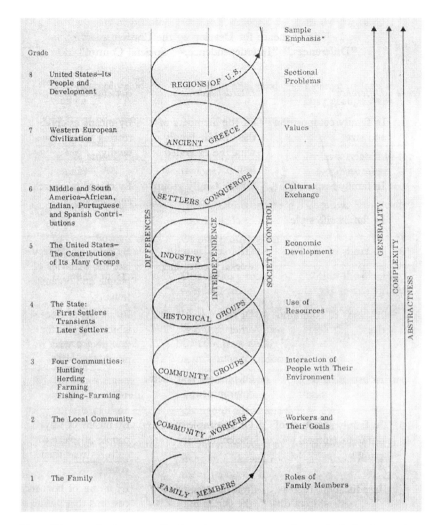

Note: The sample shown on this chart does not represent the emphasis for the year's program.

Figure 2.3.   The spiral development of three key concepts.

Figure 2.3 above (Taba et al., 1971, p. 21) illustrates the spiral curriculum. The chart examines three *key concepts* located on the vertical axes from left to right: differences, interdependence, and social control. The vertical arrows on the right side of the diagram illustrate that these concepts increase in terms of *generalizability, complexity,* and *abstraction* across the years of study. The specific subjects of study appear on the left side of the chart while the content samples are to the right of the spiral.

This emphasis is made even clearer when analyzing the development of a main idea in the curriculum: In this case, the interaction of people and their environment. The main idea is stated as an abstract generalization at

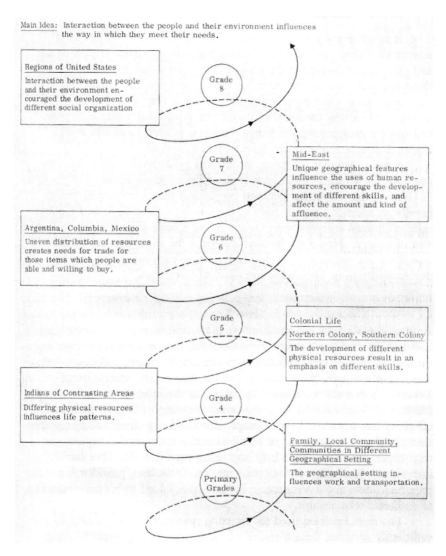

Main Idea: Interaction between the people and their environment influences the way in which they meet their needs.

Grade 8 — Regions of United States
Interaction between the people and their environment encouraged the development of different social organization

Grade 7 — Mid-East
Unique geographical features influence the uses of human resources, encourage the development of different skills, and affect the amount and kind of affluence.

Grade 6 — Argentina, Columbia, Mexico
Uneven distribution of resources creates needs for trade for those items which people are able and willing to buy.

Grade 5 — Colonial Life
Northern Colony, Southern Colony
The development of different physical resources result in an emphasis on different skills.

Grade 4 — Indians of Contrasting Areas
Differing physical resources influences life patterns.

Primary Grades — Family, Local Community, Communities in Different Geographical Setting
The geographical setting influences work and transportation.

Note: Note that the similarity in the processes of development of key concepts and main ideas stems from the fact that main ideas are contained within and are therefore a part of the key concepts.

Figure 2.4.   The spiral development of a main idea (Taba et al., 1971, p. 29).

the top of the chart. The units of study appear in boxes at the left and the right of the spiral demonstrating the relationship of each year's curriculum unit on this idea to the making of meaning, that is, the deep understanding of the generalization over the years. And, it should be noted that several of the basic concepts will be explored in any of these units. For example, the *key concept* of interdependence includes the following two *generalizations*: "All persons and groups of persons depend upon other persons and groups for satisfaction of needs." and "Behavior of each person and group affects other persons and groups in important ways. These effects on others are often indirect and not apparent" (Taba et al., p. 25). The curriculum guide lists multiple generalizations for each key concept (pp. 24–27) although this is not an exclusive list and would be revisited by teachers as the curriculum developed over time.

Once the concepts, generalizations and units of study have been determined, the students learning experiences or activities would be decided upon by the teacher(s). Taba firmly believed that each learning activity required pedagogy appropriate to the achievement of the generalization that students were supposed to acquire. In almost every case the pedagogy of choice was active and inductive—concept development and concept attainment are two of the instructional strategies (models) most often associated with this curriculum approach. To reiterate, the instructional strategies used by the teachers to facilitate the acquisition of the specific content, skills and attitudes defined by the curriculum are of paramount importance and are not seen as separate from the curriculum.

Figure 2.5 (Taba et al., 1971, p. 94) illustrates how students move from specific facts to generalizations by examining situations and through questioning techniques taught to teachers during intensive staff development, students would develop ever more sophisticated generalizations. If one refers back to Figure 2.1 on economic development, the specific situations are the Latin American nations being studied and the students will arrive at new generalizations as they compare and contrast different nations under study. At the close of the unit, students will have a deeper understanding of economic development.

It should go without saying that the testing or evaluation of this sort of curriculum would need to be focused on the ability to use the understandings, i.e. skills, knowledge and attitudes in ways consistent with today's construct of authentic assessment tasks (NCSS, 1996; Newmann & Associates, 1996). Simple multiple choice tests, so popular in our current political environment, focus on basic acquisition of knowledge—the Taba curriculum is based on much more depth and understanding to assist students in making sense of and creating meaning for the world around them. The *Handbook* has considerable guidance (see Taba et al., 1971, chapter 8, pp. 138–154), towards developing what we now call rubrics to

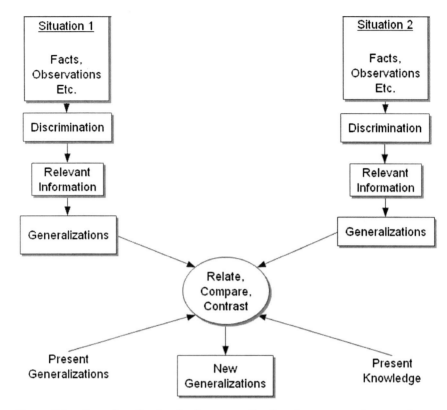

Figure 2.5.   Procedure for developing generalizations by means and comparison.

evaluate the multiple objectives that the curriculum strives to achieve. These evaluation techniques call for both qualitative and quantitative measures of student performance in order to assess the whole developmental picture. In addition there are multiple suggestions for the kinds of activities that would provide the evaluation data necessary to evaluate student learning. These activities are integrated throughout the curriculum to assist teachers in seeing evaluation as a constant process rather than as a single test at the end of a unit of study. These ideas are currently reflected in backwards design with its emphasis on formative and summative assessment throughout lessons (Wiggins & McTighe, 2005).

Linking to the Ideas of the New Social Studies

How does the Taba social studies curriculum project align with the fundamental goals and objectives of the movement known as the New Social

Studies? This is easily demonstrated in the introduction to *The Teacher's Handbook to Elementary Social Studies* (Taba et al., 1971) which states in chapter 1:

> A new perspective is appearing on the content to be used, with emphasis being placed on the content believed most durable (such as concepts and generalizations) rather than on the acquisition of essentially factual information alone. A major emphasis has been placed on identifying basic concept, principles, and methods of investigation in history and the social sciences, and then using these elements as a basis around which to organize the curriculum. More and more we see an emphasis on an in-depth study of fewer topics and a reduction of the superficial "coverage" aimed for in the past. (p. 1)

The chapter goes on to discuss the learning process as a call is made for a shift from learning as mere acquisition of knowledge to one of utilization of knowledge; focused on the processes required for a more inquiry based learning approach geared toward the discovery of relationships and principles inductively according to the procedures, skills and ways of thinking in the social sciences (p. 1).

Although Taba et al. (1971) was deceased when this chapter was written, the author team stated that "New social studies curricula show a growing concern for developing such skills as conceptualizing, generalizing, hypothesizing, and applying previously learned generalizations in new situations, and in techniques of independent inquiry" (p. 2). Middu-agh and Perlstein (2005) discuss Taba's curriculum as part of the movement to reform social studies and refer to New Social Studies advocate James Oswald by state his belief that "the new social studies inquiry approach would not only develop children's understanding of social scientific concepts; it also would encourage students' 'conscious development of coherent individual world views based on reality, flexible toward future change' " (p. 252). This surely aligns with Taba's approach.

When one reviews the variety of instructional strategies and learning activities, it is clear that the fundamental goals of the New Social Studies, both from the point of view of constructivist, conceptual learning (the outcome of the disciplines based approach espoused by Bruner as an outcome of the Woods Hole conference) as well as the goal of wrestling with the persistent questions that face the citizens of our democracy and the world (Newmann & Oliver, 1970; Oliver, 1968) are encompassed by the Taba curriculum developed in Contra Costa, California.

Nonetheless, an analysis of the differences between the development and implementation of most New Social Studies programs points to fundamental differences. Foremost of these differences is the bottom up approach taken by the Taba team. Krull (2003) points out that from the beginning:

> the study was largely concerned with the identification and analysis of teachers' problems in the field of social studies. The teachers, after they had identified mismatches in the curricula they were using with their expectations for them, were asked to develop their own teaching/learning units. The members of the research team primarily provided this kind of in-service training for co-operating teachers. Later on, this function was gradually taken over by the county staff as their expertise through in-service training that was especially organized for them increased. Teachers who developed the new teaching/learning units first checked them in school practice. Then they underwent a critical revision and were again tried out, but this time by a larger number of teachers. This procedure was applied many times, until results satisfying the needs of teachers at different schools were achieved. Usually, the curriculum for an entire grade involved from five to eight units. (p. 486)

Taba's curriculum project began before the funding for the New Social Studies was available. Unlike most later programs, it was not developed by university professionals with little consultation with the teachers (although this varied significantly across projects) and it involved significant, continual teacher professional development through intensive workshops. In fact, there is some evidence that the idea for intensive summer workshops for teachers developed as part of the Intergroup Project headed by Taba. This workshop model was transported from Chicago to California and remains a model for teacher professional development that has long outlasted both Taba and the New Social Studies movement. And, the very longevity of the development process points to the Taba curriculum model as dynamic and never really reaching completion. The teachers and local curriculum specialists, working with consultants as requested, would be the center of curricular change based on needs arising from students in the classroom and changes in the world over time. Thus, the Taba process is, for the most part, the opposite of the process for either the New Social Studies projects or today's current reforms based on the development of standards. The students are rarely consulted and the teachers are only a small part of the process in those models.

Where Could We Be Now?

It is common now, in the wake of the standards movement unleashed by Goals 200 and the federal legislation known as No Child Left Behind (NCLB), to speak of curriculum reform. Of course, one of the most hotly contested areas of this reform has been, and continues to be, social studies where the various academic disciplines that comprise the social sciences vie with one another as well as an integrated social studies approach for time in our nation's classrooms. States like Virginia serve as a good illustration of the problem. The curriculum guide states that the courses are "History and Social Sciences" and a seemingly well-intentioned standardized curriculum guide for teachers contains columns for essential questions and essential skills in addition to essential knowledge. Yet problems abound. A few of them are: the high stakes tests that accompany the standards tend to emphasize the mere acquisition of the reams of factual material encompassed by the standards; test development and evaluation is handled by a contracted private business outside the state removing evaluation from its central role in classroom curriculum improvement, the essential questions listed are frequently not really essential; and the number of stakeholders involved in creation of the standards did not emphasize the felt needs of students or their teachers. Could modern reform move in a different, albeit, mandated by NCLB state controlled direction that would be more in keeping with the ideas of Taba and her team?

In the early 1990s the state of Florida briefly adopted a new social studies curriculum. While this K–12 Florida experiment did not flourish, *Connections, Challenges, and Choices* is a relatively nice example of the Taba conceptual approach (Florida State Dept. of Education, 1993) despite the fact the teachers were not the source of the development of the curriculum. The introductory statements paraphrase Jack Fraenkel, a member of the Taba team, in their discussion of the conceptual framework for developing the content, skills and attitudes desired by this curriculum (p. 2). Seven key concepts were selected for social studies: *interdependence, change, culture, scarcity, conflict, perspective, and responsibility.* Figure 2.6 demonstrates how the concepts would operate not only for social studies but also cut across the academic subject areas traditionally taught in schools. A true integrated curriculum approach with a mission statement in the center and the concepts and disciplines surrounded that vision. For example, as can be seen in the diagram, the key concept of *responsibility* is listed under science, social studies and physical education/health.

In the accompanying social studies guide, each *key concept* is followed by a *generalization* and related core concepts that would be explored across the K–12 curriculum. For example, the generalization under responsibility is "Democratic societies depend upon the act of participation of citizens who recognize and accept the consequences of their economic, political and social behaviors" (Florida State Dept. of Education, 1993, p. 11). Thus, this generalization operationalizes the center of the diagram containing the mission statement. The related core concepts listed under the generalization are: justice, choice, authority, rules, civic action, equality of

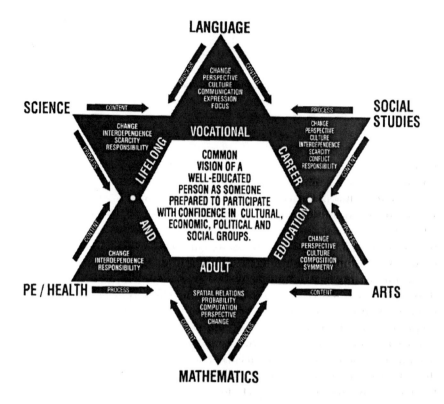

Figure 2.6.   Florida, Connections, Challenges and Choices Interdisciplinary
Schematic Diagram (Florida State Dept. of Education, 1993, p. 52)

opportunity, freedom, diversity, due process, decision making, dependabil-
ity, self control, community, volunteerism, public welfare, civic virtue,
citizenship, leadership, risk-taking, and efficacy (p. 11). It is not difficult
for teachers, students or the community to understand how these concepts
cross academic subjects both in the formal curriculum and in the co- or
extra-curriculum over a student's school career.

The document states that the social studies curriculum can be seen as a
matrix consisting of the core concepts as one dimension with the second
dimension consisting of fundamental skills including critical thinking,
problem-solving, decision-making, and human relations. The Taba criteria of developing depth of knowledge through a spiraling of key concepts
and content sampling are clear as well as the calls in the document for
intensive professional development to assist with multiple instructional
strategies, creative learning and assessment activities outlined throughout
this 53 page curriculum guide. An attempt is made in the document and

in revised versions of the document (both still available in PDF format on the Internet) which include a K-12 flow chart to explicate the matrix demonstrating how this curriculum works in concert with the traditional expanding environments course scope and sequence that most social studies educators are very familiar with.

The document is a well thought out, well executed K–12 curriculum framework. I first saw an abbreviated version of the program at a 1993 Florida Council for the Social Studies annual conference. At the time I had been a Florida high school social studies teacher beginning 1983 and the document was dated 1990. I was confused as to its origin, its adoption, and its future implementation. Sadly this introduction was the only time I ever had the opportunity as a Florida teacher to work with this curriculum. It seems to have been developed and then to have disappeared without out anyone really knowing about or trying it.

Of course, it does illustrate Taba's belief in the need to work with teachers from the bottom or ground level up. The hue and cry when this curriculum was revealed at the meeting was a very sad sight, especially given the subset of caring, enthusiastic teachers that normally attend a state conference. I wondered why people were so hostile to such an intriguing idea (and this was before I had returned to graduate school to pursue doctoral work or had ever heard of Hilda Taba or her instructional strategies).

However, in thinking it through I relate to what Jack Fraenkel told me about the reactions Taba curriculum and his work with the New Social Studies in general. During our interview he said:

> teachers are the lynchpin; they don't get respect; teaching is so difficult; they burnout; the majority of teachers are out of their disciplinary area; the models aren't there; the system is too difficult to change; the system is built against the teachers; those that were flexible—they just grabbed it, the others didn't have time to do it. (personal communication, February 2007)

Despite all of these reasons, I still believe that it can be done and that it can be done well if the commitment is present.

Causality, conflict, cooperation, cultural change, differences, interdependence, modification, power, societal control, tradition and values (Taba et al., 1971 pp. 24–26). These were the key concepts of the Contra Costa K–8 social studies curriculum. Faenkel told me that Taba's legacy is "enduring ideas." You take key concepts and develop the generalizations and ideas that explicate them. Then multiple objectives of thinking, knowing, skills, and attitudes can be developed at national or state levels. The content sampling would remain local option as students are exposed to a social studies curriculum that is powerful and durable.

But, and most importantly, the other lesson for social studies reform that can be drawn from Taba's legacy is that all of this must be percolated up from the teachers felt needs to improve the teaching and learning situations for the students in their classrooms. That is where most of the New Social Studies failed. That is why the standards based movement of today is doomed as well. If you want to reform the social studies, or education in general, you have to start where the rubber meets the road—with the teachers in the classrooms and the students they serve.

REFERENCES

Education Encylopedia. (2007a). *Dalton school.* Retrieved February 19, 2007, from http://education.stateuniversity.com/pages/1902/Dalton-School.html

Education Encylopedia. (2007b). *Hilda Taba (1902–1967).* Retrieved February 19, 2007, from http://education.stateuniversity.com/pages/2474/Taba-Hilda-1902-1967.html

Florida State Department of Education. (1993). *Improving student achievement. connections, challenges, and choices. Florida K–12 social studies program of study.* Tallahassee, FL: Author.

Hirsch, E. D., Jr. (1987). *Cultural literacy: What every American needs to know.* Boston: Houghton Mifflin.

Isham, M. M. (1982). Hilda Taba, 1904–1967: Pioneer in social studies curriculum and teaching. *Journal of Thought, 17*(3), 108–116.

Isham, M. M. (1984). *Hilda Taba: Pioneer in curriculum development.* Unpublished PhD, University of Texas.

Krull, E. (2003). Hilda Taba (1902–1967). *Prospects (Paris, France), 33*(4), 481–491.

Middaugh, E., & Perlstein, D. (2005). Thinking and teaching in a democratic way: Hilda taba and the ethos of brown. [Electronic version]. *Journal of Curriculum and Supervision, 20*(3), 234–222. Retrieved June 25,2009 from http://vnweb.hwwilsonweb.com/hww/results/external_link_maincontentframe.jhtml?_DARGS=/hww/results/results_common.jhtml.30.

National Council for the Social Studies. (1980). *The essentials of the social studies.* Washington, DC: Author.

National Council for the Social Studies. (1996). *Powerful and authentic social studies.* Washington, DC: Author.

Newmann, F., & Associates. (1996) *Authentic achievement: Restructuring schools for intellectual quality.* San Francisco: Jossey-Bass.

Newmann, F. M., & Oliver, D. W. (1970). *Clarifying public controversy: An approach to teaching social studies.* Boston: Little Brown.

Oliver, D.W. (1968). The selection of content in the social studies. In J. P. Shaver & H. Berlak (Eds.), *Democracy, pluralism, and the social studies, readings and commentaries: An approach to curriculum decisions in the social studies* (pp. 17–42). Boston: Houghton Mifflin.

Stern, B. S. (2007, Oct. 4). *Hilda Taba: A voice in the wilderness.* A paper for the symposium "Critical Times in Curriculum Thought" presented to the American

Association of Teaching and Curriculum at their annual meeting, Cleveland, OH.

Taba, H., Durkin, M. C., Fraenkel, J. R., & NcNaughton, A. H. (1971). *A teacher's handbook to elementary social studies; an inductive approach*. Reading, MA: Addison-Wesley.

Wiggins, G., & McTighe, J. (2005) *Understanding by design*. Alexandria, VA: Association for Supervision and Curriculum Development.

CHAPTER 3

FANNIE SHAFTEL AND HER NEW SOCIAL STUDIES

Jane Bernard-Powers

Dr. Fannie Shaftel, noted social educator and the subject of this chapter, was one of the first women to join the Stanford University education faculty having come as a doctoral student at the invitation of Dr. Paul Hanna in 1944. She completed her doctoral studies in 1948 and was invited to stay on at Stanford where she spent her career in curriculum and teacher education, teaching and working with MA and PhD students.

Her 1952 publication titled *Role-Playing: The Problem Story*, written in collaboration with her husband George Shaftel, featured a story about a group of boys involved in an ethical dilemma. The story, known as "The Club-House Boat," the publication, the writings about citizenship education and human relations education, and the developed processes for role-playing human dilemmas constitute Fannie Shaftel's main contributions to the social studies reforms of the 1960s and 1970s.

There have been multiple and varied characterizations of the "New Social Studies" and social studies reform in the 1960s and 1970s (Evans, 2004; Hertzberg, 1981; Nelson & Drake, 1994). In general, one dominant thread of the "new" social studies focused on discipline learning—geography, anthropology, history, sociology, and economics—and innova-

The New Social Studies: People, Projects, and Perspectives, pp. 63–73
Copyright © 2010 by Information Age Publishing
All rights of reproduction in any form reserved.

tive combinations of strategies with resource materials to engage students (Hertzberg, 1981, p. 116). A second dominant thread characterized by Evans as "the newer social studies" focused on contemporary issues and innovative strategies— problems and process (Nelson, 1994). The passions and promise of the 1960s' political and social issues such as futurism, racism, the war in Vietnam and multicultural education were wrapped into the programs and rhetoric of social studies. Values education, role-playing and simulations were among the instructional strategies of the period that were linked to reform, relevance and empowerment of social groups (Engle, 1960).

Shaftel's work on role-playing for "social values" and "intelligent concern for others" is appropriately associated with the newer social studies. Shaftel focused her academic attentions on citizenship education and specifically the requisite interpersonal skills necessary for compassionate resolution of conflicts and ethical dilemmas that children face in their daily lives. She was both an advocate for social education and a critic of discipline based social studies curricula with its privileging of the structures of knowledge over social education which emphasized "personal-social problems," caring, and valuing (Beyer, 1994; Shaftel, 1969, 1970).

Focusing on Shaftel's work in relation to other social studies educators presents a challenge in two respects. First, Shaftel was a scholar whose work was enacted and articulated in professional contexts. She was often called on to speak about her work, and to demonstrate the power of role-playing that is taught and developed well. However, she was not a prolific writer and thus there are limited academic writings that can be consulted for the record. Therefore, the main sources for this chapter on Fannie Shaftel and the New Social Studies are her dissertation, "Role-Playing in Teaching American Ideals" (1948); two publications, *Role-Playing the Problem Story* (1952) and *Role-Playing for Social Values* (1967/1982) co-authored with her husband, who was a professional writer; a small group of articles; and a life history interview, conducted by this author over the course of 2 years (1991–1993).

A second challenge is that her maturation as a scholar, thinker, and activist, was prior to the 1960s and 70s. Shaftel's evolution as a teacher and scholar began with her mentor, Corinne Seeds, a prominent progressive educator at UCLA's Laboratory School in the 1920s. Shaftel studied at Teachers' College Columbia in the 1930s. Then, she moved to Stanford University in the 1940s and developed her role-playing processes and rationales by the early 1950s when concerns about racial, ethnic, and religious conflicts were on the rise. Thus, her work was significantly influenced by her own biography and the contexts and people she had worked with. Dr. Shaftel's passion for interactive democratic education and her skilled development of the use of role-playing in the classroom began in the seat of her family's values and developed over the course of her professional life.

The chapter considers Dr. Shaftel's work from the vantage point of the multiple influences that shaped it and established her place in the New Social Studies: her family's roots; her mentors; her attraction to the power of psychodrama and sociodrama; her network of colleagues that included Hilda Taba, Jean Grambs, and Lavonne Hanna; and her work for the National Conference of Christian and Jews on Intergroup Relations.

Embedded in this discussion are two points about social studies reforms of the 1960s and 70s. One is that Fannie Shaftel's work on roleplay, in relation to the newer social studies, is best understood in the context of the twentieth century. Progressive educators' notions about education for democracy found sustenance in the intercultural education movement and human relations emphasis of the 1940s and 50s, as well as the renewed concerns about racism that developed in the 1960s.

The second point is about gender. While the vast majority of educators associated with the New Social Studies were males, there were female educators who provided leadership for social education. The personal and professional connections enjoyed by these women and their mutual interests in social education distinguish them from their discipline-oriented colleagues in the New Social Studies. The distinction between the two was articulated by Crocco who wrote in 1999 that social studies is a more narrow term than social education which "Seeks to address ... the skills and knowledge individuals need to live effectively in a democracy" (p. 1).

Family Origins and Social Responsibility

In an oral history interview conducted in 1991, Dr. Shaftel discussed her family roots. With a clarity that is characteristic of a mature individual—she was 83 years old in 1991—she traced the sources of her social education orientation to her family background (F. R. Shaftel, personal communication, February 17, 18, 1991, April 13, 14, 16, 1992, September 11, 1992, September 28, 1993). Her mother was from Poland, and her father was from Russia. She was first generation Jewish American and was raised in an ethnically diverse section of Los Angeles and in a household that took the "improvement of society" seriously. In the interview, she explained that her family came from "a socialist tradition in Europe" and they migrated to the United States to escape from the oppression of Czarist Russia. It was in the family circle that Shaftel's notions of global connections, responsibility to community and the connection between belief and actions were fostered. From Shaftel's perspective there was a fluid connection between her family's sense of social responsibility, social justice, and the centerpiece of her life's work—role-playing in the elementary school for the development of a sense of caring, connection, and habits of democratic habits, attitudes and behavior.

Progressive Education Roots

Shaftel's work in the UCLA Laboratory Schools working under the supervision of Corinne Seeds and her pursuit of an MA at Teacher's College Columbia constitute another chapter in the development of her approach to elementary social studies and the advent of role-playing (F. Shaftel, personal communication, April, 1992).

Corrine Seeds, the head of the University Elementary School at UCLA from 1925 to 1957 and a professor of education, was a passionate and creative advocate of progressive education and Fannie Shaftel's mentor. Shaftel enrolled in the teacher training program at UCLA the year that Seeds had returned from to LA from her work at Teacher's College (Shaftel, 1982). John Dewey and William Heard Kilpatrick were Seed's mentors. The curriculum approaches that they espoused, experiential child centered education that integrated multiple disciplines in interactive experiences, so inspired Shaftel that with Seed's urging she went to Teacher's College in 1934 to finish her BA (bachelor of arts) and pursue a master's degree. Her work with Seeds, her teaching experience in Pasadena, which involved considerable freedom to design curriculum, and her subsequent work at Teacher's College, inspired by Dewey, Counts, and Childs (F. Shaftel, personal communication, February 17, 18, 1991), reinforced her commitment and passion for teaching democracy through interactive experiences. The extensive dioramas and role-playing that Fannie incorporated into her teaching were building blocks for the work she did at Stanford as a PhD candidate and full-time faculty member.

Shaftel's narrative identified two additional sources of information and inspiration for her work on role-playing. Virginia Axeline, principal author of a book on play therapy, and Jacob Moreno, an advocate for psychodrama and sociodrama who, from Shaftel's perspective, enthralled audiences at the Pasadena Play House. Dr. Jacob Moreno was especially motivating and helpful to Shaftel in demonstrating group problem solving, which is a fundamental aspect of the role-playing process. She named Dr. Moreno in acknowledgments for a monograph titled, *Building Intelligent Concern for Others Through Role-Playing*, published by the National Conference for Christians and Jews, noting his pioneering work in human relations research (Shaftel & Shaftel, 1967).

Stanford School of Education and the Development of Role-Playing

Role-Playing for Social Values: Decision Making in the Social Studies was published in 1967 by Prentice Hall, the same year that the projects on the New Social Studies reached the numerical high point of 50 (Evans, 2004, p. 127) While the factors which influenced Fannie Shaftel's work have been identified in the previous sections, the development of the processes and the writing of the stories took place at Stanford University over the course of 2 decades.

Shaftel was invited by Professor Paul Hanna of Stanford University to be a consultant on a curriculum project in Southern California, and he subsequently invited her to apply to Stanford as a doctoral student. She came with her husband and eventual co-author George Shaftel and began her work in 1944. Her dissertation, *Role-Playing for Teaching American Ideals* (1948), was the first significant writing she had done on role-playing and it was accomplished with support from a project identified as Education for American Ideals. The project was funded by private donors who wanted to support curriculum projects for teaching democratic ideals and behavior to 5th and 6th and 11th and 12th grade students (p. 1).

The introduction to Shaftel's dissertation provides insight into the context for her work at Stanford and her professional relationship with the National Conference on Christians and Jews and the Intercultural Education Movement. While this work on teaching democratic ideals and democratic behaviors through carefully designed role-playing of problem stories came to fruition in the 1960s, when the Civil Rights movement, racial profiling and violence in urban areas were on the rise, the genesis of the work was in the late 1940s. The 40s gave rise to facism and totalitariam regimes in Europe, racism, shifting urban demographics, anti-Semitism and general concerns about national unity in the United States. These concerns were the impetus for the establishment of the National Conference of Christian and Jews (NCCJ), and the Intergroup Education in Cooperating Schools Project that her friend Hilda Taba directed (Shaftel, 1948 p. 28) Support for education for democratic behavior was evident in Conclusions and Recommendations of the Commission on Social Studies of the American Historical Association (p. 26) and in a subsequent publication by the National Education Association according to Shaftel's citation (p. 26). Shaftel drew these sources into her dissertation to establish a sense of the breadth of the Intergroup Education Movement.

Along with an ambitious agenda established by the Commission on Education Organizations of the NCCJ that focused on the schools, teacher training, and curricula, the development of a new field—human relations—was on the rise (Pitt, 1955). Graduate programs were established at Teacher's College, Columbia and a handful of universities followed suit (p. 179). Human relations, intercultural education, and the teaching of American ideals were incorporated into curriculum vernacular and, in some instances, into the objectives of American Schools (p. 180).

Shaftel was influenced by the Intergroup Education Movement and she contributed to it. The timing of her development as a teacher in Pasadena, the influence of her professors at Teacher's College, and the timing of her work at Stanford amounted to a fortuitous confluence of factors that gave Shaftel the means to develop role-playing in the context of social studies generally and intergroup education specifically.

The Role-Playing Process

Paraphrasing Shaftel, teaching American ideals must be accomplished by providing children with authentic, interpersonal experiences stimulated by life situations that are emotionally and intellectually evocative and developmentally appropriate. To achieve this, Dr. Shaftel, mapped out developmental needs of 10- and 11-year-olds, collected problems faced by children of that age, and worked with her husband, a professional writer, to devise dramatic problem stories that involved American Ideals (Shaftel, 1948, p. 42).

The choice of language-role-playing was a matter of expedience. Dr. Shaftel was really using sociodrama techniques that provide for problem resolution in a supportive climate (F. Shaftel, personal communication, February 18, 1991). A critical aspect of the process was that children engaged the issues explored values and conflicts through successive enactments. The language Shaftel used to characterize the process was that of "sensitive tools for exploring human transactions and looking at value dimensions of the decisions that are made" (personal communication, February 18, 1991).

In her study, the developmental tasks of 10- and 11-year-olds were derived from the work of Daniel Prescott and Robert J. Havighurst, among others (Shaftel, 1948, pp. 39–40). The developmental tasks of 10- and 11-year-olds were augmented with problems faced by children in real life situations. The procedures to be implemented for successful role-playing (or sociodrama) were detailed by Shaftel and she provided some specific scripts of role-plays from the classrooms of teachers in the Palo Alto Area. The problem stories, which were unfinished stories conceived of by Fannie and George and written by George Shaftel, were based on developmental needs and real life problems. The categories included family relations, education, personal development, race and ethnicity, and legal rights. A typical problem story and one that was included in subsequent publications was "Clubhouse Boat," a story of a conflict between the requirements of a peer group and restrictions forced on the student by a parent who knew little of the friendship context.

The dissertation involved both the design and the evaluation of the problem stories in classrooms in and around Palo Alto. Trained observers took notes on the role-plays, the reenactments, and teacher and student growth in discussion and deliberation. Shaftel concluded that socio-drama was an effective tool for classrooms in focusing on human relations (p.186). Her conclusion stated:

> Children, under optimum conditions, can cope with an[d] devise solutions to their problems in ways that truly develop respect for personality and skill in democratic human relations. (p. 189)

"Role-Playing in Teaching American Ideals" was submitted to the College of Education and approved in August of 1948. While the completed work launched her professional work, the materials from The American Ideals Project became embroiled in a dispute over funding and ethics and they were confined to a vault for many years at the behest of college administrators. A new provost rescued them several years later and they were included in the book, *Role-Playing for Social Values* (1967) (F. Shaftel, personal communication, April 4, 1992).

Continuing her dissemination of role-playing processes and materials, Shaftel and her husband, George, wrote *Role-Playing: The Problem Story, an Approach to Human Relations in the Classroom,* which was published by the National Conference of Christians and Jews (1952), and *Building Intelligent Concern for Others through Role-playing* (NCCJ, 1967). Shaftel taught role-playing in her classes at Stanford where she was awarded tenure and promotion shortly after completing her PhD. She taught in the Elementary Credential Program, supervised students in the field and maintained a heavy speaking schedule (F. Shaftel, personal communication, April 4, 1992). Additionally, she was first reader on a number of dissertations which she shared with her mentor Dr. Paul Hanna.

It is significant that Shaftel's relationship with her mentor at Stanford, Paul Hanna became both troubled and distant over time. At the heart of the tension was the relationship between subject matter and child development: the great divide in New Social Studies. While social studies educators, including Hanna, moved aggressively toward subject matter definitions and scope sequence in the 1950s and 60s, Shaftel was tenacious in her support for social studies education that was problem-centered and child-centered (Stallone, 2002, p. 85). If support for her position was not forthcoming from Hanna, Shaftel found support for her work and her ideas in the Stanford community and in her friendships with two prominent social studies educators, Dr. Jean Grambs and Dr. Hilda Taba, with whom she shared values and ideas about social studies, human relations education and the changing American landscape (F. Shaftel, personal communication, 1991–1993). The gender of this group and the shared beliefs are a remarkable phenomenon. Beth Rubin, a Shaftel biographer, noted that Shaftel was part of "A cohort of like minded women social studies educators" that included Taba (Rubin, 2002, p. 118).

Feminine/Feminist Networks of Social Educators

Shaftel knew of Taba's work at the University of Chicago, but her first face-to-face meeting with Taba was in the Bay Area when she was asked by the National Conference on Christian and Jews to review the monograph titled *Role-Playing: The Problem Story.* Taba had come to San Francisco State University in 1951 after directing the Intergroup Education in Cooperating Schools Project and the University of Chicago Intergroup Education project (1945–1948). She continued to work on Intergroup education matters and supported Fannie's appointment as director and facilitator for the NCCJ Western Workshop, held over a period of summers. Taba was particularly appreciative of Fannie's ability to capture an audience through a carefully orchestrated role-play that provided powerful teaching about topics related to social justice, racial sensitivities and human relations generally.

Grambs was in the doctoral program at Stanford during the same period as Shaftel. In Fannie's words, they shared dinners, camping trips, and sometimes money when budgets were tight. Grambs was interested in psychodrama, the subject of her dissertation; following the awarding of her PhD in 1948, she informally collaborated with Shaftel on roleplaying. She stayed on at Stanford for several years, providing more time for informal collaboration. However, when job offers did not develop, in 1953 Grambs took a job at the University of Maryland. Despite some distance in miles, Grambs remained close to Fannie George Shaftel throughout their careers (personal communication, 1991, 1992)

Both women shared Shaftel's commitment to classrooms where carefully designed interactions among students was a central point of growth and both were committed to social action.

It is important to note for the record that Taba had turned seriously to cognition, learning and teacher training in social studies when she moved to the San Francisco Bay Area in 1951, and joined the San Francisco State College Faculty. While she was interested in the interactions of people from different cultures, and believed that the social interactions of children in the classroom were critical, she also became enamored of the idea that a carefully developed system of questioning and reasoning—a step by step for teachers engaged in inquiry—was both possible and desirable. Shaftel and Taba had lively discussions which involved Jules Henry, an anthropologist, on this particular point. Taba changed her mind on the notion of scripted lessons for teachers and said to Shaftel in 1967 just prior to her death, "I know now Fannie that if teachers are to guide this [conversation] they have to experience it themselves. Air tight systems won't work" (Bernard-Powers, personal communication, 1993).

The professional relationships between Shaftel and Taba and between Shaftel and Grambs constitute a significant phenomena in social studies education. The consonance between cognitive and affective was not "bifurcated" for these women who were social educators (Hertzberg, 1981, p. 113). Their mutual interest in human relations and intercultural education challenged notions of subject matter dominated social studies, and enhanced the profile of the New New Social Studies.

The contemporary works of Margaret Crocco and O. L. Davis Jr., *Bending the Future to Their Will* (1999) and *Building a Legacy, Women in Social Education 1784-1984* (2002), has validated the work of women who were pioneers in social education as well as the idea of social education as a main thrust of social studies.

CONCLUDING COMMENTS

In the short term, Shaftel and the social education circle she was part of contributed to the notion of school and social studies education as a site for "reforming the social order." Photographs and teachers' guides for teaching democratic understandings through role-play were published by Holt Social Studies in 1970 and were subsequently included on the California State Supplementary Materials listing. The book, *Role-playing for Social Values* was reprinted in 1982, and it is still cited in methods text books for elementary social studies (Martorella & Beal, 2002; Nelson, 1992; Sunal & Haas, 2002). Shaftel has an impressive list of doctoral candidates she taught at San Francisco State, which includes Millard Clements, William Fielder, Robert Tabachnick, Murray Nelson, Thomassine Sellers, Jane Stallings, and the late Violet Robinson. Clements, Fielder and Tabachnick dedicated their 1966 social studies methods book, *Social Study: Inquiry in Elementary Classrooms* to Fannie Shaftel, "teacher and friend."

In the long run, the significance of role-playing for social education is that it has claimed a place in the catalog of effective strategies for the elementary class room. Progressive education strategies that employ drama continue to be appreciated and referenced by elementary social studies educators. Shaftel's work on *Role-playing for Social Values* occupies a significant place in that work.

Moreover, citizenship education curricula for diverse student populations can readily embrace Shaftel's role-playing, and social education goals for schooling. As Shaftel recounted:

> The main thrust of my professional work was Social Education. I saw schooling as a way to develop the socially sensitive, socially responsible individual who can function in a democratic society.... Not only did you have to be an interpersonally sensitive person, but a socially committed person ... and as a result I saw social studies as the core of the curriculum. (personal communication, 1993)

REFERENCES

Beyer, B. (1994). Gone but not forgotten-reflections on the New Social Studies. *Social Studies, 85*(6), 251–256.

Clements, M., Fielder, W. R., & Tabachnick, B. R. (1966). *Social study: Inquiry in elementary classrooms.* New York: Bobbs-Merrill.

Crocco, M. (1999). "Introduction." In M. Crocco & O. L. Davis (Eds.), *Bending the future to their will: Civic women, social education and democracy* (p. 1). Boulder, CO: Rowman & Littlefield.

Crocco, M., & Davis, O. L. (Eds.). (2002). *Building a legacy, Women in social education 1784-1984.* Silver Spring, MD: National Council for the Social Studies.

Evans, R. (2004). *The social studies wars: What should we teach the children.* New York: Teachers College Press.

Hertzberg, H. (1981). *Social studies reform 1880–1980.* Boulder, CO: Social Science Education Consortium.

Martorella, P., & Beal, C. (2002). *Social studies for elementary school classrooms* Columbus, OH: Merrill, Prentice-Hall.

Nelson, L., & Drake, F. (1994). Social Studies teachers reactions to the "New Social Studies." *Theory and Research in Social Education, 22*(1), 44–46.

Nelson, M. (1992). *Children and social studies* New York: Harcourt Brace Jovanovich.

Pitt, J. E. (1955). *Adventures in brotherhood* New York: Farrar, Strous.

Rubin, B. (2002). Fannie Raskin Shaftel. In M. Crocco & O. L. Davis, (Eds.), *building a legacy, women in social education 1784-1984.* Silver Springs, MD: National Council for the Social Studies.

Shaftel, F. (1948). *Role playing in teaching american ideals.* PhD dissertation, Stanford University.

Shaftel, F. (1969). The Stanford evaluation of nine elementary teacher training models. U.S. Department of Health, Education and Welfare, Final Report Project No. 08710.

Shaftel, F. (1970). *A survival curriculum in the social studies. An address to the Southern California Social Studies Council-October 1970.* Unpublished remarks.

Shaftel, F. (1982). Corinne Seeds, theorist and practitioner. *Education, the Magazine of the UCLA Graduate School of Education, 1*(1), 13, 25.

Shaftel, F., & Shaftel G. (1952). *Role-playing the problem story: An approach to human relations in the classroom.* New York: National Conference on Christian and Jews.

Shaftel, F., & Shaftel, G. (1967). *Building intelligent concern for others through role-playing.* New York: National Conference of Christians and Jews.

Shaftel, F., & Shaftel, G. (1967, 1982). *Role-playing for social values.* Englewood Cliffs, NJ: Prentice-Hall. (Original work published 1967)

Shaftel, F., & Shaftel, G. (1970). *People in action, role-playing and discussion photographsfor elementary social studies.* New York: Holt, Rinehart and Winston.

Stallone, J. R. (2002). *Paul Robert Hanna: A life of expanding communities.* Stanford, CA: Hoover Institution Press.

Sunal, C., & Haas, M. (2002). *Social studies for the elementary and middle grades.* Boston: Allyn & Bacon.

CHAPTER 4

CAN YOU STILL CATCH FISH WITH NEW SOCIAL STUDIES BAIT?

Ted Fenton and the Carnegie-Mellon (Social Studies) Project

Michelle D. Cude

INTRODUCTION

A Look at the Man Behind the Project

Caught any fish lately? Ask Edwin "Ted" Fenton that question and he will entertain you with tales like this—"A bluefish took off the end of my finger. But then I got even. I ate him for supper" (Fenton, 2001). But Ted Fenton is more than an expert fisherman. For one who has been called the "leader" or the "prophet" of the New Social Studies, his vitae lists 21 books, more than 100 articles, 64 audiovisual and supplemental materials, 22 textbooks, and 1 "personal, irreverent and informative" cookbook on bluefish (Fenton, 2007b; Flail et al., 1973; Weinberg, 2004). So in his

The New Social Studies: People, Projects, and Perspectives, pp. 75–94
Copyright © 2010 by Information Age Publishing
All rights of reproduction in any form reserved.

spare time, he fishes in the waters off Cape Cod where he lives with his wife now in quiet retirement from his prolific professorship at Carnegie Mellon? Not exactly. Interviews reveal he is busier than ever writing an academic biography, cataloging his many publications, and cooperating with colleagues on articles and books on the New Social Studies (E. Fenton, personal communication, March 7, 2007). I am grateful for his time and assistance with this chapter concerning his role in the New Social Studies (NSS) movement.

For Fenton, teaching is a lot like fishing. To really make a difference, you have to teach someone to fish for themselves, not just hand them a codfish. Similarly, it is not enough to hand students some facts, you have to teach them how to find, analyze, hypothesize, and evaluate the content themselves. This method of teaching, which Fenton popularized as "inquiry," revolutionized social studies education in America in the 1960s … or did it?

In the midst of the NSS movement, Fenton (1966), then a young history professor, wrote that we were on the verge of "a pending revolution in the teaching of the social studies" (p. v). He and others truly believed they were starting a tidal wave effect to revolutionize what went on in social studies classrooms around the country and beyond (Beyer, 1994; Fenton, 1966; Fenton & Good, 1965; Penna, 1995). Besides the scores of published works bearing witness to his centrality in the movement, there are testimonies of his work and spirit which prompted, mentored, inspired, and hosted those involved in developing the materials (D. Greenwald, personal communication, March 21, 2007; Penna, 1995). Penna states,

> Ted Fenton was the catalyst for the development of *The Americans*. He was also our mentor and our negotiator…. As friend, he opened his home to us, introduced us to his … friends, and invited us to dinners that he hosted for project directors from curriculum centers across the nation. He was the leader. (p. 156)

Fenton also hosted many summer institutes at Carnegie Mellon designed to familiarize teachers with the curriculum reforms. He was in the midst of crafting a revolution, with all the drive, single-minded vision, and productivity that requires (Domencic, 1985; Fenton, 2007b; D. Greenwald, personal communication, March 7, 2007).

Yet, now we see the faults of the NSS projects enumerated in prevalent articles (Dow, 1992; Engle, 1986; Fenton, 1991; Massialas, 1992; Rossi, 1992; Tice, 1992). While many of these sources cite the failure of the NSS, others claim it was simply "set aside" (Tice, 1992) or the movement "faded" (Goetz, 1994) or "disintegrated" (Massialas, 1992). For whatever reason, though, the materials are largely forgotten. Why did they fall into disuse? Scholars still debate the effects of the NSS movement, but Fenton's role is undeniably one of the most significant. His name still circulates today in conjunction with inquiry learning and the other aspects of the NSS movement which he created and/or chronicled (Beyer, 1994; Flail et al., 1973; D. Greenwald, personal communication, March 21, 2007; Rossi, 1992). This chapter will first overview Fenton's contributions, then look more closely at the Carnegie Mellon curriculum that he directed. By analyzing the curriculum and comparing it to a modern text, it will be possible to ascertain the lasting legacies of NSS and of Fenton's work specifically.

Background of Edwin "Ted" Fenton

Fenton graduated in 1948 from the College of Wooster with a bachelor of arts in history and political sciences, and earned his master's in history from Harvard the following year. From 1950–1954 he taught high school history in Boston at an all-girls school despite his lack of pedagogical training. Much of his dedication to improving curriculum and engaging students in the historical process stemmed from the stilted, antiquated curriculum he was required to teach at this school (Fenton, 2007a). He was then hired to join the history department at Carnegie Institute of Technology. In 1958 he earned a doctoral degree from Harvard in history under Oscar Handlin's advisement. Six years later he became a full professor at Carnegie Institute (Carnegie Mellon University Archives, n.d.; Fenton, 2007a).

Overview of Fenton's Main Contributions

Fenton's contributions form the foundation for much of what the public came to know about the NSS. Though there were many experts and professionals involved in the many curriculum projects, Fenton's text, *The New Social Studies* (1967), introduced the projects to the general public— the teachers on the front lines, the parents, and the school board members in small towns and large cities all across America. Fenton himself considers this book his real introduction to the NSS as a whole and the way he put his finger on the heartbeat of the whole movement. He recalls,

> I had a grant from the Ford Foundation, to write a little book—only 135 pages—called *The New Social Studies* which was published by Holt, Rinehart and Winston in 1967. This gets cited all the time. I visited and met with directors and talked with them, and drew conclusions. This little book sold 30,000 copies and got into colleges and school systems.

As advice to a novice NSS researcher, Fenton continued, "To start, read that 1967 book. That's what got me known all around" (E. Fenton, personal communication, March 7, 2007). William Goetz (1994), a teacher at the time, remembers how the thin paperback book was circulated to all the social studies teachers in his district to introduce them to the latest developments in the field. Smith (2004) even credits Fenton (and John Good) with the first use of the term "New Social Studies" in their article in *Social Education* in 1965. Fenton himself does not recall with certainty, stating in an interview, "I don't know. I just read someplace that our article was the first time the term was used. It may be" (E. Fenton, personal communication, March 7, 2007). It was that year, 1967, when Fenton won the Middle States Council Gold Medal for a major published contribution to social studies education (Carnegie Mellon University Archives, n.d.).

While this was perhaps the most widely circulated of his published works, Fenton made many other contributions by way of publication. Several of his main ideas, which later became the heart of the NSS, originated in earlier curriculum projects such as his advanced placement course designed in conjunction with the Pittsburgh Public Schools (Fenton, 1961). Also, his first major published work, *32 Problems in World History* (Fenton, 1964), outlined his approach to teaching the inquiry method of an historian within a concept-based course. Fenton was already becoming the chief advocate for cooperation and collaboration between the college and the local school district. Therefore, when Carnegie Mellon received a grant from the U.S. government to open the curriculum center there as one of more than 50 funded social studies curriculum development centers around the country, he was asked to direct the project (E. Fenton, personal communication, March 7, 2007).

Overview of the Carnegie Mellon Curriculum Project

The Carnegie Mellon Social Studies Curriculum represents Fenton's major contribution to the NSS movement. He was the general editor and director of the curriculum center that produced this series, published by Holt, Rinehart, and Winston (1967–1973). It included seven courses for high school students, Grades 9–12 for average and above-average students. For each course, there were five components: the text, the teacher's manual with lesson plans, the audiovisual kit, the individual/group activity set, and an evaluation program. These courses were designed so that "each course builds carefully upon the preceding ones" to provide "sequential and cumulative learning" (Fenton, 1971, as reprinted in Fenton, Penna, & Schultz, 1973, p. viii). Each volume contains readings designed to be done each night in preparation for class discussion the next day.

These primary source documents (though not referred to by Fenton as such) provide the core material for his inquiry research method. With these, Fenton expects students to pose questions about evidence, make hypotheses, test them, and finally draw conclusions or revise hypotheses based on those test results. Inquiry requires an active search, not a passive transfer of information. It also presupposes that the inquirer has some interest, some motivation to dig for the answers—to pull back the layers and reveal the truth (Beyer, 1994; Sanders & Tanck, 1970). One must *do* inquiry, be engaged in the process, in the search. This engagement leads to the type of active classroom Fenton describes as powerful for the learners (Fenton, 1966). Defined this way, inquiry has been around for a long time, ever since people have been asking questions and seeking answers to problems (Fenton, 1971). Therefore, some researchers put Fenton in the category of problem-based learning theory; either way, he clearly theorized from an inquiry perspective. With problem solving, there is a certain solution the teacher is leading the students to reach; whereas, with inquiry, there is no predetermined outcome (Engle, 1986; Rice, 1992). Inquiry is done for intellectual development, not just for the solution to a problem (Rice, 1992).

The front of each of the teacher's editions contains an elucidation of 13 principles of the inquiry classroom written by Fenton along with Judy deTuncq, a Holt, Rinehart and Winston social studies consultant. It describes the key elements in Fenton's instructional theory—teaching through inquiry—a theory which was actually tested and proven effective earlier in the *Indiana Experiments in Inquiry* (Massialas, 1965). What does Fenton's version of inquiry look like? How does it measure up to the current National Council for the Social Studies (NCSS) guidelines for active and powerful social studies? The following section examines the evidence, allowing the reader to make his/her own determinations regarding Fenton's version of inquiry versus problem solving, the impact of the project, Fenton's lasting legacy, and the success or ultimate failure of his Carnegie Mellon Curriculum Project.

EVALUATION OF CARNEGIE MELLON CURRICULUM PROJECT [TED FENTON, CURRICULUM EDITOR]

While the faults of the NSS curriculum projects as a whole have been aired on laundry lines across the media, each project had its own strengths and weaknesses (Beyer, 1994; Engle, 1986; Fenton, 1991; Massialas, 1992; Rice, 1992; Sanders & Tanck, 1970). Was the Carnegie Mellon project really a failure? Or did it just fail to reach its potential? In order for the reader to make his/her own determination, in true inquiry style, the evidence is presented here from both the original sources of the textbooks, as well as contemporary and recent reviews of the program. In preparation for this chapter, I reviewed the literature on the NSS movement concerning its effectiveness and legacy. Then, focusing on Ted Fenton, I read many of his published works, some of his unpublished autobiography, and interviewed him and several colleagues in the Carnegie Mellon curriculum project.

Methodology and Frame of Reference

Given that NCSS is the primary national organization in the field, their standard seems an appropriate measure of any curriculum. While their curriculum guidelines were not written and accepted by the NCSS board of directors until 2002, they still offer a model of "best practice" which meets the goal of engaging, effective curriculum—a goal shared among the NSS writers such as Fenton. According to NCSS, social studies teaching and learning are powerful when they are meaningful, integrative, value-based, challenging, and active (NCSS, 2002).

How does the Carnegie Mellon curriculum hold up to these accepted standards of excellence in the field? In the following section, each of the five standards is summarized. Then, quotes and observations from several textbooks represent the whole Carnegie Mellon curriculum, providing evidence to evaluate Fenton's work by the NCSS curriculum standards: (1) *Comparative Political Systems: An Inquiry Approach*, student text (1973) and teachers' guide (1973); (2) *The Shaping of Western Society: An Inquiry Approach* (1974); (3) *The Americans: A History of the United States: Teacher's Manual* (1970); and (4) *Teacher's Guide for a New History of the United States: An Inquiry Approach* (1975). This evidence allows the reader to draw his/her own conclusions, and determine whether the Carnegie Mellon Curriculum Project was a failure. Fenton himself would be pleased with nothing less than the inquiry approach to this problem.

Standard 1: Meaningful

"Meaningful" curriculum, according to NCSS, relates to students' lives and leads students to analyze social and global problems and offer solutions. It should be "based on the developmental and psychological needs of the student," involving them in the selection and assessment of the curricular activities (NCSS, 2002).

Is the Carnegie Mellon curriculum meaningful to the students in the way that NCSS defines "meaningful?" Does Fenton's work relate to student lives? Looking at his world history text (Fenton & Good, 1974), we find 10 out of 30 (approximately 33%) of the chapter activities relate to the modern social world. Of these, however, the real-world connection may be quite weak or limited, as in the following examples. Students are asked to interview a Protestant and a Catholic priest about their views of the Reformation, or the comparison of modern church music with medieval cathedral music. While they do incorporate the student's modern world and neighborhood, they are not likely to capture the engagement of all teenagers (Beyer, 1992; Fenton, 1991; Massialas, 1992; Rossi, 1992). Nor do they lead to discussion of current issues in religious tolerance in Ireland the Middle East or here in the United States. Some of the projects at the end of the chapters tend to focus more on the world of the student, such as "survey of the characteristics of school leaders;" however, the link back to the topic of study (national and local political leaders) is left to the student to make on his/her own. There is no directed reflection to aid in making those connections.

In his rationale for the Holt series, Fenton described his efforts to touch the real lives of the students: "We have chosen content to fit the interests and needs of adolescents in American society" by using, for example, "words of a number of popular and folk songs, as well as a collection of graffiti from the walls of New York coffeehouses" (Fenton et al., 1973, p. xxvi). While these are two samples of "The Diffusion of the West: A Picture Essay" in the last chapter, the effort of connection may come too late (Beyer, 1992; Massialas, 1992). His priority seems to lie in the content rather than in the connection, according to his disclaimer:

> Our occasional discussions of current affairs were deliberately chosen to help our students transfer structure from a historical situation to their own world, and assurance of this transfer is difficult if the teacher permits the latest outbreak of violence to determine the subject of discussion every Friday. (Fenton, 1961, p. 36)

Does it give opportunity for students to debate social problems, and to reach toward solutions? One of the criteria for "meaningful" extends the real-life connection to broader global problems, soliciting discussion and critical thinking about potential solutions. In the world history text, for example, the social problem of overloaded jails and reforming criminals is brought up by the illustration on page 161 of a galley in Louis XIV's navy rowed by criminals. The question above the picture prompts debate: "Do you think criminals should be condemned to hard labor? What should the purpose of sentences given to criminals be?" According to some reviewers, however, the current hot topics of debate in the 1960s were not integrated into the discussions thus contributing to their ineffectiveness (Flail et al., 1973, Fenton, 1991; Massialas, 1992).

Does Fenton's curriculum meet varying developmental and psychological student needs? Curriculum "based on the developmental and psychological needs of the students," as NCSS requires, attends to more than the cognitive development of the student. Evidence of Fenton's commitment in the higher-order thinking and moral reasoning development is embedded in the questions throughout the text. For example, in a lesson on seventeenth century science and Copernicus, he asks: "Do you feel that everyone has the right to challenge accepted beliefs? How should people go about trying to change beliefs they do not accept?" (Fenton & Good, 1974, p. 173). Yet, Fenton agrees that "the concern for the structure of the disciplines overlooked the interests and abilities of the child" (Rossi, 1992, *The Failure* section [online]).

One of the criticisms of the NSS movement in general was the way the curriculum caters to the advanced students, forgetting the diversity and range of learners in the typical classroom (Flail, et al., 1973, Massialas, 1992; Sanders & Tanck, 1970). Fenton recognized this error in all of the social studies projects and included this explanation in *The New Social Studies* (1967):

> Most of the teachers involved in them [social studies curriculum experiments] are above average in ability and training because experimental work requires rare creative abilities and writing skills. Most of the schools where field-trials of materials take place are located in the more fortunate suburbs which tend to attract better teachers and more flexible administrators and to have community support for new ways of doing things. Moreover, must [sic] of the students enrolled in experimental classes seem to be above average in ability. (p. 4)

Fenton's own curriculum materials suffered the same fate, despite his awareness of the shortcomings. A student who was in a course using the *Comparative Political Systems* textbook remarked years later that the NSS course was "completely different" from any class she had had previously, adding that it followed a "story," was based on "concepts," and prompted the students to ask questions of the sources (Goetz, 1994). Goetz also reports interviewing another student who struggled to understand the structure of the course. He concludes that the positive effect of the Carnegie Mellon curriculum was restricted to the average or above-average students, leaving the slower achievers in the dust of confusion. Charles Flail, Jr., a teacher in Duxbury, Vermont who was asked to review the materials, used portions of the 11th grade U.S. History textbook with his students and found the struggling learners to be quite perplexed by the structure of the chapters and the more fast-paced learners to tire of the repetitive nature of the structure and therefore neither group would participate fully in the discussions (Flail et al., 1973).

In part, Fenton met the former need through a specially designed separate curriculum for struggling learners. Readings were on a lower-reading level, and the whole focus of the curriculum was shifted from content to developing the skills and affective attributes of a learner. "The major objectives of this course for slow learners lie in the affective domain. They stress the development of constructive attitudes toward learning, the growth of a positive self-concept, and the clarification of values" (p. 1).

Standard 2: Integrated

"Integrated" curriculum draws together all areas of the social studies, including economics, geography, philosophy, political science, religion, sociology, and others. In doing so, it develops "proficiency in methods of inquiry and analyzing, organizing and using data" (NCSS, 2002). Students' own social environments should be balanced by the examination of the larger social world, incorporating multiple viewpoints on social issues. Finally, the powerful social studies classroom should "promote critical, creative, and ethical thinking on problems faced by citizens and leaders" (NCSS, 2002).

Does Fenton's concept-based instructional model reach the goals of an integrated curriculum? Fenton's textbooks are integrated in that they focus on developing that "proficiency in methods of inquiry" which NCSS describes. Although at first glance, Fenton's Holt textbooks appear to have similar content to most contemporary texts, upon deeper examination, one finds they are arranged not merely chronologically, but also thematically. Each chapter is opened with a summary of the "big ideas" of that chapter such as absolutism, nationalism, and economics in the market economy. Beyond the thematic approach, the skills of inquiry, student-based learning, and critical thinking operate as unifying threads, tying the multiple courses and texts together with a systematic approach to the subjects.

Each of the texts focuses on a different one of the social sciences, rather than an amalgamation of them all. Yet, still, the integrity of the curriculum is most clearly expressed in the developmental patterns linking all four years of high school history together. Fenton asserted that much of the criticism of his curriculum could be answered by the fact that it was never tested in its entirety as a full series (E. Fenton, personal communication, August 3, 2007). He explained: "The curriculum has been planned so that each course builds carefully upon the preceding ones, and hence, provides for sequential and cumulative learning" (Fenton et al., 1973, p. viii). Yet, the designed integrity of the full program was compromised by its usage in isolation.

Does the Carnegie Mellon curriculum develop students' skills in inquiry and problem-solving, as well as "promote critical, creative, and ethical thinking?" In the introduction, Fenton warns students that this textbook differs widely from ones he has probably used in the past (Fenton et al., 1973):

> Instead of merely memorizing facts or generalizations, you will be asked to use them to identify problems, develop hypotheses or tentative answers to questions, gather information, and come to your own conclusions. Throughout this course, you will be challenged to think for yourself and to make up your own mind. (p. xiv)

Inquiry-based learning lies at the core of the Fenton texts. In his words, "More than any other goal, the Carnegie Mellon Social Studies Curriculum stresses the development of a variety of inquiry skills" (Fenton, as cited in Judd, 1975, p. xii). Specifically, Fenton (1971) explains that his curriculum supports three types of inquiry: analytical inquiry (making valid hypotheses), valuing inquiry (helps students decide own values), and policy inquiry (problem solving of public issues). "All analytical inquiry begins with the identification of a problem" (p. 33).

A look inside the *Shaping of Western Society* text provides an example of analytical inquiry learning (Fenton & Good, 1974, pp. 293–300). First, the section opens with a one-page historical essay on attitudes toward modern war. Following this, there is a collage of photographs along with reprinted letters from two German soldiers in the early months of World War I. Next there are two excerpts from literature about war; one is a poem. No further instruction is given. In blue print (as are all questions) the book asks: "What hypothesis would you make on the basis of the evidence in this reading about the effect of the war on European attitudes toward war" (p. 300)? The tools of inquiry learning have been taught in previous chapters and here students implement them themselves.

In another example, chapter 9 of *Comparative Political Systems* (Fenton et al., 1973) introduces the topic of political decision making through an expose of Nixon's decisions during the Cambodian Crisis in 1970. Students are taught the five steps of decision making, then asked to analyze whether these were used in the decisions discussed in the sources. Thus, they are providing "critical and ethical thinking on problems" though some argue that these big ideas seemed to rarely touch upon the students' personal lives or to stretch to broader themes such as migration, racism, or how geography affects history (Sanders & Tanck, 1970).

Standard 3: Values-Based

Students in a powerful social studies classroom will be engaging in critical thinking, values-based decision making, and consideration of multiple views on controversial issues. The curriculum will support the democratic development of future citizens, helping students realize the significant role values play in policy and decision making. Finally, NCSS guidelines state that "the program should encourage students to develop a commitment to social responsibility, justice, and action" (NCSS, 2002).

While some argue that Fenton's inquiry system overlooks the affective development of a student in favor of the cognitive development (Flail et al., 1973; Massialas, 1965), evidence from the textbooks seems to point otherwise. As stated in the introductory material, the foundational objective of the Carnegie Mellon Social Studies Curriculum is divided into six main categories, including "the growth in the ability to use analytical inquiry skills ... the development of constructive attitudes toward learning, the growth of a positive self-concept, and valuing." Thus, three of the six main objectives for the course materials stress affective growth and development, leaving the remaining three to support cognitive skills. A survey of the texts reveals numerous values-based questions printed in blue in the margins prompting real and deep discussions within the class after individual reflection by the reader. In *The Americans* (Fenton, 1970), students encounter this question in the margin "What would make you revolt?" (p. 50) as they begin to read about the American Revolution. In the *Shaping of Western Society* (Fenton & Good, 1974), students evaluate a medieval "how-to" manual on how to run a manor in order to identify the values it represents. Then, the text asks them to respond: "How do these values compare to your own" (p. 47)? Questions such as these appear frequently [mean average of eight per chapter], sprinkled in the margins of the texts to stimulate self-reflection and values-identification. Sanders and Tank (1970) concur that the Carnegie Mellon Social Studies Project does a better job than most other projects in the "values orientation often neglected in previous curricula" (p. 397). Fenton explains, "The inquiry technique helps students to clarify their values. The objective ... is to have each child think the issues through in order to arrive at a defensible position for himself ... with evidence to support it" (Fenton, 1971, p. 35).

A comparison of the Holt *The Shaping of Western Society* with a popular world history textbook (Beck, Black, Krieger, Naylor, & Shabaka, 2003) illustrates Fenton's unusual emphasis on values education. The questions in the Holt text probed much deeper, causing the student to think more deeply about his/her values, express his/her opinions on controversial matters often, and to grapple with the consequences of historical events/decisions. For example, in a lesson on equality and citizenship, students are prompted by this question: "To what extent do you believe that the things people have in common are more important than the things that sometimes separate them, such as color, faith, income, or national origin" (p. 251)? These types of questions spawn frequent, meaningful discussions in the world history classroom. When such questions were found in the modern text, they were often only in the teacher's manual or they occurred much less frequently within the text (Beck et al., 2003). Additionally, the moral dilemma presented for the study of China in *Comparative Political Systems* asks students to decide whether a son, Li, who has just become a communist residing in a city should take away his father's land back in the village when asked by the authorities to do so. Teachers are directed to stimulate their students' moral development by presenting these real-life dilemmas which require students to use valuing inquiry skills.

However, there are recognized limitations to the values education included in the Holt curriculum. Fenton himself showed a growing appreciation for the role of values clarification and moral development in education through his career. In later years, he worked closely with Lawrence Kohlberg on materials dealing with cognitive moral development (D. Greenberg, personal communication, March 21, 2007 and May 10, 2007). Although the second editions of all the Holt texts provided far greater emphasis on values and moral development (Social Science Education Consortium, 1978), it still remained a personal growth issue, rather than a social responsibility. Herein lay fertile soil for frustration and disengagement by students and teachers once the social climate of the 1960s called for greater commitment to social justice and action.

Standard 4: Challenging

According to NCSS (2002), the powerful social studies program will challenge students in a learning environment which includes *opportunities to discuss and reflect* upon each others' ideas. It will also *provide sources with conflicting viewpoints* on controversial issues. Student products will include both written and oral discussion of content, and students will be assessed on their progress not only academically, but also developmentally in values, thinking skills, and social participation. Assessments will be both traditional and alternative designs.

Opportunities to discuss and reflect are at the heart of the inquiry-based classroom (Fenton, 1967). In lesson #13 in the *Comparative Political Systems Teacher's Edition (1973)*, one of the objectives is to find a question for class discussion which is so controversial that mutual consensus will be impossible to reach. Many times throughout the teacher's guide, the following instruction appears: "They should not be asked to come to agreement on this matter." Although this open atmosphere is stressed by Fenton in the introductory materials to his texts, the word *community* is not found. Instead, the emphasis is on the tone which the teacher sets in teacher-student relationships. The students' peer-to-peer relations are not emphasized, nor are the points of potential and active controversy. For example, two teacher reviewers, William Crowell and Robert Barret, agreed that "The entire course would be strengthened by the inclusion of materials which present conflicting historical argument" (Flail et al., 1973, p. 179). The absence of controversy in the course materials and the consistency of the historical documentary evidence presented, according to some reviewers, provided an inaccurate, rosy image of history as a "neat and tidy" account to be discovered by the students—free from the disorderly and controversial nature of history (Flail et al., 1973).

Standard 5: Active

Finally, NCSS (2002) encourages a "varied and rich range of learning activities" which will stimulate students to "investigate and respond to the human condition in the contemporary world." Activities should be varied and meet the needs of all types of learners. Teachers should act as *"fellow inquirers"* with their students, gathering and analyzing data, forming and testing hypotheses (NCSS, 2002).

To what degree is the curriculum "active" with varied, student-centered and rich elements as NCSS defines an active curriculum? In comparison to the practices of the time, Fenton (1970) claims: "The wide range of teaching strategies appropriate to all this material represents still another departure from stereotyped practices" (p. 2). And yet he continues on to say that "most class periods revolve around discussion," with variation only in the types of discussion which are used. Saunders and Tanck (1970) reviewed the curriculum and found the preponderance of teacher-directed discussion to be the "much overworked teaching strategy" of the program. A closer look at the lessons themselves indicates a very prevalent pattern with only slight variations: read the assigned reading for homework, take notes on it, and come to class prepared to discuss it. Where does the teacher draw the balance between spontaneity to fight boredom and consistent routines to provide support? Engle (1986), however, espouses a different view. According to him, the Holt series and the MACOS (Man: A Course of Study) were two examples of exceptional curriculum where students were given "full and active control of the learning process" (p. 23) rather than having adults (teachers) explaining what was to be learned. In his words, the students are in amongst the birds in the hen yard to learn about poultry firsthand themselves, rather than having adults (teachers) on the outside of the hen yard delivering expose on the finer points of a chicken [or having today's teacher show a poultry PowerPoint].

Fenton's "Introduction" to the teacher's guide for the *Comparative Political Systems* (1973) course, explains his approach to inquiry teaching where the teacher acts as a learning partner, joining the students in pursuit of answers to their questions rather than a "repository of facts" for the students to memorize. Reading #8 (p. 131) in the *Comparative Political Systems Teacher's Guide* gives evidence of a typical approach to inquiry learning. The teacher is instructed to say to the students: "Rather than give you a definition of model as social scientists use it, let's work out our own definition by looking at some examples." Here is the co-inquirer in action.

Meeting individual student needs within the learning community is another goal of NCSS powerful social studies teaching. Fenton does instruct teachers of inquiry to "take individual differences into account" (Fenton, 1971, as reprinted in Fenton et al., 1973, p. xxxvii) realizing that students learn differently. How to do this seems to be left in the hands of the teacher. And, while some of the projects in the textbooks invite interaction with the community around them, real student engagement seems artificial and unexpected. Yet, Fenton agrees that "investigating and responding to the human condition in the real world" makes the curriculum relevant, as he concurs:

> The materials in the Carnegie Mellon Social Studies Curriculum are designed to foster investigations which students find meaningful and relevant. Even such historical topics as the development of the idea of equality in the West, of the treatment of black people after the Civil War emphasize issues of continuing concern to young people.... Occasionally students become deeply concerned about a vital contemporary issue. (p. xxxviii)

CONCLUSION: WAS IT A FAILURE?

The results of the study are in the reader's own conclusions regarding the worth and success of the Carnegie Mellon curriculum. Nevertheless, some concluding comments follow. Was the NSS a "failure" or simply a step along the continuum of curriculum change and development over the years?

Impact of Carnegie Mellon Curriculum Project

The impact of the NSS movement is still being debated as is evident in the many chapters within this book. Some scholars actually count the materials created by the NSS teams as one of the most beneficial legacies.

Beyer (1994), himself a NSS teacher, estimates "at best, ... only about a third" of teachers in America were affected by the NSS. According to Rice 1992), the results of the NSS movement had "limited impact beyond the field-test schools." He concludes only about 10% of classrooms across America were affected. Some argue that the immediate effect was hampered by a dissemination lag (Dow, 1992) while others contend that was the least of the problems (Beyer, 1994; Fenton, 1991; Rossi, 1992). There seems little agreement in the field of whether the NSS movement was successful or not, and why it faded.

In some of the qualities of a powerful curriculum proposed by NCSS, Fenton's curriculum ranks higher than most. In other areas, it falls short of expectations. However, results in the schools showed students scoring as well or better on the standardized tests than those taught with the traditional textbooks (Fenton, Good, & Lichtenberg, 1969; Flail et al., 1973). In one test on world history, students using Fenton's semester-long, inquiry-based course scored as well as their counterparts who took a year-long traditional world history course in the content area. In the use of inquiry skills, they greatly outshone their peers (Social Science Education Consortium, 1971). As Fenton himself noted, though, there is no real data for the full implementation of his curriculum since it was never adopted and used sequentially (E. Fenton, personal communication, August 3, 2007). Still, his influence on the field of social studies remains.

Implications for Practice

In today's classrooms full of heterogeneously grouped students, Fenton's course would work well *some* of the time for *some* of the students because it is a single-method approach. Sanders and Tanck (1970) as well as other reviewers (Flail et al., 1973) have proposed using portions of the Holt materials, adding a variety of other methods and activities. Fenton's more lasting contribution, then, is the tool of inquiry, used as one tool among many in the social studies classroom. In the world of standardized tests where teachers are so often driven to the coverage of multitudinous facts, the inquiry method is a welcome change to offer students. We need a rebirth of such approaches which encourage a deeper understanding of social studies, focus on broader concepts, and teach students to think for themselves (Engle, 1986).

Fenton's Legacy

According to several education specialists, Fenton's legacy can be traced in areas as diverse as constructivism, case-based research, use of primary sources, preservice teacher training, as well as inquiry. Some have proposed that constructivism is NSS inquiry revisited. If this be the case, then Fenton's legacy lives on. In an interview, Fenton described writing "a rationale for the NSS and their connection to constructivism—which is, I think, the new name for them (for NSS methods), a repackaging.... Constructivists have discovered the curriculum artifacts in the NSS which fit their needs" (E. Fenton, personal communication, March 7, 2007). Beyer (1994) claims that "much of the NSS ... was constructionist long before constructivism became popular" (p. 3).

A review of the literature highlights other instances where scholars trace trends and influences of Edwin Fenton. Apparently, he was one of the first handful of professors (in 1967) using case-based research as an instructional tool for teachers. At least one professor, Alan Kirchner, PhD. (2003), attributes the current movement of critical thinking to Fenton's emphasis on inquiry. And Kathleen Steeves (2007) reports Fenton among the lineage of thinkers and historians who have shaped the history in our schools today: "Inquiry learning, advocated by Edwin Fenton in the late 1960s and early 1970s—from which so much of what is being done today in history education has evolved—has been reinforced by James Banks and others in the 1990s" (www.historians.org/pubs/Free/Steeves/theory.htm, section 5, para. 2). Rice (1992) contends that inquiry had been around earlier in the form of problem solving, but Fenton re-birthed it into the more intellectual, pure form.

And yet, Fenton's contributions have stretched beyond inquiry. A teacher, Ivan Frank of Taylor Allderdice High School, uses Fenton's formula of inductive, inquiry learning in designing lessons where students read primary sources to determine for themselves the causes of the Great Depression. In his article, "Primary Sources: A New Old Method of Teaching History," Canadian scholar Ken Osborne (2003), heralds Fenton's use of primary sources as opening the door to a whole new interest in teaching with documents. According to another teacher, Anthony Napoli of New York, these sources provide exactly what is needed when teachers attempt to do inquiry in the classroom without enough raw materials (Flail et al., 1973). But then, much is left to the willingness, innovation, and skill of the teacher in drawing out investigatory questions and in restraining from doling out answers so students will be required to investigate and hypothesize on their own (Beyer, 1994; Flail et al., 1973).

As an historian, Fenton's dedication to the public school system— where theory meets the seventh grader—set him apart from most of his Ivy League colleagues. Perhaps his innovative practice to go into the schools as a teacher inspires other teacher educators to strengthen their determination to spend time in the classroom and learn again what the teachers are facing firsthand today (E. Fenton, personal communication,

March 7, 2007; Fenton, 1961, 1991). Some (Dow, 1992; VanSledright, 2007) see the involvement of scholars in the efforts of teaching students as fundamental to closing the research to practice gap and influential in raising the intellectual rigor and vitality of the subject for the students. Bruce Van Sledwright points to the foresight of Fenton's priority on social studies content for preservice teacher preparation.

One other major component of Fenton's legacy is the preservice methods course. To address methods, he wrote a text, despite the fact that he was opposed to teaching from a text. Therein, he outlined his proposal for how teachers should be trained for the next generation. Though of his contributions this one perhaps had a smaller circle of influence, it is noteworthy to see the imprints in my copy which I ordered at a used book distributor online. The book bears the library seal from the Llyfrgell Normal College in Bangor, Wales. Clearly Fenton's work had international effect.

The methods text itself received mixed reviews (Rundell, 1967), yet we might still consider what is worth applying to our own methods teaching. The text outlines the inquiry approach as it is applied to teacher education: "If teachers are to improve steadily at their craft, they must master the principles upon which good teaching rests. This book has been designed to encourage students to discover those principles for themselves" (p. 7). Could we redesign methods courses upon the inquiry principle? Rather than a textbook, this is a collection of resources for that purpose. The entire text has been focused around three essential questions: why? how? and what? The questions for guided student reflection ask basically those same three questions: "1.) *Why* should we teach Chapter 3 to a fifteen-year-old American high school student? ... 2.) ... *What methods of teaching (How)* ...? and 3.) *What* content emphases are most important to teach" (Fenton, 1966)? These three questions remain at the heart of what it means to be a reflective teacher of social studies, certainly a viable organization for implementing an inquiry-based methods course.

Dale Greenwald, closely involved in the movement as a student, then as a colleague of Fenton's, summarized it best:

> In many ways the NSS was successful. Textbooks today reflect the use of data and original sources, and at least pay lip service to higher level thinking skills and having students synthesize information in order to draw conclusions, [though] they are very different from 1950s texts. Prentice Hall recently released ancillary materials to support their history texts that provide students with original sources and ask them to act as mini historians.... So while the NSS materials did not take hold, the strategies they exposed were incorporated into many commercial materials and continue to be there today. It's somewhat similar to saying that third party movements in U.S. history have been failures because the parties themselves did not survive;

yet, many of their platforms were incorporated into one of the two major parties. (personal communcation, March 7, 2007)

And so, while the Holt social studies textbooks may be growing moldy in high school basements, the concepts and inspiration contained within their covers lives on. Even decomposing matter becomes fertile soil for future growth. Perhaps it is true, then, that what we have today, or what we hope for, is a resurrection of the NSS. In this, Ted Fenton has made a significant contribution.

ACKNOWLEDGMENT

The author wishes to thank Dale Greenwald for his assistance in this research project.

REFERENCES

Beck, R. B., Black, L., Krieger, L. S., Naylor, P. C., & Shabaka, D. I. (2003). *World history: Patterns of interaction.* Evanston, IL: McDougal Littell.

Beyer, B. K. (1994). Is the old New Social Studies back? [Electronic version]. *Social Studies 85*, 251–255.

Carnegie Mellon University Archives, Faculty and Staff Collections. (n.d.). *Fenton, Edwin, Papers, 1955–1994.* Retrieved December 17, 2008, from http://www.library.cmu.edu/Research/Archives/UnivArchives/Fenton.html

Domencic, R. J. (1985). *Edwin Fenton and the New Social Studies: A study in curriculum development and publication* [microfische]. Unpublished doctoral dissertation, Carnegie Mellon University.

Dow, P. B. (1992). Past as prologue: The legacy of Sputnik [Electronic version]. *Social Studies 83*(4) 164–168.

Engle, S. (1986). Late night thoughts about the new social studies. *Social Education, 50*(1), 20–22.

Fenton, E. (1961). *College/High school cooperation: Instituting the Advanced placement program in Pittsburgh.* Pittsburgh, PA: Carnegie Institute of Technology.

Fenton, E. (1964). *32 problems in world history: Source readings and interpretations.* Chicago: Scott, Foresman.

Fenton, E. (1966). *Teaching the New Social Studies in secondary schools: An inductive approach.* New York: Holt, Rinehart, and Winston.

Fenton, E. (1967). *The New Social Studies.* New York: Holt, Rinehart, and Winston, Inc.

Fenton, E. (1968). In the audio-visual world: Using audio-visual materials to teach history [Electronic version]. *The History Teacher, 2*(1), 43–47.

Fenton, E. (Ed.). (1970). *The Americans: A history of the United States: Teacher's manual.* New York: Holt, Rinehart, and Winston.

Fenton, E. (1971). Inquiry techniques in the New Social Studies. *The High School Journal*, *55*(1), 28–40.

Fenton, E. (1991). Reflections on the "New Social Studies." *Social Studies, 82*(3), 84–90.

Fenton, E. (2001). *Laugh the blues away: A bluefish cookbook*. As reviewed by Parrish, M. (2002, Feb. 24). *Cookbook connects with the lore and allure of bluefish*. Pittsburgh Post Gazette [Electronic version].

Fenton, E. (2007a). *My academic autobiography*. Unpublished manuscript.

Fenton, E. (2007b). Curriculum Vitae: Edwin Fenton. Unpublished manuscript.

Fenton, E., & Good, J. M. (1965). Project Social Studies: A progress report [microfische]. *Social Education, 29*(4), 206–208.

Fenton, E., & Good, J. M. (1974). *The shaping of Western society: An inquiry approach*. New York: Holt, Rinehart, and Winston.

Fenton, E., Good, J. M., & Lichtenberg, M. P. (1969). *A high school social studies curriculum for able students; an audio-visual component to a high school social studies curriculum for able students* (Final Report). Pittsburgh, PA: Social Studies Curriculum Center at Carnegie Mellon University & the U.S. Department of Health, Education, and Welfare, Office of Education.

Fenton, E., Penna, A. N., & Schultz, M. (1973). *Comparative political systems: An inquiry approach. Teacher's guide*. New York: Holt, Rinehart, and Winston.

Flail, C. M., Jr., Napoli, A. J., Hunt, D. G., Kendikian, L., Crowell, W. G., & Barret, R. L., et al. (1973). Inquiry into inquiry: An examination of the Fenton 11th grade U.S. history materials [Electronic version]. *The History Teacher, 6*(2), 169–190.

Goetz, W. W. (1994) The New Social Studies: The memoir of a practitioner [Electronic version]. *Social Studies 85*(3), 100–105.

Judd, B. (1975). *Teacher's guide for a new history of the United States: An inquiry approach*. New York: Holt, Rinehart, and Winston.

Kirchner, A. (2003). *Memorandum: Self-evaluation*. Retrieved March 6, 2007, from http://www.kirshnerisms.com/Self-Evaluation/2003.html

Massialas, B. G. (1965, October). Reactions to the reports on Project Social Studies [Letter to Editor]. *Social Education, 29*(6), 356–357.

Massialas, B. G. (1992). The "New Social Studies"—Retrospect and prospect. *Social Studies 3,* 120–124.

National Council for the Social Studies. (2002). *Curriculum guidelines (for social studies teaching and learning)*. Retrieved May 15, 2007, from http://www.socialstudies.org

Osborne, K. (2003). Primary sources: A new old method of teaching history. *Canadian Social Studies, 37*(2). Retrieved March 5, 2007, from http://www.quasar.ualberta.ca/css/ Css_37_2/CLvoices_from_the_past.htm

Penna, A. N. (1995). The New Social Studies in perspective: The Carnegie Mellon Slow-Learner Project. *The Social Studies 86*(4), 155–161.

Rice, M. J. (1992). Reflections on the New Social Studies [Electronic version]. *Social Studies, 83*(5), 224–231.

Rossi, J. A. (1992). Uniformity, diversity, and the "New Social Studies" [Electroni version]. *Social Studies, 83*(1), 41–45.

Rundell, W., Jr. (1967). Teaching the New Social Studies in secondary schools: An inductive approach [Book Review] [Electonic version]. *The Journal of American History, 54*(1), 93–95.

Sanders, N. M., & Tanck, M. L. (1970). A critical appraisal of twenty-six national social studies projects. *Social Education, 34*(4), 397–401.

Smith, R. E. (2004). *Development of the secondary social studies 1960 to 1987.* Retrieved March 5, 2007, from http://www.siue.edu/~resmith/chapter2.htm

Social Studies Curriculum Center, Carnegie Mellon University. (1970). *The Americans: A History of the United States: Teacher's Manual.* New York: American Heritag.

Social Science Education Consortium. (1978). *Social studies curriculum materials: Data book* [Looseleaf binder]. Boulder, CO: Social Science Education Consortium, Inc.

Steeves, K. A. (2007) Building successful collaborations to enhance history teaching in secondary schools [Section 5]. *Learning Theory and Teaching History.* Retrieved March 6, 2007, from http://www.historians.org/pubs/Free/steeves/theory.htm

Tice, T. N. (1992). Social studies reform [Electronic version]. *Education Digest, 0013127X, 57*(6).

VanSledright, B. (2007). *Why should historians care about history teaching? Teaching column of the February 2007 Perspectives of American Historical Association.* Retrieved March 6, 2007, from http://www.historians.org/pubs/Free/steeves/theory.htm

Weinberg, S. (2004). Crazy about history. *Journal of American History Textbooks & Teaching* [Endnotes] [Online]. Retrieved March 5, 2007, from http://www.indiana.edu/~jah/ textbooks/2004/wineburg.shtml

CHAPTER 5

"THE QUEST FOR RELEVANCY"

Allan Kownslar and Historical Inquiry in the New Social Studies Movement

Elizabeth Yeager Washington and Robert L. Dahlgren

INTRODUCTION

Allan O. Kownslar, Professor of history at Trinity University in San Antonio, Texas, conceptualized and wrote about inquiry in American history during the New Social Studies movement of the 1960s and 1970s. He authored many articles in professional journals, including *Social Education*, and was general editor and one of the authors of a yearbook for the National Council for the Social Studies titled *Teaching American History: The Quest for Relevancy* (1974). He was a Danforth Fellow, a writer for the Amherst College Committee on the study of history, and a presenter of a series of inquiry-oriented lessons for teachers in over 300 U.S. school districts as well as for workshops sponsored by such organizations as the Institute of Texan Cultures, the Texas Education Agency, and the National Council for History Education. He created a series of television programs for PBS (public broadcasting service) affiliates using the inquiry method in teaching history, served as president of the Texas Association

The New Social Studies: People, Projects, and Perspectives, pp. 95–110
Copyright © 2010 by Information Age Publishing

for the Advancement of History, was a member of the Texas Commission on Standards for the Teaching Profession, and served as chair of the Trinity University history department. At Trinity, he taught courses in American history, methods of teaching history, and Texas history.

The curricular reform movement that came to be known as "The New Social Studies" had its roots in the flood of discussions that followed the launching of the Soviet *Sputnik* satellite probe in 1957. Evans (2004) has characterized this movement as emanating from the material and ideological concerns and needs of the Cold War machine, describing the September 1959 Woods Hole conference as

> a reaction to Sputnik and the complaints of critics such as Vice Admiral Rickover and was funded by a range of federal agencies. In a sense what was emerging was a manufactured consensus, paid for by the stakeholders with an interest in education conducted on behalf of national security. It was a direct outgrowth of the cold war and of the war on social studies. (pp. 123–124)

Despite these inauspicious origins, it is clear that the atmosphere of anti-Soviet fear that produced an electoral victory, largely based on the myth of a "missile gap," for John F. Kennedy in 1960 also produced a wealth of federal funding for curricular reform projects. These projects, often federally funded at the behest of the 1958 National Defense Education Act (NDEA), would come to provide the material foundations for the emergence of a far more progressive second-wave of social studies curriculum programs in the mid-60s. That NDEA could produce both an early call for a "Back to Basics" approach similar to that proposed by the 1983 A Nation at Risk report, as well as a range of humanistic, progressive reform movements, is an irony not lost on Gerald Gutek (2000), who refers to the period of the early 60s as "a push-pull tug of war between two sets of educators" (p. 189). It is in the context of this renaissance of progressive methodology in the social studies that the remarkable work of Allan Kownslar must be situated. The following article explores the seminal role played by Kownslar and his associates in the coalescence of the New Social Studies Movement of the 1960s. By tracing the roots of this pedagogical movement, we will argue that the Cold War conflict temporarily opened an avenue for progressive educators to revive the traditions of child-centered methodology and to pioneer new techniques that would greatly influence the social studies classroom.

BACKGROUND:
HISTORY IN THE "NEW SOCIAL STUDIES" MOVEMENT

A number of scholars in the 1950s and 1960s, as a direct response to the Cold War/national security agenda and to criticism of the public schools by such figures as Hyman Rickover and Arthur Bestor, developed curriculum projects advocating a social science-based, inquiry approach to social studies and history. Flowing from the curriculum reform initiatives of the 1950s funded by the National Science Foundation and the U.S. Office of Education (USOE), and from Jerome Bruner's (1960) *The Process of Education*, the "New History" also emphasized the structure of its academic discipline and the assertion that learners at any age were capable of intellectual inquiry. According to Evans (2004), the clearest introduction of the New Social Studies era came with Charles Keller's 1961 article in the *Saturday Review*, in which he claimed that school social studies was in the doldrums because of its confusing array of subject areas and its overemphasis on textbooks and pedantic teaching. Keller proposed a reform movement in social studies similar to those in mathematics and science, starting with substituting the term "history and the social sciences" for "social studies" (Evans, 2004).

The earliest stirrings of the New Social Studies can be seen in the 1959 Amherst history project. Spearheaded by Van Halsey (1963), the dialogues surrounding the project eventually led Halsey to propose a new high school American history course in *Social Education*. In October 1962, *Social Education* published an announcement for "Project Social Studies," whereby the USOE would fund research projects, curriculum study centers, and conferences geared towards improving research and teaching in the field (Evans, 2004). Another early leader was Edwin Fenton, a historian at Carnegie Institute of Technology who taught preservice teacher education courses who "was bothered by the pat assertions found in high school history textbooks and by the boredom and loathing of his own students for many history … courses" (Evans, 2004, p. 125). Fenton introduced the use of primary source documents into his courses in order to generate more enthusiasm among his students and to engage them in the actual work of historians (Evans, 2004). His experiences resulted in his book *32 Problems in World History* (Fenton, 1964).

Evans (2004) reports that by 1965, around two dozen projects that constituted the "New Social Studies" had been funded either by the USOE, National Science Foundation, or private foundations such as Ford and Carnegie, by 1967 more than 50 national projects were in progress. However, Haas (1977) asserts that the projects created after 1967, while claiming to be consistent with the New Social Studies, were in fact heading in numerous, divergent directions. Evans (2004) states that the movement and its funding peaked in 1967, with its topics dominating both *Social Education* and the National Council for the Social Studies conference; "the years after 1967 would be spent dealing with publication, dissemination, and diffusion of materials" (p. 127).

ALLAN KOWNSLAR AND THE "NEW HISTORY"

Allan Kownslar (1967) emerged as a leader in the New Social Studies movement's early initiative phase through the publication of his first major textbook, *Discovering American History*. His involvement with the movement began while he was working for the Amherst School District in Massachusetts and built upon the work of Halsey in the Amherst history project and of Fenton at the Carnegie Institute. There he was approached by Halsey—director of Amherst College's Committee on the Study of History—to participate in the committee's writing projects. This affiliation led to the publication of two small, innovative high school texts —*Manifest Destiny and Expansionism in the 1840s* and *The Progressive Era: Tradition in a Changing Society, 1900–1917*.

Kownslar's early work bears the unmistakable imprint of the social reconstructionist movement of the Depression era, as well as the contemporary vogue for "inquiry-based" methodology shared by 1960s theorists such as John Holt and Neil Postman. Kownslar's and Frizzle's (1967) *Discovering American History*, for example, reflected the priorities of social reconstructionists George Counts and Harold Rugg, while doubtlessly updating the concerns of these earlier writers. Social reconstructionism, as Lawrence Dennis (1989) noted, grew out of the view that schools in an era of crisis for industrial capitalism could not merely train students for future jobs in a failed economic system. In the immediate aftermath of the stock market crash of 1929, many American intellectuals became disenchanted with the political economy of the United States and looked to the innovative economic programs of the nascent Soviet Union for inspiration. Counts and other social reconstructionists were particularly impressed by the dynamism of the Soviet economy. As Dennis wrote, Counts, after a lengthy and inspirational visit to the Soviet Union in 1929,

> came to believe that a planned economy had to be an essential feature of any well-run industrial society, and that view was reinforced on his return to America early in 1930, when he saw at first hand the effects of capitalism gone amok. (p. 37)

Counts (1934) believed that schools could play an integral role in promoting collectivism as a means of social change. Writing during the depths of the Depression in 1934, Counts stated:

> Any completely satisfactory solution of the problem of education therefore would seem to involve fairly radical social reconstruction. The fact is that for the most part contemporary society is not organized primarily for the education of its children or for the achievement any other humane purpose. Such matters are largely subordinated to the processes of wealth production and accumulation. (p. 562)

In the same way that Counts (1934) and others (e.g., Harold Rugg) emphasized the analysis of the Communist Party and the concerns over poverty prevalent during the 1930s, Kownslar's (1967) text *Discovering American History*—written in conjunction with Donald Frizzle—undeniably promoted the concerns of the 1960s social movements around civil rights and the U.S. military involvement in Vietnam. For example, the Civil Rights Movement was highlighted in a section that included excerpts of the landmark *Plessy v. Ferguson* and *Brown v. Board of Education* Supreme Court decisions (p. 728). By choosing an "oral history" approach, using personal testimony of activists who had taken part in sit-in protests at lunch counters in Knoxville, Chattanooga, and Montgomery, rather than a dry secondary source analysis of the movement, Kownslar and Frizzle tried to appeal to the natural empathy of students and to encourage them to see themselves as future activists. The authors, however, took care not to be overly didactic in their methods. In an intriguing section of the unit, they included extensive quotations from residents of Southern towns on both sides of the conflict, such as a Montgomery building contractor who equated civil rights activists with Communists, a Presbyterian minister who feared that the sit-in protests antagonized White Southerners who might otherwise be disposed to support the struggle, and a former president of the Alabama State Bar Association who hinted at threats of police violence against activists (p. 732).

In a unit titled "The Vietnam Debate," Kownslar and Frizzle (1967) constructed a roundtable of opinions on the Vietnam intervention from excerpts of published works and speeches by individuals such as President Lyndon B. Johnson and General William Westmoreland, as well as critics of the policy such as Senator Frank Church. At the conclusion of this section, Kownslar and Frizzle asked students to consider each of the statements and to explain which were most and least convincing (pp. 771–781) In this manner, Kownslar and Frizzle sought to engage students in the very debate that was dominating Capitol Hill at the time, rather than continue the condescending pattern of one-way transference of information encouraged by most mainstream history textbooks. Their work also provided teachers with a means of adding supplementary materials to classroom discussions rather than relying upon the often obsolete and deliberately uncontroversial material in traditional textbooks.

This critical approach was continued in *Manifest Destiny and Expansionism in the 1840s* (Kownslar, 1967), a slim volume intended for high school use. In this text, Kownslar employed a historical discussion about the philosophical concept of "manifest destiny" to explore the imperial desires of the American leadership class in the eighteenth and nineteenth century. The book was structured once again around profound questions such as: "Is superiority of race or superiority of institutions implicit in the idea (of manifest destiny)?" (p. 1). Kownslar provided key quotations from individuals such as John Adams (p. 10), Thomas Hart Benton (p. 22), and Stephen A. Douglas (p. 41) to answer these questions. Working on this text inspired Kownslar to think in a profoundly different way about creating social studies textbooks. He explained:

> Since those of us with the Amherst College Committee were consciously or subconsciously really using the inquiry method in our curriculum development, why not expand that to be incorporated not only in limited in-depth case studies but instead for a year long school segment? Thus, within an hour I had outlined what became *Discovering American History*. (Kownslar, 2006)

The importance of asking the right questions in inquiry-based history instruction was emphasized again most recently by Barton and Levstik (2005), who argued that posing questions that merely ask students to recall decontextualized dates and battle sites is a self-defeating exercise; it at once deprives students of the ability to use prior knowledge in order to investigate the topic as well as reinforces the sense that studying history is irredeemably dull. Instead, Barton and Levstik argue that, "The point of these questions is not to see whether students have read a particular text; rather, it is to provide direction and motivation for the rigorous work of doing history" (p. 30). The questions Kownslar used in his early texts clearly fit within the best tradition of inquiry-based instruction.

Indeed, much of Kownslar's textbook work was written in the style of the project-based materials, emphasizing inquiry skills. This methodology, based on the concept of scaffolding instruction by using previously acquired information from a child's own experiences, owes much to the romantic, humanistic tradition of such Enlightenment figures as Jean Jacques Rousseau and John Locke. These ideas were taken up in the early 1960s by a new group of romantics led by John Holt. In books such as *How Children Learn* (1967), Holt castigated traditional pedagogy while promoting a new variant of the Pestalozzian "discovery method." He argued:

> The child is curious. He wants to make sense out of things, find out how things work, gain competence and control over himself and his environment, do what he can see other people doing. He is open, receptive, and perceptive. He does not shut himself off from the strange, confused, complicated world around him. (pp. 184–185)

Holt and other radical educators of the day stressed that an inquiry-based pedagogy could open up children who had been previously closed down emotionally and intellectually by traditional pedagogy in traditional schools.

The movement toward using inquiry-based techniques came to its full flowering in the late 1960s as Kownslar's texts were being published. In their influential 1969 book *Teaching as a Subversive Activity*, Postman and Weingartner described this new methodology:

> The inquiry method is very much a product of our electric age. It makes the syllabus obsolete; students generate their own stories by becoming involved in the methods of learning. Where the older school environment has asked, "Who discovered America?," the inquiry methods asks, "How do you discover who discovered America?" The older school environment stressed that learning is being told what happened. The inquiry environment stresses that learning is a happening in itself. (p. 29)

In a middle school text that reflected this methodology, *Inquiring About American History* (1972), Kownslar and Fielder used a juxtaposition of images and probing questions to challenge young students to confront their own misconceptions about history. "Did Columbus Really Discover America?" the authors ask in the text's early pages: "How do we know Columbus sailed to the New World with three ships in 1492? How do we know he thought he had reached the East? How can we be sure that these things are true?" (p. 9).

Kownslar and Fielder (1972) followed this questioning by stressing the use of historical evidence, especially primary source documents such as Columbus's own diary of his voyages, a portion of which was reproduced in the text (p. 11). In a later section on the immigrant experience in the United States titled "The Neighborhood," Kownslar and Fielder used Jacob Riis's stark photographs of New York's immigrant neighborhoods in a manner reminiscent of Harold Rugg's popular textbook series of the 1930s and 1940s (pp. 250–253). The photographs were accompanied by the following text:

> Many immigrants who arrived in America spoke no English and knew no Americans. Imagine how such an immigrant must have felt when he first met people who understood the same language and made him feel more at home. He didn't feel lost or alone anymore. (p. 250)

The "social problems" focus of the *Inquiring About American History* (Kownslar & Fielder, 1972) text was continued in its final unit—"Regions and Cities"—which reflected the concerns of the period's nascent environmental movement while encouraging students to play the roles of contemporary urban planners. In a section titled "Working on a Problem," Kownslar and Fielder addressed the issue of solving the transportation crisis around metropolitan New York City. The authors began the discussion by posing the dilemmas involved in the different options facing urban planners. They wrote:

> If the state tried to improve the city's transportation by itself, then there would not be enough money for other needs. And other states were involved in the problem, too. For example, New York State could not build a bridge between New York City and a town in New Jersey unless the New Jersey town agreed. (p. 305)

Having scaffolded the lesson—again employing rich photographic images to provoke a visceral response from students—Kownslar and Fielder then asked:

> What was to be done? Would transportation around New York City just get worse and worse until the great city stopped? It was clear that people from different cities and different states would have to get together and agree on a plan for the whole area if they wanted to save the city. (p. 306)

The intention of the authors was clear, and one can imagine a creative classroom teacher using this material in order to launch a role playing exercise or perhaps an introductory discussion to be followed by a lengthy project on urban planning.

THE NEW SOCIAL STUDIES: CRITICISMS

Evans (2004) argued that

> events in the society, many of which impinged directly on schools, may have diluted teacher enthusiasm for the New Social Studies and its general focus on inquiry based in the disciplines, a step removed from the conflicts and dilemmas of the social world. (p. 127)

In fact, Evans explained, "the profession was far from united behind the new reform movement" (p. 128). For example, he pointed out that Shirley Engle and others, including Byron Massialas and Lawrence Metcalf, in an April 1963 themed issue of *Social Education* article titled "Revising the Social Studies," were already beginning to take the New Social Studies in a different direction than that of historians, discussing the "possible structures for a discipline of social studies as a unified field of study" (p. 131). Various articles called for an integrated social studies curriculum focused on social problems and issues, the study of value conflicts, and the reflective examination of beliefs about race, class, and gender, with history and social science content as simply a vehicle for inquiring about these broader questions.

Later, in letters published in a 1965 issue of *Social Education*, Fred Newmann, Byron Massialas, and Richard Gross cautioned against overemphasis of "inductive thinking" and "discovery methods" based on the structure of only one discipline, and against the overuse of "teacher-proof" materials developed by social scientists with little understanding of the normative and affective aspects of learning (Evans, 2004, p. 128; Newmann, Massialas, & Gross 1965). More specifically, Mark Krug (1966) criticized the movement for its conceptual weaknesses and lack of logical structure, questioning the need for children to become "mini-historians" and arguing that they needed traditional historical knowledge. Albert Anthony (1967) argued that the "new history" curricula lacked clear objectives and a sound rationale, and that historians had involved themselves in this initiative primarily out of fear that history would become extinct in the school curriculum.

Evans (2004) concluded that the New Social Studies movement led to the production of materials that frequently omitted citizens' questions and perennial social issues. He wrote:

> Discipline-based experts were lionized as the main source of knowledge. This approach ignored or minimized student knowledge, community resources, issues, and problems. It also served to undermine the possibility of interdisciplinary study and to reify education and power relationships endemic to the institution of schools. (p. 129)

Only one published critique appears specifically focused on Kownslar's work. In an essay on recent U.S. history textbooks' treatment of the Cold War and the role of veterans, Fournier (2004) cited a 1978 study by Herz (1978) of the Ethics and Public Policy Center on how the Cold War was presented in six textbooks that were written while the Cold War was underway. Herz concluded that *Discovering American History* was "the worst.... Of the chapter's 28 pages, fully 43% were devoted to 'McCarthyism' and to the Left's all-encompassing criticism of U.S. actions during the Cold War" (Fournier, 2004). Herz accused Kownslar and Frizzle of being apologists for communism. Specifically, he criticized them for whitewashing communism, indoctrinating the reader, and giving the Soviet system the complete benefit of the doubt, while ignoring the Soviet conquest of Eastern Europe, the policy of containment, the Berlin blockade, and the lack of human rights in communist regimes. Moreover, Herz criticized the authors for provided "ideological cover" to dictators such as Fidel Castro, whom they described as a "nationalist." Therefore, objections to Kownslar's work were rooted both in his training as an historian and in his ideology (Herz, 1970).

KOWNSLAR'S LATER WORK

As Joel Spring (1998) pointed out, the flowering of progressive pedagogy in the late 1960s and early 1970s was short-lived and provoked an intense conservative reaction during the Nixon era that would soon profoundly affect Kownslar's work. According to Spring, "the conservative and political and educational patterns of the 1970s emerged in reaction to the student protest and civil rights demonstrations of the 1960s and the policies of the War on Poverty" (p. 312). It is ironic that the very successes of these campaigns ushered in a period of conservative backlash, leading directly to the "Back to Basics" prescriptions of the Reagan administration's *A Nation at Risk* report. Certainly, by the 1970s the New Social Studies movement seemed to have run its course.

According to Earle (1982), Kownslar's textbooks changed over the years to incorporate features enhancing the relevance of history and fostering students' mastery of basic historical knowledge and skills. Earle also noted in Kownslar's work a transition from scientific inquiry to basic information mixed with more reflected inquiry. The 1980 *American Government* text by Kownslar and Terry L. Smart, for example, looks to the casual observer to be a mainstream text. Its organization of units – from "Our Political Heritage" to units covering the three branches of the U.S. government—follows that of most civics texts on the market today (Kownslar & Smart, 1980). However, a more careful analysis reveals that the focus on social problems and commitment to inquiry-based learning that marks Kownslar's seminal work is still intact. In a unit on "Local Government," Kownslar and Smart include a section on "The Special Problems of Big Cities" (pp. 402–415). This section is introduced with an inquiry-based lesson that asks students to put themselves in the role of urban planners (p. 410). Kownslar's later texts, thus, represent a duality of approaches; they could equally be used by those teachers committed to either progressive or more traditional pedagogies.

O. L. Davis, Jr. (personal communications, November 9, 2006) observed that Kownslar did not disavow or abandon the New Social Studies; he simply went on to his next project, sometimes by himself, on other occasions with colleagues. Davis explained:

> Allan was utterly practical in this regard. For example, he knew quite well that almost all teachers, among other things, had or believed they had no adequate knowledge of "inquiry," nor, they believed, did they have "time to teach" such that inquiry ... could be a part of their courses. So, in the first edition of his Texas history textbook, he alternated chapters that focused on "typical textbook presentation" and "inquiry-based presentation".... That first edition, as I recall, took most of the adoptions for the next five years [period of adoption].   But teachers, as differentiated from central office

supervisors/administrators, did not like the "inquiry chapters," so, in subsequent revisions, Allan simply excised or rewrote the inquiry chapters.

In fact, in 1974 Kownslar edited the 44th Yearbook of the National Council for the Social Studies, in which he seemed to take great care to emphasize the practical aspects of the New Social Studies, the cognitive and skills-based orientation of historical inquiry, and the importance of developing students' critical thinking capabilities—while at the same time incorporating values clarification, the affective dimensions of historical understanding, and the dismantling of historical myths and stereotypes. Titled *Teaching American History: The Quest for Relevancy*, the yearbook included Kownslar's (1974) essay on "Why the Teaching of American History Should Remain a Vital Part of the Quest for Relevancy Within the School Curriculum" (p. xiii). He explained that he agreed to take on the project only if it would mainly contain inquiry-oriented lessons for classroom use, and New Social Studies agreed (A. Kownslar, personal communication, 2006). In the introduction to *Teaching American History* Kownslar wrote:

> Perhaps shortcomings in the presentation of materials are responsible for the cry of irrelevance – a protest repeated all too often during the past two decades by many students who believed that teaching strategies in history classes fostered a senseless examination of the past. If such criticism has validity, then the quest for relevance should not suggest the abolition of history courses but rather alteration in the ways history classes have been taught. Students must be led to understand how and why a study of the past does have meaning and practical application as they face a difficult present and an uncertain future. (1974, p. 12)

Perhaps most importantly, Kownslar pointed out that social studies teachers from numerous school districts around the state of Texas had reviewed the book and provided ample suggestions and critiques, resulting in a lesson plan format for each chapter that included an introduction and rationale, a suggested time frame and student audience, a description of materials needed for the lesson, lesson objectives, teaching suggestions and activities, and an annotated bibliography.

Consequently, the *Teaching American History* yearbook (Kownslar, 1974) featured a "History in the Classroom" section with detailed lesson plans focused on helping students understand the nature of the discipline of history and historical inquiry, including a lesson on early American Indian life that illustrated the "incomplete and interpretive aspects of history" (pp. 19–39) a lesson on conditions of life during the Civil War to help students "utilize a process of inquiry as they try to piece together what may have transpired in the past" (pp. 41–56) a concept development lesson on "women's liberation" (pp. 57–80) a simulation involving Appalachian coal miners designed to develop students' historical empathy skills (pp. 81–112) and a case study on the formation of historical myth and its application to Black culture and the validity of the "melting pot theory" (pp. 113–148).

The yearbook's final section emphasized the use of historical topics to help students "cope with issues which may arise in the future" (Kownslar, 1974, p. xiii). For example, "The American City in the 19th Century: Questions We Can Ask" (pp. 149–168) focused on "helping students learn what questions they can ask about a historical topic" and "how to utilize those questions in the future when processing information, arriving at conclusions, and judging the appropriateness of those conclusions" (p. xiv) A lesson on "Who is Qualified for the Presidency?" used objective historical data to help students analyze their opinions and concerns (pp. 169–188) Further, a lesson on environmental issues asked students to consider their own relevance to history by examining how their actions might affect the future of their country (pp. 189–216). Finally, Kownslar included a questionnaire developed by teachers to be used as a means of evaluating history teaching materials (pp. 217–234).

Ultimately, Kownslar (1974) asserted that good social studies teachers had been using engaging practices long before they had even heard of a New Social Studies movement and that they were in an advantageous position with regard to "counteracting student boredom and the discipline problems so often associated with it" (p. 12). He explained:

> Long before the advent of *Sputnik* or before the New Social Studies even had a name, those teachers, instead of pretending to represent a walking set of encyclopedias, remained the experienced teacher, director, and a constant and constructive critic to student opinions. These teachers found ways to actively involve students in long-lasting learning processes. They somehow managed to find the time and energy to use their own imagination and initiative in developing new materials and teaching strategies which presented factualdata in an appealing, challenging, and effective way to their pupils. (p. 12)

Kownslar (1974) also stated his belief that the students themselves could "provide some of the many ways to begin the restoration of history as a relevant academic discipline" (p. 11). He suggested that they also could bring "what Jerome Bruner calls social relevance to personal relevance and vice versa; to bring knowledge and conviction together; to link directly a historical issue with personal conviction" (p. 11). In what he then termed "the 'New' New Social Studies," teachers and students could link historical data and critical thinking with clarification of values and attitudes—a "developmental interplay between objectives within the cognitive and affective domains" (p. 11).

Finally, Kownslar argued that anything teachers undertook in the history or social studies classroom must withstand the rigors of what he called the "Five Year Test"

> In other words, much of what we teach students should continue to affect or to have an impact on them five years thereafter. Having students absorb large doses of historical data will not provide us with a very satisfactory evaluation. But history taught as a quest for relevancy, incorporating the best qualities of the Old, the New, and the "New" New Social Studies, should not only improve our rating but make the teaching of history more challenging each year. For wherever it appears in the school curriculum, a study of history can readily serve as a vehicle by which students can acquire an applicable mode of inquiry, develop useful concepts, successfully empathize with the past, continue to clarify values, learn to recognize and to cope with suspected myths and stereotypes, and to ask critical questions about the past, present, and future.... Students should need never ask: "What good's all this gonna do me?" They'll already know. (p. 12)

CONCLUSIONS

"The New Social Studies Movement" was a broader progressive movement that attracted many educators outside the field of social studies. According to Davis, Kownslar was not a social studies educator per se, nor was the National Council for the Social Studies a prominent professional reference point for him. Rather, his professional identity was as a historian and experienced teacher "who wrote textbooks as a serious means of influencing positively the teaching of school history" (O. L. Davis, personal communication, November 6, 2006). Using the intellectual opening and funding opportunities provided by the national crisis that the *Sputnik* satellite launch had provoked in 1957, Kownslar and his colleagues created a body of work that revised the "problem-based" curriculum frameworks and inquiry-based methods for a new generation of social studies students and teachers. However, Kownslar stated that he did not give the Cold War much consideration when he became involved in the New Social Studies movement. Instead, he explained, he simply sought ways for students to further develop their critical thinking skills and writing skills, as well as clarification of their values by using the inquiry method through the study of social studies—in other words, to "exploit" the social studies content in order to accomplish such goals (A. O. Kownslar, personal communications, 2006).

When the New Social Studies movement faded, Kownslar believed he had satisfied his goal to attempt various ways to try to somehow introduce the inquiry method to as many teachers and students as possible (A. O. Kownslar, personal communications, 2006). Indeed, some of his publications are inquiry-oriented throughout, such as *Discovering American History: Inquiring About American History* (1967), *The Americans, Manifest Destiny, The Progressive Era, Teaching About Social Issues in American History,* and the Department of Defense Dependents Schools Honors World History Program. Others, such as *The Texans,* are about one-half inquiry-oriented, and still others such as *World History: A Story of Progress, American Government,* and *Civics: Citizens and Society* are about one-third inquiry-oriented. Kownslar explained that the idea of the latter works was "to provide options to the more lecture-prone teachers to use some inquiry-oriented materials, but only if it suited their purposes and teaching personalities" (A. O. Kownslar, personal communications, 2006).

Upon moving to Texas in 1970, Kownslar devoted time to working with social studies teachers to further introduce the inquiry method in their classrooms as well as to research and write other types of works in the field of history and biography. For example, his *Texas Iconoclast: Maury Maverick, Jr.,* published by Texas Christian University Press, his *European Texans,* one of a five-volume series on ethnic Texans, as well as his authoring chapters in the *Black Cowboys of Texas* and *Texas Women on the Cattle Trails* (all published by Texas A&M University Press) represented efforts to bring to light new evidence about such topics for use by teachers and future scholars (A. O. Kownslar, personal communications, 2006).

Kownslar explained that his history and methods courses at Trinity University have remained totally inquiry-oriented, and that he "writes the textbooks with a pro-con or point-counterpoint values conflict approach for his American history and Texas history courses" (A. O. Kownslar, personal communications, 2006). Yet he also stated:

> My overall experience in presenting social studies inquiry strategies has been that students are much more adaptable to them than are some teachers. Probably that is because use of the inquiry method is more time-consuming than the lecture method and generally requires more effort on the part of already vastly overworked classroom teachers. Even more daunting is the problem regarding greater emphasis today on standardized testing for social studies content, which leaves even less time for teachers to stress little else in the classroom. (personal communications, 2006)

Kownslar concluded that, while those in the New Social Studies movement did manage to make some needed changes, he did not think anyone got enough teachers involved to make a tremendous or significant difference in how social studies was taught. And although he continued to receive inquiries from teachers from all over the country wanting him to revise some of his publications, such as *Discovering American History,* he believed that publishers of elementary and secondary social studies text-books are not interested in doing extensive inquiry-oriented ventures, "preferring instead to place primary focus on the safer and more lucrative traditional-narrative materials" (A. O. Kownslar, personal communications, 2006).

Nonetheless, despite the obvious pressures, Kownslar's commitment to progressive education and inquiry learning has remained consistent. Ultimately, he reflected on his work thusly:

> Throughout, I realized there are many effective ways to teach, the inquiry approach being only one of them, but it is a very vital one. Use of the inquiry method as part of social studies instruction stresses the very essence of sound critical thinking and writing, which are among the very important skills students should utilize to be informed citizens.

REFERENCES

Anthony, A. S. (1967). The role of objectives in the "new history." *Social Education, 31*, 574, 580.

Barton, K. C., & Levstik, L. S. (2005). *Doing history: Investigating with children in elementary and middle schools*. Mahwah, NJ: Erlbaum.

Bruner, J. (1960). *The process of education*. Cambridge, MA: Harvard University Press.

Counts, G. S. (1934). *Social foundations of education*. New York: Charles Scribner's Sons.

Dennis, L. J. (1989) *George S. Counts and Charles A. Beard: Collaborators for change*. Albany, NY: State University of New York Press.

Earle, D. D. (1982, February). *Allan Kownslar and the New Social Studies*. Paper presented at the annual meeting of the Southwest Educational Research Association, Austin, TX. (ERIC Document ED221419)

Engle, S. H. (1963). Thoughts in regard to revision. *Social Education, 27*, 182.

Evans, R. W. (2004). *The social studies wars: What should we teach the children?* New York: Teachers College Press.

Fenton, E. (1964). *32 problems in world history*. Glenview, IL: Scott, Foresman.

Fournier, R. (2004). *Political correctness pervades history textbooks*. Retrieved from http://www.vfw.org/index.cfm?fa=news.magDtl&dtl=2&mid=2360

Gutek, G. L. (2000). *American education: 1945–2000*. Chicago: Loyola University Press.

Haas, J. D. (1977). *The era of the new social studies*. Boulder, CO: Social Science Education Consortium.

Halsey, V. R., Jr. (1963). American history: A new high school course. *Social Education, 27*, 249–252.

Herz, M. F. (1978). *How the Cold War is taught: Six American history textbooks examined*. Washington, DC: Ethics and Public Policy Center, Georgetown University.

Holt, J. (1967). *How children learn*. New York: Pitman.

Keller, C. R. (1961, September). Needed: Revolution in the social studies. *Saturday Review, 16*, 60–62.

Kownslar, A. (1967). *Manifest destiny and expansionism in the 1840s.* Boston: D. C. Heath.

Kownslar, A. O. (Ed.). (1968). *The Progressive era: Tradition in a changing society. 1900–1917.* Boston: D. C. Heath.

Kownslar, A. O. (1972). *The Texans. Their land and history.* Boston: McGraw-Hill.

Kownslar, A. O. (1974). *Teaching American history: The quest for relevancy* (44th Yearbook of the National Council for the Social Studies). Washington, DC: National Council for the Social Studies.

Kownslar, A. O. (1975). *The Americans: A history of the United States.* New York: Holt, Rinehart, and Winston.

Kownslar, A. O. (1978). *Teaching about social issues in American history. Four demonstration lessons.* Boulder, CO: ERIC Clearinghouse for Social Studies/Social Science Education.

Kownslar, A. O. (1982). *American government.* New York: MacMillan.

Kownslar, A. O. (Ed.). (1997). *Texas iconoclast. Maury Maverick, Jr.* Fort Worth, Texas: Texas Christian University Press.

Kownslar, A. O. (2000). Robert Lemmons: A Black Texan mustanger. In S. R. Massey (Ed.), *Black cowboys of Texas* (pp. 325–342). College Station, TX: Texas A&M University Press.

Kownslar, A. O. (2004). *The European Texans.* College Station, TX: Texas A&M University Press.

Kownslar, A. O. (2006). Mary (Molly) Catherine Dunn Bugbee: Mrs. Thomas Sherman Bugbee. In S. R. Massey (Ed.), *Texas women on the cattle trails* (pp. 79-88). College Station, TX: Texas A&M University Press.

Kownslar, A., & W. Fielder. (1972). *Inquiring about American history: Studies in history and political science.* New York: Holt, Rinehart and Winston.

Kownslar, A. O., & Frizzle, D. B. (1967). *Discovering American history.* New York: Holt, Rinehart, and Winston.

Kownslar, A. O., & Smart, T. L. (1980). *American government.* New York: McGraw-Hill.

Kownslar, A. O., & Smart, T. O. (1982). *Civics: Citizens and society.* New York: MacMillan.

Kownslar, A. O., & Smart, T. O., Perez-Abreu, M. L., Larios, R., Michaud, S., & Michaud, R. (1987). *World history: A story of progress.* New York: Holt, Rinehart and Winston.

Krug, M. M. (1966). Bruner's new social studies: A critique. *Social Education, 30*, 400–406.

Newmann, F. M., Massalias, B. G., & Gross R. E. (1965). Reactions to the reports on Project Social Studies. *Social Education, 29*, 356–360.

Postman, N., & Weingartner, C. (1969). *Teaching as a subversive activity.* New York: Delacorte Press.

Spring, J. (1998). *American education* (8th ed.). Boston: McGraw-Hill.

CHAPTER 6

LEADER-WRITERS

The Contributions of Donald Oliver, Fred Newmann, and James Shaver to the Harvard Social Studies Project

Chara Haeussler Bohan and Joseph R. Feinberg

English author Graham Greene wrote in *The Quiet American* that "God exists only for leader-writers" (Oxford, 1979, p. 236). In the field of social studies education, Donald Oliver, Fred Newmann, and James Shaver were leader-writers. These three Harvard education intellects engaged in the luxury of thinking about ways to improve social studies education. From their position of advantage, they were able to create exemplary materials that were part of the New Social Studies movement in the 1960s and 1970s, which arguably transformed the social studies curriculum in America. Indeed, all three made notable contributions to social studies education throughout their careers, and cultivated their relationship during the Harvard Social Studies Project.

A series of pamphlets published in the 1960s and 1970s, the Harvard Social Studies Project was a collaborative effort by Harvard education professor, Donald Oliver, his many graduate students, including Newmann

The New Social Studies: People, Projects, and Perspectives, pp. 111–132
Copyright © 2010 by Information Age Publishing
All rights of reproduction in any form reserved.

and Shaver, and 7th–12th grade Boston area school teachers. The curriculum materials that were developed from the project became known as the Public Issue Series (Stern, 2006). Although the materials may never have been widely adopted, many of the intellectual concepts and instructional methods produced a lasting legacy on social studies education (p. 267). Oliver, Newmann, and Shaver's writings about instructional methods and their conceptual understanding of social studies education are unique and worthy of contemporary examination, as the Harvard Social Studies Project is "hailed as one of the best" of the New Social Studies curricula (Woyshner, 2006, p. 29).

Throughout the past century, social studies education faced division between supporters of a discipline-centered approach and advocates of inquiry-based social education methods (Fallace, 2008; Lybarger, 1991; Ross, 1997; Thornton, 2005). The Public Issue Series demonstrated that Oliver, Newmann, and Shaver favored an inquiry-based, interdisciplinary approach to social studies education. Established as topic-oriented case studies, the pamphlets centered on persistent political-ethical questions in history and, as active participants, teachers and students were encouraged to employ rational decision making for addressing complex problems that did not have established, correct answers.

The focus of this research is an analysis of the Harvard Social Studies Project and an exploration of the contributions by Donald Oliver, Fred Newmann, and James Shaver to that project and to social studies education, writ large. All three giants in social studies education served as leader-writers in the field. Oliver, Newmann, and Shaver's writings about instructional methods and their conceptual understanding of social studies education are unique and worthy of contemporary examination. The Harvard Social Studies Project not only established all three men as influential leaders in social studies education, but also laid the groundwork for their subsequent work in broader areas of education. Furthermore, as standards-based testing currently sweeps across the nation in the wake of the No Child Left Behind Act, test creators would be well served to examine the publications that resulted from the Harvard Social Studies Project. These pamphlets were designed to encourage students to appreciate multiple perspectives, to evaluate historical understandings, to compare and contrast past historical events with contemporary issues, and to foster student evaluation of persisting questions in history through weighing of factual claims and values. In other words, reading traditional textbooks and answering end-of-chapter questions were abandoned in favor of multiple perspectives, higher order thinking, evaluation, and dialogue. Oliver, Shaver, and Newmann intended to change traditional social studies education through the Harvard Social Studies Project. Indeed, after more than 40 years since initiating the Harvard Social Studies Project, their work supported pedagogical approaches for social studies teaching and learning similar to models advocated by current researchers, such as Wineburg, Mosborg, Porat, and Duncan (2007), Thornton (2005) Barton and Levstik (2004), VanSledright (2002), and Foster (2001), and Stearns, Seixas, and Wineburg (2000).

WHO WAS DONALD OLIVER?

When asked to analyze the significance of Donald Oliver's contributions to the Harvard Social Studies Project, James Shaver responded, "Don Oliver didn't 'contribute' to the project. He *was* the Harvard Social Studies Project" (personal communication, May 10, 2007). Although Donald Oliver directed the project single-mindedly, it was a cooperative endeavor between professors, graduate students, and classroom teachers to change traditional social studies teaching, and to promote analysis of societal problems.

Born in 1929, the year of the infamous stock market crash, Donald Oliver was a product of the Great Depression. Oliver's family was of working class origin, and he attended a one-room schoolhouse in Connecticut during his primary grades. In later years, he excelled as a public high school student, and earned a scholarship to Amherst College in Massachusetts (Stern, 2006). In 1952, Oliver graduated from Amherst with a bachelor's degree in psychology. He continued his studies at Harvard Graduate School of Education, earned a doctorate in 1956, and subsequently joined the faculty at Harvard. Despite an elite background in higher education, Oliver possessed strong anti-elitist sentiments, in large part due to his working class and Depression era origins.

Donald Oliver was a complex individual described as brilliant, distant, acerbic, confrontational, insecure, and analytic (Stern, 2006). His success in education can be attributed, in large part, to his intellectual prowess and his bulldog nature. He was known for obstinate behavior in an argument. He conducted class as Socratic discussion, and the intensity of the debate brought more than one graduate student to tears. Indeed, the author of his obituary wrote in *The Harvard University Gazette* that he was "known for conducting marathon discussion classes, lasting four hours or more," and his students remembered him for his, "confrontational discussion style" (Gewertz, 2002, p. 1).

During the course of his lifetime, Donald Oliver mellowed and changed. At the height of the Harvard Social Studies Project, however, he was a brash, young assistant professor with bold ideas. Oliver described the foundation of his ideas for the Harvard Social Studies Project in a 1957 article published in the *Harvard Educational Review* (repinted in

Oliver, 1968). In this seminal article, he discussed the value of an inquiry approach to social studies education. This 1957 article, on the selection of content in social studies, broke new ground in the field (Newmann, personal communication, May 15, 2007). Yet, it took a decade for such ideas to be realized in social studies classrooms and textbooks.

The Harvard Social Studies Project was one of several New Social Studies projects implemented throughout the nation. For example, Edwin Fenton of the Carnegie Institute of Technology published a textbook series with Holt, Rinehart, and Winston in the late 1960s and early 1970s, which also became renowned for promoting an inquiry approach in social studies education. In a book titled *The New Social Studies,* Fenton described the various social studies curriculum reform projects throughout the United States, the quality of their work, and their comprehensiveness (Shaftel, 1968). Perhaps, Fenton's series made a larger impact because his work had a large national publisher supporting the endeavor. However, Donald Oliver had established the innovative intellectual basis for such work as early as the late 1950s.

Donald Oliver's inquiry approach provided specific instructional strategies that sought to nurture discussion in the classroom. He loved classroom debate, so it is not surprising that he would foster such methodology in social studies classrooms and textbooks. He wanted teachers and students to think about persistent questions in history, and these questions did not have clear-cut, right or wrong answers. His analytical approach to social studies education contrasted sharply with the post-Sputnik emphasis on content knowledge, especially in science and math. Despite "new math," "new science" and "new social studies," traditional teaching methods often prevailed. Critics, such as Arthur Bestor, challenged the intellectual rigor of progressive educational methods, and emphasized the need for strong content knowledge. Paradoxically, the funding for the New Social Studies, with its avant-garde methodology, came from the U.S. Office of Education (Shaver, 2006), in the wake of concern that Russian students were better educated than American students in the post-Sputnik era (see e.g., Davidow, 1977; Flesch, 1955).

Donald Oliver became more radical in his beliefs about education as his career progressed. When he worked on the Harvard Social Studies Project, Oliver employed Deweyan beliefs about education and Jeffersonian perspectives on society. By the mid-1970s, however, he adopted a critical theory educational stance (Shaver, 2006). Student unrest at Harvard—the counter culture movement—profoundly impacted Oliver's beliefs. He lost faith in authority, and believed real learning occurred when students rejected obedience and questioned hierarchical structures. At the same time, Oliver's 20 year marriage dissolved (Stern, 2006). In a break from traditional norms of the time, reportedly, he had much of the childcare responsibilities and household chores, and had been unhappy in his marriage. Oliver and his first wife divorced. Later he married Pauline "Polly" Anderson. According to Polly, Oliver was happy in his second marriage. Oliver had four children from the two marriages, two boys and two girls, and three stepsons (Gewertz, 2002).

Personal and professional events of the early 1970s led Oliver to change the focus of his studies. He began to engage in broader intellectual interests rather than the more narrow interest in social studies. Oliver's most important book, *Education and Community: A Radical Critique of Innovative Schooling* reflected his changing attention. In *Education and Community*, Oliver (1976) critiqued the helping professions to act as agents of social change. He described various different cultures, such as Kibbutzes, Hutterites, the Highlander Folk School (a social action community), the Marathon House (a therapeutic community), and Japanese Americans. He also discussed human experiences, such as varied dimensions of the quality of life. Oliver employed these descriptions of cultures and human experiences as a means to develop a theory of community. His expansive study of community led him to reject traditional public schooling and assumptions of progress. He came to believe that true learning, and real cultural exchanges occurred in ordinary places, such as coffee shops and hair salons, where people talk informally. This belief in learning in everyday locations guided him to spend his 1978 sabbatical studying hairdressing at a beauty school in Lowell, Massachusetts.

Oliver continued to write throughout the remainder of his life. And, he sustained his questioning of assumptions and his probing at the meaning of life. Two more important books followed, *Education, Modernity, and Fractured Meaning* (1989), and *The Primal, the Modern, and the Vital Center* (2002). In *Education, Modernity, and Fractured Meaning*, Oliver continued to question the assumptions of advanced industrial societies and posited that the age of "modern scientific-materialistic culture" would end because technical achievements failed to fulfill human beings and provide "deep meanings" (Oliver, 1989, p. 2). Toward the end of his life, he no longer believed that human beings were exceedingly rational, and he no longer thought that the secular state could provide solutions to problems, such as citizenship, public issues, or social issues (Stern, 2006). He focused on small formal and informal communities, spirituality, and religious communities. His last book was dedicated to "the domicile at 18 Willow Street," his home address. Donald Oliver died at the age of 73, on June 28, 2002. He had made significant intellectual contributions, not only to social studies education, but also to education in general, and more broadly to the study of humans, culture, and community.

Who is James Shaver?

James Shaver was one of the first of Donald Oliver's graduate students to collaborate with him on the Harvard Social Studies Project. Shaver was born almost 5 years after Oliver, in 1933, also a product of the Great Depression. However, Shaver was raised across the country from Oliver. Born in Wadena, Minnesota, James Shaver moved to the state of Washington when he was in fourth grade (personal communication, May 10, 2007). He claimed that his career in social studies education was "Happenstance-Based," but the body of his work suggests that chance was not the only factor affecting his career path (Shaver, 2006). Intelligence and determination also must have been at play. At high school in Sumner, Washington he was class valedictorian. Subsequently, he earned a bachelor of arts degree, magna cum laude, Phi Beta Kappa from the University of Washington in 1955.

Similar to Oliver, Shaver's parents had not attended college, but Shaver believed that his parents expected he and his siblings would continue their education at the university level. Finding much academic success as an undergraduate, Shaver explored the possibility of law school. When Louis A. Toepfer, the Secretary of the Harvard Law School, visited the University of Washington, Shaver was curious to see what a Harvard man looked like and he interviewed with Toepfer. Shaver was accepted and enrolled, but found that Harvard Law School did not suit his interests and temperament, and switched to the master of arts in teaching program at the Harvard Graduate School of Education (HGSE). Having married in 1953, Shaver believed that becoming a social studies teacher would be a good way to support his growing family and utilize his political science degree (Shaver, 2006). At HGSE in 1957, Shaver met Donald Oliver and began studying with him.

Don Oliver was Shaver's social studies methods instructor, and he served as Shaver's master teacher at the Peter Buckley Junior High School in Concord, Massachusetts, where Shaver worked as a student teacher and which served as the location of the first implementation of the Harvard Social Studies Project. Although Shaver was unaware at the time, Oliver had already begun his highly influential 1957 article about content selection in social studies. Shaver was certain that Oliver was one of the brightest intellects with whom he had ever been acquainted. Oliver challenged assumptions, raised questions, and helped Shaver think about teaching, curriculum, social studies education, and societal issues.

According to Fred Newmann, who succeeded James Shaver at HGSE and who became an instrumental collaborator, Shaver was "Oliver's key colleague" from 1957 through 1961 (personal communication, May 15, 2007). Shaver reported that his early schooling did not affect his ideas about social studies education, but perhaps it impacted him more than he realized, and materialized in the form of his desire to be a different kind of teacher than those who had educated him. Shaver's educational experiences in K–12 schooling may have served as a non-example of the kind of teacher he aspired to become. He knew he wanted to teach in a more interesting fashion than the methodology he had been exposed to: "the read, answer end-of-chapter questions, recite, test teaching" (personal communication, May 10, 2007). Shaver credited Don Oliver with changing his understanding of social studies education. Shaver wrote,

> The major influence on my approach to social/societal issues was certainly Don Oliver. My involvement in the Harvard Project and other exposure to his probing intellect as a student and colleague affected me profoundly. There could be only one Don Oliver, but the commitment he exuded to the relentless probing of assumptions and their relations to teaching and curricular decisions reinforced an analytic bent in myself that other people had sometimes labeled as overly aggressive or too negative (Shaver, 2006, p. 165).

James Shaver's work with Donald Oliver was the start of a significant academic publishing career. Shaver was instrumental in assisting with the first grant that funded the Harvard Social Studies Project, and his first significant publication was a direct result of the project. He co-authored with Don Oliver (1966) *Teaching Public Issues in the High School*. In this book, Oliver and Shaver discussed social studies education in general, provided the conceptual framework for teaching analysis of public issues, elaborated on the application of the jurisprudential framework to the teaching of public issues, and offered a description of an experimental curriculum project carried out within the jurisprudential framework (pp. v–vi). The authors stated that the book was a progress report of the first 5 years of the Harvard Social Studies Project and meant for the book to be "an open challenge to current efforts to redefine the social studies in narrow academic terms" (p. xii). Review of the *Public Issues* work was favorable in the academic community. The author of an approving review in the *Teachers College Record* wrote that

> the authors effectively attack the prevailing myth, that the function of the social studies teacher is simply to teach "the facts" and let the students form their own "opinions," by pointing out that this ignores the "complex problem of teaching the student to relate fact to opinion or value." (Burton, 1967, p. 2)

Indeed, the reviewer believed that the book demanded a "radical change in educational orientation" (p. 3).

After earning his EdD from Harvard in 1961, James Shaver returned to the Western United States and began his work as a member of the faculty at Utah State University (USU) in the summer of 1962. Aside from the *Public Issues* book, Shaver stated that he and Oliver worked very little afterwards. He believed that Oliver was an "out-of-sight out-of-mind" kind of person, who did not like to venture away from New England. Shaver, on the other hand, seemingly independent by nature moved in his own academic direction. In addition, like Oliver, Shaver seems to have moved in a different direction from his first wife. He divorced in 1969, and remarried in 1976, the same year he served as National Council for the Social Studies President. He had three children from his two marriages, and one stepdaughter (personal communication, May 10, 2007).

Shaver expanded the work of the Harvard Project in the Utah Analysis of Public Issues Project, and developed the idea of qualified decision making (Shaver, 2006). After a 1 year stint to direct the Social Studies Curriculum Center at The Ohio State University in 1964, Shaver returned to the comfort of Utah State University. Upon his return, however, he began teaching statistics and research design. Shaver has called his dual interests in social studies and statistics "schizophrenic," but his expertise in both likely helped broaden his understanding of each content area and education in general (Shaver, 2006, p. 171). His capabilities in both areas also guided his career as he accepted increased responsibility within the university, first as the chairman of the Bureau of Educational Research, and in 1977 as associate dean for research in the College of Education. During the nation's bicentennial, Shaver was the president of the National Council for the Social Studies (NCSS), and in characteristic "Don Oliver style" delivered a critical analysis of the state of social studies education.

Shaver's academic interests broadened, just as Donald Oliver's had, but in different areas. Although he remained committed to social studies education, despite disappointment at the pace of school reform and the redundant nature of NCSS programs over the years, Shaver edited the *Handbook of Social Studies Teaching and Learning* in 1991. When Charles Curtis came to work with Shaver at USU in the mid-1970s, he became interested in the potential of social studies to improve attitudes towards persons with disabilities and began a project conducting a meta-analysis with funding from the Office of Special Education and Rehabilitative Services (Shaver, 2006). This research resulted in several significant publications on social studies and special education, such as "Improving Slow Learners Self-Esteem in Secondary Social Studies Classes" (Curtis & Shaver, 1981). Curtis won the NCSS exemplary dissertation award for his research on social studies and special education. Considering the changing attitudes towards special education students that have evolved over the past 30 years, with the development of laws to protect special education students, the inclusion movement, and the Americans with Disabilities Act, Shaver and Curtis shaped perceptions towards special education students.[1] Shaver also worked with Carol Strong on investigations of short-term ability cohesion scores for spoken narratives of language-impaired and normally developing school-aged children (Strong & Shaver, 1989). Clearly, Shaver also became an expert on the relationship between special education and social studies education.

Shaver also developed an interest in law related education (LRE), and became involved in LRE work at the national level. Once again, when he presented a critical analysis of LRE's claims to reduce juvenile delinquency, à là Donald Oliver, he received negative feedback about his presentations and findings (Johnson, 1984). The educational community typically does not warmly receive negative criticisms of educational endeavors. Shaver, however, has always been willing to present difficult findings throughout his career, even when his analysis confronted a hostile audience. Indeed, at the start of his career one reviewer of a 1965 *School Review* article claimed that Shaver had

> dealt the textbooks a really thorough pasting. The carnage is so complete that I have responded by putting down [my] his (sic) own ax, looking around at other critics of textbooks, and wondering just what it is that we are about. (Joyce, 1966, p. 319)

Shaver, in typical academic fashion, responded in his 1966 article "The Evaluation of Textbooks: A Continuous Responsibility," by highlighting fallacies in Joyce's argument. Throughout Shaver's career, he was willing to engage in difficult academic debate. He learned debate from the master, Donald Oliver.

Nonetheless, Shaver's career continued to blossom, as he was appointed graduate dean of Utah State University in 1993. He lamented that this position pulled him further away from thinking about social studies education and public issues that had given him purpose at the start of his career (Shaver, 2006). Yet, in retrospect, James Shaver seems to have been cut from the same type of tree as Donald Oliver, although the trees grew in different geographical areas and assumed different shapes. Throughout his career and into retirement, Shaver sought to put his interest in social studies education and public issues, in particular, into practice through social activism. He took a more traditional route than Donald Oliver, by becoming involved in supporting local and state political candidates and typically liberal causes, such as the Sierra Club, Defenders of Wildlife, the ACLU, and the NAACP. Shaver believed that his "analysis-of-public-issues conceptual framework that grew out of [his] work with Don Oliver" served him well in his commitment to social activism throughout his life (personal communication, May 10, 2007).

Who is Fred Newmann?

Similar to James Shaver, Fred Newmann was another graduate student prodigy of Don Oliver. Also similar to Oliver and Shaver, Newmann was born during the Great Depression era in January 1937. Yet, in contrast, Newmann had a relatively privileged background, and during his teenage life in the 1950s, he had little involvement with social issues. However, when he was a freshman in high school, his interest in government and civic responsibility was cultivated by his civics-government teacher. An American studies major at Amherst College in Massachusetts, Newmann's interest in social issues was further developed through a critical analysis approach that used case studies in U.S. history (Newmann, 2006). After graduating in 1959 from Amherst College, which was Oliver's alma mater 7 years earlier, Newmann began the Harvard MAT program the same year. Oliver was his social studies methods instructor and the persuasive structure of the class that was "later published as the Oliver-Shaver rationale" (p. 121) had a profound impact on Newmann's conception of social studies education. Although Fred Newmann was the youngest co-creator of the Harvard Social Studies Project, his contribution to the project was indispensable.

Early in his teaching career, Newmann became frustrated with the traditional discipline-based curriculum that did not offer opportunities for students to arrive at reasoned positions about public issues (Newmann, 2006). He realized during his semester-long internship at Winchester High School, in Winchester, Massachusetts (fall 1959) and his first year of teaching across the country at Capuchino High School in San Bruno, California (1960–1961) that it was difficult to engage students using the conventional chronological framework. Newmann saw the Oliver-Shaver public issues approach as a solution to the problems he encountered as a teacher. He preferred to emphasize and use public issue over social issue because social issue "can be construed to include almost any disagreement between two or more people," whereas, public issue is limited to disputes that are political or legal in nature (p. 122). Thus, the public issues approach entails events that impact politicians and legislative policy and entitle citizens to become actively influential and involved in a direct manner.

After completing his MAT degree in 1960, Newmann was awarded Amherst Fellowships for graduate study at Harvard University (1960–62) and Lehman Fellowships (1962–64) for his doctoral studies at Harvard

University. He married in 1963 while in the throes of working on his EdD degree and the Harvard Social Studies Project. After Newmann completed his dissertation with distinction and earned a doctorate in 1964, he continued working with Oliver as an assistant professor of education at Harvard (1964–1968). During his career, he had two children and three grandchildren. In 1990, he shared another commonality with Oliver and Shaver by remarrying (personal communication, May 15, 2008).

Newmann initially collaborated with the Harvard Social Studies Project when he was still a graduate student and he was a key contributor to the second grant, which was successfully funded through co-sponsorship by Harvard University and the Cooperative Research Branch of the U.S. Office of Education from June 1963 to June 1968 (Newmann & Oliver, 1970). In cooperation with Don Oliver, several Harvard graduate students, and teachers at Newton High School (Newton, Massachusetts), Newmann "conceptualized, developed materials for, taught experimentally, and conducted research on a three-year curriculum focusing on the analysis of public controversy" (p. vi). Thus, he embraced and diligently worked with the Harvard Social Studies Project that evolved into the Harvard Public Issues Project. With the assistance of Don Oliver, Newmann wrote *Clarifying Public Controversy: An Approach to Teaching Social Studies*. He focused the book on "the clarification of public controversy" and he hoped a diverse audience beyond high school social studies teachers would embrace the book (p. v). Interestingly, the text evolved from his association with the Harvard Social Studies Project and direct work with Oliver, but Shaver's name only appears in a long alphabetical list of acknowledged contributors. The detachment of Oliver and Shaver appears to contribute to the limited interaction between Newmann and Shaver. In a written communication (May 26, 2007), Newmann expressed great respect for Shaver, although they had no direct relationship, they maintained cordial and professional relations throughout their careers.

During 3 of his 6 years of public school teaching experience in Massachusetts, California, and Wisconsin, Newmann worked with "the Harvard Public Issues Project teaching students to analyze public controversy, and two years with Madison's Community Issues program sending students into the community to take action" (Newmann, Bertocci, & Landness, 1977, pp. ii–iii). In 1968, he became an associate professor of curriculum and instruction at the University of Wisconsin. At the University of Wisconsin, Newmann's passion for public issues evolved into a desire to extend "the Oliver-Shaver approach beyond classroom study/discussion to students' acting on their beliefs in their communities through volunteer service and social action" (Newmann, 2006, p. 123). The result was several publications that Newmann (2006, p. 127) cited as some of his major contributions to the field, such as *Education for Citizen Action: Challenge for*

Secondary Curriculum (1975) and *Skills in Citizen Action: An English-Social Studies Program for Secondary Schools* (1977). However, in the early 1980s and after almost 20 years of working to develop social studies curriculum, Newman became frustrated with the structural and cultural barriers of public education that inhibited the adoption of reflective and participatory social studies curriculum (Newmann, 2006). In addition, funding was no longer readily available, so he changed his research direction and focused on how schools functioned. He reasoned that learning how schools operate would lead to more effective implementation of curriculum innovations for participatory citizenship. Thus, Newmann began a new research path with another "twenty years of work on how schools function, what makes some more effective than others, and how schools change" (Newmann, 2006, p. 125). From 1985–1990, Newmann directed the National Center on Effective Secondary Schools, and researched "how and why some high school social studies departments promoted higher order thinking more than others" (p. 126). His publications in *Theory and Research in Social Education* (see Newmann, 1991a, 1991b) that resulted from his higher order thinking research were significant contributions to the field of social studies. When he directed the Center on Organization and Restructuring of Schools (1990–1996), he studied authentic pedagogy in a similar manner. He also conducted a national study from 1996 to 2000 to study the use of professional development to enhance organizational capacity in low-income schools. From 1996–2001, Newmann culminated his professional career by working with the "Consortium on Chicago School Research to understand the impact of the Chicago Annenberg Challenge in Chicago's elementary schools" (Newmann, 2006, p. 126).

In recognition of his powerful research, Newmann received numerous awards and distinctions, which include the Distinguished Career in Research Award in 1988 and the Exemplary Research Award in 1991 from the National Council for the Social Studies. In addition, he was awarded the Distinguished Paper Award from the Special Interest Group in Social Studies Education of the American Educational Research Association. After his retirement, he also received the American Education Research Association's Presidential Citation in 2002, for his work on authentic instruction. Finally, he was recognized in 2003 with the American Educational Research Association Palmer O. Johnson Award for his article, "Instructional Program Coherence: What It Is and Why It Should Guide School Improvement Policy" in *Education Evaluation Policy Analysis, 23,* 4 (2001).

Beyond his rich research career, a common interest with Shaver is Newmann's passion for social activism. In Boston, during the 1960s, he actively organized tenants to improve low-income housing and promoted faculty unionization at the University of Wisconsin in the 1970s. In addition, he worked on local elections and he has contributed to a number of activist organizations, such as Southern Poverty Law Center, Children's Defense Fund, and Habitat for Humanity. One of the reasons he retired in 2001 from the University of Wisconsin was to become more active in community affairs, because he believed professional work, family, and other personal interests had isolated him from the local community (Newmann, 2006). Indeed, soon after retirement he worked on Wisconsin Governor Doyle's education platform, U.S. Senator Feingold's 2002 reelection, and volunteered for Habitat for Humanity.

General Background of the Harvard Social Studies Project

In his seminal 1957 *Harvard Educational Review* article on content selection in social studies education, Donald Oliver launched the innovative conceptual framework for the Harvard Social Studies Project. He advocated for a change in traditional social studies curriculum, teaching, and textbooks, and for social studies educators to develop a more analytic approach to pedagogy and content knowledge. In creating a theory to undergird social studies education, Oliver relied on the work of previous influential educational and political theorists, such as Thomas Jefferson, John Dewey, and Gunnar Myrdal (Oliver & Shaver, 1966; Stern, 2006; Shaver, 2006). Jefferson, famously established the theoretical rationale for representative democracy, but also unsuccessfully advocated for public education (Milson, Bohan, Glanzer, & Null, 2004, see "Jefferson's Bill for the More General Diffusion of Knowledge," pp. 61–68). Jefferson recognized that an educated populace was critical to the success of democratic government. Dewey's progressive educational philosophy coupled with Jefferson's enlightenment philosophy, and Myrdal's path breaking work on normative concepts such as the American creed, served as the foundation for Oliver's creation of a social studies curriculum in which public issues provided the focus of debated topics in social studies classrooms.

The Harvard Social Studies Project first received private funding, and later won federal funding from the U.S. Office of Education. In the post-Sputnik era, the federal government poured considerable money into education. Indeed, Urban and Wagoner (2004) report that the most significant consequence of Sputnik was not the space race or the attention to academic studies, but "the impetus it gave to federal financing of public education" (p. 293). Donald Oliver was a fortunate recipient of federal funding for the Harvard Social Studies Project, and he was able to provide the project direction with the theoretical framework he established.

The first phase of the Harvard Social Studies Project was implemented at Peter Buckley Junior High School in Concord, Massachusetts, and

James Shaver participated as a teacher-researcher. Don Oliver believed in the importance of "teacher involvement and public school experiences in developing curricula" (Shaver, personal communication, May 10, 2007). He rejected the idea of "teacher proof" materials, and valued the authenticity of a curriculum that was developed and implemented in actual schools. The second phase of the project was facilitated by Oliver and Newmann and implemented at a High School in Newton, Massachusetts. Again, all participants were Don Oliver's graduate students, teachers who taught at these schools, or students in the Boston area. Although Oliver guided the project, clearly the work that resulted was a collaborative effort. According to Fred Newmann, during the development phase of the Newton Project, the Harvard staff worked consistently with six to ten teachers on the many details of the project (personal communication, May 15, 2007).

The Public Issues Series that was published by American Education Publications (a Xerox Company) derived from the actual implementation of the Harvard Social Studies Project in the schools. Oliver and his colleagues created approximately 30 pamphlets in the series on an assortment of social studies topics. The idea for developing individual, short (50–75 pages) staple bound pamphlets was that they would be fairly inexpensive, easy for teachers and students to use (not heavy hard bound books), and teachers could select and flexibly implement individual units as they desired. More important than the ease and convenience of use, however, was the innovative approach to teaching social studies that the pamphlets facilitated. The thirty pamphlets listed on the back of the 1972 The American Revolution pamphlet include the following titles:

The American Revolution: Crisis of Law and Change
The Railroad Era: Business Competition and the Public Interest
Taking a Stand: A Guide to Clear Discussion of Public Issues
Religious Freedom: Minority Faiths and Majority Rule
The Rise of Organized Labor: Worker Security and Employer Rights
The Immigrant's Experience: Cultural Variety and the "Melting Pot"
Negro Views of America: The Legacy of Oppression
Municipal Politics: Interest Groups and the Government
The New Deal: Free Enterprise and Public Planning
Rights of the Accused: Criminal Procedure and Public Security
The Lawsuit: Legal Reasoning and Civil Procedure
Community Change: Law, Politics, and Social Attitudes
Colonial Africa: The Kenya Experience
Communist China: Communal Progress and Individual Freedom
Nazi Germany: Social Forces and Personal Responsibility
20th Century Russia: Agents of the Revolution

The Civil War: Crisis of Federalism
Race and Education: Integration and Community Control
Science and Public Policy: Uses and Control of Knowledge
Status: Achievement and Social Values
Revolution and World Politics: The Search for National Independence
The Limits of War: National Policy and World Conscience
Organizations Among Nations: The Search for World Order
Diplomacy and International Law: Alternatives to War
Privacy: The Control of Personal Information
The Progressive Era: Abundance, Poverty, and Reform
Population Control: Whose Right to Live?
Jacksonian Democracy: The Common Man in American Life
Moral Reasoning: The Value of Life
Social Action: Dilemmas and Strategies

In order to understand the approach to social studies education that Oliver developed with the Harvard project, a detailed examination of selected pamphlets is warranted. The pamphlets are worthy of contemporary examination and, in fact, a few have been updated and adapted for current use. Updates by the Social Science Education Consortium include: *The Progressive Era* (1989), *The Railroad Era* (1991), and *Science and Public Policy* (1993). *The Railroad Era* and many of the other pamphlets in the series opens up with a section titled, "The Necessary Questions." In this section students were asked if social studies typically covers answers and leaves out important questions, as the authors believed. The authors hoped to draw students into the drama of history, in order for students to recognize that they were part of a "living dimension of history" (Oliver & Newmann, 1970, p. 3).

The next section of *The Railroad Era* provided background information in the form of a description of a state legislature meeting on a proposal to consider the benefits and harms of bringing the railroad to the state. Indeed, the pamphlets often provided introductory background that demonstrated varying perspectives on a particular historical issue. Rather than provide historical detail as facts that happened, students were helped to realize that multiple perspectives were at play, even with respect to historical events. Authors carefully portrayed conflicts of interest. Subsequently, students were instructed to answer persisting questions of history including making value judgments about the conflicts. Students also identified various interest groups, explained why a particular person would support or oppose the railroad, and made parallels to similar modern problems. In this modern analogy, a community wrestled with the idea of constructing a solar energy facility (Oliver & Newmann, 1970, p. 17).

In another section of *The Railroad Era* (1967) students were invited to participate in a simulation game called "The Railroad Game." Teachers were to divide students into four groups, representing different railroad lines. Each group was asked to compete for the business of carrying ore between mining towns on the railroad. Rules of the game were provided, as well as a sequence of competition. The simulation game was followed by a description of "Three Faces of Competition," that included stakeholders in railroad development. One was an ordinary California farmer; a second was a New York merchant, and the third was William H. Vanderbilt, head of the New York Central railroad system (Oliver & Newmann, 1970, pp. 37–50). Interestingly, Fred Newmann reported that one of the problems of developing the public issues series was the "lack of adequate history of the common man" (personal communication, May 15, 2007). Despite such challenges, the authors clearly created a different kind of historical narrative—one that included competing interests and the perspective of ordinary people in events.

In another pamphlet, *The American Revolution*, students were introduced to "A Crisis of Youth" and asked to contemplate, not only how Revolutionary events unfolded, but also how resolution of the differences between the colonists and the British might have been different and better (Oliver & Newmann, 1972, p. 5). After a basic overview of events leading up to the Revolution, students read a case study of George Watkins, a fictional character, caught in the middle of two views of authority. By reading this case study, students could develop an understanding of multiple perspectives, as they follow a discussion between a British supporter and a colonial supporter. Later in the narrative, students continued to explore differing perspectives by reading about a speech given by Sam Adams, a famous revolutionary, and Dr. James Cartwright, a minister and loyalist. Students subsequently determined their own values about the role of government as they assessed and classified the values of the historical characters in the reading. Persisting questions of history followed, which required students to define terms such as patriotism and legality, and to assess individuals such as Patrick Henry to determine whether they were lawmakers or lawbreakers. Students were expected to provide reasons to support their positions. Finally, students made judgments about methods of protest. In reviewing these activities, the authors likely considered Bloom's taxonomy when creating the pamphlets. The aim of the Harvard Social Studies Project was to encourage students to understand differing perspectives, evaluate, make judgments, and clarify values which are all ideas that represent high levels of human thinking. In the closing section, students read short biographies of several individuals and were asked to evaluate the likelihood the person was a patriot, loyalist, or undecided. Many of the pamphlets closed with a section of contemporary analogies, and The American Revolution asked students to compare the Revolution to a modern case. The modern analogy was the incident at Pettus Bridge, which was a Civil Rights protest in Selma, Alabama that led to violence between protestors and city officials and police (pp. 55–60). The unit concluded by asking students to review, reflect, and research.

The Public Issue series was pioneering in facilitating discussion of social studies topics by providing unique historical background of events, but also in giving readers multiple perspectives, including that of ordinary people. The pamphlets encouraged student opinions, supported by evidence. Teachers were able to foster critical analysis by helping students understand connections between facts, values, and judgments, and by encouraging rationale discussion in classrooms. The ultimate goal was for students to clarify and justify their views on persisting questions of public policy. For example, students were to consider hypotheses as in the case of the American Revolution, "Under what conditions would citizens be justified in using violence to overthrow a government?" Or they were asked to think about issues related to organized labor: "In what situations should the rights of private property and private enterprise be limited to insure certain rights or benefits to workers?" The pamphlets stood in sharp contrast to textbooks that provided simple narrative of events from one voice.

More than 8 million copies of the Harvard Social Studies Project/Public Issue Series sold during the 20 years of initial publication, not counting subsequent adaptations (Newmann, 2006). The extent of their use and the effect on methodology in social studies classrooms throughout the United States is open to interpretation, rationale discussion, and multiple perspectives.

Lasting Legacy of the Harvard Social Studies Project

Early in his career, Donald Oliver set in motion the intellectual framework for inquiry-based social studies education in his 1957 Harvard Educational Review article. The article launched the "New Social Studies Movement," which profoundly affected social studies education during the late 1960s and early 1970s (Lybarger, 1991). Within the New Social Studies Movement, the Harvard Social Studies Project confronted basic beliefs about how K-12 students should learn social studies.

Oliver's creation of the Harvard Social Studies Project commenced the academic careers of James Shaver and Fred Newmann. These icons profoundly impacted the direction of scholarly activity in social studies education. Although the Harvard Social Studies Project may not have impacted the broader audience, the influence of the authors was not limited. For example, the Fenton series, Man: a Course of Study (MACOS), and the Amherst Project were all popular reforms that comprised the New Social Studies Movement (Lybarger, 1991). Fenton, MACOS, and the Amherst Project consequently benefited from Oliver's framework and, of course, Sputnik helped with financing.

The New Social Studies movement grew so rapidly that there were more than 50 national curriculum projects by 1967 (Haas, 1977). Three years later, a comprehensive appraisal of the New Social Studies movement reported more than 100 projects (Sanders & Tanck, 1970). Some common characteristics pertained to most New Social Studies projects, such as greater emphasis on ideas from the disciplines of sociology, anthropology, psychology, and political science as well as stronger interdisciplinary approaches to curriculum development. A 1970 issue of Social Education highlighted twenty-six national social studies projects and critically appraised each (Sanders & Tanck, 1970). Most New Social Studies projects, nonetheless, promoted inquiry-based learning.

However, as New Social Studies projects grew in popularity, critics arose. For example, Edwin Fenton's textbook series with Holt, Rinehart, and Winston became renowned for promoting an inquiry approach in social studies education. In a book titled *The New Social Studies*, Fenton described the various social studies curriculum reform projects throughout the United States, the quality of the work, and each projects' comprehensiveness (Shaftel, 1968). Fenton, a respected academic from Carnegie Institute of Technology, nonetheless, became a target of criticism. In Georgia, his 1972 textbook on American history was banned by the Georgia State Board of Education (Anon, 2007).

Shaver surprisingly joined the critics and in his 1976 NCSS presidential address declared that the curricular reforms and projects of the 1960s were "a fad that exemplified our long standing and unthinking subservience to professors in the academic disciplines" (Shaver, 1977, p. 305). Shaver also asserted that most educational research was useless and had little effect on teaching. Not surprisingly, Shaver's views were not warmly received. Newmann may have agreed as he examined the structure of schools to implement authentic learning.

Yet, Newmann found positive implications that resulted from the Harvard Social Studies Project. He believed one legacy of the project was its relationship to graduate education in social studies. According to Newmann, "The purpose of the Harvard project has been not merely the creation of a curriculum or product. Perhaps more important has been the improved training of graduate students in social studies through intensive clinical experience in writing, teaching, and evaluating curriculum" (Newmann & Oliver, 1970, p. vi). However, Newmann recently argued that the lasting legacy was the creation of a "positive teaching experience for the teachers who were philosophically committed to the approach and used the materials, most of whom are probably retired by now, and for professors of education who are interested in the history of social studies" (personal communication, May 26, 2007).

Indeed, the Harvard Social Studies Project sought to promote inquiry-based learning through a variety of methods, such as reading multiple perspectives, learning about the history of the common man, participating in interactive games, making comparisons to contemporary events, critically analyzing materials, conducting classroom discussion and debate, and forming opinions and making value judgments. Barton and Levstik (2004) noted that a long tradition of inquiry exists, as the term history derives from the Greek word *historein* meaning "to inquire," but they observed that inquiry is not common in schools. VanSledright (2002) attributed history's interpretive paradox to presenting challenges for teaching, but he believed the benefits outweigh the negatives. Teaching about multiple perspectives, helping students form opinions and make value judgments is messy business. And certainly, high stakes standardized tests more readily evaluate student's content knowledge than skill at reading multiple accounts of an event and ability to form an opinion based upon all available evidence. Document based questions on Advanced Placement examinations evaluate the later, but thousands of teachers, rather than Scantron machines, are required to read the AP examinations.

Nontheless, Thorton (2005) argued that social studies reform efforts that were sensitive to methodology concerns generally achieved more widespread adoption than the myriad of government reform projects that predominantly focused on content knowledge. Indeed, current programs such as History Alive are praised by teachers because they foster creative and engaging methods for teaching content knowledge. Despite the relevance of reflecting on the curricular ideas and methods advocated by the Harvard Social Studies Project, Foster (2001) cautioned that the past represents a very different time. The concepts and methods of the Harvard Social Studies Project would need to be adapted for the contemporary generation of social studies students, who Wineburg et al. (2007) remind us, learn common beliefs and cultural curriculum from a variety of media —cell phones, Ipods, Internet sources such as Google, YouTube, MySpace, Instant Messenger, and Wikipedia—sources that did not exist 40 years ago when Oliver, Shaver, and Newmann conceptualized the work of the Harvard Social Studies Project.

NOTE

1. On a personal note, one of the authors of this article is the parent of a special education student in both Texas and Georgia school systems, and has personally witnessed changed attitudes and improved assistance to our most vulnerable public school students.

REFERENCES

Anonymous. (2007). *Georgia history textbooks. The new Georgia encyclopedia.* Retrieved July 19, 2007, from www.georgiaencyclopedia.org/nge/Article.jsp?id=n-859

Barton, K. C., & Levstik, L. S. (2004). *Teaching history for the common good.* Mahwah, NJ: Erlbaum.

Burton, H. (1967). Review of Teaching Public Issues in the High School. *Teachers College Record.* Retrieved May 23, 2007, from www.tcrecord.org

Curtis, C., & Shaver, J. (1981). Improving slow learners' self-esteem in secondary social studies classes. *Journal of Educational Research, 74,* 217–223.

Davidow, M. (1977). *Why Johnny can't read and Ivan can.* Moscow: Novosti Press Agency.

Fallace, T. (2008). Did the social studies really replace history in American secondary schools? *Teachers College Record, 110*(10), 2245–2270.

Fenton, E. (1974). *Tradition and change in four societies.* New York: Holt, Rinehart and Winston.

Flesch, R. (1955). *Why Johnny can't read.* New York: Harper & Row.

Foster, S. J. (2001). Historical empathy in theory and practice. In O. L. Davis Jr., E. A. Yeager, & S. J. Foster (Eds.), *Historical empathy and perspective taking in the social studies* (pp. 167–181). New York: Rowman & Littlefield.

Gewertz, K. (2002, July 18). GSE professor Donald Oliver is dead at 73 [Electronic version]. *Harvard University Gazette, 1–2.*

Giese, J. R. (1989). *The Progressive Era: The limits of reform.* Boulder, CO: Social Science Education Consortium.

Greenawald, G.D. (1991). *The Railroad Era: Business, competition, and public interest.* Boulder, CO: Social Science Education Consortium.

Haas, J. (1977). *The era of the new social studies.* Boulder, CO: Social Science Education Consortium.

Johnson, G. (1984, April). *When law-related education is a deterrent to delinquency: A preliminary response to James P. Shaver's paper, "The law-related education evaluation project: A methodological critique of the 'impacts on students' findings."* Presentation at the Rocky Mountain Regional Conference of the National Council for the Social Studies, Phoenix, AZ.

Joyce, B. R. (1966 Autumn). Please stop beating the textbooks. *The School Review, 74,* 319–322.

Lybarger, M. B. (1991). The historiography of social studies: Retrospect, circumspect, and prospect. In J. P. Shaver (Ed.), *Handbook of Research on Social Studies Teaching and Learning* (pp. 3-15). New York: Macmillan.

Milson, A. J., Bohan, C. H., Glanzer, P. L. & Null, J. W. (Eds.). (2004). *Readings in American educational thought: From puritanism to progressivism.* Greenwich, CT: Information Age.

Newmann, F. M. (1975). *Education for citizen action: Challenge for secondary curriculum.* Berkeley, CA: McCutchin.

Newmann, F. M. (1991a). Promoting higher order thinking in social studies: Overview of a study of 16 high school departments. *Theory and Research in Social Education, 19*(4), 323–339.

Newmann, F. M. (1991b). Classroom thoughtfulness and students' higher order thinking: common indicators and diverse social studies courses. *Theory and Research in Social Education, 19*(4), 409–431.

Newmann, F. M. (2006). My experience with social issues and education. In S. Totten & J. Pederson (Eds.), *Addressing social issues in the classroom and beyond: The pedagogical efforts of pioneers in the field* (pp. 121–130). Charlotte, NC: Information Age.

Newmann, F. M., Bertocci, T. A., & Landness, R. M. (1977). *Skills in citizen action: An English-social studies program for secondary schools.* Skokie, IL: National Textbook.

Newmann, F. M., & Oliver, D. W. (1970). *Clarifying public controversy: An approach to teaching social studies.* Boston: Little, Brown and Company.

Oliver, D. W. (1957). The selection of content in social studies. *Harvard Educational Review 31,* 437–448.

Oliver, D. W. (1968). The selection of content in social studies. In J. P. Shaver & H. Berlak (Eds.), *Democracy, pluralism, and the social studies, readings and commentaries: An approach to curriculum decisions in social studies* (pp. 17–42). Boston: Houghton Mifflin.

Oliver, D. W. (1976). *Education and community: A radical critique of innovative schooling.* Berkley, CA: McCutchan.

Oliver, D. W. (with Gersham, K. W.) (1989). *Education, modernity, and fractured meaning: Toward a process theory of learning.* Albany: State University of New York Press.

Oliver, D. W., Canniff, J., & Korhonen, J. (2002). *The primal, the modern, and the vital center: A theory of balanced culture in a living place.* Brandon, VT: The Foundation for Educational Renewal.

Oliver, D. W., & Newmann, F. M. (1967). *The Railroad Era. Public Issue Series/Harvard Social Studies Project.* Middleton, CT: American Education Publications.

Oliver, D. W., & Newmann, F. M. (1972). *The American revolution: Crisis of law and change. Public Issue Series/Harvard Social Studies Project.* Middleton, CT: American Education Publications.

Oliver, D. W., & Shaver, J. P. (1966). *Teaching public issues in the high school.* Boston: Houghton, Mifflin.

Oxford Dictionary of Quotations. (1979). 3rd edition. New York: Oxford University Press.

Ross, W. (1997). The struggle for the social studies curriculum. In E. W. Ross (Ed.), *The social studies curriculum: Purposes, problems, and possibilities.* New York: State University of New York Press.

Sanders, N., & Tanck, M. (1970). A critical appraisal of twenty-six national social studies projects. *Social Education, 4*(34), 383–388.

Shaftel, F. (1968). Review of The New Social Studies. *Teachers College Record 69*(7), 618.

Shaver, J. P. (1966, Autumn). The evaluation of textbooks: A continuous responsibility. *The School Review, 74,* 323–331.

Shaver, J. P. (1977). A critical view of the social studies profession. *Social Education, 40,* 300–307.

Shaver, J. P. (Ed.). (1991). *Handbook of Research on Social Studies Teaching and Learning.* New York: Macmillan.

Shaver, J. P. (2006). A happenstance-based social issues career. In S. Totten & J. Pederson (Eds.), *Addressing social issues in the classroom and beyond: the pedagogical efforts of pioneers in the field* (pp. 67–289). Charlotte, NC: Information Age.

Singleton, L. R. (1993). *Science and public policy.* Boulder, CO: Social Science Education Consortium.

Stearns, P., Seixas, N. P., & Wineburg, S. (Eds). (2000). *Knowing, teaching, and learning history: National and international perspectives.* New York & London: New York University Press.

Stern, B. S. (2006). Donald Oliver: the search for democratic community. In S. Totten & J. Pederson (Eds.), *Addressing social issues in the classroom and beyond: the pedagogical efforts of pioneers in the field* (pp. 67–289). Charlotte, NC: Information Age.

Strong, C. J., & Shaver, J. P. (1989). Stability of cohesion in the spoken narratives of language impaired and normally developing school-aged children. *Journal of Speech and Hearing Research, 34,* 95–111.

Thornton, S. (2005). *Teaching social studies that matters: Curriculum for active learning.* New York: Teachers College Press.

Urban, W. J., & Wagoner, J. L., Jr. (2004). *American education: A history.* New York: McGraw-Hill.

VanSledright, B. (2002). *In search of America's past: Learning to read history in elementary school.* New York: Teachers College Press.

Wineburg, S., Mosborg, S., Porat, D., & Duncan, A. (2007). Common belief and the cultural curriculum: An intergenerational study of historical consciousness. *American Educational Research Journal, 44,* 40–76.

Woyshner, C. (2006). *Notes toward a historiography of the social studies: Recent scholarship and future directions.* In K. C. Barton (Ed.), *Research methods in social studies education: Contemporary issues and perspectives* (pp. 11–38). Greenwich: CT: Information Age.

CHAPTER 7

HAROLD BERLAK AND THE METROPOLITAN ST. LOUIS SOCIAL STUDIES PROJECT

Cultivating Social Studies at the Local Level

Carol Klages

"Return the government to the people" is not the battle cry of a weary Civil War soldier or political slogan of Civil Rights activists, but that of social studies educator, Harold Berlak (personal communication, July 5, 2007). What exactly does Mr. Berlak wish to be returned to the people: education and the democratic right to decide educational curriculum as reflected in the needs and desires of local communities. Local communities should know what is in the best interest of its children. Presidents Clinton and Bush, along with other supporters and No Child Left Behind (NCLB, 2002) advocates, may encourage the reliance of standardized tests to determine what students ought to know, Harold Berlak does not. He believes that education, including social studies education, should be cultivated at the local community level. Parents, teachers, and all members of the community should be part of the process of how the young are

The New Social Studies: People, Projects, and Perspectives, pp. 133–145

educated and what assessment practices are to be utilized. Harold Berlak worked with his community in the late 1960s to the early 1970s to address the needs of social science educators and their students by directing the Metropolitan St. Louis Social Studies Center.

THE METROPOLITAN ST. LOUIS SOCIAL STUDIES CENTER

Social studies education is based upon the relationship one has to the world. This relationship's development is based upon citizenship education, which is one of the central tenets of social studies education. The board of directors for National Council for the Social Studies (2001) "has defined an effective citizen as one who has the knowledge, skills, and attitudes required to assume the 'office of citizen' in our democratic republic." True social studies education allows for the student to understand others as a means for understanding one's self. The educated citizenry is willing and able to think critically regarding the issues of the day because its people have been prepared to scrutinize what the media asserts. According to Hobbs (2007), a specific type of media, for example, a newspaper, requires students to bring his/her cognitive abilities, as well as reading abilities, when reading its contents. On the same level, civic education ought to prepare students to be the type of citizens who eagerly seek multiple ways of knowing about the world (Leland & Harste, 1994).

In a conversation with Harold Berlak, he shared an example from his early years as a social studies teacher in which he encouraged students to think critically about history. When studying a particular event in history, the students read from two different sources about the same event. They soon discovered that there were glaring differences in how this particular historical event was described. Berlak's students asked questions about which of the versions were true. These students had a difficult time understanding that no one right answer existed for this historical event. To prove his point even further, Berlak had each student write down a personal history of what took place the previous day in class. As the students began to read each other's accounts, they soon determined that everyone had his/her own version of the same event. Berlak encouraged this process of questioning history: social studies education is about raising questions. The job of social studies educators is to provide students with the means and opportunities to help them answer the questions they pose. The investigations conducted by students are a way for them to use their intellectual capacities instead of promoting the learning of social studies abstractions.

Social studies education must be concrete—connected to something. This something is the knowledge that students already possess and how they see themselves as a part of the world around them. Berlak asserts that one of the reasons that social studies education is trivialized and looked down upon when compared to the Big Three—reading, writing, and mathematics—is that too many social studies classrooms have been boring and students were not able to connect the social studies information with what they already knew about the world. Make no mistake; students do come to classrooms with knowledge. Sometimes teachers may not know what students know, but to prepare properly an educated citizenry, teachers ought to utilize what students already know as a means for making the important personal connections to the content. As a social studies educator for over 30 years, Harold Berlak understands the importance of using opportunities for learning rather than strictly adhering to a government-mandated curriculum.

Berlak investigated and promoted the idea of what social studies issues students ought to know by working in the late 1960s and early 1970s as the director of the Metropolitan St. Louis Social Studies Center. In his efforts as director, he was assisted by Washington University's Timothy Tomlinson, Judson Shaplin, and numerous other educators and educational community members. This center had three purposes. They were to create and maintain a social studies center; to prepare, revise, and disseminate an elementary social studies curriculum under the heading of the Elementary Social Studies Project; and to serve as a research partner into the field of social science education. This agency's curriculum goals were established (1) to analyze, execute, and disperse new social studies curriculums in the St. Louis area and (2) to develop a unified elementary school social science curriculum for Grades 1–6 (Berlak & Tomlinson, 1973). Berlak analyzed the problems of implementing and disseminating curriculum and innovations in the social sciences and created a plan to establish an interschool innovation agency, analogous to agricultural field stations. The plan yielded for four field stations which included 28 school systems. The new program was created to rectify the shortcomings of elementary social studies curriculum. Children were not prepared to cope with the continuing social and economic change. This new program highlighted a curriculum that focused on teaching students an understanding of contemporary democracy and the social and economic changes of a democratic society as well as non-demoocratic societies. Students involved with this curriculum were provided with the social science knowledge and the critical thinking skills necessary to analyze social, economic, and political controversies.

In his role as director, Berlak worked with fellow educators, both at the university and public school levels, to identify, prepare, and teach a series of social studies unit or case studies for first through sixth grades which were intended to allow students to investigate various social issues that people faced in a changing society. One case study required students to determine if a Mexican family from a rural area should move the family to an urban area. This case study was titled *A Village Family* (Berlak & Tomlinson, 1973). In another case study, *Changing Neighborhoods* (Berlak & Tomlinson, 1975), students study an African American family that must decide whether or not to move to a new neighborhood in the midst of changing racial residential patterns in the inner city and suburbs. Each social studies unit was designed to emphasize personalized case studies while promoting social science concepts and understandings through the vessel of critical thinking. The materials for these case studies included recordings, filmstrips, and texts. The texts consisted of a teacher's edition, a children's text, an activity book, and audiovisual components. The text provided both a lesson plan sequence, as well as a source of readings and study materials that were applicable to the unit.

The teacher's edition provided a lesson plan sequencing guide. This guide consisted of seven fundamental components: the lesson overview, materials list, the social science concepts that pertained to the lesson, skills taught in the lesson, a suggested teaching schedule, a list of performance objectives, and suggested teaching strategies in order for students to meet those objectives. These lessons were not meant to be taught in isolation. If the school personnel believed that curriculum integration was integral to student learning, the lessons could fit easily into the school's established curriculum rather than stand as an isolated learning opportunity.

The units were not the standard social science materials. These units emphasized students' active involvement in the investigation of change through the use of role play, simulations, discussions, literature, news articles, and photographs. The use of diagrams, artifact creation and analysis, and maps were included as well. What made this social studies curriculum so different from the curriculum that went before it and even after it was that students were encouraged to think critically about a changing society. According to Vogler and Virtue (2007), in today's social studies classrooms, students are not taught how social studies fits in with the bigger picture of the world. Instead they use low-cognitive abilities in order to collect small pieces of trivial information. While each unit provided various strategies that could be used, ultimately it was left to the professional educator to decide what would work best for the students. No predetermined script was necessary or even provided. These units were curricularly integrated and cross-cultural and they would span history and geographical regions while promoting skills within the context of what the students were learning. Students were not taught social studies abstractions or even social studies ideas in isolation. Rather, students were encouraged to think and make judgments about issues that confronted them personally in a shifting society. These judgments were determined based upon how the student would solve or make a decision about an issue after gathering enough data to support that judgment. In other words, these social studies units were innovative both about how social studies were viewed as a content area as well as how citizenship education was promoted. At one point, these units were so popular that over 7,000 students in the St. Louis area were engaged with them (H. Berlak, personal communication, July 5, 2007).

The Metropolitan St. Louis Social Studies Center served not only as a provider of social studies units, but also as a central location where social studies educators could come to locate and utilize various social studies resources. These educators worked within their own schools and districts to evaluate their social studies programs and make determinations about their needs. They would use these resources to create their own personal development workshops that were based upon their students' needs in terms of social studies education. Social studies educators were not only allowed, but also encouraged to use their professional knowledge and skills to provide a social studies curriculum that served student needs. This encouragement was all but curtailed by political intrusions when a significant push for standardization of curriculum and assessment began at the national level.

Justification for the St. Louis Project

To state a well-known cliché, the world is changing. The founders of the Metropolitan St. Louis Social Studies Center believed strongly that children must have not only an awareness of this change, but also possess an ability to think and understand how change impacts them and their environment. In order to prepare children for thinking about change, their teachers must have easy access to useful resource materials for the classroom. As such, the concept of change was identified as the basic premise for the teaching and learning in these case studies. Societal changes may confuse people who previously were quite stable. As most societies experience some changes whether they be technological, political, social, or some combination of the thereof, tensions can occur that make one's thinking unstable. These case studies were designed to provide students with learning opportunities rather than to watch passively as the changes occur. The concern for social science education then was *how to* or even *if to* make children think about these changes. The St. Louis Project compelled teachers to encourage students to understand and think about the tensions and conflicts that change produces. Thus it provided teachers and schools with practical, purposeful, interesting, and diverse resources to address this issue.

Since the teachers had case studies that included an incredible amount of teaching and learning resources, the role of assessment had to be addressed. Ideally, no pre-made, multiple choice tests were included in the St. Louis social studies project. The creators of the program state up front that, "Such tests would not be consistent with the goals of this program" (Berlak & Tomlinson, 1975, p. T-6). Continuous evaluation was necessary and encouraged, though. The creators endorsed an assessment that utilized carefully recorded anecdotal records for the performance of each child. With teacher observation and feedback, the student received a purposeful record of how he/she performed on various activities. As such, the teacher would also use these anecdotal records to determine which teaching strategies and activities to use that would best fit the needs of the students. The originators of the program emphasized that the goal of teaching, learning, and assessment was not to learn isolated facts, but to be consistent with the overall objectives of the project.

Positive Aspects of the Metropolitan St. Louis Social Studies Center

The developers of this project spent 7 years working with teachers, social scientists, and educational researchers. It was not about one group of people trying to impose their political or education views on the educational masses. Neither was it another "worksheet-based, don't encourage the students to think" solution to social studies curricular needs. This project allowed much time for field testing the case studies and lessons. This process occurred prior to the actual implementation rather than afterward. The lessons were all taught in a series of three phases. In the first phase the project director and co-directors would teach the lessons. This process allowed for working out any significant errors in information or process. The second phase was led by teachers who had been selected as project teachers. Phase three was taught by a group of about 30 volunteer teachers—found throughout the community and in various teaching situations—throughout the nation. These volunteer teachers were not associated with the St. Louis project in any fashion. As a result, The Metropolitan St. Louis Social Studies Project promoted an authentic social studies curriculum with appropriate social science concepts and thinking skills that students needed.

The case studies used in this project provided a humanistic side of social science learning. Each case study focused on a small group of people for the students' learning opportunities. Therefore, students had an intimate experience with how the people lived, worked, interacted with other people, and expressed their personal concerns. The students were able to view the people in the case study as real people via role play, readings, filmstrips, and other vehicles of instruction. This intimacy allowed students the opportunity to care about the people they were studying. As each case study is based upon the concept of change and how people respond to change, it was important that the studies of change were historical, cross-cultural, and modern day. Students who studied in the manner presented by the curriculum were better prepared to examine how change affects people rather than to viewing people in abstract generalizations. This humanistic approach allowed for a more authentic approach to learning social science concepts and critical thinking skills.

The thinking skills played a vital role in this social studies project because students not only needed to understand the human aspect of change, but they also needed the ability to reason while thinking reflectively. These reasoning skills were presented in a systematic manner. Value analysis, listening, and inferential thinking were all aspects of the reasoning skills that the case studies supported. Several value analysis skills were presented each in case study unit. A value analysis skill was based upon a student taking a personal stance on an issue identified within the case study. In order for the student to establish his/her position on an issue, each lesson in the unit provided ample opportunities for the students to read, identify, and discuss what the actual issues were, thus providing them with reasons for their position. The material and various resources were vital to develop the student's ability to use his/her value analysis skills. One example of a value analysis skill from the case studies is that of "stating a clear position and using specific data to support a position" (Berlak & Tomlinson, 1973, p. ix). Students were also required to work in small groups as a means for developing their listening skills. Class discussions, as well as small group discussions, were emphasized to teach students how to listen to each other and then how to respond. From the case study, *Changing Neighborhoods*, some examples of listening skills were paraphrasing and then learning how to ask a question that related to what the previous speaker stated (Berlak & Tomlinson, 1975).

For inferential thinking, the teachers were provided a description of when these skills were to be included in the lesson. A specific objective and overview would point out the skill and when it was most appropriate to have students use it. Examples of the inferential skills were making decisions from available data and identifying when important data was missing. An example of how this thinking skill was identified for the teacher in the overview of a lesson was "For children to make generalizations and to provide information to support their statement" (Berlak & Tomlinson, 1973, p. ix).

These case studies incorporated various types of learning activities and opportunities for students such as role play, reading, writing, group discussion, and artifact creation, and photograph analysis at least ten years before Howard Gardner (1983) identified and promoted the importance of the multiple intelligences. The lessons did not focus all the learning opportunities on linguistic and logical intelligences; equal opportunities were provided for students to experience and demonstrate their knowledge in other forms.

Short Term Impact of the Metropolitan St. Louis Social Studies Center

The Social Studies Center was deemed a success by all involved (personal communication, July 8, 2007). The teachers who taught the case studies in the field were constantly observed, not to look for criticisms, but for ways to revise and examine the lessons for improvement. The students showed an interest in the case studies as observed by the members of the Social Studies Center. No longer was social studies taught in a pedestrian manner, but a manner that promoted more active engagement from the students. From the very beginning of the project, the Metropolitan St. Louis Social Studies Center was utilized by all the principal players. It was not a center in name only. It was an active place for social science discourse and engagement. All research, case study creation, implementation, and revision came from this center. The Elementary Social Studies Project, working under the auspices of the Metropolitan St. Louis Social Studies Center, completed its part of the working contract with Random House Publishers by completing 12 case studies for the social studies classrooms in St. Louis. However, the publishing company withdrew from its contract with the Center due to profitability issues. As a result, Random House published only three of the case studies materials for teachers or researchers to use. According to Harold Berlak (personal communication, July 8, 2007), social studies "didn't go away. It was pushed away due to testing," a call for high-stakes testing that required teachers to focus on other content areas rather than social studies. Berlak sees these tests as a political intrusion.

What Does Social Studies Mean for Today's Students and Teachers?: Political Intrusions

Berlak states (personal communication, July 5, 2007) that schools must be protected from political intrusions. The national government is leading the charge for standardized curriculum and standardized assessment for all states to follow. This charge to test is the governmental leaders' strategy for improving education for all students. The problem is that the type of assessment, standardized testing, is not conducive to teaching, learning, diversity, and curricular issues. The United States, more than any other industrialized nation, relies on the information generated from these tests. Unfortunately, the test results are used inappropriately to measure school competence, teacher aptitude and student achievement (Berlak, 1985b). Problems abound with these forms of assessment. Teachers are so concerned with students' passing the test that the only material they teach is what is specifically on the test. As a result, social studies education takes a backseat to reading, writing, and mathematics. If social studies is taught at all, it is at a minimal level where a student may practice a skill or work with knowledge that is found on the test while a social studies reading or concept is haphazardly thrown in as way of saying, "Yes, we teach social studies at our school."

Learning for students is reduced to being able to take an objective-based test (Berlak, 1985a) that requires the mere filling in of a small rectangle without scratching beyond the line. Basically, students learn and are tested on many abstract notions, such as a timeline of major battles in a world war. If students actually do possess the knowledge, these standardized tests are not designed to determine to what extent they understand the information (personal communication, July 5, 2007). The student who does well in the liberal arts is not given the opportunity to demonstrate what he/she knows. These students may understand the battles of the war very well, but need to show their understanding through a visual media like poetry or art project. Students are rid of the opportunities to look at historical events and people in multiple ways, thus limiting their thinking about social studies concepts. So, it is possible for a student to be denied a high school diploma based on the denial of alternative means to demonstrate understanding. In the content area of social studies, there is no one way to answer a question or understand a historical event. Questions should be asked that allow and encourage that students can answer questions in a different manner. According to Berlak (personal communication, July 5, 2007), judging a student's performance based on standardized testing is too punitive. Thus, the education system has become punitive to students, teachers, and community members because the federal government believes the only way to show educational progress is in quantitative measures.

The standardized testing movement plays a significant role in promoting a lack of diversity in social studies education. This testing process provides a ranking of schools based upon test results. Unfortunately, more African-American, American Indian and Hispanics are found at schools that were ranked low in math and reading (Berlak, 2001). These rankings affect academic opportunities for students. Students in schools ranked low in reading and math have fewer opportunities to take gifted and talented classes. Another aspect of diversity that is affected by standardized testing is that of whose truth is taught in social studies classes. If students are limited to learning that only one right answer is possible on the multiple choice standardized test, they will not acknowledge that more than one viewpoint is possible and even logical.

As such, the curriculum is dramatically affected when high-stakes tests are used for educational policy making. To the national government, testing is a means for driving the curriculum. Harold Berlak believes otherwise. In order to change the system, we must change the testing system. Policymakers base decisions on test results, which often have often irreversible life-altering consequences. Berlak believes instead of using the test results as a gatekeeper, pupils should be given opportunities to demonstrate what they know in a variety of methods. It is a cultural myth that in order to show educational progress, only one method is best and that is quantitatively. People either cannot or will not change from what they are used to doing. In this case, the federal government takes advantage of this myth as a means of perpetuating the testing process and all within it stands (personal communication, July 5, 2007). The testing process pushes for uniformity of what is taught, what and how it is tested, and how the test results are used. Anything that pushes for uniformity is going to eliminate the multiple voices.

The students have to take the test, using only one voice—the voice that will allow them to pass the test so they can get on with their lives (personal communication, July 5, 2007). By emphasizing the importance of standardized testing, the national government is relying on short term academic gains to serve as a guide for not only what to teach, but also who should be teaching it and where it should be taught. Such heavy reliance on short-term gains has a damaging impact because teachers are fired, schools are closed, and students are left with out high school diplomas. Some pupils may take longer to grasp concepts (Gruber, 1995), so to pigeonhole these students and hold them accountable because a governmental entity says that they must be tested on a certain date is preposterous (personal communication, July 5, 2007). In the business world, if an investor has not seen a significant increase in stock returns after a year, it may be time to move onto another investment. However, education is not that cut and dry. Students learn at different rates (Gruber, 1995) and in different styles (Gardner, 1983). Good educators know that information, but apparently the federal government does not. No Child Left Behind (NCLB, 2002) is a current example of how the federal government views education; they push for a standardized curriculum that is developed based upon standardized test scores.

Social Studies and the Standardization Movement

Social studies education must change. This change does not take place due to test results, but due to people being made aware of and open to diversity: the diversity of ideas and people. In social studies education, socials studies learning and assessment are inseparable. To change the system, one must understand it. Particular forms of tests and assessments represent particular forms of discourse. This discourse generates specific ways of talking and communicating with others about the instruction and the schooling- process. However, the general public and educators have been pushed away from the dialogue (personal communication, July 5, 2007). The reason the general public and educators have been pushed away from the discussion of social studies education, or any type of content area for that matter, is that school control has become a top-down management system. This type of school control has "led to an increasingly restrictive view of knowledge, learning, literacy, and the nature of human talents and capacities; and to abandonment of the commitment to public schools that educate all children" (Berlak, 1985a). Unfortunately, those in power do not like to release that power to people and groups who have a vested interest in seeing the system not only be successful, but thrive. This power is really about who gets to decide—decide on curricular matters, decide on assessment matters. Teachers are spending more and more class time preparing students to take the required tests—time that would, could, should be spent on social studies education is forgotten or trivialized. Thus, teachers, have become functionaries of a bureaucratic system which views test results as more significant than what a student actually knows and can do. Of course, this system leads to teacher burnout, lack of student commitment and concern for learning, and the decline of educational standards. In other words, what goes into social studies education is what comes out.

Coming Full Circle

To social science educators, Harold Berlak played a significant role in the creation of purposeful and child-centered social studies curriculum from the early 1960s into the early 1970s with his direction of the Metropolitan St. Louis Social Studies Center. The curriculum that was created served as the vehicle through which social studies educators needed to provide the much needed concrete connection that social science concepts require for student unawareness and understanding. The elementary social studies project supported the social science premise that questions must be asked and investigated in order to study the social sciences because the curriculum was based upon providing students with social science knowledge and critical thinking skills through the analysis of social, economic and political controversies. Such curricular usage had been unknown to that point. No longer were students encouraged to passively receive social science information only for it to be regurgitated for some mindless test and then forgotten.

The Metropolitan St. Louis Social Studies Center acknowledged the social studies teacher as a professional by providing useful and relevant classroom resources, such as role-playing and simulations. However, if the educator believed a better method to be available, he/she was encouraged to utilize it. The curriculum was not an all or nothing program. The educator's knowledge and expertise was respected. With such a positive relationship established, the teachers utilized the many resources at the center on a regular basis which in turn served the learning needs of the students. The program was not scripted, nor was it entirely mandatory for each teacher in every school. This level of educator respect and child-centered curriculum was a new approach to social science education. Of course, this approach is almost unheard of in today's social studies classroom since federal financial support is based upon meeting the guidelines of No Child Left Behind (NCLD, 2002) and standardized tests scores.

Any curriculum, not just social sciences, is drastically affected once high-stakes tests are used to determine educational policy. Test scores should not be in the driver's seat when it comes to curricular decisions. Harold Berlak sees the community and professional educators as those who should be steering the wheel. When a community determines the needs of its students, diversity becomes part of the equation, as well as academic opportunities for students. The system in place currently is not one conducive to student learning, thinking, or social science awareness. Instead, standardized test results are a major negative factor in determining many students' academic fates. As director of the Metropolitan St. Louis Social Studies Center, Berlak guided the creation of a curriculum not based upon high-stakes testing, but on the learning needs of students. Tests results were not the impetus for curricular decisions, they were not even the choice for student assessment within the elementary social studies project. Students were given opportunities to demonstrate their learning a variety of ways. Harold Berlak does not see the purpose in pigeonholing students for short-term academic gains on a high-stakes test that does nothing but distort the educational process while insulting community members by ignoring their needs and input. Social studies learning has been increasingly limited for today's students due to school focus on standardized test preparation and a restrictive view of social studies learning and human talents. Returning the government to the people so they can determine the educational needs of its students is vital to the renewed success of social science education. The advocates of standardized testing are not qualified to determine the academic needs of students, but the community and its people should have the democratic right to determine the best interests of its members. Social studies education is based upon citizenship education. Therefore, let the citizens use their rights and knowledge to determine how best to prepare its future citizens. This idea led Harold Berlak as director of the Metropolitan St. Louis Social Studies Center and the creation of a social studies curriculum that included a variety of learning opportunities for students while considering the needs of the community and its members.

REFERENCES

Berlak, H. (1985a, June). *Democratic school reform and the social studies.* Paper presented at the annual meeting of the Social Science Education Consortium, Racine, WI.

Berlak, H. (1985b). Testing in a democracy. *Educational Leadership. 43,* 16–17.

Berlak, H. (2001). *Academic achievement, race, and reform.* Oakland, CA: Applied Research Center. (ERIC Document Reproduction Service No. ED464973)

Berlak, H., & Tomlinson, T. (1973). *A village family.* New York: Random House.

Berlak, H., & Tomlinson, T. (1975). *Changing neighborhoods.* New York: Random House.

Gardner, H. (1983). *Frames of mind: The theory of multiple intelligences.* New York: Basic.

Hobbs, R. (2007). *Reading the media: Media literacy in high school English.* Newark, DE: Teachers College Press.

Leland, C. H., & Harste, J. C. (1994). Multiple ways of knowing: Curriculum in a new key. *Language Arts, 71*(5), 337–345.

National Council for the Social Studies. (2001). *Creating effective citizens.* Retrieved July 8, 2007, from http://www.socialstudies.org/publications/effectivecitizens/

No Child Left Behind Act of 2001, 20 U.S.C. § 6319 (2008).

Gruber H. E. (1995). *The essential Piaget: An interpretive reference and guide* (H E. Gruber & J J. Voneche, Eds.). Lanham, MD: Jason Aronson.

Vogler. K. E., & Virtue, D. (2007). "Just the facts, Ma'am": Teaching social studies in the era of standards and high stakes testing. *The Social Studies, 98*(2), 54–58.

SECTION II

PROJECTS

CHAPTER 8

A RED HEADED STEPCHILD OF SOCIAL RECONSTRUCTION

Sociology and the New Social Studies

Karen L. Riley

Over the past 2 decades, educational researchers of social studies have wrestled with finding answers as to the storied failure of the New Social Studies Movement. After all, a sweeping curricular movement of this magnitude should have resulted in fundamental changes in American educational practice. Yet, the New Social Studies Movement quietly slipped into the dustbin of obscure curricular initiatives carrying with it perhaps the most obscure of all social studies curricular areas—sociology. The story of sociology and the New Social Studies begins in the fall of 1961, when the American Sociological Association (ASA) established a Committee on the Social Studies Curriculum of American Secondary Schools (Switzer, 1993). Sociologists like historians and other disciplined-based experts, likely hoped to "cash in" on the many educational grants offered by the National Science Foundation (NSF), whose members in the early 1960s could still hear the faint pinging of Sputnik I. With the weight of massive funding at the national level and the involvement of distinguished researchers from

The New Social Studies: People, Projects, and Perspectives, pp. 149–165
Copyright © 2010 by Information Age Publishing
All rights of reproduction in any form reserved.

every area of social science located at some of America's top colleges and universities, why and how did the sociology project of the New Social Studies Movement fail to make a lasting impact?

This chapter, as part of this book on the New Social Studies, seeks to chronicle the rise and fall of the sociology project in general, and the fate of the *Sociological Resources for the Social Studies* (SRSS) in particular. It also offers a look at the important individuals involved with the development of SRSS along with the secondary course entitled "Inquiries in Sociology." The background for this chapter emanates from a score of period literature (articles and books written at the height of the New Social Studies Movement) as well as books and articles from later decades which examine from a distance "what was" and "what went wrong." The promise and possibility for sociology to play an important role in the secondary social science curriculum faded more quickly from view perhaps than other curriculum projects of the New Social Studies Movement. The Social Reconstructionist nature of the sociology curriculum—an examination of social problems—challenged the timelessly popular American history curriculum with its emphasis on documenting progress and success. Hanvey (1961) in illuminating for readers the shift from social studies to social science offers a compelling look at the academic tensions within such a shift:

> History's pre-eminence in the curriculum has been supported not only by the important functions it served but by the unpopularity of potential competitors. History served the culture; the newer social sciences struck at its very roots. The ideas of the sociologist and the theories propounded by the Freudians, if not scorned as pompous pedantry, were long treated as blasphemies or left-wing laments. Sociologists, like social reformers, seemed to be preoccupied with national shortcomings: urban disorganization, intergroup conflict, divorce, crime, mental illness. This predilection for pathology generated little public sympathy. (pp. 15–16)

A few years later, in an edited book that some might call an "apology," Page (1964) sought to examine the nature, structure, content, and methodology of the discipline and perhaps "rehabilitate" the image of sociology and to a larger extent social science.

Hence, the story of the 1960s sociology projects runs parallel with those of history, geography, economics, and other curricular areas of the social studies that sought to reform the school curriculum, but in the end, failed to make a lasting imprint on American education. One reason might be, as Mehlinger (1988) bluntly put it, the New Social Studies was little more than old wine in a new bottle, unable to dislodge or truly change the social studies reform movement of 1916. Yet Thornton's (1994) assessment is that the New Social Studies should not be viewed as a sort of stand-alone-curricular phenomenon, but rather, as part of a broader curriculum reform movement influenced by Jerome Bruner and the concept of process and nature of the disciplines. However, in general, most educational scholars consider the New Social Studies to have been a curricular reform movement of great promise, unfortunately, with disappointing results.

But why, one might ask, is a study of failed curricular projects important? Why should educators concern themselves with the past? After all, isn't the most important research in education that which involves statistics, classroom experiments into this or that strategy, and the latest theories of neuroscience and how children learn, rather than historical treatments of where We were and what We did in terms of educational practice? The answer is that educational historians believe otherwise. As Edward Gibbon, the renowned historian of the Enlightenment and author of *The Rise and Fall of the Roman Empire* once stated, "I have but one lamp by which my feet are guided, and that is the lamp of experience. I know no way of judging the future but by the past." Therefore, our educational past is our experience. The distance of time is important because it offers us an opportunity to examine without responsibility for the outcome, our past educational practice, so that as a people we might determine for current curricular initiatives how best to avoid the slippery slope of failure and ultimately, obscurity.

BACKGROUND TO SOCIOLOGICAL RESOURCES IN THE SOCIAL STUDIES (SRSS)

The social and political crises of the 1960s and 1970s—which included a rebellion of America's youth to traditional perspectives on just about everything, a presidential assassination, and an unpopular war in Southeast Asia—called for strong solutions to growing problems. However, long before these troubled decades, American educators had advocated a new rationale for public schooling. Educators like Harold Rugg, George Counts, Theodore Brameld and countless others from the 1920s, well into the 1950s, called for an overhaul or reconstruction of society through the use of the scientific method in identifying and solving America's social ills, especially economic inequality (Evans 2008; Ponder, 1971; Riley, 2006; Riley & Stern, 2003/04; Stern & Riley, 2001). While their "cause" attracted any number of listeners, social reconstruction as an educational philosophy never enjoyed the status of educational policy.

The turbulent decades beginning with the 1960s caused federal lawmakers to search for educational answers to social, political, and economic problems. Because one cannot separate public school systems from their respective systems of government, U.S. lawmakers and those who influence public policy backed their search for answers with funds through organizations such as the NSF. Thus, the quest to ramp up American education in order to battle domestic problems helped to usher in the "New Social Sciences" of the 1960s and 1970s. Smith and Cox (1969) identified more than 50 social studies curriculum projects in existence in the late 1960s. In fact, Malone (1968) described curriculum development during this period as being in a "healthy state" of transition, a state of change that should last well into the next decade (pp. 111–112). Indeed, the next decade proved highly productive. Goldsmid and Goldsmid (1980) compiled an impressive list of resource initiatives regarding sociology teaching at the undergraduate level. They concluded that "more significant advances in understanding the teaching and learning of sociology were seen in 1975–1979 than in any short period in the history of sociology" (p. 392). The flurry of activity during this five year period produced the following: publication of some 309 articles, three dozen workshops, three national surveys, the ASA *Teaching Newsletter*, and the Teaching Resource Center, to name but a few. But what is interesting about the findings of the Goldsmids' article is that they failed to link the activity and interest in teaching sociology at the undergraduate level between 1975–1970 to the ASA's initiatives on teaching sociology and curriculum development for secondary education as part of the New Social Studies.

Despite the promise of exciting social science curriculum initiatives in the 1960s and 1970s, secondary sociology and other social studies reform curricula soon joined a long list of other forgettable educational reform projects from an earlier vintage. Sociology likely took top billing in terms of ultimate lack of allure and failure.

In the fall of 1961, the ASA dispatched a proposal to the "course content improvement section "of the NSF offering to develop curriculum materials for secondary schools, with Neal Gross as Chair of the ASA Curriculum Committee" (Short & Matlock 1982, p. 313). Perhaps Grupp's (1961) stinging article of the same year, "The Status of Teaching Sociology in High Schools," in which he pointed out the ASA's inattention to high school sociology and/or the training of teachers, prompted the ASA's enthusiasm for involvement with secondary curriculum development. Grupp (1962) also found the school sociology program to lack clear instructional goals. DeCesare (2002) considers Grupp's 1961 assessment regarding the status of sociology in the high school to be relatively unchanged. Whatever the reason, in May of 1964, the NSF notified the ASA that funding was available as of August 1964 with an annual renewal. Hence, the ASA established Sociological Resources for Secondary Schools as an official project of the New Social Sciences, but in 1968 renamed the project Sociological Resources for the Social Studies or SRSS. The project lasted until 1971 (Switzer, 1993). According to one "eyewitness account" (Switzer, 1993), the project began at Dartmouth College under the direction of Robert Feldmesser as executive director, but Felmesser's scholarly pursuits forced him to turn over the project in 1966 to Distinguished Sociology Professor and past President of the ASA, Robert Angell at the University of Michigan at Ann Arbor. Switzer asserts that high turnover rates plagued all of the New Social Studies Curriculum projects to one degree or another for the same reason:

> Many discipline-based scholars at the peak of their careers found it difficult to justify devoting time to work on curricular materials for elementary and secondary schools. Contributing to such materials brought little recognition to the scholar and did nothing to bring prestige to the scholar within the academic field. Work on curricular materials for use in elementary and secondary schools was and remains today outside the reward structure of the academic disciplines. Angell, fully established within his discipline and nearing the end of his academic career, could afford to take on the direction of SRSS as his final contribution to the field of sociology. Feldmesser, a relatively young man, could not afford a long-term commitment to the low-prestige pursuit of developing *social studies* curricular materials. (Switzer, 1993)

In short, the SRSS project failed to attract more than a handful of sociologists who stayed the course out of what they hoped would be unique opportunities for upward advancement. Those who remained, unknowingly or unwittingly developed materials laced with social reconstruction methodology and Progressive Era educational goals, something they would have known had there been participation of professors of education on the team.

The Sociology Resources for the Social Studies project consisted of three initiatives: (1) A one semester high school course titled "Inquiries in Sociology;" (2) A series of paperback units to be used in courses other than sociology; and (3 A set of paperback books on topics related to the field of sociology. The basic design for SRSS was developed by Robert Feldmesser and included collaborative efforts of both sociologists and classroom teachers throughout the design, implementation, and refinement process of curriculum development. The overarching objective of the SRSS project was for students to engage in a sort of detached inquiry thereby mimicking the type of research and study conducted in the real world by practicing sociologists. On the surface, one might ask, "How could something so seemingly promising fail so miserably?" After all, what could be wrong with teaching students how to examine the problems of their world and then find solutions to fix them? And, shouldn't methodology take center stage in an authentic curriculum experiment? If yes to the above questions, then why the failure?

Jarolimek (1973), writing at the height of the New Social Studies movement, pointed out that professional educators (professors located in schools of education) were largely cut out of SRSS projects as they were viewed by disciplined-based practicing sociologists as part of the problem with education in the first place. Moreover, "this omission was not an accident. Many of the discipline-based scholars simply felt that professional educators had little to contribute to the development of cutting-edge curricular materials in their discipline" (Jarolimek, 1973). Therefore, sociologists and classroom teachers formed the collaborative groups that worked on design, implementation, and field testing sans education faculty. Smarting from the sting of rejection, a number of faculty from schools of education, in turn, became critics of those engaged in the SRSS projects (Switzer, 1993).

Textbook publishers also joined the ranks of New Social Studies critics as they were unsure if and when there would be a role for them to play in this latest education reform movement. Yet, the world of textbook publishing would never be the same after the New Social Studies. The introduction of multimedia, primary materials, case studies, data analysis, and the like, became common offerings in textbooks of the future thanks to curricular innovations emerging from the New Social Studies projects. The richly colorful textbooks with their graphs, charts, short biographies, and the like of today, owe much to the New Social Studies. However, if one were to judge the success of the New Social Studies, one measure might be the sales figures of instructional materials throughout the 1960s and 1970s. In terms of sales, instructional materials developed by New Social Studies researchers, at least according to one study (Hahn, Marker, Switzer, & Turner 1977), dominated about 30% of the market in the 1970s. Perhaps an unintended positive outcome of the sociology projects of the New Social Studies were the professional sociologists involved with the projects who stated that their teaching methods were forever changed as a result their collaboration with secondary teachers and students. The activities approach found in these classrooms likely inspired professional sociologists to return to the university classroom with a renewed senses of excitement. Teachers, on the other hand, appeared far less enthusiastic. One period study of the early 1970s demonstrated that materials and activities for sociology, geography, and economics, were used far less in the classroom that those of world history or American history, which measured a higher rate of usage (Guenther & Dumas 1972, p. 50 Table 2).

Sociologists looking to apply their theories and ideas to the K–12 classroom throughout the period of the New Social Studies, namely the 1960s and 1970s left themselves open to criticism for their inattention to developmental theories. One such curricular innovation emanated from sociologists working in the field of gaming-simulation and moral development. In fact, the era of the New Social Studies coincided with the then fascination with gaming theory. According to Tamminga (1977), the use of gaming-simulation for teaching is increasing in elementary schools, junior and senior high schools, colleges and universities, professional institutes, and community organizations. Since the early 1960s, the subject of gaming-simulation has received increased attention in curriculum resource centers (such as the Social Science Education Consortium in Boulder, Colorado), summer workshops for teachers, symposiums and meetings of professional associations of educators and social scientists, and professional journals (almost every issue of *Teaching Sociology* contains an article regarding gaming-simulation) (p. 255). Yet gaming simulation was not without its critics. Rest (1974) felt compelled to draw attention to the "pitfalls" of moral development through gaming simulation when he stated that

> Kohlberg and Lockwood have more generally questioned whether the new social studies and the structure-of-the discipline approaches (those inspired by Jerome Bruner) to curriculum revision are to be faulted on the same point, namely that the level of reasoning presupposed by these curricula is inappropriately high for most students for whom it is intended. According to Kohlberg, such new curricula often presuppose Piaget's stage of formal operations or Kohlberg's stages 5 and 6, and high school students typically are not there yet, thus students miss the fascination and relevance that their teachers see in the new curricula. (p. 244)

The End of a Reform Movement

In the world of academe—the unwritten rule, well-known secret, or whatever one wishes to call something that is common knowledge—the players all agree that when the funding dries up, it's time to call it quits. Euologies in the form of articles filled academic journals for years covering all aspects of the "autopsy." Certainly, such is the case of the New Social Studies. Researchers then and now offer the same question, "how could such an exciting project with participants from some of the most prestigious universities across the land rocket onto the educational stage only to descend with hardly a vapor trail?" Many of course will point to funding or lack of funding as a primary cause. To be sure, projects of all stripes come and go at the whim of funding agencies. But in the case of the New Social Studies, a combination of factors coalesced to create an educational climate that was not conducive to the implementation of this new reform effort.

If this chapter were a law brief, "our" side would simply admit that dwindling funds played the major role in the "death" of the New Social Studies. Yet funding had a few accomplices. One, school culture. Those most familiar with school culture, teacher educators, had been "cut out" of the movement from the beginning. Professionals from the disciplines along with classroom teachers developed and implemented curriculum projects, although some claim that the SRSS project was dominated by academic sociologists who only used classroom teachers to lend credibility to what they developed (Smith, 1979, p. 27). The teachers and the newly developed materials were the supposed agents of change, despite the fact that any number of sociologists associated with the evaluation of the project judged the participating teachers to be incompetent, while the teachers judged the curriculum materials developed by sociologists to be over the heads of their students. As for school culture, it is highly complex and multi-layered, with school boards, principals, department chairs, parents, students, and the like, playing a vital role in the success or failure of reform measures.

Another problem that added to the already burgeoning reasons-for-the-failure-of-the-New-Social-Studies-roster was the lack of any real consensus in school districts about the need for reforming the social studies. Perhaps those professionals located in history departments, sociology departments, or geography departments believed that because these materials were developed by folks from the disciplines in higher education, they were naturally superior to materials developed by their colleagues in schools of education and therefore would be received with greater fanfare. This did not happen. Too many gaps in the complex world of school culture existed.

And too, regardless of the quality of the materials developed, one must have a way to get the materials from the drawing board and into the hands of the teachers. In the case of the sociology project, the materials were handed over to Allyn & Bacon to publish and market. Switzer (1973) represented the eastern half of the United States. Following is his assessment of the marketing relationship with Allyn & Bacon:

> Allyn and Bacon was the only publisher to present a serious bid for distribution of the SRSS materials. Although the Allyn and Bacon Company had many well-intentioned and professional employees, their system was not well suited for distribution of project materials. It was my assignment to introduce the Allyn and Bacon sales force from the eastern half of the United States to the SRSS materials they were to market. At that briefing, a salesman expressed reality very clearly when he said, "Remember, we take out of our case only those things that will sell." Given the rather limited market for curricular materials stressing a *sociological* perspective, the

future of SRSS materials in the hands of Allyn and Bacon sales force did not seem promising.

The publishers also had difficulty understanding the nature of inquiry-oriented teacher materials. Editors frequently made changes in the text or inserted photographs with captions that destroyed the inquiry emphasis of the materials. At conventions, multiple copies of student materials would be displayed, but one had to search hard to find a single copy of the teacher's manual without which the materials for students made little sense. Salespersons used to marketing textbooks did not understand the integral nature of the teacher's manual to inquiry-oriented instructional materials. This is not to lay blame on Allyn and Bacon for limited marketing of the SRSS materials. Their system and the norms that drove it were simply incompatible with distribution of the SRSS materials. Unfortunately, there was no other option.

A common thread that runs throughout the literature on sociology at the high school level is the complaint by academic sociologists that high school teachers were underprepared to teach the subject—the reader might recall earlier that often the term incompetent was used to describe the abilities of classroom teachers to adequately teach sociology (Angell, 1971; Bain, 1926, 1931; Bohlke, 1964; Dennick-Brecht, 2000; Dorn, 1986; Dykstra, 1967; Fraser & Switzer, 1970; Friedman & Howery, 1995; Gillette, 1913; Gray, 1993; Grupp, 1961; Hering, 1967; Howery, 1985; Kelly, 1969; Landis, 1942, 1947; Lashbrook, 2001; Leavitt, 1982; Meyer, 1936; Short & Matlock, 1982; Short, Watts, & Matlock 1986; Switzer & Wilson, 1969; Weber, 1978; West, 1930). If true, "we" in the field of teacher education have not learned very much from out past curriculum mistakes as even today, preservice teachers are required to take little more than two courses in sociology (one of which is usually an *Introduction to Sociology* course, yet this subject area is often a course offering at most medium to large high schools). If two courses were the norm then as now, it is little wonder that practicing sociologists complained about the underpreparedness of high school sociology teachers.

Primary SRSS Source Materials, an Analysis

The comprehensive *Social Studies Curriculum Materials Data Book* published by the Social Science Education Consortium, Inc., organized all of the various social science projects according to materials, textbook, and games and simulations. Each project contained a summary data sheet, which provided abbreviated details such as required course time, available materials, and user characteristics. The sociology project consisted of three distinct components: (1) A secondary high school course titled

Inquiries in Sociology; (2) A reading series titled Episodes in Sociology; and, (3) A set of paperback units that could be used to supplement other social studies courses with sociology content. The grade levels designated for the course of study were Grades 10–12. According to the summary data sheet, "Episodes [was] supposed to provide students a brief but dramatic first-hand experience with social data These experiences place them in a position to analyze the data and draw conclusions based on a scientific process of sociological inquiry" (Social Science Education Consortium 1974, Summary Data Sheet by Michael Radz). What strikes this writer about the data sheet's description of the project is how closely it resembles descriptions of materials produced by Harold Rugg some 30 years prior.

The *Inquiries in Sociology* course was designed as a one-semester course. The suggested time for each "episode" was 3 weeks. Paradoxically, the literature base for the sociology project is replete with complaints by sociologists involved with the project over the lack of preparedness of teachers to teach the sociological concepts and content of the newly developed materials; yet, the summary data sheet states the following: "Teachers need not have an extensive background in sociology because the instructor's guides provide detailed teaching procedures as well as background readings" (Summary Data Sheet, 1974). The underlying objective of the sociology project was to teach social science methods to students so that they might avoid conclusions based upon what they, the practicing sociologists, referred to as value judgments rather than conclusions that were based upon observable measures or evidence. Technique was the cornerstone of the project.

The *Episodes* were stand alone units that explored a variety of social problems, from social mobility, social stratification, poverty, and discrimination, to prejudice, social institutions, urban problems and social status (Summary Data Sheet, 1974). Teachers assumed the role of facilitator rather than classroom authority figure in order to create an environment in which students felt comfortable enough to explore ideas and in what way/s they understood the problems under study. The goal for students, according to the SRSS developers, was "not to acquire a grasp of the entire field of sociology, but rather that they learn the kinds of questions sociologists ask about society and recognize contrasting approaches to reaching conclusions" (Summary Data Sheet, 1974). Although the intentions of the developers appeared, at first, to be less focused on creating "mini" sociologists, the materials developed for the course and goals for student participation suggest otherwise. What remains unclear is how university sociologists, with at least 8 to 10 years of advanced study in sociology "under their belts" could expect a high rate of performance from students whose teachers were, in their words, incompetent.

The teacher's guide for the course, *Inquiries in Sociology*, is daunting. The introduction makes it clear that the researchers believe that learning occurs best when students are actively engaged in the process and are not simply playing the role of passive learner. Despite this claim, when one examines the teacher's guide, it becomes readily apparent that even an experienced teacher would have had difficulty executing the lessons developed by the planners. The curriculum guide is filled with complex charts that require extended study in order to extract meaningful information from them. Moreover, a number of the lessons incorporate complex psychological concepts and presuppose that the teacher and student body have already acquired the necessary background in order to engage in the lesson. Additionally, some lessons actually reinforce or introduce negative stereotypes. Lesson #18 on prejudice, for example, provides the following example.

In the teacher's guide, students are asked to examine two case studies. In case study A, students are asked to determine whether or not the author of a statement was showing prejudice. According to the author of the statement, she asserted that "she is not prejudiced." She also asserts that "blacks are uneducated and unclean and have not, therefore 'earned their place in the average community.'" While Jews do not suffer these alleged deficiencies ("they fit in most any place"), still they "are underhanded and sneaky." We ask: Is the author of the statement showing prejudice? Or we might put the question: Is this an overgeneralization or a faulty generalization that irrationally depreciates an ethnic group? (Social Science Education Consortium, 1972, p. 172). What is doubtful about this example is whether or not the teacher would have had any way to deal with the problem or stated questions much less high school students. Little wonder that practicing sociologists felt that teachers were unable to teach the program successfully owing to incompetency while participating teachers complained that the materials were far over the heads of their students.

Of the materials developed for SRSS, the small paperback booklets on topics such as "Contemporary Soviet Society," "Images of People," "Values in Mass Communication," to name but a few, appear more inviting, although they too burden the reader with an over abundance of statistical data. While the goal or objective of the designers, as they have previously stated, was to have students engage in the methods of evidence gathering, analyzing and interpreting like practicing sociologists, the narrative, which serves as a foundation for the study is often lost in a sea of charts, graphs, and columns of words and numbers. Additionally, when one examines the teacher designers involved with the pamphlets, one is struck by their affluent locations: Arlington, Virginia; New Haven Connecticut, and Brookline, Massachusetts, to name only three. Teachers from affluent areas writing about social problems struck the author of this chapter as problematic. In recalling these words of Elie Wiesel, Nobel Prize Winner for Literature, at a conference from more than 20 years ago, "how can one imagine the unimaginable," this writer wondered about the question of authenticity in terms of SRSS materials.

After an examination of the literature base on the New Social Studies, along with an evaluation of the primary sources themselves (SRSS materials), what can be said for the SRSS project as part of the 12 projects of the New Social Science program is that its scope was impressive. Its materials were innovative. Its commitment to curriculum reform was encompassing. Switzer (1993), whose first-hand involvement with the sociology projects of the New Social Studies offers readers a keen summary of lessons that should be gleaned from this monumental curriculum reform movement. As he succinctly stated, "Here are a few of the things we learned or should have learned.

1. Periodically a national effort is needed to reform the *social studies* curriculum with an infusion of major funding by the federal government and private sources. The most creative minds in the field must have the opportunity to transfer current best thinking about teaching and learning and about the disciplines into innovative curriculum materials free of the constraints of profit making or barriers within the current educational system.

2. We must develop a far more sophisticated, systemic model for change in classrooms involving the development, distribution, and infusion of innovative curricular materials. Innovative, high-quality, curricular materials are a necessary but not sufficient component in bringing about change in teacher behavior.

3. The reward structures in both schools and in higher education must change before teachers and scholars will make the commitment necessary for the development and implementation of innovative curricular materials. We must come to the collective realization that all segments of the educational system must be mobilized and pursue goals of quality education in elementary and secondary schools.

4. For innovative curricular materials to find their way into classrooms, major efforts must be made in teacher training both inservice and preservice. This training needs to extend to college and university instructors who teach *social studies* methods courses to preservice teachers.

5. We need a system for the dissemination of innovative curricular materials to school systems that does not rely on the profit-moti-

vated commercial publishing industry. This is not a criticism of the publishing industry but a realization that the need for profit makes a publishing industry basically conservative. Their task is more to identify an existing market niche and appeal to it than to attempt to create a new market through innovative materials. (p. 26)

The time in which the New Social Studies curricular projects flourished was an exciting period in the history of *social studies* education. It was a time of ferment and change; a time for bold experimentation. The old debate over the success or failure of the New Social Studies movement should be laid to rest. Of course, it was a failure. Of course, it was a success. It was a part of history: a period in time. As in all things, it was evolutionary, leading to the next period of time when I hope we can put into practice what we have learned. We learned a great deal.

CONCLUSION

The New Social Studies movement for secondary schools in the United States streaked across the educational landscape like the famed Silver Meteor of 1939, gathering excitement and generating interest in creating a new way to learn the traditional social studies subjects and displacing outmoded methods and strategies of teaching and learning. The New Social Studies Movement brought on board a host of educational notables from Harvard to Stanford and from Michigan to Utah. Twelve projects in all were developed by teams of professional and practicing sociologists from across the United States. Secondary teachers too played a role in the development of programs and materials. What reform movement could fail with all of the seemingly right ingredients: professionals at the helm accompanied by classroom teachers? Whether failure is the correct word for the fate of The New Social Studies movement or not, one of the greatest curriculum reform movements of the twentieth century derailed nearly as quickly as it began its journey in 1961.

Since the end of the era of the New Social Studies, educational historians and others have attempted to discover the reason or cause for loss of interest, collapse, or rejection of a reform movement that promised to unlock the secrets of the disciplines for scores of American secondary students. This chapter has looked at the failure of the sociology project, SRSS, in particular. The evidence examined for this study includes literature from the period, written by those who enjoyed a front row seat. It also includes primary source materials, including the Data Book of the New Social Science project, a teacher's guide from 1972 for the one semester course *Inquires in Sociology*, and, a set of pamphlets from *Episodes in Social Inquiry Series*, along with secondary source material.

Any number of causes have been advanced by this or that sociologist involved with the project. More than a few lay the blame for the failure of the project at the feet of the teacher participants. The word "incompetent," referring to the high school teachers who used the materials, was a recurring theme throughout the literature on the sociology project. Equally accusing were those teachers who attempted to use the materials, often complaining that the program was "over the heads" of their students. After an examination of the primary materials themselves, this writer concludes that the materials were likely over the heads of the teachers as well. But, accusations aside, the question remains, what happened to such a promising reform movement?

First, when the funding dried up, the passion that moved so many to mobilize their creative energies began to wane. In a perfect world, professors or teachers would not have to be concerned with something so pedestrian as money. However, the world is not perfect and when the funding went away, so did the interest of many of those involved. Second, the "war" between the disciplines versus professional schools played a role in weakening the momentum and sustainability of the New Social Studies. While practicing sociologists courted classroom teachers in order to put together a credible team, professors in schools of education who would have been the ones to advise on important elements of curricular change such as the nature of school culture, were left out of the project. This rebuke backfired, propelling teacher educators into the camp of the New Social Studies critics. And third, the structure and traditions of public schools and the curriculum acted as a barrier to change.

Curriculum, in some ways, is like a language. It is not a dead or static language. If it were, one could easily pass its understandings from one generation to the next. No, curriculum is like a living language, which contains words that change meaning, and whose philosophical underpinnings change depending upon the social makeup of our communities and schools. With sweeping change comes opposition. Also, when the natural leaders of teacher preparation are left out of the reform process, opposition arises. When parents can no longer help their children with the learning process because its content and methods seem insurmountable, opposition arises. When students have no role to play in the reform process, opposition arises. The failure of the New Social Studies movement was not a subject matter failure. Those who pushed for curriculum reform of our secondary schools throughout the 1960s and 1970s in discipline areas such as social studies, mathematics, and other subject areas did so without understanding that school culture and the structure of our schooling traditions will only allow for superficial change. John Dewey, like most of our important educational philosophers, understood that real change must be structural. Otherwise, educators of all ranks will simply chase after the latest grant in order to secure the funding for what they hope will be the next big opportunity for curriculum reform.

REFERENCES

Angell, R. C. (1971). Sociology instruction, secondary schools. In *The Encyclopedia of Education* (Vol. 8, pp. 308–311). New York: Macmillan.

Bain, R. (1926). Sociology in Washington high schools. *The School Review, 34*, 535–542.

Bain, R. (1931). High school sociology. *The High School Teacher, 7,* 134–137, 153–155.

Bohlke, R. H. (1964). The teaching of sociology in secondary schools: Problems and prospects. *Social Forces, 42,* 363-734.

DeCesare, M. A. (2002). The lesson to be learned: The past troubles and future promise of teaching high school sociology. *Teaching Sociology, 30*(3), 302–316.

Dennick-Brecht, M. K. (2000). *A Status report on introductory sociology courses in public high schools in Pennsylvania.* EdD dissertation, School of Education, Duquesne University, Pittsburgh, PA.

Dorn, D. S. (1986). High school sociology: A view from California. *Footnotes, 14*(4), 13-14.

Dykstra, J. W. (1967). The high school sociology course. *Social Education, 3*(1), 487–489.

Evans, R. (2008). *This happened in America: Harold Rugg and the censure of social studies.* Charlotte, NC: Information Age.

Fraser, G. S., & T. J. Switzer. (1970). Inquiries in sociology: Responses by teachers and students. *Social Education, 34,* 922–926, 930.

Friedman, S., & C. B. Howery. (1995). *Report on a Survey of State Credentialing Standards and Textbook Selection in High Schools.* American Sociological Association Committee on Sociology in the Elementary and Secondary Schools, Washington, DC. Unpublished manuscript.

Gillette, J. M. (1913). Sociology as a high school subject. *The Educational Review, 45,* 256–262.

Goldsmid, C. A., & Goldsmid, P. L. (1980). The great leap forward?: The teaching of sociology 1975-1979, and beyond. *Teaching Sociology, 7*(4), 373–395.

Gray, P. S. (1993). Sociology in the schools. In Virginia S. Wilson, J. A. Litle, and G. L. Wilson (Ed.), *Teaching Social Studies: Hand book of Trena's, Issues, and Implications for the Future* (pp. 187–200). Westport, CT: Greenwood.

Grupp, S. E. (1961). The status of teaching sociology in high schools. *Sociology and Social Research, 45,* 327-331.

Guenther, J., & Dumas, W. (1972). N. S. S. project material in the classroom: A survey. *The History Teacher, 5*(3), 47–50.

Hahn, C. L., Marker, G. W., Switzer, T. J., & Turner, M. J. (1977). Three studies on perception and utilization of "The New Social Studies" materials. Boulder, CO: Social Science Education Consortium.

Hanvey, R. (1961). Augury for the social studies. *The School Review, 69*(1), 11–24.

Hering, W. M. (1967). Sociology and the high school: What and why? *Indiana Social Studies Quarterly*, pp. 4–12.

Howery, C, B. (1985). Sociology in High School. *Footnotes, 13*(1), 4.

Jarolimek, J. (1973). In pursuit of the elusive New Social Studies. *Educational Leadership, 30*, 596–599.

Kelly, P. E. (1969). Sociology in the secondary-school curriculum: Problems and prospects. *The High School Journal, 52*, 281–289.

Landis, J. T. (1942). Sociology in Illinois high schools. *The Social Studies, 33*, 354–55.

Landis, J. T. (1947). The sociology curriculum and teacher training. *American Sociological Review, 12*, 113–116.

Malone, W. C. (1968). Civic education. *Peabody Journal of Education, 46*(2), 110–114.

Mehlinger, H. D. (1988). The reform of social studies and the role of the National Commission for the Social Studies. *The History Teacher, 21*(2), 195–206.

Landis, J. T. (1942). Sociology in Illinois high schools. *The Social Studies, 33*, 354–55.

Landis, J. T. (1947). The sociology curriculum and teacher training. *American Sociological Review, 12*, 113–116.

Lashbrook, J. (2001). Sociology in high school: A profile of New York State. *Teaching Sociology, 29*(3), 354–359.

Leavitt, L. A. (1982). *Varieties of teaching experience: An analysis of the teaching of sociology in four divergent academic settings.* Unpublished dissertation, University of Massachussetts.

Meyer, H. D. (1936). The correlation of the teaching of sociology in high schools and colleges. *Social Forces, 15*, 221–222.

Page, C. H. (Ed.). (1964). Sociology and contemporary education. *American Sociological Review, 29*(6), 941–942.

Ponder, G. (1971). The teacher as activist. *Theory Into Practice, 10*(5), 363–367.

Radz, M. (1974). *Summary data sheet. Sociological Resources for the Social Sciences.* Boulder, CO: Social Science Education Consortium.

Rest, J. (1974). Developmental psychology as a guide to value education: A review of "Kohlbergian" programs. *Review of Educational Research, 44*(2), 241–259.

Riley, K. L. (2006). *Social reconstruction: People, politics, perspectives.* Charlotte, NC: Information Age.

Riley, K. L., & Stern, B. S. (2003/2004). A bootlegged curriculum: The American Legion vs. Harold Rugg. *International Journal of Social Education, 18*(2), 62–72.

Short, A. P., & Matlock, D. T. (1982). Sociology programs in U.S. high schools: Current findings with a national sample. *Teaching Sociology, 9*(3), 313–322.

Short, A. P., Watts, W. D., & Matlock, D. T. (1986). Sociology in the high school: Perceptions of those who teach it. *Sociological Spectrum, 6*, 211–219.

Smith, D. W. (1979). *Assessing the impact of the "New Social Studies" upon school curriculum: A case study of high school sociology.* PhD dissertation, Social Studies Education, Northwestern University, Evanston, IL.

Smith, F. R., & Cox, B. (1969). New strategies and curriculum in *social studies.* Chicago: Rand McNally.

Social Science Education Consortium. (1972). *Inquiries in sociology* (2nd ed.). Boulder, CO: Author.

Sociological Resources for Secondary Schools. (1966). *A sociology course for secondary schools. A report of the 1966 Summer Workshop.* The American Sociological Association.

Stern, B. S., & Riley, K. L. (2001). Reflecting on the common good: Harold Rugg and the reconstructionists. *Social Studies, 92*(2), 56–59.

Switzer, T. J. (1993, Sep/Oct). In retrospect: Sociological resources for the social studies curriculum project. *Social Studies, 84,* 5.

Switzer, T. J. (1973). *Factors associated with adoption and rejection of the course "Inquiries in Sociology" by teachers who participated in the classroom evaluation.* Unpublished doctoral dissertation, The University of Michigan, Ann Arbor.

Switzer, T. J., & E. K. Wilson. (1969) Nobody knows the trouble we've seen: Launching a high school sociology course. *Phi Delta Kappan, 50,* 346–350.

Thornton, S. J. (1994). The social studies near century's end: Reconsidering patterns of curriculum and instruction. *Review of Research in Education, 20,* 223–254.

Tamminga, H. L. (1977). Moral education through gaming-simulation in sociology courses. *Teaching Sociology, 4*(3), 251–270.

Weber, M. (1978). Sociology in the secondary schools of Wisconsin. *Wisconsin Sociologist,* 156-113.

West, J. C. (1930). *An analysis of senior high school sociology.* EdD dissertation, University of North Dakota, Grand Forks, ND.

CHAPTER 9

GEOGRAPHY AND
THE NEW SOCIAL STUDIES

The High School Geography Project and the
Georgia Geography Curriculum Project

Joseph P. Stoltman

INTRODUCTION

The decade of the 1960s had significance for academic disciplines ranging from physics to literature. In the midst of the space race and the Cold
War, experimentation was occurring within social programs, theater, literary interpretation, and the arts. The discipline of geography made a
major change in its scholarly focus, from descriptive to analytical and spatial analysis of both the human and physical Earth systems, giving rise to
the "New Geography." The 1960s were also the period of the "New Social
Studies," which grew out of the deep concern for the state of education in
the United States and the prospects of teaching both to and for a new
generation of students. The children of the post-World War II baby boom
would soon be enrolling their own children in school; the cohort of new

The New Social Studies: People, Projects, and Perspectives, pp. 167–191
Copyright © 2010 by Information Age Publishing

students entering kindergarten and first grade each year was larger, and the expectations of parents and society for their future well-being were greater than for prior generations.

Geography and social studies responded to the social and academic changes of the time in similar, yet conceptually different ways. Within geography, the change was referred to as a quantitative revolution whereby the discipline made the transition from dominance of descriptive research to the inclusion of analytical research using quantitative methods. Geographers became familiar with and gained expertise in using analysis of variance and multivariable correlations with data that just a few years earlier were presented and analyzed as graphs. It was truly a revolution in the discipline's research methodology applied to many of the very same geographic phenomena that descriptive analysis had been used to explain prior to the application of sophisticated quantification.

A second development in the geographic revolution was the increasing accessibility of computers to research geographers in research universities. Geographers asked spatial questions: Where is it located? Why is it there? What else is located there? What are the advantages of that location compared to other locations? Those questions are readily answered using maps, and map analysis had a long tradition in geographic scholarship (Haggett, 1990). The availability of the computer did two things. First, it enabled more rapid processing and mapping of spatial data; once the software program was written, the labor-intensive methods of traditional cartography were not necessary for particular types of maps. Second, computers enabled geographers to use considerably larger databases than were practical using mechanical computing methods. Those larger data sets of geographic information, along with more powerful computers and appropriate software programs, enabled geographers to not only analyze data, but also to use those same data to model possible spatial patterns on Earth and to increase the probability of predictive models of urban/ suburban change, atmospheric conditions, industrial location, and retail shopping centers. These monumental changes in the discipline were occurring at the same time the High School Geography Project (HSGP) was being conceptualized.

The "New Social Studies" was conceptualized beginning in the 1960s, partly as a result of the publication of a twentieth century classic, *The Process of Education* (Bruner, 1960). The book, based on a 1959 Woods Hole conference in which 10 of the leading scholars in various disciplines participated, had profound effects on the way professional educators viewed teaching and learning. Among the results of the Woods Hole conference were two that had greater importance for social studies. The initial book and a subsequent publication (Bruner, 1966) brought considerable attention to the structure and syntax of the discipline as important elements in learning. The structure of disciplines called for students to learn content by asking the same types of questions that scholarly theorists ask, but at a level appropriate to the age of the learner. Those types of educational experiences, it was believed, would impress upon students that knowledge was not simply a collection of information, but was based on underlying concepts, principles, and theories that were used in a discipline, such as geography. Syntax learning was intended to engage students in studying the content of a discipline just as professional geographers, anthropologists, and other scholars pursued knowledge. The student studying geography should use maps, spatial data, models, photographs, and geographic field study reports to test theories and examine relationships between the environment and people in much the same way as professional geographers carried out their research.

A world historian at Carnegie Mellon University, greatly interested in the changes that were occurring in scholarship in the 1960s in various disciplines, was one of the first to apply the suggestions from Bruner's writing. Edwin Fenton (1967) initiated a world history project based largely on the student using archival and primary documents in the study of history. While the project was interesting, Fenton's greatest impact on the social studies resulted from a book that reflected on a new paradigm for teaching. Titled *The New Social Studies* and addressing specifically the issues facing the teaching of social science content, the book became influential with curriculum developers and funding agencies interested in promoting change in the teaching of social studies. The consequence was that the HSGP and the New Social Studies entered the stage of curriculum development at approximately the same time. The influence of the Burner and Fenton ideas for teaching and learning were to have profound effects on HSGP.

Geography's Entry to New Social Studies Movement

Geography instruction in the United States developed largely as a memory-intensive subject with compendiums of factual information as textbooks. Layered onto much memorization were the tools of the geographer, comprised of maps and photographic evidence, which represented the investigative elements of the discipline developed in decades prior to the 1960s. New technologies, such as aerial photographs and visual correlation in spatial analysis, were seldom included in textbooks. While generalizations about a school subject can be dangerous, on the eve of the 1960s there was generally a 1- or 2-year sequence of geography in the junior high school (since reinvented as the middle school) in which students studied the eastern and western hemispheres from largely a regional geographic approach. Some high schools offered world regional geography courses while others taught a course in commercial or economic geography.

This was certainly the case in the Chicago Public Schools in the mid 1950s, when Sargent Shriver, then chairman of the city's board of education, began searching for a new approach to the commercial geography taught in the public schools and contacted Gilbert F. White about the problems facing classroom geography (Pratt, 1970). White was professor of geography at the University of Chicago. While not able to make much progress in reforming geography in Chicago's public schools, the challenge did ignite an interest in K–12 geography that White pursued passionately for the rest of his career. The Chicago experience led him to confer with Clyde Kohn, Professor of geography at the University of Iowa. Kohn was the author of a widely adopted school textbook on world geography as well as a spokesperson for the new geography. White and Kohn together formed the Joint Committee on Geographic Education that was supported by the National Council for Geographic Education and the Association of American Geographers with assistance in its initial years from the Fund for the Advancement of Education (Vuicich & Stoltman, 1974). The committee decided that its task was the improvement of geography education through updated and improved classroom instructional materials. Coincidentally, the revolution in geography as a discipline, the Bruner book, and the attention of two highly regarded professional geographers, White and Kohn, came together in a period of a few years. The new geography planned by the committee was destined to join the new social studies movement.

Geography and the New Social Studies

The influence of the Woods Hole conference and the developments in physics and biology education were early influences in the development of the HSGP. William Pattison, a historical geographer with a keen interest in geography teaching, was appointed director of HSGP and commissioned by the Joint Committee on geographic education to prepare an advisory paper that would assist high school teachers with teaching the subject (Pattison, 1962a). Pattison, a Chicago PhD in geography, was on the faculty of the University of California, Los Angeles and was an articulate spokesperson for the discipline. Highly regarded as an up-and-coming scholar, he served as director of HSGP from 1961 to 1964, clearly putting his mark on the project through his precise writing of the Advisory Paper and his vision of geography relative to what Bruner, and later Fenton, were proposing within education and social studies. The Advisory Paper, which became known as "the geographer's way," was to geography what Burner's *The Process of Education* (1960) was to the education community.

The Advisory Paper was the blueprint for HSGP. Pattison presented the concept that geography should focus on a particular set of objectives that would result in positive attitudes toward and appreciations for the subject. He intended to present a view of geography that would be practical for teachers, recognizable as representative of the cutting edge of the discipline to professional geographers, and widely embraceable for education officials and curriculum leaders responsible for determining school policy at local, state and national levels. It was within Pattison's writing of objectives that the conceptual structure of the discipline and the concepts of geography education were codified as they related to HSGP. Pattison wanted the discipline's approach to be as innovative as those being developed by the new physics and biology curriculum projects. It would present the case for high school students to conceptualize "the geographer's way." As author of the Advisory Paper, he emerged as the initial architect for HSGP (Pattison, 1962a).

The Advisory Paper was written in 1961 and published in 1962, following major curriculum developments in science education and preceding the new social studies by several years. However, discussions were underway regarding social science education, and Pattison was familiar with the developments at Purdue University under the direction of Irving Morrissett, Professor of economics. Morrissett and other social scientists were deeply concerned that an equivalent effort be devoted to the content of the social sciences as was being devoted to physics, biology, chemistry, earth science, and mathematics. Morrissett's early organizational efforts eventually became the basis for establishing the Social Science Education Consortium. Pattison reviewed a huge amount of new curricular activity among the sciences and social sciences in searching for a conceptualization of and convenient role for HSGP (Fraser, 1992); that role was to straddle the sciences and social sciences—a role that geography was accustomed to filling due to its natural and human content, and their interactions, that scholars in the discipline studied and researched. The objectives reflected a new role in the curriculum, but would it function effectively in the high school curriculum? HSGP was to be the experiment.

A New View of Objectives and Concepts in Geography: HSGP

The Advisory Paper addressed three types of objectives in geography: (1) attitudes and appreciations; (2) knowledge; and (3) skills. Two aspects of the selection of objectives reflected the thinking that was beginning to emerge in the new social studies. First was attention to attitudes and appreciations. Pattison did not use the word values except with regard to the student recognizing the value of observation, for example. (Note: Values, in the context of social values instilled in students or clarified within instruction, became a prominent part of the new social studies in their 1980s iteration). The second objective Pattison cited was directed towards student interaction with the content of the social science disciplines and became more widely referred to as inquiry. It is notable that the final report by HSGP to its funding agencies was titled *From Geographic Discipline to Inquiring Student* (Patton et al., 1970). The eventual commitment of the project to inquiry was set in motion from the very start.

Pattison launched the introduction to the new geography with six objectives he classified as attitudes and appreciations:

1. The winning of knowledge: prepare students who "respect calm, orderly and objective methods of scientific investigation."
2. Seeing things for oneself: prepare students to recognize the value of observation—both first hand and by vicarious means.
3. Location and distance: develop a curiosity for knowing about places and an atlas habit that will last throughout a lifetime of learning.
4. Uniqueness of places: prepare students to recognize that places reflect a complex interrelationship of many elements—both natural and human.
5. Natural environment: link students to human life and its sources in nature, with a major emphasis on respect for the natural environment.
6. World societies: assist students to develop responsibility in their own society and an intelligent interest in and concern for other people and environments in the world.

In hindsight, the attitudes and appreciations objectives were a mixture of cognitive and affective concepts. Natural environment is recognized as a cognitive concept; whereas the value of observation is an affective concept, the gathering of information through observation is a cognitive objective. It was Pattison's intention that the student would come to have a positive attitude or appreciate (accommodate a positive personal or social value) as a result of studying geography.

The concepts that were identified as essential to HSGP reflected the new scholarship of geography as well as the traditions of the discipline. They included:

1. Map representation: the map is a visual means for transmitting information.

2. Region: an area of Earth's surface that is different from surrounding and adjacent areas and is uniform in one or more aspects, such as language, economy, physical terrain, climate, etc.

3. Man-land relations: the interrelationships between natural and human elements of Earth provide a unique, but necessary bridge between them.

4. Spatial relations: the interaction between location, distribution, association, and movement on Earth's surface.

Pattison further stated that the concepts of geography must be firmly grounded on knowledge of specific facts. Among those important for a high school course were:

1. Place locations: a knowledge of locations on Earth so that the student has a reasonably accurate context for considering news, travel destinations, major cities, and the types of geographic information that the general public expects students to learn in a geography class.

2. Order of magnitude: rules of thumb for figures, such as the highest mountain is about 40,000 feet rather than 75,000 feet high, and the Great Lakes hold about 20% of Earth's fresh water, Earth is about 25,000 miles in diameter at the equator, it takes about 20 inches of precipitation annually to grow a tree in natural conditions, etc. For a geographer, these rules of thumb are similar to the student placing the U.S. Civil War in the nineteenth century rather than the seventeenth century.

3. World patterns: knowledge of the significant physical, economic, social, and political features of Earth necessary for global context-setting. Prior knowledge enables a student to point to any location on a world map and suggest, with modest proficiency, what combination of geographic elements are there.

4. Content of areas: basic information about several specific areas of the world that also demonstrate the types of geographic questions that people should ask. For example, geographic questions about language, religion, climate, human-environment interaction, influences on or by other cultural groups, and so forth, represented the geographic inquisitiveness desired of all students.

The third set of objectives formulated in the Advisory Paper focused on geographic skills. This topic was of particular importance to Pattison, since his firm belief was that the skills (referred to also as methodology) represented the "geographer's way." Central to the skills was the geographer's reliance on maps and a spatial attribute of the information that was of significance to geographers. The two were complementary, since mapping was the geographer's way of representing, visually interpreting, and presenting spatial information. The geographic skills that Pattison proposed were:

1. Map reading: the ability to read and comprehend maps is central to the geographic enterprise, including the elements of scale, symbols, direction, coordinates, and projections.

2. Map interpretation: the analysis of locations, patterns, and densities on maps provides the means for explanation and gives a foundation for the prediction of changes on Earth.

3. Comprehension of geographic literature: geography literary materials, in addition to maps, include a rich variety of materials that require a technical vocabulary and working familiarity with narratives that describe and explain the interaction of Earth elements.

4. Production of creative geography: the student studying geography should be able, within reason, to demonstrate skills in doing the types of study and research that are completed by professional geographers. This was viewed as the syntax of geography and became a significant component of HSGP.

The Advisory Paper was a newly developed concept paper on the teaching of geography using a spatial analysis approach. The question remained, however: Would the paper resonate for teachers? An often overlooked early component of HSGP was to determine through work with teachers in classes if it did resonate. Ten high school geography teachers in different locales in the United States were selected to apply the concepts, objectives, and skills presented in the Advisory Paper in their classrooms. An additional 20 high school teachers worked with the Advisory Paper, but in a less formal way. They provided limited feedback and reflections on the Advisory Paper. Each of the 30 teachers was teamed with a nearby university faculty member in geography who served as a resource and liaison to the project. The teachers made extensive notes and comments based on their classroom trials, providing a large amount of feedback from different professional and personal perspectives (Pattison, 1963). The inclusion of classroom teachers early in the process was to be maintained through the development of HSGP, a positive indication that classroom use and suitability were important considerations for the materials being developed.

William Pattison made an indelible imprint during the initial years of HSGP. Numerous attributes of the Advisory Paper were evident as HSGP continued to develop under a new group of geographers. In reporting to professional geographers about the development of HSGP, he indicated that "educators are welcoming assistance from … the disciplines of higher education and research" as they work towards improving the American high school experience (Pattison, 1962b, p. 282). He viewed it as a unique opportunity for geography education to benefit high school students, teachers, and the nation as the country addressed issues ranging from national security to career education in the early 1960s.

The People and the Organizations

During the period from 1959–1964, the HSGP was governed by the Joint Committee representing the National Council for Geographic Education (NCGE) and the Association of American Geographers (AAG), with funding from the Ford Foundation's Fund for the Advancement of Education. In 1964 the National Science Foundation (NSF), a quasi-independent governmental agency created to improve the capacity for scientific research and learning, made the judgment that geography was eligible for science education awards similar to those that had been awarded for the development of educational materials in physics, biology, earth science, and mathematics. Since geography included both natural and social science content, the human-environment, Earth science, and spatial elements of the discipline were especially notable for NSF. The AAG was named as the sponsoring scholarly organization for HSGP, and the NCGE was largely removed from the Project. While there was little collaboration between the professional societies of geographers, the geographers who became principal decision makers and participants in HSGP post-1963 were active members of both organizations. The future benefits, both in terms of recognition and monetarily, of HSGP went largely to the AAG because, as Pattison had noted, assistance was requested from the disciplines in higher education and research. AAG was the foremost professional society in that role.

The proposal for the development of a high school course based on recent developments and methods in geography was submitted and funded beginning in 1964. The availability of funding resulted in new leadership for the project. Directing HSGP was to be a full time commitment, and the project sought a geographer with administrative skills and scholarly credentials, as well as the commitment to relocate to Boulder, Colorado, which was to become the headquarters for the project. The geographer who was eventually selected for the directorship was Nicholas

Helburn, Professor of geography at the University of Montana, Bozeman. A specialist in soil and agricultural geography, Helburn had established his credentials as a proponent of the new academic geography that was transforming the discipline. Gilbert White, serving as Chair of the AAG Steering Committee for HSGP from 1964–69, had known Helburn for some years and recognized his ability to engage successfully in such a significant role as director. In 1965 the offices of HSGP moved from Bozeman to Boulder, Colorado, in order to be near the newly developing Earth Science Curriculum Project (ESCP) and the Biological Sciences Curriculum Study (BSCS) project.

Helburn selected as his associate director an early career faculty member from the University of Wisconsin, Eau Claire. George Vuicich had graduated from the University of Iowa with an MA in geography and then accepted a position teaching geography at University High, the laboratory school affiliated with Western Michigan University in Kalamazoo, MI. After teaching high school for several years, he returned to complete his doctorate at Iowa and then accepted the position in geography at Eau Claire. The addition of Vuicich, with his classroom experience, made for a strong central team leading HGSP.

The remainder of the development team for HSGP consisted mainly of early career faculty members from geography departments that were recognized for scholarship. Younger faculty members dominated, since they were the professional geographers who had either led or benefited from the 1950s revolution in the discipline. They brought a strong belief that geography's future was as an analytical discipline, rather than continuing the largely descriptive role of the past.

The newly formed Steering Committee and staff responsible for building HSGP into a widely used high school curriculum were faced with several major issues. One of the most urgent was to determine the type of course to be developed. Two major proposals were considered: (1) a world regional course that was familiar to geographers and geography teachers and (2) a course that would follow a systematic treatment of the discipline, reflecting more accurately the new geography. While that debate was continuing, the project staff continued to work on the overall criteria for the high school course. NSF had several criteria to which the project had committed in preparation of the proposal, and the staff had several additional items. The criteria that were developed included: (1) solid geography that was accurate, significant, and representative of the discipline; (2) satisfying to students in the sense that the content was important to their lives, (3) attractive to teachers so that the materials would be engaging and compatible with the many classroom contexts that occur in the United States; (4) reflective of contemporary trends in education that are being set by other projects for innovation, conceptual/cognitive skills, and a wide range of classroom procedures; and (5) commercially publishable by a major producer and distributor of educational products (Helburn & White, 1969).

While the criteria set the larger parameters of the project, the decision about whether it would be a systematic or regional approach continued to face the project staff and Steering Committee. Preston James, Professor of geography at Syracuse University was an articulate spokesperson for the regional tradition of geography. The geography teachers in the high schools, for the most part, were familiar with the regional paradigm and would find comfort in adjusting their courses to incorporate new geographic methodologies within the study of regions. The majority of members of the Steering Committee were in favor of the new geography that used statistical methods, visual map correlations, modeling geographic decision making, and role playing human environmental relationships. In addition, HSGP should do no less in formulating inquiry as an essential part of the course, in keeping with the new NSF-sponsored courses in other disciplines in the sciences. It was finally decided that HSGP must rely upon the support of the entire discipline of geography, and a compromise was reached: components of the course would represent systematic materials devoted to a particular topic, such as urbanization, and at least one component would be a regional study.

The Steering Committee was crucial in reaching compromises and disseminating information about the project. It consisted of the most prominent scholars in geography at the time, representing the major research universities in the United States. Edwin Fenton (1967), often referred to as the father of the new social studies, served as a member of the committee. James Marran, who served as a school trials teacher at New Trier High School, Winnetka, Illinois, became a well known social studies and geography educator, serving as a member of the writing committee for the Geography National Content Standards (Geography Education Standards Project, 1994). Salvatore Natole, who later served as editor of *Social Education* for the National Council for the Social Studies, served on the project staff during 1969–70. However, the director, Helburn, and associate director, Vuicich, served for nearly the duration of the project and were responsible for both the day-to-day operations and the long-term goals of HSGP.

Helburn and Vuicich were acutely aware that the new social studies would have a major impact on the curriculum where world geography had traditionally been taught—in the social studies. In order to find a niche within that changing curriculum, the new geography represented by HSGP would require not only relevance to the students, but also a means to extend intellectual curiosity to explain the world outside of school. The pragmatic attributes of geography were challenged by the inquiry process that was emerging from both science and social studies projects.

The attention to the structure of the discipline proposed by Bruner (1960) was attractive to professional geographers, who believed few people outside the discipline knew what the new geography was all about. The structure of geography would, or should, enhance inquiry into the kinds of questions that geographers studied. In October 1965, HSGP introduced limited school trials of an instructional unit based on the structure of the discipline. The unit included six activities developed from a concept paper by Edwin Thomas, a geographer whose specialty was quantitative spatial analysis. For geographers who knew the discipline, the structure of geography was a brilliant unit with which to begin the study of the new geography for high school students. For teachers and students, the classroom trials demonstrated that the unit was not teachable. The theoretical position regarding the structure of the discipline was justifiable, but with geography it was not practical. Another approach was needed so that the tension between those who proposed a regional course compared to a systematic course would not be magnified.

The HSGP staff and Steering Committee deliberated the organizational aspects of the content. Then, in 1965, Robert McNee, Professor of geography at the University of Cincinnati, proposed a theme for HSGP that was based on settlement, a widely accepted systematic approach in geographic scholarship. After going through two drafts with editorial guidance from the Steering Committee and the HSGP staff, a third draft that was acceptable was published (McNee, 1966). The settlement topic began with the study of urban settlements, then proceeded to manufacturing and agricultural settlement patterns, and then to the cultural, physical, and political considerations that affect settlements. McNee argued that the settlement theme was well suited to inquiry, since the students would have to use geographic methods in the analysis of problems that they could encounter in the future. The exception to the settlement topic was one part of HSGP dedicated to regional geography, the result of the compromise within the two schools of geographic thought represented on the Steering Committee. McNee later reflected on the symbiotic relationship between the structure of the discipline and the settlement theme that was accommodated by the project (McNee, 1967).

Helburn had, during this period, been conceptualizing a graphic model that presented the new approach to teaching geography as compared with the conventional course. He believed that in the conventional geography classroom the interaction was minimal, being mainly reception learning by the student and information delivery by the teacher (Figure 9. 1). In the HSGP classroom, he envisioned students engaged in asking geographic questions such as: Where is it? What is the relationship to other human and

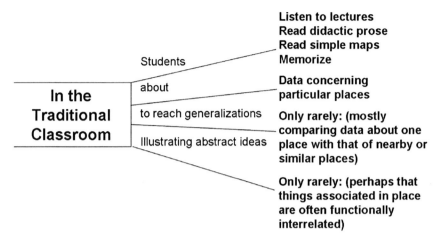

Figure 9.1.   Traditional Geography Teaching.

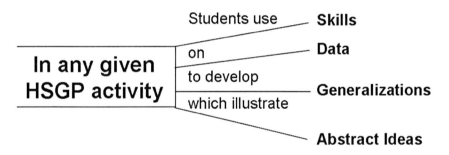

Figure 9.2.   Inquiry Based Geography Teaching.

physical elements that are nearby? What generalizations can be forwarded from its location and relationships? The HSGP materials would function in a much different manner (Figure 9.2 above) (Helburn, 1968).

Following the acceptance of the settlement theme, the project moved forward quickly on some fronts and at a snail's pace on others. The McNee settlement themes specified eleven separate units that would comprise the year-long course in geography. Authors with the particular specialty were needed for each of the units, and the geographers were nearly all young scholars in the discipline. They included geographers, who in 2008, read like a who's who in American geography during the second half of the twentieth century. Nearly all went on to become prominent in the discipline, and nearly all continued to reflect on the importance of geography for high school students long after HSGP ended.

HSGP: The Published Course

HSGP developed and field tested six units of instruction that eventually were published in 1970 under the title *Geography in an Urban Age* (HSGP, 1970a). They included:

Unit 1: Geography of Cities—six activities that developed concepts and principles of urban geography using site and situation, aerial photos, models, and city function.

Unit 2: Manufacturing and Agriculture – nine activities that examined the location and spatial analysis of the assembly and distribution of products used in manufacturing. The agricultural activities included interviews with farmers, the game of farming, and making decisions regarding enough food for the world.

Unit 3: Cultural Geography—five activities using sports, religion, cattle, and a culturally homogeneous region. The spread of cultural ideas was presented in a game format.

Unit 4: Political Geography—five activities using spatial political concepts of school redistricting, voting patterns, a London comparative study, and the political aspects of Point Roberts, Washington.

Unit 5: Habitat and Resources—seven activities that addressed people using Earth's mineral and water resources and the consequences of living in hazardous locations.

Unit 6: Japan—four activities that compared Japan's traditional and modern landscapes and regional characteristics.

In keeping with the richness of the materials being produced with the new science and social studies projects, each unit in HSGP included a teacher's guide, student resources, student manual, and transparency masters. The materials were numerous: units included hands-on components such as tables of census sheets, maps, aerial photographs, models constructed with Lego blocks, simulation games, filmstrips, vinyl records, role playing scenarios, case study vignettes, and student readings. The project set the context for geographical issues analysis, problem solving, and decision making. By providing the students with ready-to-use data and tools, the students were to ask the questions and discover the answers or plausible solutions.

Each of the units was field tested by high school teachers. The field trials were extensive, being completed by individuals or groups of teachers in nearly every state. For example, Unit 1 was field tested by 75 classroom teachers with slightly more that 3000 students. The Educational Testing Service (ETS) of Princeton provided considerable guidance in the early design and assessment of student learning from the HSGP activities. After 1966, the assessment shifted to two project evaluators, Dana Kurfman and Robert Richburg. Students responded to paper-and-pencil tasks and tests to assess pre to post changes in knowledge and in their dispositions to discuss geographic issues and examine the value considerations underpinning many of the topics presented in the classroom activities.

Considerably more materials were developed by HSGP than could be comfortably used by teachers in a year-long course in geography. Some of the materials were developed in teacher training kits and others found their way into resource books. *The Local Community: A Handbook for Teachers* (HSGP, 1971) was a collection of resources and suggestions for studying the local community. In its early stages, HSGP personnel had expressed a high regard for local knowledge and action. This interest was sustained in many of the supplementary materials assembled by the project, but never used as part of the six units or their classroom activities. The second book was titled *Sourcebook of Information and Materials: Maps and Aerial Photographs* (HSGP, 1970b). The sourcebook was to geography as the archival documents were to the world history project (Fenton, 1966) and the public issues case studies were to the Harvard Social Studies Project (Oliver & Shaver, 1966). Both relied on the study, interpretation, and analysis of documents, and geography's archival and contemporary documents were maps and aerial photographs. The documents added another specific link to the new social studies.

The Macmillan Company published a revised edition of HSGP in 1979. While some of the changes were cosmetic, substantive changes were made in segments of the materials. Geographic content that was not in the mainstream of the discipline in the 1960s had gained research and scholarly significance by the late 1970s. Increased interest in climate change in urban regions and the heat island effect was one of the new topics included in the revision (Stoltman & Eichenlaub, 1979). The format, inquiry structure, and methodology for classroom use followed the earlier model established for HSGP.

Not all six units of HSGP were adopted and used equally by secondary schools in the United States. Geography of Cities sold far more units than did Japan, the unit that was used least from the project (Stoltman, 1980). Activities from HSGP were quickly identified as favorites by teachers and used in geography and other classes. The Game of Farming was a good example: the simulation was used in geography, United States history, and an array of social studies electives. The National Science Foundation sponsored numerous summer teacher conferences and institutes for HSGP beginning in 1968. Teachers, curriculum specialists, and school leaders were invited to participate in workshops designed to disseminate HSGP. While the developers realized early in the project that teacher background in the content of geography and preparation to teach a new type of geography would present challenges, the relatively modest adoption of the year-long course in high schools was disappointing to the profession.

The HSGP received support from two main sources during its development. The first was the Fund for the Advancement of Education, which provided $178,000 between 1961 and 1963. The NSF funded the project for a total of $2,309,463 between 1964 and 1970 (Patton et al., 1970). The new science and the new social studies projects supported by the federal government were well funded, and HSGP was no exception. They were intended to make a difference within the American educational system.

HSGP: Positives and Negatives

All projects have positive attributes and most have some aspect of their existence that are less positive, or perhaps negative. While HSGP was able to resolve many of the differences regarding the nature of the high school course among professional geographers, there remained a tension between those geographers who were principal authors of high school geography textbooks and the intended outcome of the course. That tension extended to beginning university geography textbooks and courses, since it was claimed that a successful HSGP would make obsolete the way in which geography was being taught not only at the high school, but also at the university level (Patton et al., 1970). Such a claim immediately captured the interest of geographers inside academia since HSGP was envisioned to make huge and lasting changes in the way geography was taught at secondary and collegiate levels of education. There was considerable anticipation, which eventually materialized as the positives outcomes of HSGP:

First, the professional geographers engaged in the project reached agreement fairly early on an integrating theme of settlement. Whereas the traditional conceptual division between regional and systematic geography could have been problematic, the compromise was reached relatively easily for a topical, systematic treatment of the discipline with one regional unit on Japan.

Second, a substantial number of geographers were engaged in the development of HSGP, with over eighty being involved directly (Patton et al., 1970). That resulted in substantial support for the project within the largest scholarly organization in the United States, the Association of

American Geographers. NSF was interested in scholarly, research-based support, and it was provided by the participation in HSGP.

Third, there was a genuine engagement between students and materials in doing geography. Within the project it was often referred to as the geographer's way, a phrase coined by William Pattison early in the project. The geographer's way meant asking questions about spatial observations and then using maps, air photos, field research, and written accounts to answer the questions. In those ways geography was more a science than a social study, but its inclusion of relationships between people and the environment provided it with a cross-disciplinary, synthesizing role in academe. While the content was recognizable as systematic geography to most teachers, the methods that were used by students to study the content were new. The instructional methods and the methods of inquiry in HSGP were cutting edge in the 1970s.

Fourth, syntax geography was both challenging and transferable to the world outside the classroom. The geographic issues and problems introduced to students in HSGP were similar in content and context to many of the issues that students living in an urban age faced. In the 1960s, manufacturing was a major employer, and pull factors that attracted workers to factories in specific locations were analyzed and discussed in HSGP. Location and cost of production were studied as significant factors in where to locate the hypothetical company called MetFab. HSGP was farsighted, in that the topics proposed for high school geography in the 1970s were very similar to those that highlighted the outsourcing and off shoring of industry during the 1990s and 2000s and which American workers were not able to explain or comprehend.

The negative aspects of HSGP were primarily in the newness of the concept that the systematic study of topics in geography, such as urban geography, was as valid as the traditional regional geography represented by textbooks. Further, the engagement of students doing geography rather than simply studying geography was a new concept. It was comparable to the new social studies whereby students undertook the study of anthropology, sociology, history, economics, and political science much as the scholars in those disciplines were engaged with their research. Jerome Bruner claimed it was not only possible, but also it was necessary in order for the student to discover the content and structure of a subject (Bruner, 1960).

HSGP had three major negative aspects from the viewpoint of either those who used its materials in the classroom or were involved in teacher preparation. First, only a small segment of the geography and social studies teachers in the United States were reached through summer institutes and conference presentations about HSGP. Many teachers continued with their traditional textbook approach to teaching geography, remaining unaware of the availability of HSGP. Often when they became aware of HSGP, it was a challenge to make the transition from textbook to HSGP without professional development workshop assistance. Topics such as urban geography, manufacturing and agriculture, and political geography were not often included in the preservice preparation of most teachers who were teaching geography. Unfamiliarity with the materials and the content of the new geography presented a problem for the diffusion and adoption of the new course.

Second, HSGP had many different parts, making it a major transition from a textbook course. Unit one, Geography of Cities, had more than 200 individual pieces of equipment, data sheets, maps, aerial photographs, and model components. Japan, the unit with the smallest number of pieces, still had ten pieces of equipment. It was overwhelming for a teacher who was not well versed in the content, the materials, and classroom management of the materials. Teacher kits were prepared to ease teachers through the transition to the new geography, but they were largely dependent on participating in a professional development workshop.

Third, the sales force that the publisher, Macmillan, had in the field to service HSGP was accustomed to selling textbooks. Five sample books in a briefcase was what they traditionally carried into the school for a demonstration and a straight-forward adoption. HSGP with its kits and models required a major transition in the sales approach, and the sales force did not respond well. For example, the author of this chapter interviewed several Macmillan salespeople in the Midwest and learned that they left HSGP in the trunk of the car when they visited a school. They seldom took samples of the teacher's or student's material to demonstrate or display since it would require a major effort and many materials to demonstrate this new approach to teaching geography. To offset this problem, Macmillan prepared teacher demonstration kits that provided samples of the HSGP materials.

Despite the difficulty with a sales force that was more intent on selling textbooks, HSGP did reach classrooms. Macmillan was reluctant to release information about schools that purchased HSGP because they did not want such information to become available to competitors in the school publishing business. One indication of the success was the royalty that was paid to the Association of American Geographers, holders of the copyright, during the initial 5 years of publication. Royalties indicated that HSGP was finding a welcome market with teachers and school districts in the United States despite many logistical difficulties described above.

The Short-Term Impact of HSGP

The 1970s saw numerous workshops on HSGP sponsored by universities with funding from NSF. Larger school districts undertook initiatives to provide district-wide content preparation for teachers designated to use HSGP. While never quantified entirely, it was apparent to participant observers in the process of providing professional development that there was an increased interest and attention to the new geography within the high school curriculum. This was a different approach to teacher training for many mid-career teachers who selected HSGP for their classroom (Patton et al., 1970).

It was also apparent to the observer that teachers at earlier grades, especially the middle school and upper elementary grade levels, were making age-appropriate adjustments and adaptations of the HSGP materials so they could be used with younger students. This was particularly true on an activity-by-activity basis: for example, the Game of Farming and Portsville, the urban model, were used outside the context of HSGP. The result was that more teachers became interested, and many upgraded their skills in teaching geography.

HSGP was diffused to undergraduate instruction in geography in the United States. Often this entailed the use of the more engaging components of the materials: the multimedia, filmstrips, and the role playing. Availability of the HSGP materials enabled higher education geographers who were innovative in the classroom to try new materials that they could be relatively certain their students had not experienced in secondary school, since HSGP had only recently been distributed. In some cases, those innovations in the use of aerial photos, simulations, role playing, decision making, and political geography were adapted to local applications of similar conditions. Overall, the collegiate faculty was made aware of, if not directly introduced to, a new way to teach geography that resonated with undergraduate students. Early career faculty were often those who used HSGP in their classrooms.

While there was some, but by no means universal, use of HSGP in introductory geography classes at the university, uptake and use in the instructional methods courses offered by education faculty members was especially low. The majority of students who graduate in preservice teacher education receive their methods course from the faculty of the school of (or college of) education rather than in the disciplines that comprise the social sciences. As a result, a large proportion of new graduates in secondary education received their certification to teach geography as part of the social studies curriculum with no knowledge of or praxis with HSGP materials. The practical problems and costs associated with reaching in-service teachers made it prohibitive to reach all classroom teachers;

thus, the dissemination theory was that newly certified teachers would have gained the experience either in the content or teaching methodology courses leading to their certification. This was not the case. While institutes and workshop provided a major jump start, the professional development component was not sustainable. Successful dissemination would have required several generations of new teachers to ask the question: Where are the HSGP materials that I want to use to teach the new geography? That did not happen.

The unintended consequences of HSGP occurred beyond the geographical boundaries of the United States. Transitions in disciplinary and educational thinking about students and learning were occurring in many other regions of the world. A 1972 forum on high school geography at the International Congress of the International Geographical Union featured reports and discussions by representatives from the German Federal Republic (GFR), Israel, the United Kingdom, and the Netherlands regarding initiatives to adapt or replicate the content and methodologies from HSGP within national curricula (Gunn, 1972). Discussions in Finland continued the dissemination within Europe (Rikkinen, 1973); by the mid-1970s there were instructional materials in schools in England and Wales that resembled HSGP (Kent, Rolfe, Dearden, Rowe, & Grenyer, 1974) in their methodological approach to teaching. Since 1972, the author of this chapter has been a regular participant in the Commission on Geographical Education, where it is often commented that HSGP had a greater impact on geography instruction outside the United States than within the country. Considerable empirical evidence in curriculum materials have been produced in many countries to support that claim.

The Georgia Geography Project

While the HSGP was capturing most of the attention due to its NSF funding and the sponsorship by the Association of American Geographers, another project was making headway in geography curriculum development for the elementary and middle schools: the Georgia Geography Curriculum Project. The person behind the development and success of the Georgia Project was Marion Rice, Professor of Social Science Education. Rice began his appointment at Georgia in 1960 and retired in 1986; during his tenure, he became widely known both nationally and internationally for his role as director of the Georgia Geography Curriculum Project and the Georgia Anthropology Curriculum Project.

Marion Rice found the message of *The Process of Education* (Bruner, 1960) agreeable. He had long believed that understanding the structure of the discipline was essential to student learning and applying the content. Further, he was suspicious that, as Bruner had proposed, appropriately designed material could be used to teach complex content to students at an early age. Many of Rice's philosophical beliefs and positions regarding educational theories were recorded in a doctoral dissertation titled *Marion Jennings Rice, Philosophy and Praxis: The Professional Biography of a Georgia Educator* (Sorrells, 2001). Two curriculum projects directed by Rice, one in anthropology and the other in geography, are well documented by the dissertation.

While Rice was responsible for the design of the Georgia Project, the HSGP was initiated from the educational perspective of William D. Pattison and the Advisory Paper (Pattison, 1962a). However, HSGP was eventually reshaped by the Steering Committee and the professional geographers who authored the units of instruction. The product's philosophy and focus was created by Pattison, but the final materials reflected many others. The Georgia Geography Curriculum Project was largely Marion J. Rice from initial conception to completed materials. That was accomplished by the engagement of doctoral students writing and researching the results of the project's theories, geographic concepts, and classroom methodologies.

The Georgia Project was in alignment with the new social studies in three ways. First, it was devoted to the presentation of geographic content in both big ideas and supporting concepts. For example, Earth as the Home of Man was the topic of the kindergarten unit (W. Imperatore, 1968; W. A. Imperatore, 1970). The topic was represented by concepts that were geographic, but which could be readily conceptualized by children five and six years of age. The second way that the Georgia Project fit the new social studies was the agreement that any student at any age could be taught the legitimate content of the discipline at an appropriate level. Marion Rice was a firm subscriber to that theory proposed by Bruner. Third, Rice also believed that the structure of the discipline was a significant part of learning and applying content knowledge, principles, and theories. That philosophy was very much in keeping with the new social studies and presented a similar interest in structure as was demonstrated in the planning phases of the HSGP.

The Georgia Project differed from the new social studies and from HSGP in two significant ways. The first was the belief that student learning was not restricted to inquiry, and that language and reception learning were a powerful means to teach content in an efficient and effective manner. The project experimented with the reception learning proposed by David Ausubel, a noted expert on verbal learning (Ausubel, 1963), as an instructional methodology. Several of the classroom units were based on Ausubel's theory of meaningful verbal learning, which proposed the use of advanced organizers. The advanced organizers provided the learners with a referent, such as a concept, model, or map, into which subsequent information could be assimilated. Rice and his graduate students experimented with the use of different types of advance organizers.

Second, the Georgia Project was researched at nearly every step. Graduate students enrolled in the doctoral program in social science education were supported by the project to either author or co-author a unit of instruction. The units' contents were closely related to a conceptual design that reflected the structure of the discipline of geography. The experimental component was the preparation of a research design and the use of the units with students in schools. Experimental and control group design was most frequently used to analyze the differences in the learning of geographic content based on methodology and structure of the delivery. One group of students received the unit designed in the project and the control group received another appropriate methodology. The content was held consistent for the groups.

The research component in combination with the classroom trials provided data that allowed the Georgia Geography Curriculum Project to achieve both credibility and practicality. However, the project materials were never disseminated nationally since a commercial publisher was not involved in the development process. This was a disadvantage for the Georgia Project. The University printed units, they were marketed, and the proceeds were used to support graduate students through assistantships. Its dissemination was largely through the project philosophy and research studies that doctoral graduates carried with them into their careers. Some were able to insert the philosophy of the Georgia Project as they taught classes, presented workshops for teachers, and participated in the writing of textbooks. The funding for social studies projects became more difficult in the early 1970s; by the late 1980s, the Georgia Geography Project was known to few in social studies education who had not been directly associated with it in prior years.

The Impact of Geography Projects on Teachers and Students Today and in the Twenty-First Century

The final report of the HSGP included a section titled *Next Steps*, written by Gilbert F. White (Patton et al., 1970). White suggested that the project would have to undergo an assessment of its impact compared to a baseline that should also be collected at the conclusion of the project. His concern was that the enthusiasm for HSGP would wane once the newness of the content and the instructional methodology was gone. He envisioned the assessment extending to university faculty members who enrolled preservice teachers in their classes, recognizing the need to prepare new generations of teachers while in their initial teacher education years and the futility of trying to achieve content proficiency with HSGP solely through teacher workshops and institutes. Those suggestions never came to fruition, little assessment data were collected, and the impact of HSGP was never fully documented. The institutional memory of HSGP rests largely in the literature, some of which is cited in this paper, and in the experiences of only a few professional geographers and teachers who worked directly with the project. In the author's 36 years of involvement in geography education in Michigan, the most recent students enrolled in geography undergraduate courses that had used HSGP in their classes in high school were enrolled in about 1986. Similarly, the Georgia Project ended when Marion Rice retired from full-time teaching at the university. No other faculty member was interested in continuing the project after his retirement in January 1986. The institutional memory for both HSGP and the Georgia Geography Curriculum Project has lapsed and will be gone in a few short years.

Not all is lost, however. Two examples of ideas similar to, and reflective of HSGP, are evident in 2006. The first is in the Activities and Readings in the Geography of the United States (ARGUS) (Association of American Geographers, 1997) and Activities and Resources in the Geography of the World (ARGWorld) Project of the Association of American Geographers (Association of American Geographers, 2002). The materials include three activities shaped largely by HSGP. One is an activity that entails the concepts of site and situation and is very similar to the site selection Activity from HSGP. In the activity, students use the conditions of site and situation to locate a settlement. The second is a computer simulation of farming in Russia and Central Asia that is reminiscent of the Game of Farming in HSGP. The ARGWorld version uses drag-and-drop of crop symbols based on growing season and precipitation patterns. The third is a print ARGWorld activity titled Land Use Decisions in the Gold Coast. The land use materials in the print activity are modeled after the HSGP Game of Farming, with brochures to attract new settlers with lavish promises of soil fertility, climatic suitability, and markets for products. Students assume the role of a farmer, are allocated a farm, and provided basic geographic and economic information that is useful in determining what crops to plant or the type of animal husbandry to begin. The economic ledger for each farm is based on outcomes that reflect weather, pests, and markets locally as well as in other parts of the world. The students in 2006 become engaged in the simulation, make rational decisions, and compete against geographic factors of the region as well as with each other to achieve both survival as a farmer and apply geographic knowledge to a practical problem.

A final interesting note on the impact of the geography projects is that while social studies and geographic educators in the United States have little knowledge of or perceived interest in HSGP and the Georgia Project any longer, the author continues to attend conferences with colleagues from Europe, Australia, Asia, and Latin America who inquire about the availability of the projects and use in schools. *International Research in Geography and Environmental Education* (IRGEE), which the author serves as co-editor, will include in one of its numbers during 2007 a research article analyzing the impacts of HSGP on geography in the schools of Finland. While geography in the new social studies achieved minimal recognition as having a clearly identifiable presence in the schools of the United States, it did fit a niche in the curricula in other countries. One might conclude that its impact was quantitatively small, yet qualitatively significant over the past three decades. Perhaps, as Gilbert White speculated, it would no longer have "the dominant imprint of any one nation or culture ... [but] would draw from the range of scientific and humane thinking about the earth and would encompass a wide diversity in method, material, and presentation" (Patton et al., 1970, p. 71). While the hard evidence is not readily available, I tend to believe that has been the role of HSGP and the Georgia Project in the new social studies movement.

REFERENCES

Association of American Geographers. (1997). *Activities and readings in the geography of the United States* (ARGUS). Washington, DC: Association of American Geographers.

Association of American Geographers. (2002). *Activities and resources in the geography of the world* (ARGWorld). Washington, DC: Association of American Geographers.

Ausubel, D. (1963). *The psychology of meaningful verbal learning: An introduction to school learning*. New York: Grune & Stratton.

Bruner, J. (1960). *The process of education*. Cambridge, MA: Harvard University Press.

Bruner, J. (1966). *Toward a theory of instruction*. Cambridge, MA: Belkapp Press.

Fenton, E. (1966). *Teaching the new social studies in secondary school: An inductive approach*. New York: Holt, Rinehart and Winston.

Fenton, E. (1967). *The new social studies*. New York: Holt, Rinehart and Winston.

Fraser, D. (1992). *Current curriculum studies in academic subjects*. Washington, DC: National Education Association.

Geography Education Standards Project. (1994). *Geography for life: National geography content standards 1994*. Washington, DC: National Geographic Society.

Gunn, A. M. (Ed.). (1972). *High School Geography Project: Legacy for the seventies*. Montreal: Centre Educatif et Culturel.

Haggett, P. (1990). *The geographer's art*. Cambridge, England: Basil Blackwell.

Helburn, N. (1968). The educational objectives of high school geography. *Journal of Geography, 67*(5), 274-281.

Helburn, N., & White, G. (1969). *A strategy for change in geography education*. Boulder, CO: High School Geography Project.

High School Geography Project. (1965). *Teacher's guide for introductory materials: Limited school trials 1965-66*. Boulder, CO: Author.

High School Geography Project. (1970a). *Geography in an urban age*. New York: Macmillan.

High School Geography Project. (1970b). *Information and materials: Maps and aerial photographs*. Boulder: Author.

High School Geography Project. (1971). *The local community: A handbook for teachers*. New York: Macmillan.

Imperatore, W. (1968). *Earth man's home: A beginning geography unit*. Athens, GA: University of Georgia Geography Curriculum Project.

Imperatore, W. A. (1970). *Evaluation of a conceptual geography unit for kindergarten*. Athens, GA: University of Georgia.

Kent, A., Rolfe, J., Dearden, R., Rowe, C., & Grenyer, N. (1974). *Oxford geography project: The local framework*. Oxford, England: Oxford University Press.

McNee, R. (1966). *Settlement theme course outline*. Washington, DC: Association of American Geographers.

McNee, R. (1967). An approach to understanding the current structure of geography. In I. Morrissett (Ed.), *Concepts and structure in the new social science curricula* (pp. 57–63). New York: Holt, Rinehart and Winston.

Oliver, D., & Shaver, J. (1966). *Teaching about public issues in the high school*. Boston: Houghton Mifflin.

Pattison, W. (1962a). *Advisory paper for teachers associated with the High School Geography Project*. Los Angeles: University of California.

Pattison, W. (1962b). Geography in the high school. *Annals of the Association of American Geographers, 52*(3), 280–284.

Pattison, W. (1963). *Response paper: Suggestions from teachers associated with the High School Geography Project*. Los Angeles: University of California.

Patton, D., Carswell, R., Helburn, N., Kurfman, D., Pattison, W., Richburg, R., et al. (1970). *From Geographic discipline to inquiring student*. Washington, DC: The Association of American Geographers.

Pratt, R. B. (1970). *A historical analysis of the High School Geography Project as a study in curriculum development*. Unpublished doctoral dissertation, University of Colorado, Boulder.

Rikkinen, K. (1973). Geografin in Finland's förändrande skola [Geography in Finland's School Curriculum. Geographical Notes]. *Geografiska Notiser, 2*, 61–65.

Sorrells, R. (2001). *Marion Jennings Rice, philosophy and praxis. The professional biography of a Georgia educator*. Unpublished doctoral dissertation, Georgia, Athens.

Stoltman, J. (1980). Round one for HSGP: A report on acceptance and diffusion. *Professional Geographer, 32*(2), 209–215.

Stoltman, J., & Eichenlaub, V. (1979). Climate and the city. In S. Natoli (Ed.), *Environment and resources: Geography in an urban age* (pp. 78-94). New York: Macmillan.

Vuicich, G., & Stoltman, J. P. (1974). *Geography in elementary and secondary education*. Boulder, CO: Social Science Education Consortium.

CHAPTER 10

ECONOMICS AND THE NEW SOCIAL STUDIES

Beverly J. Armento

INTRODUCTION

Events in the *real world* provide much of the content of the social studies curriculum, and events have also, over time, come to stimulate changes in the social studies curriculum. For example, panic in the United States over the Soviet Union's 1957 beach-ball sized Sputnik I (Dow, 1992) prompted a national response unlike any other. Fears that the nation was failing to maintain its world position as leader, that we would be, could be, and were embarrassed by our rival, a communist country; that the Cold War had indeed evolved into a real war where the best and brightest could win on scientific rather than on military fronts—such fears resulted in heretofore unheard of actions. Money flowed from the national coffers, from the U.S. Office of Education, from the National Science Foundation (NSF), and from organizations such as the Charles Stuart Mott Foundation, the Carnegie Foundation, and the Joint Council on Economic Education (JCEE, now the Council for Economic Education,) into the hands of academicians who would create curriculum that would make

The New Social Studies: People, Projects, and Perspectives, pp. 193–212
Copyright © 2009 by Information Age Publishing

the nation's children brighter, smarter, more scientific, and more able to compete in this new world.

Thus dawned the *New Math*, the *New Science* and eventually, the *New Social Studies* curricula (Beyer, 1994, 1995; Fenton, 1967b, 1970; Haas, 1977; Krug, Poster, & Gillies, 1970; Massialas, 1992; Morrissett, 1967; Sanders & Tanck, 1970; Shaver Davis, & Helburn, 1979; Smith & Cox, 1969; Wiley & Morrissett, 1972; Wiley & Superka, 1977). Inspired by John Dewey's ideas of experiential learning (Dewey, 1938); Jerome Bruner's hypothesis that any child could learn any idea if presented in a developmentally appropriate way (Bruner, 1960); Hilda Taba's notions that conceptual knowledge was the most enduring type of knowledge and that a meaningful curriculum was one that spiraled (Taba, 1967; Taba, Durkin, McNaughton, & Fraenkel, 1967); Richard Suchman's ideas that higher level thinking and inquiry processes should be taught to children (Suchman, 1966); and Joseph Schwab's ideas that one could organize curriculum around the structure of a discipline (Schwab, 1962), geographers, anthropologists, sociologists, and economists created development teams to invent better curriculum, more substantive, more inquiry-focused, conceptually-framed ways of teaching and learning the social sciences (Rice, 1992; Rossi, 1992; Tice, 1992; and Wiley & Morrissett, 1972). Since historians and political scientists were generally pleased that their fields were well-represented in the existing K–12 curriculum, these academicians "remained largely aloof" (Hertzberg, 1981, p. 100) from the reform efforts. Convinced that learning the academic structure of their social science discipline—and learning the inquiry processes of their discipline—were, at least in part, the answers to the national crisis in education, these social scientists and their teams gave birth to the many curricular projects known as the *New Social Studies*.

By the time these social studies projects were developed, field-tested, and taken on by large publishing houses for marketing and dissemination, the times had changed. By the late 1960s, we had seen the assassinations of a President, a U.S. Senator, Malcolm X, and Martin Luther King, Jr.; the Civil Rights Movement, Women's Movement, War on Poverty, Farm Workers Movement, and the antiwar movements engaged young and old alike in the struggles for rights and equality. By 1969, the United States had scored another notch in the space race by landing the first humans on the moon. Again the events of the *real world* signaled changes in the social studies curriculum. But these changes had little to do with learning the structures and inquiry processes of the academic social science disciplines. By the time the New Social Studies projects were published as textbooks, many school systems were structuring their social studies curriculum around minicourses, with titles such as Black History, Law-Related Education, Women's Studies, Environmentalism, Urbanization, Global Education, and Consumer Education—courses that were deemed more interesting, more relevant and more applicable to the burning social issues of the 1970s.

The changing social environment is but one reason the New Social Studies projects did not take hold in the schools. There are other factors; but, more about that later. This chapter is about what happened in Economic Education during this dynamic period of curriculum development. There was quite a flurry of activity and curriculum development in Economic Education during the 1960s, the creation period of the New Social Studies, in part spurred on by the historical lack of attention to economics in schools. In their various committee reports on the Social Studies, the National Education Association (NEA) had heretofore diminished the role of the social sciences in schools, in favor of the study of history and political science. *Political Economy* had been rejected as a separate course by the NEA's History Ten committee, urging that the economics principles be functionally integrated into history, government, and civil government classes (Hertzberg, 1981, p. 11). The NEA's 1916 Committee gave a nod to the social sciences by inventing the Principles of Democracy (POD) course for high school seniors, that was to focus on issues, and to examine them in their political, economic, and sociological aspects (Hertzberg, 1981, p. 28).

After World War I, several professional social science associations were formed, including the American Economic Association (AEA) that soon recommended a number of economics and business education courses for the high school. By World War II, the AEA had turned its attention to the post secondary curriculum; however, the Joint Council on Economic Education, founded in 1949, took over the battle cry for including economics in the K–12 curriculum. By the 1950s, there were many in the academic community who were sure children needed a firm grounding in the study of economics in order to make better decisions in a democratic and capitalistic society. Thus, a number of university level economists applied for and received grants, and led exciting curricular development projects during the 1960s, each contributing ideas that lay the foundation for the state of economic education today.

Two major New Social Studies economics instructional projects focused on elementary school learners: the Lawrence Senesh project, Our Working World, Grades 1–6 (Senesh, 1973), and the Elementary School Economics Program, Grades 4–8, developed at the University of Chicago's Industrial Relations Center by William Radar, a student of Professor Senesh (Rader, 1995, 1996). Teaching sophisticated economic concepts to young children was really unheard of at this time—but Senesh and Rader and their teams—persisted and developed creative materials, inspired by Bruner's idea that it was possible and Schwab's idea that the major concepts of the discipline constituted the proper focus for powerful learning. Today, the ideas of these pioneers can be seen reflected in the K–12 economic education focus taken by the Council on Economic Education, the inclusion of economic concepts in the National Council for the Social Studies Standards, as well as the inclusion of economic concepts in many state social studies standards for elementary schools, and in well-used elementary school textbooks (Armento, 1980, 1986; Armstrong & Burlbaw, 1991; Buckles, 1987; Davis, 1987; Schug & Armento, 1985; Taba, 1966; Walstad & Soper, 1991; and Wentworth, Hansen, & Hawke, 1977).

At the secondary school level, at least three major economics projects are usually identified as part of the New Social Studies movement: (a) The Manpower and Economic Education Project, Ohio University at Athens, Meno Lovenstein, Director (Darcy & Powell, 1966; and The Ohio University Research Foundation, 1966); (b) the Carnegie-Mellon University Social Studies Curriculum Project, directed by Ted Fenton (1967a), that included a major economics component; and (c) the San Jose State, ECON 12 or Economics in Society project, under the direction of Suzanne Wiggins Helburn (1977; Helburn, Sperling, Evans, & Lott, 1974).

There is one other economics project that is identified as a *New Social Studies* program: that is the Developmental Economic Education Program (DEEP) (supported by a U.S. Office of Education grant), an innovative idea developed by the Joint Council on Economic Education. DEEP, still very much in existence, is a *process* for change, an adoption and diffusion of innovations process designed to provide a structure for school systems to use when considering how to reform their curriculum and in-service training, particularly in terms of the economics dimension of the curriculum.

In the late 1940s, the Committee for Economic Development (CED) and a group of New York University professors sponsored a 3-week workshop for educators, teaching them economics, so that they could integrate this knowledge into their classrooms. The participants were so energized by this new knowledge, and so concerned that schools were generally ignoring the teaching of economics, that they proposed the establishment of an organization that would assist educators with economic education. The result was the founding of the Joint Council for Economic Education in 1949; State Councils and Centers on Economic Education were soon established in most of the states (Kim & Kratochvil, 1972).

By 1964, DEEP was born, conceptualized as a process for effecting economic education curricular change through a structure that included a system of committees, consultants, staff development, and materials assessment, selection, and development (Watts, 1991). The general aims of the DEEP process were to:

build economics into the existing school curricula at all grade levels; improve teacher preparation in economics; develop and evaluate new teaching materials for economics for all grade levels; identify diverse models of curriculum revision in economic education; and disseminate the results of the experiment. (Kim & Kratochvil, 1972, p. 2)

The DEEP program provided financial and consultant resources to school systems as they made the commitments to integrate economics throughout their curriculum, K–12.

Interestingly, one of the major criticisms of the new social studies projects is that the developers knew little about change in schools, and that they ignored the "adoption of innovations process" (Hahn, Marker, Switzer, & Turner, 1977). However, in economics, the field had the DEEP project, explicitly designed to promote change in schools, to aid schools in focusing on the processes of change, and to facilitate the embracing of economic education innovations. In terms of the economics curricular projects, the JCEE actually financially supported the development of some of these projects, and at least Senesh and Helburn had professional linkages with the JCEE. However, when it came time to support the adoption of Our Working World or ECON 12, the JCEE and its DEEP process did not overtly embrace these projects and did little to support their adoption by participating DEEP school systems. According to Suzanne Helburn (1997),

the JCEE mostly ignored our materials. They had their own materials and programs to promote. Our work was important to know about, to discuss and criticize, possibly to copy, but not to adopt. If I remember correctly, the JCEE could not take positions on the materials of other groups, although they did promote their own. (p. 274)

Thus, DEEP, a *new social studies* project, a process explicitly designed to promote economic education in schools, failed to support the adoption of any of the economics *new social studies* content projects. Perhaps the lives of projects such as Our Working World and Econ 12 would have been longer had there been deeper professional relationships, collaboration with the primary economic education association at the time, JCEE, and the many economists who were working to develop effective economic education materials for schools. Needless to say, collaboration and consensus building with other relevant professionals, namely the social studies educators active in the National Council for the Social Studies (NCSS) and its College and University Faculty Assembly (CUFA) were also missing, and this lack of support from key gatekeepers minimized the likelihood that the New Social Studies economics projects would be successful.

Given the space constraints of this chapter, I shall focus on the work and contributions of Lawrence Senesh and Suzanne Helburn, key leaders and innovative thinkers during this period. Each of the major economics instructional projects moved curriculum development along, from a focus on generalizations to a focus on major concepts of the social sciences; from social studies as topical and descriptive to topical, conceptual, inquiry and spiraling, becoming more sophisticated as students matured; from teacher dominated to more student focused, incorporating more student-centered discussions and activities; from narrative textbooks to student readings, case studies, audiovisual and other materials. These economics projects questioned old, traditional and well-established ways of thinking about and teaching social studies, and established innovative curricular patterns that persist to today.

LAWRENCE SENESH AND ELEMENTARY ECONOMICS EDUCATION

Professor Lawrence Senesh, "a living example of the power of a committed Renaissance man" who loved art, music, and "the highest forms of human expression in every field" (Howe & Singell, 2003, Senesh obituary), was truly a man ahead of his time. Born Lazslo Szenes in 1910 in Nagybecskerek, Hungary, he received a degree in economics from the University of Berlin in 1932 and a master's degree in law from the University of Budapest in 1938. Fleeing Hungary at the beginning of World War II, he worked as a manual laborer in a lumber mill in Birmingham, Alabama before he was inducted into the U.S. Army in 1942. By 1950, Senesh was studying at the London School of Economics, and in 1952 he became the first staff economist at the Joint Council on Economic Education. In 1957, Senesh joined Purdue University's economics faculty where he became the nation's first professor of economic education.

Long before Sputnik I, Senesh (1967) imagined the relevance of economics and the social sciences for the lives of young children. Highly influenced by Dewey (his father was the director of a Deweyian school in Hungary), Senesh placed children and their life experiences at the center of the curriculum. The child lives in the

> real world, where s/he is exposed to all kinds of experiences—brutal social realities of poverty, violence, discrimination, and so on. Life is the curriculum, not economics or political science. But, to understand life, the individual social sciences have to be used, for the sole reason –that there is no unified social science theory yet. (p. 150)

Senesh wanted to design curriculum that helped students "discover the design underlying the seemingly chaotic world" and that aided the development of social competence, awareness, and a respect for analysis from kindergarten through the twelfth grade (Senesh, 1981, p. 65).

Senesh is perhaps best known for his ideas about the *organic* curriculum (Blanchard, Senesh, & Patterson-Black, 1999) *orchestration* of the social sciences, and the *community social profile*. Fundamentally, Senesh truly believed that sophisticated, complex concepts could be introduced to young children, if illustrated by the rich experiences in their own lives. While teaching at Purdue University, Senesh realized his freshmen were less than excited about the introductory economics course, and they seemed to understand and retain little from the course. Some of Senesh's colleagues wanted to wait until the college students were more mature to schedule the class, perhaps during the sophomore year. But Senesh was reminded of his work with elementary school students when he was at the JCEE: "an idea took hold in my mind and refused to go away. Instead of waiting until college to teach seemingly complex concepts, might it be possible to introduce such ideas earlier, perhaps even in the primary grades?" (Senesh, 1993, p. 93). Senesh attributed the birth of this idea to his colleagues at JCEE: "JCEE was at the forefront of revolutionizing economic education—long before anyone else thought that children might be able to learn about the economic system or about economic theory" (Senesh, 1977, p. 228).

Professor Senesh tested out these ideas himself by working with children in urban areas, from the Cardozo neighborhood in Washington, DC to Elkhart, Indiana, and with Native American children in reservation schools in the Southwest (Senesh, 1993). He was so well known for his work with children and for his commitment to creating a more substantive, exciting, issues-focused, and meaningful curriculum for children, that his colleague and fellow economist, Kenneth Boulding, formulated *Senesh's Law*. This law proposes that anything you can't explain to fourth graders is unlikely to be true (Howe & Singell, 2003). Senesh had a passion for children and for Democracy, believing that the key to active citizenship resided in a strong social studies program. His goal was to develop such a curriculum.

Out of Senesh's work with children came the elements of what he called the *organic* curriculum. The foundation of such a curriculum was the fundamental concepts of each of the social sciences, and in this case, economics. Senesh believed that the central ideas of economics could be incorporated at every grade level; these ideas included:

- Scarcity is the central idea of economics, namely that every society faces a conflict between unlimited wants and limited resources.

- Because of scarcity, people have learned to produce more with fewer materials, in less time; people specialize geographically, occupationally, and technologically.
- Because we specialize, we are interdependent; interdependence demands monetary and transportation systems.
- Buyers and sellers interact in markets, where prices are determined; prices determine the pattern and method of production, income distribution, and the level of spending and saving, which, in turn, decide the levels of total economic activity. The economic system is a part of political society.
- Market decisions are modified by public policies, carried out by government, to assure social welfare objectives. Such goals aim to accelerate growth, promote stability, assure economic security, promote economic freedom, and promote economic justice. (Senesh, 1967, pp. 24–26)

Senesh saw the structure of the economics discipline as a pedagogical tool for teachers, to be "engraved on the mental screen of teachers" (Senesh, 1967, p. 46). He did not think that children should study the structure, but rather that the "structure of knowledge should slowly evolve as a child moves from grade to grade. By the ninth grade, students should be ready to ask: What holds society together? Then, the teacher could help students 'discover' the analytical tools of economists and other social scientists" (Senesh, 1967, p. 46). Thus, by increasing the depth and complexity of the conceptual ideas and thinking skills at each grade level, the *organic* curriculum would grow as the child matures (Senesh, 1967, p. 24).

The social sciences were the keys to understanding and analyzing social issues, thought Senesh; he saw students asking relevant values questions about important issues, and applying social science concepts to an issue-focused curriculum. That is, public policy issues, important questions—should be at the center of the curriculum. Disciplinary content was needed mainly to inform students about such issues. Students should "analyze gaps between societal goals and social realities and should question the relationships between such things as materialism and the quality of life." Students should learn, not by rote, but through thinking, analyzing, and creating (Senesh, 1981, p. 65). Thus, Senesh saw *social issues* as the curricular core, not the social sciences; the social sciences were merely analytical tools to help students understand, analyze and tackle important societal issues.

While we tend to think of Larry Senesh as an economist, and his major project, Our Working World, as an economics project, he did not believe we should focus on teaching the individual social science disciplines.

Rather, the focus should be on an "*orchestration* of all the social sciences, showing their relationships to each other. The disciplines should be used as they are needed, usually with one or another discipline, playing the chief role at one particular time" (Senesh, 1967, p. 67). Thus, depending on the topic, if some economic analysis were needed, like a flute, economics concepts would play a solo, then the entire orchestra, or all the other social sciences, would resume playing. Then, needing some political science analysis, that discipline, like a cello, would be highlighted (Armento class notes, Purdue University, Senesh lecture, 1968). This integrated, *orchestrated* social science approach could be developed by starting "with any social issue—and by drawing on facts, concepts, and analytical tools from each of the social science disciplines to address the problem" (Senesh, 1967, pp. 72–73).

Senesh's multidisciplinary and issue-focused curricular ideas were truly ahead of the times. The visual image of the orchestra provides a useful metaphor for social studies curriculum development—that could be helpful even today as we continue the ages-old battles over whether the social sciences/social studies should be taught as individual disciplines or as some interdisciplinary curriculum that few have been able to actually create.

True to his interdisciplinary beliefs, Senesh proposed cooperation among disciplinary academicians in the solving of social problems, in the development of curriculum, and in the preparation of teachers; that cooperation should extend to the social studies methods professors. "There is practically no relationship between people in methodology and people in subject matter" (Senesh, 1967, p. 68). Hilda Taba, participating in the same Social Science Education Consortium (SSEC) conference at Purdue, agreed:

> The content and methods people have ignored each other's knowledge during the development of the *new social studies projects* and now hostile criticism and rivalry exist. The Social Science Education Consortium is the best mechanism for bringing content and process people together. (Taba, 1967, p. 90)

While the SSEC did much to mend these wounds, the alienation between social scientists and social studies educators never truly healed then, and is still evident today. The lack of involvement of social studies educators on the new social studies project teams and their subsequent lack of support for many of the projects was another major reason for the short shelf life of the *new social studies* programs.

Senesh saw the *Community Social Profile* as an instructional mechanism that drew on all that he thought was important in the teaching and learning process:

- Start with experiences in the child's own life: the community in which the students live;
- Start with issues: real issues that are current in the community;
- Actively involve the learners: students should actively and cooperatively investigate aspects of their own community, identify, analyze, and apply data to understanding and addressing the issues; and
- Make the investigation multi-disciplinary: have students analyze the historic, social, economic, geographic, and political dimensions of the community.

Senesh proposed such a curriculum for high school students, but he did think students from the lower grades could also benefit from such a project, and he built many community investigations into his elementary project, Our Working World. Not only would the community social profile actively engage students in the workings of their own surroundings, but it would give them a sense of participation and ownership in the community and its problems (Senesh, 1980, 1981). Senesh reasoned that students would be less alienated and rebellious if they were actively studying relevant and important topics, values issues, and social problems that were evident in their own lives. In addition, students would be more likely to be active participants, good citizens, if you will, in a community that they knew well, and one in which they had a vested interest.

Our Working World, Senesh's project for Grades 1–6, was comprised of textbooks, resource books, audio recordings, and other supplementary materials. These materials were widely used for a time in the late 1960s and early 1970s, but eventually lost their appeal. The textbook series, published by Science Research Associates (SRA), focused on topics at each grade level not dissimilar to the widely-popular expanding horizons approach:

- Grade 1: Families
- Grade 2: Neighborhoods
- Grade 3: Cities
- Grade 4: Regions of the United States
- Grade 5: The American Way of Life
- Grade 6: Regions of the World.

Our Working World was designed by Senesh to illustrate his major beliefs about curriculum and children. The series was interdisciplinary, drawing on all the social sciences, not merely economics. The program employed a spiraling, conceptual approach, with major concepts and themes becoming more complex with each added year of maturity. The lessons were framed in time and space, emphasizing history and geography. The focus was community-oriented, with activities calling upon students to be engaged with their families, their neighborhoods, their communities, and for them to see their local community as a microcosm of the world community. Senesh stressed an interdependent, interrelated systems analysis approach (Boulding, Kuhn, & Senesh, 1973) to the studies of families, neighborhoods, regions, and so on—and all of this was done within a problem-solving approach, that called upon students to not only identify with social issues—but to be actively engaged with the problems of society. Senesh also believed that language arts, literature, art, mathematics, science, and music should be related to social studies, and he designed activities explicitly to draw upon and extend these areas of the curriculum.

The design of each unit was carefully crafted to reflect not only the philosophy of Our Working World but also to be teacher and student friendly, and to actively engage students in ways that would culminate in meaningful learning. Each unit in the early grades opened with a photo essay to arouse curiosity about one of the major concepts of the unit. Following the *photo essay*, was a *case study*, based on a real world application of the central ideas; then, an *episode*, emphasizing inner thoughts or affective aspects of the characters under discussion. Senesh wrote letters to the students, and these were included in the student text also. Many engaging student activities, literature, and art suggestions, as well as assessment tasks rounded out each unit.

The teachers' resource guide carefully presented the objectives, major conceptual ideas to be developed, the range of short term and longer term student activities, assessment tools, literature, and other resources correlated with each unit. All of the teacher and student ideas had been crafted during extensive pilot testing in the Elkhart, Indiana Public Schools, under a grant from the Carnegie Corporation.

The fifth grade curriculum, rather than presenting a strictly chronological approach to U.S. History, was, rather, a "study of how we came to think and act as Americans" (Senesh, 1973, p. 14, fifth grade Teacher Resource guide)—a systems approach (Boulding et al., 1973). The four units were named: Shaping the Social System; The Emerging Social System; Testing the Social System; and The Social System: Present and Future. Senesh felt that the structure and successful implementation of Our Working World would result in students' understanding of their family, community, nation, and world as social systems: goal-oriented, changing, interdependent, cybernetic systems with economic, political, sociological, and cultural subsystems. He felt that young people would "come to see themselves in proper perspective to the world around them—and to develop the skills and attitudes to become captains of their fate" (Senesh, 1973, p. 1).

Some say the Senesh materials, Our Working World, were too sophisticated for both students and teachers; the reading and conceptual levels
too high. Others blame the failure of the materials on the content weaknesses in the preparation of elementary school educators, and on the lack
of widespread specific preparation for the use of the approach employed
by Senesh. Whatever the reasons, this well-crafted, brilliantly-designed
curriculum had too short a life.

"Teachers' commitments to their students have become mine. Chil-
drens' commitment to intellectual honesty has become my highest ideal"
(Senesh, 1973, Grade 1, acknowledgements). Senesh never wavered in his
focus on an interdisciplinary, orchestrated, issues-focused social science
curriculum as the vehicle for effective citizenship education in a democratic society.

SUZANNE HELBURN AND SECONDARY ECONOMIC EDUCATION

Suzanne Wiggins Helburn, a visionary like Senesh, was also influenced by
the leading cutting edge thinkers of the day: Richard Suchman's (1966)
inquiry and learning theory notion; Hilda Taba's (1967) ideas about the
conceptually-spiraling curriculum; Joseph Schwab's (1962) structure of
the academic disciplines approach; Jerome Bruner's (1960) proposition
that young students could learn sophisticated concepts if presented
appropriately; and even Larry Senesh's (1967) audacity to actually build
an economics-based curriculum for elementary social studies programs.

Helburn, earning a PhD in economics from Indiana University in
1963, was one of only a handful of female economists at the time. Interested in public policy issues, and recognizing the need for young people
to be better informed in order to act responsibly in their roles as citizens,
Helburn saw the high school curriculum as the proper target for her creative energies. As a professor and the director of the Center for Economic
Education at San Jose State University in California, Helburn received
grants from the U.S. Office of Education Project Social Studies and the
Joint Council for Economic Education for the development of ECON 12.
In addition, the SSEC provided assistance with school implementation
trials and with teacher training workshops.

Working with fellow San Jose State colleague, John Sperling (who later
went on to become the founder of the University of Phoenix, where he
incorporated many of the instructional strategies Helburn and he developed), Helburn applied progressive ideas to the creation of a six unit
innovative curriculum to be used either as a full-year course or as modules for a semester course. The overall goal was to use the economics curriculum as a vehicle toward civic education, a mechanism for stimulating

youth to care about important social issues—and to be able to analytically comprehend and address issues such as poverty, unemployment, income distribution, and the environment (Wiggins & Sperling, 1967). Helburn and Sperling saw their economics project as a wide departure from the standard descriptive economics curriculum of the day whose aim was to impart the virtues of a market economy (Warmke, 1970; Warmke & Draayer, 1969). With the focus on public policy controversies, Helburn and Sperling used conceptual knowledge as the foundation for helping young people build the cognitive tools and the affective willingness to analyze serious economic issues and to be actively involved in society.

The ECON 12 project eventually became Economics in Society (EIS), a curricular textbook series of five units (each comprising a textbook): Concepts and Institutions; Industry Organization; National Economy; Third World Economics; and Communist Economies. The sixth unit, Economic Justice, developed for the ECON 12 project, was never published. The EIS series was published by Addison-Wesley Publishers in 1974, a decade after the 1964 initiation of ECON 12. By 1974, the energy from the New Social Studies movement was waning, times had changed, and another expertly designed, creative and potentially powerful set of economics curricular materials bit the dust.

The major characteristics and themes evident in Helburn's economics projects include: a *systems* approach to (Boulding et al., 1973) the economy and to learning; *inquiry* as well as *programmed learning* approaches to methodology; and the incorporation of a *spiraling* approach to curriculum. Helburn's conceptualization of the structure of the economy took the form of a dynamic, multi-dimensional cybernetic system. Called the *Economics in Society* model, the graphic representation portrayed the interactions between and among the physical world, society, and the economy. The economy uses resources from the physical world; and derives its goals and values from the society. Changes in any of the three systems affect changes in the other spheres (Helburn et al., 1974). Such a model served to portray, in simple terms, the complexities of the real economy—and served as a guide for curricular development. Like Senesh, Helburn did not believe in teaching the model to students, but rather thought that engaging learning activities would help students construct their own cognitive structure, their own model of the economic system.

Borrowing from Schwab's (1962) ideas about the structure of academic disciplines, Helburn believed there was a conceptual as well as a syntactical structure of economics. The conceptual structure was to be developed in a systematic, spiraling way so that students could comprehend, apply, and continue to build upon these major ideas. The syntactical structure, or the analytical tools of the discipline, were methods economists used to discover new content, and were to be developed in tandem with the conceptual ideas (Helburn, 1997). Thus, students would learn measurement and other analytic tools, and most importantly, would learn how the economic system is a "cybernetic system, one that self-corrects to achieve a given set of objectives" (Helburn, 1997, p. 270).

Contra Costa County, California was the locus of much curriculum development activity in the mid-1960s: both Hilda Taba and Suzanne Helburn were developing and pilot testing their New Social Studies projects there. As colleagues and friends, along with Richard Suchman, then the New Social Studies Project Director at the Office of Education, they shared ideas and provided support for each other's projects. Taba and Suchman influenced Helburn's ideas about inquiry teaching and the nature of the learning process. Suchman (1966) saw learning as a cybernetic flow of action from the initial perception or encounter with a new stimulus, to the ways that encounter interacts with conceptual organizers (or prior knowledge content structures) the person already holds in memory. One's conceptual organizers build, change, and become more refined and more useful as one learns over a lifetime. Motivation is a major key in learning, for motivation controls incoming stimuli. Helburn et al. (1974) applied Suchman's language and ideas to her material, using her *Core Essays* to "introduce the major new organizers" to students. "The organizers are the ideas, theories, and descriptions of economic life that make up a knowledge base" (p. v). Taba's (1967) ideas of the conceptually spiraling curriculum, inquiry learning and use of case studies influenced Helburn to structure student exercises and readings in such a way as to build, reinforce, and apply key concepts, and to build activities that engaged students' natural inquisitiveness about the economy.

Helburn's notions that the economy was a system and that learning was a system guided the design of ECON 12 and then EIS. Helburn wanted students to hold a dynamic view of the economy, and to ask unconventional questions about its operation. There was nothing static in her views about teaching economics or her views about high school students. Like Senesh, Helburn believed in starting with students' "concrete life experiences and gradually adding more and more dimensions, always fitting them into a more complete view of the whole" (Helburn, 1976, p. 533). If students could learn the vocabulary, the facts, concepts, theories (the organizers) of economics, they would start to develop a way of thinking about economics. In addition, Helburn, believed, students needed economic reasoning skills, or abstract, analytic skills useful for addressing real world economic problems (Helburn, 1976, p. 533). But, Helburn also realized that the common thought amongst students and teachers was that teaching and studying economics was both difficult and boring (Davis, 1977; Fenton, 1968; Keller, 1974; and Warmke, 1970). Thus, the initial hurdle in designing a successful high school economics program was to tackle the motivational and the success factors. Students had to realize the relevance of economics for their lives and had to experience enough interest and success in their studies that they could sustain motivation. And, teachers needed a program they could teach easily and with enthusiasm.

Helburn turned to a programmed learning approach to help achieve the instructional goals of teaching a large quantity of economic content/organizers efficiently and with a high rate of student success. The use of behavioral objectives and programmed learning provided an unlikely and interesting juxtaposition to the more expansive inquiry approach also employed. Helburn (1997) felt that this eclectic approach drew on the best thinking of the day to attack the multiple and complex goals of an effective economics course. Thus, students could work their way through a step-by-step development of a complex skill or concept, completing carefully sequenced questions and then uncovering the correct answers. This instant feedback provided part of the success factor Helburn was seeking for students. Following each series of frames (developing such concepts or skills as: index numbers, measuring price level changes, the process of economic development, and the law of diminishing marginal returns) the student would complete a criterion test for a final assessment of the objectives.

The use of programmed instruction allowed students to build an extensive repertoire of basic concepts and skills that were then applied to the more teacher-directed lessons where inquiry exercises were incorporated, including extensive use of case studies illustrating real life applications of the topics being studied, and many interactive tasks.

As brilliantly as ECON 12/EIS were designed and as popular at they were amongst many teachers in the pilot trials—these projects, also, had short lives. But "invention is not innovation" (Helburn, 1997, p. 268) and the "conscious and unconscious competition among innovators and their allies created a kind of prisoner's dilemma in which no one, in the end, won" (p. 272).

CONCLUSION

Needless to say, contemporary economic educators are still faced with the same questions Senesh and Helburn tried to tackle: namely—how can one build a curriculum to help young people think logically about economic policy issues? How can we tap into the natural curiosity of youth, challenge their imaginations, and facilitate the development of intellectual faculties? How can we promote a sense of economic efficacy in young people? Today's educators seek insights in cutting edge learning theories in much the same ways Senesh and Helburn did in the 1960s to build the best curriculum imaginable to achieve such goals.

Today's Economic Education movement (Chandler, 2007) reflects many of the themes and constructs promoted by Senesh and Helburn in spite of the fact that their particular curricular projects did not survive intact. While the lineage of many ideas cannot be definitely traced to these early giants, it is clear that they employed provocative ideas of the time that were based in sound curricular and learning theories—and, they were among the first to effectively apply these ideas to real curriculum projects that were used by real teachers and students in many classrooms. Ideas such as the use of student-centered inquiry strategies, the conceptually-spiraling curriculum, the issues-oriented focus to economic problems, and the need to provide supplemental teacher preparation to K–12 educators in economic education are all components of today's economic education arena, led by groups such as the Council for Economic Education, Junior Achievement, and the National Council for the Social Studies.

Student-centered methodology, inquiry, case studies, and issues-oriented curriculum were actively employed by the New Social Studies economics projects. These effective pedagogical tools, of course, are evident in today's economic education materials, and would have survived on their own strength and integrity. However, Senesh and Helburn's projects provided important stepping-stones to later curriculum development.

Senesh and Helburn, both charismatic individuals, influenced many educators, graduate students, and others who went on to promote, use, and apply their mentors' ideas. It is difficult to trace the direct influence of such persons in the field, but the list is long of contemporary leaders in the Social Studies and Economics Education fields who were students of either Senesh or Helburn.

National and state standards in economic education currently promote a K–12 focus; the elementary emphasis must be attributed, at least in part, to the efforts, enthusiasm, verve, and energy of Senesh. Today, few question the viability of teaching basic economic concepts to young children, and today many creative, developmentally-appropriate economics materials and lessons exist for the early grades, even kindergarten. This was really unheard of before the New Social Studies movement, and the work of Larry Senesh. Today's elementary social studies curriculum is much more cognitively substantive, thanks, in part, to Senesh's work. And, economics is clearly established now as a legitimate part of the social studies curriculum, thanks, in part, to the work of Senesh and Helburn.

Perhaps the most obvious contribution of the New Social Studies movement on today's economics curriculum is the Structure of the Disciplines approach. The structure of the economics discipline has provided the major framework for standards and curriculum design in the field consistently since the 1960s. Actually, a neoclassical approach to economics has been and continues to be the major and dominant emphasis in economic education curriculum development. While this approach is the "mainstream" approach to economics, Helburn points out that other political schools of thought (Keynesian, Marxian, Public Choice, for example) have much to offer in the analysis of public policy issues (Helburn, 1997). However, there is little evidence in the contemporary economic education movement that anything other than the neoclassical structure of the economics discipline will be evident in classrooms any time soon.

Senesh and Helburn went against the prevailing ideas of their time to develop innovative, groundbreaking curricular projects. Their lofty goals—to use economics as a vehicle for citizenship education and to build economically literate young people—resonate with social studies educators today. The search continues for the best program and the best ideas. Perhaps a glimpse at the ideas of the 1960s will spark the candle of innovation by one of today's pioneers.

REFERENCES

Armento, B. J. (1980, April). Experiencing economic concepts: Formal and informal concept learning. *Peabody Journal of Education, 57*(3), 160–162.

Armento, B. J. (1986). Learning about the economic world. In V. Atwood (Ed.). *Elementary School Social Studies: Research as a guide to practice.* Washington, DC: National Council for the Social Studies.

Armstrong, D., & Burlbaw, L. (1991, July). Cashing in on students' interest in money. *Social Studies, 82*(4), 143.

Beyer, B. K. (1994, Nov–Dec). Gone, but not forgotten—reflections on the new social studies movement. *Social Studies, 85*(6), 151–156.

Beyer, B. K. (1995, April). Is the old "new social studies" back? *Education Digest, 60*(8), 67–70.

Blanchard, R. A., Senesh, L., & Patterson-Black, S. (1999, March–April). The organic social studies curriculum and the 1994 NCSS standards: A model for linking the community and the world. *Social Studies, 90*(2), 63–67.

Boulding, K., Kuhn, A., & Senesh, L. (1973, June). *System analysis and its use in the classroom.* Boulder, CO: Social Science Education Consortium.

Bruner, J. S. (1960). *The process of education.* New York: Vintage Press.

Buckles, S. (1987). What is—and isn't—economic education? *Theory into Practice, 26*(3), 163–170.

Chandler, M. A. (2007, August 9). High school seniors test well in basic economics. *Washington Post,* p. D-01.

Clark, J. R., & Davis, W. L. (1992, Jan-Feb.). Does high school economics turn off too many students? *Journal of Education for Business, 67*(3), 152–156.

Darcy, R., & Powell, P. (1966). *Manpower and economic education: Opportunities in American Life*. Athens: Ohio University.

Davis, J. E. (1977). Needed materials in pre-college economic education. In D. R. Wentworth, W. L. Hansen, & S. H. Hawke, (Eds.), *Perspectives in Economic Education* (pp. 157–180). New York: Joint Council on Economic Education.

Davis, J. E. (1987). *Teaching economics to young adolescents: A research based rationale.* San Francisco: Foundation for Teaching Economics.

Dewey, J. (1938). *Experience and education.* London: Collier-Macmillan.

Dow, P. B. (1992). Past as prologue: The legacy of Sputnik. *Social Studies, 83*(4), 164–172.

Howe, C., & Singell, L. (2003). *Obituary, Lawrence Senesh.* Retrieved September 14, 2006, http://www.colorado.edu/econ/news/fall04-newsletter/ fall-04-senesh.htm

Fenton, E. (1967a). *Developing a new curriculum: A rationale for the Holt Social Studies Curriculum: Comparative economic systems: An Inquiry Approach.* New York: Holt, Rinehart & Winston.

Fenton, E. (1967b). *The new social studies.* New York: Holt, Rinehart, & Winston.

Fenton, E. (1968). *Teacher's guide for comparative economic systems: An inquiry approach.* New York: Holt, Rinehart & Winston.

Fenton, E. (1970). The new social studies reconsidered. In M. M. Krug, J. B. Poster, & W. B. Gillies, III. (Eds.), *The New Social Studies: Analysis of theory and materials.* Itasca, IL: F. E. Peacock.

Fenton, E. (1991). Reflections on the "New Social Studies." *Social Education, 82*(3), 84–91.

Haas, J. D. (1977). *The era of the new social studies.* Boulder: CO: The Social Science Education Consortium.

Hahn, C. L., Marker, G. W., Switzer, T. J., & Turner, M. J. (1977). *Three studies on the perception and utilization of new social studies materials.* Boulder, CO: Social Science Education Consortium.

Helburn, S. W. (1976). How to develop your own social studies tests in economics. *Social Education, 40*(7), 533–537.

Helburn, S. W. (1977). Response. In D. R. Wentworth, W. L. Hansen, & S. H. Hawke (Eds.), *Perspectives in economic education* (pp. 189–194). New York: Joint Council on Economic Education.

Helburn, S. W. (1997). ECON 12 and the new social studies: Love's labor lost? *Social Studies, 88*(6), 268–277.

Helburn, S. W., Sperling, J. G., Evans, R. G., & Lott, E. (1974). *Economics in society: Concepts and institutions; industry performers; national economic policy; communist economies; and Third World economies.* Menlo Park, CA: Addison-Wesley.

Hertzberg, H. (1981). *Social Studies Reform: 1880–1980.* Boulder, CO: Social Science Education Consortium.

Keller, C. W. (1974). *Involving students in the new social studies.* Boston: Little, Brown & Co.

Kim, Y., & Kratochvil, D. W. (1972). *Developmental economic education program (DEEP).* Product Project Report No. 16, Palo Alto, CA: American Institutes for Research in the Behavioral Sciences.

Krug, M. M., Poster, J. B., & Gillies, W. B. III. (1970). *The new social studies: Analysis of theory and materials.* Itasca, IL: F. E. Peacock.

Massialas, B. G. (1992). The "new social studies"—retrospective and prospect. *Social Studies, 83*(3), 120–125.

Morrissett, I. (1967). The new social studies curriculum. In I. Morrissett (Ed.), *Concepts and structures in the New Social Studies curricula.* New York: Holt, Rinehart, & Winston.

Rader, W. D. (1995). The elementary school economics project at the University of Chicago. *Social Studies, 86*(2), 85–90.

Rader, W. D. (1996). Toward a philosophy of economics education. *Social Studies, 87*(1), 4–7.

Rice, M. J. (1992). Reflections on the new social studies. *Social Studies, 83*(5), 224–232.

Rossi, J. A. (1992). Uniformity, diversity, and the "New Social Studies." *Social Studies, 83* (1), 41–46.

Sanders, N. M., & Tanck, M. L. (1970, April). A critical appraisal of twenty-six National Social Studies Projects. *Social Education, 34*(4), entire issue.

Schug, M. C., & Armento, B. J. (1985). Teaching economics to children. In M. C. Schug (Ed.), *Economics in the School Curriculum, K–12.* Washington, DC: National Education Association.

Schwab, J. J. (1962, July). The concept of the structure of a discipline. *The Educational Record,* 197–205.

Senesh, L. (1967). Organizing a curriculum around social science concepts. In I. Morrissett (Ed.), *Concepts and structure in the new social science curricula.* New York: Holt, Rinehart & Winston.

Senesh, L. (1973). *Our Working World* (Textbook Series). Chicago: Science Research Associates.

Senesh, L. (1977). Response. In D. R. Wentworth, W. L. Hansen, & S. H. Hawke (Eds.), *Perspectives in economic education* (pp. 43–60, 225–230). New York: Joint Council on Economic Education.

Senesh, L. (1980). The community profile: A tool to improve economic competence. *Peabody Journal of Education, 57*(3), 163–166.

Senesh, L. (1981). The new social studies movement of the 1960's. *Educational Evaluation and Policy Analysis, 3*(5), 63–73.

Senesh, L. (1993). Our working world and the birth of the organic curriculum. *Social Studies, 84*(3), 92–99.

Shaver, J. P., Davis, O. L., & Helburn, S. W. (1979). The status of social studies education: Impressions from three NSF studies. *Social Education, 43,* 150–153.

Smith, F. R., & Cox, C. B. (1969). *New strategies and curriculum in social studies.* Chicago: Rand McNally.

Suchman, J. R. (1966). A model for the analysis of inquiry. In J.R. Suchman (Ed.), *Analysis of concept learning.* New York: Academic Press.

Taba, H. (1966, Feb.). *Teaching strategies and cognitive functioning in elementary school children.* Comparative Research Project No. 2404. San Francisco: San Francisco State University.

Taba, H. (1967). Roundtable. In I. Morrissett (Ed.), *Concepts and structure of the new social science curricula*. New York: Holt, Rinehart, & Winston.

Taba, H., Durkin, M. C., McNaughton, A. H., & Fraenkel, J. R. (1967). *Teachers' Handbook for Elementary Social Studies*. Menlo Park, CA: Addison-Wesley.

The Ohio University Research Foundation. (1966). *Final Report, Development of Economics Curricular Materials for Secondary Schools*. Cooperative Research Project, No. HS-082 Contract No. OE-4-10-063, Columbus, OH.

Tice, N. (1992). Social studies reform. *Education Digest, 57*(6), 45–47.

Walstad, W. B., & Soper, J. C. (Eds.). (1991). *Effective economic education in the schools*. Washington, DC: National Education Association.

Warmke, R. F. (1970). High school economics: Problems and prospects. *Journal of Economic Education, 2*(1), 89–99.

Warmke, R. F., & Draayer, G. F., (Eds.). (1969). *Selected readings in economic education*. Athens: Ohio University Press.

Watts, M. (1991, Feb.). Research on DEEP: The first 25 years. In W. B. Walstad & J. C. Soper (Eds.), *Effective economic education*. Washington, DC: National Education Association.

Wentworth, D. R., Hansen, W. L., & Hawke, S. H. (1977). *Perspectives on Economic Education*. New York: Joint Council on Economic Education.

Wiggins, S., & Sperling, J. G. (1967). *ECON 12. Final report on Project Social Studies grant No. H-153, U. S. Office of Education*. Washington, DC: Government Printing Office.

Wiley, K., & Morrissett, I. (Eds.). (1972). New in-depth evaluations of twenty-six curricular projects, programs, and materials. *Social Education, 36*(7), 711–782.

Wiley, K. B., & Superka, D. P. (1977). *Evaluation studies on new social studies materials*. Boulder, CO: ERIC Clearinghouse for Social Studies/Social Science Education and Social Science Education Consortium.

CHAPTER 11

ANTHROPOLOGY AND THE ANTHROPOLOGY PROJECTS, LONG AGO IN A GALAXY FAR AWAY

Murry Nelson

It seems hard to believe but there was a time, not long ago, when anthropology was held in great favor by educators, especially as a part of the school curriculum as it was reshaped and refined to meet the needs of an ever changing world. During the 1960s and 1970s, it seemed like a natural confluence of schools, curriculum, and society, but viewed from the perspective of the early twenty-first century, the events and attention were an aberrant moment in time. There was an excitement and a promise of greater cultural exploration and understanding that would lead to greater student appreciation of the cultural complexities of the world. Today, this seems cruelly idealistic and makes one's views border on cynicism, but the period and the goals need to be more fully contextualized in order to appreciate how such idealistic notions could have been so widely accepted.

Anthropology, or the concepts of anthropology, can be traced back to early observers of cultures visited as part of trade or war. Thucydides and

The New Social Studies: People, Projects, and Perspectives, pp. 213–230
Copyright © 2010 by Information Age Publishing
All rights of reproduction in any form reserved.

Ibn-khaldun are two examples of this early observation, although the concept of culture, as defined by anthropologists did not exist until around 1750, this according to Alfred Kroeber and Clyde Kluckhohn (1952), two classically respected anthropologists. Anthropology is a relatively young social science and the first official position in the field in an American university was not created and held until 1888 when Franz Boas was awarded this honor at Clark University in Worcester, Massachusetts. He was an anthropology professor, however, without an anthropology department, and he left Clark in 1892 over an academic freedom dispute. The American Anthropological Association was not founded until 1900.

This was the period of creation and recognition of social science organizations, and anthropology was viewed as a social science with concepts and perspectives that could significantly affect human learning. Thus, it was not surprising that there would be some suggestions that there might be a place for anthropology in the lower school curriculum. In 1903, Frank Russell of Teachers College, Columbia, made such an observation in a brief article in *Education*, but his notion was not influential enough to result in any insertions of anthropology into the school program.

From then until post-World War II, anthropology languished as a school subject, even though many elementary texts made some efforts at viewing other cultures in an academically legitimate manner. One of the best of those was the elementary textbook series co-authored by Harold Rugg and Louise Krueger, especially the third grade text, *Nature Peoples*, and the fourth grade text, *Communities of Men*, both published in 1936. There were infrequent suggestions for anthropology's acceptance as part of the school curriculum, but it was not until the 1960s that anthropology was "re-discovered" and proposed for school inclusion.

The impetus was that which spurred the New Social Studies and most of the attention in this book, that is, the launching of Sputnik in 1957 and the subsequent September, 1959 Woods Hole conference, which culminated in Jerome Bruner's *The Process of Education* in 1960. National Science Foundation (NSF) money flowed to a number of new projects. Other projects were underwritten by professional organizations or foundations. In regard to anthropology these materials included Man: A Course of Study (MACOS), which was really an interdisciplinary science/social studies curriculum for the fifth grade; materials from the Boston Children's Museum called MATCH (Materials and Activities to Teach Children History); and a number of materials that were published later as textbooks. Marion Rice mentions a number of these in a short review of materials for teaching anthropology in elementary school appearing in *Social Education* (Rice, 1968). Rice's article was one of five that was in a special section on anthropology and the elementary school in the March, 1968 *Social Education*. Rice was the coordinator of the Anthropology Curriculum Project located at the University of Georgia and initially funded in 1964 by the U.S. Office of Education. This project was the largest, best funded and developed of any anthropology project for the elementary schools.

As noted in my opening comments, there was a thrilling optimism among many educators and anthropologists at the time, most decidedly among the anthropologists. They believed passionately that this was the time for anthropology in schools, that its presence in schools would make a better world and that they should be doing all that they could to assist the schools in implementing sound curriculum materials in anthropology. A surprising number of outstanding anthropologists "signed up for the cause" and the results were primarily seen in two distinct federally supported projects. The remainder of this chapter will describe these two projects, the Anthropology Curriculum Project (ACP) developed at the University of Georgia and the Anthropology Curriculum Study Project (ACSP) developed by the American Anthropology Association.

Anthropology Curriculum Project

The Anthropology Curriculum Project was originally conceived by Wilfred Bailey, the Chair of the Department of the University of Georgia, and Marion Rice, a Professor of social studies education at the University of Georgia and a former elementary school teacher. Bailey and Rice sought to improve the teaching of social studies in the elementary school and saw this as an opportunity to do so ("University has 'first' " 1965).

The project was initially conceived to have month-long units for each of the Grades 1–7. "The structure of each unit is designed to convey a scientific conception of the field and methods of anthropology" (Rice, 1968). This was consistent with two of the major characteristics of New Social Studies, that is, an emphasis on the processes of social science investigation and the use of raw social science data (Searles & Nelson, 1976). Many social studies educators of the 1960s had noted a decided lack of academic content from the social studies in the elementary school curriculum and contended that "the need for increased content was a matter of high priority" (Rice & Bailey, 1971, p. 6). The ACP was funded by the U.S. Office of Education from 1964–69 under the aegis of "Project Social Studies" (p. 1). It then received continued funding for 2 more years under the auspices of the University of Georgia.

Although the original intent was to limit curriculum materials to Grades 1–7, the project did end up producing kindergarten and secondary units, also. The materials were developed by Rice, Bailey, and their evolving team of graduate students, many of whom were able to get data and access to the schools in which the materials were field-tested in order to do dissertation studies (Clawson & Barnes, 1973; Frech, 1975; Green, 1965; Potterfield, 1968; Wash, 1967). Schools in Savannah—Chatham County Public Schools were the most utilized in field-testing. The graduate students involved in the project sought evaluative data on the project's efforts through quantitative assessments, almost exclusively, which struck some observers as ironic, considering the content and techniques of cultural anthropology and its reliance on qualitative data gathering. Throughout the project a panel of six professors in anthropology and three local educators were utilized as consultants.

The materials that were produced included student "texts," pupil study guides, teacher materials, and tests. Many of the materials, including tests, for the lower grades had a minimum of words, so much of the interpretation and understanding depended on the teacher's understanding of the concepts and purposes of the materials. The intent was to produce curricula in anthropology that could be used in connection with existing social studies programs, a difficult task, considering the entrenchment of the expanding communities model, which dominated (and still dominates) the elementary curricular structure of social studies. Prior studies had indicated no systematic anthropology content in the elementary curriculum and this project tried to improve that while also reducing the heavy dosage of history and geography in the curriculum, especially in the intermediate grades. To try and integrate important anthropological concepts, Rice and Bailey designed a spiral curriculum in which each major topic would be presented twice, first at a primary grade, then at a more advanced level several grades later ("University has 'first,' " 1965). These major topics/concepts were "the concept of culture," introduced at Grade 1 and revisited in Grade 4; "the development of man and his culture," introduced in Grade 2 and reinforced in Grade 5; "cultural dynamics," introduced in Grade 3 and revisited in Grade 6. "Cross cultural views of the life cycle" were to be addressed in Grade 7 only, kind of a capstone to the prior 6 years of study. Subsequently, the units were never developed under contract for Grades 3 and 6, "cultural dynamics," but unit materials for Grades K, 8, and 9 were created and used. The high school unit was on "Race, Caste and Prejudice." All of the material was developed in a similar manner, namely, teacher essay (done by graduate students in anthropology), pupil text (based on the teacher essay and written by education members of the staff), teacher guide, pupil guide (done under the supervision of a curriculum specialist), and finally, the anthropology achievement tests (done under the supervision of the measurement specialists) (Austin & Potterfield, 1966; Bailey & Clune, 1968).

The pupil texts for the primary grades were relatively simple line drawings with limited text on each page. Maps located the cultures to be examined. The comparison of Kazak, Arunta, and American grew increasingly more complex and detailed as the text progressed (Anthropology Curriculum Project, 1965a, 1965b, 1965c, 1965d; Anthropology Curriculum Study Project, 1970, 1972a, 1972b; Anthropology Curriculum Study Project Proposals, 1968). The fourth grade pupil text on the concept of culture had no illustrations and focused on five major themes. These were (1) how an anthropologist studies cultures, (2) what is meant by culture, (3) how cultures differ, (4) how people acquire their culture, (5) how cultures change. Many key words were introduced, defined, and illustrated including enculturation, acculturation, cultural universals, cultural continuity, cultural diffusion, syncretism, cultural lag, and cultural stability. The text (of 54 pages) was dense, but interesting. Most of the evaluation studies showed that students could learn this material, although the overall rate of retention was never tested and with little reinforcement in future grades, the material may have been "lost" quickly, as much of school information often is. The Pupil Guide was meant to maximize student understanding of material. Each chapter had a word list, a summary of key ideas, suggested activities, thought questions and review questions. It was foreseen that these guides would help students learn key material, whether their teacher had been trained for using the materials or not.

Initially, the project began with 60 classrooms as field-testing sites, all in Georgia. Eventually, they hoped to test in 150–175 classrooms throughout the United States in order to draw conclusions about the use and acceptance of the materials. In order to ensure greater acceptability and understanding of the materials, the project developers held a series of summer institutes, most of which ran 6 weeks. These were divided into two components, one emphasizing "knowledge" and the other "application."

From early on the developers noted their distinct differences from the other early 1960s social studies curricula. Some of these distinctions would be the very problems that helped lead to the demise of the ACP. ACP objectives were specific to anthropology. As anthropology was continually remarginalized in the elementary school curriculum, there would be no room for a project that emphasized that social science as primary. Many 1960s projects emphasized problem solving, but ACP emphasized the techniques of anthropological research and taught these explicitly. Many 1960s social studies materials made use of stories or trips, but ACP produced "simple, attractive, ethnographies in which the anthropological concepts and facts were made explicit." This would also limit the interest of teachers and schools in the 1970.

In addition, the manner of presenting the materials was seen as crude and unacceptable by many teachers and critics. The illustrations were simple line drawings, nicely done considering the medium, but not very "eye-catching" to teachers and students. Both these groups desired more realistic, preferably color, illustrations. There was a plan to take photographs, but this proved financially unfeasible. Georgia and experimental classes were supplied with back issues of *National Geographic* which had Kazak, Arunta, and other ethnographic illustrations. It was too demanding of teachers to try to find appropriate photos. Without this medium and the lack of good visuals, ACP looked rough and unfinished. Later, there was a suggestion to provide real artifacts to accompany the materials, but this also proved to be economically unrealistic. A feasibility study done by the ACP also did not find that pupil learning seemed to increase as a result of the use of such artifacts.

Evaluation of ACP

As noted earlier, much of the evaluation, which was a prime component of the project was done by doctoral students in the Social Science Education program at the University of Georgia. Their evaluative goals, generally, were rather modest and, almost exclusively, "restricted to cognitive evaluation. This results not only from a particular educational commitment, but also experience with the costs of conducting even very limited types of evaluation" (Rice & Bailey, 1971, pp. 54–55). Thus, one of the two stated objectives for the project, evaluation of the materials, was seriously hampered by ideological bias and financial limitations. Many of the evaluations sought to determine the effectiveness of materials in promoting student learning of anthropology and the effect of special training in anthropology for teachers. All of the studies indicated that students could learn the material at any of the elementary grades. The training of teachers in anthropology, however, did not necessarily lead to more successful student learning of the materials. Many of the doctoral studies came to the same conclusions, using different grade levels and geographic locations (Green, 1965; Wash, 1967).

Two school people who used the materials in Savannah as part of the experiments, made their own assessments, not necessarily statistical in nature, but rather more qualitative, based on their observations and participation. They drew a number of useful inferences, based on their classroom work in the first and second grades. They noted that young children were fascinated with archaeology, that they could and did learn to be accurate reporters and that they could appreciate cross-cultural comparisons. Students were able to see how similarities in environment lead to similarities in using that environment, not startling revelations, but insightful for youngsters of that age to be able to discern. "In studying about a culture, young children prefer topics that have some kind of concrete referent, such as tools, ways of making a living, or house types," an observation that reinforced the notion that a kit for students might have been a good idea, despite the determination of the developers, noted earlier (Emmons & Cobia, 1968, p. 249).

Dissemination and Success

The ACP developers and staff made presentations at professional meetings, published articles in professional journals and "disseminated the materials to potential users, even in tentative experimental form" (Rice & Bailey, 1971, p. 56). Ultimately, the materials were used in schools throughout Georgia, as well as in districts in 36 states, the District of Columbia, two districts in Ontario, and in the Overseas School of Rome, Italy. Nevertheless, the use of the materials was nearly nonexistent within ten years. One major reason was the lack of a commercial publisher.

> No contract has been made with a commercial publisher for the distribution of the material. Two reasons may account for the failure to attract commercial marketing and distribution: the highly cognitive content of the materials, which is contrary to the common practice of limiting content by rigid vocabulary control, and the supplementary nature of the materials. (p. 33)

It is this latter reason that seems most telling. The cognitive content, per se, was not a drawback, when viewed in the light of continual calls for more content in the elementary school, particularly in social studies. The content that was favored, however, was history with dollops of government and geography added. Anthropology was and is seen as supplemental, as noted by the developers. Overcoming that barrier simply proved impossible.

The Anthropology Curriculum Study Project (ACSP)

At the same time as ACP was being developed, tested and utilized in elementary schools, so, too was the ACSP undergoing a parallel process in and for American secondary schools. The American Anthropological Association (AAA) first expressed interest in secondary schools and the role of anthropology study in schools at their annual meeting in November of 1960. A Committee on High School Anthropology was established, and this was followed by an advisory committee to aid in the shaping of what would be the ACSP. In 1962, funds were awarded to AAA from NSF to prepare materials for high school anthropology instruction and in March of that year the new "ACSP staff began full-time preparation of materials" (Memo from ACSP Advisory Committee to AAA Executive Board, 11/24/67, National Anthropological Archives).

The problem of staffing and a director was resolved early on in the ACSP history through the appointment of Malcolm Collier, a professor of anthropology at the University of Chicago. Most of the staff work then was done there under her direction. Collier was a well-respected cultural anthropologist who had received her PhD from the University of Chicago, whose field work and research were undertaken among the Navaho culture of the Southwestern United States. She also served as associate editor of *American Anthropologist* (1952–55), assistant editor of *Current Anthropology* (1958–60), and served as a research associate at the University of Chicago. At the time of her appointment as director of ACSP, she was 54 years old and served the project for its ten year "life" as director.

In a piece published in *Current Anthropology* in 1964, Collier summarized the findings and activities of the project up to that time. She noted that her analysis of the high school curriculum led to the conclusion "that both in its methodology and concepts and in some particular areas of research, anthropology can make a distinctive contribution to the intellectual capabilities and knowledge of high school students" (p. 102). She also conceded that anthropology did not have a place in the traditional high school curriculum, but she felt that it certainly could, when one considered how it was easily connected to the biology, social studies, and humanities curriculum. These were notions that she and her staff had in mind as they designed and developed the ACSP materials. They did have a caveat, i.e. that the materials were, in a sense, "prepared for use by the teacher who understands them and can adapt them to the needs of the students" (Collier, 1964, p. 102). She noted that the first unit on "Comparative Analysis of Early Civilizations" would be ready for trial teaching in the fall.

"Case Studies of Preliterate Societies" would be a second area of work and several anthropologist-authors were already engaged in this writing, so Collier (1964) noted. A connection to state history was being tried, specifically in New York, regarding the study of three (unnamed) cultures within the state. Reflective of the new science work like Biological Sciences Curriculum Study (BSCS), Chem 12, and Physical Science Study Curriculum Physics (PSSC), all funded by NSF, Collier saw ACSP as aiding in new ways of viewing social science.

> Just as the new high school science courses acquaint students with the concepts and theories of the working scientist, so, also, the conceptual tools of the social scientist can give new meaning to the bewildering quantity of facts of the social studies. (p. 103)

Collier's view was reiterated, with more supportive data and experience, in a 1968 article co-authored with Ed Dethlefsen, Unit Director for

"The Study of Early Man." In referring to what anthropology could do for citizenship, broadly defined, they draw from Robert Hanvey, who observed that

> The high school graduate who has been taught to expect regularities in the affairs of the physical universe will never have heard of the search for regularities in the affairs of men…. It will be in the context of such a development that Anthropology may find a role in the schools. (pp. 11–12)

They then go on to present four steps to developing this contribution and illustrate those steps with examples from the unit on Early Man. The first is the selection of significant topics from the mass of anthropological data. Second was identifying the relevance of each topic to high school students. Third was isolating the essential aspects of each topic, while fourth was developing methods to aid students in understanding and using the data and concepts.

Developing the Materials

During 1966–67 three experimental units were written, titled "The Study of Early Man," "The great Transformation" and "Studying Societies." Preparation was begun for the writing of the 16-week course, "The Transformation of Human Societies." Even at that early date concern was expressed by the advisory committee about whether the materials would be used and, if so, how; they were not very sanguine about the outcome. The advisory committee was effusive in their praise of the staff, however, especially Robert Hanvey, Edwin Dethlefsen, and Kurt Johnson. The committee felt that these folks were the "best qualified in the country in developing materials for the social sciences" and under the leadership of Malcolm Collier "they are an exceedingly productive team." They strongly advised the continuance of project activities through at least July of 1970 (Advisory Committee to AAA Executive Board, 11/24/67). The advisory board signatories were Stephen Boggs, Chair of the Anthropology Department at the University of Hawaii; Paul Bohannon, Professor of Anthropology at Northwestern University and a vocal advocate for the presence of anthropology in the high school curriculum; Fred Gearing, Professor of Anthropology at the University of California-Riverside; and Charles Frantz, Executive Secretary of the American Anthropological Association.

Bohannon had co-developed an anthropology course for high school use at the exclusive North Shore Country Day School in Winnetka, Illinois. He and his co-developers, anthropology graduate students Merwyn

Garbarino and Earle Carlson, worked to create appropriate materials for high schoolers in anthropology in the mid-1960s, but began using the ACSP materials as soon as they were available on an experimental basis in 1967–68. Bohannon endorsed them as "the best prepared materials we know for teaching anthropology in secondary schools" (Bohannon, Garbarino & Carlson, 1969, p. 419).

Even as the materials were being developed, there were parallel plans for providing teacher support, especially for those interested teachers who did not seem to have a very strong foundation in anthropology. Two films were to be made available (for a very low fee) that illustrated classroom use of the materials, a selected annotated bibliography was being compiled and a slide tape on ACSP aims, materials and pedagogy was made. In addition there was great elation in the journal of the National Council for the Social Studies, *Social Education*, having an upcoming issue with a dedicated focus on anthropology with an article prepared by the ACSP staff (ACSP, 1972).

Still, this concern for training teachers to use the materials "properly" would continue to trouble the staff and director for the rest of the project's life. In 1968, the ACSP proposed to NSF that additional funds be allocated to the project in order to offer a series of three week workshops for teachers in the summers of 1968 and 1969. The workshops would be taped on-site (Minneapolis, Atlanta, Oakland) for replay by groups and interested individuals. The success of the workshops would be measured through ACSP evaluation forms and through devices of the participants' own design. Another issue that always seemed to plague the project was the budget. It wasn't that the staff and director were profligate spenders as much the fact that new, unexpected issues would arise that needed to be addressed and ACSP would have to return to NSF for more funding requests. It obviously didn't help that initial funding requests were almost never met at the requested amounts. This problem began as early as 1966 and continued through 1972.

The Curriculum and the Use in Schools

Early Man was the first unit topic developed and it was tested for use in 36 schools, 60 teachers and 5,805 students in 14 states (NAA, Box 158, Appendices ACSP Folder). The unit had a number of emphases that included evolution as a change process, the emergence of language and comparative anatomy in the study of human evolution. All were interrelated and often focused on race and race classification. There is a general skepticism among cultural anthropologists as to the significance of race itself as a factor in human functions and this was before more advanced genetic work has shown the minute differences in various races, except as the esoteric specialist studying human adaptations and evolutionary prehistory. In describing the teaching of this unit, Collier and Dethlefsen (1968) note that its use has not led to sweeping reforms in the curriculum or in teaching, itself. They do point out that the materials led some teachers to realize that students can think. So, too, with students, some of whom commented that "they are relieved to be 'allowed' to think" (p. 16).

The Great Transition was tested in that same academic year (1966–67) in 342 schools, 54 teachers, and 5,025 students in 14 states (NAA, Box 158, Appendices ACSP folder). This unit focused on nomadic pastoralism, peasant cultures, and the movement into early urban civilizations. For both units, the materials included pamphlets, maps, charts, transparencies, slide tapes and/or film strips, and records. Also planned were tests and quizzes for teachers and students (Tenenberg & Dethlefsen, 1972).

Following these field tests, the ACSP staff had a meeting with a number of representatives from publishing companies since any success for the ACSP would only come through mass-produced, commercial publication. The publishing meeting included representatives from Laidlaw, Xerox, SRA, Rand McNally, McGraw-Hill, American Book, Silver Burdett, Prentice-Hall, Van Nostrand, Grolier, Holt, Rinehart and Winston, Cowles Communication, D.C. Heath, McMillan and Scott, and Foresman & Co. Ultimately, Macmillan was agreed upon as publisher of the ACSP materials and, over a period of years, published materials for ACSP before finally bringing out the course in book form as *Patterns in Human History* in 1971.

During the next academic year, 1967–68, nine teachers from six schools in Illinois, Massachusetts, New Hampshire, Oregon, Pennsylvania, and Washington field tested part of the course that would become *Patterns in Human History*. This was called "Studying Societies" and was "designed to familiarize the student with how an anthropologist looks at people" (Bailey, Tate, & Dumbleton, 1973, p. 963). Also, part of the materials used in school were three books that Macmillan published for ACSP. These included (1) *The Great Tree and Longhouse: The Culture of the Iroquois* by Hazel Hertzberg with an accompanying teacher's manual by Hertzberg; (2) *Kiowa Years: Study in Cultural Impact* and *Profile of a People* by Alice Marriott, with a teachers manual by Rachel Reese Sady; and (3) *Annotated Bibliography of Anthropological Materials for High School Use* by James Gallagher. Further evaluations done in 1970 in Northern California with 1,200 10th graders concluded that ACSP material "increased student ability to draw inferences about societies from artifacts and written anecdotes and to process and apply ideas from anthropology to social realities" (Parsons, 1970, p. 19).

Meeting in 1969 in Chicago, the ACSP Advisory Committee had a limited but important agenda. First was a hoped for report from a Macmillan staff person who could update the committee on the progress on the *Patterns of Human History* text. Archival data does not indicate if that person did, indeed, appear. A second item was the recurring concern of the preparation of teacher service materials related to *Patterns*. These included film, teacher self-evaluation forms, sample tests, and answers to FAQs by school personnel regarding the ACSP materials in their schools. Publicity was another ongoing concern, as well as implementation of ACSP materials. The advisory committee had also changed in its 5 or so years of existence, losing Fred Gearing who was becoming the co-director of ACSP, and adding a number of additional anthropologists, including Solon Kimball of the University of Chicago, Ernestine Kyle of SUNY-Buffalo, Conrad Reining of the Library of Congress and the University of Minnesota, and sociologist Edward Lehman of Columbia University.

Patterns in Human History

Patterns in Human History was due for publication in late 1969 or early 1970. In February of 1971, Malcolm Collier indicated her continuing frustration at the failure of Macmillan to publish the work at that time. She lamented Macmillan's "quite incredible slowness and general inefficiency of handling of the problems of publishing the ACSP course" (Collier, 1971). In April, Ed Lehman (1971) noted that "One of the great problems of ACSP has been lack of awareness about it." But finally, after a number of delays on the part of Macmillan, the text and multimedia course, *Patterns in Human History*, was finally published in June of 1971. The product consisted of four kits, all based on the prior work. These were now titled *Studying Societies, Origins of Humanness, The Emergence of Complex Societies, and Modernization and Traditional Societies*. Each kit contained a book of student readings, a teaching plan and either records, filmstrips, transparencies, photographs, artifacts or a combination of these. The rationale was, as always in the project, the acquisition of better understanding of human behavior.

Reviews of the material appeared in *Social Education* and *American Anthropologist*. The former review, which was part of an issue dedicated to New Social Studies projects, examined the objectives, content, methodology, implementation conditions, and evaluation of ACSP. Accurately noted was the notion that ACSP had as primary instructional strategy the acquisition of skills of scientific investigation. It was also noted that the teacher plans were very complete and intended to be followed as written, all of which reinforced the notions that had been in place in ACSP since its first curriculum endeavors. The reviewer had no access to the evaluation data (which were internal or shared with the sponsor, NSF), but it was noted that the materials were "an exciting, enriching addition to any social studies classroom at the junior and senior high level" (ACSP, 1972, p. 726). The final note was telling in its unintended forecast of the ACSP's demise, that is "In a time when people are searching for ways to understand human complexities, these materials afford an interesting and significant learning experience" (p. 726).

The *American Anthropologist* review presented what the authors called two points of view, one pedagogical, the other anthropological. In examining the former, they felt that ACSP would be best taught as a prelude to world history, acknowledging, at least tacitly, the stronghold that history had on the curriculum and seeking a entry to the curriculum through that history dominance. A fear that the reviewers had was that the entire package, which held together very well, would be too expensive for some schools to purchase or that some teachers would use the materials in a selective manner, negating the teaching plan. "Potential users need to remember that without the teaching plan the other materials will be floating odds and ends without much meaning" (Bailey, Tate, & Dumbleton, 1973, p. 963).

The reviewers thought that the ACSP would prove useful to social studies teachers because of the provocative topics which "should capture the interest of secondary school students" through very readable texts (page number?). The reviewers saw three potential obstacles in the wide adoption of ACSP in the schools nationally. These were aforementioned cost, flexibility of use (alluded to earlier) and a lack of guidelines for evaluation of pupil performance (an area of emphasis for the parallel developed ACP). Ultimately, these would be significant in the lack of the ACSP and anthropology to become embedded in the social studies curriculum.

Aftermath of ACSP

With the agreement of Macmillan to publish the ACSP materials, the project began to shut down. NSF funding was needed to establish archival placement for the ACSP data and that was allowed through remaining funding. The Social Science Education Consortium (SSEC), located in Boulder, Colorado, had been visionary in seeking to acquire materials from a number of the NSF projects and brokered a deal; whereby, the archival data would be stored in a separate collection in the University of Colorado archives. SSEC, under the guidance of Nick Helburn, an economics professor at Colorado and SSEC executive board member, was able to acquire the archival material from the High School Geography Project (HSGP) and Sociological Resources for the Social Sciences (SRSS); this acquisition influenced Collier in determining where the ACSP material might go (Collier, 1971a). In December, Collier sent a letter to Lehman detailing a list of materials sent to the University of Colorado library and those materials sent to the American Anthropological Association. The latter are now located in the National Anthropological Archives in Suitland, Maryland.

The *Patterns in Human History* materials were never updated and as the interest in their use waned, Macmillan made no effort to create a second edition. By the 1980s evidence of the ACSP was found only in pieces in limited schools throughout the U.S. Today they only exist hidden in storage areas in schools.

What Happened to Cause the Demise of ACP and ACSP?

Before examining the details of the ACP and ACSP "failures," it seems best to contextualize those projects and the time period in which they flourished. As initially noted, anthropology never had much of a place in the school curriculum. By the time anthropology has legitimated itself as a social science, the school curriculum in social studies was to include history, government, and economics with some cognates of them appearing at times. Geography had sealed its own fate in 1894 when, as a part of the Committee of Ten reports of the National Education Association (NEA), the leaders of geography chose to emphasize the physical, hard science, aspect of the field and eschew efforts at human geography as part of the school curriculum. Anthropology and sociology were latecomers to this process, not just in the school curriculum, but in the curriculum of higher education. For many years, these social sciences were wedded as one department in a number of colleges and universities. This conflation was, ultimately, not to be beneficial to anthropology or sociology as they were considered for inclusion in the regular school curriculum.

Anthropology was not part of a traditional social studies curriculum, and as long as there was such a curriculum, anthropology would be excluded. The uncertainty of American educational superiority that came about in the early 1960s was the initial entrée for anthropology to be considered for school inclusion. Couple that with the enthusiasm and hope of a number of eager anthropologists to proselytize about the great ecumenical possibilities that anthropology could yield, as well as with a populace increasingly wondering about how the rest of the world thought (as a result of the confusion and frustration that permeated thoughts of the war in Vietnam), and anthropology was given new credence in its quest for school relevance.

The ACP and ACSP projects were relatively modest in their major goals. ACP wanted to see if children could learn anthropological concepts and if they found them of interest and ACP staff found that the answer was "yes" to both questions. Unfortunately, that affirmative answer was not deemed as truly relevant to a more traditional curriculum, one that returned in the 1980s and has remained steadfast since then. Even the relative ease of using the materials was not to be enough to "save" these project materials. As Cawelti had noted in 1967, innovations perceived by potential adopters as difficult to understand or use or requiring particular skills or equipment lessened the likelihood of adoption of those materials (as cited in Turner & Haley, 1977, p. 60). Recognizing that, the ACSP and ACP materials were developed to minimize such problems and all indications from users and evaluators were that the projects staffs had succeeded in this effort.

ACSP staffers seemed to recognize from early on that anthropology would need some way to gain a foothold, albeit modest, in the high school curriculum. There, every course was seen as having some potential utility for college admission and proof of vital and "testable" learning. Thus, the ACSP tried to connect the concepts and content of ACSP to world history, with the notion that world history would be better absorbed and understood with anthropology as a "precursor." As the testing and standards movement grew, most aspects of social studies (even history) have been marginalized with anthropology and sociology, further marginalized by the already marginalized field of social studies. World history has yielded ground to American history, more and more, and anthropology is viewed almost as a "luxury" that history and the social studies curriculum cannot afford in either time invested or conceptual understandings.

Studies of the New Social Studies conducted in the 1970s noted a number of interesting aspects of ACSP. First, not surprisingly, it was the least used of most of the New Social Studies projects studied, since anthropology classes were the least found in American high schools. But, of those teachers sampled who *did* teach anthropology, they had the largest percentage aware of the ACSP materials and actually using them, compared to other New Social Studies projects included in studies (Switzer, Lowther, Hanna, & Kidder, 1977, p. 51; Turner & Haley, 1977, p. 95). Hahn noted in her study, however, that most of the New Social Studies projects went unheard of in rural and small schools (Hahn, 1977, p. 26), making adoption in most of these areas unlikely without a significant outlay of cash for publicity by publishers or developers.

All of social studies field has been subject to reassessment and scrutiny that question the relevance of the field of social studies to the school curriculum and student learning. The new and current buzzword is citizenship education, a term that is not well defined. In Pennsylvania, the notion of social studies was removed from the schools by the State Board of Education, under pressure from the governor, and replaced by two certification areas, citizenship education (not defined, but confined to history, geography, economics, and government/political science) and social sciences (consisting of anthropology, sociology, and psychology). In schools, the latter three would only count as electives, not required courses for graduation, essentially consigning these fields to having no new teachers certified to teach them and eventually leading to their demise in schools. The phase-in of these areas and the phase-out of social studies were to be done over a 3-year period, but months before the change was to take effect, a change in administrations gave social studies a reprieve and it continues in Pennsylvania. For the purposes of this chapter, this example illustrates the continued indifference or disdain with which anthropology is viewed in some political quarters, making any required or recommended work in anthropology highly unlikely in Pennsylvania, if not all of the United States.

Thus, the demise of the anthropology projects, ACP and ACSP, was no real surprise (the "scandal" around *Man: A Course of Study* [MACOS] in the 1970s also contributed to the suspicion of all NSF-funded materials). These materials had been developed at an exceptional time in American educational history by an enthusiastic and passionate group of anthropologists and educators. The limited scope of the materials would doom them, unless there were to be seismic shift in the American school curriculum and, ultimately, that would not occur. The entrenchment of the traditional curriculum was, and is, a continual obstacle to real reform and increased understanding in social studies. The anthropology projects had neither the scope, nor the "clout" to alter that.

REFERENCES

Anthropology Curriculum Project. (1965) *The Arunta* (Publication No. 6.) Athens: University of Georgia.

Anthropology Curriculum Project. (1965, 1968 revision). *Arunta Kazak American* (Publication No. 6 and 7 revised). Athens: University of Georgia.

Anthropology Curriculum Project. (1965). *The concept of culture: Pupil text* (Publication No. 16). Athens: University of Georgia.

Anthropology Curriculum Project. (1965) *The concept of culture: Pupil study guide* (Publication No. 17). Athens: University of Georgia.

Anthropology Curriculum Study Project Patterns in Human History. (1972, November). *Social Education, 36*(7), 724–726.

Anthropology Curriculum Study Project Proposals. (1968). National Anthropological Archives, Smithsonian Institution, Box 158 (Formerly Box 169)., Museum Support Center, Suitland, MD.

Austin, C., & Potterfield, J. (Preparers). (1966, March). *The development of man and his culture, pupil guide, grade two* (Publication no. 33). Athens: University of Georgia.

Bailey, W., Tate, B., & Dumbleton, D. (1973). Studying societies: Teaching plan. Readings, review. *American Anthropologist*, 962–964.

Bailey, W., & Clune, F., Jr. (1968, Spring). Preparation of elementary school units on the concept of culture. *Human Organization*, 27(1), 6–10.

Bohannon, P., Garbarino, M., & Carlson, E. (1969, June). An experimental ninth grade anthropology course. *American Anthropologist*, 71, 409–420.

Bruner, J. (1960). *The process of education*, Cambridge, MA: Harvard University Press.

Collier, M. (1964). *A brief summary of the findings and activities of the Anthropology Curriculum Study Project.* Chicago: Current Anthropology

Collier, M., & Dethlefsen, E. S. (1968, Spring). Anthropology in the pre-collegiate curriculum. *Human Organization*, 27(1), 11–16.

Collier, M. (1971a, February 2). *Letter to Edward Lehman.* NAA Box 158, Correspondence folder.

Collier, M. (1971b, September 10). *Letter to Edward Lehman.* NAA Box 158, Correspondence folder.

Clawson, E., & Barnes, B. (1973). *Journal of Experimental Education, 42,* 11–15.

Emmons, F., & Cobia, J. (1968, March). Introducing anthropological concepts in the primary grades. *Social Education, 32*(3), 248–250.

Frech, W. (July, 1975.) The effect of cognitive training in anthropology on ethnocentric attitudes. *Psychology in the Schools, 12,* 364–370.

Georgia, University of, Anthropology Curriculum Project. (1972, November), *Social Education, 45*(7), 747–748.

Gonzalez, N. (with J. Haefner & R. Fitch). (1973, Fall). Applied anthropology and the grade schools. *Human Organization, 32,* 295

Green, W. W., Jr. (1965, November). *Evaluation of the Anthropology Curriculum Project for Grades one and four as measured by selected and prepared test instruments* Washington, DC, National Council for the Social Studies (ED 132 069).

Hahn, C. L. (1977). Familiarity with and perceived characteristics of "New Social Studies" materials." In C. Hahn, G. Marker, T. Switzer, & M. J. Turner (Ed.), *Three studies on perception and utilization of "New Social Studies" materials* (pp. 9–27). Boulder, CO: Social Science Education Consortium,.

Hahn, C., Marker, G., Switzer, T., & Turner, M. J. (1977). *Three studies on perception and utilization of "New Social Studies" Materials.* Boulder, CO" Social Science Education Consortium.

Kroeber, A., & Kluckhohn, C. (1952). *Culture: A critical review of concepts and definitions.* Papers of the Peabody Museum of American Archaeology and Ethnology, Harvard University, MA.

Lehman, E. (1971, April 15). *Letter to Theodore Parsons* (University of California-Berkeley). NAA, Box 158, Correspondence Folder.

Parsons, T. (and others). (1970). *Report of the Anthropology Curriculum Study Project Research Program* Washington, DC, National Science Foundation (ED 179 446).

Potterfield, J. E. (1968, March). Analysis of elementary children's ability to learn anthropological content at grades four, five, and six. *Journal of Educational Research, 61*(7), 297–299.

Rice, M. (1968, March). Materials for teaching anthropology in the elementary school. *Social Education, 42*(3), 254–256, 260.

Rice, M., & Bailey, W. (1971). *The development of a sequential curriculum in anthropology, grades 1-7,* Athens: Anthropology Curriculum Project, University of Georgia.

Russell, F. (1903, May). Anthropology in American high schools and after. *Education, 23*(9), 530–537.

Searles, J. E., & Nelson, M. (1976, November/December). The state of the New Social Studies: I. In Pennsylvania. *The Social Studies, 67*(6), 254–257.

Switzer, T. J., Lowther, M. A., Hanna, W. M., & Kidder, R. D. (1977). Dissemination and implementation of social studies materials. In C. Hahn, G. Marker, T. Switzer, & M. J. Turner (Eds.), *Three studies on perception and utilization of "New Social Studies" materials* (pp. 29–52). Boulder, CO: Social Science Education Consortium.

Tenenberg, M. S., & Dethlefsen, E. S. (1972). *"Anthropology Curriculum Study Project" Teacher service material. Students and teachers: Strategies for discussion. What is anthropology? Four samples.* Washington, DC, American Anthropology Association, National Science Foundation (ED 062 263).

Turner, M. J., & Haley, F. (1977). Utilization of "New Social Studies" curriculum programs. In C. Hahn, G. Marker, T. Switzer, & M. J. Turner (Eds.), *Three Studies on perception and utilization of "New Social Studies" materials* (pp. 54–101). Boulder, CO: Social Science Education Consortium.

University has "first" in anthropology project. (1965, November 11). *Athens Banner Herald,* p. 10.

Wash, J. (1967, February). *An evaluation of the Sequential Anthropology Curriculum Project.* Washington, DC, American Educational Research Association (ED 132 070)

CHAPTER 12

MAKING SENSE OF IT ALL

A Research Synthesis on the Impact of
Man: A Course of Study

Chrystal S. Johnson

INTRODUCTION

Forty years ago, the *Man: A Course of Study* (MACOS) curriculum entered elementary classroom across the United States. This curriculum brought forth the nature of humanness and of human behavior. Students applied inquiry skills in an effort to make sense of the human condition. Teachers received training on how to effectively teach the content and use the materials. For the most part, MACOS exemplified the progressive ideals of the "New Social Studies," which focused on the cognitive realm and sought to "transform ... students into junior historians and social scientists" (Evans, 2004, p. 123). Perhaps, this "New Social Studies" gave birth to social science education (Barnes, Stallings, & Rivner, 1981).

MACOS, as with the other Project Social Studies endeavors, came to pass as a reaction toward Russian advances in science and mathematics and criticism of public schooling in the United States. The MACOS curricular reform movement, moreover, served as "one of the most important efforts

The New Social Studies: People, Projects, and Perspectives, pp. 231–260

of our time to relate research findings and theory in education psychology to the development of new and better instructional materials" (Dow, 1975, p. 395). Not long after implementation, empirical studies emerged that examined the project's effectiveness and impact on elementary teachers and learners. Eventually, these empirical studies would not only investigate the MACOS experiment, but also employ research data to quell those arguments raging against the curriculum (e.g., Barnes et al., 1981; Cole & Lacefield, 1980; Tredwell & Zedikoff, 1975; Wilson & Taylor, 1978).

A substantial body of research on the MACOS project exists. Yet, most of the contemporary literature on MACOS catalogues the sociopolitical context and curricular flaws that precipitated its decline (e.g., Dow, 1991a, 1991b, 1992; Evans, 2004; Latno, 1998; Ross, 2001). More recent MACOS studies bring to the forefront how a troubling curricular squall left an indelible mark on the social studies field from which it has yet to recover (Dow, 1976; Evans, 2004). As such, historians now view the MACOS period as a turning point in the history of social education (Dow, 1991a; 1992; Evans, 2004; Fenton, 1991; Massialas, 1992). Current scholars fluidly describe the partisan rancor associated with the project, thus generating a usable past. Their interpretations incorporate varied theoretical perspectives and historical methods to present distinctive ways of understanding how a national curricular project could falter so easily (e.g., Dow, 1992; Evans, 2004; Gunnarsson, 1990). Ultimately, each historical presentation put forth the notion of an intersection of curricular thought and cognitive science amongst a growing neoconservative tide.

Controversy in all forms is interesting. Yes, the MACOS story is a compelling narrative of ideological differences and curricular postulating. What is missing, though, is a cogent synthesis of actual research on MACOS itself. No exhaustive review of studies on MACOS has, however, to my knowledge appeared. Because of the persistence surrounding the MACOS controversy and the numerous studies generated by this debate, a synthesis of such research makes sense.

NATURE OF THIS CHAPTER

By its nature, a research synthesis involves the collection of information describing the key results and various attributes of the studies under investigation. A descriptive analysis is one statistical approach to a research synthesis. It makes available a constructive representation of the nature of a research literature. Published works, dissertations, and conference presentations reflect the state of our knowledge on MACOS For better or worse, methodological issues confine how we appreciate the impact MACOS had on teachers and learners. By examining this corpus of knowledge, we can better identify gaps in the literature that need additional study (Lipsey, 1994). An examination may also yield strengths, which stimulate meaningful curriculum projects that advance powerful social studies teaching and learning.

This chapter seeks to analyze key results and important attributes of all research conducted on the MACOS curriculum experiment from 1965–2008. Of particular interest were studies that examined the impact MACOS had on teachers and learners. Descriptive characteristics further examined in published works, dissertations, and conference presentations included: publication type, use of theory, type of research, methodologies used, and methodological quality. With this goal in mind, the first section is devoted to a description of the MACOS curriculum and provides a historical perspective for the chapter by detailing the rationale and theory behind the MACOS project. The second section describes the methods used to conduct the research synthesis. I then provide an overview of the research on MACOS by addressing the descriptive characteristics. From there, I focus on the guiding questions:

(a) What impact did MACOS have on teachers and learners?
(b) Did MACOS meet its overall goal?

To address each question, I evaluated empirical studies from three research categories, program evaluation, student attitudes, and student academic achievement. The fourth section discusses the results and couples gaps in the research with additional questions to identify directions for future research.

WHAT EXACTLY WAS MACOS?

This was progressive education, 1960's style ... I firmly believed that the curriculum was working, that the children were mastering the materials, and that we were witnessing the first intimations of a revolution in how children would come to understand the social and psychological world. (Howard Gardner, as cited by Dow, 1992, p. 166)

Gardner's statement signaled the promise of progressive education many curriculum specialist and researchers witnessed in MACOS. On one hand, MACOS is regarded as the most elegant, scholarly, and ingenious curricula ever produced (Herlihy, 1974; Posner, 1992). On the other, the curriculum is also regarded as one of the most disastrous attempts by the federal government to develop and design curriculum (Dow, 1992; Ross, 2000). The MACOS experiment, in a way, logically connected the content selected for study with the process of thinking. Based on Jerome Bruner's theories of learning and development, MACOS incorporated intuitive learning strategies for Grades 4–6. Bruner (1965) suggested that "The more 'elementary' a course and the younger its students, the more serious must be its pedagogical aim of forming the intellectual powers of those whom it serves" (p. 3). Through inquiry, learners could raise questions relative to man and his environment (Cort & Peskowitz, 1977b; Fraser, 1975; Wilson & Taylor, 1978). Such questions sought to explain social behaviors and customs across varying groups.

√   MACOS employed anthropology to compare the social and behavioral patterns of humans and animals in diverse settings. MACOS, Bruner (1965) suggested, embodied a curriculum where students could learn "wherein man is distinctive in his adaptation to the world, and wherein there is discernible continuity between him and his animal forbears" (p. 4). The course work consisted of 9 teacher's guides, 30 children's booklets, 16 films, 4 records, 5 filmstrips, 3 games, 44 artifact cards, 2 wall sized maps, a caribou hunting strategy chart, a kinship chart, a sea-ice camp chart, 11 enlarged photographs taken from the Netsilik films, several poster-sized photo murals, and a three-dimensional seal (Dow, 1991b; Latno, 1998). In their review of the course materials, Dynneson and Taylor (1972) noted that overall the films were superbly executed and very rich in ethnographic detail. They suggested, however, that all levels of education could incorporate the films easily.

By and large, MACOS illuminated the nature of humanness and of human behavior. Course objectives sought to:

1. To give our pupils respect for and confidence in the powers of their own mind.

2. To extend that respect and confidence to their power to think about the human condition, man's plight, and his social life.

3. To provide a set of workable models that make it simpler to analyze the nature of the social world in which we live and the condition in which man finds himself.

4. To impart a sense of respect for the capacities and humanity of man as a species.

5. To leave the student with a sense of the unfinished business of man's evaluation (Fraser, 1974).

Bruner, who wanted to include scholars and scientist in curriculum development, collaborated with anthropologists, biologists, and social psychologists to craft the discipline-based curriculum. This gave the project an air of scientific credibility. The specific content was selected based on the availability of usable materials from social science research, with heavy reliance on DeVore's study of baboons, Balicki's study of the Netsilik Eskimos, and Dr. Nikolaas Timbergen's study of herring gulls, among others (Posner, 1992). These eminent scientists contributed directly to the development of the curriculum. Course materials entered classrooms by September of 1969 (Latno, 1998). At its height, MACOS was in 1,700 schools in 47 states. Though problems existed with the project (Caputo, 1971; Hanley, Whitla, Moo, & Walter, 1970), both teachers and students enthusiastically received the curriculum. The American Educational Research Association (AERA) and the American Educational Publishers Institute cited the general excellence of the program. As such, both organizations presented Bruner with awards (Latno, 1998).

A Question of Man and His Nature

Three basic questions structured the curriculum: (1) What is human about humans (2) How did they get that way, and (3) How can they be made more human (Joyce, 1971). Bruner (1965) found that it was more useful to pose the three questions directly to students so that "their own views can be brought into the open and so that they can establish some points of view of their own" (p. 4). Questions helped students make reasoned inferences about the content—man. Students could form concepts as they began to sort different objects (ideas, events, etc.) that they observed or identified into a meaningful set of categories. Such classification permitted students to organize or arrange patterns out of their diversity. In general, the MACOS curriculum sought to have students respond to questions which required them to:

(a) Observe a situation (read a book, watch a film, listen to a recording, and so forth.
(b) Describe that which they have observed (list items);
(c) Find a basis for grouping those listed items which are similar in some respect;
(d) Identify the common characteristics of the items in a group;
(e) Label the groups they have formed;
(f) Subsume additional items that they have listed under those labels; and
(g) Recombine items to form new groups and to create even larger and more inclusive groups (Cole & Lacefield; 1980; Tredwell & Zodikoff, 1975).

Comparing and contrasting man with other groups served an integral part of the curriculum. Cognitive psychologist suggested that students did not comprehend individuals, ideas, objects, events, locations or characteristics clearly unless they compared and contrasted these phenomena in terms of their similarities and differences (Bruner, 1966a).

The first question, "What is human about humans?" addressed the characteristics of human beings. To expand on this topic, young learners considered other species in order to compare and contrast with the various behaviors of humans. Later in the curriculum, students reviewed another human culture, the Netsilik Eskimos. With the Netsilik, they applied these principles to a specific human setting (see Hanley et al., 1970b; see also Posner, 1992). The second question, on the other hand, dealt with the distinctive features of human adaptation to their environment. This was achieved to a large extent through the vehicle of culture. Young learners studied such concepts as acquired and innate behavior, natural selection, and adaptation. Through concept development, children developed comprehension of some of the forces influencing human behavior and human society (Bruner, 1966a; Cole & Lacefield, 1980).

The third question challenged children to integrate previously learned information to draw new conclusions. Related to the study of values, of self, and of humanity, this topic allowed children to engage in inquiry processes, such as defining a problem, formulating and testing hypotheses, and drawing conclusions. These processes were an integral part of the curriculum (Bruner, 1965). Like the other two topics, this topic question enabled children to state their own views. From there, students could subject their views to the challenge of an open forum discussion in the classroom. This was done for the purpose of bring to light students' own insights and perspectives (Lewis, 1976).

Key Anthropological Concepts That Structured MACOS

Tool-making, language, social organization, child-rearing practices, and world view were among the cultural behaviors expanded on throughout the curriculum. Why should learners explore these five areas? Bruner (1965) explained that:

> It has been our first lesson in teaching that no pupil, however, eager, can appreciate the relevance of, say, tool-making in human evolution without first grasping the fundamental concept of a tool or what a language is or a myth or social organization. These are not obvious matters. So we are involved in teaching not only the role of tools or language in the emergence of man, but as a necessary precondition for doing so, setting forth the fundamentals of linguistics or the theory of tools. (p. 4)

Tool-making represented a process by which human beings strengthen their capabilities and implemented their activities. This concept was studied particularly in the Netsilik Eskimo units to show how tools affect life, culture, and social organization (Bruner, 1965; Herlihy, 1974). For example, students observed how the Netsilik constructed specific tools to survive in their harsh environment. In this way, they developed a cross-cultural reference point. Most important, the Netsilik were not studied to see "primitive or uncivilized people. Their culture demonstrated how humanity met and adapted to the adversity of a particular surroundings (Lewis, 1976; Posner, 1992).

The study of language included consideration of what constituted communication. The concept was developed by distinguishing how humans and animals manage sent and received messages. All forms of communication were considered. Types of communication ranged from the tactile contacts of bees to facial mannerisms to literature. For example, one unit in the animal section dealt with baboon communication. Warning cries and even emotions were communicated. The students learned why some anthropologists believed that grooming was a form of communication and mutual respect. Learners then compared and contrasted the needs for baboon communication with the way the Netsiliks' harsh environment necessitated the generational transmission of survival information (Bruner, 1966a; Lewis, 1976; Posner, 1992).

Students discovered that social organization represented an important feature of both animal and human life. They realized that society is structured. The structure, however, is not fixed. It is an integrated pattern, and a change in one part of the pattern affects other parts—in fact, affects the whole of society. This social pattern establishes values and attitudes. The method of comparison and contrast was used again to help the child understand these ideas in new settings (baboon and Eskimos), where the children's own involvement would not lead them to accept views uncritically (Bruner, 1966a; Herilhy, 1974). In summarizing the facts gleaned from DeVore's field notes and the materials on the Netsilik students would then infer reasons for things happening as they did. They would identify similarities and differences. Students would then explain these similarities and differences and infer reasons for similarities and differences identified. Students would then state an inference or a conclusion which applies to both items under consideration.

✓ The general purpose for examining child-rearing practices was to examine the extent to which, and the way in which, offspring learned from their parents. Salmon, whose parents die before they are born, were contrasted with human beings, who have a long period of dependency. Students also studied the mechanisms by which baboons learn behaviors necessary to become good members of a troop and to keep their positions in this survival group (Fraser, 1974; Posner, 1992). Likewise, through the use of authentic ethnographic films utilizing only natural sounds, students observed the behavior of children in the Netsilik household. Through this comparison students learn the methods and procedures whereby children become acculturated.

The concept "world view" was used in MACOS to account for the human drive to explain the human condition and the world, and to devise ways to represent the world. MACOS explored art, myth, legend, and how cultures attempted to account for those elements of the world that people could not dominate. The curriculum taught that one kind of explanation is not more human than another (Maranda, 1965).

MACOS: A CURRICULAR (RE)EVOLUTION?

To frame the historical context from which the MACOS project emerged, I identified one seminal work as an "anchor" text. The curricular theory behind MACOS can be traced to the publication, *The Process of Education*. Written by Jerome Bruner, *The Process of Education* (1962) summarized the findings of the Woods Hole Conference (Evans, 2004). The National Academy of Sciences called the 10-day meeting to address concerns for the quality and intellectual aims of education. To meet the needs of rapidly changing world, 35 scientists, scholars, and educators discussed how to improve primary and secondary level science education. Their thoughts and ideas reflected a new spirit emerging from the scientific revolution at that time. Attendees, however, did not favor discarding citizenship development. For them, education served as a means to train well-balanced citizens for a democracy.

Overall, *The Process of Education* articulated an approach to curriculum design and development that fused a cognitive psychological perspective with specific content. Four ideas structured the text: (a) structure of the disciplines, (b) readiness of learning, (c) intuitive and analytic thinking, and d) motives for learning. The central premise, though, revolved around structure of the disciplines. Bruner (1962) asserted that (a) transfer of training and (b) transfer of principles and attitudes foster learning that serves us in the future. Transfer of training referred to the extension of habits or associations whereas transfer of principles and attitudes consisted of "learning initially not a skill but a general idea, which can be used as a basis for recognizing subsequent problems as special cases of the idea originally mastered" (p. 17). It was this type of transfer, though, that resided at the heart of education.

Transfer of principles and attitudes required mastery of the structure of a discipline (Bruner, 1962). In a sense, a person could not recognize the relevance of an idea to a new condition if he did not possess general understanding of the phenomenon.

When we understand the key concepts, principles/generalizations, and facts of a subject, we are better able to comprehend it. It is uneconomical to teach specific topics or skills without first situating them in the fundamental structure of a discipline. In the first place, such teaching makes it exceedingly difficult for the student to generalize from what he has learned to what he will encounter later. In the second place, learning that has fallen short of a grasp of general principles has little reward in terms of intellectual excitement. Bruner (1962) argued that detail should be placed in a structured pattern. If not, it would be rapidly forgotten. Understanding key concepts, principles/generalizations, and facts leads to adequate "transfer of training. Bruner suggested that:

> To understand something as a specific instance of a more general case—which is what understanding a more fundamental principle or structure means—is to have learned not only a specific thing but also a model for understanding other things like it that one may encounter. (p. 23)

Through a spiral curriculum, information presented in elementary and secondary classrooms would narrow the gap between advanced knowledge and elementary knowledge.

However, Bruner (1962) realized that constructing a curriculum based on the structure of the discipline would pose problematic. The first and most obvious problem was how to construct curricula that could be taught by ordinary teachers to ordinary students and that at the same time reflect clearly the basic or underlying principles of various fields of inquiry.

The second theme of the text dealt with the hypothesis that any subject could be taught to any child at any stage of development. A bold hypothesis, this position suggested that curriculum be built around "the great issues, principles, and values that a society deems worthy of the continual concern of its members" (Bruner, 1962, p. 25). From there, Bruner examined intuitive and analytic thinking. In teaching, emphasis upon the structure or connectedness of knowledge increases facility in intuitive thinking. Bruner suggested that, "A good intuiter may have been born with something special, but his effectiveness rests upon a solid knowledge of the subject, a familiarity that gives intuition something to work with" (pp. 56-57) For the most part, comprehension of structure facilitated learners to effectively deal intuitively with problems. The development of self-confidence and courage in the student advanced effective intuitive thinking. As for motives for learning, Bruner suggested that they are situated in arousing interest and must be kept broad and diverse in expression.

RELEVANCE OF BRUNER'S THEORY TO MACOS

So then, how did Bruner apply his theory to the MACOS project? In particular, one application Bruner's teaching and learning theory in the MACOS project signified the selection and use of teaching materials. Extensive use of a wide variety of media, such as booklets, films, sound recordings, and simulation games, broadened students' experiences. Teachers' guides recommended ways these materials could foster learners' ability to ask questions, comprehend concepts, and spawn a sense of discovery as they contemplated core questions (Barnes et al., 1981).

In addition, Bruner's idea of arranging concepts according to a spiral curriculum permeated MACOS (Bruner, 1965; Barnes et al., 1981; Fraser, 1974). The concepts of life cycle, parenting, innate and learned behavior, adaptation, language and communication, social organization, culture, environment, and values and belief systems were introduced in basic terms at first. After which, concepts were presented in more involved ways as learners investigated salmon, herring gulls, baboons, and finally, a human society—the Netsilik Eskimos (Barnes et al., 1981).

The MACOS curriculum epitomized progressive ideals inherent in social education. A product of the period, MACOS jettisoned a traditional behaviorist curricular approach for one steeped in cognitive psychology. While such an approach was en vogue at the time, it did raise concerns regarding evaluation. Specifically, Lowrie (1974) asserted that because MACOS course objectives were not listed in behavioral terms, the difficulty of evaluation increased. Such evaluation concerns, however, did not stem the tide for measuring the impact of MACOS on teachers and learners.

WHAT VALUE IS THERE IN SYNTHESIZING THE RESEARCH ON MACOS?

A research synthesis concentrates on empirical studies, where investigators engage in a disciplined inquiry in a systematic manner. It coherently summarizes past research by drawing overall conclusions from many separate investigations that address related or identical hypotheses. Systematically, the research synthesist expects to put forward the state of knowledge concerning a phenomenon. Such was the purpose of this chapter.

MACOS epitomized the curriculum reform movement of the 1960s. One of the most recognizable of the "New Social Studies" projects, MACOS related research findings and theory in education psychology to design and implement powerful instructional materials (Dow, 1975). What is, however, the validity of our knowledge on MACOS? Can we, as a field, describe the impact of MACOS on teachers and learners? My answer to each question is NO.

An ample body of research on the MACOS project exists. To my knowledge, no exhaustative review of the research on MACOS has appeared. In a nutshell, a paucity exists affirming a knowledge base for the project. What we know is confined to the several contemporary pieces that catalogue the sociopolitical context and curricular flaws that precipitated its decline. A research synthesis of MACOS findings is fruitful as it establishes a firm foundation for the state of our knowledge on MACOS. A solid foundation bolsters our conceptions of those theoretical and methodological issues that confined the project. Current discourses on MACOS colorfully describe the troubles and controversy surrounding the project. Unfortunately, these discussions have provided a one-dimensional perspective of how we come to know and understand this massive curricular project. Herein resides the problem.

METHODS

As stated in the introduction, this chapter seeks to unearth the impact of MACOS on teachers and learners. Two questions structured the review process. The guiding questions were:

(a) What impact did MACOS have on teachers and learners?
(b) Did MACOS meet its overall goal?

A method for review of MACOS research incorporated four phases: searching, reviewing, sorting, and confirming. This procedure ensured thorough classification of materials. Initially, the topic framed the review of MACOS research. No single database provided access to the full research corpus. As such, a number of databases were selected to offer access across the literature.

The searching phase included three steps. To start with, I conducted a broad search across three databases, Educational Resources Information Center (ERIC) database, PsycINFO, and Dissertation Abstracts International (DAI). Initially, my search sought all published and non-published works on MACOS. For this review, ERIC, PsycINFO, DAI supplied access to both published and non-published MACOS literature. Included were refereed journal articles, dissertations, conference proceedings, research reports, and U.S. Department of Education and contractor reports.[1] Every attempt was made to locate all relevant studies on MACOS.

Additional criteria, such as availability and relationship to the guiding questions, condensed the searches to a manageable size. The narrowed searched focused on refereed journal articles, dissertations, conference presentations of research, and research and evaluation reports of federally and privately funded programs. To ensure that established researchers in the field were represented, I developed a cross-checking analysis approach. A cross-checking analysis approach also provided a way to ensure the degree to which each database presented convergent results as well as unique results. In addition, I contrasted materials that listed research presentations, along with names of contributors identified from reference lists. This second level of the search led to the identification of 50 potential references.

The second phase consisted of reviewing the documents gathered to gain a comprehensive understanding of the MACOS project. Sorting the documents, the third phase, was undertaken as a method for organizing the 50 published and non-published works. This process produced five general categories: (a) single program descriptions that included evaluation reports, (b) issues in measurement and research, (c) research-based advice for educators, program designers, and policymakers (d) historical interpretations, and (e) opinions/commentaries.

Descriptive Analysis

Research syntheses are valuable because they can facilitate the gathering of evidence and generate new evidence (Hall, Tickle-Degnen, Rosenthal, & Mostellar, 1994). Descriptive analysis offers an indispensable portrait of the nature of the MACOS research literature. First, it identifies the issues that have already been sufficiently studied and those gaps in the literature that need additional study. Second, it brings into relief common methodological practices and provides a basis for assessing he areas in which improvement is warranted.

Coding Schema. Each work was coded for its descriptive characteristics: The country of the first author, the affiliation of the first author (university, government agency, or nongovernmental organization), publication date, and the research question of the work.

Publication type. Publications were reviewed to determine whether they fell into one of three mutually exclusive categories (give the constructs): a research study, a program description, or a commentary or opinion papers. Research studies were defined as those articles that included original data collection and analysis, secondary data analysis, or reviews of published literature. Works coded as program descriptions illustrated a promotion or synopsis of the MACOS curriculum. Opinion papers were defined as brief presentations of a point of view with limited or no references.

Use of theory. Works were reviewed to determine whether they used a theory or theoretical model to drive their research. Works could receive one of four codes: no theory or theoretical constructs used; use of one theory as the basis of their article/research; use of multiple theories. All articles marked as using theory also were coded as whether it was the original presentation of the theory or theoretical model to explain the MACOS experiment.

Type of research. Those articles identified as research studies were further coded to assess whether they were an empirical study, rhetorical study, or a review. Empirical studies included work that described a research study and presented findings using either qualitative or quantitative data. Rhetorical studies included critical and historical research. Reviews were those works that summarized published research using extensive references but with no original data presented.

Methodology used in empirical research. Additional coding was done on those works defined as empirical. All were classified according to the methodology used in the work. In the case where more than one method was used, I identified the primary method and reported this for the classification. Quantitative methods coded included the following: experimental or quasi-experimental design; surveys or interviews discourse analysis observation; (that were not part of an experimental or quasi-experimental); content analyses; meta-analysis, and studies that focused on scale/metric development or methodological testing. Additional descriptive characteristics coded included the year of publication and the duration of research study (to determine if short-term and long term studies resulted in different findings, and methodological quality of study (to determine if quality of study resulted in different findings).

RESULTS OF REVIEW

What is the history of research on *Man: A Course of Study*? The answer to this question is a complicated one; various published and non-published works have measured the impact of MACOS, detailed its curricular objectives, and articulated why the project failed. Yet, there exist no known attempts to synthesize the research on MACOS curriculum. With this in mind, there are two objectives for this section. First, I outline the descriptive characteristics associated with all ($n = 50$) MACOS research reviewed for this synthesis. The research reviewed focused on MACOS from various perspectives. These perspectives included course description, program evaluation, impact on teachers and learners, and historical interpretations. To my knowledge, research has brought into relief the content of published works, dissertations and conference presentations on MACOS;

therefore, this section provides a constructive representation of the nature of the research literature. Each work was dissected to generate key results and assess what the field knows regarding the research on MACOS.

Descriptive Characteristics

Much of the research on MACOS peaks in 1975 and all but disappears by 1980. Contemporary research on MACOS, from 1980 to the present, is almost exclusively rhetorical in nature and does not examine the impact of the curriculum (e.g. Dow, 1991a, 1991b, 1992; Edelstein, 1987; Latno, 1998). That means studies focused on critical or historical perspectives of the curriculum rather than impact on teachers and learners. Moreover, the majority of the research oriented MACOS literature was empirical in nature (e.g. Barnes et al., 1981; Cole & Lacefield, 1980; Cort & Peskowitz, 1977; DeNike, 1975; Fanthorpe & Longstaff, 1975; Fraser, 1975; Hanley et al., 1970, 1970b, 1970c; Holmes & Davis, 1972). Empirically grounded MACOS research, then, utilized quasi-experimental or qualitative methods to ascertain: a) the impact of MACOS on teachers and learners and b) whether or not MACOS met its overall goal?

Typical methods used included surveys/questionnaires. Fanthorpe and Longstaff (1975), though, employed a case study approach to examine the intricacies of MACOS at one school The majority of the research selected for this synthesis were published works (journals, books, etc.). A review of unpublished works, particularly dissertations and conference meetings, suggested that notable findings on MACOS were present but not subjected to peer review. Tables 12.1 and 12.2 depict the descriptive analysis results of this research synthesis.

IMPACT ON TEACHERS AND LEARNERS

The second goal of this section is to excavate the impact MACOS had on teachers and learners, thus distinguishing whether or not the curriculum met its objectives. Because MACOS was driven by a structure of the disciplines and a cognitive psychological perspective, quasi-experimental studies sought to determine the impact MACOS had on thinking, reasoning, mental development, and perception.

Almost all of the empirical studies reviewed detailed the influence of MACOS on student attitudes and learning. Of the research studies that articulated the influence of MACOS on student attitudes and learning, more than half were classified as dissertations or conference meetings. These classifications forced a conservative interpretation of the results as

**Table 12.1.   Descriptive Characteristics of
MACOS Research**

Characteristics	Studies (n = 50)
Publication Type	
Published (journal, book, reports)	33
Unpublished (dissertations, conference meetings, etc.)	17
Research Studies	38
Opinions/Commentary	4
Program Description	8
Year of Publication	
≤ 1975	35
1976–1980	10
> 1980	5
Research Studies (n = 38)	
Type:	
Empirical	28
Rhetorical	10
Reviews	0
Methods Used	
Survey/Questionnaire	25
Case Study	1
Mixed	2
Use of Theory	4

the unpublished data may not have received a thorough review (as compared to refereed journal articles).

Each of the "impact on learners" oriented studies reviewed were, in essence, attempts to legitimize MACOS. Each study challenged the criticisms aimed at the project. Some researchers utilized comprehensive (large scale) and or longitudinal investigations. Every attempt was made to gather empirical research published in peer reviewed, scholarly journals. However, this proved to be a difficult task. For the sake of space, all studies reviewed for this synthesis were not included in the following subsections. Those listed are meant as a representative sample of studies reviewed. This representative sample highlights methodological issues pertaining to MACOS research as well as overall findings.

**Table 12.1.   Selected Student Impact Studies:
Research Questions and Methodology Used**

Author(s) (Year)	Research Questions	Methodology
Barnes et al. (1981)	What is the influence of MACOS on the attitudes of children toward six practices: cruelty to animals, divorce, cannibalism, murder, senilicide, and female infanticide?	Measured attitudinal change of students toward the most objectionable practices associated with MACOS.
Tredwell and Zodikoff (1975) THE REFERENCE ENTRY HAS 1975 AS THE PUBLICATON YEAR.	What achievement changes occurred in fifth grade children after studying MACOS as their social studies curriculum?	Compared the academic achievement of MACOS and non-MACOS classrooms. Results were based on the "Sequential Tests of Education Progress (STEP): Social Studies.
Cole and Lacefield (1980)	What are the empirical effects of MACOS on fifth grade students as compared to the House of Ancient Greece (HOAG) curriculum and traditional social studies courses?	Measured the impact of a well-designed process curriculum on teacher and student attitudes and classroom behaviors as compared to another process curriculum and a traditional social studies curriculum. Results were based on upon national samples of MACOS and control classroom.
Wilson and Taylor (1978)	What effect did MACOS have on children's behavior as evidenced by their responses to selected statements?	Measured student response to selected statements. Results were based on no measures of behavior changes only on selected student responses.
Fraser (1975)	What impact did MACOS have on students' self-concept?	Measured a significant increase in motivation with the experimental group, particularly African American males
DeNike (1975)	To what extent does a students educational cognitive style (ECS) relate to learning from a simulation game?	Measured ECS to determine that those students likely to derive maximum cognitive knowledge from a simulation game also gathered information from listening and peer group interaction. Results were based on a small sample.

Impact on Student Attitude

MACOS impact on student attitudes have also been subjected to study. Fraser (1975) investigated the self-concept and motivation of students enrolled in MACOS. He then compared those results with students enrolled in traditional social studies classrooms. Seven-hundred and twenty-one MACOS students and 736 non-MACOS students in Atlanta public elementary schools participated in the survey. Participants were measured for total self-concept as a learner, motivation, task orientation, concept of themselves as problem solvers, and how they saw themselves in relation to other students in the class. Findings pointed toward a significant increase in motivation with the experimental group. Most important, the MACOS materials significantly affected African American students. Black males indicated that they were more motivated by the MACOS curriculum. Black students in the sixth grade perceived themselves as significantly better problem solvers and black males saw themselves as stronger members of a class.

Calvert (1970) though, examined whether fifth grade students developed more positive attitude toward social studies as the result of being introduced to MACOS. Students ranked their five major subjects in order of personal preference and in order of personal difficulty, and to circle descriptors which best reflected how they felt about social studies. Based on pre- posttests, students had a more positive "perceptual set" toward social studies and also increased their selection of positive terms toward social studies after having taken MACOS. Social studies courses markedly increased in popularity and declined as a subject of difficulty among both males and females, the magnitude of change being greater for males than females.

Cort and Peskowitz (1977b, 1977c) also found that MACOS students tended to express a more favorable attitude toward social studies. In their study, Cort and Peskowitz conducted a summative evaluation of MACOS. It focused on motivation and achievement of students using the MACOS curriculum. The major purpose of the 2-year study was to compare MACOS as it was taught in 57 fifth and sixth grade classes in 15 school districts with other social studies curricula taught in 51 comparison classes at the same grade levels. Classes selected for the study exhibited similar racial and socioeconomic characteristics, and were taught by persons with similar teaching experience.

Wilson and Taylor (1978) investigated the influence of MACOS on young minds and hearts. Specifically, they sought to determine the effect of MACOS on behavior's and attitudes as evidenced by their responses to selected statements. These researchers found that a profound study of a given culture did not significantly lead to more open attitudes toward culturally determined behaviors on a wider scale. Even when the study had results in more positive feelings toward that particular culture, it did not follow that these feelings generalized to all behaviors of that culture, or other cultures and behaviors. Students enjoyed the group work and pair work on projects, but the experience did not necessarily develop either an improved self-concept or a greater respect for their peers' contributions to class.

Barnes et al. (1981), though, investigated the influence of MACOS on the attitudes of children toward six practices: cruelty to animals, divorce, cannibalism, murder, senilicide, and female infanticide. Ninety-five fourth grade students from one suburban school in a southeastern city participated in the study. Most of the students were predominantly White, with an approximate equivalent numbers of males and females. Findings indicated no significant attitudinal change of children toward cruelty to animals, divorce, murder, senilicide, and female infanticide when each of these topics was tested separately or when they were grouped together. The MACOS group did, however, seem slightly more tolerant of "repugnant" activities than did the non-MACOS group.

Impact on Student Learning

For academic achievement, some researchers found little to no significant difference between MACOS and non-MACOS classrooms. Tredwell and Zodikoff (1975) investigated achievement changes that occurred in fifth grade students using the social studies curriculum program MACOS. The experimental group consisted of 103 students in MACOS classrooms. The control group was comprised of 103 students in classrooms that used a traditional social studies curriculum. Based on their findings, Tredwell and Zodikoff (1975) suggested that students did not suffer by using innovative, inquiry-oriented curriculum. They encouraged teachers to incorporate the MACOS project in their classrooms. Holmes and Davis (1972), for example, found that sixth grade students who participated in MACOS did not differ significantly in creativity nor in the achievement of social studies skills as measured by the "Sequential Tests of Education Progress (STEP): Social Studies." A pattern, however, emerged from the data that indicated the MACOS materials may produce greater verbal creativity.

Cort and Peskowitz (1977c) findings also indicated similarity between MACOS and non-MACOS groups of classes on generalized tests of social studies and inquiry skills, and differences on tests that were curriculum specific. Findings pointed out that MACOS students scored significantly higher than non-MACOS students on the MACOS-specific posttest; scored similarly on more generalized tests of social studies skills; learned more about facts and terms than abstract concepts; and tended to like social studies more than non-MACOS students. Analysis of tallies of data from interviews indicated that teachers in both groups had problems working with groups of students and felt that additional inservice training would be helpful. Although students developed similar social studies skills, inquiry skills, and attitudes toward other cultures in both MACOS and non-MACOS classes, MACOS students tended to express a more favorable attitude toward social studies.

Few MACOS studies investigated the impact of simulations/games on learners. DeNike (1975), though, conducted an exploratory study to determine if a student's educational cognitive style (ECS) related to learning from a simulation game. With a sample of 24 fifth grade students, DeNike divided students into two groups. Each group participated in two simulation games from the social studies curriculum Man a course of study. Group 1 played three rounds of the bow and arrow hunting game, followed by the crossing place hunting game. Group 2 played the games in reverse order. Knowledge gain was measured by identical pre- posttests. After the gaming, an ECS test was administered to all participants. ECS elements were classified as to their frequency within the high-or low-achieving student groups. Results indicated that those students likely to derive maximum cognitive knowledge from a simulation game were those who gathered information by listening, preferred peer group interaction, and tended to reason on the basis of rules. Students who tend to receive the least benefit from games derived information from both reading and listening and prefer independent activities.

Impact on Teachers

Teaching is a mediated activity, where race, gender, and historicity produce particular consequences and conditions (Johnson, 2007). Teachers deliberately alter their curricular and instructional practices to create new knowledge based on their race, gender, and historicity. Based on their experiences as both students and educators, teachers enact a curriculum that produces doubt about assertions of knowledge, whether some opinions are treated as facts while other opinions are discounted as unworthy of consideration (Ross, McCutheon, & Cornett, 1992). Such teacher beliefs and attitudes probably impacted the type and extent of MACOS instruction made available to students.

In terms of curricular development, the MACOS project excluded the ideas and perspectives of teachers. The scholars and scientists who created and championed the MACOS endeavor assumed that teachers would serve as "active implementers" (Ross, 2001). As active implementers, teachers are assumed to have a bearing on the implementation of curricular ideas. There is, however, no space at the curriculum planning table for teachers! Curriculum developers style implementation strategies aimed at "helping" teachers understand the curricular project. The MACOS project served as an exemplar of this role for the teacher. Teachers were viewed as active implementers but not as full partners in the creation of the curriculum. Strategies for promoting the use of the MACOS materials focused on preparing teachers to faithfully implement the developers' curricular ideas.

Review of relevant research demonstrated issues and concerns associated with teacher as "active implementer" of MACOS. Bumstead (1970) argued that teachers and students failed to comprehend the major concepts associated with the curriculum. His analysis reported that students often did not have sufficient grasp of the MACOS concepts in that they had no "utility beyond the subject under study." One explanation, he countered, represented the difficulty teachers encountered when comprehending the MACOS concepts—therefore they would be generally unaware of the student's comprehension of the concepts.

Caputo (1971) evaluated MACOS curriculum in the Florida Migrant Compensatory Program. Seven of 14 self-contained fifth and sixth grade classrooms were taught by National Science Foundation Institute trained teachers and 7 were taught by teachers trained in local schools' in-service workshops. Significant gains in achievement on the Man and other Animals unit were obtained by students taught by both groups of trained teachers. The pretest was an initial reading comprehension score, and the post test a recall of information score. There was a significant increase in mean post-test scores on Man and other Animals unit. Girls scored better on the pretest and boys on the posttest, though not significantly.

Students taught by teaches trained in the National Science Foundation summer institutes failed to make significant gains over students taught by teachers trained in in-service workshops.

Attitudinal changes were measured for four concepts, ARCTIC, ESKIMO Families, Cooperation, and American families by pre- posttest differences on the Netsilik Semantic Differential Scale. There was no significant change in pre-post semantic results. Male students showed a significant positive attitudinal shift toward the concept of COOPERATION.

An analysis of student attitudinal changes with teacher training differences revealed that students of in-service workshop trained teachers changed their attitudes toward American families, though not significantly, and students of National Science Foundation summer Institute teachers had no significant shifts toward cooperation.

Summarizing the study, Caputo (1971) concluded that the MACOS curriculum can be taught successfully without requiring teachers to attend summer institute training programs. Teachers can feel confident of adequate success in teaching MACOS by studying the teacher's manuals and handbook.

A typical example of an evaluation that investigated learning gains, learning problems, and pedagogical climate related to the elementary school social studies curriculum MACOS is Hanley et al. (1970a, 1970b, 1970c). The four volume report summarized the project's development and objectives, specified evaluation questions, utilized various data sources and analysis techniques, and provided information for how the evaluation could improve the MACOS experience. Findings indicated that MACOS teachers were more open with their students than were other teachers and that MACOS lessons were more often aimed at conceptual development than non-MACOS lessons were. Teachers stressed that working with MACOS made them understand the importance of active listening, communicating, observing, sharing in group exchanges, and expressing ideas orally. In addition, films, stories of other cultures, and simulation games were closely associated with high student interest in MACOS and with increased knowledge about subjects covered in the MACOS curriculum.

My examination raised a number of issues and questions. For example, research findings did not conclusively suggest a significant impact on learners' attitudes or academic achievement. In essence, the research on learners' impact represented a mixed bag. Some empirical studies were conducted by researchers with ties to project. This brought into question issues of objectivity and conflict of interest. Moreover, I noticed a peak in empirical research between 1975 and 1976. Why was there a peak in empirical research at this point? Did it have anything to do with responding to those critics who charged the curriculum as being anti-American?

METHODOLOGICAL QUALITY

Because the majority of research studies on MACOS focused on quasi-experimental design. It was important to focus on methodological quality. Methodological quality deals with the issues and criteria for assessing worth in the primary studies that comprise this research synthesis. Methodological quality was determined by using Campbell and Stanley's typology of experimental and quasi-experimental research. The validity of a study reflects to the accuracy of the results. How confident are we that what we have seen is what is really happening? Can we actually attribute the changes observed to participation in the program? While the issue of validity can be technical and highly complex, the principal concerns of validity are straightforward and must be considered in every investigation.

There are two threats to validity: internal and external. Internal validity means that the changes observed in the dependent variable are due to the effect of the independent variable, not to some other unintended variables (known as extraneous variables, alternative explanations, or rival hypotheses). If extraneous variables are controlled, the results can said to be due to the treatment, and therefore the study is internally valid. External validity refers to the degree to which the findings can be generalized to other settings.

Campbell and Stanley (1966) identified eight extraneous variables that can threaten internal validity.

1. History: events that happen during the course of the study that can influence the results
2. Maturation: biological or psychological changes in the participants during the course of the study
3. Testing: becoming "test-wise" by having taken a pretest that is similar to the post-test
4. Instrumentation:
5. Statistical Regression: The movement of posttest scores toward the mean, independent of any treatment effect
6. Differential Selection: results of the study may be due to group differences, not necessarily to the treatment or the independent variable
7. Experimental Mortality
8. Interaction Effects: produce effects which may be mistaken for the effect of the treatment variable

Campbell and Stanley (1966) identified four threats to external validity:

1. Reactive or Interaction Effects of Testing: the sensitization effects of pretesting which may cause the results obtained from the treatment groups to be different from what would have been obtained.
2. Interaction of Selection and Treatment: the results observed in the treatment group are due in part to selection biases.
3. Reactive Effects of Experimental Arrangements: the experimental environment is so different from the real world that generalization is not possible.
4. Multiple Treatment Interference: occurs when multiple treatments are applied to the same cases.

Of those research studies examined, the most frequent outcome measures assessed student and teacher attitude toward MACOS. Attitude change was a program goal and important to assess. It was, nonetheless, too often used at the exclusion of other outcome measures. This was problematic because attitude measures are often easily influenced by social pressure to support program initiatives. Moreover, expressed attitudes can be quite inconsistent with actual behavior. Sometimes, the evaluation of student change is assessed by teacher perceptions of the students. Admittedly, measuring most psychological and social concepts that have broad, real-world meaning in student populations is difficult. However, this difficulty is increased dramatically when researchers assess outcomes in one population (e.g. students) using the perceptions of others who might have different goals, motives, and experiences (e.g., curriculum developers, scholars, and teachers). Such is the problem when attempting to measure difficult to observe constructs such as motivations and attitudes.

Many of the research studies used a quasi-experimental, pre/post test design using a treatment group and control group, and MACOS as the treatment. A pre- posttest design controlled for differential selection and mortality somewhat by the use of a pretest. What was not provided, however, were statements concerning how history or specific events, such as MACOS adoption and community concerns with the curriculum, influenced the results or in this case interpretation of the results. Moreover, few studies articulated whether a difference existed between the pre- and posttests.

Few, if any, indicators were given as to what specific steps were taken to ensure the treatment, MACOS, was implemented as planned. Investigators stated that MACOS classrooms engaged in the curriculum. But, how? This brought about questions arose concerning issues of treatment fidelity or treatment integrity. Were there differences associated with teacher implementation?

After review, several studies brought forth issues concerning methodological quality. For example, Tredwell and Zedikoff's (1975) raised concerns of treatment fidelity or treatment fidelity. In addition, no statements were given as to where the sample population emerged. There is no indication if two separate schools were part of the sampled population. Fraser's (1975), who controlled for reading level and IQ, investigation appeared sound as he accounted for differential selection, experimental mortality, and instrumentation; I could not account for whether Fraser controlled for experimental treatment diffusion or compensatory rivalry by the control group. DeNike (1974) utilized a low sample population, which raised issues of external validity. Buckley et al. (1981), Cole and Lacefield (1980), and Cort and Peskowitz (1977) were examples of were threats to validity were little or nonexistent.

Another concern with the several of the studies represented the possibility of a conflict of interest on the part of the researchers. Hanley, in particular, as well as others either aided in the curriculum development for the project or received funding from the National Science Foundation. Of the studies covered in this review 80 per cent were supportive the MACOS curriculum. For example, Cole and Lacefield (1980) and Wilson and Taylor (1978) sought to use their findings to quiet the criticisms associated with MACOS.

DISCUSSION

If the science of social studies teaching and learning is to meet new challenges, we must systematically forge ahead. Part of making progress entails examining questions related to our collective past. The synthesized research on MACOS allows us to construct a profile of the typical work on the topic. It is an empirical study, more likely to use a quasi-experimental design, rather than naturalistic inquiry methods. It probably is not driven by theory. It was published or presented in or before 1975. The research question focused on the influence of MACOS on learners' attitudes and/or academic achievement.

Whether and how MACOS impacted learners' attitudes and/or academic achievement produced a mix bag. Findings indicated that some populations displayed slightly significant increases in achievement as compared to their non-MACOS counterparts. On average, learners in MACOS classrooms fared no better than their counterparts in non-MACOS classrooms. The findings do not suggest, however, that MACOS learners outperformed their non-MACOS counterparts. This suggests that MACOS, despite intense government and scholarly involvement did not shift student thinking or knowledge acquisition. This could be due to the convoluted nature of the curriculum and the use of teachers as active implementers.

It is of interest, however, that African American students, particularly males (Fraser, 1974, 1975) responded favorably to the MACOS curriculum. This review indicated that MACOS, a largely process oriented curriculum engaged African American students. Whether because of its focus on culture or its focus on inquiry, one thing is certain. This opens up a great deal of discussion when it comes to educating black students. The field should consider the benefits of a process oriented curriculum on the learning styles of African American students

Findings indicated that MACOS did positively influence students' attitudes towards social studies. Students were given the opportunity to engage in a "novel" curriculum that utilized various media and materials.

In addition, the evidence indicated that, despite their interest and support of the project, MACOS teachers had problems with implementation and knowledge acquisition of the content. Curriculum development is best when its local and emerges from the bottom up. When teachers have input there is ownership.

Simulations/role play stands as an important instructional tool in social studies. Simulations/role play promotes acquisition to knowledge, skills, and dispositions covered in social studies. Though there was little research on the internal dynamics of simulations/role play in MACOS classrooms, one study did find that students likely to derive maximum cognitive knowledge from a simulation game were those who gathered information by listening, preferred peer group interaction, and tended to reason on the basis.

A well-conceived curriculum is one in which the objectives are completely specified and met. The evidence suggests that several of the MACOS objectives were not met. Studies were inconclusive as to whether students left their MACOS classrooms with a sense of the unfinished business of man's evaluation. Wilson and Taylor's (1978) findings also suggest that the MACOS model did not provide a simpler way to analyze the nature of learners' social world. Some studies suggested that learners did gain a respect for and confidence in the powers of their own mind. But whether this new found respect and confidence led to a reevaluation of the human condition, man's plight, and his social life is left to question.

There may be two reasons why the research on the impact of MACOS on learners was mixed. First, there were several questions concerning methodological quality. Dissertations and conference proceedings did not go through a peer review process. Moreover, issues of design, particularly a pre-post test design created several questions related to validity. Second, several authors were attempting to demonstrate the legitimacy of MACOS. Study rationales included such statements as "to answer the critics' charges" and to "encourage to teachers to use an innovative, inquiry oriented curriculum. Such statements suggest that investigators positions may have influenced study design.

Moreover, findings call into question the inquiry dispositions and skills associated with social studies research. The state of our knowledge reflects the scientific progress of our field. This research synthesis suggests that because of mediocre and, to some extent, poor methodological quality, our comprehension of MACOS is limited to rhetorical perspectives. So, where do we go from here? I suggest that we plow further into the MACOS research in order to ascertain effect sizes. The summaries of the results of these studies, however, may not have been nearly as informative with respect to summarized significance levels or with respect to summarized effect sizes. It is worth noting that a meta-analysis of key MACOS studies might further unearth the complexities associated with the impact of MACOS on teachers and learners.

NOTE

1.   Studies used in the research synthesis are indicated with an asterisk*.

REFERENCES

*Arends, R. I. (1972). *A summative evaluation of "Man: A Course of Study": A study of its human effects*. Doctoral dissertation, University of Oregon, Eugene, Oregon. Retrieved February 10, 2008, from ProQuest Dissertations & Theses database (Publication No. AAT 7313722).

*Barnes, B., Stallings, W., & Rivner, R. (1981). Are the critics right about MACOS? *Theory and Research in Social Education, 9*(1), 35–44.

*Bruner, J. (1965). *Man: A course of study* (Occasional Paper No. 3, Social Studies Curriculum Program). Cambridge, MA: Educational Development Center, Inc.

*Bruner, J. (1966a). *Toward a theory of instruction*. Cambridge, MA. Harvard University Press.

*Bruner, J. (1966b). *The growth of mind* (Occasional paper no. 8, Social Studies Curriculum Program). Cambridge, MA: Education Development Center.

*Bruner, J. (1962). *The process of education*. Cambridge, MA: Harvard University Press.

*Bumstead, R. (1970). Man: A course of study. *Educate, 3*, 22–29.

Campbell, D. T., & Stanley, J. C. (1966). *Experimental and quasi-experimental designs for research*. Chicago: Rand McNally.

*Calvert, J. F. (1970). *Change in student perceptions of the "social studies" following the introduction of MACOS*. Syracuse, NY: Eastern Regional Institute for Education.

*Caputo, E. M. (1971). *The effects of "Man: A Course of Study," an experimental social science course, upon the achievement, attitudes, and anxiety of improverished children in selected Florida schools*. PhD dissertation, The Florida State University, Tallahassee, FL. Retrieved February 10, 2008, from ProQuest Dissertations & Theses database. (Publication No. AAT 7213493)

*Cohen, K. C. (1970). *An evaluation of the Iowa test score difference between six classes of students using the MACOS curriculum for a year and six classes receiving traditional instruction* (Project Social Studies). Cambridge MA: Education Development Center.

*Cole, H. P., & Lacefield, W. E. (1980, September). *MACOS: Its empirical effects versus its critics*. Paper presented at annual meeting of the American Psychological Association, Montreal, Quebec, Canada.

*Conlan, J. B., & Dow, P. B. (1975). The MACOS controversy. *Social Education*, 388–396.

*Cort, H. R. Jr., & Peskowitz, N. (1977a). *A longitudinal study of Man: A course of Study. Summary Report* (Social Studies Research Project). Washington, DC: National Science Foundation.

*Cort, H. R. Jr., & Peskowitz, N. (1977b). *A longitudinal study of Man: A Course of Study. Volume 1: Summary, background and design* (Social Studies Research Project, Final Report). Washington, DC: National Science Foundation.

*Cort, H. R. Jr., & Peskowitz, N. (1977c). *A longitudinal study of Man: A Course of Study. Volume 2: Quantitative results* (Social Studies Research Project, Final Report). Washington, DC: National Science Foundation.

*Cort, H. R. Jr., & Peskowitz, N. (1977d). *A longitudinal study of Man: A Course of Study. Volume 3: Interviews* (Social Studies Research Project, Final Report). Washington, DC: National Science Foundation.

*Cort, H. R. Jr., & Peskowitz, N. (1977e). *A longitudinal study of Man: A Course of Study. Volume 4: Appendices* (Social Studies Research Project). Washington, DC. National Science Foundation.

*Davis, Y. A. (1977). *The relationship between pupils' participation in "Man: A Course of Study" and their achievement in social studies*. EdD dissertation, University of California, Los Angeles, CA. Retrieved February 10, 2008, from ProQuest Dissertations & Theses database. (Publication No. AAT 7806467)

*DeNike, L. (1975, April). *An exploratory study of cognitive style as a predictor of learning from simulation games*. Paper presented at the meeting of the Association for Educational Communications and Technology Annual Convention, Dallas Texas.

*Dow, P. B. (1992). Past as prologue: The legacy of Sputnik. *Social Studies, 83*(4) 164–71.

*Dow, P. B. (1991a). *Schoolhouse politics: Lessons from the Sputnik ear.* Cambridge: Harvard University Press.

*Dow, P. B. (1991b). *MACOS and the Global Perspective.*

*Dow, P. B. (1975). MACOS revisited: A commentary on the most frequently asked questions about Man: A Course of Study. *Social Education, 388* 393–396.

*Dow, P. B. (1979). *Innovation perils: An account of the origins, development, implementation, and public reaction to "Man: A Course of Study."* EdD dissertation, Harvard University, Cambridge, MA. Retrieved February 10, 2008, from ProQuest Dissertations & Theses database. (Publication No. AAT 7927944)

*Duhs, L. A. (1979). MACOS/SEMP debate in Queensland, 1978: Some central issues. *Australian Journal of Education, 23*(3), 270–283.

*Dynneson, T. L., & Taylor, B. L. (1972). *The review of and reaction to selected anthropology projects by professional anthropologists.*

Evans, R. W. (2004). *The social studies wars: What do we teach the children?* New York: Teachers College Press.

*Falkenstein, L. C.(1977). *"Man: A Course of Study:" A case study of diffusion in Oregon*. PhD dissertation, Stanford University, California. Retrieved February 10, 2008, from ProQuest Dissertations & Theses database. (Publication No. AAT 7725661)

*Fanthorpe, D., & Longstaff, D. (1975). MACOS at one school. *Forum for the Discussion of New Trends in Education, 17*(2), 44–46.

Fenton, E. (1991). Reflections on the "New Social Studies." *Social Studies, 82*(3), 84–89.

*Fraser, L. A. (1975, November). *Effect of "Man: A Course of Study" on urban students' self concept as learners.* Paper presented at the meeting of the National Council for the Social Studies, Atlanta, GA.

*Fraser, L. A. (1974). *The effect of "Man: A Course of Study" materials and inservice activities on teacher attitudes and self-concept, knowledge, and thinking processes.* PhD dissertation, Georgia State University, GA. Retrieved March 17, 2008, from ProQuest Dissertations & Theses database. (Publication No. AAT 7423171)

*Gunnarsson, T. V. (1990). *Controlling curriculum knowledge: A documentary study of the Icelandic Social Science Curriculum Project (SSCP), 1974-1984.* PhD dissertation, Ohio University, OH. Retrieved March 17, 2008, from ProQuest Dissertations & Theses database. (Publication No. AAT 9024120)

*Hager, R. A. (1971). *Transfer effects of "Man: A Course of Study" (MACOS) to other elementary school subjects.* PhD dissertation, Michigan State University, Lansing, MI. Retrieved March 17, 2008, from ProQuest Dissertations & Theses database. (Publication No. AAT 7208680)

*Harrison, R. S. (1971). *Regional center for the improvement of instruction in elementary school social studies. Final Report* (Social Studies Research Project). Washington, DC: National Science Foundation.

Hall, J. A., Rosenthal, R., Tickle-Degnen, L., & Mosteller, F. (1994). Hypotheses and in research synthesis. In H. Cooper & L. V. Hedges (Eds.), *The handbook of research synthesis* (pp. 15–28). New York: Russell Sage Foundation.

*Hanley, J. P., Whitla, D. K., Moo, E. W., & Walter, A. S. (1970a). *Curiosity, competence, community, An Evaluation of Man: A Course of Study* (Project Social Studies). Cambridge, MA: Education Development Center.

*Hanley, J. P., Whitla, D. K., Moo, E. W., & Walter, A. S. (1970b). *Curiosity, competence, community, An evaluation of Man: A Course of Stud, a summary of the original Two-Volume edition* (Project Social Studies). Cambridge, MA: Education Development Center.

*Hanley, J. P., Whitla, D. K., Moo, E. W., & Walter, A. S. (1970c). *Man: A Course of Study: Evaluation strategies* (Project Social Studies). Cambridge, MA: Education Development Center.

*Herlihy, J. G. (1974). Man: A Course of Study, An exemplar of the new social studies. *Social Education, 38*(5), 442–443, 455.

*Holmes, J. L., & Davis, R. M. (1972). *A comparative study of the effects of a traditional social studies curriculum at the sixth grade level and "Man: A Course of Study." Final Report* (Regional Research Program). Washington, DC: National Center for Education Research and Development.

*Joyce, W. (1971). MACOS: A report from the inner-city. *Social Education, 35*(3), 305–309.

*Kraus, L. L. (1977). *Curriculum, public policy, and criticism: An analysis of the controversies surrounding "Man: A Course of Study."* PhD dissertation, The University of Texas at Austin, TX. Retrieved May 19, 2008, from Dissertations & Theses database. (Publication No. AAT 7722979)

*Latno, M. R. (1998). *Institutions under siege: The rise of the New Right and the 1975 congressional attack on the social sciences curriculum projects.* MA dissertation, California State University, Dominguez Hills, CA. Retrieved March 17, 2008, from ProQuest Dissertations & Theses database. (Publication No. AAT 1392125)

*Lewis, D. R. (1976). Anyone for MACOS? *Independent School, 36*(2) 40-43.

Lipsey, M. W. (1994). Identifying potentially interesting variables and analysis opportunities. In H. Cooper & L. V. Hedges (Eds.), *The handbook of research synthesis* (pp. 111–124)). New York: Russell Sage Foundation.

*Ludes, M. J. (1971). *A comparison of the cognitive emphasis of the intended and practiced questioning strategies employed in the Herring Gull unit of "Man: A Couse of Study."* EdD dissertation, State University of New York at Buffalo, NY. Retrieved May 19, 2008, from Dissertations & Theses database. (Publication No. AAT 7128817)

*Macfadyen, D. L. (1974). *A descriptive study of the implementation of "Man: A Course of Study" as revealed through ethnocentrism.* EdD dissertation, Michigan State University, Lansing, MI. Retrieved May 19, 2008, from Dissertations & Theses databases. (Publication No. AAT 7507206)

Massialas, B. G. (1992). The "New Social Studies: "Retrospect and prospect. *Social Studies, 3*, 120–124.

*Mazza, P. (1971). Social studies in the second generation. *Indiana Social Studies Quarterly, 24*(2), 32–35.

*Morgan, R. (1973). *Man: A Course of Study. Forum for the Discussion of New Trends in Education, 16*(1) 15–17.

*Otto, R. (1979, November). *Implications of Piaget's research for the inquiry process of learning.* Paper presented at the meeting of the National Council for the Social Studies, Portland, OR.

Ross, E. W. (2001). The struggle for the social studies curriculum. In E. W. Ross (Ed.), *The social studies curriculum: Purposes, problems, and possibilities* (pp. 19–42). Albany: State University of New York Press.

Ross, E. W., Cornett, J. W., & McCutcheon, G. (1992). Teacher personal theorizing and research on curriculum and teaching. In E. W. Ross, J. W. Cornett, & G. McCutcheon (Eds.), *Teacher personal theorizing* (pp. 3–18). Albany: State University of New York Press.

*Rocca, M. A., Jr. (1971). *A study of the effects of Man: A Course of Study on reading achievement at the intermediate-grade level.* EdD dissertation, The Pennsylvania State University, State College, PA. Retrieved January 9, 2008, from Dissertations & Theses database. (Publication No. AAT 7213920)

*Schaar, K. (1975). MACOS: The controversy continues. *APA Monitor, 6*(1), 5.

*Smith, R.A., & Knight, J. (1978). MACOS in Queensland: The Politics of educational knowledge. *Australian Journal of Education, 22*(3), 225–248.

Stock, W. A. (1994). Systematic coding for research synthesis. In H. Cooper & L. V. Hedges (Eds.), *The handbook of research synthesis* (pp. 125–139). New York: Russell Sage Foundation.

*Tredwell, L., & Zodikoff, D. (1975, December). *A study of the effects of Jerome Bruner's Man: A Course of Study on social studies achievement in fifth grade*. Paper presented at the Asian American Conference, University of Massachusetts.

*Walters, R. A. (1976). An investigation of the educational effects of "Man: A Course of Study." PhD dissertation, University of Missouri, Kansas City, MO. Retrieved January 9, 2008, from Dissertations & Theses database. (Publication No. AAT 7628350)

*Wilson, J. R. H. (1973). *An analysis of selected affective student response to an intermediate "Man: A Course of Study" program*. EdD dissertation, University of Colorado at Boulder, CO. Retrieved January 9, 2008, from Dissertations & Theses database. (Publication No. AAT 7323309)

*Wilson, J., & Taylor, B. L. (1978). The effects of MACOS on intermediate-grade children's attitudes. *Education, 98*(3) 359–364.

*Youngers, J. C. (1972). *A descriptive study of the cognitive emphases expressed in "Man: A Course of study" social studies classes*. EdD dissertation, The University of Rochester, NY. Retrieved January 9, 2008, from Dissertations & Theses database. (Publication No. AAT 7228816)

CHAPTER 13

AMERICAN POLITICAL BEHAVIOR

The Project and the People

Carole L. Hahn

In this chapter I tell the story of the development and diffusion of one of the most widely known projects of the New Social Studies, *American Political Behavior*. This is a personal story, as well as a historic case study. I worked with the program as a teacher, a researcher, and a graduate student assigned to help with its dissemination. In writing this chapter, I drew on project reports and I interviewed the project director, Howard Mehlinger, and the associate director, John Patrick. Both men are now professor emeriti at Indiana University and they have remained my friends and wise counselors for over 35 years. In this chapter I describe the history of *American Political Behavior,* known to many social studies educators as APB, and my experiences with it. I reflect on research conducted on APB at the height of the New Social Studies era and I compare the project to recent efforts to reform civic education.

THE DEVELOPMENT OF *AMERICAN POLITICAL BEHAVIOR*

On September 1, 1964, Indiana University Professor of Education Shirley Engle and Professor of Government Byrum Carter submitted a proposal to the U.S. Office of Education to establish the High School Curriculum Center in Government (HSCCG). After extended negotiations, the Center officially began work July 1, 1966. The primary purposes of the Center were:

1. To identify broad topics and problems in political science... and to select and present topics suitable for study in junior and senior high school courses in civics and government;
2. To develop materials and teaching procedures which would incorporate the most recent findings in political science, psychology, and education. (Engle & Carter, 1965)

The project proposal listed additional objectives including: familiarizing students with the process of developing and testing hypotheses pertaining to the political world; enabling students to handle questions of public policy; and encouraging university scholars in the social sciences to work with high school teachers in the development of a social studies program. These objectives, while focusing on political science, were similar to those of many other projects of the New Social Studies that emphasized other social sciences.

The Developers

In May 1966 the HSCCG advisory board invited Dr. Howard Mehlinger to be the director of the HSCCG. Soon after that the board hired a graduate student in Indiana University's School of Education, John Patrick, to be a half-time graduate research assistant on the project. Later Patrick became associate director of the HSCCG. Although other people worked on the 5-year project, these two individuals were responsible for turning the general objectives in the proposal into the unique curriculum project *American Political Behavior*. The two men had come to the project as experienced high school social studies teachers and curriculum writers.

Mehlinger was born and spent his early years in Marion, Kansas, a small farming community. After completing his freshman year in high school, his family moved to McPherson, Kansas, where he graduated from high school in 1949 and subsequently attended McPherson College, a small Brethren Church related college. His junior year he began dating a young woman, Carolee, who grew up in McPherson. They were married in 1952 and he graduated from college in 1953. Mehlinger began his career teaching high school world history to sophomores at Lawrence High School in Lawrence, Kansas from 1954–1963. In addition to teaching world history, he taught a course in American government and one on the modern history of China and Japan to gifted seniors. He also served as an assistant coach in football, basketball, and track at various times. While teaching at Lawrence, Mehlinger completed an MS degree in education and began working on a PhD in Russian history at the University of Kansas. Years later he recalled that his goal in pursuing a PhD had been "to be the best prepared world history teacher I could be" (H. Mehlinger, personal communication, January 12, 2008).

In 1963, Mehlinger, his wife Carolee, and their two young children, Brad and Barbara, left Kansas for Pittsburgh, Pennsylvania where he had accepted a job as co-director of one of the earliest and most widely known New Social Studies projects, the Carnegie Mellon project, directed by Ted Fenton. Having been hired for the co-director position by the Pittsburgh Schools, during the day Mehlinger taught two high school world history classes and wrote and edited lessons for the course *Comparing Political Systems*; at night he worked on his dissertation in Russian history (H. Mehlinger, personal communication, January 12, 2008). Mehlinger later explained that he brought from that experience to his later work with *American Political Behavior* not only experience developing curriculum, but also a desire to use greater variety in lesson types than were used by the Carnegie Mellon Project, a commitment to working as an equal partner with John Patrick, and a recognition that he and Carolee felt more at home in a Midwestern university town than an eastern city (H. Mehlinger, personal communication, January 12, 2008).

After 1 year, in Fall 1964, Mehlinger left Pittsburgh, with his completed PhD and his family that now included a third child, Susan. He went to work for James (Jim) Becker on the North Central Association of Schools and College's Foreign Relations project, based in Chicago. The project staff sought to stimulate interest in teaching about American foreign relations in secondary schools by writing curriculum and conducting professional development workshops for teachers throughout the Midwest. After less than a year with Becker's project Mehlinger accepted another job and in June, 1965, moved his family once again—this time to Bloomington, Indiana, which became home for more than 40 years. He had accepted a "soft money" job as deputy chairman of the Inter-University Committee on Travel Grants. The Committee on Travel Grants handled the academic exchanges of faculty and advanced graduate students from universities across the country with universities in the USSR, Bulgaria, Hungary, and Czechoslovakia. Previously Mehlinger had published a book of readings for high school students entitled *Communism in Theory and Practice* and in 1966 he was completing a teachers' guide on teaching about totalitarianism for the National Council of the Social Studies (NCSS) (Engle, Mehlinger, & Patrick, 1972).

John Patrick, like Howard Mehlinger, had both teaching and writing experience before working on *American Political Behavior.* John Patrick lived in East Chicago, Indiana, from the time he was 8 years old. After graduating from Roosevelt High School (RHS) in East Chicago, he attended Dartmouth College, and subsequently returned to teach civics and U.S. history at RHS (1958–1962), his alma mater. In the fall of 1962, Patrick began a new job teaching eighth grade U.S. history at the University of Chicago Laboratory School, where Gerald Marker and Robert Hanvey (later widely known for writing *An Attainable Global Perspective*) were also teaching. While teaching in East Chicago, Patrick had been enrolled in an MA program (completed 1961) at Indiana University, Bloomington, when he met Dr. Fred Smith, a professor of social studies education. Later, at the University of Chicago Lab School Patrick got to know professors Mark Krug, Byron Massialas, and Bob Hanvey, who were faculty members at the University of Chicago's Graduate School of Education, and whose student teachers worked in the Lab School. Massialas had received his doctorate from Indiana University, under the direction of Professor Shirley Engle, while working with C. Benjamin Cox, Jack Cousins, and R. T. Elsmere on the Indiana Studies in Inquiry Project. Patrick (2008) later recalled that he first met Howard Mehlinger in the Fall of 1964, when Marker and Patrick attended professional development workshops sponsored by the North Central Association's Foreign Relations project. Mehlinger then learned that Patrick had used his book on Communism with students at the Lab School and was interested in making a visit to see Patrick teach, which he subsequently did. Patrick (J. Patrick, personal communication, May 28, 2008) explained, "so we already were acquainted before I went to IU to begin my doctoral work."[1]

For several years Fred Smith had been trying to recruit Patrick to Indiana University's doctoral program in social studies, but Patrick was newly married to his wife, Pat, and felt a need to continue earning his teaching salary. He did work with Smith one summer coordinating a program to encourage high school students to go on to college and become teachers. Gerald Marker left the Chicago Lab School for Bloomington in 1964 (to replace Jack Lunstrum as the Coordinator for School Social Studies, housed in the College of Arts and Sciences). Patrick, as well as Mehlinger, moved to Bloomington a year later. Patrick (J. Patrick, personal communication, May 28, 2008) recalled that he first learned about the proposed project for a High School Curriculum Center in Government from Byron Massialas, as Massialas wrote the project proposal and had hoped to return to Indiana to direct it. In the meantime, however, while the U.S. Office of Education was negotiating with Indiana University, Massialas was offered and accepted a tenure-track appointment at the University of Michigan. As a result, Patrick explained, the project was "on ice" for 1 year. Engle had other commitments and did not want to be the project director, but he also did not want to return the grant. By Spring 1966, Mehlinger agreed to leave his position with the University Travel Grants position to be the director of the HSCCG; he hired Patrick as his graduate research assistant on the project.

Patrick, like Mehlinger, was not only an experienced social studies teacher, but also a published author. He had written a book on African American history targeted to high school libraries and adolescent readers, titled *Progress of the Afro American*. He also wrote a review of high school civics textbooks titled "Civics: Relating Social Study to Social Reality," which became a chapter in the book *Social Studies in the United States* edited by Cox and Massialas.

The Development Process

In the summer of 1966, when Mehlinger and Patrick were to start work on the HSCCG project, Mehlinger had to complete an earlier commitment he had made to visit West German research institutes specializing on the Soviet Union. Before leaving he suggested to Patrick that he see what he could find out about research on political socialization—some of which had been cited in the HSCCG proposal. When Mehlinger returned from Germany, he found that Patrick's review "was so good" that they decided to publish it as the first occasional paper of the new HSCCG (H. Mehlinger, personal communication, January 12, 2008). Subsequently, they offered the manuscript to NCSS, which published it as a research bulletin (Patrick, 1967) and as an article in the NCSS journal *Social Education* (Engle, Mehlinger, & Patrick, 1972; Patrick, 1969a). Thus, the first product of the HSCCG was a synthesis of research on political socialization, which became the foundation for the research-based curriculum development project *American Political Behavior*. That summer of 1966 Mehlinger and Patrick also asked a government professor, Leroy Reiselbach to talk to them about the new behavioral approach to politics that was gaining much attention in political science. Professor Reiselbach agreed to write a paper that became the third of the Center's occasional papers; Mehlinger wrote the second occasional paper on designing the APB course (Engle et al., 1972; H. Mehlinger, personal communication, January 12, 2008).

In the early months of the project, Mehlinger and Patrick made the decision to develop a 9th grade course first, postponing the development of a 12th grade course until later. The first part of the course would center on the role of individuals as citizens—what citizens actually do (as opposed to the moralizing of traditional textbooks). The second part would focus on formal roles, including the role of the President, Congressional representatives, and Supreme Court justices (see the Appendix for Table of Contents).

Mehlinger later recalled that the first 6 months, he and Patrick spent conceptualizing the project; they "would talk, write, argue, and share ideas" (H. Mehlinger, personal communication, January 12, 2008). In the 1967–68 year they wrote the lessons. Patrick (J. Patrick, personal communication, May 28, 2008) recalled that he took the lead in writing the lessons for units 1 through 3 and Mehlinger took the lead for Units 4 and 5. "Both of us interacted with each other in doing our primary tasks," editing each other's early drafts. Patrick emphasized that he learned much about good writing style from Mehlinger, who was a good "wordsmith." He explained that they developed a true "writing partnership" and noted that because of their close interaction, they were able to achieve a comprehensive tone and style throughout the program.

In the Fall of 1966 an incident occurred in Terre Haute, Indiana, which they thought had the potential for a case study. To make the point that the American flag, despite it's power as a symbol, was only a piece of fabric, a professor at Indiana State University (ISU) burned an American flag. Subsequently, a high school teacher in the town of Bloomfield referred to the flag burning incident in his class, for which he was fired. Mehlinger decided to spend several days in Bloomfield gathering information for a case study, which he later recalled was the first of several original case studies that became an innovative feature of the course (H. Mehlinger, personal communication, January 12, 2008).

By the Spring of 1968, Mehlinger and Patrick were running out of time, so they hired others to help them write unit 5 on unofficial political experts, the media, and political party leaders (H. Mehlinger, personal communication, January 12, 2008).[2] In the summer of 1968 they conducted a workshop to train 40 pilot teachers to use the experimental version of APB in the 1968–69 academic year.

An important and often overlooked aspect of *American Political Behavior* was the carefully planned and executed formative evaluation of the project (Mehlinger & Patrick, 1971). First, a panel of political scientists reviewed the content of the experimental version and social studies specialists reviewed the pedagogical strategies and sequencing of lessons. Second, teachers administered multiple-choice type tests at the end of each instructional sequence, approximately every 2 weeks. Third, the teachers completed a questionnaire at the end of each instructional sequence. Fourth, at the end of the pilot, in June 1969, the developers met with about half of the teachers in a 3-day meeting to debrief the year's experience. Finally, and perhaps most unusually, John Patrick taught the course to a ninth-grade class at a local school to obtain first-hand impressions of strengths and weaknesses in the course. Mehlinger and Patrick made revisions in the course based on the feedback they received from these multiple sources. As a result, they asserted that by 1971, "the course *American Political Behavior* is a far different course today than the one used by the 40 pilot teachers" (Mehlinger & Patrick, 1971, p. 892).

After the initial years of development and pilot testing, Mehlinger and Patrick worked with a film company to develop four instructional films that drew upon APB course content, including one on The Role of the Congressman. Judy Gillespie joined the project to develop simulations and games for APB. Also during this period, John Patrick and Gerald Marker wrote their doctoral dissertations on APB. Patrick (1969b) examined the effects of the course on students' political knowledge, skills, and attitudes and Marker (1970) examined the association between APB teachers' levels of dogmatism and student attitudes. Near this time the Center staff was also busy securing a publisher for APB. One of the conditions of the U.S. Office of Education (USOE) funding the HSCCG was that when curriculum development (including evaluation) was complete, the project would be published by a commercial publisher and the royalties would be divided between Indiana University and the USOE. Consequently, the HSCCG invited publishers to submit proposals to publish the program. Three publishers competed for the contract, which was granted to Ginn and Company for a 5-year period; after 5 years, the materials would be in the public domain and could be used by anyone free of charge.

The Completed Project

Over the life of the project three slightly different versions of the program were produced. The first, or experimental, version was used by approximately 100 pilot teachers and 10,000 students during 3 years of field tests (1968–71). That version was the basis for the summative evaluation of the project and the dissertations written by Marker and Patrick. The second version was the first edition published by Ginn and Company in 1972. It was published as a single hardback textbook (black cover showing a display of campaign buttons) designed for a year-long course. It was also published in two soft back textbooks (yellow and black covers), which could be used separately for single-semester courses. Both hard and soft covered books contained sepia toned drawings. Mehlinger (in press) later wrote that the 1972 commercially published edition was "faithful to the experimental version." The third version was the revised edition published by Ginn and Company in 1977; it was a blue hard back book or two paperbacks and unlike the earlier version, it contained color photographs and drawings. Accompanying both the 1972 and 1977 editions of the student books were a teachers' guide containing masters for student worksheets and a set of color transparencies. The masters for two forms of each test, a package of simulations ("City Hall" and "Influence"), and a box containing two games ("Bottleneck" and "Ninth Justice") were sold separately.[3] Four films, referred to earlier, were developed to tie in with the course and were also sold separately.

When I compared the 1972 and 1977 commercial editions of the program, I found that: (1) some of the material, particularly lessons teaching social science methods were reorganized, (2) a few of the original case studies were dropped, (3) new information was added, including material on recent elections, and (4) the word "Negroes" was changed to "Blacks," reflecting a cultural change (Mehlinger & Patrick, 1972, 1977). The main change in content, however, was that the final unit was replaced. In the first edition Unit 5 focused on unofficial political roles and contained chapters on experts as unofficial political specialists, the media, and political party leaders. In the revised edition, Unit 5 focused on state and local decision makers (containing chapters on the nature of American state and local government, chief executives in state and local government, legislative bodies in state and local government, courts in state and local government, and state and local bureaucrats). Apparently, the feedback from government teachers and textbook adoption committees to the publisher's representatives were that APB needed to fit their (traditional) curriculum, which included state and local government—rather than the media, unofficial political specialists, and political party leaders. Reflecting on the change, Mehlinger (H. Mehlinger, personal communication, January 12, 2008) recalled that he and Patrick recognized they needed to add material on local government because the teachers wanted it and he thought that the original Unit 5 was the least strong part of the first edition. They could use the behavioral approach to teach local government and still remain different from traditional textbooks like the dominant one in the market, authored by Magruder.

I entered the APB story in a minor role during the year of field testing, 1968–69. As a young social studies teacher at The Lincoln School in Kentucky (a residential school for bright students from low-income families and communities), I attended the November 1968 convention of the NCSS in Washington DC. At the convention I met George McClellan (a friend of my high school social studies teacher, Jack Curtin), who in turn introduced me to Howard Mehlinger. When Howard told me about the new project *American Political Behavior* I showed interest in using the program. He explained that the project already had all the pilot teachers they needed. However, he offered to let me use copies of the materials with my students, which I did the following Spring. I had been enthusiastic about the New Social Studies projects since first hearing about them from Richard Gross, my social studies methods professor at Stanford University, when he returned from the 1966 NCSS convention. Thus, it was the excitement of the New Social Studies projects, and the experiences of meeting Howard Mehlinger and working with a draft copy of *American Political Behavior* that led me to apply to graduate school at Indiana University (as well as two other centers of the New Social Studies) when The Lincoln School closed in 1970.

In my first year of graduate school at Indiana University, I worked as a doctoral associate on another project based at the Social Studies Development Center, co directed by Howard Mehlinger and Gerald Marker, The Social Studies Field Agent Training Program. Based on the model of agricultural extension agents, the purpose of the program was to train a cadre of experienced social studies teachers to be change agents, disseminating information about innovations in social studies. Marker and Mehlinger envisioned that similar to agricultural extension agents introducing innovations in farming, the social studies field agents would introduce innovations like the New Social Studies projects into their departments. The 11 field agents and two doctoral associates learned about APB, as well as the many other New Social Studies projects. We also learned about the importance of research-based curriculum development and the process of educational change. But that was not the end of my part in the APB story; indeed for me, "the best was yet to come."

THE DIFFUSION OF *AMERICAN POLITICAL BEHAVIOR*

Through my work with the field agent program and Gerald Marker's course on educational change, I developed an interest in the dissemination of innovations in social studies. In the spring of 1971, Mehlinger proposed that I put my theoretical knowledge of the change process to the test by spending a year "on the road" disseminating an innovation— APB. He had proposed to Ginn and Company that they pay the Social Studies Development Center an amount that would cover my university tuition and a stipend for the year. In return, as the APB "demonstration teacher" I would meet with textbook adoption committees, make presentations to create awareness of the program, conduct 1-day training sessions in districts that had bought the program, and meet with individual teachers, social studies supervisors, and others who might be involved in the decision to adopt the program at a school or district level.

Traveling With APB

While I was still taking courses in my doctoral program on campus, I made a few presentations. On September 9, 1971 in Chicago, I and the program were "launched" at the annual convention of the American Political Science Association. Mehlinger, as the project director, gave an overview of the project, its objectives, and a summary of the evaluation of the experimental version. I then demonstrated a lesson with a group of high school students I had never seen before. Later that semester, I gave presentations on my own to social studies teachers and supervisors in Ft. Wayne, Indiana; Dayton, Ohio; and Baton Rouge, Louisiana.

It was, however, from January through May 1972 that I lived, breathed, and dreamed APB. I was assigned to the Ginn and Company (which had recently been purchased by Xerox) sales force in a particular region, usually for a week at a time. On Sunday afternoon I would fly from Bloomington to my destination, where a Ginn representative would meet me and drive me from the airport to my Holiday Inn of the night and preview my schedule for the week. In a typical day I might meet with a social studies supervisor in one town, then ride along with the "Ginn rep" to another town where I would give a demonstration lesson to a class of students in one school, and then on to another school to give an after-school in-service session to a group of teachers. That night or early the next morning I might ride across the state with the Ginn rep to the next day's venue and mid week I would fly to another city in the region.[4]

In the journal that I kept I often complained of exhaustion, getting into a hotel near midnight and departing the next morning for a flight or drive at 7 A.M.; I expressed frustration with less than ideal conditions for conducting after-school presentations to tired teachers. Looking through my correspondence from those days, I found a handwritten note by one Ginn representative that said, "the point at which you can't sleep unless you have a Holiday Inn sign on your lawn, or when you sit at your family's breakfast table and request breakfast #3, you know you are in trouble." Additionally, he noted "incidental intelligence: orders for APB look really fine" (personal communication, March 30, 1972). Looking back more than 35 years later I continue to be grateful for this amazing opportunity; I gained incomparable knowledge about the diffusion of innovations in social studies and I was introduced to the national network of leaders in social studies education, many of whom remain my friends many years later.

Modeling my presentations on ones I had observed Mehlinger give and making variations depending on the audience and the length of time I had, a typical presentation included the following components, which reflect what the developers thought was important about the program at the time: I would give some background as to why the course was created, an overview of the content, a description of the pedagogy used in the course, teach a lesson from the course, and point out several unique features including the simulations and testing program based on the ideas of mastery learning.

In terms of why the course was created, I explained that that there were many indications that a new approach was needed to civics instruction. As I had observed Mehlinger saying in his presentations, I said,

> Teachers were concerned that kids weren't interested in their courses when they felt the subject was so important. There was criticism from the discipline that pre-collegiate instruction didn't reflect the latest knowledge in political science; legal historical approach dominated, and no attention was given to the newer behavioral approach to the study of politics. (C. Hahn's, personal communication, January, 1972)

I cited political socialization research indicating that for many students what was taught in school merely reinforced what students already learned from family and the media—yet there was still much that students did not learn. I explained that it was for that reason the High School Curriculum Center in Government attempted to create a course that:

1. Would reflect the latest knowledge in political science;
2. Have high interest for students;
3. Teach ideas, information and skills that weren't learned elsewhere and that were important to act effectively within the American political process; and
4. Would be usable by teachers who had limited time and resources to develop such a course on their own. (C. Hahn's, personal communication, January, 1972, pp. 1–2)

In my presentations I noted that I had taught a pilot version of the course in Kentucky to a heterogeneous class that contained white and African American students from low-income families in inner city and rural Appalachian communities. I recalled that my students and I "were continually applying the concepts and skills taught in the course to the kids' particular experiences" and to current issues within the school, or in Kentucky, or issues of current national concern.

Next I would give an overview of the sequence of unit topics followed by descriptions of the four lesson types. I highlighted the different role of the teacher in each type: the confrontation lesson (to focus attention, motivate, and generate hypotheses usually at the beginning of a topic), the rule-example lessons (to systematically develop concepts or skills, and to test hypotheses), the application lesson (to practice the use of concepts and skills), and the value judgment lessons (to explore value issues and require reasoned value judgment, often with issues in case studies).

After a brief break for coffee, I would demonstrate a lesson to a group of students or to teachers and other adults. I used the political symbols confrontation lesson most often, because no prior reading was required and it illustrated clearly a behavioral approach to politics. I showed a series of symbols (from the package of transparencies), including the American flag, Soviet flag, peace symbol, Statue of Liberty, the Democratic Party's donkey, the Republican elephant, a Nazi swastika, a Lenin medal, and the Viet Cong flag. I asked students (or teachers) to respond to each symbol using a 5-point Likert scale. I asked how many had a very bad feeling, bad feeling, little or no feeling, good feeling, or very good feeling? I tallied the responses on an overhead transparency. Next I asked the students (or teachers) to hypothesize about how they thought a comparable group in the Soviet Union would respond, and how they thought they got their feelings toward these symbols. I then introduced the concepts of "political culture" and "political socialization," which were the focus of Unit 2. Another lesson I frequently used to demonstrate the behavioral approach to politics asked participants to hypothesize about how a number of individuals pictured on transparencies might vote.

In the final part of the presentation, I explained the idea of criterion referenced mastery learning that underlay the testing program. Additionally, I described the games and simulations.

In addition to the many workshops that I conducted when the program was first published, for several years before and after that Mehlinger and Patrick gave speeches about the program at many social studies conferences and summer workshops for teachers. The Ginn marketing division and their sales team worked with individuals and school districts to promote sales. These dissemination activities were occurring at the same time that the staffs of other New Social Studies projects were promoting their projects. As a result, by the mid-1970s a number of social studies educators developed an interest in the dissemination and adoption of innovations in social studies. Several young scholars conducted research on the topic (see Hahn, 1977a, 1977b; Hahn, Marker, Switzer, & Turner, 1977; Kissock & Falk, 1978).

Research on the Diffusion of APB

In 1973–75 several researchers surveyed teachers and social studies department heads in random samples of high schools in selected states. I sent questionnaires to social studies department heads in Indiana, Ohio, Georgia, and Florida; Switzer and his colleagues sent questionnaires to principals to distribute to social studies teachers in Michigan, Ohio, Illinois, Indiana, and Wisconsin; and Turner and Haley sent questionnaires to be distributed to social studies teachers in California, Texas, Colorado, and Connecticut (Hahn, Marker et al., 1977). Although the researchers used slightly different lists of New Social Studies projects and focused on different aspects of diffusion,[5] several findings related to APB were consistent across studies.

First, I found that 40% of responding social studies department heads in Indiana and Ohio in 1973 and 49% in Georgia and Florida in 1974 were not familiar enough with any of the 21 New Social Studies Projects on the list I provided to be able to answer questions about them. In contrast, Switzer found that only 13% of responding teachers in the 5 Midwestern states he surveyed in 1973 reported never having heard of any of the 10 New Social Studies projects he listed (Hahn, Marker et al., 1977).

In my survey, the project that the most respondents said they were familiar with was the Carnegie Mellon project (most frequently cited in Indiana and Ohio; and the second most frequently cited in Georgia and Florida) (Hahn, 1977a; Hahn, Marker et al., 1977). The Harvard Public Issues series was most widely cited in Ohio and Florida but not in Georgia and Florida, where it was not on the official state textbook adoption lists. *American Political Behavior* was the third most frequently cited project in the four states in my study. In Switzer's study of five Midwestern states, the Carnegie Mellon project was the project respondents were the most likely to report they were familiar with; followed by *Law in a Free Society*, the Harvard Public Issues series, and *American Political Behavior*. Importantly, Switzer and colleagues established that 58% of the government and political science teachers had heard of APB and 43% of those teachers had examined the materials. That is, although relatively small percentages of teachers or department heads in general were familiar with APB, more than half of the teachers who taught courses that might use APB were familiar with the program. Reinforcing the other studies, Turner's respondents reported they were most likely to be using the Carnegie Mellon project materials, published by Holt, followed by the Harvard Public Issues series. The Indiana University project, *American Political Behavior*, was the third most frequently used project by respondents in three of the states, and first in Texas, where it was on the state textbook adoption list. Furthermore, of the 264 respondents who actually taught courses in

American government, 21% used APB (27% in Texas). Across the three studies other projects that were listed were used far less and fewer respondents were familiar with them (Hahn, Marker et al., 1977). Clearly, although APB was not the most famous of the New Social Studies projects, it was widely known and used in the early 1970s.

Researchers who studied the diffusion of the New Social Studies projects used two models of the change process to situate their work (Hahn, 1977b). Most of those researchers and many of the project developers viewed the New Social Studies in terms of the Research, Development, Dissemination, and Adoption (RDD & A) model that had guided federally funded projects in science and technology, as well as education. In the first phase, Research, *American Political Behavior* built on research in political science, educational psychology, and educational change. The developers began by surveying the research on a behavioral approach to politics, political socialization, and learning theory. The content of APB reflected their understanding of the behavioral approach in political science transformed for young people. The confrontation and rule-example lessons took account of research on motivation and concept development. The testing program was based on research on mastery learning. Reflecting the second stage of the model, Development, Mehlinger and Patrick spent months reading, talking, and conceptualizing the course before they started writing (Mehlinger, 1970). Mehlinger (H. Mehlinger, personal communication, January 12, 2008) described this period as "one of the most creative periods" of his life. The course was field tested and revised twice. Formative and summative evaluations were important components of the development stage. Project staff deliberately planned for the third stage, Dissemination, by holding summer dissemination workshops in Bloomington and speaking at numerous teacher workshops and conferences where many of the New Social Studies projects were featured. Between 1966 and 1971 Mehlinger alone gave more than 100 talks about efforts to improve civics and government instruction, highlighting the goals and progress of APB and both Mehlinger and Patrick wrote numerous articles for journals (Engle et al., 1972, p. 14). Further, the idea of sending a graduate student/demonstration teacher "on the road" for a year reflected purposeful planning for dissemination. Additionally, although the requirement to turn the program over to a commercial publisher may have been made on financial grounds, so the federal government could recover some of its investment in development, it had the advantage of building on commercial publishers' experience in disseminating textbooks. Most of the other New Social Studies projects similarly followed the RDD & A model in terms of research and development. However, few were as purposeful as APB in planning for dissemination. Most of the project directors had assumed that the final stage, adoption, would follow because their programs were well designed; as one developer told me, we "assumed that if we designed a better mousetrap, people would buy it" (Hahn, 1977b).

A second model of change that had some influence on developers of the New Social Studies projects was the social-interaction model made popular by Everett Rogers (Hahn, 1977b). Growing out of research in rural sociology, this model viewed the diffusion of innovations as following a bell-shaped curve. At first only a few innovators who were risk takers would try an innovation; the next group of early adopters would observe early trials of an innovation, then decide to try it for themselves. Over time, late adopters, and eventually laggards would try and eventually adopt an innovation. Researchers working in this tradition studied characteristics of the various types of adopters and their perceptions of innovations, including researchers who studied the New Social Studies (Becker & Hahn, 1975; Hahn, 1977a, 1977b; Hahn, Marker et al., 1977). APB and several of the other New Social Studies Projects were successful in being widely adopted by social studies teachers and school districts that were innovators and early adopters. However, it is not clear that many of the projects were adopted by late adopters and laggards. Additionally, with time, the innovators and early adopters shifted their enthusiasm to new innovations.

THE LEGACY OF APB

The Indiana University High School Curriculum Center in Government (HSCCG) began its work near the end of the "curriculum development decade" (Engle et al. 1972). The three major projects funded by the National Science Foundation to teach anthropology, geography, and sociology had been in existence for several years and nearly all of the special projects that formed "Project Social Studies" and were funded by the U.S. Office of Education (USOE) were moving toward final publication when the HSCCG began work. When the project ended "it was probably the last USOE curriculum development project of its kind" (Engle et al., 1972).

Over the 5-year period July 1, 1966 through June 30, 1971, the HSCCG spent $348,220 "designing, developing, producing, and testing alternative approaches to instruction in high school civics and government courses" (Mehlinger, in press). This was one small part of the investment that the federal government made in educational reform through the development of school curriculum following the launch of Sputnik and the subsequent Woods Hole conference when Jerome Bruner (1962) stimulated the search for the "structure of the disciplines" to teach students in an "intellectually honest form" (p. 33). Now, with 35 years hindsight, it is appropriate to ask, what were the returns on the investment over the long run?

The objectives of the project, as stated in the original proposal were clearly met. The HSCCG identified topics and problems in political science that were suitable to teach junior and senior high school students. They developed materials that incorporated the most recent findings in political science (a behavioral approach), educational psychology (motivation, concept learning), and education (mastery learning approach to testing, the use of simulations as instructional strategies). They successfully taught social science concepts (political behavior, political culture, political socialization) and familiarized students with the process of developing and testing hypotheses pertaining to the political world; they enabled students to handle questions of public policy in ethically and intellectually defensible ways and maximized the ability of students to understand the conditions under which political decisions are made. Evaluations of the project demonstrated that students acquired political knowledge and skills (Patrick, 1972).

While acknowledging that APB did not transform high school civics and government courses, Patrick (J. Patrick, personal communication, May 28, 2008) estimated that it did have some partial influence on textbooks, supplementary materials, and the content of some state-level standards for teaching civics and government. He noted that,

> We were pioneers in using case studies to teach about government and citizenship. We also were among the first to bring more realistic and controversial content and public issues into civics and government courses. We treated in depth such topics as race, social class, and gender in relationship to government and politics long before it became fashionable to do so. No book of that era, other than APB, treated the civil rights movement in such depth as we did. Now, no middle school or high school textbook in government or civics fails to treat such topics, although to this day none of the standard books has treated race-related issues as pervasively, deeply, and realistically as we did. We also emphasized the application or use of knowledge by students—concepts and facts—o analyze and interpret realistic political events and government decision making. (J. Patrick, personal communication, May 28, 2008)

Reflecting back, Mehlinger (H. Mehlinger, personal communication, January 12, 2008) recalled that when APB was conceived textbook adoption committees selected textbooks that were similar to the ones they had used before. State guidelines were written to fit the traditional textbooks and textbooks were selected to fit the guidelines. "We wanted to break out of that cycle, to offer an alternative that reflected what social scientists know" and "we wanted to make something that teachers could use that included what they wanted their students to know." "We showed that you could teach a social science course, a behavioral approach to politics, to high school students" and "I think we were successful in that" (H. Mehlinger, personal communication, January 12, 2008).

The publishers' idea of success was slightly different, Mehlinger (2008) noted; their goal was to make state textbook adoption lists and sell many books. The first edition made the adoption list in Texas and made "very healthy" sales. Even though most teachers continued to use traditional civics books like the one by Magruder, a sizeable number of teachers used the APB alternative. The second edition (1977) did not have as many sales as the first. By then, Jack Fraenkel, a professor at San Francisco State University, had written another similar book incorporating the same topics and using case studies. Fraenkel's book competed with APB for the segment of the market that wanted an alternative approach (H. Mehlinger, personal communication, January 12, 2008).

Additionally, Mehlinger recalled, by the late 1970s the "Back to Basics" movement had taken hold and selection committees wanted to know the reading level of books. The formulas that they used were based on a list of common words and sentence length. A book that taught concepts like 'political socialization' and taught students how to test social science hypotheses appeared to have a higher reading level than competing books. From Ginn's perspective, the program was no longer a success when sales figures for the second edition declined. Yet, as Mehlinger recalled, "we kept hearing that many teachers would reproduce parts of the text to use as a supplement to their traditional textbook. We once referred to it as the most successful supplementary text for civics and government" (H. Mehlinger, personal communication, January 12, 2008).

The final report of the project points to another factor that may have affected widespread implementation. In discussing the fact that APB was one of the last projects of the New Social Studies, the report authors noted that "the agenda of national priorities in American education had begun to shift from concerns about the academic validity of curriculum content (expressed as "the structure of the discipline") and the need to include scholars in educational reform to "new concerns including the education of disadvantaged youth, problems of inner-city schools, and the education of ethnic minorities" (Engle et al., 1972, p. 3).

Four decades later I am struck by the fact that a curriculum project that focused on understanding the political world was being field tested the same year that Martin Luther King Jr. and Bobby Kennedy were assassinated, protests outside the Democratic convention in Chicago turned into bedlam, and protests spread demanding that the United States get out of Vietnam. Additionally, on college campuses, activist youth demanded relevant instruction and called for ethnic studies courses and programs. As the APB developers explained, they and others working on the New Social Studies projects had tried to address problems identified in the later 1950s and early 1960s, but schools and society had moved on to new concerns (Engle et al., 1972). Given that context, it is remarkable that APB and other New Social Studies projects were implemented in as many classrooms as they were in the 1970s. Federal funding had not taken into account the need to continually revise curricular offerings to fit a changing society.

Yet even though their presence in schools lasted no more than a decade, I believe that the New Social Studies projects had an important impact on the field of social studies education that lasted well beyond those years. For example, teachers who field tested projects and who attended workshops on the New Social Studies projects, such as myself, were socialized to the ideas of connecting recent scholarship to school curriculum, promoting research-based teaching and teacher education, and using variety in instruction with an emphasis on student inquiry and engagement. Teachers and teacher educators who experienced the New Social Studies took those lessons to their work in subsequent years as can be seen in their writing in civic education, history education, economic education, multicultural education, global education, and social studies teacher education.

Looking at civic/political education in particular, I can view the glass as either half empty or half full in 2008. I see the glass as half empty as I note that textbooks still reflect the institutional framework that was prevalent before APB was developed. In the IEA Civic Education study, students and teachers in the mid-1990s reported teaching and learning about the three branches of government, and the levels of national, state, and local government (Hahn, 2002). No one mentioned teaching or learning about concepts like "civic culture" or "political socialization" and no one mentioned experiences testing hypotheses. Students of today do learn about variables that relate to voting behavior—but primarily from the pollsters and political commentators who fill the media during election periods.

With the exceptions Patrick cited, for the most part civics and government textbooks have changed little. But textbook content does not reflect all that has occurred in civic and political education. In the period following the publication of *A Nation at Risk* in 1983, through the years of accountability and the standards movement for educational reform, numerous organizations provided classroom materials for students and professional development opportunities for teachers under the umbrellas of "law-related education" and "civic education." Most notably, the Center for Civic Education received grants from Congress to develop curriculum and to develop *National Standards for Civics and Government* (Center for Civic Education, 1994).

In 2002 political scientists, political socialization researchers, representatives from varied organizations working in civic education, and individuals working in the area of service learning held a series of meetings that led to the publication of *The Civic Mission of Schools* (Carnegie & CIRCLE, 2003), which reflected a revival of interest in civic education. Unlike the period of the New Social Studies, reformers at the beginning of the twenty-first century did not seek funds for curriculum development. Rather, they sought to create a movement to promoted changes in school district policies and classroom practices. They drew attention to numerous indicators of declining civic engagement and called for states to re-institute required courses in civics. They encouraged teachers to engage their students in discussions of current events and controversial public issues and they urged schools to implement well conceived programs in service learning tied to the study of public issues (Carnegie & CIRCLE, 2003). Such reform efforts require a partnership of social studies teachers, school administrators, civic-related organizations, and communities. Whether this broad—or diffuse—approach to reform will have more lasting effect than did that of the New Social Studies remains to be seen.

Finally, readers might wonder what happened to the characters in my story of one New Social Studies Project, *American Political Behavior.* Howard Mehlinger was elected President of the National Council for the Social Studies in 1977 after serving a term on the NCSS Board of Directors and having been the NCSS vice-president and president-elect. He remained Director of the Social Studies Development Center until 1981 and during that time he secured many more grants for the Center. In 1981 he went on to serve for 9 years as Dean of Indiana University's School of Education. During his tenure as Dean, Mehlinger undertook his "ultimate development effort;" raising approximately $25 million to build a new building for the School of Education and to establish a new research and development center, the Center for Excellence in Education (CEE), whose mission was to study the applications of computers and other electronic technology in education. In 1990 Mehlinger resigned the deanship to become CEE director. He held this position until he retired from Indiana University in 1999. During his tenure as dean and CEE director, he also directed several research and professional development projects with Russian educators, including an Indiana University partnership with Ryazan State Pedagogical University.

John Patrick served as director of Indiana University's Social Studies Development Center for 18 years from 1986 until his retirement from the university in 2004. During that time, he coordinated the writing of the proposal to the U.S. Office of Education for the ERIC Clearinghouse for Social Studies/Social Science Education and he served as the director of the ERIC Clearinghouse until his retirement. After his experience with

APB he went on to become one of the leading experts in civic education in the United States, writing numerous books on Constitutional history, as well as textbooks for civics and United States history. He explained,

> The ABP project provided an extraordinary opportunity for me to develop competency as a curriculum developer and writer of instructional materials. It was a launching pad for my subsequent career as a writer of books for teachers and students on topics in American history, government, and civics. Through the APB project, I formed my deep and abiding commitment to the conjoining of solid academic content with processes of cognition and inquiry in the development of instructional materials for adolescent learners. (J. Patrick, personal communication, May 28, 2008)

In the 1990s Patrick served on committees that developed the *National Standards for Civics and Government* (Center for Civic Education, 1994) and the *National History Standards* (Center for History in the Schools, 1996). From 1992–2006 he was a member of the framework development and the standing committees for the National Assessments of Educational Progress (NAEP) in civics and U.S. history. From 1991 through 2006 he worked on several democracy education projects in Eastern Europe, including Latvia, Estonia, Lithuania, Poland, and Bosnia-Herzogovina, as well as in several Latin-American countries. At the time of this writing, he remains active assisting with professional development programs related to those projects.

As for myself, as I noted earlier, the experiences I had traveling the country with APB brought me into the national network of leaders in social studies education. I was elected to two terms on the Board of Directors of NCSS in the 1970s and was subsequently elected vice president, president-elect, and eventually president of NCSS in 1983. Importantly, working with APB stimulated my own interest in understanding politics and political socialization. After my initial research on the diffusion of innovations, which was rooted in the New Social Studies, I have spent most of my career researching political socialization and civic education in the United States and internationally (Hahn, 1996, 1998, 2002, 2008; Hahn & Alviar-Martin, 2008). I remain fascinated by American political behavior, from a global and comparative perspective.

NOTES

1. Mehlinger (H. Mehlinger, personal communication, January 12, 2008) similarly noted that he had met Gerald Marker and Jack Thompson, an IU history professor, through the North Central's Foreign Relations project before he joined them as colleagues at IU.

2. By this time also, in 1968, Indiana University had established the Social Studies Development Center (SSDC), with Howard Mehlinger as director. The HSCCG, which developed APB, was one of the first of many social studies projects housed at the SSDC. For example, the SSDC had a National Science Foundation grant, sponsored by the American Political Science Association to develop a 12th grade government course, which eventually became the text *Comparing Political Experiences* by Judy Gillespie and Stuart Lazarus. Lee Anderson from Northwestern University spent a year at the Center working on the political science education project with the American Political Science Association. Indiana University history professor Jack Thompson directed the World History project, which published a textbook, *People and Civilizations: A World History*. In 1971 James Becker came to the Center to work on projects on educational change in social studies. In the 1970s, the Center also housed a global studies curriculum project for middle school students.

3. The hardback text sold for $5.22 per copy and each paperback sold for $2.40. The teachers guide, containing masters for transparencies and worksheets was $3.96. Estimates of the average per-pupil cost for purchasing separate components of the course, based on a class size of 30 students was: tests $1.12, transparencies, $1.41; worksheets, .45; two simulations, .40, and games, $1.65 (Indiana University, 1972).

4. My travels over the 5 months covered, in order: Oklahoma, the Washington DC/northern Virginia/Baltimore area, Michigan, Massachusetts, New York, Louisiana, Georgia, West Virginia, Pennsylvania, Wisconsin, Missouri, Ohio, Oregon/Washington, California, Iowa, and a return to the Maryland/northern Virginia area.

5. Hahn focused on how potential adopters of innovations perceived the characteristics of 21 of the New Social Studies Projects. The research teams headed by Switzer and Turner analyzed characteristics of individuals and school districts that were familiar with and adopted 10 of The New Social Studies Projects.

Appendix: Table of Contents From the
1977 Edition of American Political Behavior

REFERENCES

Becker, J. M., & Hahn, C. L. (1975). *Wingspread workbook for educational change*. Boulder, CO: Social Science Education Consortium.

Bruner, J. (1962) *The process of education*. Cambridge, MA: Harvard University Press.

Carnegie Corporation of New York and CIRCLE the Center for Information & Research on Civic Learning & Engagement. (2003). *The civic mission of schools*. New York: Carnegie Corporation of New York.

Center for Civic Education. (1994). *National standards for civics and government*. Calabasas, CA: Author.

Center for History in the Schools. (1996). *National standards for history.* Los Angeles, CA: University of California, Author.

Engle, S. H., & Carter, B. E., Jr., (1965). Unpublished manuscript. Bloomington, IN: Indiana University.

Engle, S. H., Mehlinger, H. D., & Patrick, J. J. (1972, March). *Report of the high school curriculum center in government.* Final Report. Project No. H-223, Contract Nu. OE-6-10-274. US Department of Health, Education, and Welfare, Office of Education.

Hahn, C. L. (1977a) Attributes of new social studies curriculum materials and the adoption of those materials. *Theory and Research in Social Education, 5,* 19–40.

Hahn, C. L. (1977b). Research on the diffusion of social studies innovations. *Review of Research in Social Studies Education, 1970–75* (pp. 137–178). Washington DC: National Council for the Social Studies and Boulder, CO: ERIC Clearinghouse for Social Studies/Social Science Education.

Hahn, C. L. (1996). Gender and political learning. *Theory and Research in Social Education, 24,* 8–35.

Hahn, C. L. (1998). *Becoming political: Citizenship education in comparative perspective.* Albany, NY: SUNY Press.

Hahn, C. L. (2002) Education for democratic citizenship: One nation's story. In W. C. Parker (Ed.) *Education for democracy: Contexts, curricula, assessments* (pp. 63–92). Greenwich, CT: Information Age.

Hahn, C. L. (2008). Research on civic education in the United States. In J. Arthur, I. Davies, & C. L. Hahn (Eds.), *Handbook of education for citizenship and democracy* (pp. 263–278). London: SAGE.

Hahn, C. L., & Alviar-Martin, T. (2008). International political socialization research. In L. Levstik & C. Tyson (Eds.), *Handbook on research in social studies* (pp. 81–108). Mahwah, NJ: Earlbaum.

Hahn, C. L., Marker, G. W., Switzer, T. J., & Turner, M. J. (1977). *Three studies on perception and utilization of "new social studies" materials.* Boulder, CO: Social Science Education Consortium.

Indiana University High School Curriculum Center in Government. (1972). *Social Education, 36,* 752–754.

Kissock, C., & Falk, D. R. (1978) A reconsideration of "Attributes and adoption of new social studies materials." *Theory and Research in Social Education, 6,* 56–70.

Marker, G. W. (1970). *Teacher dogmatism and its impact upon the political attitudes of students.* Doctoral dissertation, Indiana University.

Mehlinger, H. (1970). Development as a creative activity. *Viewpoints, 46*(2), 69–77.

Mehlinger, H. (in press). American political behavior. In G. Scheurman & R. Evans (Eds.), *Constructivism and the new social studies.* New York: Information Age.

Mehlinger, H. D., & Patrick, J. J. (1971). The use of "formative evaluation in an experimental curriculum project: A case in the practice of instructional materials evaluation. *Social Education, 35,* 884–887, 892.

Mehlinger, H. D., & Patrick, J. J. (1972). *American political behavior.* Lexington, MA: Ginn & Co.

Mehlinger, H. D., & Patrick, J. J. (1977). *American political behavior* (Rev. ed.). Lexington, MA: Ginn & Co.

Patrick, J. J. (1967). *Political socialization of American youth: Implications for secondary school social studies*. Research bulletin 3. Washington, DC: National Council for the Social Studies. Occasional paper. Bloomington, IN: High School Curriculum Center in Government.

Patrick, J. J. (1972) The impact of an experimental course APB on the knowledge, skills, and attitudes of secondary students, *Social Education, 36*, 168–179.

Patrick, J. J. (1969a). Implications of political socialization research for the reform of civic education. *Social Education, 33*, 15–22.

Patrick, J. J. (1969b). *Democratic political orientation of ninth-grade students in four community types*. Doctoral dissertation, Indiana University.

CHAPTER 14

SMALL PROJECTS OF THE NEW SOCIAL STUDIES

(Bring Back the Best)

John D. Hoge

Well-informed college social studies instructors should have some knowledge of the most famous New Social Studies (NSS) projects and the individuals who developed these groundbreaking curriculum materials. These projects and individuals are the subjects of most of the other chapters in this volume and they richly deserve the recognition that they have received as icons of the NSS movement. However, what may not be known so widely now is that the NSS included an outpouring of many hundreds of innovative curriculum designs and products that spontaneously sprang from the ferment of the movement and the fertile soil of the era's optimism. The spirit of this outpouring of curriculum experimentation suffused all grade levels and content areas of the social studies and it provides many examples of ideal NSS practice. Indeed, the full flavor of the NSS movement may well be represented better in the array of these hundreds of small projects than in the few NSS projects that received wide distribution, were converted into commercial products, or became the

The New Social Studies: People, Projects, and Perspectives, pp. 285–305
Copyright © 2010 by Information Age Publishing

subject of public controversy. Beyond being more representative of the NSS movement, these small projects may also serve as a source of inspiration to future social studies educators who seek to innovate and exceed the bounds of established contemporary curricula.

PURPOSE AND METHOD

My purpose in this chapter is to give readers some insights into the hundreds of small projects that spontaneously appeared during the era of the NSS.[1] In doing this, I have been forced to be selective in my review for several reasons. First, many of these projects are now little more than a memory documented only by a brief ERIC abstract or a summary that exists in the dusty pages of old issues of Social Education.[2] Because of this, I was limited to resources that I had personally collected over the years, to items that had been deposited into the ERIC microfiche system, or to lessons that were featured in *Social Education* during the 1960s and 1970s. Another factor limiting the material presented here was my desire to exemplify the best curriculum products and practices of the NSS and not merely relate a jumbled collection of mixed-quality items.[3] Finally, I was limited in my ability to locate NSS curriculum materials by the search capabilities of the ERIC system and the fact that one cannot simply search Google to locate these materials. To locate NSS curriculum materials I conducted a large number of ERIC searches using several different descriptors and date boundaries. For example, using the ERIC descriptors "social studies" and "units of study" with pre-1966 to 1980 dates, I located 1,428 *potential* NSS resources. Restricting the end date to 1975 reduced this number to 983 *potential* resources. Restricting the date range further to 1970 resulted in only 387 *potential* resources. Searches using the keyword phrase "new social studies" and the ERIC Descriptor "units of study" yielded only 12 (1980 end date), 10 (1975 end date) and 4 (1970 end date) *potential* resources.

The point of sharing this information is to emphasize that there are, very likely, many hundreds of NSS curriculum materials deposited in the ERIC microfiche collection. However, there is no direct way to identify these materials since "new social studies" never became an ERIC Descriptor that could be used to tag NSS curriculum materials, research, or journal articles. As a result, curriculum researchers will have to make personal judgments about each individual piece of curriculum deposited in the ERIC microfiche collection in order to determine if it qualifies as a manifestation of the NSS. Of course, microfiche collections, microfiche display machines, and microfiche printers are outdated technology compared to the easy digital storage and retrieval offered by modern computer technologies. Anyone who has used ERIC microfiche understands the limitations of this form of data storage, retrieval, and display. The only thing that could be worse would be attempting to access the original paper versions of these documents. Easier access in the future may become possible, however, as a result of the ERIC system's drive to digitize its several hundred thousand pieces of microfiche.[4] As this happens, it may become possible to conduct key word and phrase searches of the entire contents of each piece of microfiche, not just the ERIC Descriptor and other database fields. In the interim, researchers who wish to report on the NSS would be well advised to examine each of the almost 1,500 pieces of microfiche that appear when searching for NSS instructional units if they want to gain a comprehensive picture of curriculum development activities during the NSS era.

After identifying a large collection of NSS curriculum resources, I needed a set of criteria to guide my selection of "small NSS projects."[5] The criteria I used for selecting small NSS projects were quite simple. First, the project had to be developed during the NSS era, and to never have become widely distributed or converted into a commercial product. Second, I looked for a variety of materials that spanned across the grade levels and typical subjects of the social studies. Third, I selected materials that exemplified the best features of the NSS. Sanders and Tank (1970) offered a list of 17 essential NSS characteristics in their critical appraisal of 26 national projects. Among these 17, the most salient for this report were: (a) an emphasis on the ideas and methodologies of the behavioral sciences, (b) the use of an integrated, multidisciplinary approach with clear delineation of concepts and generalizations, (c) provision of a variety of instructional resources needed for active, inductive, inquiry-oriented teaching, (d) an explicit representation of social realism and attention to conflict, (e) a focus on social and personal values questions and decisions, (f) the provision of cross-cultural materials and an added emphasis on non-Western societies, and (g) a significant emphasis on instruction that requires higher order thinking skills.[7] All in all, these traits or characteristics fit rather nicely with the *Expectations of Excellence* (NCSS, 1994) statement which asserts "social studies teaching and learning are powerful when they are meaningful, integrative, value-based, challenging, and active" (p. 158).

Of course, it is important to also note what I have not done. In particular, I have made no attempt to completely describe the selected pieces of curriculum or to justify that the entire curriculum product should be considered exemplary. Instead, I selected just those aspects of the projects that exemplified outstanding NSS instruction. My purpose is to demonstrate that models of outstanding social studies instruction came from the NSS movement as it was manifested in schools and classrooms across the nation. My goal is that contemporary readers will be inspired by what they see here and recognize that what was advocated by the NSS is still worthwhile in today's classrooms. Finally, my presentation of the following NSS exemplars follows no particular order that might convey that the first case, for example, is better than the last. I have simply attempted to keep the reader intrigued and engaged as I report these pieces of exemplary "small project" NSS curricula.

Secondary Exemplars

Daniel Klassen (1973) presented a paper on the potential of computer simulations in the social studies at the 1973 annual convention of the Association for Educational Data Systems. His report detailed how three currently used high school level simulations (MARKET, USPOP, and ELECT) demonstrated the power of the NSS to "subordinate mere mastery of factual content to the recognition of and ability to deal with the social imperatives of the future" (p. i). MARKET placed students in the position of entrepreneurs who were competing for sales of racing bicycles, USPOP helped students examine how population growth variables such as infant mortality and the timing of the birth of the first child interact to influence projected U.S. population growth, and ELECT allowed students to simulate local, state, and national elections varying factors such as candidates' personalities, experience, party affiliation, issue positions, voter turn out, and media distortion. The ELECT simulation also included data on seven U.S. presidential elections conducted between 1828 and 1896 and allowed students to "replay" these elections manipulating each campaign's emphasis on the candidates' images, party affiliations, and issues. Klassen's paper states that he was a classroom teacher as well as a researcher, held a PhD in political science, and was developing computer-based social studies materials at SUNY-Stony Brook. Readers of this first exemplar should note, among other things, this early and sophisticated use of computers, the focus on substantial, enduring conceptual content, and the linking of history to present day and potential future realities. Readers should also be impressed to see a content area PhD functioning both as a classroom teacher and researcher. To what degree does our current curriculum and schooling milieu support similar practices today? I think the likely, truthful answer is "not much."[7]

Mary Jane Turner prepared a paper for the American Political Science Association titled: "Political Science in 'New Social Studies' Curricula: State of the Art—1970" in which she described and evaluated 46 NSS curriculum development projects of the 1960s (Turner, 1970). While a few of the projects became commercially viable, at least for a period of time,

Turner reviewed the general trends present in the whole collection, which she separated into four categories, (a) those ($n = 14$) that were primarily interdisciplinary (but with a political science component), (b) those ($n = 18$) that focused on a single discipline (history, geography, or anthropology) and included a political science component, (c) those ($n = 10$) that had a predominantly political science content focus, and finally (d) those ($n = 4$) that were essentially area studies that included, of course, political science content. Turner noted that as a group these materials were profoundly influenced by the rise of a behavioral research focus within the discipline of political science, the ever-increasing flows of new information, knowledge, and theories that were sweeping across virtually all modern societies, the realization of global interdependence, and the demands that these trends placed upon the education of new and future citizens. These projects moved away from prior World War II era civics/government instruction that was primarily focused on the mechanical aspects of government, and teaching a dull, factual, coverage-oriented chronology of events in an effort to build political allegiance "that did little to lead students to a productive understanding of political activity" (p. 2). NSS curricula with political science content focused instead on "new methods of organizing facts so that they related to other knowledge in ways which contribute to perspective and understanding, and new ways of teaching skills" (p. 5). These new methods structured instruction so that students could "critically examine the values inherent in the American political system and in their own personal belief system" (p. 7) and confront both social and political controversies. Turner closes her paper by recounting the 16 cognitive and affective instructional goals advocated by the California Political Science Advisory Panel and noting which curricula most readily helped students to achieve these ends. Specific projects were recognized for their provision of instruction that would help students recognize the tentativeness of policy decisions, learn how to analyze and peacefully resolve complex value conflicts, and develop an appreciation for the roles and limitations of laws. Other projects were praised for helping students recognize the "shifting dividing line between public and private acts" (p. 15), helping students develop "an awareness of the rules of the political game" (p. 15), and understand "the nature and mechanisms of membership in a polity" (p.15). Turner recognized that the content of these projects was more extensive, but the real change in the material was in *how* this content was to be taught. On a more critical note, Turner noted that these curricula lacked a significant focus on international relations and failed to provide a significant multicultural perspective.

Turner's 1970 review of 1960s era NSS curricula with political science content should impress readers in several ways. First, she has documented the direct impact of what were then influential disciplinary advances in political science theory and research on the content composition and instructional approaches used in secondary social studies, civics, and government courses. Beyond this, she has highlighted the origins of several key tenets of postmodern, constructivist orientations to education, namely the centrality of context and position as these influence learners' ability to make sense of complex social/political phenomena and tentative and imperfect "solutions" that we attain through government and personal actions. In these exemplary new curricula, learners are not just recipients of information but agents who must actively engage content in inductive and problem-focused learning. Finally, Turner appropriately predicted the need for greater emphasis in international understanding as our global interconnections grew in number and significance.

Speaking at the 1973 Hawaii Conference of the Joint Committee on United States-Japan Educational and Cultural Cooperation, Robin McKeown (1973) reported on six newly developed secondary social studies projects that teach toward international understanding. McKeown characterized the earlier pre-NSS high school curriculum in social studies as limited to generally "helping students become aware of the diplomatic, economic, and military relations among European nations" (p. 1). She states:

> Often the approach was to teach what was 'newsworthy' without seriously attempting to generate an organized body of concepts and principles. More often than not, students were required to learn the names, dates, and events associated with wars, governments, and political events through a chronologically arranged history textbook which focused almost exclusively on Europe. (p. 2)

The decade of the 1960s, however, with the rise of the NSS, produced significant movement toward an improved global orientation to instruction often fueled by a variety of the more widely available audiovisual and print materials designed to supplement the textbook.

> For a select group of social studies teachers, the 1960s period was an innovative, exciting, and productive period. Academicians and school administrators alike encouraged the concept of inquiry-oriented instruction. Many teachers were required to develop courses allowing students to encounter documents, articles, issues, and problems conducive to the learning of "inquiry-techniques," "thinking skills," or "value conflict resolution procedures." (p. 3)

While in the past teaching for international understanding remained "ethnocentric, nationalistic, and pragmatic" (p. 3) now it became more common to help students recognize their cultural biases and develop empathy for people in other nations. McKeown states:

> Teachers are beginning to believe that exposure to the personal values and responses found in other cultures and societies is the most effective way to assist students to comprehend the human condition and thereby better prepare themselves for choosing among alternatives to life. The consequence of this view is that teachers now want students to study the world's people as much as possible from the "inside." (p. 4)

Students wanted to know about common people's lives, thoughts, and aspirations and teachers had begun to grasp their responsibility to prepare students for rewarding lives within pluralistic, internationally connected societies where they would have "to cope with the continuing change, complexity, and ambiguity to be encountered throughout their lives" (p. 5). Other than the six projects she reviewed, McKeown notes that there were very few exciting or effective materials for classroom teachers to use and that there were no serious curriculum development projects underway. Among her recommendations for improvement were pleas for a "world systems" approach to international understanding, the need for "tangible, concrete, imaginative, student-motivating materials to use in the classroom" (p. 7), and the infusion of global education across all subject areas and grade levels. Contemporary readers will doubtlessly resonate with much of what McKeown reported because much of this is still being advocated. With the globalization of the world economy and the rise of the Internet and sophisticated instructional tools, teachers can no longer justify providing instruction that presents a single cultural view, neglects large areas of the world, or is starved for the lack of significant content. Of course, there may be other causes for the neglect of education for international understanding, among them probably the biggest and most pernicious being high stakes accountability testing that is heavily U.S./Eurocentric and restricted to low level thinking processes.

As I mentioned in the introduction, another source of NSS curriculum materials are the issues of *Social Education* that were published in the 1960s and 70s. Unfortunately, this material does not exist in electronic format and probably never will.[8] In addition, as of result of ERIC not including *Social Education* among the journals that it indexed prior to November, 1970 (volume 34, Number 8 was the first) it is also impossible to even know of the existence of NSS articles that appeared in *Social Education* by searching the ERIC database. Of course ERIC generally did not reproduce copies of journal articles on microfiche, but instead simply indexed journal articles to help users determine the existence of relevant material—which was then obtained by (HORRORS) physically going to the library to find the desired paper-based journal articles. With this context understood, let me present a few examples of outstanding NSS curriculum materials that existed in the pages of *Social Education* during the 1960s and early 1970s.

Perhaps most emblematic of the NSS was the October 1967 issue of *Social Education* that contained, among other things, articles titled: "The Right to Privacy—A Case Study" (Cleary, 1967), "Charles A. Beard and the Commission on the Social Studies, 1929–1933: A Reappraisal" (Soderbergh, 1967), "Local Planning for Revision of the Social Studies: The Use of Federal Assistance Programs" (Portzline, 1967), "Reinvigorating the Social Studies Program" (Ryan, 1967), "Urban Schools and the Negro" (Cuban, 1967), "A High School Sociology Course" (Dykstra, 1967), "A Directory of Social Studies Projects" (USOE, 1967), "Familiarity and Contrast as Curriculum Principles" (Preston, 1967), and "Total Involvement in Student Government" (Morganti, 1967) as featured pieces. While the article titles are significant in themselves because they speak of a fundamental reconceptualization of the social studies curriculum, some information about their content is also enlightening. The first article, on the Constitutional right to privacy, featured the case, *Camara vs. San Francisco Municipal Court,* in which a bookstore owner who lived at the rear of his first floor business refused to allow an inspection of the premises. The U.S. Supreme Court reversed lower court decisions that had upheld the city's business inspection authority. This insert, complete with eight pages of students' material and four pages of teachers' guide, carefully reviews the story of *Camara* within the context of seven other U.S. Supreme Court cases on the right to privacy. The students' material begins,

> The venerable protections of the Bill or Rights must continually be reinterpreted by the needs of modern society. In this case, two problems confronted the Supreme Court. The first was implicit: what is the real purpose of the Fourth Amendment protection from unreasonable searchers and seizures. The second is explicit: what weight must be given to the increasing problem of a local government's need and desire to maintain safe and healthy residential areas, when each move toward this goal involves a corresponding retreat from freedom for the individual citizen.

The student material then reviewed the essential facts of the case and presented the majority and dissenting opinions of the Justices. A *Washington Post* cartoon used in the student material showed a pot-bellied, armed, and helmeted police officer confronting an apron-wearing woman with the caption reading "Under Precedent Established by King George III We Are Hereby Granted The Right to Forcible Search and Seizure" The teachers' guide states:

This case study marks the beginning of a third year for this series, which now numbers nine studies. This fact allows the teacher to consider a new approach to the use of JUDGMENT [the name of this series] which has not been practical to date, and that is the development of a major unit, or even a course, around the series. (Three additional cases will become available during this school year.)

While each case is distinctive, and intended to stand independently as a teaching device, those who are searching for innovative, but significant, ways to utilize the inquiry and related "new" methods could find these cases an excellent vehicle.

Each one highlights a different Constitutional issue, and in-depth study of the series would provide students with a thoughtful and practical background to our governmental system. Teachers are urged to plan at least as much time for consideration of the issues raised in the Discussion Questions as they do for a study of the facts of the case (not paginated).

Eight review questions (all requiring higher order thinking) and six discussion questions followed for teachers' use. The other JUDGMENT issues available at the time addressed Bible Reading and Prayer, Constitutional Reapportionment, Right to Legal Counsel, Privilege Against Self-Incrimination, Citizenship, Fair Trial versus Free Press, State Loyalty Oaths, and the use of a Poll Tax as Voting Requirement. Thirty copies of any one issue sold for $5. Contemporary readers should realize that these materials creatively illuminated enduring issues, actively engaged students in higher order thinking, and provided an essential opportunity for in-depth learning, all of which are hallmarks of persistent pronouncements concerning the essential nature of high quality social studies. Despite being over 40 years old, the JUDGEMENT materials could be dropped directly into any contemporary high school government class with confidence of positive learning results. Creative teachers might want to go beyond these materials to include the development of a mock trial, small group work aimed at exploring cases that have arisen since 1967, and use of one or more of the excellent legal research resources provided on the Internet.

Some comment is due the other articles in this October 1967 issue of *Social Education*. For example, in the article on Charles Beard we learn that although Beard was a great historian and immensely popular, his leadership of the Commission failed to achieve a practical vision of the social studies that could guide classroom instruction. In *Reinvigorating the Social Studies Program* we are told how the Union-Endicott Central School District of New York used a Special Purpose Grant under Title II of the Elementary and Secondary Education Act of 1965 to transform its secondary social studies program. Among the changes: the purchase of heretofore unaffordable supplemental materials placed into a special resource center located near the school's library; additional teachers to free up more time for the planning of creative lessons and team teaching; the provision of a summer curriculum development workshop; and the retrofitting of classrooms with special wiring, sliding partitions, black-out drapes, and filing cabinets. In Larry Cuban's (1967) *Urban Schools and the Negro*, the Civil Rights Movement is credited with exposing the massive discrimination suffered by Black children in inferior, underfunded urban schools that largely exist as they do because they have a government monopoly that "crushes initiative and stifles experimentation" (p. 479). Cuban calls for more experimentation, decentralizing the school system, changing the role of the teacher, and eliminating neighborhood schools in order to overcome "inferior instruction, antiquated curricula, [and] obsolescent organization" (p. 481). All of this probably sounds quite familiar to the contemporary social studies teachers who are reading these pages. Who among us is not aware of the battles fought over the inclusion of particular courses, content, or topics within the social studies curriculum? Who is unaware of many attempts to reform public education and to achieve a higher quality of education for our most needy families? And what teacher has not longed for more planning time, more resources, and more flexible control over his or her classroom instruction?

Of course, just as it is difficult to briefly and adequately characterize this 1967 issue of *Social Education* and it is even more difficult to convey the essence of the many hundreds of secondary NSS small curriculum projects that never achieved recognition within professional organizations or became publications in state, regional, or national social studies journals. However, some insights into NSS innovations can be gained through inferences drawn from what was presented and published. For example, the February 1973 issue of *Social Education* was entirely devoted to teaching world history through science fiction (Roselle, 1973). Individual articles offered clear instructional plans and complete, professionally written short stories to foster thinking about traditional and nontraditional topics. For example, Gertrude Bacon's *The Gorgon's Head* was used to promote high school students' thinking about ancient Greek myths; Ray Bradbury's *The Smile* was reprinted as a vehicle for opening deep thought about Leonardo da Vinci's Renaissance Era "Mona Lisa" and the meaning and importance of beauty in the lives of individuals no matter where or when they lived; and Judith Merril's compelling space tale, *Survival Ship*, provoked dialogue about women's liberation. Other science fiction stories augmented instruction on the Age of Charlemagne, relationships between East and West, the expanding impact of science and technology, the rise of modern dictators, the use of atomic bombs and radiation, the generation gap, and dehumanization that results from overattention to clock-like precision in the workplace.

The December 1973 issue featured, among other items, articles on teaching for ethnic literacy (Banks, 1973), the plight of the migrant (Mahood, 1973), clarifying sexist values (Sadker, Sadker, & Simon, 1973), and a 2-week mock-trial-based unit focused on examining the conflicting interests surrounding environmental protection and development (MacLagan, 1973). As another example, a complete fold-out simulation board-game of the difficulties of life in and escape from the ghetto (Nay, 1971) and a unit on how to use authentic slave songs as a historical resource (Lord, 1971) were featured in the November 1971 issue of *Social Education*.

In addition to these examples, many issues of *Social Education* in the era of the NSS contained brief descriptions of the curriculum revisions taking place in schools across the nation. Dorothy Fraser, for example, edited this section for the April 1968 issue that included descriptions of comprehensive curriculum guides that had been recently developed for the St. Louis MO, Brooklyn NY, Cedar Grove IA, Ridgefield NJ, Nederland TX, and Little Rock AR school systems. These curriculum guides were described as offering new behavioral science content, including raw data that would lead students to do inductive, scholarly thinking, and featuring comprehensive listings of skills that were to be acquired. As an example of what was taking place around the nation, consider the 1967 curriculum change implemented in the Los Angeles city schools where the middle school social studies curriculum was transformed (Perryman, 1967). Using the California state guideline that 1/5 of the social studies curriculum should be related to current events, the 26 social studies teachers at Mark Twain Junior High School developed a sequence of two-week current event "focal points" that spanned seventh through ninth grade. The titles of these NSS curriculum units tell the story, as they featured a current events focus on world hunger, free trade, welfare programs, the Arab-Israeli conflict, separation of church and state, value conflicts over how children should be educated, crime, the space race, freedom of speech, politics and political power, conservation, the status of Blacks in American society, labor conflicts, value conflicts that arise between government (the public interest) and business (private interests), combating poverty, the authority of the United Nations, promoting democratic governance in Latin America, disputes over science and technology, Vietnam and U.S. imperialism, and nuclear disarmament.

Somewhat rhetorically, I ask the reader to consider, wouldn't it be refreshing to have many of these same topics addressed in today's middle and high school social studies classrooms? And, isn't it perplexing that we still live with many of these same problems, and that today's youth seem no better prepared—perhaps even less prepared—to engage, these topics than their grandparents[9] were over two generations ago? Whether you agree or disagree with my rather pejorative characterization of our present education circumstances, it is still necessary to turn our attention briefly toward how the NSS affected elementary social studies since efforts to change this area of the established curriculum also influenced professional teaching practices during this era and hence help us to understand the fullness of the NSS curriculum reform era.

Elementary Exemplars

Elementary social studies in the United States was widely following an "expanding environments" or "widening horizons" scope and sequence by the mid 1950s. Elementary teachers, school boards, and administrators were generally comfortable with this familiar pattern of topics and their contentment spawned skepticism regarding the necessity of any changes supposedly dictated by the NSS movement. Some teachers and administrators doubtlessly saw the NSS as being something more properly directed toward middle and high schools, where the first developments occurred, rather than little children, their judgments also being buttressed by the nearly ubiquitous presence and acceptance of the widening horizons curriculum. In addition, the existing widening horizons curriculum was, after all, already interdisciplinary, it was often taught with a variety of methods that actively engaged young learners, and it was typically supported by a variety of project-oriented learning experiences. There were, however, notable attempts to infuse NSS content and methods into the K–6 curriculum and an examination of these efforts is necessary to fully characterize the NSS movement.

Dorothy Frazier's "Review of Curriculum Materials" in the April 1968 issue of *Social Education* included descriptions of six new elementary social studies curriculum guides being implemented in Richmond VA, Miami FL, Minneapolis MN, Mount Vernon NY, Fort Knox KY, and Beaumont TX. Several of these guides offered new and increased emphasis on the teaching of economics content, a subject area that had often been neglected in the widening horizons curriculum, which tended to stress mostly history, geography, and citizenship and to focus on local communities, the home state, and the United States. One of the guides emphasized the study of non-Western nations and included the provision of audiovisual kits that contained numerous reproductions of cultural artifacts, a representation of the NSS-born drive to include the humanities and an anthropological focus to elementary social studies instruction. And one guide offered an emphasis on law-related education, an aspect of citizenship education that had been neglected in the typical implementation of the widening horizons curriculum.

The NSS movement included substantial support for adding anthropology as an important content area for study in the elementary social studies. This development is best represented in the University of Georgia's Anthropology Curriculum Project (Rice, 1975, 1992) covered elsewhere in this book. However, there were also many small anthropology curriculum development projects that fall within the scope of this chapter and also help to illustrate the content of this aspect of the NSS. For example, five articles on the teaching of anthropology in the elementary school appeared in the March 1968 issue of *Social Education*, and the April 1969 issue of *Social Education* contained four articles with a significant anthropological emphasis on the study of minority groups in American society: Hispanics (Valdez, 1968); Blacks (Harris, 1968); Orientals (Inn, 1968); and American Indians (Misiaszek, 1968). As another example, the December 1972 issue of *Social Education* contained a series of three articles that examined early adolescent drug use and offered a drug education unit for upper elementary school. The unit concluded with a set of guidelines for instruction that was decidedly anthropological and behavioral, among them, "assess the level of your students," "include all drugs," "compare drug use and abuse," "don't sensationalize," and "emphasize motivational factors" (Schweiss, 1972, pp. 875–876).

The subject area of economics also received substantially increased attention in the NSS revision of the widening horizons elementary social studies curriculum. Here, the work of Lawrence Senesh at Purdue University, covered in-depth in a separate chapter of this volume and later published by Science Research Associates under the title *Our Working World*, was instrumental in expanding this strand of the typical widening horizons curriculum beyond its stereotypical inclusion of community helpers and playing "grocery store" to include, among other things, such concepts as division of labor, economic interdependency, production, consumption, and market forces. True to the spirit of the NSS, Senesh (1968) offered seven guidelines for the inclusion of economics study in the elementary grades, among them: "the curriculum should be reality-oriented," "the curriculum should be problem-oriented," "the curriculum should be structure-oriented," and "the economics curriculum should be interdisciplinary" (pp. 48–49). At the University of Chicago, William Rader directed another elementary school economics curriculum project that produced fourth through sixth grade economics units. The three sixth grade units were focused on exchange, the first being a conceptual introduction to the topic while the second and third focused on domestic and international trade. Earlier I mentioned that one of the characteristics of many of the NSS projects was planned inclusion of authentic field tests of materials with in-depth evaluations of the "teach-ability" of the materials and the level of student learning attained through their use.

Rader's Chicago program (Sander & Tank, 1970) was revised five times prior to being made available for national distribution in 1964, and Sanders and Tank reported "The sixth-grade materials are currently in their third field-test in California, Connecticut, and Texas schools with two thousand students in experimental classes and fifteen hundred students in comparison classes" (p. 422). Contemporary readers should be impressed with the high level of conceptual learning advocated in both the anthropology and economics curriculum additions to elementary social studies. They might also reflect on the care that was given to authentic field tests of these curriculum materials, field tests that included not only numerous cycles of revision but also quasi-experimental research designs that could yield credible claims about the educational effectiveness of these materials.

CONCLUDING THOUGHTS

This brief exploration of small, now nearly forgotten, projects of the NSS was undertaken in the belief that the spirit of the NSS movement could be more fully characterized by examining "small fry" projects rather than viewing the movement through the larger projects. It was hoped that recounting this story would inspire contemporary teachers, perhaps motivating them to exceed the bounds of the contemporary status quo and especially to confront the particular burdens of their present-day instructional regimens that teachers say too often serves only to stifle creativity and stultify higher order learning. Throughout the chapter I have attempted to draw out the insights that would help readers see the better aspects of the NSS curriculum movement. It may be helpful, however, at this point to go a bit further into a few of the many published critiques and reflections on the NSS in order to bolster contemporary teachers' thinking and hearten their spirit for taking independent or collaborative actions to improve their social studies instruction.

C. Fredrick Risinger (1974) reminded thousands of high school principals of the best characteristics of the NSS when he reviewed the largely spontaneous and voluntary changes being made to social studies instruction in ten different high schools for the 1974 issue of the NSSP's Curriculum Report. Spontaneous and voluntary are important words to be used in this context for they convey an essential trait of education within our particular form of representative democracy, namely the value we place on the importance of exercising local control over what actually happens in classrooms and the need to honor teachers', parents', and students' judgments concerning both the contents and methods of instruction. The ERIC abstract for Risinger's publication (ED 093 773) states:

Four major content changes include the trend away from expository history and toward the behavioral science, attention to the analysis of individual values, systematic and realistic study of public issues, and closer concern with local needs, resources, and problems. New instructional strategies emphasize experimental learning, the use of role-playing activities, group discussions, student selection of courses and assignments, and other inquiry oriented activities (not paginated).

Concerning changes in content, the report states that "when implemented with care...the examination of values can be both an exciting and a meaningful addition to social studies education" (Risinger, 1974, p. 3) and that this examination of values complements the serious, rational, and structured study of public issues with "the overall objective ... to help students develop command of rational decision-making processes, which they can use when confronted with personal and public dilemmas" (p. 3). Risinger notes,

the past few years have witnessed a more intimate and action-oriented concern with local needs, resources, and possible solutions to local problems than formerly was true of social studies courses and content. Global topics are still the major components, but they, too, are frequently related to community-based issues. (p. 3)

Methods of NSS instruction were also reviewed by Risinger (1974), who stated,

Common to all of these trends in instructional strategy is the effort to make the student an active participant not only in the teaching/learning act but in the social scene itself. Increasingly, social studies courses call upon students to be citizens in a complete sense, not just readers and talkers about citizenship. (p. 3)

Recognizing that social studies has traditionally not been among students' most favorite subjects, Risinger noted that

a radical reversal of attitude has been observed in most schools where some or all of these innovative changes in social studies programming have been made. This alone is not convincing proof of the value of the changes, but it certainly is consistent with the judgment of both classroom teacher and scholars in the social sciences that the newer social studies programs are both more appealing and intellectually more substantial than those more conventional in content and methodology. (p. 4)

I wish space would allow me to characterize in more detail the exciting descriptions of NSS curriculums developed in the 10 school districts described in the second part of Risinger's (1974) curriculum report. Here, for your consideration, are just three brief examples. The St. Louis Park Schools, for example, had developed a one-semester world religions course that examined major faith traditions and religious stereotypes as well as the interface between religion and public policy and religion and cultural change. Or consider Bell Junior High School in Golden, Colorado, where the social studies curriculum

> was one of the outcomes of a major all-school effort to create a democratic environment, and experiment to see if and how a junior high school could become more open, democratic, and humane in fact and practice as well as in principle" (p. 5).

And think about the fact that Parker Senior High School in Janesville, Wisconsin, had developed an integrated three-year program for which the overarching goal was "to observe, interpret, and evaluate man as a total, many-sided being [using] knowledge and viewpoints of the six social sciences ... the arts, history, and various value-belief systems for our course content" (p. 4). I contend that the quality of education obtained in these schools was enhanced by these local, voluntary NSS developments and I am also willing to bet that the students and their teachers were energized by this professional work.

Jan Tucker's (1970) research on social studies teacher educators/methods professors holds some other insights that may prove valuable to today's teachers and curriculum leaders. Tucker surveyed a national sample ($n = 94$) of methods professors to determine their views on the impact of the NSS. Among other things, he concluded that methods professors mainly associated the NSS with the major projects that had gained national recognition rather than the small projects. He wrote,

> In summary, teacher educators reject the [big] project notion that curriculum development should take place outside of particular educational situations. As a corollary, teacher educators, particularly those holding appointments in a school of education, tend to prefer an interdisciplinary curriculum designed around the interests, beliefs, values, and life experience of students. They see project-centered NSS over-emphasizing such characteristics as separate academic disciplines, homogeneous grouping, and cognitive goals; in short, too much emphasis on "the structure of a discipline" approach. (p. 5)

Tucker (1970) noted that the kind of social studies instruction favored by methods professors was "not easily packaged" (p. 12) and that "preservice social studies teachers need to learn [the] broad principles of developing a student-centered, community-oriented curriculum, not the specific details of a large number of pre-packaged curricula" (p. 12). He pointed out that social studies methods professors were largely bypassed by the NSS movement; that the majority of the grant money went to alert local school districts to fund curriculum development and revisions of their social studies programs (p. 8). Thus, it seems that Tucker's sample of social studies methods professors were mainly critical of the few large NSS curriculum projects that attempted to pre-package teacher-proof, highly-academic, structure-of-the-discipline curriculums. Philosophically, they were much more supportive of the kinds of small projects that I have reported on in this paper, the locally developed projects that infused new content and made use of creative, student-centered instruction.

As yet another example of where the small projects of NSS were on target, Jonathon McLendon (1970) reported on his survey of 400 research and curriculum development projects, which were identified as being specifically designed for minority groups in American society. His analysis suggested nine key traits that were associated with effective social studies instruction for these groups. Among them, that (a) subject matter is more appropriate when it is specific in nature and is dealt with through a "real-people approach;" (b) that the most successful content tended to include elements of law, culture, and social issues; (c) that multimedia and simulation games facilitated more learning; and (d) that teachers' participation in curriculum development and teachers' positive attitudes were important to success. Matthew Downey's (1983) postmortem on the NSS arrived at somewhat similar conclusions: the NSS did influence the teaching of social studies by making teachers more aware of the need to use diverse methods for diverse learners and empowering teachers to do local history studies, which to many teachers "was just another inquiry strategy" (p. 7). He also judged that the NSS had positively influenced the content and presentation of history textbooks and had given rise to a "deluge of documents collections, edited historiographical anthologies, and paperback history books" (pp. 8–9). Herlihy and Strahan's (1984) study of elementary social studies teachers drew similar conclusions, stating that 60% of the teachers that they surveyed "demonstrated a student-centered/process-oriented approach to teaching" (p. 469) and "used a wide range of teaching resources, devoted class time to exploratory learning and active discussion" (p. 469). Readers should reflect on the fact that these three reviews revealed teachers' enduring quest to provide authentic learning experiences tailored to their learners' interests and needs and to local conditions within their communities. Pre-packaged curricula intended to be universally and uniformly implemented—as well as all learning assessments tied to such curricula—often fail to accommodate these desirable goals for social studies education.

Marion Rice in his 1992 reflection on the NSS identified three important legacies that he considered worthy of future study and reflection.

First, he contended that the NSS "showed that the content of subject instruction could be substantially increased and that students at all levels, even those in kindergarten, could learn more" (p. 229). However, Rice noted, reversion to traditional lower-level content learning and concomitant less-demanding teaching methods was an easy and all-too-acceptable fallback for many teachers and students. Second was the legacy of inquiry-based instruction which went far beyond prior, social and personal problem-solving activities "to show its relevance to the development of intellectual abilities within the pursuit of school subjects … [which] … shifted the emphasis from immediate utility to the process of acquiring a deeper understanding and intellectual skills, independent of practical effects" (p. 229). Third, according to Rice, was "the legacy of the curriculum artifacts themselves" (p. 229) which should be studied not as "monuments for adulation" but as "creative product[s] of a given period" that come with an extensive explanatory, analytical, and evaluative literature (p. 230).

In summary, these authors' reflections and the exemplars reported earlier demonstrate that there was much of value to the NSS. The NSS was indeed a curriculum movement and this movement is best represented in the hundreds of small projects that were the products of the intellectual and instructional innovations of the NSS. What we clearly see, I think, is educators, students, and their parents involved in formulating challenging and meaningful learning experiences where instruction went far beyond lower level outcomes and often pushed into multidisciplinary inquiries of contemporary issues. Having experienced this era first hand, I can attest to the sense of energy that was generated by the ability to address instruction from an inquiry perspective and the freedom that came from working in a professional environment that encouraged the exploration of new content. Without doubt, the largest impediment--back then—to effective instruction was the limited body of knowledge that could easily be tapped. Encyclopedias, newspapers, prepared "data banks" and other traditional media center resources were the limited tools we used to support inquiries into questions about the past, present, and potential futures or our world. Information age technologies have effectively eliminated this impediment so that there is no longer any practical roadblock to the realization of the best practices of the NSS save retrograde demands for an artificial uniformity of learning outcomes and the draconian testing programs that seemingly "justify" this industrial-era thinking about pedagogy. Clearly, if we deeply care about our professional practice and we hold ourselves accountable for achieving all that we desire for every student who entrusts their learning potential to us, we must attempt to learn and benefit from the lessons of the NSS as they are clearly displayed in the many hundreds of small NSS projects that now have slipped over the rim of many teachers' conscious remembrance. We are living with a legacy that provides clear guidelines for effective instruction and it is a shame that all too often teachers feel compelled to abandon these practices for promoting advanced learning and more positive attitudes toward social studies. I would suggest that contemporary teachers might profit from exceeding the bounds of any social studies curriculum that binds their creative instincts or diminishes their students' lust for social learning. Carefully listening to students' questions and supporting their search for better understanding of the complex world they will inevitably inherit can achieve a beginning toward this goal.

NOTES

1. Bob Taylor and Thomas Groom described 111 NSS projects in their 1971 ASCD publication, *Social studies education projects: An ASCD index.*
2. *Social Education* annually published a section that reviewed curriculum materials. For example, the April 1968 issue, edited by Dorothy Fraser, contained reports on 44 curriculum projects developed in school districts across the United States. Fraser noted, among other things, that 44 projects, taken as a whole, tended to show continued evidence of NSS trends, including the "desirability of employing the inductive approach," and "increasing study of peoples and cultures of the non-western world" (p. 363).
3. The NSS is no different from any other curriculum phenomenon or teaching practice in that individual manifestations and implementations will always fall along a continuum of fidelity.
4. ERIC's "Microfiche to Megabytes" digitization project is described on the www.eric.ed.gov Web site. Information retrieved on April 6, 2007.
5. In addition to presenting individual pieces of curriculum, I also have included published reviews of noteworthy and meritorious small projects.
6. It should be noted that many of the NSS materials also contained features such as a spiral development of core concepts, behavioral objectives, and carefully matched assessments of students' learning. In addition, many of the projects had conducted field tests of their materials and some offered various forms of teacher training. These characteristics were not used in my selection process.
7. While I realize that there are, indeed, many high quality contemporary social studies programs sprinkled across the nation and throughout the grades, the overall impact of federal and many states' policies has been to narrow the social studies curriculum and even to reduce the time devoted to social studies instruction
8. The National Council for the Social Studies archives only go back to 1991 and there has been little talk of trying to digitize pre-1991 articles.
9. Yes, I meant grandparents: a generation is roughly 20–25 years and this was over 40 years ago!

REFERENCES

Bacon, G. (1973). The Gorgon's head. *Social Education, 37,* 96–101.

Banks, J. A. (1973). Teaching for ethnic literacy: A comparative approach. *Social Education, 37,* 738–750.

Bradbury, R. (1970). *S is for space.* New York: Bantam Books.

Cleary, R. E. (1967). The right to privacy—A case study. *Social Education, 31,* (n.p.).

Cuban, L. (1967). Urban schools and the Negro. *Social Education, 31,* 478–482.

Downey, M. T. (1983). Beyond the era of the new social studies: Putting the present in perspective. *Social Studies, 74*(1), 6–9.

Dykstra, J. W. (1967). The high school sociology course. *Social Education, 31,* 487–489.

Fraser, D. M. (1968). Review of curriculum materials. *Social Education, 32,* 362–372, 381–385.

Harris, N. H. (1968). The treatment of Negroes in books and media designed for the elementary school. *Social Education, 33,* 434–437.

Herlihy, J. G., & Strahan, D. B. (1984). Social studies innovations—A decade later. *Social Education, 48,* 466–469.

Inn, A. M. S. (1968). The Orientals. *Social Education, 33,* 443–446.

Klassen, D. L. (1973). *Computer simulation in the social sciences/social studies.* Paper presented at the Association for Educational Data Systems Annual Convention, New Orleans, LA. (ERIC Document Reproduction Service ED087429)

Lord, D. C. (1971). The slave song as a historical source. *Social Education, 35,* 763–767, 821.

MacLagan, R. (1973). *Environmental issues: A courtroom simulation.* (ERIC Document Reproduction Service No. ED082982).

Mahood, W. (1973). The plight of the migrant. *Social Education, 37,* 751–755.

McKeown, R. J. (1973). *Toward international understanding in the American secondary schools.* Paper presented that the Hawaii Conference of the Joint Committee on United States-Japan Educational and Cultural Cooperation, Hilo, HI. (ERIC Document Reproduction Service No. ED083079)

McLendon, J. C. (1970). *Social studies and the disadvantaged. Targeted communication (interpretive) study of research and development; phase 1, analysis and implications.* Final report. National Council for the Social Studies, Washington, DC. (ERIC Document Reproduction Services No. ED049956)

Merril, J. (1973). *Survivor ship and other stories.* Toronto: Kakabeka Publishing.

Misiaszek, L. (1968). The cultural dilemma of American Indians. *Social Education, 33,* 438–439, 446.

Morganti, M. D. (1967). Total involvement in student government. *Social Education, 31,* 4493–4494.

National Council for the Social Studies. (1994). *Expectations of Excellence: Curriculum Standards for Social Studies.* Washington, DC: Author.

Nay, J. (1971). "ESCAPE": A game. *Social Education, 35,* 746-761.

Perryman, D. (1967). Emphasis on basic issues. *Social Education, 31,* 693–697.

Portzline, D. B. (1967). Local planning for revision of the social studies: The use of federal assistance programs. *Social Education, 31,* 469–474.

Preston, R. C. (1967). Familiarity and contrast as curriculum principles. *Social Education, 31,* 491–493.

Rice, M. J. (1975, December). *The development of a sequential curriculum in anthropology, Grades 1–7.* Paper presented at the American Anthropology Association, San Francisco, CA. (ERIC Document Reproduction Service No. ED132071).

Rice, M. J. (1992). Reflections on the new social studies. *Social Studies, 83,* 224–231.

Risinger, C. F. (1974). New social studies programs. *Curriculum Report, 3*(6). (ERIC Document Reporduction Service No. ED093773)

Roselle, D. (1973). Teaching about world history through science fiction, an anthology compiled by Daniel Roselle. *Social Education, 37,* 96–150.

Ryan, M. J. (1967). Reinvigorating the social studies program. *Social Education, 31,* 475–477.

Sadker, D., Sadker, M., & Simon, S. (1973). Clarifying sexist values. *Social Education, 37,* 756–760.

Sanders, N. M., & Tanck, M. L. (1970). A critical appraisal of twenty-six national social studies projects. *Social Education, 34,* 383–446.

Schweiss, E. (1972). Case study: Developing a drug education curriculum for the upper-elementary grades. *Social Education, 36,* 874–878.

Senesh, L. (1968). The pattern of the economic curriculum. *Social Education, 32,* 47–50, 59.

Soderbergh, P. A. (1967). Charles A. Beard and the commission on the social studies 1929-1933: A reappraisal. *Social Education, 31,* 465-468, 477.

Taylor, B. L., & Groom, T. L. (1971). *Social Studies Education Projects: an ASCD Index.* Washington, DC: The Association for Supervision and Curriculum Development.

Tucker, J. L. (1970, November). *Social studies projects and teacher educators: Creative tension?* Paper presented at the meeting of the College and University Faculty Assembly of the National Council for the Social Studies, New York. (ERIC Document Reproduction Service No. ED045507).

Turner, M. J. (1970). *Political science in "New Social Studies" curricula: State of the art—1970.* Paper prepared for the Political Science Education Project, American Political Science Association. (ERIC Document Reproduction Service No. ED062218)

United States Office of Education. (1967). A directory of social studies projects. *Social Education, 31,* 509–511.

Valdez, D. T. (1968). The U.S. Hispano. *Social Education, 33,* 440–442.

SECTION III

PERSPECTIVES

CHAPTER 15

THE FIGHT OVER MACOS

Larry Kraus

"This is simply not the kind of material Congress or any federal agency should be promoting and marketing with taxpayer's money" (Conlan, 1975). This statement, made by Rep. John Conlan from the floor of the United State House of Representatives in April, 1975, concisely defined two major areas of debate that came out of the controversies surrounding *Man: A Course of Study* (MACOS), one of the more prominent federally-funded curriculum programs developed by the National Science Foundation (NSF) in the 1950s and 1960s. Not only was the content of MACOS unusual and a bit controversial, the manner in which it had been funded raised issues that were even more intense to some groups. And, while the issues related to the content of the program were somewhat specific to MACOS, the funding issues cut a broader swath through political, social, and educational issues. To understand MACOS and the attendant controversies, we must also understand the political and educational climate.

As Stephen Ambrose (1983) was later to chronicle, in the late 1930s the United States was not a technological power, nor was there any real political pressure for it to become one. And, in the area of education, the vast majority of funds spent on curriculum development came from private and commercial sources. Federal policy related to educational goals was essentially nonexistent. The bombing of Pearl Harbor by Japan in 1941,

The New Social Studies: People, Projects, and Perspectives, pp. 309–339

though, put the United States into a war with enemies that were developing technologies and were using them against us. Ambrose points out that, had Hitler been more aware of the advantages his jet propulsion research was providing and had he used these resources better, the outcome of World War II might have been significantly delayed or possibly even altered. At the conclusion of the war, President Harry Truman (and later President Dwight Eisenhower) recognized the need for a national scientific and technological research effort and influenced federal policy toward this goal. One result of these efforts was federal funding of pre-college curriculum, something which had never been done before in the country's history.

In September 1959, approximately 35 nationally recognized scholars from the areas of the natural sciences, history, classics, cinematography, and psychology met at Woods Hole, Massachusetts to discuss the math and science projects that had been developed with funding from the National Science Foundation (Bruner, 1960). The conference, co-chaired by Harvard psychologist Jerome Bruner (who later served as project director for MACOS) and Jerrald Zacharias, a physicist from MIT, was called to review and examine the early results of projects, such as the Physical Sciences Study Committee (PSSC) physics program (headed by Zacharias); the Biological Science Curriculum Study (BSCS), headed by Addison Lee at the University of Colorado; and the School Mathematics Study Group (SMSG), headed by Edward Begle of Yale University. These projects had sprung forth from concerns after the peacetime draft following World War II. While many trace these changes to the years immediately following Sputnik (1956), Goodladd (1964) states that the actual beginnings occurred ten years earlier:

> But the roots of change go back further, to the years immediately following World War II. The recruitment of young men for the armed services had revealed shocking inadequacies in the science and mathematics programs of high school graduates. The problem was partly the limited quantity of work in these areas, partly the quality of what had been taught. The secondary school curriculum too often reflected knowledge of another era, instead of the scientific advances of the twentieth century. Recognizing their responsibility for this unhappy state of affairs, scholars in a few fields began to participate actively in what has now become a major curriculum reform movement. (p. 9)

The need for scientific research and education was recognized as a national need as early as 1944, when President Roosevelt became especially interested and concerned with the development of scientific education. In a letter to Vannevar Bush, the Director of U.S. Office of Scientific Research and Development, Roosevelt exhibited his interest:

Can an effective program be proposed for discovering and developing scientific talent in American youth so that the continuing future of scientific research in this country can be assured on a level comparable to what has been done during the war? (U.S., Congress, House Subcommittee on Science, 1975)

Many in the nation's scientific community shared Roosevelt's concern. After Roosevelt's death, steps were taken to create a national foundation, charged with fostering scientific research. This foundation, known as the National Science Foundation, was established by Congress in 1947, but was vetoed by President Harry Truman (NSF Bill Vetoed, 1947), who feared too little political control over the foundation. The scientific community, on the other hand, feared government control and refused to endorse any agency not given a pledge of independence. After almost three years of debate, President Truman finally withdrew his objections and signed the legislation creating the National Science Foundation in 1950 (U.S., Congress, House Subcommittee on Science, 1975).

When NSF was authorized, in 1950, the assumption was that activities would be restricted to the collegiate and graduate levels. A short statement in *Science*, in 1957, changed that:

The National Science Foundation has announced that it will accept proposals to support, on an experimental basis, about 15 in-service institutes for secondary teachers of science and mathematics to be held in the academic year 1957–58. ("NSF to Support", 1957, p. 294)

According to Goodladd (1964), the national curriculum reform movement was already active by the time NSF entered the picture. The movement began in 1951 with the University of Illinois Committee on School Mathematics (UICSM), which was supported with funding from the University of Illinois, the United States Office of Education, and the Carnegie Corporation (p. 13). NSF participation in this project began in 1957 with the funding of summer institutes, although there was a great deal of reluctance on the part of the NSF Board to become involved with pre-college science education, partly because of funding problems and partly because of a feeling that the need was not that great (U.S. Congress, House Subcommittee on Science, 1975).

Not until 1956 was the lack of scientific manpower generally considered to be a threat to the United States. There had been reports that the USSR was making great scientific strides, especially in Nicholas DeWitt's (1955) book, *Soviet Professional Manpower,* but there was a general hesitance in the scientific community and by some members of Congress to believe these reports. With the growing realization that U.S. technology was being bypassed, an urgent movement to correct the situation became visible. Dr. Detlev Bront, an early opponent of overreacting to Soviet claims of scientific superiority, reversed his stand in 1956 when he introduced the subject of education of teachers to the Subcommittee of the House Committee on Appropriations:

> I am one of those who has said that I think we should not say we are going to do this or we are going to do that, because the Russians are doing it. I think we are a country that can stand on our own feet and make our own decisions.
>
> But, nevertheless, having been one of five representatives to Geneva at the Peace Conference last year, I feel I have an obligation to say that I was shocked by the necessity for reversing my previous opinion.
>
> I had thought that the Russians were so crude in their approaches to education and science that we did not have anything very much to worry about from them. I thought that a lot of people had said much more than the Russians deserved with regard to their competence. But I was certainly impressed by the fact that they had been able to do many things that I did not think they could do.
>
> Furthermore, I was impressed by the fact that we heard over and over again that they were increasing more and more the number of students who are taking science and are being trained in science and engineering. I think that this is almost a necessity for any country which desires to hold itself high in a modern scientific and technological age.
>
> Every new development unfolds other developments, and the only way we can cope with these new scientific and technical developments is to have people who are competent to deal with them. (Goodladd, 1964, p. 52)

As Russian superiority in scientific and technological matters became more and more of a concern, a corresponding increase in the NSF budget and, perhaps more importantly, a willingness to remove the legislative limitation of $15,000,000 per year imposed on the NSF were evidenced. This increase in funding, beginning in fiscal year 1957, opened the door to grants for the development of school curricula.

The first move in this direction was the funding of the work of the Physical Sciences Study Committee (PSSC). The grant, in the amount of $303,000 (a relatively large sum for NSF grants at the time), was intended to cover the "study phase" of the program (Goodladd, 1964, p. 59). From this initial grant, in 1956, the NSF expanded in the curriculum field rapidly, funding programs such as the Chemical Bond Approach (CBA) in 1957; the Biological Sciences Curriculum Project (BSCS) and the Elementary School Science Project, both in 1959; and the University of Illinois Elementary School Science Project in 1960 (Goodladd, 1964, pp. 13–41).

According to Spring, NSF involvement in curriculum development received vital support from President Dwight Eisenhower in a special message to Congress in January 1958. Eisenhower, concerned about the effect of the Russian Sputnik on national defense, tended to view education as one way of meeting the Soviet challenge. In the message, Eisenhower called for a five-fold increase in appropriations for science programs, increased spending for summer institutes to train high school science and mathematics teachers, increased funding for improving content in science programs, and expanding programs encouraging students to consider careers in scientific fields (Spring, 1976, pp. 7–36). All of these programs were under the control of the National Science Foundation. Another section of the message called for an educational package to be under the jurisdiction of the Office of Education in the Department of Health, Education, and Welfare. These recommendations resulted in the passage of the National Defense Education Act (NDEA) in November 1958 (p. 100).

The total NSF budget in 1952 was $1.5 million. By 1959, this had increased by over $62 million to a total appropriation of almost $64 million. With this increase in funding occurred a drastic increase in curriculum development. In 1975, the Foundation listed 54 curriculum projects receiving funding, at a cost of approximately $106.8 million, with an additional $79.8 million paid for implementation costs. In the 20 years between 1956, when PSSC was first funded, and 1975, over $186 million was spent on developing and implementing pre-college curricula (Science Curriculum Review Team, 1975).

Considering the expense, a reasonable question seems to be: How successful were they? Sweeping generalizations are impossible, of course. Some were more successful than others. Ausubel, discussing Biological Sciences Curriculum Study (BSCS) (cited by Goodladd, 1964, p. 52) as perhaps the most successful of the federally funded programs), described two of the three divisions of the program as being "admirably thorough, accurate, and up-to-date, but so ineffectively presented and organized, and so impossibly sophisticated for their intended audience, as to be intrinsically unlearnable on a long term basis" (Ausubel, 1966, p. 176). BSCS, along with many of the other projects, is also frequently criticized for ignoring social problems insofar as those problems related to the subject matter (p. 176). Other problems encountered by the federally funded curricula included teacher variability, the argument of purity versus application, a softening of emphasis placed on "subject-centered" curricula, and the difficulty of keeping subject matter current in the midst of a technology and knowledge explosion (p. 176).

While the preceding discussions of the quality of the NSF programs were primarily held within the scientific and educational communities, a seemingly minor decision by the U.S. Congress, in 1963, was to lay the groundwork for a much broader discussion in the general public in later years: The NSF would expand its work into the social sciences. In November of that year, the NSF approved a proposal for a 6-year elementary social studies program titled *The Human Past*. The prototype for the project, a fifth-grade program called *Man: A Course of Study*, would cost $4.6 million and, more importantly, set the stage for a heated and wide-ranging controversy, which would change the way the National Science Foundation participated in pre-college curriculum development.

Man: A Course of Study (MACOS) asserted a five-fold purpose:

1. To give our pupils respect for and confidence in the powers of their own minds.

2. To extend that respect and confidence to their power to think about the human condition, man's plight, and his social life.

3. To provide a set of workable models that make it simpler to analyze the nature of the social world in which we live and the conditions in which man finds himself.

4. To impart a sense of respect for the capacities and humanity of a species.

5. To leave the students with a sense of the unfinished business of man's evolution (Bruner, 1966, p. 101).

To accomplish these purposes, the students are exposed to three basic organizing questions throughout the materials of the MACOS program:

What is human about human beings?
How did they get that way?
How can they be made more so? (Bruner, 1966, p. 101)

Five topics are used to consider these questions and to provide comparisons and contrasts between different organisms and social structures. These subjects include tool making, language, social organization, the management of man's prolonged childhood, and man's urge to explain his world (P. B Dow, personal communication, May 14, 1976).

The first half of *Man: A Course of Study* was devoted to a study of non-human species, including salmon, herring gulls, and baboons. Students compare and contrast the behavior of these species with human behavior to determine some basic characteristics about the nature of being human. For example, while studying salmon, students were exposed to a species that does not have an overlap in generations. By examining and comparing the life-cycle of the salmon with the life-cycle of humans, students make generalizations about the nature of man and are able to understand human-kind's humanness more fully.

The second half of the program was devoted to the study of a less-developed human culture, the Netsilik Eskimo. Students were asked to compare the life and culture of the Netsilik with their own lives and cultures. Through this comparison, the students were exposed to the interaction of values and culture. Whereas the first part of the course, comparing humans to other animals, might have logically been considered the more controversial aspects of MACOS, due to the materials dealing with evolution and comparing humans to lower animals, the materials about the Netsilik Eskimo evoked the most strident, and the greatest amount of, protest.

As mentioned earlier, MACOS was developed as the prototype of a larger project, *The Human Past*. The original project director, Douglas Oliver, left the project in 1964, to be replaced by Jerome Bruner, who had served as project evaluator from the beginning of the project. Bruner made several key decisions in the program, including designing the course for fifth-grade students (P. B. Dow, personal communication, May 14, 1976). Bruner also decided to wait until the program neared completion before involving a commercial publisher. Finally, Bruner was primarily responsible for the choice of content in the program.

Bruner's ideas about the course differed greatly from those of Douglas Oliver. According to Peter B. Dow, who became MACOS project director in 1966 after Bruner stepped down to become a consulting scholar and the guiding spirit of the program, Oliver looked upon the program as a vehicle for anthropological research, with little emphasis on an elementary curriculum, except as it related to this research (P. B Dow, personal communication, May 14, 1976). Bruner's primary interests also were not in curriculum; however, he was attracted to developing the program in order to study stages of development within the learning process. Dow comments about his perception of Bruner's interest:

> His notion was very different from Oliver's. He was a psychologist, of course. He was more interested in the stages of development within the learning process and he saw the whole anthropological study more as a vehicle for inquiring about what kids could and couldn't do; what they could and couldn't learn about human behavior. As you know, he'd written a book in which he said you could teach anybody anything at any age. But I don't think Bruner was really persuaded that that was true, at least not so persuaded that he didn't want to test the assumption. (P. B Dow, personal communication, May 14, 1976)

Bruner served as project director of MACOS until 1966, when Dow became the director. Bruner (personal communication, April 12, 1975) later described the development of MACOS:

> When we started on MACOS, the teaching of social studies was dominated by commercial textbooks produced by professional textbook writers who

wrote for a set market; books that were out of touch with contemporary knowledge and research on the nature of man, his evolution, and the structure of human societies. These books made huge profits for their publishers and their authors. We brought together a mix of first-class teachers, distinguished scholars, sensitive artists and writers and film-makers with the hope that we could bring students the best that was available in scholarship, presented in a way that was lively and challenging. We wanted students to develop a sense of what was uniquely human about man, how he had become human in his long evolution in the animal kingdom, and how man, by his efforts, could become even more human. Those were the professed aims and they animated our work. The people who worked on the project did so out of the conviction that it was worth taking instruction in the human sciences seriously. They gave of their time and their efforts with generosity and a devotion to duty—giving up time, renouncing profits (for none of us ever had a penny profit from the sales of these materials), learning how to do things that were intellectually challenging for young students.

Several observations about the development of MACOS must be made, not only to summarize, but also to provide a needed frame of reference for the controversies that followed. First, by design (as Bruner infers above), no commercial publishers were involved in the development. Publication of the program was never seriously considered until completion of the project was near. Those involved with the development had no publishing experience. An argument could be made that earlier involvement of a publisher might have altered the program in such a manner that the controversies concerning content could have been largely avoided. However, an opposing argument could also be made that, had a publisher been involved, MACOS would have not had the same passion and the same intellectual challenge for which the program became known.

A second factor that could have been impacted by earlier intervention of a publisher was the ultimate cost of the program to schools. No indications exist that the developers ever considered program costs. MACOS was a very expensive program, costing approximately twice the amount of competing programs at the time. (For comparative purposes, MACOS cost in excess of $3,000 (in 1969 dollars) per classroom set. Adjusted for inflation, it would have cost almost $16,000 per classroom set in 2005 (Friedman, n.d.).

A third factor could have been the choice of the fifth-grade as the target grade level. Almost all commercial social studies programs in existence in the late 1960's introduced American history at this grade level. This prevented integration of MACOS into the scope and sequence of existing programs. Some publishers who might have considered adding MACOS to their existing offerings might have been hesitant to do so because of this. Using MACOS to replace fifth-grade American history also left the program open to criticism from those like George Weber (1975, p. 82), the executive director of the Council for Basic Education (CBE) in 1975, who felt that the program might have been acceptable as a high school elective, but would not be acceptable as a replacement for instruction in American culture.

The developers of MACOS were aware that certain parts of the program were controversial. They were not aware, however, of just how controversial the program would be (P. B Dow, personal communication, May 14, 1976). They believed a course was needed which would give pupils another way of looking at the study of behavior. MACOS was their attempt at creating such a course. In the years immediately following publication of the program, MACOS became the center of a maelstrom of controversy that both put a damper on future curriculum development and also fundamentally changed the involvement of the federal government in curriculum funding.

Of course, not all of the attention to MACOS was negative. In fact, much of the early discussion was highly favorable. *Time* magazine (January 9, 1970) called the program "intriguing" and devoted its entire "Education" section to a positive report on MACOS. *Time* also reported in that same issue that "few parents have objected to the course, even though it contains rather fundamental information on mating habits and some of the bloodiest film imaginable on the slaughtering of seals" ("Teaching Man," 1970).

More positive publicity came from the May, 1970, issue of *American Education,*" which called MACOS "the successful realization of one aim of Jerome Bruner" (Ferber, 1970). The article also reports enthusiastic teacher response to the program and very favorable response from students.

Ironically, the first attacks on MACOS also occurred in 1970, in the town of Lake City, Florida. In that year, Lake City was in the process of desegregating its schools and had chosen to use a "grade-center" concept (students at each grade level attending one school). In preparation for this change, three social studies teachers in the district, who had heard about the MACOS program, went to the Tallahassee, Florida MACOS training center. These teachers, one White, one Black, and one American Indian, hoped that the program could help them provide a non-racial social studies program. The teachers liked MACOS and, with the approval of their principal and superintendent (but without the approval of the local school board), purchased the program and brought it back to the Lake City sixth-grade center (P. B Dow, personal communication, May 14, 1976).

The program was implemented at the beginning of the school year with no immediate reaction from parents or the community. At Christmas, however, the quiet was disrupted. Peter Dow related that:

One day a local Baptist minister named Glenn took airtime on the local radio station, sponsored by the hardware store, I believe. Glenn had just been in the community about six months; he'd just come in as a new Baptist minister. How he'd gotten a hold of the *Man: A Course of Study* materials, I don't quite know; perhaps a parent had shown him the materials. In any case, he went up to the school building and got the teacher's manual and went on the air reading selected passages from the background readings for teachers. Well, you can imagine what happened in that community that was looking for a reason why it should have a controversy over schooling, anyway. (P. B Dow, personal communication, May 14, 1976)

The result was a loud school board meeting, with each side defending its view of MACOS. MACOS, which had been the only social studies curriculum in use at the sixth-grade center, was kept at the school, but became one of several programs available. The program was eventually dropped on the premise that it was too expensive. However, some teachers felt the controversy was more responsible for removing the program than the cost (P. B Dow, personal communication, May 14, 1976).

The next location for controversy was Phoenix, Arizona in 1971. This confrontation between pro-MACOS and anti-MACOS forces marked the first involvement of John Conlan with the program. The man who was to lead the fight against MACOS on the floor of the U.S. House of Representatives was, at the time, a state senator from the Phoenix suburb of Scottsdale. While Conlan's involvement in 1971 was minimal, it clearly laid the groundwork for his subsequent attacks on MACOS 4 years later. As a result of the controversy in Phoenix, MACOS was banned from all Arizona public schools, except those supported by the federal government, primarily Bureau of Indian Affairs schools (George Archibald, personal communication, May 10, 1976).

Other protests erupted in Maryland, Texas, Washington, and New York. In each of the situations, the complaints surrounding the content of MACOS fell into one or more of the ten categories listed by Rep. Conlan in his April, 1975 speech on the floor of the House: Cruel murder of old people or senilicide; female infanticide; gore and excessive blood being shown in scenes of killing and butchering of animals in vivid detail on film; teaching sex education; murder and cannibalism; divorce, trial marriage, polygamy, and polyandry, and wife-swapping; religion treated as a myth; evolution taught as fact; murder and revenge; and bestiality (Conlan, 1975). For a more complete discussion of each of these controversies, see Larry L. Kraus (1977), *Curriculum, Public Policy, and Criticism: An Analysis of the Controversies Surrounding Man: A Course of Study*. While many different charges were leveled against MACOS, several of the main ones will be discussed below. Note should be made that, in addition to the student materials included with MACOS, teachers also had materials. The MACOS developers realized that the information included in the program was, in all likelihood, beyond the scope of the training most teachers received. Therefore, a nine volume teacher's guide was included with the program, along with a requirement that teachers using the program must receive training from a MACOS Training Center. This is important, as many of the controversies, although certainly not all, arose from materials contained solely in the Teacher's Guides.

CONTENT ISSUES

While a detailed discussion of all 10 of the categories is not possible in the context of this narrative, note should be made that most of the criticisms were based on second or third-hand information, rather than witnessed by the person making the protest. For example, MACOS was heavily criticized for including the topic of senilicide in the materials. In the story of Arfek and his family, a dilemma occurs when the mother-in-law became too frail to travel with the family on their hunt. A family meeting is held and the mother-in-law volunteers to stay behind. Arfek knows that leaving her behind means that she will die; however, he must think of his wife and children. The old woman is left on the ice.

Critics essentially ignored some of the facts when condemning the story. For example, nationally syndicated columnist James J. Kilpatrick (1975) quoted a letter he had received:

> The price of survival is killing; the lesson is reinforced by the story of the old woman who was left on the ice to die because she could not contribute to her society.
>
> The book word for this is senilicide, a tough word for fifth-graders, but they got it. They approved and defended the abandonment of the old woman.

Kilpatrick was an opponent of MACOS from almost the very beginning of the controversy. Yet, there was little evidence that he had actually seen or been exposed to the program in any way other than hearing other people discuss it. For example, he was one of the first to state that MACOS had been jointly developed by Jerome Bruner and B. F. Skinner (Kilpatrick, 1975). Although Skinner's non-involvement was well documented, Kilpatrick never recanted his story. The passage cited above is another example of his lack of familiarity with the program. Had he seen the materials, he would have known that the elderly woman was not left because she could no longer contribute to her society, but rather because her presence on the journey would have caused more death.

Peter Dow (n.d.) replied in a paper prepared to respond to charges against MACOS:

> Arfek's dilemma, namely the choice between the care of his wife and children and the care of his aging mother-in-law, is presented to children as a problem not only central to the Netsilik society ("No one wishes to harm old people. We too may be old some day."), but also the central problem for any society, including our own. Children are fascinated by this issue, they identify with old people, and they are conscious that the problems that Arfek faces are problems for their own families as well. It is the moral dilemma posed by Arfek's plight that *Man: A Course of Study* seeks to raise.

One major criticism of the MACOS program, exemplified by the discussions of the Arfek story, was that many of the questions posed in the materials were too large and abstract to be considered by elementary school children and would have been better approached in the upper grades (Weber, 1975). Major questions were raised as to the appropriateness of the materials for younger children, even if the assumption were made that they could handle them intellectually. O. L. Davis, Jr. (1976), commented that "children can learn some things earlier than once thought," but continues that the " 'can' has been translated quite illogically to 'should' " (p. 9).

Some of the other criticisms of the program seemed to come from people who were willing to stray from the facts when making their complaints. For example, included in the MACOS program were several graphic films of Eskimo hunting and fishing practices. Norma Gabler (personal communication, March 10, 1976), a nationally known textbook critic at the time of the MACOS controversies, stated that the films included "four and one-half hours of bloody gore, showing the stoning to death of a bird tied by one leg, the braiding of bloody guts, etc., with no narration."

A television show aired in Reston, Virginia provided an interesting view into the film controversies. The program, billed as an investigative study of MACOS, showed approximately 2 minutes of the films. According to Marcia Fram, these 2 minutes consisted of what the commentator admitted were the "uglier parts," including the skinning of a seal, the stabbing of a giraffe, a child eating the eye of a caribou, and a deer-like creature being dragged ashore by an Eskimo (Fram, 1975).

The final scene presented in the television program is a seal kill, which ended with the Eskimos' efforts to bring the animal's carcass up through the hole in the ice, showing blood on the previously white surface. In the MACOS materials, this scene is unnarrated. In the television program, however, the film is given a voice-over by Guyford Stever, the director of the National Science Foundation, saying "Everything I've seen indicates it's the kind of course I'd like to have my children take" (Fram, 1975).

In her own investigation of the television program, Fram discovered that the reporter who had researched the series specifically requested the film showing the killing of the seal and the caribou. When offered the entire package of films used in the MACOS program, the reporter refused them. The killing of the giraffe by a Kalahari Bushman was described in the television program as coming from films available as supplemental materials. However, Jack Gentry, at Curriculum Development Associates (publisher of the MACOS program), points out that the films in question were never sold by his firm, which was the only company allowed to distribute MACOS materials (Fram, 1975).

The films were an integral part of MACOS. They provided the closest approximation of actual events. And, while some of the films were graphic, most were not. Contrary to Mrs. Gabler's claims of 4½ hours of gore, the vast majority of the films showed rather placid occurrences, including many day-to-day non-hunting activities of the Netsilik. The 4½ hours of film was approximately the total amount of films included in the program.

Although the above accounts of the controversies are abbreviated, a study of the controversies reached several conclusions (Kraus, 1977). First, much of the cited material (especially those that discuss cannibalism, divorce, trial marriage, polygamy and polyandry, wife-swapping, and the treatment of religion as myth) was located only in the teachers' manuals. In as much as these were the most frequently leveled charges against MACOS, there is a temptation to wonder why the program should be dismissed on those grounds. Opponents of the program argued that much of this material found its way into the hands of students and that the program encouraged dissemination of this information to children. While it was true that some of the material included in the teachers' manuals can be used with students, Dow pointed out that, to a great extent, the decision to use this information rested with individual teachers, based on their perception of the students' maturity and ability to deal with the information (personal communication, May 14, 1976). Note should be made that part of the requirement for purchasing the MACOS program was that the materials not be used unless the teacher had undergone training prior to teaching the program. While this requirement did not guarantee that the program was used properly, an attempt was made to minimize teacher misuse.

A second conclusion is that many of the negative comments about MACOS were based on statements taken out of context. These statements, if examined in this manner, would have seemingly made a case against the program. Statements taken out of context and given sensational media exposure can be shocking and have a greater effect than the reasoned responses made in professional journals.

Many of the materials used in the MACOS program were criticized as immoral. The question of teaching morals and values has long been a controversy in American schools. MACOS clearly presented a view that values and morals differ from individual to individual and did not attempt to establish a set of values for students. MACOS was very clear in its attempt to show that values are cultural, while asking students to identify the sources of their own values and the reasons for these values. Those who see the school as an extension of the home, including training in values (namely, those of the parents), often resist any efforts to expose students to other value systems.

Some critics even accused MACOS of attempting to "brainwash" students into holding values counter to the "traditional" values of the culture. An examination of the program, its claims, and supporting materials, revealed that no values were given preference. If a student, after considering one of the dilemmas presented in the course, decided that a "traditional" response was best, materials in the course did not attempt to sway this opinion. The attempt throughout the course was to ask what makes a person "human." It is, indeed, human to disagree with either majority or minority positions and to hold intellectually warranted or unwarranted beliefs.

MACOS was also criticized for dealing with subject matter which was too advanced for students at the fifth and sixth grade levels. While this charge was, perhaps, valid in relation to some of the content, reactions from teachers using the materials indicated that it was not valid across all materials. Teachers using the program consistently praised it, citing student interest and grasp of the concepts in the program.

An indication of how well a program accomplishes the goals it sets and how well it is accepted by students lies in the results of evaluation studies. The evaluations of the MACOS program indicated that, in several areas, MACOS was equal to, or superior to, other programs which were available to schools at the same time for elementary social studies. In a survey published in 1975, MACOS ranked number two among 24 programs evaluated by the Curriculum Information Network of the Social Sciences Education Consortium and first among those receiving federal funding (Curriculum Information Network, 1975). These rankings were based on teacher opinion of how well various programs worked with students.

Two studies of the cognitive emphasis found in MACOS both indicated that students in the program were exposed to more emphasis on higher cognitive processes than students in non-MACOS classrooms. The first study, by Matthew Ludes (1971), analyzed teacher questions and questions found in the "Herring Gull" unit of the MACOS program, using

Bloom's Taxonomy. The study indicated that the cognitive emphasis of the MACOS program was higher than traditional social studies textbooks and that questions in the MACOS materials were on a higher cognitive level than questions traditionally asked by teachers in the classroom.

The second study, by John Youngers (1972), compared 20 MACOS classrooms to 20 non-MACOS classrooms for differences in cognitive levels, using the Aschner-Gallagher categories for classifying thought processes. This study indicated that non-MACOS teachers asked a higher percentage of memory questions (42%) than did MACOS teachers (23%). Additionally, talk patterns in non-MACOS classrooms showed teacher emphasis on factual materials; non-MACOS teachers tended to present information and follow it with a memory level question more frequently than MACOS teachers.

Another study, by Richard Arends (1972), indicated that MACOS classrooms were slightly less competitive than non-MACOS classrooms, that more student satisfaction existed in MACOS classrooms, and that students in MACOS classrooms believed that they could increase their achievement in social studies. The study also reported that social studies was the preferred subject among students using MACOS, as compared to the least preferred among students not using MACOS.

MACOS was also included in a study of several programs representing the new social studies in Marin County, California, in 1970. Several findings in the evaluation had particular significance for MACOS. Field tests indicated the "new" social studies programs were superior to traditional materials in teaching students how to deal with concepts, and that only MACOS could be called superior to the other new social studies programs. With the exception of MACOS, teachers were determined to have been a more crucial variable than the materials. Other findings in the study showed an increase of 50% in students' use of higher cognitive processes and a 20% increase in student-initiated dialogue. One key effort of the new socials studies was to increase students' positive attitudes toward social studies. Findings from this study show that this had not occurred, except in the MACOS classrooms. Finally, the study showed that, with the exception of the MACOS program, teacher-designed curriculum materials were generally superior to commercially distributed materials (*A Social Studies Curriculum for a Modern World*, 1971).

To summarize the content controversies, MACOS was the target of many strident attacks. Most of these attacks were based on materials located in the segment of the program dealing with the Netsilik Eskimo, and in the Teacher Materials, rather than in the Student Materials. Opponents of the program often misstated the context or quoted passages out of context. The content of MACOS was not typical of that generally found in schools in the late 1960's in social studies classrooms. For this reason, among others, MACOS was especially vulnerable to attack.

Evaluation studies did indicate that MACOS was successful in what it attempted to do. Students' use of higher cognitive processes and their grasp of content were increased significantly.

Funding Issues

Had *Man: A Course of Study* simply been the target of those concerned with exposing children to content they deemed inappropriate, the program would have been little more than a footnote in curriculum history books. While the content was somewhat controversial for the late 1960s, the culture at that time was in a state of open conflict between the counter-culture and the so-called "Silent Majority." Flag burnings and physical confrontations between radicals at the political nominating conventions easily trumped issues of senilicide and seal blood on ice in the political discourse of the day.

However, those who were protesting the program in the beginning apparently were not aware that funding for MACOS came from the National Science Foundation, a branch of the federal government. In the final analysis, MACOS will likely not be judged on its success or failure in the classroom or the results of the evaluation studies. Rather, MACOS will be discussed for the impact it had on federal curriculum development policy. The issues in this debate centered around questions of the role of the federal government in the development of curriculum and the preservation of local prerogatives in educational decisions, dissemination practices of the NSF, and questions of oversight and review of programs developed with federal funds.

Prior to 1950, federal involvement in curricular matters was advisory in nature. Some programs, such as the Smith-Hughes Act of 1917, provided federal funds to vocational programs, but did not attempt to control the content or development of the programs. Instead, the act provided for supporting salaries of teachers and supervisors, who then designed the curricula for their own school or class. Other federal involvement came through the support of policy commissions, such as the Commission on Life-Adjustment Education (1951), supported by the Office of Education. These commissions, while exerting influence, had no power to determine the direction or content of a program.

Beginning with the funding of the Physical Sciences Study Committee (PSSC) in 1956, federal involvement in curriculum development increased steadily, both in influence and the amount of money spent. Spring (1976) states that the first direct involvement of the federal government was based on national defense. Beginning with the Truman Administration, the nation's scientists perceived a need for increasing the number of competent scientists and were very influential in the creation of the National Science Foundation in 1950. During the Eisenhower Administration, this need was stimulated by both the Cold War and the launching of the Soviet satellite Sputnik. Sputnik led almost directly to the passage of the National Defense Education Act (NDEA) of 1958 (Spring, 1975). As time passed, further justification for federal involvement in education was found in the civil rights movement of the late 1950s and 1960s, as well as in the Johnson Administration's War on Poverty (Spring, 1975). The Civil Rights Act of 1964, while not directly related to curriculum, did lay the groundwork for increasing federal involvement in all areas of education. The War on Poverty not only extended federal involvement, but created programs which would exert, either directly or indirectly, great influence over the curricula of the schools. Programs such as Project Head Start, Upward Bound, and the Job Corps were federal programs, developed and funded by the Office of Economic Opportunity (Spring, 1976). While not curricular projects, they did influence curriculum development.

Throughout this period of increasing federal involvement in educational matters, the National Science Foundation supported the development of a wide variety of curriculum projects. NSF also actively supported the dissemination of these projects following their completion. Although some concerns about federal involvement in both development and dissemination were voiced from the beginning, these were seen as minor and had little impact on the growing federal expenditures for education and curriculum (U.S. Congress, House Subcommittee on Science, 1975).

These concerns could not be submerged, however, and became prominent at least as early as 1970. Beginning in that year, the first serious questions related to what was being done, and why, were given serious consideration. Some members of Congress, along with several members of the scientific community, questioned the expense of the pre-college science programs being developed by NSF, believing that the money could have been better spent on research for applied science (U.S. Congress, House Subcommittee on Science, 1975).

These debates became more and more common over the next several years, evolving from a discussion of the amount of money diverted from applied research, to a discussion of the role of the federal government in curriculum development. The evolution of this discussion was, to some extent, given impetus from other debates concerning the role of government in education. These discussions, revolving around forced busing, increasing federal requirements concerning civil rights, and other governmental actions, added to suspicions that the federal government was trying to take control of the schools (Spring, 1975).

The MACOS controversies emerged from these roots. Obviously controversial in content and supported by grants from a federal agency, *Man: A Course of Study* provided the perfect opportunity for opponents of federal involvement in curriculum to bring their concerns to the attention of the nation.

Federal Funding and Local Prerogatives

A major reason for the questions regarding the role of the federal government in curriculum development can be traced to a clear lack of objectives for American education. The 1918 report of the Commission on the Reorganization of Secondary Education, *Cardinal Principles of Secondary Education* (1918), was the first major attempt at defining national purposes for public schools. This report, however influential, was written as an advisory statement by the Commission. Although printed and distributed by the U.S. Bureau of Education, it had no force of law behind it. The *Cardinal Principles* was followed by other advisory statements through the years, including *Purposes of Education in American Democracy* (Education Policies Commision, 1938), *Ten Imperative Needs of American Youth* (Education Policies Commision, 1944), *The Central Purpose of American Education* (Education Policies Commision, 1961), and *Imperatives in Education* (Education Policies Commision, 1966). All of these reports, like the *Cardinal Principles,* were advisory statements only and carried no power in determining the objectives for the nation's education.

As the debate over national involvement increased, Paul R. Hanna (1962) noted a lack of national policy, a situation that was responsible for some degree of confusion. Hanna pointed out that two groups were dominant at that time in determining policy, but that these groups were diametrically opposed concerning what this policy should be. The first group, according to Hanna, viewed education as a consumer-oriented product. This consumer demand (parents and students) would dictate curriculum. The second group saw education as an investment. Individuals in this group believed that education was the answer to national survival. In the latter view, goals would be set using national priorities, rather than the desires of parents or students.

Richard Hofstadter (1963) saw another source for controversy in determining national policy. He believed that American society was basically anti-intellectual and that this characteristic greatly influenced national policy. Hofstedter drew a distinction between the terms "intellect" and "intelligent." Intellect, according to Hofstedter, is the "critical, creative, and contemplative side of the mind." Intelligence, on the other hand, is the "excellence of mind that is employed within a fairly narrow, immediate, and predictable range" (pp. 24–25). Hofstadter stated that the American people looked upon the intellectual with suspicion or resentment, while intelligence was consistently praised and, therefore, was to be cultivated.

This preference for intelligence, as opposed to intellect, was considered by Hofstadter (1963) to be a major force behind the movement toward "practical," that is, vocational and professional, education. Because of the emphasis on vocational training and individual freedom in the classroom, along with a "soft" curriculum designed to "adjust to life," Hofstadter cites the progressive education movement as being strongly anti-intellectual in practice. Hofstadter asserted that life adjustment education, as he termed progressive education, ignored intellectual development, while devoting all energies to social development.

Citing Hofstadter's work as documentation of an anti-intellectual bias, Spring (1975) asserted that the establishment of the National Science Foundation and the passage of the National Defense Education Act was a reaction to progressivism and consumer-oriented education. These two events, according to Spring, were the first major attempts at moving the nations schools in a direction that would serve national interests. During the cold war and the space race, some discussion of educational policy occurred, but it was minimal. Fear of Soviet superiority in science and technology not only suppressed opposition to federal aid in education, it also alarmed the nation to the point that long denied federal aid was granted.

As the cold war thawed and joint Soviet-American space exploration occurred, questions arose, both in Congress and in several public sectors, of the need for continued federal involvement in education. Spurred by the controversy surrounding forced busing, all areas of federal involvement were faced with questions. A special task force of the National Institute of Education (NIE) questioned the role of the federal government in curriculum specifically. In its 1976 report, the broad range of feelings among those interviewed was evident:

> Briefly, interviewees' positions on federal involvement in curriculum development ranged from the belief that increased government support and leadership had benefited the nation and should be maintained or further increased, to the belief that the government's efforts in the past two decades have been highly successful, but that the need for such direct involvement has decreased because so many new curricula are now available, to the view that the government should alter the nature of its role (e.g., by moving toward the provision of guidelines and technical assistance to local and private developers or toward the development of only exemplary curricular

"modules" or toward the provision of only "thin market" programs for special needs and populations), to the belief that all federal involvement in curriculum is an infringement on local and private rights, that all government "interference" thus far has harmed the practice of education, and that the government should immediately terminate its role in this area. (Schaffarzick, 1976)

Former Rep. Robert Krueger saw a role for the federal government, but expressed some reservations:

I think the federal government can assist in certain kinds of curricular programs. [The science programs developed after Sputnik], according to scientists I've spoken to, were helpful at the university level. They were helpful in getting people farther along faster ... I thought those were legitimate undertakings.

The political problem, and the real problem of having educational programs that accord with the community's interest, is that science is considered to be neither immoral or moral, but amoral. Since science does not run in conflict with the local values structure, you are less likely to run aground on specific cultural values when you are dealing with scientific programs. Once you get into the humanities, you are not in an area where there is, perhaps, a broader feeling that this is fluff and something of no great value, but you also can run afoul of the local and cultural traditions and values. (Personal Communication, May 11, 1976)

A statement issued from the National Council for the Social Studies (NCSS) in 1975, authored by Brian Larkin, pointed out that the only entity with sufficient funds to truly underwrite the development of innovative curriculum was the federal government. According to Larkin, individual local schools and state educational agencies did not have the funds or, in some cases, the professional expertise, to bring about needed curriculum change. Larkin (1975) also pointed to the high cost of research and the high financial risk as deterrents to the involvement of the commercial publishing sector in creating innovative programs.

Opponents of federal funding generally were of the view that education had always been a locally-controlled enterprise and that federal funding eventually led to federal control. They were fearful of losing control of their schools. As Onalee McGraw stated in testimony before the U.S. Senate Special Subcommittee on the National Science Foundation in 1975:

in recent years parents have virtually lost control of what is taught and done in their elementary and secondary schools. Their inherent right to decide how schools can best serve the educational needs of their children has been usurped by a highly powerful organization of educators and the National

Education Association. This well-organized, heavily financed educationist complex is now virtually dictating education policy throughout America.

McGraw stated that federally-funded curricula were imposed on local school districts in five ways: NSF's funding of promotion conference to market materials; NSF's lobbying of federal, state, and local officials; using federal funds to finance university-based promotion and marketing networks in at least 85 regions in the country; training teachers to use these programs and offering graduate credit to those taking the training; and reducing the costs of federally-funded materials to give them an advantage in the market place (McGraw, 1975).

McGraw's (1975) conclusion that parents had lost control of what their children were taught may have been true, but she seemed to have overlooked an important historical context. Shortly after the launching of Sputnik, the scientific community, professional organizations, and large numbers of citizens were concerned about our national future. In effect, the nation seemed to be willing to turn over its schools to the federal government, because the government appeared to, at least, be trying to make improvements. The federal government had resources not available to the states and local districts, and it was willing to use them.

Dissemination and Implementation

Closely related to the issue of federal involvement in curriculum development were issues surrounding the dissemination and implementation of those materials, once they had been developed. Programs developed by the National Science Foundation were generally seen as being the responsibility of the developers, who were charged with negotiating contracts with commercial publishers. Few requirements existed to guide developers in negotiating contracts. NSF required that materials be made available in a manner that would ensure educational benefits took precedence over other considerations, including generation of revenue; that public and private interests must be safeguarded (including the continuing availability of the materials); the avoidance, in so far as was possible, of interference with normal commercial practices; NSF's financial interests would be proportional to the support the Foundation provided; and, NSF had the right to review any contracts before they became binding (U.S. General Accounting Office, 1973).

The policies of the National Science Foundation toward implementation and dissemination activities were based on the perceived necessity and scope of the activities. This view was outlined in the report of the Science Curriculum Review Team (1975):

The Foundation has increasingly recognized that the development of innovative curriculum materials is not of itself sufficient to assure utilization. Implementation is a complicated undertaking which begins soon after the development process is initiated. Creators of new educational materials start providing information about their activities to engender an awareness of the expected products. Another step in the development process—field testing and trial using of materials, contributes to early dissemination efforts. Thus, there is no clear line separating materials development and materials implementation—they overlap and both are to some extent parts of a single process.

Normally, implementation is considered to encompass (a) dissemination of information about, and (b) activities which may lead to adoption by schools and schools systems of new educational materials and techniques.

Many of the controversies in the MACOS debate, as well as with other programs, revolved around those activities designed to encourage adoption of a program by schools.

A study of NSF implementation policies found no evidence of aggressive NSF policies or behavior exerting exceptional influence on local school boards (Kraus, 1977). No NSF policy encouraged or permitted circumvention of normal school district policies. Several individuals, who claimed that NSF pressure had resulted in the adoption of NSF-funded materials, were asked to cite instances of pressure exceeding legal limits during hearings before the Special Subcommittee on the National Science Foundation of the Committee on Labor and Public Welfare of the U.S. Senate in March and April, 1975. None of the witnesses was able to do so (A. Strauss, personal communication, May 12, 1976).

A second question related to dissemination/implementation activities concerned the effects of those efforts on commercial publishers. Did federal involvement in promotion and marketing of materials provide unfair advantages to those who were selected to participate in NSF dissemination activities?

On this question, the publishing community was divided. It is important to keep in mind that, at this time, this was basically new ground. For years, publishers had absorbed all of the development and marketing costs of school materials. Increasing the development costs either meant a lower profit or high prices (and possibly lower sales). Having a significant amount of the product produced with the help of large federal grants would make a major impact on any company's bottom line. Robert L. Barnes (personal communication, March 5, 1975), former Vice-President and Director of Marketing, Educational Publishing Division, J. B. Lippincott Company, stated this concern forcefully:

Since any company taking over the distribution of a federally funded program already has benefited to a very considerable extent through not having to use private investment funds, it would only serve to compound the inequity by allowing them also to use federal funds of any kind to implement the program by developing a market for it. Let's keep our private enterprise system intact.

John T. Riordan (personal communication, August 12, 1975), former Vice-President and Director, School Division, Houghton Mifflin Company, disagreed:

We are naturally interested in the work of the House Committee on Science and Technology as it relates to the National Science Foundation. We have cooperated with numerous National Science Foundation activities, including specific curriculum projects. We feel that in the areas of mathematics and sciences, particularly, NSF's sponsorship of summer workshops and implementation conferences has contributed in a large way to the advancement of mathematics and science education in the nation, and, indeed, the world.

Riordan did suggest that NSF refrain from becoming involved in the development of instructional materials for later commercial distribution unless publishers were part of the development from the outset.

As might be guessed, the attitudes of the two publishers might have been influenced by their level of participation in NSF projects. A search of NSF publishing contracts, conducted in 1976, found that Lippincott had not published any NSF programs, while Houghton Mifflin had been one of the more active publishers of NSF materials, including the Blue Edition of the *Biological Sciences Curriculum Study* (BSCS), the *Earth Science Curriculum Project,* and the *High School Course Modern Coordinate Geometry.* The most active publisher of NSF materials was the Webster Division of McGraw-Hill, which published the *Chemical Bond Approach, Elementary Science Study, Secondary School Science Project,* and *Engineering Concepts Curriculum Project* (Science Curriculum Review Team, 1975, pp. 171–176).

BMCA Associates, in a report commissioned by the National Science Foundation, stated that, while there was opposition to NSF competition at the beginning, a compatible working relationship between NSF and the publishing community was achieved. The report also stated that NSF participation in curriculum development had stimulated the publishing community to become more innovative. The report continued:

In reviewing today the developments in the industry, el-hi [school] publishers are likely to take a different point of view about federally funded curriculum projects from the point of view they held less than two decades ago. For one thing, educational publishing continues to be very much alive and even thriving. For another, the industry has transformed itself from publishers of textbooks to publishers of programs of many components. Today, publishers generally tend to be interested in publishing programs of excellence wherever they are developed. It can be said with some confidence, we believe, that any curriculum project that meets the demands of the educational marketplace is likely to find a publisher.

To this we add our personal opinion that the earlier a developer of a curriculum project can reach an agreement with a publisher, the better it will be for both parties and for the program. (Science Curriculum Review Team, 1975, p. 165)

Note should be made that, of the 54 programs developed with NSF funding after 1956, 25 were either unpublished or unavailable by 1975. These projects, which were funded at a total cost of $45 million in development and implementation funds, were not used in classrooms or were used only for a limited time (Science Curriculum Review Team, 1975, pp 171–176).

In 1976, due to the controversies surrounding *Man: A Course of Study*, all funds for dissemination and implementation of curriculum projects were removed from the federal budget. The following year, a small amount ($800,000 as compared to $12.5 million in 1975) was restored to complete contractual obligations that had been established prior to 1976 (G. Archibald, personal communication, May 10, 1976).

Oversight and Review

If the most basic question to arise from the MACOS debates concerned the role of the federal government in the development, dissemination, and implementation of curricula, questions of oversight and review (which some labeled as "censorship") would be, perhaps, the most visible. Censorship is generally regarded as having two distinct connotations, one legal and one pragmatic. The legal definition refers to prior review and restraint of publication. This type of censorship is addressed in the First Amendment to the U.S. Constitution, which states that "Congress shall make no law ... abridging the freedom of speech, or of the press."

Pragmatic censorship, on the other hand, concerns attempts at restricting the availability of materials, including print materials, video materials, pictures, or recordings. This was the type of censorship encountered in the MACOS controversies. Most of the debates concerning this type of censorship occurred in the areas of oversight and review. Oversight is defined as activities which direct action while they are in progress; review is the examination of the results of those actions. Applied to curriculum development activities, oversight consists of giving guidelines, requirements, and suggestions during the development process. Review would be the examination of the materials, after they had been developed, to determine that the policies and procedures were followed correctly.

Two issues were central to the oversight and review of the NSF programs: How much oversight and review, and by whom? Early fears of political dominance led to the initial reluctance on the part of Congress to establish NSF. Fear on the part of President Harry Truman that there would not be enough political control led to his initial veto of the NSF in 1947 (Spring, 1976, p. 76). The scientific community, meanwhile, refused to endorse an agency controlled by the federal government. The ensuing debate resulted in a 3-year additional wait before NSF was founded. In the end, the battle was won by the scientific community and by Congress. The government would not control NSF.

Upon establishment by Congress in 1950, NSF calmed fears that federal involvement would mean federal control by adopting a policy of not reviewing grants after they had been awarded. This policy was meant to ensure academic freedom for those involved in research and to insure that these projects would not be controlled by the federal government. While originally intended for those receiving research grants, this policy was extended to curriculum projects when NSF ventured into pre-college science programs (U.S. Congress, House Subcommittee on Science, 1975, pp. 15–39).

Although most Foundation documents stated that the policy remained in effect, the report of the Science Curriculum Review Team (1975) stated that procedures for oversight and review "appear to be unique to each of the cases studied" (p. 63) in their report. In the case of *Man: A Course of Study,* the report states that NSF involvement in pre-award oversight was minimal, primarily because of the reputation of the scholars involved. The report also states that oversight was much more common during the development of CHEM study. Apparently, the policy of not reviewing curricular programs was not always closely followed.

As a result of the MACOS controversies, the Division of Pre-College Education within NSF, which awarded all grants for curriculum development, instituted a five-phase review program. The new policy required two reviews of initial proposals (one each by the NSF staff and the National Science Board); an oversight committee, which studied the content and methodology; a series of status and content reviews of existing programs; and an advisory committee. This program was designed to answer critics of the former NSF policy of non-review, according to Joel Snow (personal communication, May 10, 1976), former Special Assistant to the Director of the NSF.

The revised policy was not without critics. Gerard Piel, former publisher of *Scientific American,* recalling the historical reasons for not reviewing programs after funding, Piel (1976) stated that NSF had:

promulgated onerous second-guessing review procedures that are intended to anticipate and avert controversy in future curricula; they are bound to discourage the kind of volunteer enterprise that fired up the science curriculum reform movement. Worst of all, these procedures promise to burden a federal agency, the National Science Foundation, with the responsibility that it should not have for the content and substance of the curricula it finances.

Piel supported a return to the peer review system of oversight and review, a position also favored by Sen. Edward M. Kennedy. In the report of the Senate Committee on Labor and Public Welfare, which accompanied the National Science Foundation Authorization Act of 1976, Kennedy stated that the peer review system established by NSF was an integral and necessary part of evaluating programs. Writing as Chairman of the Special Subcommittee on the National Science Foundation of the Committee on Labor and Public Welfare, Kennedy (U.S. Congress, Senate, 1975) said:

> It is the firmly held conviction of the committee that the peer review system is vital to the success of the National Science Foundation's mission—the support of research which is of the highest quality and which addressed priority national research needs.

The section concludes with an admonition to NSF to strengthen the peer review system by seeking broad representation of the scientific community and to make the system open, encouraging the entry of new and diverse reviewers.

The second question of oversight concerned the level at which this function should occur, were it to be deemed proper. In the mid-1970s, this discussion was particularly active in the U.S. Congress, where some members believed that oversight should be the responsibility of elected officials. Other members, however, believed that oversight should rest with the funding agency, with Congress only establishing broad policies.

Former Rep. Robert Bauman (1975) represented those who wanted oversight to be in Congress. While offering an amendment to the NSF appropriations bill, Bauman stated that "my legislation would place the responsibility for these uses of taxpayers' money right where it belongs--in the Congress of the United States." The amendment would have required NSF to submit proposals for funding to Congress, which then had 30 days to consider them. If opposed by any member of either house of Congress, funding for the bill would have been withheld until appropriated through resolution. Although passed by the House, Bauman's amendment was later removed from the final appropriations bill by a House-Senate Conference Committee (G, Archibald, personal communication, May 10, 1976).

In a 1976 interview, former Rep. Robert Krueger asserted both philosophical and practical reasons for his opposition to the Bauman amendment. Arguing that members of Congress were simply too busy to oversee specific programs of the NSF, as well as other agencies, Krueger (personal communication, May 11, 1976) continued:

> The Congress is a body that this year is going to be spending about $400 billion. This is better than a billion dollars a day, Saturdays and Sundays included. Now, the Congress, then, in my judgment, should not be deciding that this particular textbook should be offered or should not be offered.
>
> I don't want the government, particularly the Congress, to get into the business of saying this book should or should not be approved because I've sat through Congress and watched them vote on hundred billion dollar bills knowing very little about them. Certainly, we don't want Congress to become a kind of review body and censor for specific textbooks.

CONCLUSION

Many factors combine to make a controversy significant, including timeliness, events, context, personalities involved, and the issues being debated. A consideration of these factors could easily lead to the conclusion that the debate surrounding *Man: A Course of Study* was the proverbial "tempest in a teapot." Federal involvement in curriculum had been a fact of life since the mid-1950s. In that respect, the MACOS funding controversies occurred some 20 years after the fact. Events in the MACOS controversies were by no means unique. Other programs, as well as novels and scientific theories, had caused heated discussion before MACOS. No schools were bombed, nor were any shots fired at school buses, as had happened in Kanawha County, West Virginia in 1974. The protests lodged against the MACOS program raised few, if any, issues that had not previously been confronted in some fashion in other controversies. What, then, made the MACOS controversies significant?

To provide an answer to the question, the controversies must be examined from two perspectives: the content issues and the funding issues. Both were significant, but for different reasons. The content issues were important because they served as a reminder that previous battles concerning values and curriculum content were not finished. The accusations that *Man: A Course of Study* undermined the value structure and political system were, to some extent, very similar to those waged in the 1920s and 1930s against Harold Rugg's *Man and His Changing Society* and Paul R. Hanna's *Building America,* two highly controversial curricula of that time.

The most significant factor in the MACOS debates was arguably the fact that MACOS had received federal funding for both its development and implementation. Although federal funding had been occurring for several years before MACOS, two factors combined to make this important. First, when the National Science Foundation made it's first grant to PSSC, in 1956, there was a feeling of urgency in the country. Not only had we just emerged from a World War, but the Soviet Union was taking the lead in science and technology. This urgency led to a national demand that education be improved. At the time, the best, and quickest, method of doing so seemed to be by using the best qualified people in the various fields to develop improved courses for pre-college students. It would be expensive, perhaps beyond the means of most states or commercial publishers, so the federal government was expected to help. National goals were developed and national resources were provided to meet these goals.

In spite of this, as stated earlier, due to the MACOS controversies all pre-college curriculum funding came to a halt in 1976. Tensions were too high and the protests were too loud for politicians to try to justify their earlier efforts. However, the 1983 publication of *A Nation at Risk* by the National Commission on Excellence in Education once again brought education to the forefront of American politics and, once again, brought the National Science Foundation back into the discussion. According to Bob Tinker (2006):

> The NSF Education Directorate was eliminated in 1980 and then, as a result of a storm of critical reports culminating in *A Nation at Risk,* was created anew in 1983 with a mission to address K–12 education through curriculum and TPD (Teacher Professional Development). By starting fresh, the NSF education effort did not have multiple demands on its funding and it was able to concentrate its limited resources on a few large initiatives, such as the investigations project, which eventually received $12M and became self-sufficient from royalties and fees. Investigations was one of three NSF projects that now dominates elementary mathematics education. A parallel effort was made in elementary science education, with similar results—a few projects that were funded in excess of $10M created exemplary materials that are the best available now. This initial NSF effort in elementary mathematics has been a huge success and we are currently enjoying the results of a successful investment from two decades ago.

In the end, most questions about the efficacy of federal funding and its impact on local control, dissemination, and implementation policies, as well as issues related to oversight and review, lost their edge when the MACOS controversies ended the NSF's curriculum activities in 1976. And, as frequently happens in Congress, once the specific problem was "solved," the sticky policy issues were left to die of neglect. Although times seem a bit different today, the potential for controversy still exists. The questions of appropriateness still have not been resolved and agreements on federal policy goals still have not been reached.

REFERENCES

Ambrose, S. E. (1983). *Eisenhower: Soldier, General of the Army, President-Elect, 1890-1952.* New York: Simon & Schuster.

Ausubel, D. P., (1966, March) An evaluation of the BSCS approach to high school biology. *American Biology Teacher,* p. 176.

Arends, R. I. (1972). *A summative evaluation of Man: A course of study: A study of its human effects.* Unpublished doctoral dissertation, University of Oregon.

Bauman, Rep [MD]. (1975, April 19). Speaking against the amendment to the National Science Foundation Appropriations Bill, Congressional Record 94th Cong., 1st Sess.

Bruner, J. S. (1960). *The process of education.* Cambridge, MA: Harvard University Press.

Bruner, J. S. (1966). *Toward a theory of instruction.* New York: W. W. Norton.

Cardinal Principles of Secondary Education. (1918). *U.S. Bureau of Education, Bulletin,* 35.

Conlan, J. (U.S. Congress, House Rep.). (1975, April 9). The Amendment to the National Science Foundations Appropriations bill. *Congressional Record.*

Curriculum Information Network. (1975, February) *Social Education.* pp. 96–99.

Davis, O. L., Jr. (1976). Prologue: Curriculum across two hundred years of independence. *Perspectives on Curriculum Development, 1776-1976.* Washington DC: Association for Supervision and Curriculum Development.

DeWitt, N. (1955). *Soviet professional manpower—Its education, training, and supply.* Washington, DC: National Science Foundation.

Dow, P. B. (n.d.). Mimeographed paper answering charges against *Man: A Course of Study,* p. 1. (Copy in the files of the author)

Education Policies Commision. (1938). *Purpose of education in American Democracy.* Washington DC: Author.

Education Policies Commision. (1944). *Education for all American youth: A further look.* Washington DC: Author.

Education Policies Commision. (1961). *The Central Purpose of American Education.* Washington DC.: Author.

Education Policies Commision. (1966) *Imperatives in education.* Arlington, VA: The Association.

Ferber, E. (1970, May). What Makes Humans Human? *American Education.*

First Commission on Life Adjustment Education. (1951). *Vitalizing secondary education.* Washington, DC: Office of Education, Bulletin 1951, #3.

Fram, M., (1975, May 8). MACOS report: Opportunity for distortion, abuse. *The Reston Times.*

Friedman, S. M. (n.d.). *The inflation calculator.* Retrieved from http://www.westegg.com/inflation/infl.cgi

Goodladd, J. I. (1964). *School curriculum reform*. New York: The Fund for the Advancement of Education.

Hanna, P. R. (1962) Education: An instrument of national purpose and policy. In P. R. Hanna (Ed.), *Education: An instrument of national goals* (pp. 1–3). New York: McGraw-Hill.

Hofstadter, R. (1963). *Anti-intellectualism in American life*. New York: Alfred A. Knopf.

Kilpatrick, J. J. (1975, April 27). Bay State fifth-grade teacher calls new study system lethal brainwash. *Boston Globe*.

Kraus, L. L. (1977). *Curriculum, public policy, and criticism: An analysis of the controversies surrounding man: A course of study*. Doctoral dissertation, The University of Texas at Austin.

Larkin, B. J. (1975, November-December). The MACOS Question: A Statement by the National Council for the Social Studies. *Social Education*, 448–449.

Ludes, M. J. (1971). *A comparison of the cognitive emphasis of the intended and practiced questioning strategies employed in the Herring Gull Unit of Man: A course of study*. Unpublished doctoral dissertation, State University of New York at Buffalo.

MACOS Program: Student Material. (n.d.) *A Journey to the Artic*. p. 21.

MACOS Program: Teacher Material. (n.d.). *The Netsilik Eskimos on the Ice*. p. 188.

MACOS Program: Teacher Material. (n.d.). *Talks to Teachers*. p. 101.

McGraw, O. (1975, April 21). Statement before the Senate Special Subcommittee on the National Science Foundation. pp. 1, 7-8. (Prepared statement in the files of the author.)

National Commission of Excellence in Education. (1983). *A Nation at Risk: The Imperative for educational reform*. Washington, DC: U.S. Government Printing Office.

NSF Bill Vetoed. (1947, September 15). *Higher Education*.

NSF to Support In-Service Training for High School Teachers (1957, February 15). *Science* p. 294.

Piel, G. (1976, March 21). *Congress Shall Make No Law….* Address to the National Science Teachers Association, Philadelphia, Pennsylvania. (Abridged version of this speech appeared under the same title in *Educational Leadership*, November, 1976.)

Schaffarzick, J. (1976) *Current issues, problems, and concerns in curriculum development*. Washington, DC: The National Institute of Education.

Science Curriculum Review Team. (1975, May). *Pre-college science curriculum activities of the National Science Foundation*. Washington, DC: National Science Foundation.

A Social Studies Curriculum for a Modern World. (1971, June). The Marin Social Studies Project [Abstract].

Spring, J. (1976). *The sorting machine: National Educational Policy Since 1945*. New York: David McKay.

Teaching man to children. (1970, January 19). *Time*, p. 50.

Tinker, B. (2006, August 4). *NSF and K12 Reform*. Retrieved November 27, 2006, from http://blog.concord.org/archives/14-NSF-and-K12-Reform.html

U.S., Congress, House Subcommittee on Science, Research, and Technology of the Committee on Science and Technology. (1975). *The National Science Foun-*

dation: 1950-1975. By Dr. Landon T. Crane, Committee Print, Serial T. Washington, DC: Government Printing Office.

U.S. Congress, Senate. (1975). *National Science Foundation Authorization Act, 1976.* S. Rept. 94-111 to accompany S. 1539, 94th Congress, 1st sess., 1975.

U.S., General Accounting Office. (1973, October 14). *Administration of the Science Education Project Man: A Course of Study* (MACOS). Report of the Comptroller General of the United States to the House Committee on Science and Technology.

Weber, G., (1975, October). The case against "Man: A Course of Study." *Phi Delta Kappan,* p. 82.

Youngers, J. C. (1972). *A descriptive study of the cognitive emphasis in Man: A course of study social studies classes.* Unpublished doctoral dissertation, The University of Rochester.

CHAPTER 16

THE "HISTORY PROBLEM" IN CURRICULAR REFORM

A Warning to Constructivists From the New Social Studies Movement

Geoffrey Scheurman and Keith Reynolds

The New Social Studies (NSS) movement of the 1960s and 1970s hoped to effect lasting reform to the social studies curriculum. This chapter begins with the premise that the principles and processes of inquiry learning suggested by that effort were, by and large, a good thing—then, at the time of this writing, and at any foreseeable time in the future. While others have offered myriad reasons for the apparent failure of the NSS to reform teaching in explicit or permanent ways, few have considered how the movement failed to fully accommodate itself to the unique nature of history as both a scholarly pursuit and a curriculum domain. Specifically, the rigors of historical scholarship ultimately left teachers and materials inadequately prepared to introduce inquiry into the classroom—a failing magnified by the nature of history education which mandates a chronological narrative and multiple curricular goals based in divergent conceptions of citizenship. These failings significantly contributed to the

The New Social Studies: People, Projects, and Perspectives, pp. 341–359

movement's failure in the history classroom and, given the continuing centrality of history in the social studies, contributed to the overall demise of the movement. Despite its relatively short lifespan, there is, however, evidence that the NSS movement left a legacy of some success in the design of curriculum and instruction based on principles of scientific method. If any reform efforts, including those informed by the so-called "constructivist" movement of the late twentieth and early twenty-first centuries, are to effect lasting changes in social studies education, they must recognize that legacy and address the unique challenges posed by history education illuminated by the NSS movement's failure to overcome those challenges.

CONTEXT OF THE PROBLEM

Traditionally, the social studies curriculum has been dominated by a model stressing teacher-centered information transmission, memorization, and recitation of discrete information—the names, dates, places, theories and interpretations of the various social studies disciplines. Attempts to reform that curriculum beyond simply updating the lists of names and dates deemed important have periodically pushed their way to the forefront of professional discussion. These reform movements desire, generally speaking, to create a more student-centered curriculum stressing discipline correct methods of inquiry and critical thinking skills. A history of these reform movements represents more than periodic pedagogical discussions; they represent a persistent tension between two fundamentally competing approaches to social studies education. The traditional model stresses delivering to students the products of the social studies—those names, dates, and places and, at most, perhaps a clear transmission of values consistent with good citizenship. The latter stresses student mastery of the fundamental concepts, assumptions and procedures of a discipline in hopes that the students themselves might discover what is important in the world around them or develop abilities and dispositions for addressing real world problems.

   In the parlance of social studies educators, the tension between these two models is often referred to simply as the "product versus process" debate. Frustrating to anyone in the profession long enough to have witnessed a full cycle, this debate seems to have produced a "pendulum effect" as prevailing attitudes within the profession periodically shift from valuing one model over the other only to then shift back again after a few years. The very nature of this debate and its perennial, almost cyclical appearance every few years seems to indicate two somewhat disquieting realities of social studies education. First, many in the profession are left with a nagging dissatisfaction with the traditional social studies curriculum—hence the periodically felt need to reform that curriculum. Second, that the resulting reform movements have generally failed to effect lasting improvement—hence the pendulum effect as support for the traditional curriculum inevitably seems to return.

The 1980s and 90s witnessed a unique reinvigoration of the process-product debate. Across the nation, states and school districts sought to increase product accountability with intensified testing and multicultural content standards. Simultaneously, methodologies and attitudes informed by constructivist learning theories became popular, if not exclusive, throughout many university teacher preparation programs. These methodologies relied heavily on "process" and became formulated by experts under such names as "authentic pedagogy" (see Newmann, Marks, & Gamoran, 1996; Scheurman & Newmann, 1998). Emerging from the culture wars of the 1980s and in the midst of the constructivist methodology discussions of the 1990s, Edwin Fenton and the journal *Social Studies* reopened in 1991 an investigation into the rise and fall of a curricular reform movement known as the NSS. By expanding on the insights generated from that investigation led largely by the creators of the movement itself we can, in the best tradition of our art, learn from the past and effect meaningful and lasting curricular reform (Fenton, 1991, p. 85 ff).

THE NSS AND A VOTE FOR "PROCESS"

During the 1960s and into the early 70s the best hope for those wishing to move the social studies curriculum away from its traditional mimetic model of information transmission was embodied in the New Social Studies. NSS was largely premised on the ideals articulated by Jerome Bruner in 1960 in a classic treatise titled *The Process of Education*. Itself a product of the educational reform culture spurned by a perceived "education gap" with the Soviets after the launching of Sputnik, Bruner's (1960) *Process* stands as the rallying document for a flurry of curricular development activities as scholars and experts engaged in one of the most zealous reform frenzies in education history. Following the lead of scientists and science educators, the goal in social studies was to create curricula and materials, which would develop in students the ability to appreciate and manipulate the structures, concepts, and procedures of the social science disciplines. Although an oversimplification, the hope of NSS was to create a new curricular synthesis between process and product and, specifically, a synthesis giving dominance to the former (Oswald, 1993).

Bruner's *Process* would make three significant contributions to the NSS movement. First, it firmly established the desirability of the discovery teaching and learning model as the most effective means to promote student mastery of a discipline's conceptual and structural knowledge base—including the inquiry skills necessary to develop such understandings. As Barry Beyer (1994), an influential NSS practitioner and critical thinking expert would later note, by "a process called discovery learning or inquiry, students generated and tested hypotheses to develop conclusions, concepts, and generalizations" (pp. 94, 251). Richard Brown (1996), an Amherst History Project director, more specifically and emphatically noted, "we hitched our star to the concept of 'discovery' learning" in hopes that students "would learn 'history' [and], of even greater importance, [that] they would learn how to learn" (p. 268).

Process was never intended to be a detailed how-to manual. However, its second contribution to the NSS movement was the identification of several general prerequisites necessary for the development of any discovery-learning model hoping to achieve student mastery of conceptual and structural knowledge. According to Bruner (1977), curricula had to be "rewritten and their teaching materials revamped in such a way that the pervading and powerful ideas and attitudes relating to [a discipline] are given a central role." Furthermore, "the levels of these materials [had to be matched] to the capacities of students of different abilities at different grades in schools" (p. 18). In short, the structures and concepts of a discipline had to be identified and then made age appropriate.

A third prerequisite articulated in *Process*, and a means to achieving the first two, was the necessity of a "mastery of the knowledge to be communicated" embodied in both curriculum producers and deliverers (Bruner 1977, p. 88) In other words, if students were to be led down the garden path of discovery in a particular domain, the materials and instructors serving as guides along that path had to be steeped in the very conceptual and structural understandings which were the journey's rewards. For social studies teachers, this meant they must not only understand the process of education; they must also have a deep understanding of the process of political science, geography, or history, and so forth.

WHY NSS FAILED I: HISTORY AS A DISCIPLINE[1]

Having "hitched [their] star to the concept of discovery learning," the NSS movement made progress in creating materials for teachers to invite students into the inquiry process. Unfortunately, many of these materials failed to fulfill the prerequisites for the successful development of such a model as outlined by Bruner—fundamental structures and concepts identified and made age appropriate with teachers and curriculum developers steeped in that knowledge. In attempting to identify and distill the structures of the social sciences (Senesh, 1993), NSS developers were particularly thwarted by the unique nature of history as a discipline. With its origins and a continuing legacy derived from the humanities and its modern striving for veracity and objectivity, history maintains a home in both the arts and the sciences and, yet, is somewhat uncomfortable in either. Beyond the pale of reductionism, without the ability to conduct replicable experimentation, and forced to draw upon an evidentiary base that will always remain incomplete and haphazardly preserved, nothing so readily identifiable as the scientific method provides structure in history. These realities of history as a discipline would create significant difficulties in both preparing teachers and materials and thereby greatly reduced the reforming potential of the NSS history materials.

Teacher Competence

To fuel the movement with materials, the NSS successfully recruited scholars with Bruner's required mastery of the conceptual and structural knowledge to be communicated. Unfortunately, the mastery of those charged with trying to implement the curriculum never matched the mastery of those who developed it. During the movement itself, research by Zevin (1973) revealed that many classroom teachers, having had little contact with live models and few opportunities to participate in authentic disciplined inquiry during their own education, lacked the skills and dispositions necessary to conduct such inquiries. Stephen Thornton (1994), echoing concerns voiced by later NSS commentators, noted that many classroom teachers, even those with advanced degrees and teaching upper level classes in secondary schools, lacked grounding in the concepts and structures of the disciplines they taught.

Extensive conversations regarding structures and concepts developed soon after the NSS movement set sail (e.g., see Allen, Fleckenstein, & Lyon, 1967—especially Fenton, 1967b; Morrissett, 1967; Schwab, 1962). However, as Rice (1992) later remarked, these conversations were "generally ignored by educators as being esoteric and remote from the practical issues of teaching and learning" (p. 228) and Goetz (1994) simply noted that "the jargon of ... 'structures' and 'concepts' was not the stuff of teacher talk" (pp. 100–101). Lacking mastery of the concepts and structures of their disciplines, and unprepared, unable, or unwilling to incorporate the developing professional conversations into their teaching, "even the best teachers," according to Richard Brown (1996), an Amherst Project director, "needed more help than we were giving them" (p. 269).

Inexplicit Materials

Unfortunately, as Brown's comment above alludes to, shortcomings in teacher preparation to handle the structures and concepts of history were compounded by the shortcomings of the materials themselves. The problem was not the inability of expert curriculum developers to prepare materials steeped in conceptual knowledge and procedure. Rather, it appears that the problem was in the inability to translate their expertise into materials readily usable by classroom teachers. In attempting to identify and distill the structures of the social sciences, NSS developers were particularly thwarted by the unique nature of history as a discipline. Some authors, most notably Fenton, provided elegant opportunities for inquiry learning based on similarities between empirical processes in science and those in history. His opening lessons in the *Shaping of Western Society: An Inquiry Approach* provide a classic example of inviting students to consider "what is history," including the way experts make observations, offer hypotheses, decide what is a fact, interpret raw materials and revise conclusions as evidence evolves (Fenton, 1968). In fact, a cumulative and sequential curriculum designed at Carnegie Melon University, demonstrated that there *were* elegant and effective templates for inquiry learning. The Holt Social Studies Curriculum, which was the progeny of Project Social Studies, guided students and teachers through disciplined examination of "issues" across multiple fields of inquiry – comparative economic and political systems, global cultures, American history, and behavioral sciences. The curriculum culminated with a fascinating course called "The Humanities in Three Cities" where students engaged in a constructivist exploration of ancient Athens, Renaissance Florence, and modern New York City (see Fenton, 1971).

Although such approaches shaped Western education, it is not clear whether the importance of these lessons stuck with teachers. For example, the primary means of assessing historical understanding in our experience have remained focused more on the conclusions or "products" of historical scholarship rather than on the "process" by which those conclusions were derived. Before long, these "process" features that appeared in the Carnegie Melon materials gave way to the facts of history and soon textbooks were, at best, relegating such activities to the dreaded heap of "supplementary materials."

One reason may be the unique processes that comprise the "doing" of history. The role and value of "conceptual theorems" which can be delineated from a set of specifics, made into generalizations, and used to inform later investigations—the identification of which are often the very goal of discovery learning—are more questionable in history than they are in other disciplines. Nothing akin to Newton's Laws in science—so easily made age appropriate and "discoverable" through experimentation and thereby valuable as conceptual models—emerges from the study of history. Even other social science subjects—most notably psychology, sociology, anthropology, and even political "science"—have a stronger affinity for thinking and methods that mirror those in the natural and physical sciences, at least in the minds of teachers.

In short, the uniqueness of history as a discipline helped prevent the NSS movement from producing ready-made materials with age appropriate concepts and a structure for teachers to guide their students along the path of discovery towards a better understanding of the historian's process and the past itself. To remedy this shortcoming, many NSS developers sought to utilize the classroom teacher as an additional resource. Ideally, teachers themselves were to be "models of inquiry" as student and teacher alike pored over documents, attempted to develop hypotheses, formulate additional questions, search for evidence, and draw conclusions (Brown, 1996). No one would discount the value of such intellectual role models. However, given the inexperience and unpreparedness of teachers to conduct disciplined historical inquiries, this reliance upon the classroom teacher to "fill-in the blanks" created a fatal flaw in the NSS approach. For, while appearing to fulfill the highest goals of the discovery learning process, if both student and teacher are engaging in disciplined inquiry for the first time and without the proper guidance from materials, they could only be doing so in appearance.[2]

An Example

This is not to say that NSS curricula lacked the potential for powerful discoveries in history using inquiry learning. For example, Goetz referred to one of the Amherst Project's units, *Hiroshima: A Study in Science, Politics, and the Ethics of War* (Harris & Schreiber, 1970), as "the most impressive inquiry lesson that I have ever seen" (Goetz, 1994, p. 103). However, a close analysis of the *Hiroshima* unit highlights not only its potential but also the inherent difficulties faced by many of the NSS materials. Like all the Amherst units, this one consists primarily of a collection of primary documents from a wide variety of sources with brief narrative comments inserted for context, all of which is organized around some very general questions—for example "Was it [the decision to drop the bomb] a military decision?" Guided by these questions students are, in accordance with the highest goals of inquiry and discovery learning, to comb the documents, formulate their own questions, develop hypotheses, pursue evidence, and construct conclusions. In other words, they are to assume the roles of amateur scholars "doing history" (see Holt, 1990). Yet, as noted above, the unique nature of history makes doing history in a disciplinarily correct manner an extremely difficult task. For those not trained as historians, as articulated by one of the current leading commentators on history education, "thinking historically" can constitute nothing less than an "unnatural act" (Wineburg, 1999, p. 488).

To aid the students, the unit's teachers' manual provides additional guiding questions, a slightly extended narrative for deeper context, and some general discussion about how to handle the issues raised in historical investigations such as moral relativism and multiple-causation. Unfortunately, a brief manual is not enough to transform a teacher from someone engaging in an unnatural act into someone with a mastery of the material to be presented, as called for by Bruner. The manual correctly notes, for instance, "the exploration of the question [regarding the dropping of the bomb] should give the student some awareness of the possibility of multiple-causality in historical events" and warns the classroom teacher to require "reasonably sound logic and solid evidence [usage] in support of opinions" (Teacher's Manual, 1970, p. 15). Yet, nowhere in the *Hiroshima* materials is found a discussion on the complexities of dissecting multiple-causation in history and the points of clarification regarding the use of evidence are too few and too brief to adequately inform a teacher unversed in the use of historical evidence. Even if it had, how many teachers have the time or inclination to pursue such disciplinary questions themselves, let alone endure what they perceive as the headaches of extended inquiry among children with limited attention spans?

And so the problem persists: If the classroom teacher lacks the skills and motivation of the historian, then the best we can hope for is that student and teacher alike may participate in an opinion forming exercise—albeit one with the trappings and appearance of a disciplinary correct historical inquiry.

WHY NSS FAILED II: HISTORY AS A CONTENT AREA

The combination of ill-prepared teachers and inexplicit materials resulting from the unique challenges posed by history as a scholarly discipline greatly limited the reforming potential of the NSS materials. If these were the only problems, our recommendations, and the NSS movement's guiding legacy for new attempts at curricular reform, might be a simple and familiar refrain—steep teachers more deeply in the concepts and structures of a particular discipline and provide them with more explicit materials. However, because of the contention that surrounds its very purpose of fostering citizenship, history education suffers something of an identity crisis—further complicating the matter. This crisis mandates the inclusion of a narrative as a curricular minimum and creates competing curricular needs corresponding to history education's various "identities." The failure of the NSS movement to accommodate itself to these challenges sped the abandonment of materials whose reforming potential was already limited by shortcomings in teacher and material preparation.

The Narrative in the History Curriculum

For better or worse, many commentators have noted the intransigence of "the narrative" as the dominant paradigm of history education (e.g., see Shemilt, 2000). At a minimum, an apparently unalterable minimum, history courses are expected to provide a chronological story. Regardless of how valuable teaching the processes of history and the historian might appear at any given moment in time, the profession and society at large have proven unwilling to envision, at least for very long, history courses which exclude the products of those processes—namely the historical names, dates, and interpretations offered by the narrative (Whelan, 2001). Therefore, whatever synthesis between teaching product and process currently holds sway, it must always remain a synthesis of the two and the narrative seems to be a component of the curriculum here to stay (Thornton, 1994).

Its intractable nature as a component of the curriculum positions the narrative and its chronology as the primary provider of structure in history courses. This condition significantly affected the NSS movement as many of its projects were ultimately evaluated in terms of how much they enhanced traditional subject matter (Nelson & Drake, 1994). Furthermore, the types of new curricula even possible were largely limited to those that would meaningfully inform, rather than replace, a chronologically based narrative. As Massialas (1992) would later note, the maintenance or return within the profession of the sense that "chronology was the most important basis for organizing and sequencing content" presented a nearly insurmountable challenge for those hoping to transform the history curriculum into one based on topical or thematic courses (p. 122). As the chronology of history grows, it also represents an increasingly tenacious barrier to those who would favor a measure of "depth" even at the cost of "breadth" in the delivery of historical information.

Rather than a thematic replacement of the narrative, various NSS projects did, in fact, hope to provide an enhancement to narrative based courses.[3] According to Brown (1996), Amherst Project creators "hoped our units [would be] plugged into a larger narrative" which "would enable students to read [the narrative] with both new interest and new critical power" (p. 272). The Harvard Social Studies Project's *Public Issues Series* was based largely upon the investigation of thematic "Persisting Questions of History" and was less intended to be used as narrative supplements than the Amherst Project materials. However, even this project followed enough of a chronology internal to each pamphlet and as a series to be plugged into a chronology-based course. Ultimately, many teachers attempted to utilize the NSS materials as depth achieving supplements to their narrative based courses (Nelson & Drake, 1994).

Post-holing—achieving depth by occasionally plugging in NSS units within the larger context of the narrative—was a viable construct (Beyer, 1994; Brown, 1996). Ideally, through the units students would be able to develop conceptual generalizations, structural insights, and procedural understandings that would inform later learning—even, and especially, when returning to the narrative. However, even the Amherst units, which were intended to be used as such supplements, "offered teachers little or no help in seeing how this might happen" as it was "left entirely to teachers to deal with such knotty problems as what should link the post-holes, what to do once a unit was completed, or what the relationship was between the units and the narrative of American history" (Brown, 1996, p. 272). It was to be the classroom teacher's responsibility to foster the development and application of disciplinary appropriate conceptual generalizations to inform the narrative. Unfortunately, as mentioned above, classroom teachers inadequately trained as historians were too often simply incapable of generating the necessary conceptual generalizations—let alone the more difficult task of using those generalizations in a disciplinary appropriate manner to inform later learning.

Again, a weakness of many classroom history teachers—the inability to develop and utilize conceptual generalizations—was left unaided by inexplicit curriculum materials. However, now actualized by the necessity of returning to the narrative, a condition mandated by the uniqueness of history as a content area, these failings were compounded and the use of depth-achieving and process-oriented materials, if only as post-holes, became worse than unsuccessful—they tended to become an unproductive drain on the time demanded by a narrative trying to cover a chronology. Typically, a focus on standards and standardized testing only exacerbates this rift between process and content.

The Identity Crisis and Mismatched Roles

Competition for time between teaching the chronology of the narrative and the processes that produce that narrative is only a symptom of the larger pedagogical identity crisis perennially affecting history education. While few contest the idea that the purpose of such education is to foster citizenship, there exist several ideas regarding what constitutes citizenship and how it should be fostered. It is from these divergent definitions—citizenship as a nationalistic celebration of the past, as the ability to fully develop one's own sense of self and clarify one's own values within the context of a pluralistic or global society, or as the ability to make the observations and decisions required by a democratic society in an informed, rational, and disciplined manner—that the profession's contention over purpose and its identity crisis arise as each definition mandates a fundamentally different approach to teaching.

Over the years, various authors have articulated general approaches to teaching as they correlate with these enduring views of citizenship (Barr, Barth, & Shermis, 1977; Rossi, 1992; see also Ross, 2001). In his review of the history of social studies education, Thornton (1994) outlined these approaches as follows: (a) the citizenship transmission model in which the instructor provides students with a (presumably nationalistic) canonical narrative; (b) the reflective thinking model in which students are expected to clarify their own ideas and beliefs about the present through investigations of the past; and (c) the disciplined inquiry or "social sciences simplified for pedagogical purposes" model in which students are expected to develop the habits of mind possessed by social studies scholars (borrowed from Wesley, 1937, p. 6). Naturally, efforts at curricular reform tend to be grounded in one of these views of citizenship.

Unfortunately for the New Social Studies, these conceptions of citizenship, the corresponding teaching style, and the movement's desired outcomes were frequently improperly aligned. The citizenship transmission view stems from an essentially imitative or "mimetic" conception of curriculum (Jackson, 1986, p. 117). Facts, conclusions, and even the morals of history are presented to students via two dominant instructional tools— the textbook and the lecturing teacher. Additionally, such an approach often entails what Ryan (1973) identified as a "hidden curriculum" stressing the primacy of facts, hierarchical teacher-student relationships, and the infallibility of "experts." Clearly, the NSS materials, with their focus on student led investigation and open ended questioning, were poorly suited to this approach. However, NSS materials were, in fact, implemented in classrooms where the transmission approach dominated. As early as 1973, Ryan described how attempting to implement NSS materials and methods in such settings—threatening both the security of a canonical narrative and the "hidden curriculum"—positioned the citizenship transmission view of social studies education as antithetical to NSS.

The NSS movement was better suited to the latter two curricular approaches—the reflective thinking and disciplined inquiry, or social sciences, models. Both stress the importance of student-centered processes and both aim to achieve thinking of the highest taxonomical order. In fact, both could be thought of as "inquiry" based models. Unfortunately, however, history education again posed a unique condition that the movement was unable to fully accommodate. Most of the history specific projects hoped to address both the reflective thinking and disciplined inquiry traditions of social studies education, resulting in an internal tension that was never resolved. Oliver and Newmann's *Public Issues Series* (1967) provides perhaps the best example. The series authors "believe[d] that most of the important current events can be clarified by reference to public issues in other places and other times" (Oliver & Newmann, 1988, p. 1)— the very definition of reflective thinking. However, the units intended that the necessary understanding of "public issues in other places and other times" would be derived through analysis and evaluation of primary documents—a hallmark of disciplined inquiry.

Unfortunately, these two approaches are not as complementary as one might hope. Using history as a guide to clarify one's values in the context of contemporary issues, as the reflective thinking view prescribes, requires the exact moral relativism that historians and even the Amherst *Hiroshima* unit caution against when engaging in authentic historical scholarship. Furthermore, conclusions derived from the two approaches fundamentally differ—one being a relative value claim, the other a scientific truth claim. If either is to be considered valid, students must be able to differentiate between the two. Unfortunately, in his 1984 generalized survey of schools, Goodlad (1984) found lacking anything "to suggest ... [student] understanding of the difference between [moral judgments] and decisions based upon scientific fact" (p. 242). This is not to say that the two approaches were mutually exclusive. However, when coupled with the time required to pursue both approaches simultaneously—we conservatively concluded 23 days would be necessary to complete the single *Public Issues Series* pamphlet on the American Revolution and at least 1–2 weeks to do justice to *Hiroshima*—the inability of students to differentiate between value and truth claims certainly created a degree of competition and misdirection of efforts between the two approaches.

The tension would become significant as the sociopolitical turmoil of the later 1960s and early 1970s re-invigorated contention regarding the role of social studies and, specifically, history education (Greenawald, 1995). To many, the relativistic and often revisionist explorations of history and society induced by the reflective thinking model added fuel to a perceived cultural revolution undermining the stability of society. To others, the necessity to accept the past on its own terms required by the disciplined inquiry approach detracted from the need to address the pressing social issues of the day (Nelson & Drake, 1994). In short, and once again, no one got to where they wanted to be and the pressure to find materials better suited to one's immediate needs soon found the NSS materials replaced and gathering dust. Many never left the safety of a narrative, while others who dared to try something different beat a hasty retreat back to the transmission model of citizenship education.

A Final Example

We have already mentioned the efforts undertaken at Carnegie Melon University as part of the U.S. Office of Education's Project Social Studies. Under the direction of Edwin Fenton, a cumulative, sequential social studies curriculum was developed for 9th through 12th grade. This Holt Social Studies Curriculum stands as the best example of a concerted effort to address the "warnings" addressed in this paper. Beginning with "Comparative Political Systems" and "Comparative Economic Systems" as separate semester courses at the freshmen year and ending with "Introduction to the Behavioral Sciences" and "The Humanities in Three Cities" in the Senior Year, every core text in the series took an "Inquiry Approach." The texts for two history courses—"The Shaping of Western Society" (sophomore) and "A New History of the United States" (junior)—bore striking similarities to those for other social science disciplines. Namely, these materials were chock full of raw materials with the opportunity for students to analyze and evaluate them in a guided inquiry that is consistent with the process of the discipline.

For example, in the 11th grade text, *A New History of the United States: An Inquiry Approach* (Bartlett, 1975), chapter 12—"Civil War and Reconstruction: 1850–1877"—begins like all chapters in the entire Holt series, by "Stating an Issue." Along with an historical essay titled "The Failure of Compromise: 1850–1859," a series of pictures used to illustrate several versions of *Uncle Tom's Cabin* are presented with a question for students to consider how they would have reacted if they were from the north or from the south. The essay provides a historical narrative and the context for John Brown's attack on a government arsenal at Harper's Ferry in 1859. At this point the chapter becomes more like a miniature Amherst unit, with an "Exercise in Historical Inquiry" inserted for students to dig a post-hole on this particular event. The extended exercise begins with students assigned to view a collection of documents through the perspective of one of eight biographical excerpts (Southern reporter, U.S. Army officer, abolitionist teacher, elderly Black servant etc.). Then students are confronted with an impressive array of documents, including autobiographical accounts, letters, testimonies, artistic representations, and commentaries on John Brown "as others have seen him" (Garrison and Benet to Lincoln and Davis).

Step-by-step suggestions for provoking student analysis are provided for the teacher who cares to consult the comprehensive Teachers' Guide, and the student is ultimately left to question and defend whether "war between the North and the South was the *inevitable* consequence of John Brown's raid on Harper's Ferry." The chapter concludes with two more historical essays, with both the war itself (1860–1865) and Reconstruction (1865–1877) covered in six pages with one map in each essay. In our judgment, the materials of the Holt curriculum reflect the best attempt to accommodate both the spirit and practice of inquiry while preserving the nature of chronological narrative, all in one text. Throughout the book, students pause to interpret data, analyze primary documents, and consider "big questions" that serve to deepen their understanding of the narrative as it is "covered" in small spurts or short historical essays, if at all.

The approach taken by the Holt Curriculum reflects an effort by its creators to accommodate both the demands of repeated practice with inquiry learning while not abandoning the coverage of a narrative to the separate expertise of individual teachers. In addition, it took a hearty stab at addressing all three varieties of citizenship education. It celebrates the story of American history in chronological fashion, inserts opportunities for students to consider moral questions and to reflect on personal values, and clearly emphasizes the process of history as a structured disciplinary activity. As evidence of this, teachers' guides in the series include objectives not only for knowledge and skills, but "affective" and "method of inquiry" objectives as well. To purists of chronological coverage, the history books would simply be woefully inadequate in terms of content. And even to the inquiry aficionado, the rigor of dealing with one open-ended posthole after another, chapter after chapter, would probably wear most social studies teachers down during any era. The point of this example is that even the "best" exemplar for dealing with the issues raised in the paper failed to capture a lasting audience among practitioners, with concerns about the teaching of history leading the way.

This example also illustrates that the specific factor contributing to the demise of NSS was not the positioning of one competing vision of history education as wholly better than the other two. In fact, the reality necessitated and the opportunity provided by history education creates a catch 22: Namely, to achieve multiple instructional goals mandates that any sound curriculum incorporate multiple approaches, but when curriculum reformers dare to do that very thing, they risk doing too much and leaving teachers frustrated and unable to manage it all. What becomes relevant is that student-centered, process-oriented, and depth-seeking materials must be carefully matched to specific goals. In the end, even the best attempts to implement NSS materials in classrooms dominated by a transmission model resulted, as Ryan noted, in the abandonment of those materials and, obviously, any hope that those materials would fundamentally alter the curriculum. Similarly, confounding the reflective thinking and disciplined inquiry approaches invited, from a variety of practical and political viewpoints, a reactionary accusation of wasting time and misdirected efforts—also resulting in the abandonment of materials and their reforming potential.

CONCLUSION AND (HOPEFULLY) PREAMBLE

In failing to fully accommodate its attitudes and methodologies to the unique challenges posed by history as a scholarly discipline, the NSS movement too often produced outcomes in the history classroom generating more the appearance of discovery learning than any actual substantive discovery learning. When such activities failed to inform a larger narrative and detracted time from other curricular needs, challenges posed by history as a component of the curriculum, many teachers concluded that NSS simply failed to get them where they wanted to be and were abandoned. And, in doing so, a generation's chance at fundamental reform in the social studies curriculum was lost.

The attitudes and methodologies informed by the learning theories of constructivism provided another chance to reform the social studies curriculum at the turn of the twenty-first century. Since the demise of NSS, pedagogical and epistemological research has reinforced such principles as the relevance of prior knowledge and the sociopsychological dimensions of teaching and learning—all of which was lacking in the NSS movement (see Beyer, 1996; Rice, 1992; Scheurman, 1998; Wineburg, 2000). We have mentioned several efforts to translate this research into meaningful models for curricular design (e.g., "authentic pedagogy"). If combined with the lasting legacy of the NSS movement—the need for conceptual and structural knowledge, the potential of post-holing, and the viability of an inquiry model—such methods promise to foster a social studies curriculum friendly to the processes of interpretation and intuition and hospitable to the goals of conversation and invention.

Additionally, if one looks closely enough, a legacy of inquiry methods strikingly similar to the NSS can still be found in many history classrooms. Many Advanced Placement classrooms contain a strong component of "doing history" as students pore over primary and secondary documents to form conclusions in preparation for the Document Based Question. These activities are crafted around a guiding question and students are to construct a disciplined argument rather than memorize a set of facts. One still finds copies and recopies of the Amherst originals *Hiroshima* and *Lexington Green* in use. More recent efforts include document-rich units based on specific questions in American and World History. For example, invoking the spirit of A.P. History and the importance of disciplinary procedures inherent to that curriculum, one curriculum designer refers to his commercially available units in American and World History affectionately as "DBQ for the rest of us" (Roden, 2004).

Certainly, if we are to transform the history classroom through constructivist informed methodologies we must learn how to overcome the challenges posed by history as a discipline and a content area. Equally important, given the perennial tension between process proponents and those who favor a focus on the knowledge products of history, it may well again prove true that "at every stage of the development of the social studies the field of history has been at the center" (Jennes, 1990). If we are unable to reform the way we teach history, we may ultimately lose ground in the other social studies.

Practitioners of every generation must proceed with a solid grounding in their discipline and a firm understanding of constructivism. For social studies teachers, there is no better place to hone their constructivist skills than in the treasure trove of curricular examples left behind by the NSS movement. Curriculum developers must produce materials that explicitly extrapolate the implementation of theory. Additionally, teachers must be taught explicit methods to immerse students in historical inquiry in ways that are time efficient, enhance coverage of the narrative, and appropriately match methodology, hopeful outcomes, and one of history education's identities. Otherwise, constructivist history classrooms, like inquiry classrooms of yesteryear, will be so only in appearance—perhaps with students actively moving around the room or navigating their way through an Internet "Webquest," but not necessarily thinking critically or learning anything about the disciplinary processes of history and social science. If true, then such constructivist methods, currently the best hope to reform the social studies curriculum, will again fail to get teachers where they need to be and do so at the expense of other curricular needs. And, not surprisingly, the momentum to reform the curriculum toward a more student-centered, depth-achieving, and process-oriented focus will be lost each time the cycle returns.

The NSS movement came very close to providing a lasting model of curricular reform. If we can resolve the "history problem" before the next cycle commences and ends, we might just get even closer.

ACKNOWLEDGMENTS

The authors would like to acknowledge Dr. O.L. Davis and Dr. Barry Beyer for their valuable feedback on earlier versions of this paper.

NOTES

1. As mentioned earlier, a great deal of analysis has already been devoted to the failure of the NSS movement. It is perhaps important to note that our purpose here is not to provide a definitive postmortem of the movement or even review the analyses and arguments presented by other commentators. We have limited ourselves to the discussion of the unique challenges posed by history because we feel it is a relevant and pertinent factor that has been somewhat overlooked in past analyses.

2. In fairness to the vast amount of literature and materials produced as part of the NSS movement, this section criticizing NSS curricula for their lack of explicitness excludes a few obvious exceptions. Some resources went to great lengths to spell out and provide examples of disciplinary structure and conceptual explicitness—exemplified by the rigorous works of Edwin Fenton—*The New Social Studies* (1967a) and *Teaching with New Social Studies in Secondary Schools; An Inductive Approach* (1966). In fact, the Amherst Project and Public Issues Series, the two projects we have most relied upon here—due to their history specific nature, longevity, popularity, and continued commentary by their creators—also contained many examples of disciplinary structure and conceptual explicitness. However, explicitness must be measured in the context of the degree required by the users of the materials. In this case, the literature suggests that for many teachers the curriculum may have contained more than enough disciplinary depth but too little pedagogical guidance which, as we have pointed out, is interrelated with the need to have expertise in the processes of doing history, not just the processes of teaching it.

3. One project stands as a notable exception to this rule, and that is the aforementioned Holt Social Studies Curriculum developed at Carnegie Melon University. This project created a cumulative, sequential curriculum grounded in inquiry approach while maintaining a respect for chronological narrative. We discuss this in more detail later. See "Final Example."

REFERENCES

Allen, R. F., Fleckenstein, J. V., & Lyon, P. M. (Eds.). (1967). *Inquiry in the social studies: Theory and examples for classroom teachers.* Washington, DC: National Council for Social Studies.

Barr, R. R., Barth, J. L., & Shermis, S. S. (1977). *The nature of the social studies.* Palm Springs, CA: ETC.

Bartlett, I. (Eds.). (1975). *A new history of the United States: An inquiry approach.* New York: Holt, Rinehart and Winston.

Beyer, B. K. (1994). Gone but not forgotten: Reflections on the new social studies movement. *The Social Studies, 85,* 251–255.

Brown, R. H. (1996). Learning how to learn: The Amherst project and history education in the schools. *The Social Studies, 87,* 267–273.

Bruner, J. (1960). *The process of education*. Cambridge, MA: Harvard University Press.

Bruner, J. (1977). *The process of education* (Preface to the second edition). Cambridge, MA: Harvard University Press.

Fenton, E. (1966). *Teaching with new social studies in secondary schools; an inductive approach*. New York: Holt, Rinehart and Winston.

Fenton, E. (1967a). *The New Social Studies*. New York: Holt, Rinehart and Winston.

Fenton, E. (1967b). Structure and inquiry. In L. J. Hebert & W. Murphy (Eds.), *Structure in the social studies* (pp. 75–81). Washington, DC: National Council for the Social Studies.

Fenton, E. (1971). *A rationale for the second edition of the Holt Social Studies Curriculum*. New York: Holt, Rinehart and Winston.

Fenton, E. (1991). Reflections on the "New Social Studies." *The Social Studies, 82,* 84–90.

Fenton, E. (1968). *The shaping of Western society: An inquiry approach*. New York: Holt, Rinehart and Winston.

Goetz, W. W. (1994). The New Social Studies: The memoir of a practitioner. *The Social Studies, 85,* 100–105.

Goodlad, J. I. (1984). *A place called school*. New York: McGraw-Hill.

Greenawald, D. (1995). Maturation and change. *Social Education, 59,* 416-428.

Harris, J., & Schreiber, P. D. (1970). *Hiroshima: Imperialism and the dilemma of power.* Boston: Addison-Wesley.

Holt, T. (1990). *Thinking historically: Narrative, imagination, and understanding*. New York: The College Board.

Jackson, P. W. (1986). *The practice of teaching*. New York: Teachers College Press.

Jenness, D. (1990). *Making sense of social studies*. New York: Macmillan.

Massialas, B. G. (1992). The "New Social Studies"—retrospect and prospect. *The Social Studies, 83,* 120–124.

Morrissett, I. (Ed.). (1967). *Concepts and structure in the new social science curricula*. New York: Holt, Rinehart and Winston.

Nelson, L. R., & Drake, F. D. (1994). Secondary teachers' reactions to the New Social Studies. *Theory and Research in Social Education, 22,* 44–73.

Newmann, F. M., Marks, H. M., & Gamoran, A. (1996). Authentic pedagogy and student performance. *American Journal of Education, 104,* 280–312.

Oliver, D. W., & Newmann, F. M. (1967). *Cases and controversy: Guide to teaching the Public Issues Series/Harvard Social Studies Project*. Middletown, CT: American Education.

Oliver, D. W., & Newmann, F. M. (1988). *American Revolution: Crisis of law and change Teacher's Guide*. Boulder, CO: Social Science Education Consortium.

Oswald, J. M. (1993). The social studies curriculum revolution. *Social Studies, 84,* 14–19.

Rice, M. J. (1992). Reflections on the New Social Studies. *The Social Studies, 83,* 224–231.

Roden, P. (2000). *Document based questions in American history*. Evanston, IL: The DBQ Project.

Ross, E. W. (Ed.). (2001). *The social studies curriculum: Purposes, problems, and possibilities*. Albany, NY: State University of New York Press.

Rossi, J. A. (1992). Uniformity, diversity, and the "New Social Studies." *The Social Studies, 83,* 41–45.

Ryan, F. L. (1973). Implementing the hidden curriculum of the social studies. *Social Education, 37,* 679–681.

Scheurman, G. (1998). From behaviorist to constructivist teaching. *Social Education, 62,* 6–9.

Scheurman, G. (1998). Revisiting Lexington Green. *Social Education, 62,* 10–18.

Scheurman, G., & Newmann, F. M. (1998). Authentic intellectual work in social studies: Putting performance before pedagogy. *Social Education, 62,* 23–25.

Schwab, J. J. (1962). The concept of the structure of a discipline. *The Educational Record, 43,* 197–205.

Senesh, L. (1993). Our working world and the birth of the organic curriculum. *The Social Studies, 84,* 92–98.

Shemilt, D. (2000). The caliph's coin: The currency of narrative frameworks in history teaching. In P. N Stearns, P. Seixas, & S. Wineburg (Eds.), *Knowing, teaching &learning history: National and international perspectives* (pp. 83–101). Albany, NY: New York University Press.

Teacher's Manual. (1970). *Hiroshima: Imperialism and the dilemma of power.* Boston: Boston: Addison-Wesley.

Thornton, S. J. (1994). The social studies near century's end: Reconsidering patterns of curriculum and instruction. In L. Darling-Hammond (Ed.), *Review of Research in Education* (pp. 223–254). Itasca, IL: Peacock.

Wesley, E. B. (1937). *Teaching the social studies.* New York: Heath.

Whelan, M. (2001). Why the study of history should be the core of social studies education. In E. W. Ross (Ed.), *The social studies curriculum: Purposes, problems, and possibilities* (pp. 43–56). Albany, NY: State University of New York Press.

Wineburg, S. (2000). Making historical sense. In P. N. Stearns, P. Seixas, & S. Wineburg (Eds.), *Knowing, teaching & learning history: National and international perspectives* (pp. 306–326). Albany, NY: New York University Press.

Wineburg, S. (1999, March). Historical thinking and other unnatural acts. *Kappan,* 488–498.

Zevin, J. (1973). Training teachers in inquiry. *Social Education, 38,* 310–316.

CHAPTER 17

WE WON'T GET FOOLED AGAIN; WILL WE??

Teacher Perceptions of the New Social Studies

Mark A. Previte

"Meet the new boss, same as the old boss."

"We Won't Get Fooled Again"

The Who (1971)

INTRODUCTION

Social studies teachers during the 1960s were witnesses to a curriculum revision movement that was unparalleled since the heyday of the Progressive Movement in the 1930s (Social Education, 1965). The launching of Sputnik in 1957 had cast a pall over America and her schools. How could a nation that was economically, politically and educationally inferior to the United States pull off a feat of such technological magnitude? After

The New Social Studies: People, Projects, and Perspectives, pp. 361–377
Copyright © 2010 by Information Age Publishing
All rights of reproduction in any form reserved.

much soul searching, the nation's leaders concluded that one area that should be upgraded or overhauled was education. The federal government began the funding of projects in science and mathematics producing the next generation of scientists that would propel the United States to a first place finish in the 1960s Space Race. This placed the social studies in a precarious place: once again math and science were placed front and center in the educational debate and social studies did not want to be left behind at the train station.

Scores of perspectives have been published and dissected regarding the successes and failures of the New Social Studies movement. Curriculum specialists, social studies coordinators, university professors and educational historians all have weighed in with their expertise relevant to the triumphs and tragedies of that movement. Statistics have been gathered and scrutinized, curriculum documents have been probed and dissected, and the appropriate commentary has been rendered for public consumption and reflective discussion. At this moment in time, we possess a fairly satisfactory understanding that the failures of the movement outweighed the successes (Berkwits, 1973; Engle, 1986; Haas, 1977; Hertzberg, 1981).

One specific voice of this movement that has been diminished and underrepresented in this discussion is that of classroom teachers; the final vital link in a chain of events that would determine the success of social studies education that sought to move away from a teacher centered classroom dependent upon lecture and rote memorization to a student centered environment that focused on inquiry and discovery learning. This chapter will not seek to conduct an all encompassing study but rather to review a number of studies and reflections that indicate how classroom teacher perceptions of the New Social Studies influenced the course of the movement and the lessons to be assimilated for the future.

Origins of The New Social Studies

In the fall of 1959, 35 scientists, scholars, and educators met "to discuss how education in science might be improved in our primary and secondary schools" (Bruner, 1960, p. vii). From this convocation of experts, Jerome Burner (1960), a Harvard cognitive psychologist, penned his work *Process of Education*. The new curricular projects of the 1960s owe their existence to this work that summarized the basic principles of curricular reform in mathematics and science and exemplified the forces that supported them. Bruner provided the guiding principles of the movement: curriculum can be taught to any student, and each social science discipline can facilitate learning through its own method of inquiry. Change in the social studies would discard committee recommendations in favor of curriculum development. According to Bruner:

> The teaching and learning of structure, rather than simply the mastery of facts and techniques, is at the center of the classic problem of transfer.... The foundations of any subject may be taught to anybody at any age in some form.... Intuitive thinking, the training of hunches, is a much-neglected and essential feature of productive thinking not only in formal academic disciplines but also in everyday life ... [and] interest in the material to be learned is the best stimulus to learning, rather than such external goals as grades or later competitive advantage. (pp. 12–14)

What did this mean for the social studies? In searching for a methodology to create an exciting learning environment for students, the focus would be placed on the individual disciplines to provide the methods, skills and information necessary to teach students how to work like an historian, geographer, or economist. It would be 2 years later that the "revolution" in the social studies would receive further marching orders from Charles Keller (1961):

> We should begin by eliminating the term "social studies" which is vague, murky, and too all-inclusive and substitute for it the term "history and the social sciences," which is exact and hence meaningful. Such a change is necessary. (p. 61)

As a professor of history, Keller proposed a new plan to replace other curricular blueprints that were modeled after the 1916 Report of the Committee on Social Studies of the Commission on the Reorganization of Secondary Education of the National Education Association (Dunn, 1916). Upon reviewing some of the more salient points of the Committee's report he proposed two categories of ideas that would revolutionize the face of social studies education. First, history and the social sciences would replace the social studies. The good citizen goal of social education would be expunged. Taking its place would be continued reinforcement and development of skills and habits that contribute to student knowledge and thinking. Second, a single, vertical plan would become the new scope and sequence. No history or social sciences would be taught until grade 5. His scheme proposed a greater focus to be spent on studying the past, utilizing biography, writing, primary sources, and in-depth pedagogy. A 10th grade class on the "Introduction to the Social Sciences" was a unique addition to this program. He concluded that greater planning should be phrased in academic rather than structural terms.

Instead of citizenship education being the major objective of the social studies, students would be taught the disciplines to understand how social scientists go about their work. Learning would be defined as the acquisition of important facts and concepts of the disciplines, their application to important questions, weighing evidence and forming conclusions. (Keller, 1961, p. 62) To Keller, the concept of citizenship education did not make any sense since he felt that democratic attitudes cannot be taught in the schools. The seeds had been sown for one of the major movements of social studies curriculum change that would be known as "the New Social Studies" (Dougan, 1988–1989, p. 22)

Responding to the charges made by Arthur Bestor, *The Social Sciences and The Social Studies*, a joint publication of the National Council for the Social Studies and the American Council of Learned Societies, reported on the condition of social studies education during the late 1950s (American Council of Learned Societies/National Council for the Social Studies, 1962). This report responded to the confusion that was generated by a lack of direction in social studies. A scholar from each of the social science disciplines was selected to report on the relationship of his discipline to the social studies objectives. The intent of the study was not to mandate a national curriculum in the social studies but to suggest possible guidelines to be chosen and followed by individual districts within the framework of the individual disciplines. Producing responsible citizens, scholarship, issues-centered education, organization of social studies education, in-depth analysis, and cooperation between public and higher education were some of the issues that were confronted and supported in this work.

The National Council for the Social Studies (NCSS) began to fall in line with the social science camp through two publications. *Interpreting and Teaching American History*, the 31st NCSS yearbook, was "to encourage critical thinking through the interpretive approach" (Cartwright & Watson, 1961, p. 4). This theme was presented in a series of essays by prominent historians who covered interpretations of successive periods in American history. Bestor's presence no doubt reflected the efforts of NCSS to bring its erstwhile critics into camp. In 1962, the National Council for the Social Studies solidified its position when it published its definition of the social studies:

> The social studies are concerned with human relations. This content is derived principally from the scholarly disciplines.... The ultimate goal of the social studies is the development of desirable socio-civic and personal behavior....Knowledge and the ability to think should provide the basis on which American children and youth build the beliefs and behavior of free citizens. (National Council for the Social Studies, 1962, p. 315)

Joseph Schwab substantiated the need for the study of the structure of the disciplines due to their vast complexities. With great clarity, he submitted that education would be the recipient of two consequential results generated by the disciplines: better planning of the intended curriculum and pedagogy and the meshing of the disciplines with the real curriculum. Schwab was convinced that schools must not fall prey to the embedded belief that the goal of education is knowledge transmission. The disciplines generate knowledge but the interpretation of that knowledge yields meaning to what has been uncovered. Interpretation demands that knowledge can not be taken as unchanging or final. He believed that inquiry must remain as an open-ended process where new questions and new information may cast doubt on what is considered to be the truth (Schwab, 1962, p. 197).

The beginning of the new discipline movement had not been kind to the social studies. Merrill Hartshorn (1961), NCSS executive secretary, presented a letter to the Chairman of the House Rules Committee stipulating the membership's displeasure with the amendments being added to the 1958 National Defense Education Act. These amendments did not include any funding for the social studies. It was the organization's position that the social studies deals with problems and issues that other curriculum areas omit. A balance of funding must be maintained so that U.S. students would receive a well-balanced education.

In 1962, the financing of 12 curriculum projects by the Cooperative Research Branch of the Department of Health, Education, and Welfare under a program called Project Social Studies was completed (Fenton & Good, 1962). In order to stem the movement toward a national curriculum each social studies center was left to its own devices in developing themes and materials. Using the writings of Jerome Bruner as the overarching framework, several themes are emphasized among the projects: structure, inductive teaching, integration of concepts from the disciplines, sequential learning, and materials development.

Proponents of the new social studies, mostly university professors and curriculum developers, were convinced that subjects could be taught to any child at any time, that learning could be heightened through the teaching of the disciplines and that higher order thinking could be attained through student development of hypotheses and utilizing evidence to support those hypotheses. However, there was a solitary voice that was overlooked during the developmental and implementation stages that was one of the more significant reasons for the demise of the New Social Studies.

The Newness Syndrome

The 1960s was a decade that featured "the newness syndrome": the New Frontier, The New School, The New Politics, the New Look and the

Now Generation (Berkwits, 1973, p. 18). The designers of the New Social Studies programs were excited about the prospects of keeping pace with their math and science brethren but what of the classroom teacher? This section will review and critique a select number of studies and reminiscences that will investigate the perceptions of classroom teachers during the New Social Studies era.

The new social studies movement had not only spawned the well-publicized curriculum projects developed on campuses across the nation but it had spread into the nation's public school districts that were interested in joining the bandwagon. In 1965, the North Eugene School District located in Eugene, Oregon was seeking to revise their scope and sequence and methodology of the social studies curriculum in the direction of Edwin Fenton's philosophy of inquiry. Fenton's philosophy of curriculum was based on four specific themes: inquiry skills, attitudes, values, and knowledge. The key to unlocking discovery learning for the student would be to imitate the process used by social scientists:

1. Recognizing a problem from data
2. Formulating hypotheses
    Asking analytical questions, based on concepts
    Stating hypotheses
    Remaining aware of the tentative nature of hypotheses
3. Recognizing the logical implications of hypotheses
4. Gathering data
    Deciding what data will be needed
    Selecting or rejecting sources on the basis of relevance to the hypotheses
5. Analyzing, evaluating, and interpreting data
    Evaluating sources
        Determining the frame of reference of the author of a source
        Determining the accuracy of statements of fact
    Selecting relevant data from sources Interpreting data
6. Evaluating the hypotheses in light of the data
    Modifying the hypotheses, if necessary
        Rejecting logical implications unsupported by data
    Restating the hypotheses
    Stating generalizations (Judd, 1969, pp. 10–11).

Marvin L. Jaegers, the North Eugene social studies department chairman, had recommended to his superiors that Shirley Engle, a social studies professor from the Indiana University and noted advocate of an issues centered education in the social studies, come and talk to the administration and teachers about the new movement. There was a special connection here for Jaegers had studied under Engle as an undergraduate student at Indiana University (K. W. Jaegers, personal communication, May 8, 1968). Jaegers remembered that Engle's speech had an inspirational quality reminiscent of the methods class he had taken as an undergraduate at Indiana.

Engle made only one trip to Oregon and that was to outline the philosophy behind social studies curriculum development that was in the middle of a revolution. But that one trip swayed the thinking of the committee:

> As you look over the proposal, I think you will see considerable evidence of the impact you have had on the thinking regarding social studies curriculum in this state. In the event that the project is funded, we are certainly thinking in terms of your involvement in its development. (M. F. Harriger, personal communication, December 3, 1965)

The new program would take its content and structure from the disciplines of anthropology, economics, sociology, psychology, social psychology, political science, geography, history, philosophy, and ethics. Inquiry would take the place of memorization. Critical thinking, especially decision making skills that had been forgotten, would now be stressed. Teacher-centered classrooms dominated by the teaching of facts would be replaced with a student-centered environment focusing on concept development and student inquiry.

Engle's influence over the development of this curriculum would persist over the next 3 years. Jaegers sent Engle a status report on the progress of their program. He reported that their scope and sequence had been drastically revised, textbooks were abandoned, curriculum methodology was now based on the Fenton inquiry model, and units based on the conceptual approach were developed for about 50% of the instruction at each grade level (K. W. Jaegers, personal communication, May 8,1968). Jaegers also reported that local reaction to the curriculum was mixed:

> Needless to say, some of the principals and some of the teachers do not understand it and I doubt that they ever will. But we have made a bit more progress than one would normally expect. Reaction by students and parents has been mixed, generally favorable. We have had some trouble with the extremists on both ends who seem to object to teaching people to think but who would prefer indoctrination, their own particular brand. (K. W. Jaegers, personal communication, May 8,1968)

In a similar vein, a New Jersey social studies coordinator observed that the New Social Studies movement could not be viewed as a tidal wave of reform but as a stepping stone process whereby teachers would implement the best and the brightest of NSS theory and practice into their own courses and by sheer word of mouth, teachers would pass along their triumphs and tragedies in casual conversation (Crane 1974). This also appeared to be borne out by Burgess' (1972) findings:

> This study seems to affirm that its population perceives itself as at least making some attempt to practice the new methods. In addition, it is to be concluded that the subject teachers perceive themselves comprehending theory and methods necessary to implement but are somewhat ambivalent and contradictory regarding the paradigms and characteristics defining the new social studies. (p. 141)

Did teachers possess the essential attitudes to implement and sustain a New Social Studies program? A study of 79 Utah male social studies teachers from six high schools and six junior high schools attempted to determine if teachers possessed the necessary mindset to implement and sustain a New Social Studies program. A review of the current literature at the time indicated that social studies teachers were creatures of a traditional classroom culture, dominated by the values of authoritarianism and knowledge transmission, anathema to the characteristics that are essential to an inquiry, reflective classroom culture such as nurturance, openness, independence, and change (Robertson, 1968, p. 3). Countering the stereotype of mainstream teachers, this study concluded that teachers were "strongly motivated by strong social interests, as defined by their role expectations, without being inhibited by feelings of guilt or inadequacy" (p. 67). Robertson went on to conclude that his study of Utah social studies teachers found them to possess the skills and belief systems conducive to conducting a successful implementation of New Social Studies curriculum, a decided breakaway from the authoritarian stereotype presented by his review of the literature.

Social studies teachers were not lacking any politically powerful representatives who identified with the curricular and instructional issues facing teachers during the 1960s. On one front, two presidents of the National Council for the Social Studies voiced their concerns over the development and implementation of New Social Studies Programs. Emlyn Jones, a social studies teacher from Washington and NCSS President in 1961, toured the country to find that even though there were success stories and positive movement in improving social studies curriculum and instruction, there were "some school systems where the social studies program is about as adequate for the jet age as Jack Benny's Maxwell, nor are there any signs in some systems that they want to turn it in for a new model" (Previte & Sheehan, 2001, p. 226) Samuel McCutchen (1962) argued that social studies teachers from the 1940s to the early 1960s continued to employ the disciplines as their teaching frame of reference thereby preventing any hope of attaining a unified field of social studies.

Confusion Is Growing

With the American protest movement placing the Civil Rights Movement and the Vietnam War on the front burner and Watergate simmering on the back burner, student understanding and participation was vital to the democratic movement but teachers were questioning whether a classroom environment advocating inquiry and reflective thinking would lead the country out of the turbulent 60s to a position of peaceful coexistence or create more of the same dire consequences. Van Scotter (1972) reported that students were criticizing and critiquing the relevance of NSS curriculum to contemporary affairs while Chapin and Gross (1972) were resolute in their certainty that "if students are not involved, or find their attempts to participate frustrated, increasing numbers of youth will be motivated to step outside of the system in attempts to have an impact on society" (p. 154). In spite of this dilemma, research continued to provide insight and interpretation on the progress of the New Social Studies in the classroom.

A study of sixth grade teachers in selected Texas schools investigated whether a favorable perception toward New Social Studies instructional strategies and curricula would be developed through the taking of social studies methods courses, majoring in a social science discipline, and/or participation in in-service workshops (McIntosh, 1973) Completion of a college level social studies method course, 1 day in-service training or majoring in a social science discipline in college did not provide any appreciable attitude change toward the New Social Studies (p. 127). Age, years of overall experience teaching and years of experience teaching sixth graders appeared to be a noticeable factor in the favorability of the new social studies materials. Teachers under the age of 40, or who have taught in the elementary school less than 10 years, and who have taught sixth graders for 3 to 10 years showed a more favorable attitude toward the New Social Studies (p. 128).

Hahn's (1977) study focused on teacher perceptions concerning their adoption of New Social Studies materials in the states of Indiana, Ohio, Florida and Georgia. 209 teachers responded to questions related to the following subjects: adopter familiarity with new social studies materials, adopter perceptions of those materials and their willingness to adopt, adopter perceptions of the materials and their actual adoption, and the relationship between potential adopters' willingness to adopt new materials and adoption of those materials in their schools (p. 12). The Carnegie-

Mellon University materials, directed by Ed Fenton, and the Donald Oliver led Public Issues Series (Oliver & Shaver, 1966) were by far and away the most recognizable materials due to their low cost, subject coverage and early publication date (pp. 18, 21). Her study also indicated that 40% of Midwestern respondents and 49% of Southern respondents did not have any familiarity with New Social Studies materials (p. 17). Hahn stated that "there was very little empirical evidence about diffusion in social studies, there seemed to be a growing sense among social studies educators that there should be more attention to the area; development without consideration for diffusion was insufficient" (p. 12). A lack of awareness of the NSS movement and the materials generated from the movement, led her to conclude that greater dissemination of social studies materials, especially in rural areas and small town, was essential (p. 187). As far as perceptions and willingness to adopt, Hahn concluded that there was a strong correlation between the willingness to adopt and perceptions that the material was vastly improved over previous curricula, greater student interest, greater student learning, and learning would be observable to the teacher (p. 21).

Switzer, Lowther, Hanna, and Kidder (1977) analyzed the responses of 252 teachers from Ohio, Illinois, Michigan and Wisconsin concerning the dissemination and implementation of New Social Studies materials. The Carnegie Mellon and Harvard Projects placed first and third as the project most recognizable to the respondents due to their flexibility to be used in several social science disciplines. The projects that received the greatest examination treatment and usage, once again, were the Carnegie and Harvard projects but less than half noted that they had examined none or only one of the projects (p. 37). Not surprisingly, nearly three quarters of the respondents did not receive any in-service training in the materials. Conversely, there were two bright spots to this study: first, social studies department chairs and members of the National Council for the Social Studies demonstrated greater awareness of these projects and could influence the perceptions of teachers and second, there existed a high degree of awareness of the anthropology, sociology and political science projects by the respective teachers of each discipline (p. 51).

Marker's (1980) study demonstrated how Indiana social studies abandoned New Social Studies materials even though the materials were touted to be innovative. The word "new" had little impact on teacher selection of materials. Teachers were aware that these materials would create student confusion at first but persisted in the false belief that in due time, student interest would increase at subsequently, they would raise their game to the level of the materials (p. 43). A second reason for abandonment hinged on the perception of ownership and leadership. A significant reason for dropping the materials was the departure of the school's "advocate" (p. 49).

When the advocate lost interest or departed, the followers would fall like a house of cards. Finally, the perception that materials could be adjusted by the teacher to fit the needs of the classroom did not pan out (p. 52). They were accurate in their assessment that the materials would create difficulty for student understanding but that could be overcome through teacher adaptations. Unfortunately, the adaptations became a point of teacher frustration that led to certain abandonment of the materials. Interestingly enough, teachers were able to "see" some positive results from the usage of the materials but when asked, they were unable to clearly articulate those results.

Educational journals were doing their best to keep the classroom teachers informed about the movement's inconsistency. Searles and Nelson (1976) determined

> that the new social studies has been adopted in Pennsylvania, that teachers are aware of this, and that they can be and are being trained for it. If there is dissatisfaction with the social studies, it would seem that it has to be dissatisfaction with commission rather than omission. (p. 256)

In a study conducted in California, Colorado, Connecticut and Texas, Crawford (1976) determined that "approximately forty-two percent of teachers making 'some use' of at least one of the nine specified sets of 'new social studies' materials" (p. 257).

But were teachers reading and heeding the message? In 1966, Adeline Brengle, a high school social studies teacher from Indiana and President of the National Council for the Social Studies, voiced her distress over the deficiency of classroom materials and equipment to engage the students in the New Social Studies. Teachers were spending more time accessing these items rather than focusing on professional reading and curriculum construction in the development of new social studies lessons and materials. Her hope was for classroom teachers to become more aggressive in their pursuit of lifting the social studies to an equal status to that of mathematics and science, reflecting on what the New Social Studies had to offer as opposed to their old tried and true ways, exercising more cooperation and deliberation among the ranks of social studies teachers (Previte & Sheehan, 2001, pp. 274–278.)

A case study of Virginia Beach, Virginia teacher attitudes and perceptions concerning the implementation of New Social Studies materials provided some interesting insights (Garrou, 1980). The teachers possessed above average knowledge about NSS philosophy and materials used throughout the school system but no positive connection could be made between the materials and improved classroom performance (p. 142). Changes in teacher instructional practices through the implementation of

NSS materials could not be supported by the evidence. Apparently, the district's administrators did provide general support for this program but their misinterpretation of the project's details and their inability to relinquish control over curricular and instructional decision making led to the decline of teacher advocacy and the eventual demise of the program.

Rice's (1992) reflections concerning teacher behavior demonstrated that the traditional ways of teaching continued to have a firm grip in American classrooms. Teacher perceptions of curriculum materials and instructional behavior were sometime incongruous, leading to a status quo mindset. His personal experience with teaching the Georgia Anthropology Project to minority and low income students demonstrated that teachers and students could embrace the challenging nature of the materials in an attempt to raise the intellectual bar. He also observed that teacher enthusiasm increased as they became immersed in the curriculum but that enthusiasm dissipated due to diminished student effort and a dearth of in-service training and follow up.

During his 20 years as a K–12 coordinator, Goetz (1994) experienced frustration as well. Playing the dual role of teacher and coordinator does present some interesting role conflict scenarios. Using the jargon of the New Social Studies in his conversations with department members increased his feelings of insecurity, as if one was speaking in the ivory tower of academia rather than the halls of a school. Ambiguous terminology was problematic with the dissemination, acceptance and application of New Social Studies materials. A common language that placed teachers, teacher educators and publishers on the same page was one prerequisite for a program's success (Chapin & Gross, 1972) but alas, that was not to be. The vagaries of the NSS language, particularly the multiple meanings of the term "inquiry", mystified teachers and students alike (Chapin & Gross, 1972; Van Scotter, 1972).

Goetz ascertained that compromise became his ally when dealing with his department members. The social studies faculty was ambivalent toward moving away from the textbook and using alternate sources, so a compromise was reached through the adoption of a textbook series. Additionally, the success of any education program is highly dependent on the input of its teachers. Once again, Goetz moved toward common ground by agreeing to implement teacher proposals to improve the program even though they did not exactly adhere to the underlying principles of the New Social Studies.

Nelson and Drake (1994) conducted an oral history study that included 29 interviewees selected from the states of Maine and Indiana. The most significant criteria for their study was career longevity where most of the teachers served a minimum of 25 years spanning a time period from the 1940s to 1972. Many of these individuals had grown up during the politically conservative 1940s and 1950s where obedience to authority and expertise were strongly valued. These values also became strongly embedded in their educational philosophy. During the liberal revolution of the 1960s, they reacted negatively to educational innovation that shifted power away from the teacher to the student. The authors did not find any connections between the interviewees' conception of effective social studies teaching and their high school teaching; however, there was a decided connection with their university subject professors rather than their method professors.

An Achilles heel for change in social studies education was the widening gulf between public school teachers and university professors (Leming, 1989; Mehlinger, 1981). One of the leaders of the NSS movement asserted that his colleagues neglected to identify and appreciate the mindset of the classroom teacher (Fenton, 1991, p. 86). Leming suggested that conflicting agendas existed between the liberal-minded university professors and the conservative thinking classroom teachers. He contended that the university types are bound together by a code of values which stipulate that America is beset by myriad problems that must be solved, that the role of citizenship as the primary rationale of social education has not been clearly validated and discussed, and that a balanced condition has yet to be achieved between teaching commitment and critical thought to young people. Professors show their concern for the philosophical issues that face social studies education while the classroom teachers are decidedly concerned about the nuts and bolts of teaching. One such area for debate between the two groups focused on problem conception. Mehlinger concluded that the two groups appeared to be two ships passing in the night when identifying professional issues:

> The leaders spend their time cooking up new problems for teachers or dreaming up solutions to problems teachers do not confront. A vivid example of a teacher's nonproblem is one surrounding the definition of social studies. College professors enjoy debating this issue through articles and speeches and asserting that little progress can be expected in social studies until teachers address this issue. But for high school world history teachers, the definition of social studies is not a major concern—or even a minor one. For them, social studies has been effectively defined as what is found in the world history textbook. Many problems surround the teaching of world history to fifteen-year-old students; how to make the course interesting; how to handle a wide range of academic abilities within a single class; how to vary instructional practice; how to devise challenging examinations that can be scored swiftly; and so on. Very few social studies leaders are concerned with these problems. Indeed, such problems are generally considered to be too trivial to occupy the attention of the leaders. (p. 253)

How many teachers were willing to follow the leaders in the New Social Studies? Criticism was aimed at those who were spending much of their time theorizing what the New Social Studies ought to be rather than dealing with the practical problems that were confronting classroom teachers. A former school teacher and current social studies methods professor offered his unique perspective stating that "many teachers rejected the NSS because its tenets violated their beliefs and were incompatible with the structure of their school" (Rossi, 1992, p. 44). He also criticized the curriculum developers for their oversight in not involving teachers in the development phase hence depriving teachers a sense of ownership or commitment (p. 43). Suspicion of the developer's philosophy compelled teachers to cannibalize the materials "to meet the needs of the students" (Crane, 1974, p. 25). Dow (1992) agreed with the notion that many of the university scholar-reformers involved in the design of new social studies materials were indifferent to their public school teacher colleagues but this was not the case while he and his colleagues were designing and implementing the Man: A Course of Study (MACOS) curriculum. Classroom teachers were welcomed with open arms to assist in design, development and training but Dow reiterated that teachers were not asked about their needs and concerns for their classrooms and students.

Tradition and continuity is a steady variable in the life of a classroom teacher and any kind of instructional and/or curricular change can be met with resistance and skepticism as the world of their students is fraught with change. Social studies teachers are charged with preparing their students to be effective citizens for both the present and the future and that can be hinged upon their philosophy of professional development such as attending workshops and reading professional publications to find out about the latest research that may prepare students to take their rightful place as citizens. Teachers were not working in a "culture of scholarship" (Fenton, 1991, p. 86). The problem is that the educational philosophy of many teachers is inextricably linked to the past. One educator succinctly stated this situation thusly:

> The fact of change and whirlwind growth is a central one in our and the youngsters' experience. We have to adapt our thinking and strategies to accommodate that fact for their sake. Social studies, by its essence or by a process of elimination, must be the area in which the responsibility of equipping the young for that kind of change must fall. If we are not ready and able to make accommodations for and with the young, who will bear the responsibility for our failure? (Trezza, 1975, p. 163)

Inevitably, it was the classroom teacher who has the last word on educational reform movements for they truly are the gatekeepers of the curriculum (Thornton, 1991). Once the proverbial classroom door closes, the teacher is in control of the curriculum. This was especially true during one of the more controversial educational reform movements of our times: for it was the classroom teacher who chose to incorporate, transform, or ignore NSS concepts (Nelson & Drake, 1994, p. 46)

IN CONCLUSION: A PERSONAL NOTE

During the 1960s, my father, a social studies teacher in a rural central western Pennsylvania school district, attempted to use the Fenton materials and experienced limited success. At times, the materials were too challenging even for his academic students. But he was firm in his convictions that the materials possessed great promise so he adapted them to his classroom environment. A decade later, I located the Fenton texts packed away in my parents' attic. As a rookie teacher, I tried my hand at implementing the inquiry philosophy and achieved a modicum of success but probably created more confusion and frustration in my students. Together, father and son struggled against a tide of resistance that forced us to revert back to the tried and true: tradition had yet won again!

As the movement ebbed toward its conclusion, Jerome Bruner (1971) took a circumspect glance on what had occurred. His words give us pause to consider whether or not an inquiry model would have succeeded:

> If I had my choice now, in terms of a curriculum project for the seventies, it would be to find a means whereby we could bring society back to its sense of values and priorities in life. I believe I would be quite satisfied to declare, if not a moratorium, then something of a de-emphasis on matters that have to do with the structure of history, the structure of physics, the nature of mathematical consistency, and deal with it rather in the context of the problems that face us. (p. 19)

REFERENCES

American Council of Learned Societies/National Council for the Social Studies. (1962). *The social studies and the social sciences:* New York: Harcourt, Brace and World.

Berkwits, J. (1973). The "new" social studies: its shortcomings and its prospects. *The Social Studies, 64*(1), 17–19.

Bruner, J. S. (1971). The process of education revisited. *Phi Delta Kappan 53*(1), 18–21.

Bruner, J. S. (1960). *The process of education.* Cambridge, MA: Harvard University Press.

Burgess, G. A. (1972). *A survey and analysis of teacher perception of the philosophy and methods of "the new social studies."* Unpublished doctoral dissertation. University of Illinois, Urbana-Champaign.

Cartwright, W. H., & Watson, R. L. (Eds.). (1961). *Integrating and teaching american history*. 31st Yearbook of the National Council for the Social Studies. Washington, D. C.: National Council for the Social Studies.

Chapin, J. R., & Gross, R. E. (1972). Making sense out of the terminology of the new social studies. *The Social Studies, 63*(4), 147–155.

Crane, G. L. (1974). The new social studies: recent attempts to implement it. *The Social Studies, 65*(1), 22–26.

Crawford, D. A. (1976). II. In Minnesota. *The Social Studies, 67*(6), 257–259.

Dougan, A. M. (1988–1989). The search for a definition of the social studies: a historical overview. *The International Journal of Social Education, 3*(3), 13–36.

Dow, P. B. (1992). Past as prologue: the legacy of sputnik. *The Social Studies, 83*(4), 164–171.

Dunn, A. W. (1916). *The Social Studies in Secondary Education. Report of the Committee on Social Studies of the Commission on the Reorganization of Secondary Education, United States Bureau of Education*. Bulletin, 1916, No. 28. Washington, DC: GPO.

Engle, S. H. (1986). Late night thoughts about the new social studies. *Social Education, 50*(1), 20–22.

Fenton, E. (1991). Reflections on the "new social studies." *The Social Studies, 82*(3), 84–90.

Fenton, E., & Good, J. M (1962). Project social studies: a progress report. Social Education, 29(4), 206–208.

Garrou, T. M. (1980). *Implementing the "new social studies" curriculum: A case study*. Unpublished doctoral dissertation, University of North Carolina, Chapel Hill.

Goetz, W. W. (1994). The new social studies: the memoir of a practitioner. *The Social Studies, 85*(3), 100–105.

Haas, J. D. (1977). *The era of the new social studies*. Boulder, CO: ERIC Clearinghouse for Social Studies/Social Science Education and the Social Science Education Consortium.

Hahn, C. L. (1977). Familiarity with and perceived characteristics of "new social studies" materials. In C. L Hahn, G. W. Marker. T. J. Switzer, & M. J. Turner (Ed.), *Three Studies on Perception and Utilization Of "New Social Studies" Materials* (pp. 9–27). Boulder, CO: Social Science Education Consortium.

Hartshorn, M. F. (1961). Statement on HR 6744. *Social Education, 25*. 295–297.

Hertzberg, H. W. (1981). *Social Studies Reform: 1880–1980*. Boulder, CO: Social Science Education Consortium.

Judd, B. (1969). *Teachers guide for a new history of the united states: an Inquiry approach*. New York: Holt, Rinehart and Winston.

Keller, C. R. (1961). Needed: revolution in the social studies. *Saturday Review, 44*(16), 60–62.

Leming, J. S. (1989). The two cultures of social studies education. *Social Education, 53*(6), 404–408.

Marker, G. W. (1980). Why schools abandon "New Social Studies" materials. *Theory and Research in Social Education, 7*(4), 35–57.

McCutchen, S. P. (1962). A discipline for the social studies. *Social Education 27*(5), 61–65.

McIntosh, C. J. (1973). *A study of teachers' attitudes toward the "new" social studies.* Unpublished doctoral dissertation. North Texas State University, Denton.

Mehlinger, H. D. (1981). Social studies: some gulfs and priorities. In H. D. Mehlinger & O. L. Davis, Jr. (Eds.), *The social studies: Eightieth Yearbook of the National Society for the Study of Education* (pp. 243–269). Chicago: The University Of Chicago Press.

National Council for the Social Studies. (1962). The role of the social studies. *Social Education, 26* (7), 315–318.

Nelson, L. R., & Drake, F. D. (1994). Secondary teachers' reactions to the new social studies. *Theory and Research in Social Education, 22*(1), 44–73.

Oliver, D. W., & Shaver, J. P. (1966). *Teaching public issues in the high school.* Boston: Houghton Mifflin.

Previte, M. A., & Sheehan, J. J. (2002). *The NCSS presidential addresses, 1970-2000: perspectives on the social studies.* Bloomington, IN: National Council for the Social Studies and ERIC Clearinghouse for Social Studies/Social Science Education.

Previte, M. A., & Sheehan, J. J. (2001). *The NCSS presidential addresses, 1936–1969: perspectives on the social studies.* Bloomington, IN: National Council for the Social Studies and ERIC Clearinghouse for Social Studies/Social Science Education.

Rice, M. J. (1992). Reflections on the new social studies. *The Social Studies, 83*(5), 224–231.

Robertson, J. R. (1968). *Teaching styles, teacher attitudes and the new social studies.* Unpublished doctoral dissertation. Utah State University, Logan.

Rossi, J. A. (1992). Uniformity, diversity, and the "new social studies." *The Social Studies, 83*(1), 41–45.

Schwab, J. J. (1962). The concept of the structure of a discipline. *Educational Record, 43*(7), 197–209.

Searles, J. E., & Nelson, M. (1976). The state of the new social studies: I. in Pennsylvania." *The Social Studies, 67*(6), 254–257.

Social Education (1965). Reactions to the reports on Project Social Studies. *Social Education, 29*, 356–360.

Switzer, T. J., Lowther, M. A., Hanna, W. M., & Kidder, R. D. (1977). Dissemination and implementation of social studies project materials. In C. L. Hahn, G. W. Marker, T. J. Switzer, & M. J. Turner (Eds.), *Three studies on perception and utilization of "new social studies" materials* (pp. 30–52). Boulder, CO: Social Science Education Consortium.

Thornton, S. (1991). Teacher as curricular-instructional gatekeeper in social studies. In J. P. Shaver (Ed.), *Handbook of research on social studies teaching and learning* (pp. 237–248). New York: Macmillian.

Trezza, F. X. (1975) Social studies in the seventies … and beyond. *The Social Studies, 66*(4), 162–163.

Van Scotter, R. V. (1972). A prescription for teaching social studies in the seventies. *The Social Studies, 63*(4), 170–176.

CHAPTER 18

THE NEW SOCIAL STUDIES AND THE ETHOS OF MULTICULTURALISM

Gloria Contreras

My encounter with the new social studies came in the early 70s while a graduate student at the University of Georgia. Although the era had peaked and the movement waned, I found the units produced by the Anthropology and Geography Curriculum Projects most interesting and significant. The materials bore no resemblance to my public school curriculum where instruction had been mostly bad or indifferent, never good or relevant. Another view of the social studies that I held was rooted in my own Chicana identity and Mexican American heritage; as a teacher from a barrio school of South El Paso, I struggled with an irrelevant curriculum. Hence, I experienced three different kinds of social studies instruction—the dismal standard curriculum of which I was a product, the new social studies with its limited impact, and the ethnic studies variety. In this article, I rely on this experience to show how the multiculturalism that evolved from the seventies was reflected in selected project materials. While the unprecedented ethos was implicit in the materials generated by some projects, it was never the major theme of any of the new social studies projects. I relate how selected leaders within the new social studies

The New Social Studies: People, Projects, and Perspectives, pp. 379–405
Copyright © 2010 by Information Age Publishing

movement responded to the real pluralistic structure of society. How did curriculum developers approach the issues of bigotry, race, ethnicity, and poverty that were so egregiously ingrained in American society and education?

BACKGROUND

In the 1950s the disciplinary structure of the field of curriculum switched from the teacher and curriculum specialist to the disciplinary specialists who represented the "ablest scholars and scientists in the field" (Bruner, 1961). Pinar, Reynolds, Slattery, and Taubman (2004) observe that astute critics of the curriculum reform movement "understood that military and nationalistic objectives were buried in erudite discussions of the structures of the disciplines" (p. 161). Tanner and Tanner (1980) also asserted that sociopolitical influences can have a reverse effect in educational priorities:

> In one epoch, democracy is to be saved by focusing on the academically gifted, whereas in a succeeding era it is to be saved by giving priority to the lower achiever or disadvantaged learner. Instead of realizing that a democratic society requires that educational opportunity be optimized for all children and youth, and that curriculum must be reconstructed in a balanced way so as to address the needs that the widest membership of society shares, narrow priorities are established to the neglect of the wider needs. (p. 524)

These curriculum theorists held that the failure of the billion-dollar effort should have come as no surprise since the curriculum was designed to meet narrow nationalistic aims to the neglect of practical knowledge applications in the life of the learner and the wider society. Surprising, however, was how readily educators "jumped on the discipline-centered bandwagon with only a few dissenting voices" (Tanner & Tanner, 2007, p. 273).

Harsh criticism, indeed, although today we benefit from the instructive reflections of those developers of the new social studies movement who secured federal or private foundation funds under a sense of urgency to reform the curriculum under attack by critics like historians Arthur Bestor (1955, 1953) and Charles Keller (1961). As Rice (1992) pointed out, the type of inquiry built into the discipline-oriented projects of the 1960s was "related to the logic of the discipline, not to the actual social problems that had arisen since the projects began" (p. 226). Reflections by Rice and other players in the movement are presented in another section of this essay.

The New Social Studies and Competing Rationales

John Haas (1977) reviewed the phenomenon called the new social studies, asserting that by the mid-60s several approaches to social studies education were competing for ascendancy. The status quo version was rooted in the 1916 prescription of the Committee on the Social Studies of the National Education Association. A critic of this precept and of most professors of education was Bestor (1953) who proclaimed the following belief:

> I stand for an American public school system that shall be free and demo-cratic. I stand also for an American public school system that shall be *educational*. There is an antique play on words that still seems to tickle the fancy of professional educationists. "We do not teach history," they say, "we teach children." The implication that those who teach history teach it to no one is a manifest impossibility, no classrooms being located in the empty desert. But it is a distinct possibility, alas, that educationists, following their own maxim, may succeed in teaching children—*nothing*. (p. 10)

Two reform rationales for the social studies were the structures approach, or the new social studies, and the problem/processes approach. Haas stated that the latter had "pervaded every period of social studies educa-tion in the twentieth century, distinct and significant despite its minority position" (p. 53). Advocates of the problems approach included Maurice Hunt, Lawrence Metcalf, Shirley Engle, Byron Massialas, and Benjamin Cox. It was the problem/processes rationale that focused on critical social issues that citizens in a democratic society have to confront and attempt to solve through reflective thinking, critical thinking, problem solving, and decision-making processes. And indeed contentious issues abounded—anti-war protests, the civil rights movements, clashing social values of a counter culture, and other social movements like feminism. Hepburn (1993) likewise maintained that "Although social problem solving was encompassed in the social science projects, the best boost for multicultur-alism probably came from reforms outside the mainstream that promoted an interdisciplinary secondary school curriculum based on the analysis of public issues" (p. 22). In the following section a descriptive approach is used to present retrospectives of selected scholars on the multiculturalism vis-à-vis the new social studies projects.

THE NEW SOCIAL STUDIES PROJECTS IN RETROSPECT

From 1991 to 1996 *The Social Studies* journal (TSS) published a series of retrospective articles written primarily by project directors of the new social studies movement. I begin by examining a number of those writings to glean the authors' reflections that are tangential to multiculturalism. The meaning of multiculturalism at this historical juncture targeted the exclusion and exploitation which Whites had inflicted on people of color (Blacks, Hispanics, Native Americans, and Asians). The ethos tried to speak to subordinate groups, as pointed out by Whitefield (Kallen, 1924/1998) in his explication of cultural pluralism as conceptualized by Kallen:

> Greater sensitivity to the plight of the dispossessed and to the effects of bigotry and prejudice instigated the rise of the multiculturalist ethos beginning in the 1970s. The incomplete victories attained by the civil rights movement, the emergence of women's liberation, and the spurt of Third World immigration after Congress reformed immigration law in 1965 revived—within certain limits—the case for group rights with which Kallen had once flirted. A belief in the inescapability of ethnicity is a claim that multiculturalists (who have no founding thinker) echo, though they rarely cite Kallen—and that is one sign of the distinction between cultural pluralism and the ethos that has now widely displaced it. (pp. lii–liii)

Cultural pluralism sought inclusion of Eastern, Central, and Southern European immigrants into the American mainstream without forced Americanization. It was celebratory and affirmative, while multiculturalism targeted the unfair advantage that skin color gained for White ethnic groups. Multiculturalism attacked the politics of White supremacy. In one form or another, the following reformers of the new social studies movement address that disparity of power between Whites and minorities that evolved into a multicultural ethos.

John Rossi (1992), a teacher of the new social studies, discussed the perplexity of "Uniformity, Diversity, and the New Social Studies" in an early *TSS* issue. He saw curriculum reform as forming two separate streams—Bruner and Fenton championed the knowledge structure and modes of inquiry of each of the disciplines, while Oliver and Shaver emphasized the analysis of social problems and value conflicts through reflective thinking. Rossi held that there was nothing in the rhetoric of the first stream's curriculum that suggested an interest in questioning social paradigms or social reconstruction. He alleged that the stress on above-average learners, abstract disciplinary structures, and disregard for social issues reinforced existing social inequality. What's more, Rossi argued, any potential for social change within the movement was blocked by the authoritarian structures and processes found in schools.

The second stream's concentration on the "conflict-driven nature of society, contemporary social issues, the average learner, and its de-emphasis of the abstract nature of the disciplines ... was much less bound to reproducing the social order" (Rossie, 1992, p. 43). The Harvard Public

Issues Project produced a series of 30 units designed to help students analyze and discuss enduring value dilemmas through historical and contemporary case studies. Rossi concluded that, except for the Public Issues curriculum, the new social studies projects neglected the social turmoil of the decade "in favor of the empirical rationality of inquiry. Born in the later 1950s and early 1960s, the NSS was unable to anticipate the spirit of social change about to take hold" (p. 44). However, Krug, Poster, and Gillies (1970) would later evaluate early new studies materials, including the Public Issues materials, and point out the disservice of units like the "Negro Views of America" to American history high school instruction. Their evaluation revealed how any meaningful inquiry into topics like racial issues required a systematic study of Black history. The challenge to curriculum reformers posed by the new ethos of multiculturalism was enormous. For example, FitzGerald (1979) pointed out in her analysis of history textbooks over the twentieth century that "until the mid-sixties Black Americans had hardly entered the textbooks at all" (p. 83). Following a period of tokenism, she observed how most history books had been rewritten to include Black history by the 70s. Still the "new" history basically added what was not there before. A profound modification of history was never the case. FitzGerald revealed the incongruity between scholarship in the academic world and high school textbooks.

Another article in *The Social Studies* series by Byron Massialas (1992) shows how the multicultural ethos was implicit in project goals but was never a major theme of materials. Massialas reflected on Shirley Engle's vision of what social studies ought to be. In a seminal article, "Decision-Making: The Heart of Social Studies Instruction," Engle (1960) maintained that the main goal of instruction was to foster citizens' ability to make decisions on the major issues confronting them. As Massialas explained, students were to critically analyze traditional material and contemporary events to arrive at warranted decisions based on the evidence gathered. Engle's students tested the theory that culminated in a publication: *The Indiana Experiments in Inquiry: Social Studies* (Massialas, 1963). The researchers found that "Through a proper classroom environment and teaching method, students of virtually any age could be involved in reflection and critical thinking" (p. 121). In retrospect, Massialas observed the following:

> It is interesting to note that the that the Indiana researchers pointed out as early as 1961–62 that inquiry following the methods of the social scientist does not work without adjusting the process to the prevailing social-political context of the school and the emotional stage of the students and teachers. In other words, the studies identified at the very inception of the movement that what is now referred to as the "hidden curriculum" was indeed operative and that without considering its effects, efforts at reform in the social

studies classroom were bound to fail. The exclusive emphasis of many of the reformers of the 1960s on the structure of knowledge of the organized disciplines totally neglected the social-psychological dimension of teaching and learning, the hidden curriculum, and ultimately, as Fenton (1991) pointed out in his article, contributed to the demise of the New Social Studies. (p. 121)

Another major finding of the research on inquiry pointed out the need for concept-centered and student-centered curriculum reform. Massialas noted that what students saw in a problem was mostly a function of their interest and not any concern for associating a task with any of the disciplines. The methodology for implementing a concept/student-centered curriculum was provided in *Inquiry in Social Studies* (Massialas & Cox, 1966), as well as a series of units developed for a general world history course. Accordingly, historical topics were connected with current local problems—for example, interethnic relations in the students' own community. However, Massialas does not present information about the minority students participating in these classes nor the issues of racism and social injustice they might have raised. Sadly, Massialas notes the reality behind the implementation of the ideas of the original reformers:

> The condition of cultural crisis prevailing in society notwithstanding, teachers, for the most part, are oblivious to the need for social issues instruction. Our study found that teachers willing and able to tackle current issues were in the minority. Teachers preferred to gloss over the issues or avoid them altogether. (p. 122)

Massialas (1966) concluded that the "hidden curriculum" was minimally considered by the majority of reformers. Ethnicity, class, gender, religion, and linguistic background of students hardly played a role in the development and implementation of the new curriculum. At a time when minority rights were becoming salient, social studies instruction failed to be in the forefront. Yet, the "gradual acceptance of multiculturalism as a way of life has provided a more positive climate conducive to the citizenship objectives advocated in the 1960s by our Indiana group" (p. 123). Today Massialas continues to argue that problems such as AIDS, crime, drugs, and teenage pregnancies form an integral part of the school culture that the curriculum largely ignores. "Unless these issues are attended to directly and forthrightly and the school is looked upon as a microcosm of the larger society, curricula, as in the case of the New Social Studies, will continue to be dysfunctional in the education of citizens" (p. 124).

Marion J. Rice (1992), in offering his reflection on the new social studies, remarked on issues of integration:

It was not until the fall of 1968 that integration was actually forced on southern schools by the government, using the "club" of withholding federal
funds. After that stand by the U.S. government, desegregation came very
swiftly within the next two years. This long delay since the *Brown* decision
brought two hostile populations into contact—whites who were embittered
because their long delaying tactics had failed to prevent desegregation and
blacks who were angry because of the long delay and their loss of school
identity.... In this climate of mutual distrust and antagonism, for which
schools had prepared neither students nor teachers, curriculum reform took
second place to the practical matter of keeping a lid on potential school
conflict. (p. 226)

Rice (1992) berates the simplistic model of curriculum development
and dissemination followed by the National Science Foundation and the
Office of Education. The evaluation of materials was underestimated,
undertaken in-house, and underfunded. In the Georgia Anthropology
Curriculum Project (ACP), the decision was reached "that it was much better to work with a few teachers teaching pupils of different reading abilities than it was to have an extensive try out. What was lost in number was
offset by better feedback" (p. 227). Field trials for most ACP materials
took place when the schools were still segregated, but one-third of teachers and students testing the materials were deliberately chosen from an
African American population. Project material testing revealed the usual
problems of learning experienced by low-income groups, whether White
or Black, and although the amount of learning range was wide,

it was the general consensus of both teachers and pupils that it was better to
be challenged with new ideas than to be taught the familiar. If we deprive
children with low reading levels of the opportunity to receive instruction
that brings out new ideas, we guarantee that they can never grow intellectually. (p. 227)

A 2001 dissertation by Sorrells, *Marion Jennings Rice, Philosophy and
Praxis: The Professional Biography of a Georgia Educator*, is an educational
biography of Rice that includes a description of the rise and decline of the
new social studies movement and illustrates how the University of Georgia Geography and Anthropology Curriculum Projects responded to
issues of race in the South. As noted above, a third of the participating
teachers and students were Black, and in an interview Rice explained that
"Unlike any of the projects of which I am aware, we made a definite
attempt to include blacks, even though schools in Georgia were still segregated" (p. 60). *Race, Caste and Prejudice* was a high school unit designed by
the Anthropology Curriculum Project to combat prejudice. Other units
included *Education for American Indians* and *Cultural Continuity and Change
in Mexico and the United States*. Two geography units were *Black Population*

Distribution and Growth in the U.S. and *Population Growth in the U.S. and Mexico*.

A grant proposal to the United States Office of Education for a curriculum project called "The American Ethnic Minority Series" in 1969 was not funded although the impetus for the prospectus was highly viable in view of the era's social and cultural transformation. Rice, however, did secure a grant for an Indian teacher training project from the Bureau of Indian Affairs in 1970, the "Special Secondary Social Studies Training Program for Prospective Indian Teachers of Indian Students."

In an enthusiastic retrospection on the era, James Oswald (1993), a principle investigator with the American Universities Fieldstaff International/Intercultural Studies project, called the new social studies movement a 15 year curriculum revolution when scholars like Lawrence Metcalf, James Shaver, Jack Frankel, Michael Scriven, Byron Massialas, and others made education significant, exciting, interesting, and memorable. The American Universities Fieldstaff project consisted of 18 universities that funded the salaries of professors to live abroad and to report through letters and reports termed Fieldstaff Reports. From the scholarly reports that arrived in Hanover, Connecticut from around the world, project staff developed units in the form of learning packets for teachers and students that included readings, maps, simulations, and a variety of other activities. The presumably celebratory nature of these materials were more in line with Kallen's (1924/1998) theory of cultural pluralism, an ideology that validated the traditions and values of Southern and Eastern European immigrants and their descendents who were forcibly being Americanized. The philosophy of cultural pluralism formed the foundation of the intercultural education movement and the multiethnic materials developed by early reformers like Ruth Davis DuBois, founder of the Service Bureau for Intercultural Education whose "separate group approach" to ethnic studies drew intense criticism in the 1930s and 1940s (Clark, 2004; Lal, 2004; Montalto, 1982). Oswald acknowledged that the global materials were apolitical to a fault. Of course, multiculturalism targeted the politics of exclusion.

As federal funding of projects was halted for the new social studies and re-channeled to ethnic studies with shifting national policies, Oswald (1993) astutely observed: "Although I supported funding of ethnic studies, governmental insecurity seemed transparent when we saw the figures—no project received more than a few thousand dollars. That seemed disrespectful. The revolution was over" (p. 18). Still, Oswald considers the global studies project to have been a "warm-up act before a much needed multi-ethnic revolution" (p. 19).

Moving on to a position as assistant superintendent for curriculum and instruction in 1978, Oswald plunged into what he perceived to be

America's major problem—urban social conflict. Working against provincialism and racism, he coordinated a citizen-education project aimed at achieving collaboration between African and Hispanic Americans. He described the following activity:

> We introduced student government leadership teams: black, Latino, and white co-presidents, co-vice presidents, secretaries, and treasurers. I had seen this succeed in Singapore in 1967.... We demonstrated how people can get along together. I leaped forward to where these students were headed—the new undergraduate institution, a two-year college. (p. 18)

In 1980, Oswald assumed a position as an instructional development specialist in a community college where he advanced his commitment to multiculturalism.

The new social studies movement provided the basic structure for Ted Fenton's Carnegie Mellon Slow Learner Project initiated in 1967 without federal funding. Anthony N. Penna (1995), a demonstration teacher with the Slow Learner Project, described developments leading to four, year-long courses for grades eight through eleven. The eighth-grade course, *The Americans: A History of the United States*, and the ninth-grade course, *Living in Urban America*, were published by Holt, Rinehart and Winston. The project represented a shift from the elitist focus on innovative curriculum for the "best and brightest" to students of the general classroom. Penna noted:

> Project Social Studies had extended the elite notions of excellence to the social studies curriculum. The slow-learner project became an advocate for equity, addressing the educational needs of the children of the "other" Americans—those millions of citizens who were victims of American apartheid and denied access to equal housing, employment, education, and health care (Harrington, 1962). Although it was never stated explicitly, the project fit within the context of the massive national effort during the mid-1960s to alleviate the burdens of race, class, and gender in America.... By providing an innovative curriculum to the children of the underclass, we hoped to equip them with the knowledge and skills that would create economic opportunity and a "better" life. In historical context, the slow-learner project expressed the liberal idealism of the Great Society of Lyndon B. Johnson. (p. 157)

Penna (1995) conveyed a sense of the poverty that engulfed student participants. He revealed how arbitrarily a learning deficit label could be superimposed on conditions like malnourishment, poor health care, and sleep deprivation. Student participants were drawn from single-parent households or homes with unemployed adult males. Penna admitted, "How we came to believe that meeting with these adolescents one hour each day, five days a week, could influence their lives in any substantial way remains a mystery to me" (p. 158).

Penna (1995) elaborated on another common mistake of the era—the neglect to investigate the successes and failures of earlier social studies reforms. As Rossi (1992) also pointed out, the history of social studies reform reveals the institutional and cultural obstacles that resist reform efforts in order to preserve the status quo. In the attempt to make the Slow Learner Project history curriculum relevant to the current events, project writers were shortsighted by failing to consider the political culture of the communities in which *The Americans* would be used. Failure to comprehend how those schools were reflections of a community rather than change agents advocating curriculum reform further weakened project goals. For example, material relating Vietnam War protests to those of the American Revolution era or drawing comparisons to draft evasion and desertion during the Civil War was deemed unpatriotic by detractors. Penna described other criticism the project encountered. The city of Boston rejected *The Americans* (Knowslar, 1970) because of an excerpt from Kozol's (1967) *Death at an Early Age* that described the deplorable conditions for pupils and teachers in a Boston school. *Living in Urban America* (Penna, 1973) likewise drew criticism that caught the authors by surprise. As FitzGerald pointed out in 1979, "The principle that lies behind textbook history is that the inclusion of nasty information constitutes bias even if the information is true" (p. 96).

As to the egregious use of the term "slow learner," Penna (1995) recounted the following:

> We had accepted the structure of the school as a given. We had no vision of an alternative to the modern, consolidated, bureaucratically organized school in which students are sorted and classified in the most pernicious categories. "Slow learner" is one of the most pejorative of these classification schemes. If we ignored past efforts to reform the social studies, then we were equally uninformed by social theory and social science. The eminent social scientist Talcott Parsons had discovered in the 1950s that once students were classified into academic categories in the elementary school years, they remained there throughout their entire schooling (Parsons, 1956). We were working within the confines of a closed system; there was no way out for our students. They undoubtedly knew it; they lived it from one school to the next. Why were we so oblivious to this widely cited study and the culture of the school that perpetuated this caste system? (p. 159)

Controversy similarly surrounded the curriculum materials developed by the Elementary School Economics Project at the University of Chicago, under the direction of William Rader (1995) from 1964 to 1973. In this case, the project had produced six innovative units under the overarching title of *Progress and People* that met with criticism from the publisher. One reason was the cost of reproducing the units, but mainly the units were non-traditional. The topics included the following: the development of culture, the Iroquois Indians including contemporary society, the Massachusetts Bay Colony, slavery, the Pullman strike, and families and firms. Only the unit about the Massachusetts Bay Colony was found acceptable for publication. Of course, elsewhere in the country John Hope Franklin's junior high school history textbook was drawing equally intense criticism, and the 1975 MACOS controversy loomed ahead (Wiley, 1976; Zimmerman, 2002).

Today the new social studies movement comprises an important chapter in the history of social studies reform. For one the reflections on the movement from the above cited scholars have significant implications for the national standards debate. As Richard Brown (1996) of the highly successful Amherst History Project has asserted about the *National Standards for United States History: Exploring the American Experience*:

> despite its rhetorical bows to inquiry, the *National Standards* are predicated on the idea that history is a body of knowledge. The method of studying it is to start with the facts, which are euphemistically called "understandings." To these, the student applies critical skills that will result in measurable "student achievements." The structure of the discipline, if it has one, is the old chronological narrative.
>
> The more things change, the more they remain the same. In essence, the *National Standards* approach is that of the old textbook, elaborately glossed. (p. 273)

Zimmerman's (2002) *Whose America* confirms Brown's contention in relation to the Black experience. He notes that

> Just as Black History Month was added to the school calendar, black history was tacked on to American textbooks. Presented in this detached and disjointed manner, it allowed citizens of every color to avoid the crucial question: What does the black experience tell us about America? (p. 129)

EVALUATIONS OF THE NEW SOCIAL STUDIES

In this section I focus on two very different evaluation reports from the 1970s to show how information about the new social studies project materials was disseminated to potential consumers in the schools. The annotated bibliography produced by Wiley and Superka (1977) was designed to give curriculum decision makers easier access to evaluative studies relevant to the sets of materials that they compared for possible adoption. This practical publication from the Social Science Education Consortium could save educators enormous amounts of time by providing access to published and unpublished literature on materials evaluations that could be identified for 68 sets of social studies materials. The authors relied upon 192 reports of findings from actual use of materials in teacher training and classroom situations. This was the kind of information most difficult for decision makers to locate. The three data bases searched for this study included the ERIC Collection, *Dissertation Abstracts International*, and the curriculum materials collection of the Social Science Education Consortium's Resource and Demonstration Center.

I approached the Wiley and Superka (1977) evaluation report from the hypothetical perspective of a Mexican American teacher from the Southwest in search of bilingual/bicultural or multicultural social studies materials. The following sociopolitical context serves as background to this fictitious situation. First, a revival of Mexican American consciousness was in full swing by the sixties. In the wake of World War II, the Mexican Americans of the Southwest had begun to develop a new political awareness and self-consciousness. This tendency intensified in the 50s when the minority leadership composed of the "Uncle Tom" and "Tío Tomás" variety was being contested (McWilliams, 1968; Tyack, 2003). A new generation of Chicano activists formed organizations such as Berkeley's Quinto Sol, publisher of *El Grito: A Journal of Contemporary Mexican-American Thought* in 1967. Various student organizations such as the Mexican American Youth Organization were forming throughout colleges and universities of the Southwest while militant barrio youth organized into chapters of the Brown Berets to defend community rights. In 1965, Cesar Chavez led a grape-picker strike, followed by more farm worker strikes in Texas. Luis Valdez's *Teatro Campesino* also helped to spread the new Chicano ideology. High-school students from East Los Angels walked-out of schools in 1968, demanding courses in Mexican American and Mexican history, an end to the use of corporal punishment for speaking Spanish, and the hiring of Mexican-American teachers and counselors. That same year the Bilingual Education Act was passed to address problems of underachievement and structural exclusion. In Texas, attention focused on the school boycott by parents and students of Crystal City, the base of operation for José Ángel Gutiérrez and fellow Chicano students of the Mexican American Youth Organization who later formed the La Raza Unida party, a critical vehicle for achieving political self-determination (Acuña, 1972; National Latino Communications Center, 1996; San Miguel, 2004).

In view of this background the Wilely and Superka (1977) catalog was examined for potentially relevant materials to better inform the social studies instruction of Mexican American students in our hypothetical case. The subject index of 68 sets of materials were categorized according to the following 20 different subject areas:

Affective Education (13 sets)
American Government/Civics (5 sets)
American History (8 sets)
Anthropology (5 sets)
Career Education (4 sets)
Contemporary Problems (9 sets)
Economics (6 sets)
Environmental Education (7 sets)
Ethnic Studies (1 set)
Geography (2 sets)
Humanities (2 sets)
Legal Education (5 sets)
Political Science (11 sets)
Psychology (3 sets)
Religion (1 set)
Social Psychology (1 set)
Sociology (4 sets)
Social Studies-General (17 sets)
Urban Studies (2 sets)
Values Education (11 sets)

Each set of materials was listed by title, publisher, publication date, grade level and related subject area. An index of authors of the curriculum materials, a grade level index, a project index, and a publisher index assisted the decision maker in identifying potential resources. In examining each evaluation entry, the following titles might have piqued the interest of our fictitious Mexican-American teacher: *American Political Behavior*; *Analysis of Public Issues Program*; *Cultural Change in Mexico and the United States*; *Race, Caste, and Prejudice*; *Black in White America*; *Conflict, Politics, and Freedom*; *Population Growth in the United States and Mexico*; *Public Issues Series*; and *Voices for Justice*. Only two units related directly to Mexican culture and geography, but none touched, even remotely, upon the Chicano experience. Even the most resourceful and knowledgeable teacher would have been hard-pressed to adapt and integrate any of the above mentioned units to specific social studies classes of Mexican-American students.

Minority and race issues are largely defined in Black/White terms, and, of course, African Americans did constitute the largest minority group during the era of the new social studies. Ronald Takaki (1993), a leading scholar of multicultural studies, notes how African Americans have been the central minority throughout the country's history. Indeed, the African American was at the cutting edge of the Civil Rights Movement. Today he suggests that the study of ethnic groups in isolation from the other groups and the whole be replaced with a fresh comparative, multicultural perspective. *A Different Mirror: A History of Multicultural America* is a rich compendium of shared experiences among America's different racial and ethnic groups. However, Takaki's challenge to Americans of diverse races and ethnicities to connect themselves to a larger historical narrative remains as elusive today as multiculturalism was to the new social studies curricula.

The single unit appearing under the category of ethnic studies was *Black in White America: Historical Perspectives and Contemporary Cases*, developed by Janet Hanley and Arlene Walter of the Education Development Center and published by Macmillan in 1974 for Grades 7–8. The unit's description follows:

> One of the main purposes of this study was to assess the effectiveness of Black in White America in achieving its stated goals. Using objective tests, classroom environment checklists, and open-ended interviews, the study focuses on the following cognitive and social variables: learning a conceptual structure to help understand and analyze racial relationships; learning "additional information about past relations and confrontations between blacks and whites;" legitimizing racial relations as a topic for honest, rational explorations; and directing "student attention to the racial climate and facts of life of their own community." The study also assessed student attitudes toward the program. Seven high school classes involving 125 students from the greater Boston area participated in the study during the fall and winter of 1969–70. (p. 22)

Zimmerman (2002) describes the sociopolitical reality of many African American school communities at the time of the new social studies revolution. There were instances the protests by Black high school militants against integrated history textbooks in dozens of school districts from cities like Philadelphia, Detroit, Milwaukee and even Evanston, Illinois. These protests erupted just as Whites were beginning to worry that new texts overemphasized the Black experience while Blacks argued that the textbooks underestimated their history. Students complained that teachers taught Black history from a White perspective. That is, the struggles and achievements of the African American were used to illustrate American justice, obscuring the very oppression and inequality that enveloped their lives. Zimmerman contends that Blacks were dramatically successful for a short period of time:

> In less than five years, black students effected one the most remarkable transformations of the public school curriculum in the twentieth century. By 1970 Los Angeles offered four separate electives in black history, black literature, African studies, and Swahili; a single high school in Berkeley created eight different "black-oriented" courses, including African dance, economics of African-Americans, and history of jazz. In theory, such courses were open to students of every race. In practice, though, white students avoided them. (p. 123)

In the final analysis the movement for separate Black history courses was short lived, primarily due to the lack of qualified teachers and adequate materials. Nevertheless, states started to require the study of American minorities—Hispanics, Asians, African Americans, and Native Americans—and textbook publishers expanded coverage of minorities with more accurate information. Still, Zimmerman laments that texts remain unchanged, retaining the "positive image" approach whereby minorities contribute their own favorable images to the grand narrative.

Finally, in 1970, Krug, Poster, and Gillies offered the profession a critical analysis of new social studies projects. Their evaluation criteria included the need for materials to reflect social reality and society's pluralistic value structure.

Krug, Poster, and Gillies Evaluation Study

The New Social Studies: Analysis and Theory of Materials (1970) by Krug, Poster, and Gillies provided curriculum decision makers with an evaluation study based on a theoretical framework that arguably was the closest to reflecting the multicultural ethos of the 70s. The authors set out to determine to what extent the curriculum materials met the objectives set for them by their creators and how valuable these were for classroom instruction. Their purpose was to provide the consumer a basis for selection of curriculum from already developed materials, but it was necessary, they argued, for developers

> to appreciate the pluralistic value structure of American society.... Put in more simple terms, the new social studies ought to exhibit faith in the basic worth of the individual and a desire to comprehend the contemporary human condition and an intent to improve it. (p. 16)

Krug, Poster, and Gillies (1970) accentuated the relevance of social problems to the new social studies. They stated:

> The practitioners of history and of the social sciences arebeginning to appreciate the importance of the moral relevanceof their scholarship to a society direly in need of intellectual and ethical guidance. This point has great bearingon the work of the social studies teacher who is called upon to deal with ever larger numbers of "controversial issues." (p. 38)

Krug, Poster, and Gillies illustrated how one vocal group of sociologists had challenged traditional Weberian sociology structure. These sociologists claimed that conflict and disequilibrium "are as important in the story of human society as order and equilibrium" (p. 22). Therefore, they advocated social analysis of contemporary social problems. Krug, Poster, and Gillies presumed that this new trend in sociology, as well as more fruitful collaboration between historians and social scientists, would have important implications for high school social studies. They presumed added depth for the social studies, but more importantly they presumed that most social studies teachers were willing to tackle controversial issues in the classroom.

Krug, Posters, and Gillies (1970) divided the projects they analyzed into two categories—disciplinary and integrative. The Anthropology Curriculum Study Project, funded by the National Science Foundation and sponsored by the American Anthropological Association, was judged to have made a valuable contribution to the new social studies. *The Study of Man*, developed in 1965 was a 9th/10th 8-week unit about race. *Patterns in Human History*, developed in 1969, was a semester course that addressed problems of ethnocentrism and examined culture change from various perspectives, including a study of the Bushmen of the Kalahari Desert in Africa and Hasanabad, a peasant village in Iran and case studies centered on the Iroquois and Kiowa (*History as Culture Change* was a 3-week sampler of the *Patterns* course). Although criticism was aimed at some overly-confident claims about the project's ability to make the social studies come alive for students, in the final analysis the materials earned high praise for effective use of nonverbal stimuli with students of different ability levels and for being very adaptable. Also, the project had shown "a commendable tendency to trust the teacher and to believe in fact that its materials are often handled best by good teachers with little formal training in the discipline of anthropology" (p. 78).

The Association of American Geographers and the National Council for Geographic Education, concerned over the state of geographic instruction in high school, created the High School Geography Project in 1961. Materials developed by project staff included six units with the following themes—Geography and Cities, Manufacturing and Agriculture, Cultural Geography, Political Geography, Habitat and Resources, and Japan. One conclusion about the effectiveness of materials was that beyond the first two units the course is appropriate only for able students. Although geographic educators resent having their discipline relegated to slow learners, the HSGP's lucidity in terms of geographic structure and facility in terms of verbal and visual instructional techniques fairly begs to be utilized in the creation of a course for lower ability students. The HSGP has accepted school systems asthey are. (p. 110)

The National Science Foundation funded project of the American Sociological Association produced a wide range of cross-cultural supplementary units and a series of paperback books also designed to be incorporated into existing course formats. The paperbacks consisted of sociological articles rewritten into layman's language. The first paperback on *Cities and City Life*, for example, included the following range of articles: The Urbanization of Mankind; Segregation: Where Whites and Negroes Live; Crime in the City, Town and the Country; The Negro Family Moves to the City; The Slum: Who has to Live There and Who Chooses to Live There; and Rebuilding the City. Some of the supplementary units focused on stereotypes, social mobility, the family, the sociology of religion, and leadership in American Society, including a study of careers ranging from that of Booker T. Washington to Stokely Carmichael. Of this noteworthy project, the evaluators concluded that

If the secondary schools are to make the most of this opportunity to understand society better, it is essential that they perceive sociology in a way that is relevant to today's complicated world and not a hackneyed rehash of topics like marriage and the family. (Krug, Posters, & Gillies, 1970, p. 132)

The section on the new social studies and history is the most illuminating, revealing the wide breach between multiculturalism and the new social studies. About the challenge that teaching Black history posed to teachers to students, Krug, Poster, and Gillies (1970) argued that contemporary race problems could not be understood without reasonable historical background:

A reading of U.S. history textbooks discloses that a vast majority still contain no reference to over 5,000 soldiers who fought valiantly in the Revolutionary Army. Most still do not contain an outright condemnation of slavery as degrading to human beings and contradictory to the very ideals on which America was founded. The textbooks still speak with disdain, if not outright condemnation of the abolitionists, and most leave out any mention of the black abolitionist movement. The magnificent record of the 180,000 Negro soldiers in the Union Army, who according to Lincoln's testimony, helped mightily in the victory over the South, is still the best kept secret in the textbooks. (p. 172)

Distortions and a lack of honesty in U.S. history material, the evaluators pronounced, made it difficult to instill in students an understanding and respect for the subject.

Another article was an adapted speech by Edwin Fenton given at the annual meeting of the New York State Council for the Social Studies in 1968, in which he discussed some of his more illuminating insights since his 1967 edict *The New Social Studies*. His greatest concern was for the neglect by the new social studies movement of the "slow learning child." Project directors, he acknowledged, had simply followed the lead of the scientists and mathematicians, in part due to a lack of classroom experience as well as a stubborn isolation from teacher involvement and the discipline of education. By this time, Fenton's (1967) experience with the Carnegie-Mellon project had convinced him of the need for teachers to emphasize four sets of objectives, in addition to knowledge and to inquiry skills with "slow learners."

> First, they should help these students to develop good self concepts in order to convince them that they aren't hopelessly dumb, that they can graduate from high school, that they can get a job, and that they do belong—to a community, to a nation, to mankind. Second, they should help students to develop better attitudes to learning.... Third, they should help students to clarify their opinions about the nature of a good man, a good life, and a good society.... Finally, teachers of slow learners should emphasize learning skills. (pp. 177–178)

Fenton urged educators to allow student characteristics to determine objectives, material, and teaching strategies, and he called for inquiry techniques that could lead students to investigate solutions to contemporary problems. Fenton concluded:

> Children may well learn more about making a decent society by watching what their teachers do than by listening to what they say. At this moment we must speak most clearly about two issues. The first, justice to America's minorities in a land where many of the children we teach laugh in derision at texts which ignore or falsify the bitter facts of their own lives. The second, the tragedy of Vietnam where it costs us, I've heard, a half million dollars to kill a Vietcong while children in urban and rural slums alike starve spiritually, physically, and mentally for lack of the schools, the houses, the jobs for their father, and the rodent control this money could buy. So let's make sure that everyone hears this message, loud and clear. (p. 182)

Krug, Poster, and Gillies (1970) evaluated the Carnegie-Mellon University social studies materials as previously discussed in this essay (Penna, 1995). Last there came a powerful admonishment to the profession about the teaching of "Negro History." Krug, Posters, and Gillies explored the reasons behind the phenomenon of Afro-American history courses—the battle cry of militant students across the country. The reasons for the phenomenon had to do with the expected effects of the study of Black history. Three reasons were:

1. To acquaint the students with the contributions of Blacks in America.
2. To give the Black students a feeling of group identity and group pride.
3. To correct the distortions contained in the U.S. history textbooks and history syllabi used in schools.

The following statement by Krug, Poster, and Gillies goes to the core of multiculturalism:

> High school students ought to learn about the connection between the passage of the Jim Crow legislation in the South and the period of American expansion and imperialism, and history textbooks and syllabi must give an adequate account of the Negro civil rights movement and do justice to such men as Frederick Douglass, Booker T. Washington, W. E. B. Du Bois, and Dr. Martin Luther King. The point must be made that the incessant demands by Negroes for equal rights have contributed to what-ever progress in the area of civil rights has been achieved. (p. 208)

Furthermore, they declared that either in addition to the courses on Black history, or in lieu of them, a thorough revision and updating of textbooks and materials was imperative.

Finally, the featured model of integrated social studies was the Jurisprudential approach developed by Oliver, Shaver, and Newman, also known as the analysis of public issues approach that offered an alternative to traditional history-oriented social studies instruction. Krug, Poster, and Gillies (1970) endorsed the units on the American Revolution, religious freedom, the railroad era, municipal politics, organized labor, the immigrant experience and many of the other unit books not mentioned in the essay. They recommended that the supplementary material be used as widely as possible.

The unit on "Negro Views of America," however, revealed just how unprepared the profession and students were to undertake a study of race issues. Any kind of meaningful inquiry into racial problems, the reviewers contended,

> must be preceded by a systematic study of the history of Negroes in the United States and the sequence of developments in the relationships between the white majority and the black minority. The preferred method of

sociological research in plucking out events, facts, and ideas from the past, without regard to their chronology and interrelationship, is not conducive it seems to me to an effective study of the contemporary race problem. (p. 237)

The case study, for instance, proposed two "objective" positions on slavery, one cruel and evil weighted against a favorable evaluation of the institution. Krug, Poster, and Gillies (1970) contended:

It would seem little to expect that scholars and educators would adopt a stance that slavery, whether cruel or benevolent, was an evil institution, depriving human beings of their dignity as persons and utterly in violation of the ideals on which this Republic was founded. (p. 237)

Another criticism of the conceptually flawed "Negro Views of America" unit involved the topic of racial differences. The genetic theory was accorded as much prominence as two other proposed positions on differences. The criticism of the unit was primarily to illustrate how study of some public issues by their very nature required "a thorough, systematic, and yes, chronological historical background and explication" (p. 239). *The New Social Studies: Analysis of Theory and Materials* is indeed a social studies classic worth re-reading today.

John Haas (1977) argued in his review the new social studies era that

The NSS began to decline as a movement during 1968, especially in the face of dire social upheaval. As it was aided by Lyndon Johnson's "Great Society" programs, so it was slowed by Nixon's new federalism and de-emphasis of social and educational reforms. The NSS quite accurately never expired, however, but gradually faded and blended into other emerging interests and patterns. (p. 78)

Interestingly, Cremin (1961) maintained that the most important reason for the collapse of Progressive Education was its failure to keep up with the continuing transformation of society, the same charge leveled against the new social studies movement that bears repeating again as we continue to debate national content standards that tell students what to think.

CONCLUSION

Multiculturalism displaced the theory of "cultural pluralism" because of the philosophy's failure to deal with society's pluralistic reality. Just as Oscar Handlin's (1951) classic study, *The Uprooted: The Epic Story of the Great Migrations That Made the American People*, excluded Blacks, Asians, and Latin, so, too, did Kallen's (1924/1998) theory exclude non-Whites.

Cultural pluralism attacked assimilation to protect the rights of White hyphenated-Americans but ignored inequality in connection to people of color. As Tyack (2003) observes,

> If *assimilation* was the keynote of policy for immigrants, *discrimination* was a basic theme of the education of people of color. Black, Japanese, and Chinese people were categorized as members of unassimilable and inferior "races." Until the *Brown* school desegregation decision in 1954, relatively few educators followed the lead of reformers like Horace Mann Bond, W. E. B. Du Bois, or Rachel DuBois, who demanded a frontal assault on racism in school and society. The story was different with European immigrants. (pp. 82–83)

Cultural Pluralism

In 1924 the philosopher Horace Kallen coined the term cultural pluralism to refute the prevailing theories of assimilation and Americanization. Today, it strains the imagination to think of the apprehension that diversity struck in the hearts of the native born; however, the fear of fission over mass immigration gave rise to nativism, the Ku Klux Klan, immigration restrictions, the exclusion of Chinese, and a call to schools to Americanize/homogenize the "problem" immigrants. The emphasis of cultural pluralism was not on the preservation of ethnic groups but on the right of individuals to decide to what extent they desired to remain members of their ethnic group and to participate in its cultural traditions or else not to participate. The extremely controversial ideology was to free individuals from social impositions based on ethnic heritage. Democracy implied freedom of association. An individual could not be discriminated against on the basis of his ethnic heritage, just as no ethnic heritage could be imposed upon any member of a group. Assimilation was coercion to conform to one pattern of Americanism. The dilemma of *e pluribus unum*—how to reconcile ethnicity with democracy in order to achieve unity through multiplicity—is what Kallen (1924/1998) theorized in his essay "Culture and the Klan." The "one and many" could co-exist, just as a symphony comprised of individual instruments plays in harmonious unison—Kallen's favorite metaphor for diversity. Kallen urged the following with respect to the hyphenated-American:

> The point is to see to it that the hyphen connects instead of separates. And this means at least that our public schools shall teach each factor to respect every other, and shall take pains to enlighten all as to the great past contributions of every strain in our composite make-up…. I wish our teaching of American history in the schools would take more account of the great waves of migration by which our land for over three centuries has been continuously

built up, and make every pupil conscious of the rich breadth of our national make-up. When every pupil recognizes all the factors which have gone into our being, he will continue to prize and reverence that coming from his own past, but he will think of it as honored in being simply one factor in forming a whole nobler and finer than itself. In short, unless our education is nationalized in a way which recognizes that the peculiarity of our nationalism is its internationalism we shall breed enmity and division in our frantic efforts to secure unity. (p. 124)

Multicultural Education

Kallen (1924/1998) sought to overthrow amalgamation and the melting pot theory in defense of a multi-ethnic society. In the seventies multiculturalism displaced cultural pluralism as bigotry and racist practices overshadowed urban inner-city schools. Professional educational associations began committing to social justice and educational equity. In 1973, the American Association of Colleges for Teacher Education advanced a seminal position statement, *No One Model American*, building upon a broad conception of cultural pluralism and establishing the concept of multicultural education that would later get integrated into the national accreditation process for colleges of teacher education.

More recently there came the formation of the National Association for Multicultural Education (NAME, 2003). After considering numerous definitions of multicultural education espoused by scholars, researchers and organization over a 30 year period, NAME generated its own meaning of the concept in 2003. Part of the definition reads as follows:

Multicultural education is a philosophical concept built on the ideals of freedom, justice, equality, equity, and human dignity as acknowledged in various documents, such as the U.S. Declaration of Independence, Constitutions of South Africa and the United States, and Universal Declaration of Human Rights adopted by the United Nations. It affirms our need to prepare students for their responsibilities in a interdependent world. It recognizes the role schools can play in developing the attitudes and values necessary for a democratic society. It values cultural differences and affirms the pluralism that students, their communities, and teachers reflect. It challenges all forms of discrimination in schools and society through the promotion of democratic principles of social justice.

Multicultural education is a process that permeates all aspects of school practices, policies and organizations as a means to ensure the highest levels of academic achievement for all students. It helps students develop a positive self-concept by providing knowledge about the histories, cultures, and contributions of diverse groups. It prepares all students to work actively toward structural equality in organizations and institutions by providing the knowledge, dispositions, and skills for the redistribution of power and income among diverse groups. Thus, school curriculum must directly address issues of racism, sexism, classism, linguicism, ablism, ageism, heterosexism, religious intolerance, and xenophobia. (http://www.nameorg.org/resolutions/definition.html)

This inclusive conception of equity theoretically guides educational practice today, including the social studies instruction across all instructional levels.

Multicultural Social Studies

Assimilation was the prevailing ideology guiding school instruction in the fifties when a national emergency furnished the impetus for curriculum reform. Notwithstanding the monumental desegregation ruling in *Brown v. Board of Education* (1954) and other social issues already in the making, educational priority was given to discipline-oriented projects whose conceptualization emphasized academic excellence. Tyack (2003) notes that only a small minority of Whites openly confronted racism from 1890–1954. However, that approach sought to achieve greater understanding between Blacks and Whites through prejudice reduction approaches. Later, the alternative would become to mount legal attacks against institutional racism. Thus, without adequate historical knowledge and an understanding of people of color, the social studies profession was woefully unprepared to switch from an Anglo-centric curriculum and to a multicultural ethos. For instance, not until 1973 would the National Council for the Social Studies (NCSS) publish James Banks' *Teaching Ethnic Studies*. In the yearbook's forward, NCSS president Harris Dante, observed:

> Textbooks and school curricula too often have sustained the status quo, helped entrench the stereotypes, and narrated the myth and the folklore. In some instances gestures were made to indicate that various individuals had contributed to American culture but, in general, Mark Twain's "great lie of silence" prevailed. (pp. vii–viii)

The scholars contributing to this yearbook offered a wealth of information, including analyses of racism and social justice, problems of ethnic minority groups, ways of incorporating the experiences of people of color into the social studies curriculum, and problems faced by women and White ethnic groups. Three years later the NCSS published *Curriculum Guidelines for Multiethnic Education* (Banks, Cortés, Gay, Garcia, & Ochoa, 1976) and in 1980 published *Racism and Sexism, Responding to the Challenge* (Simms &

Contreras, 1980). These and many other *Social Education* publications attacked social injustice, inequality, bigotry, and racism in contrast to merely advancing a cultural awareness approach.

Today multicultural social studies—the integration of multicultural education into the social studies—remains problematic on a practical level. Boyle-Baise (1996) shows how "The integration of discipline-based courses, such as the social studies—is truly difficult to accomplish. It assumes a working knowledge of multicultural education and a second subject" (p. 81). Multicultural education courses in most teacher education programs are taught as separate semester-long classes with research suggesting that pre-service teachers lack an understanding of how sociopolitical forces affect the achievement of minority students (Adams, Bell, & Griffin, 1997; Lawrence, 1997; Weisman & Garza, 2002). Kaltsounis (1997) also points out how enduring tensions between multicultural education and citizenship education are as problematic as the numerous tensions that exist within each field. Hepburn (1993) details more of the division that has conflicted multicultural education and citizenship education in the recent past—that is, multiculturalism as a mosaic of coexistence as opposed to a form of separatism.

In sum the history of social studies education reflects group differences and value conflicts that characterize our contentious American democracy. As competing groups turn to schools to preserve their own interests, the cycle of liberal reform countered by a conservative reaction is repeated. Progressive ideology that replaced formalism was in turn undercut by narrow nationalistic interests and a space race that resulted in an elitist national curriculum reform movement. Then the new social studies movement with its disciplinary structure was attacked for a lack of practical knowledge application. Regardless of shifting ideology, the one constant in this course of events has been the "grand master narrative" about American righteousness. Zimmerman (2002) eloquently puts forth this case in his analysis of ethnicity and the history wars that have played out in the school house:

> Ethnic groups did manage to insert new heroes like Crispus Attucks and Thaddeus Kosciusko, adding a few fresh hues to the monochromatic national story. At the same time, though, they reinforced its bland, triumphal message of English tyranny and American righteousness. The result was a history of many colors but one idea, culturally diverse yet intellectually static. (pp. 14–15)

Today's Teaching American History Grant Program from the Department of Education bears out Zimmerman's claim. Program funds are reserved for projects that raise student achievement by improving teachers' knowledge, understanding, and appreciation of traditional

American history. The Department of Education presumes that "By helping teachers to develop a deeper understanding and appreciation of traditional American history as a separate subject within the core curriculum, these programs improve instruction and raise student achievement" (Innovations and Improvements, 2005, p. 19935). Guidelines for proposing American history projects are basically a call to hero worship with an Anglo-Saxon bias. Notwithstanding all the rhetoric on multicultural education, conservative forces control the curriculum, and the goal of achieving educational access and equity for many students of color remains elusive. The profession should draw lessons from remarkable curriculum reformers like Harold Rugg, Rachael Davis DuBois, and John Hope Franklin as well as a number of other pioneers of the new social studies movement who fought the good fight to advance the ethos of multiculturalism in education.

REFERENCES

American Association of Colleges for Teacher Education. (1973). No One Model American, *Journal of Teacher Education, 24*(4), 264.

Acuña, R. (1972). *Occupied America*. San Francisco: Canfield Press.

Adams, M., Bell, L., & Griffin, P. (Eds.). (1997). *Teaching for diversity and social justice*. New York: Rutledge.

Banks, J. A. (Ed.). (1973). *Teaching ethnic studies*. Washington, DC: National Council for the Social Studies.

Banks, J. A., Cortés, C. E., Gay, G., Garcia, R. L., & Ochoa, A. (1976). *Curriculum guidelines for multiethnic education*. Washington, DC: National Council for the Social Studies.

Bestor, A. E. (1953) *The retreat from learning in our public schools*. Urbana: The University of Illinois Press.

Bestor, A. E. (1955). *The restoration of learning*. New York: Alfred A. Knopf.

Boyle-Baise, M. (1996). Multicultural social studies: Ideology and practice. *The Social Studies, 87*(2), 81–87.

Brown, R. H. (1996, November/December). Learning how to learn: The Amherst project and history education in the schools. *The Social Studies, 87*(6), 267–273.

Bruner, J. S. (1961). *The process of education*. Cambridge, MA: Harvard University Press.

Clark, M. (2004, Fall). Memories of an intercultural education 1955–1957: Multiculturalism and migration. *Nashim: A Journal of Jewish Women's Studies & Gender Issues, 8*, 129–136.

Cremin, L. A. (1961). *The transformation of the school*. New York: Knopf.

Engle, S. H. (1960) Decision-making: The heart of social studies instruction. *Social Education, 24*(7), 301–304.

Fenton, E. (1967). *The new social studies*. New York: Holt, Rinehart and Winston.

Fenton, E. (1991). Reflections on the "new social studies. *The Social Studies*, *82*(3), 84–90.

FitzGerald, F. (1979) *America revised*. New York: Vintage.

Haas, J. D. (1977). *The era of the new social studies*. Boulder, CO: ERIC Clearinghouse for Social Studies/Social Science Education and Social Science Education Consortium.

Handlin, O. (1951). *The uprooted: The epic story of the great migrations that made the American people*. Boston: Little, Brown.

Hanley, J., & Walter, A. (1974). *Black in White America: Historical perspectives and contemporary cases*. New York: Macmillan.

Harrington, M. (1962). *The other America*. New York: Macmillan.

Hepburn, M. A. (1993). Concepts of pluralism and the implications for citizenship education. *The Social Studies*, *84*(1), 20–26.

Innovations and Improvements—Teaching American History Program [Fed. Reg. 70(72), 19934-19939]. (2005, April 15). The Federal Register: Main Page. Retrieved May 1, 2005, from http://frwebgate3.access.gpo.gov/cgi-bin/waisgate.cgi?WAISdocID=0083408738+0+0+0&WAISaction=retrieve

Kallen, H. M. (1998). *Culture and democracy in the United States*. New Brunswick, NJ: Transaction. (Original work published 1924)

Keller, C. R. (1961). Needed: Revolution in the Social Studies. *Saturday Review* 44(37), 60-62.

Kaltsounis, T. C. (1997, January/February). Multicultural education and citizenship education at a crossroads: Searching for common ground. *The Social Studies 88*(1), 18–22.

Kownslar, A. O. (1970). *The Americans*. New York: American Heritage

Kozol, J. (1967). *Death at an early age*. Boston: Houghton Mifflin.

Krug, M. M., Poster, J. B., & Gillies, W. B. (1970). *The new social studies: Analysis of theory and materials*. Itasca, IL: F. E. Peacock.

Lal, S. (2004, Spring). *1930s multiculturalism: Rachael Davis DuBois and the Bureau for Intercultural Education*. Radical Teacher. Retrieved February 12, 2007, from http://findarticles.com/p/articles/mi_m0JVP/is_69/ai_n6148140

Lawrence, S. (1997). Beyond race awareness: White racial identity and multicultural teaching. *Journal of Teacher Education*, *48*(2), 108–117.

Massialas B. G. (1992, May/June). The "New Social Studies"—Retrospect and prospect. *Social Studies*, *83*(6), 120–124.

Massialas, B. G. (1963). The Indiana experiments in inquiry: Social studies. *Bulletin of the School of Education, Indiana University, 39*(3).

Massialas, B. G. & Cox, C. B. (1966). *Inquiry in social studies*. New York: McGraw-Hill.

McWilliams, C. (1968). *North from Mexico*. New York: Greenwood Press.

Montalto, N. V. (1982). *A history of the intercultural education movement, 1924-1941. Modern American history*. New York: Garland.

National Association for Multicultural Education. (2003, February 1). Definition: Multicultural education. Retrieved May 20, 2005, from http://www.nameorg.org/resolutions/definition.html

National Latino Communications Center. (1996). *Chicano! History of the Mexican American civil rights movement*. Los Angeles: Author.

National standards for U.S. history: Exploring the American experience. (n.d.). University of California, Los Angeles: National Center for History in Schools.

Oswald, J. M. (1993). Another look at the new social studies movement the social studies curriculum revolution: 1960-1975. *The Social Studies, 84*(1), 14–19.

Parsons, T., & Smelser, N. J. (1956). *Economy and society: A study in the integration of economic and social theory.* Glencoe, IL: Free Press.

Penna, A. N. (1973). *Living in urban America.* New York: Holt, Rinehart, & Winston.

Penna, A. N. (1995). The new social studies in perspective: The Carnegie Mellon slow-learner project. *The Social Studies, 86*(1), 155–161.

Pinar, W. F., Reynolds, W. M., Slattery, P., & Taubman, P. M. (2004). *Understanding curriculum: An introduction to the study of historical and contemporary curriculum discourses.* New York: Peter Lang.

Rader, W. D. (1995). The elementary school economics project at the University of Chicago. *The Social Studies, 86*(1), 85–90.

Rice, M. J. (1992). Reflections on the new social studies. *The Social Studies, 83*(5), 224–231.

Rossi, J. A. (1992). Uniformity, diversity and the "new social studies." *The Social Studies, 83*(1), 41–45.

San Miguel, G., Jr. (2004). *Contested policy: The rise and fall of federal bilingual education in the United States, 1960–2001.* University of North Texas Press, Denton.

Simms, R. L., & Contreras, G. (1980). *Racism and sexism: Responding to the challenge.* Washington, DC: National Council for the Social Studies.

Sorrells, R. T. (2001). *Marion Jennings Rice, philosophy and praxis: The professional biography of a Georgia educator.* Unpublished doctoral dissertation, University of Georgia.

Takaki, R. (1993). *A different mirror: A history of multicultural America.* Boston: Little, Brown.

Tanner, D., & Tanner, L. (1980). *Curriculum development: Theory into practice.* New York: Macmillan.

Tanner, D., & Tanner, L. (2007). *Curriculum development: Theory into practice* (4th ed.). New York: Macmillan.

Tyack, D. B. (2003). *Seeking common ground: Public schools in a diverse society.* Cambridge, MA: Harvard University Press.

Wiley, K. B. (1976). *The NSF science education controversy: Issues, events, decisions.* Boulder, CO: ERIC Clearinghouse for Social Studies/Social Science Education and Social Science Education Consortium.

Wiley, K. B., & Superka, D. P. (1977). *Evaluation studies on new social studies materials.* Boulder, CO: ERIC Clearinghouse for Social Studies/Social Science Education and Social Science Education Consortium.

Weisman, E. M., & Garza, S. A. (2002). Preservice teacher attitudes toward diversity: Can one class make a difference? *Equity and Excellence in Education, 35*(1), 28–34.

Zimmerman, J. (2002). *Whose America?: Culture wars in the public schools.* Cambridge, MA: Harvard University Press.

CHAPTER 19

LIES AND HISTORY

David Warren Saxe

FIRST WORDS

While it has been supposed that The New Social Studies died somewhere in the 1970s, its legacy is very much alive. Personally, I owe much of my professional career, including my first job, to The New Social Studies (NSS). Although schooled in traditional history and trained by traditionally minded historians in college, my education training was thoroughly immersed in NSS theory and practice. Guided by Larry Metcalf and Ben Cox, my graduate and dissertation advisors at the University of Illinois, I worked with many who modeled various elements of the NSS (Shirley Engle, Fred Newmann, James Shaver, Sam Shermis, James Barth, Peter Martorella, and many others), all stamped with direct or indirect ties to the genre's originator, Alan Griffin, in the tradition of John Dewey.

As a young man in search of his first teaching job, it was a NSS enthusiast's (Charlie Gray) suggestion that I study Ed Fenton's (1969) Carnegie works that landed me at Lincoln-Way High School in New Lenox, Illinois in 1974. With Larry Metcalf serving as the social studies consultant, Lincoln-Way was designed in the 1950s as a "new school," and sought teachers willing and able to teach progressive curricula like the NSS. Happily possessed of working knowledge of Fenton's methods, I was the winning

The New Social Studies: People, Projects, and Perspectives, pp. 407–432

candidate to teach Fenton's American history text centered on "inquiry methodologies."

While Fenton's text was designed to lead students to question everything and reserve judgment unless warranted, NSS textbooks failed to capture any segment of the market and soon disappeared even at the very progressive Lincoln-Way. By the mid-to-late 1970s, the NSS (by name) was over. However, the notion of questioning traditional content and methodologies remained particularly strong among the ranks of social studies professors.

Taking up one of the major planks of NSS ideas (exploring the underside of America and questioning America's social values) the next generation of social studies professors identified themselves with (or as) multicultural-social justice insurgents questioning the underpinnings of American society. One great consequence was the unseating of traditional history content in schools. At about the same time, in seeming opposition, America's conservative political leaders (both Democrats and Republicans) sought to return traditional basic education to America's schools via *Nation At Risk* sorts of efforts. The back to basics movement suggested that some NSS ideas might have been more successful than previously thought. Just as many social studies professionals sought to continue NSS under new banners (multiculturalism-social justice) in hopes of stemming the conservative push to recover traditional forms of history (and other social studies), the most popular history-education textbook ever written was in preparation.

First published in 1995, James Loewen's *Lies My Teacher Told Me* is not only the standard corrective on "old fashioned" traditional history, it is also one of the most popular and most discussed history-education books ever published. While not in the mold of NSS adherents, Loewen's critique of what he posited as traditional-standard American history for schools, was readily digested and embraced by the social studies profession (see Ladson-Billings, 2003; Levstik, 1996). In fact, the irony was that the NSS movement (on whose shoulders modern social studies professionals stand) was centered on the notion of questioning sacred cows of our society; the idea that citizens should challenge content, values, authoritarianism, institutions, and establishment patterns (among other things). Mixed into this questioning of society so championed by the *new* NSS professionals (and modeled by the first generation of NSS professors) were new pedagogical models (under new names) loosely drawn from the older NSS models of inquiry, reflection, and decision making. However, the only thing that Loewen's *Lies* effectively leveled were the basics of questioning, inquiry, reflection, and decision making. That is, rather *than* continuing with the best of NSS practice centered in scientific principles, arguably the most popular text in our collective professional social studies library stands NSS ideals on its head.

As much as Loewen's *Lies* remains an unreflective and unwarranted diatribe on traditional American history, American history textbooks, and American history teachers, I present this chapter not only as a much-needed serious critique of this sacred cow (since none have critically examined Loewen's *Lies*), but also to serve as a positive exemplar of the sort of work social studies professionals ought to foster, profess, and model.

Loewen's *Lies* As A Negative Example of NSS Legacy

The problem with Loewen's *Lies* is that mainstream social studies professionals accepted Loewen's conclusions without thinking, rather than thinking through how those conclusions were reached. One legacy of the NSS might have been the dismantling of traditional American history (and many argued that the focus of social studies should not be backward looking American history, but forward thinking issues-centered curricula), but Loewen's *Lies* brought the social studies profession to that conviction a lot sooner and in spite of the back-to-basis movement. Moreover, urged on by Loewen's decentering of American history, the conviction to dump (or resist) any return to traditional American history came without the necessary mental work and energy. That is, the social studies profession came to an answer (perhaps right, but maybe wrong) without doing the homework.

Proclaimed by social studies professionals as "brilliant" and "solid analysis" (Ladson-Billings, 2003; Levstik, 1996), Loewen's *Lies* attacked traditional history content as viewed through the lens of contemporary American history textbooks that Loewen claimed were both "representative" and the "most popular" found in America's public schools. However, on close examination (using the tools of NSS), this chapter makes the point that Loewen's *Lies* is neither "brilliant" nor "solid analysis" and moreover stands in opposition to the very sort of penetrating analysis that dominated NSS theory and practice.

From mainstream media outlets introducing Loewen's controversial book *Lies My Teacher Told Me* (Thomas, 1995) to respected teacher educators who made Loewen's *Lies* the number one history education textbook ever published, it seems that the entire history-social studies/teacher education industry knows and honors Loewen's *Lies*, yet no one has questioned either his methodology or conclusions. As much as history education continues to be an important educational issue, certainly we make no advancement in this contentious field without carefully scrutinizing its works, even its celebrated and honored icons. While much has been written on history education (FitzGerald, 1979; Jenness, 1990; Linenthal & Engelhardt, 1996; Moreau, 2003; Nash, Crabtree, & Dunn, 1997; Symcox, 2002; Zimmerman, 2002), this chapter tackles the scholarly aspects of Loewen's *Lies* so far ignored by historians, educators, and teachers.

Unmasking Loewen's *Lies*

One of the most popular titles in American history is not a history book at all. In fact, it was not even written by an historian. According to its author, James Loewen, a sociologist by trade, *Lies My Teacher Told Me* has sold more than 700,000 copies since its publication in 1995 (Loewen, 2005). Loewen's *Lies* can be summarized briefly as a description of what American history should be taught in schools, but unfortunately, according to Loewen, is not.

It is difficult to imagine that the best selling history education book of the past decade, that carries some of the most sweeping and damning condemnations of public school teachers, American history textbooks, publishers, and the history profession itself, has never been carefully examined. Certainly *Lies* has not escaped cursory review from those who fancy this emperor's new clothes but serious scholars have ignored Loewen's *Lies*. Obviously, to the history community, best-selling is not synonymous with scholarly, as only one professional history journal thought to review *Lies*, and that review appeared five years after publication (Zimmerman, 2000). And yet, its influence among teachers, editors, and publishers is unmistakable—not because *Lies* animated or anticipated change, but because *Lies* reflected a movement well begun. Similar to the works of Howard Zinn, Loewen is a dedicated leftist with a penchant for social justice; an activist whose political proselytizing has captured a generation of educators, stridently recasting the history of the United States from its traditional roots into a form compatible to a socialist liberal-leftist worldview.

Although it appears Loewen's real issue with textbooks and teachers is that he detests anything that conveys patriotism or smacks of nationalism (as in loyalty or reverence to the United States), according to the front-matter of his 1995 book, the pretext of Loewen's *Lies* is that history is boring because textbooks are full of lies. Supposedly, Loewen discovered this "fact" while suing the State of Mississippi for failing to adopt a state history he co-edited (Loewen & Sallis, 1980). Loewen relishes the story of *Loewen v. Turnipseed* (1980), where, with the help of NAACP lawyers, Loewen vanquishes the evil State of Mississippi for its lack of social justice wisdom.[1]

Typical of Loewen's (2005) polemical rhetoric, although he claims his suit was a "ground breaking First Amendment lawsuit" (p. 4), as case law, the legal world fixed its interest on how Courts determined litigation expenses, and specifically in Loewen's case how the Court disallowed postage and private expenses for his NAACP attorneys (see *American Home Assurance v. Phineas Corp*, 2004; *Dickinson v. Indiana State Election Board*, 1992). Nonetheless, Loewen experience was enough to push him into the realm of American history textbooks and he did not like what he saw. His response to this experience is found in *Lies*.

To make his case, Loewen's *Lies* presents an appraisal of 12 American history textbooks.[2] From the start, Loewen begins with conclusions and moves through 12 chapters of carefully presented "evidence." In the best tradition of NSS theory, Loewen's approach to dismantle traditional American history should have raised many red flags of caution and alarm. However, as presented here, the thesis, contentions/conclusions, and research methodology of Loewen's *Lies* are not only unwarranted, on the whole, the work borders on academically deception—and that is my case to prove.

Given that Loewen's *Lies* is centered on a "two-year study of American history textbooks" at the Smithsonian Institution (a point frequently mentioned in his book, publicity materials, speeches, Web site, and CD program), I begin this examination of *Lies* not with his conclusions, but the methodology centered on his 12 American history textbooks in Loewen's study as found in Table 19.1.

On the selection of his sample, at first Loewen (1995) claims the 12 were picked because they were "the most popular textbooks" available (p. 3). Then, in contradiction, Loewen tells readers that he "chose the twelve as representing the range of textbooks available for American history courses" (p. 6). For textbooks, among other things, "most popular" and "representative" sample, are not synonymous terms. Selecting the 12 "most popular" American history textbooks yields a correlation between what textbook consumers (teachers, students, school boards) hold as the best, most likeable, usable, and perhaps affordable textbooks, or more plainly, what interests buyers. In a market with millions of dollars at stake (both in textbook production and sales), textbooks that generate interest, sell. Textbooks that cannot generate interest are not published (as almost happened to Loewen's passed over textbook) or, if published, never make a second edition (the fate of Loewen's failed textbook).

"Representative" textbooks, however, are altogether another matter. Rather than examining by popularity, which may or may not reflect quality, selecting a range of textbooks, representative of what is readily available, presents a much deeper and richer conspectus of the field. A study of representative samples also provides greater opportunity to present

**Table 19.1.   Methodology Centered on
Loewen's 12 American History Textbooks**

Title	Author(s)	Publisher	Date/Edition Used By Loewen/ # Editions Issued	Total Page #
The American Adventure	Social Science Staff	Allyn and Bacon	1975/1/1 (2 volumes)	655/ 574
American Adventures	Peck, Jantzen, & Rosen	Steck-Vaughn	1987/3/4	759
American History	Garraty, Singer, & Gallagher	Harcourt Brace Jovanovich	1982/1/2	942
The American Pageant	Bailey, Kennedy	Heath	1991/9/10	1002
The American Tradition	Green, Becker, & Coviello	Merrill	1984/1/2	816
The American Way	Bauer	Holt, Rinehart, Winston	1979/1/1	726
The Challenge of Freedom	Sobel, LaRaus, De Leon, Morris	Glencoe	1990/2/2	768
Discovering American History	Kownslar, Fizzle	Holt, Rinehart, Winston	1974/3/3 (2 volumes)	424/ 424
Land of Promise	Berkin & Wood	Scott, Foresman	1983/1/3 (2 volumes)	576/ 594
Life and Liberty	Roden, Greer, Kraig, & Bivins	Scott, Foresman	1984/1/1	740
Triumph of the American Nation	Todd & Curti	Harcourt, Brace, Jovanovich	1986/9/10	1076
The United States— A History of the Republic	Davidson & Lytle	Prentice-Hall	1981/1/4	798

generalizations on the various variables studied as applicable across the field of American history.

For example, on popularity, Textbook A is detailed and scholarly, yet few districts select it. While Textbook B, despite being thin on scholarship and text, is a best seller. Perhaps Textbook B's publisher has a slicker book, a larger sales force, and a more effective sales pitch. To compete against Textbook B, Textbook A needs greater recognition—the sort that a thorough comparative study of representative textbooks would provide. For research purposes, if only what sells is examined—those textbooks that presumably cater to the curricular tastes of the widest number of schools, the research can only report the American history that sells best.

If a representative sample is examined, exploring a wide range of textbooks regardless of sales, then generalizations about the field may be made with greater inclusiveness and that information might prove extremely important to textbook consumers. A representative sample would also allow readers to discover what history textbooks are poor, good, better or best according to a set of variables such as content, coverage, story line, standards, constitutional issues, special interest concerns, among other things—substantive qualitative differences that transcend a well-packaged, "best selling," but otherwise poor textbook versus a better textbook for teachers and students waiting to be recognized.

Without an operational explanation on the selection process—since Loewen vacillates between two very different beginning points (popularity and representation), readers have difficulty correlating conclusions to applications. Readers readily recognize what Loewen considers bad about these textbooks (that they largely follow established/traditional market patterns), but we do not know if these textbooks are in fact popular, representative, or even if they are in use. All we have is Loewen's *claims* that they are popular, representative, and current, and that is not enough.

Our first task with the textbooks is to dissect Loewen's claims of popularity (best sellers), representative (sample of widest range of textbooks available), and currency (textbooks presently in use in schools).

Loewen's "Most Popular-Leading Textbook" Claim Explored

As Loewen admits what is widely known to all, as a matter of guarding trade secrets, publishers do not release textbook sales figures. Therefore, without sales figures for all or any textbook, the best barometer (and easiest to report) to judge the popularity of textbooks are the number of editions issued. Another index would be the number of schools (or states) reporting adoptions (this number is also available as public information). Surveying teachers or school districts would also provide textbook adoption information, particularly in those states that do not have statewide adoptions. Throughout the history of the field, researchers have applied these techniques (Davis, 1986; Fordham Foundation, 2004; Hefley, 1979; Pierce, 1926, Ravitch, 2004b; Tryon, 1935). In support of his popularity claim, however, Loewen provides no hard or accurate data on the number of editions issued, public adoptions, or survey information.

More problematically, Loewen's selections argue against his own assertion of popularity. Using Table 19.1, we discover that 2 of Loewen's textbooks were at least 20 years old at the time of the publication of *Lies* (Loewen, 1995). Even if we push Loewen's "publication date" back to 1994 (the latest date found in the text or references of Loewen's *Lies*), arguably, 19 and 20 year old textbooks, long out of print, cannot be considered popular or current. It is also telling that 7 textbooks were first editions (2 of which never survived to a second edition). In fact, except for the 3 first editions used by Loewen, only 2 of these were the latest editions (1 that went immediately out of print and the other 10 years old in 1994). Moreover, only two of Loewen's 12 textbooks were the latest version available of that title, one 20 years old, and the other 4. This indicates that Loewen did not bother to secure the latest edition of the textbooks in question

Amid the recognition that textbook "sales figures are trade secrets," Loewen (1995), without citation, claims, "publishers admit that" one of his 12 textbooks owns "approximately a quarter of the market" (pp. 274, 314). Also buried in the footnotes of Loewen's *Lies* is the astonishing claim that sales of 7 of his 12 textbooks comprise another 35% of the textbook market, suggesting that 7 of his 12 textbooks captured 60% of the American history textbook market at some undisclosed date.

Discounting "two inquiry textbooks [that] have gone out of print, presumably due to low sales," on "most popular" grounds, as Loewen (1995) says (1995, pp. 314, 362), Loewen's rhetoric argues a case that his textbooks are the "most popular" and/or "leading" American history textbooks. However, using 1994 as a benchmark—that is the last year in which Loewen includes materials in his book, all but 2 of the 12 textbooks had gone out of print by 1994. Therefore, had Loewen examined the publishing history of the textbooks in question, he would have discovered that by 1994 10 of the 12 textbooks in his sample could not have been considered "most popular" or "leading" textbooks in American history by any stretch of the imagination. Naturally, actual publication figures would resolve this matter, but Loewen supplies none. Ultimately, Loewen produces no evidence that seven of his 12 textbooks comprise 60% of the American history textbook market at any particular date. Without a firm copyright date-range for his study, not only are Loewen's conclusions ambiguously soft, we have nothing to benchmark his work to comparative studies.

It is also important to note that copyright/publication dates on school textbooks are more sales pitch than the actual, authentic dates of publication. That is, trade books and fiction might be published anytime during a calendar year, often reflecting the actual date of publication. However, textbooks are typically issued with copyrights that fudge reality. A textbook actually published in 2009, might carry a copyright of 2010 or even 2011. After all who wants a 2009 book in 2009, when a 2010 book is available? It is a psychological deception; later dates, convey the message of an up-to-date textbook.

For example, in one of the dozens of textbooks *not* examined by Loewen, *One Flag, One Land*, published by Silver Burdett & Ginn, supplies a

1990 copyright. On close examination, the latest date found in the text is 1989, a reference to the George Bush becoming the 41st President of the United States. Yet, that date has been fudged, as the latest verified/absolute date, corresponding to an actual event, is the reference that, "On election day 1988, George Bush was elected President"—a date nearly 14 months in advance of 1990 (Brown & Base, 1990, p. 504). If an industry-wide marketing tool, Loewen's latest textbook [1991] was probably completed and published in 1990—meaning that by 1995 *all* of the textbooks in Loewen's so-called contemporary study were dated.

In sum, as far as "most popular" or "leading" textbooks, to be charitable, that may be Loewen's *opinion* based on hearsay evidence, invention, imagination, conjecture, or whatever. However, as identified by inspecting copyright dates, drawn from the number of editions produced and from marking the last edition published, the publication records of the 12 textbooks do not support Loewen's claims. Since publishers do not share sales figures, we can safely assume that popularity (as in financially successful) is correlated to the number of editions published. That is, a textbook issued 10 times may be considered more popular than a textbook published once and subsequently put out of print. For popularity, only 2 of Loewen's 12 textbooks could be considered among the "most popular" in the field with 9 editions published inclusive of the copyright date used by Loewen: *The American Pageant* and *Triumph of the American Nation*. As for the rest: 7 were first editions.

Regardless of Loewen failing to place a date next to his claim, publishing evidence augers against Loewen since of the seven allegedly "most popular" textbooks, three were never reissued, three survived only to a second edition, and only two lived to three and four editions respectively. Still, *none* of the seven remained in print as of 1994, suggesting that by virtue of dropping out of the market, all seven were "unpopular textbooks" by the time Loewen finished his study in 1994.

In sum, under the "popular" or "leading" textbooks claim, while some of the 12 made still have been used in schools (Loewen provides no evidence of the actual use of any textbook in any single school district), only 2 of Loewen's 12 were actually still in print as of 1994.

Loewen's Representative Textbooks Claim

Although he claims these 12 textbooks as "most popular" and "leading" found in American history for schools, Loewen's *Lies* focuses his assertions on a base of representative samples of American history textbooks for schools (Grade 6 or 7 through high school).

A reasonable first measure of range or representation is that a "representative sample" should include textbooks from all major publishers of American history textbooks. In total, Loewen secured textbooks from 9 different publishers, with 3 publishers supplying 2 textbooks each (half the sample) and 6 others providing one textbook each. As the necessity to prove a textbook's popularity by some meaningful measure, Loewen's representative sample of 12 textbooks offers samples from only 9 publishers, while disregarding dozens of readily available textbooks from more than 11 other publishers. Among those publishers ignored by Loewen were Laidlaw, Ginn, Oxford, McDougal Littell, Macmillan, Silver Burdett, Coronado, Knopf, Harper Row, Houghton Mifflin, and Field Educational. Not only does Loewen fail to explain why he picked his 12, he does not explain why textbooks from these publishers were ignored. This is a significant and startling omission.

On the face of it, Loewen cannot claim a "representative" sampling without considering or explaining the absence of textbook wares from the lion's share of publishers. It is possible that Loewen might have argued a case that his nine publishers do represent the whole field, but he neither makes such a case nor supplies any evidence that might lead readers to a valid reason for his narrowing the "representative sample" to just 12 textbooks. Why these 12 textbooks? Why these publishers? Why ignore the greater number of textbooks? What makes his "representative" sample a viable sample?

Without answers to such vital research questions on sampling procedures, the findings of Loewen's *Lies* are suspect. Beyond Loewen's faulty sampling technique, whatever generalizations are suggested, Loewen cannot claim they represent any more than the 12 textbooks in question. To claim generalizations that transcend his sample to encompass the whole field of American history, Loewen would have had to provide a reasonable basis for his 12 textbooks being viable representations of the whole field. On that point, as with the "most popular" claim, Loewen supplies no argument or evidence that leads readers to his sweeping generalizations about the poor quality of American history textbooks.

Loewen's Currency Claim

It is also important to note that no popular or representative sampling of the field can be considered viable unless the textbooks in question are currently in use. The samples used by Loewen regardless of being popular or not representing the whole of the possible textbook offerings, the actual age of Loewen's textbooks is problematic. With 1994 as the benchmark, the average age of Loewen's textbooks was 11 years old in 1994, ranging from 4 to 20 years old. That fact raises the third red flag on Loewen's 12 textbook sample: currency.

As a rule of thumb, the shelf life of American history textbooks in schools runs 7 to 10 years. That said, given that his books average 11 years old, it is reasonable to conclude that the majority of Loewen's textbooks may have been replaced by 1994. Certainly, at least the older, out-of-print textbooks were long gone. So, again, making sweeping generalizations about the current state of American history textbooks in schools, regardless if based on "most popular" or "representative" samples is unwarranted unless the textbooks in question are in fact the most recently available and also actually found in use. Again, as with Loewen's lack of supports on his claims of "most popular" and "representative," Loewen offers no data to sustain the notion that his 12 textbooks were actually found in schools in 1994.

If Loewen wants to make the claim that his study reflects the current state of affairs in American history textbooks, he should have used the latest textbooks available from the widest number of publishers. The fact that Loewen chose to study out-of-date and out-of-print textbooks negates the veracity of his many sweeping generalizations on contemporary American history in schools. At best, he presents a loose and limited historical conspectus of 12 textbooks published in 1970s and 1980s.

At the heart of Loewen's *Lies* is Loewen's conviction that all American history textbooks are the same, which is why it does not bother him if he uses one, 12, or 50 textbooks. Yet, Loewen's imagined pattern of all-textbooks-as-bad theory does not work in practice. And that fact brings us to the most troubling thing about Loewen's *Lies*. The idea that he ignores, fails to recognize, or otherwise make no accounting for the most pervasive change in the history of American history textbooks: the rise and implementation of the standards movement.

The Great American History Revolution

Loewen's *Lies* is full of references to the key players in the second greatest transformation of American history textbooks[3] (see American Historical Association, Committee of Seven, 1899). Loewen mentions Gary Nash and Charlotte Crabtree, authors of the revolutionary National History Standards (1994); Lynne Cheney (1994), who savaged the National History Standards; Diane Ravitch (1987) who, co-authoring with Crabtree, wrote the first state-wide K–12 history standards, California's *History-Social Science Framework*; Arthur M. Schlesinger, Jr. (1991), who critiqued the content transformation of found in these standards in his searing commentary on multicultural education, *Disuniting of America*; and William

McNeill and Paul Gagnon, who laid much of the intellectual framework for the standards movement with the Bradley Foundation (see National Council for History Education, 1993).

Loewen also knows the institutional players. *Lies* cites Lynne Cheney's National Endowment for the Humanities, which provided the grant monies to Nash and Crabtree's National Center for History in the Schools, specifically referenced by Loewen. Loewen also mentions the landmark group that sparked the history standard movement, the Bradley Commission on History in the Schools/National Council for History Education (1988), led by McNeill and Gagnon. Loewen's references suggest that he must have been aware of the *California's History-Social Science Framework* co-authored by Ravitch and Crabtree (1987). These standards were important because they provided the basis for the first wave in the major standards to textbook transformation, the Houghton Mifflin American history textbook series also co-authored by Nash.

Had Loewen examined the new face of scholarship for schools, he would have recognized that his desired revolution had already happily arrived. Consequently, left accountable for ignoring trends and developments in K–12 education, Loewen's book contains nothing about Nash's efforts to revolutionize basic education with "new" American history that focused on race, racism, women, minorities, and the "underside" of American history—a much publicized national effort that had been underway for more than 5 years. Ironically, the very publishers Loewen savaged in *Lies* were intimately involved in accommodating Nash's new National History Standards.

The intellectual elites and mover and shakers of American history for schools comprise a small circle of individuals. Cheney, Nash, and Ravitch (and her colleague Chester Finn (1987) and the others each represent different sides on the same continuum of the standards/textbooks movement. Loewen includes nonspecific references to these people only tangentially related to his social justice themes, while completely ignoring the larger issues and movement to which these people and supposedly Loewen's *Lies* are intimately connected. Loewen's glaring omission strikes one as arrogance or incompetence.

The trail toward the release of the Nash's landmark National History Standards took place over the course of 11 years, arguably beginning with the 1983 release of *Nation At Risk* (National Commission on Excellence, 1983). Under the aegis of the United States government, *Risk* attracted a wide coalition of educators, policymakers, and other interested citizens beating the drum for traditional teaching. Building on *Risk* synergy, private funding supported a back-to-basic approach toward the teaching of American history. Consequently, as Lynne Cheney (1987), then chair of the National Endowment for the Humanities, called for history in schools, the Bradley Commission on History in the Schools (1988) took the next step by placing history on the national agenda. This group produced the first "standards" model that was later filled out in California's Blue Print history standards (1987). It is important to note that Diane Ravitch factored in the Bradley work, the California Blue Print standards, and, as an Assistant Secretary in the United States Department of Education, she pushed for the development of National History Standards.

Shortly after the Bradley report was released in 1988, President Bush convened an education summit at Charlotte, Virginia. Under the leadership of Bush and then governor Bill Clinton, the Goals 2000 program was articulated, specifically calling for the writing of history standards (Goals 2000 law signed by President Clinton in 1993). Subsequently, Ravitch enlisted the assistance of Lynne Cheney who authorized the 2.5 million dollars in grants to establish Nash's National Center for History in the Schools (NCHS) and to prepare a set of National History Standards. Immediately, Nash set to work building his coalition, soon dominated largely by liberals and leftists, a reality unhappily recognized by conservatives.

While relations were still cordial, conservatives and liberals witnessed the publication of the NCHS first effort, *Lessons From History*, a 314-page explanation of the "essentials" of history (Crabtree, Nash, Gagnon, & Waugh, 1992). After 4 years of much publicized work, the NCHS released its National History Standards in the fall of 1994. These standards, representing the state-of-the-art in history education, came under attack, ironically, by Cheney, who had signed the original standards contract over to the NCHS.

In advance of official publication, the NCHS effort had already captured the attention of the publishing community. Gathering intelligence from NCHS memos and frequent meetings, well in advance of the 1994 markets sales campaign, every major publisher would pay homage to the new National History Standards, if not specifically by name or explicit reference, certainly by providing curricular attention to NCHS themes and content (see National Council for the Social Studies [NCSS], 1990, 1992). In Chicago at the 1994 annual conference of the NCSS, the largest teacher's organization devoted, in part, to teaching history, I was eager to sample the latest American history textbooks. To a textbook, evidence of alignment to the only just released National Standards was obvious. While I recall the various publishers representatives and Gary Nash were visibly shaken by the intensity of Lynne Cheney's attack on the standards (supported by a ground swell of negative publicity generated by Rush Limbaugh's television and radio programs and a number of other conservative critics), Nash and the publishing community managed to pooh-pooh the crisis, explaining that the storm over the standards was an aberration that would soon pass. Unfortunately for them, it did not—things got worse. Eventually, 2 months later more embarrassment was to follow when the National History Standards were condemned by the U.S. Senate in a striking 99–1 vote.

Certainly, Loewen can be excused for not including the late October to November 1994 Cheney-Nash-Limbaugh National Standards debacle in his book, but only arrogance or incompetence could account for not including anything on the beginnings of the standards movement, its growth, and the direct connection established between standards and textbook publishing. For example, how could Loewen (the self-proclaimed textbook expert) have missed that *none* of his 12 textbooks had made the 1992 Texas textbook adoption list (a clear indication of popularity in Texas and the nation) (M. Gabler, personal communication, 2005) or that the 1992 Texas adoption list, led by Nash's new textbook, *American Odyssey* (2004), which offered a preview of the National History Standards, contained all new textbooks (Crabtree & Nash, 1994). Moreover, these new textbooks were not "clones" of the older textbooks, but new works tightly aligned to specific standards.

In 1990, Houghton Mifflin understood the power of standards alignment. Gambling on the hope of securing the California market would ensure increased sales elsewhere, Houghton Mifflin moved into production. The editors at Oxford University Press picked up this synergy by publishing Joy Hakim's 10 volume *History of US* in 1993—another textbook hit still going strong after more than a decade in print (American Textbook Council, 2005). These textbooks, among others, were unmistakable signals that the older "standard" textbooks, so heavily critiqued by Loewen as impervious to change, were no more. The truth is painfully clear, Loewen's *Lies* attacked obsolete textbooks.

Impervious to the changing textbook world, appearing more like Don Quixote than researcher, Loewen, insulated in his social justice crusade, flailing at phantom curricular windmills thinking them giants to vanquish.

In summary, from the *Nation at Risk* in 1983, that announced a change in the curricular winds to the 1992 Texas textbook adoptions, a new force in American history (the standards movement) had taken hold, marking a sharp and clear dividing line between Loewen's dated textbooks and those packaged according to the National History Standards. Loewen's *Lies* does not attempt to recognize or explain this mass on the national curricular radar screen (see Table 19.2).

While Loewen missed the great giant of standards, looming in his midst, others did not. In 1992, Arthur Schlesinger, Jr. lamented the institution of the strident multicultural society, commandeering the history curriculum as a weapon in the fight for social justice. Loewen saw nothing. Although Diane Ravitch did not foresee the National History Standards debacle, in her 1995 book on standards, at least she recognized the curricular potency of standards. Loewen saw nothing. As Harvey Kaye (1991) and Michael Apple (1993) recognized the efforts of conservatives investing in curricula reform as dangerous in their books respectively, fellow leftist Loewen saw nothing. When Catherine Cornbleth and Dexter Waugh reported on the progress of California's Blueprint in 1995 from ideas to textbooks published exclusively by Houghton Mifflin for the California market, again, Loewen saw nothing. And finally, Robert Lerner, Althea Nagai, and Stanley Rothman took the time to specifically acknowledge the impact of the National History Standards in their 1995 book, *Molding the Good Citizen*, which reported on 5 decades of high school history textbooks. Sadly, Loewen was silent.

Again, for Loewen to proclaim himself an expert on American history textbooks in 1995 (and to continue to make that declaration), claiming to have studied them for some "ten years," then fail to include not only significant movements, but landmark events in the field or to refresh his aging list of history textbooks with newer, more relevant textbooks. Such omissions should call Loewen into question as an academic fraud, but he is rather something else, as we shall see.

And all that before even addressing the content of his *Lies* manifesto.

The question begged is simple; it is not how Loewen might have ignored the dawn, birth, and institution of the history standards movement, so fundamental to the changing of the guard in American history textbooks but rather, why he ignored it?

Loewen's *Lies*: Selected Content Examples

The full documentation of the errors, exaggerations, and lies found in Loewen's *Lies*, would take far more space than allotted for this chapter. Consequently, I will focus on a few of Loewen's most egregious fabrications. Before tracking these content issues, it is important to speculate on why Loewen might have selected these topics. Loewen does not really examine these textbooks for what they are, or rather, for what they must be. He attacks these textbooks for something they obviously are not and, as textbooks for government schools, these textbooks can never be.

Namely, all American history textbooks destined for use in public schools start with certain expectations, beginning with the responsibility for promoting some measure of allegiance, loyalty, and/or love of country. Twenty-two states have textbook adoption laws that mandate an elected or appointed body of public officials to screen publisher submitted textbooks for adoption. Only those books selected in this process may be acquired for use in the public schools of the respective states. The largest textbook

Table 19.2.   Signposts of Change: Chronology of the Great History Transformation

1983	*Nation At Risk*, call for greater attention to basic education
1987	Lynne Cheney's *American Memory*, specific call for history in schools
1987	Ravitch and Finn's report on what our 17 years olds do not know about history (and language arts)—not much
1987	Allan Bloom's brilliant observation on the collapse of scholarship in higher education, *Closing of the American Mind*
1987	E. D. Hirsch, Jr.'s bestselling book *Cultural Literacy*, suggesting the need for a common body of knowledge
1987	Bradley Commission on History in Schools, first major articulation of history for schools since 1899
1987	California *History-Social Science Framework*/Blueprint, K–12 history sequence outlined (see Crabtree & Ravitch, 1988)
1988	NEH funds the Nash/Crabtree Center for History in the Schools
1989	Goals 2000 Summit
1989	New York promotes "A Curriculum for Inclusion"
1991	NEH Contract to Nash/Crabtree's Center for Teaching History in Schools to prepare National History Standards
1990-1995	CTHS/NCSS/NEH Activities, promoting the articulation and writing of National History Standards
1991	Houghton Mifflin Textbooks, K–12 History series tied directly to California Blue-Print
1991	New York Review and Development Committe releases the radical "One Nation, Many Peoples" curriculum
1991	Arthur Schlesinger, Jr.'s defense of traditional history, *The Disuniting of America*
1991–1994	Textbook industry retools for change, concessions and alignment to Nash's National History Standards
1993	Hakim's *History of US*
1993	Goals 2000 Law
1994	National History Standards released
October 1994	Cheney's Attack on the National History Standards, conservative backlash
January, 1995	National History Standards condemned by the United States Senate 99–1
1995	*Molding the Good Citizen*, review of History Textbooks
1995	*The Great Speckled Bird*, review of the California History Textbook
1995	Virginia's State History Standards developed (Commonwealth of Virginia, 1995)
1995	Loewen's *Lies* published

market among the textbook adoption states are California (which adopts textbooks for K-8) and Texas (which adopts books K–12). Although California is a much larger market, because Texas adopts K–12, those secondary American history textbooks (9–12) adopted for Texas typically receive a lot of attention (and sales) outside of Texas as well. Given the rules of the textbook game, within government sponsored schools, every textbook used must pass through some sort of vetting process either strictly controlled by state textbook adoption boards or through state, district, or school committees and boards—all bound to observe state citizenship laws which often mandate various forms of patriotism. Given the wide use of textbooks, the textbook is, in effect, the official curriculum.

Subsequently, even if a teacher wanted to use materials or other textbooks recommended by Loewen, no public school teacher can legally refuse to teach the official curriculum. Thus, Loewen's tirade on American history textbooks is misplaced from the start. Loewen critiques his 12 textbooks for not being the textbooks that he would like to see in schools. His type of textbook (liberal/left-wing) cannot be used in schools unless first selected. While conditions may have changed for some states and individual school districts, the odds of any American school district (or state textbook committee) recommending the sort of textbooks required by Loewen is remote, and he admits as much in *Lies*, where Loewen (1995) claims that no purely leftist American history textbook (or true conservative textbook) has ever been selected for school use (p. 274). Nonetheless, despite knowing the nature of textbook selection and the limitations placed on state/local sponsored textbooks, Loewen proceeds to dismantle his 12 textbooks for failing to measure up to his standards, a task with which none could comply.

This flaw, comparing apples to oranges, is thus an exercise in futility. Just what is accomplished by tearing into textbooks that fail to mention Woodrow Wilson's alleged racism or ignore Helen Keller's flagrant socialism (the first topics of Loewen's *Lies*). If state or local textbook reviewer/selection committees and bodies mandated such content, textbooks would have been obligated to include this information. Had Loewen's study revealed that textbooks failed to measure up to state and/or local content requirements that would be a legitimate complaint. However, since no state or local textbook policy, up to that point, mandated detailed accounts of Wilson's alleged racism or Keller's socialist activities, Loewen does the educational community no service for attacking textbooks (and teachers) for not teaching something that was never required to begin with.

As suggested earlier, if Loewen had paid any attention to the standards movement, he might have reviewed National History Standards that specifically called for an examination of Wilson's relations with the African-American community, "Standard 1B" (Crabtree & Nash, 1994, p. 167).

Here, in response to the Loewen's questions on Wilson's response to African Americans, women, and labor, textbook writers would have an opportunity to include specific information. And beginning with Nash's own text (available in 1993), following his own National History Standards, Loewen would have discovered that students were specifically guided to, "describe the attitudes of progressives toward African Americans, immigrants, and socialists" (p. 191). Here the can of alleged racism and ignored socialism (championed by Loewen) can be properly opened by teachers with the aid of textbooks. Certainly, in reading Nash's textbook, Wilson, "resented any challenging [of] his authority, particularly [coming from] a defiant African American" (p. 191). In addition, Nash makes it clear that, "few white progressives thought to challenge the racism rampant in American society," and that, "most whites, including most progressives, ignored or actively opposed the efforts of [black leaders] to achieve equality" (1994, p. 193).

Nash's textbook as supported in his National History Standards found in Standard 2A (Crabtree & Nash, 1994, p. 171) do not go lightly on Wilson's foreign policies, particularly in relation to Mexico (a target of Loewen's barbs). Nash takes these issues head on and specifically addresses U.S. intervention in Mexico and its consequences (p. 212).

Although neither the National History Standards nor Nash's (2004) *American Odyssey* mention either Keller or the American excursion to Russia in 1919, neither omission calls for lashing out at textbooks. Keller was not, as Loewen admits, a major player in socialist circles. Keller may be missing, however, both the National History Standards and Nash's textbook account for socialist activities and doctrines, specifically calling upon students to consider their impact and influence of socialism in the United States. As for the Russian affair, while Loewen (1995) claims that, "Russian history textbooks … give the episode considerable coverage … [because the action gave] Bolshevik leaders [sic] clear proof … that Western powers meant to destroy the Soviet government if given the chance" (p. 14), Loewen, now posing as a supposed expert on Soviet history textbooks, overstates his case in favor of landing a propaganda plug for the Communists. The United States took no action to oust the Soviets from power in 1919, and took no such action at any other time throughout the life of the Soviet Union. Loewen is simply planting a seed of propaganda doubt.

Without verification, Loewen (1995) claims that the 1919 U.S. "intervention" in Vladivostok (thousands of miles from the Soviet heartland), "motivated the Soviets during the Cold War" (p. 14). The Soviet Union's penchant for world domination, as demonstrated throughout the Cold War, stems not from the so-called "unknown war with Russia" (p. 14), but from the nature and dictates of Communism. For Soviet history textbooks to include "considerable coverage" of the 1919 U.S. intervention is more a reflection of Soviet propaganda than an example of Soviet excellence in scholarship.

Certainly, not everything can be included in every textbook in the United States or Russia. Curricular decisions must be made and again, without a specific mandate to include Helen Keller's socialist biography or without specific instructions to include American activities in Russia, since neither Keller's socialism nor the Vladivostok affair ranks above other pressing subjects, the matter must rest on the conscience of the textbook reviewers.

Alas, Poor Columbus, We Used to Know Him Well.

One of Loewen's favor targets is Christopher Columbus. Few figures in American history have risen so high or fallen so low as Columbus. Loewen loves to bash the hero Columbus represented in U.S. textbooks. Certainly, Columbus had not changed in 500 years, but historians of the past forty years have busied themselves with revisions. Thanks to dedicated activists, few teachers, let alone textbooks, espouse any affection toward the old mariner who dared an ocean. Since at least the 1960s, Columbus has tumbled head-first off his lofty perch. The National History Standards sealed his fate, completing Columbus's transformation from hero to villain. Every complaint lodged by Loewen had already found some niche in the National History Standards: racist's Whites stole the land, murdering hapless Indians, and laying waste to the environment. Had Loewen been willing to recognize the great textbook transformation embodied in the National History Standards, he could have saved himself much of his considerable anguish.

At issue in Nash's National History Standards and Loewen's *Lies* is the decentering (a postmodernist term used to move emphasis from where it should be to track students away from information of actual importance) of American history. Where traditional American history, (the history of the nation that becomes the United States of America), starts with the English settlement of the New World, specifically at Jamestown in 1607, the decentered American history begins with environmentally attuned Native Americans, thirteenth century sea-faring Africans, and racist Europeans struggling as equal partners. Known as the Three Worlds Theory, before they encounter the dreaded Europeans, students are forced on a wild-goose chase through pre-Columbian America and pre-seventeenth century Africa where they learn the wonders of the ancient Native Americans and Africans. Certainly, as much as such histories may be interesting and informative, there is nothing in Loewen's imagined American "history" that connects either Africans or Indians to the Continental Congress declaring on July 4th 1776, "that these colonies are and of right ought to be, free and independent states."

Loewen and Nash know that the great African king Mansa Musa has no connection to American history. For them, using the decentering process, is to keep students from prying into the history of England, to learn about the birth of freedom and liberty, to discover the beginnings of free trade, or to understand the great division and diversity of the English and Europeans, and most importantly, to reveal the centrality of Christianity in the lives of our common ancestors.

For traditional American history, Columbus holds a place of honor for being the first modern mariner to brave the ocean in quest of new markets and to the greater glory of God. That said American histories need not dwell on Columbus for the true history of the nation rests elsewhere. Properly taught, this American history turns to England. Loewen, however, labors under the false impression that American schools teach Columbus as hero. Having taught high school American history between 1974 and 1985, roughly corresponding to a portion of Loewen's study span, neither I nor my colleagues, taught the sort of Columbian myth as depicted by Loewen. Apparently, I must have been teaching in some parallel universe, because the American history taught on the Illinois prairie circa 1985, fixed the beginnings of the nation on Jamestown and Plymouth.

Loewen also labors under the misconception that high school teachers teach only from textbooks. Certainly, to a fault, undoubtedly many use the textbook religiously, however, in my recollection of teaching history before the advent of state and national standards, there was little to keep teachers from spending days or weeks off the beaten trail of textbook to present favorite topics or dwell on pet subjects. A familiar truism was that although the textbook may have ended with Vietnam (or some other point), many teachers struggled to complete U.S. history from Jamestown to the present, often getting no farther than finishing World War II (or 20 to 30 years behind whenever the textbook ended).

Loewen disregards the professionalism of teachers to research lessons and provide students with viable alternatives to textbook content. For example, I was keenly interested in challenges to traditional Columbian scholarship. Shortly after reading the startling assertions raised by Ivan Van Sertima (1976), a pre-Columbian scholar adored by Loewen who asserts that African explorers had crossed the ocean long in advance of Columbus to influence the Olmec civilization in the Americas, I jumped at the chance to learn first hand about Van Sertima's fascinating theory. By luck, Van Sertima, then a professor at Rutgers University, was offering a course in Chicago titled, "Africans in Pre-Columbian America" in the Spring of 1979. Living and teaching nearby, I happily enrolled.

However, I was quickly disabused of my enthusiasm when I discovered Van Sertima to be long on theory but short on evidence. Although Van Sertima forcefully argued his case, and Loewen was willing to believe him, no other reputable archeologists or historians accepted Van Sertima's "proofs" of Africans in pre-Columbian America. When I boldly expressed my rejection of Van Sertima's theory as without merit in my class paper, Van Sertima berated me for "throwing up to his face the prejudice of centuries" (V. Sertima, personal communication, 1979). Upon my refusal to comply with shoddy scholarship, to resubmit another paper (which he demanded), Van Sertima promptly issued a failing grade—an honor which I still carry with distinction.

Although Van Sertima taught me nothing about Africans in pre-Columbian America (primarily because there were none), he did give me invaluable insight on the importance of objective scholarship and the disasters that follow when it is lacking or missing. It is telling that Loewen (1995) relies on such allies as Van Sertima and the now infamous University of Colorado celebrity/academic, Ward Churchill (p. 355). After Van Sertima's course, in the NSS tradition, I continued to present the various theories purporting to explain the peopling of the New World, citing Van Sertima as both an example of farfetched nonsense as well as the difficulty to prove a case without verifying evidence. Still, as Loewen, my fellow students in Van Sertima's class, and perhaps many more agree, far too many prefer a manufactured past to the one history has provided.

SUMMARY

Loewen's *Lies* contains much that challenges traditional American history (and lack of space has excised pages of my further critique). As a text that challenges, Loewen's *Lies* hits hard, but it is thin on sincere scholarship. Certainly, we ought to encourage challenges; we ought insist on citizens asking questions, seeking answers; being reflective, and routinely opting to scrutinize those who would rule us or would rule in our name. All that and more is in the best of NSS traditions. But no single research project should be digested as the sole exploration into any topic.

As Nash, Cheney, Ravitch, Finn, Gagnon and the others fade from the American history scene, Loewen remains strong. *Lies* is now in its 28th printing, absolute proof of popularity (and a supposed "new" version was published in 2007).[4]

At end, we find that Loewen (1995) cannot separate politics from his teaching, an unabashed trait among social justice crusaders. Where a wall should stand between the researcher and personal beliefs, Loewen sees none. As a tragic flaw, traditional schooling, as reflected in the American history textbooks under his review, remained designed to instill and promote allegiance "to our society and its policies" (p. 300). Together with socialization, a process by which individuals are trained to respond appropriately to societal rules, "allegiance and socialization processes cause the educated to believe that what America does is right ... and good" (p. 301). Believing in your country is a bad thing according to Loewen. And given that American history textbooks allegedly promote allegiance and socialization, textbooks are bad too. More specifically, what is bad about American society and its history textbooks is that they "help perpetuate the archetype of the blindly patriotic hardhat by omitting or understanding progressive elements in the working class" (p. 303). According to Loewen, "educated Americans are likely to be Republicans, hard-liners on defense, and right-wing extremists" (p. 303). Given the wide-diversity of political dispositions found among citizens schooled by public education, such bald conclusions are patently outrageous and without foundation.

Ultimately, the problem with Loewen's *Lies* does not rest with Loewen —as he is not responsible for critiquing his own work and he should remain free to pursue scholarship as defined by him. But, in the field of scholarly inquiry, educational professionals are obligated to hold our collective scholarship to high, objective standards. The idea that our contemporary social studies professors provide an unwarranted seal of approval for Loewen's *Lies* unmasks an unacceptable professional bigotry of the very people who should uphold the standards of scholarship.

While *Lies* fails as scholarship, it is a skillfully conceived piece of propaganda, well suited to effect social and political change. *Lies* worked in 1995, and works now because it speaks to a willing audience; a pliable, gullible audience who not only agrees with the suggestion that textbooks are bad before they read one, they do not even know enough history to correct its would be errors. Loewen has a preconditioned audience who suspects their government as evil and unworthy of trust, an audience that is taught to hate their own history, an audience who has been trained to reject the founding as something good, an audience who sees evil in our past, and has learned hatred of their own blood and cultural ancestors.

In summary, *Lies* is a publishing phenomenon, not because of Loewen's prowess as a researcher, but for his ability to recognize the potent power of propaganda that relies on the undeniable human thirst for explanations, any explanations, that might lead us to discover who we are and how we came to be, even if the account is full of lies.

At end, Loewen's *Lies* reminds us that the old NSS ideals remain worthy goals.

NOTES

1. According to Loewen's publisher, Andre Schiffrin (2000), winning the case did not help sales. In fact, "our sales people discovered that when they called the Mississippi school districts [from New York] to pitch the book, the officials would simply hang up on them" (pp. 59–60). Consequently, the book quickly disappeared.

2. I personally taught from five of these textbooks while teaching American history in public schools between 1975 and 1985.

3. The first great American history textbook revolution dates back to 1899 when the famed American Historical Association's Committee of Seven issued the four-block plan for secondary history. While focused on Grades 9–12, this Committee established 11th grade for American history instruction and set specific content recommendations, many of which have been maintained for more than 100 years. Shortly thereafter, textbook publishers aligned their textbooks to the 1899 model. The transformation was so complete that Rolla Tryon, an historian of the field, wrote, "with respect to textbooks, they became as they appeared in rapid succession after 1900 imposing monuments to the Committee's efforts.... The fact of the matter is that a textbook intended for high school use in history published between 1900 and 1915 had hard 'sledding' if it failed to claim that it conformed to the report of the Committee of Seven." So pervasive was this report that 4 decades after its release, Tryon claimed that about a third of school still clung to its recommendations (see Saxe, 1992).

4. In 2007, Loewen published what was touted as a "completely revised and updated" version of *Lies*. Beyond a so-called new introduction (largely gratuitously self-congratulatory), the content is essentially identical to the original text and suffers all the more from the original's pervasive aliments, only now magnified by Loewen's inability to neither recognize nor address the 1990s revolution in textbook content, the rise of standards, and the field's many debates over the past decade.

REFERENCES

American Historical Association. (1899). *Report of the Committee of Seven*. Washington, DC: American Historical Association.

American Home Assurance Co. v. Phineas Corp., 347 F. Supp. 2d 1231 (M.D. Fla. 2004)

American Textbook Council. (2005). *Widely adopted history textbooks*. Retrieved from http://www.historytextbooks.org/adoptions.htm

Apple, M. (1993). *Official knowledge*. New York: Routledge.

Bailey, T., & Kennedy, D. M. (1991). *The American Pageant*. Lexington, MA: Heath.

Bauer, N. W. (1979). *The American way*. New York: Holt, Rinehart, Winston.

Berkin, C., & L. Wood. (1983). *Land of promise*. Palo Alto, CA: Scott, Foresman.

Bloom, A. (1987). *The closing of the American mind*. New York: Simon & Schuster.

Bradley Commission on History in Schools. (1988). *Building a history curriculum: Guidelines for teaching history in schools.* Washington, DC: Education Excellence Network.

Brown, R., & H. Bass. (1990). *One flag, One land.* Morristown, NJ: Silver Burdett & Ginn.

Cheney, L. V. (1987). *American memory.* Washington, DC: National Endowment for the Humanities.

Cheney, L. V. (1994, October 20). The end of history. *Wall Street Journal,* p. A26.

Cornbleth, C., & D. Waugh. (1995). *The great speckled bird.* New York: St. Martin's Press.

Crabtree, C., & Nash, G. (1994). *National History Standards.* Los Angeles: National Center for History in the Schools.

Crabtree, C., Nash, G., Gagnon, P., & Waugh, S. (1992). *Lessons from history.* Los Angeles: National Center for History in the Schools.

Crabtree, C., & D. Ravitch. (1988). *History Social Science Framework.* Sacramento: California State Department of Education.

Commonwealth of Virginia. (1995). *History and Social Science Standards of Learning Curriculum Framework.* Richmond: Virginia Department of Education.

Davidson, J. W., & Lytle, M. H. (1981). *The United States-A history of the Republic.* Englewood Cliffs, NJ: Prentice Hall.

Davis, O. L. (and others). (1986). *Looking at history: A review of major U.S. history textbooks.* Washington, DC: People for the American Way.

Dickinson v. Indiana State Election Bd., 817 F. Supp. 737, 746 (S.D. Ind. 1992),

Fenton, E. (1969). *A new history of the United States: An inquiry approach.* New York: Holt, Rinehart, and Winston.

FitzGerald, F. (1979). *America revised.* Boston: Little, Brown.

Fordham Foundation. (2004). *The mad, mad world of textbook adoption.* Washington, DC: Thomas B. Fordham.

Garraty, J., Singer, A., & Gallagher, M. (1982). *American history.* New York: Harcourt Brace Jovanovich.

Green, R., Becker, L., & Coviello, R. (1984). *The American tradition.* Columbus, OH: Merrill.

Hakim, J. (1993). *A history of US.* New York: Oxford University Press.

Hefley, J. C. (1979). *Are textbooks harming your children.* Milford, MI: Mott Media.

Hirsch, E. D., Jr. (1987). *Cultural literacy.* New York: Houghton Mifflin.

Jenness, D. (1990). *Making sense of social studies.* New York: Macmillan.

Kownslar, A. (1974). *Discovering American history.* Holt, Rinehart, Winston.

Kaye, H. (1991). *The powers of the past.* Minneapolis, MN: University of Minnesota Press.

Ladson-Billings, G. (2003). Lies my teacher still tells. *Critical Race Theory Perspectives in Social Studies,* 1–11.

Lerner, R., Nagai, A., & S. Rothman. (1995). *Molding the good citizen.* Westport, CN: Praeger.

Levstik, L. S. (1996). Review of *Lies my teacher told me. Theory and Research in Education, 24*(4), 416–420.

Loewen, J. W. (1995). *Lies my teacher told me.* New York: New Press.

Loewen, J. W. (2005a). *Everything you've been taught is wrong*. Barnes & Noble Audio Book (course guide).

Loewen, J. W. (2005b). *Lies my teacher told me* (10th anniversary ed.). New York: New Press.

Loewen, J. W. (2007). *Lies my teacher told me* (Revised). New York: New Press.

Loewen, J. W., & Sallis, C. (Eds.). (1980). *Mississippi conflict and change*. New York: Pantheon.

Loewen v. Turnipseed, 488 F. Supp. 1138 (N.D. Miss. 1980).

Linenthal, E. T., & Engelhardt, T. (1996). *History wars*. New York: Metropolitan Books.

Moreau, J. (2003). *School book nation*. Ann Arbor, MI: University of Michigan Press.

Nash, G. (2004). *American odyssey*. New York: Glencoe.

Nash, G., Crabtree, C., & Dunn, R. (1997). *History on trial*. New York: Knopf.

National Commission on Excellence. (1983). *Nation at Risk*. Washington, DC: GPO.

National Council for History Education. (1993). *Proceedings 1993 Conference, A five-year perspective*. Westlake, OH: Author.

National Council for the Social Studies. (1990, 1992, 1994). *Annual meeting program*. Washington, DC: Author.

Peck, I., Jantzen, S., & Rosen, D. (1987). *American adventures*. Austin, TX: Steck-Vaughn.

Pierce, B. L. (1926). *Public opinion and the teaching of history*. New York: Knopf.

Ravitch, D. (2004a). *A consumer's guide to high school history textbooks*. Washington, DC: Thomas B. Fordham.

Ravitch, D. (2004b). *National standards in American education*. Washington, DC: Brookings.

Ravitch, D., & C. Finn. (1987). *What do our 17-year-olds know?* New York: Harper and Row.

Review and Development Committee. (1991). *One nation, many peoples: A declaration of cultural interdependence*. Albany: State of New York, State Education Department.

Roden, P., Greer, R., Kraig, B., & Bivins, B. (1984). *Life and liberty*. Palo Alto, CA: Scott, Foresman.

Schiffrin, A. (2000). *The business of books*. New York: Verso.

Saxe, D. W. (1991). *Social Studies in schools: A history of the early years*. Albany: State University of New York Press.

Schlesinger, A. M., Jr. (1991). *The disuniting of America*. New York: Whittle Direct.

Sobel, R., LaRaus, R., De Leon, L., & Morris, H. (1990). *The challenge of freedom*. River Forest, IL: Glencoe.

Social Science Staff. (1975). *The American adventure*. Boston: Allyn & Bacon.

Symcox, L. (2002). *Whose history?* New York: Teachers College Press.

Thomas, J. (1995, December 12). A case of textbooks lying. *Boston Globe*, 75.

Todd, L. P., & Curti, M. (1986). *Triumph of the American nation*. Orlando, FL: Harcourt, Brace, Jovanovich.

Tryon, R. (1935). *The social sciences as school subjects*. New York: Charles Scribner's.

Van Sertima, I. (1976). *They came before Columbus*. New York: Random House

Zimmerman, J. (2000). Review of Loewen's *Lies my teacher told me*. *Journal of American History, 87*(3), 1000–1001.

Zimmerman, J. (2002). *Whose America?* Cambridge, MA: Harvard.

CHAPTER 20

THE WISDOM OF EXPERIENCE AND PRACTICE

Mary E. Haas

Like many teachers, there are days when I wonder if I have made an impact on my students or if the field of social studies and I are total failures. Most of the time I give little thought to my past and charge on to meet the next deadline, absorb some new information, or do something I really enjoy and do not feel I have to do. Once in a while I am pleasantly surprised to learn that something I have done has made an important connection with others. Upon those occasions I do reflect a bit and often think of those experiences I have had with others who taught me important lessons by what they did, said, or wrote. We all benefit from others and move forward by building on the efforts and accomplishments of others.

When asked if I would be willing to write a chapter on the New Social Studies, I replied that I had a long experience using the High School Geography Project (HSGP) texts/materials (published as *Geography in an Urban Age*) and the experience of using those materials in the classroom made an important contribution to my understanding of education. As a result of the opportunities I had with the HSGP, I first met and interacted with Nick Helburn, Geoge Vuicich, Joe Stoltzman, and Rodney Allen. The four named first encouraged me both directly and

The New Social Studies: People, Projects, and Perspectives, pp. 433–450
Copyright © 2010 by Information Age Publishing

indirectly to make conference presentations, to go on to earn a doctorate, and to publish. Had it not been for their initial encouragement and support combined with teaching the HSGP materials, I would not be the professional I am today. When I read or hear social studies educators neglecting to consider the reforms of the New Social Studies, I wonder why they do not know the history of their profession and how they can be under the gross misconception that their ideas are new. I wonder about their major professors and why there is no complete review of literature from the library and not just Internet searches. Do the demands of a fast-paced world filled with multitasking lead to repetition of the easiest tasks in hopes of progress without the necessary critical thinking and complete identification of the problem required for productive problem solving and/ or growth?

Today's educators advocate reflecting on personal experiences. Could it be that today's students are coming to view reflection as the only way to learn? I view reflection more as an important tool for evaluating research needs and findings. I resent reading another person's reflections passed off as research. I expect to see reflections that include a plan of action which seeks to affirm or change a past learning experience in ways that may lead to greater learning in classrooms. I am not trying to be a veteran with the attitude, "Been there, done that, it doesn't work, don't waste your time and energy," but someone urging the profession to apply the old adage, "Don't throw out the baby with the bath water." As much as I respect the efforts of those active in the New Social Studies, I do believe that the developers of the materials were guilty of failing to plan for teachers holding on to such an attitude. Instead the developers naively created and promoted the expectation that teachers would willingly adopt the strategies and materials to increase student learning.

When Barry K. Beyers wrote in 1994 that the New Social Studies is still around in the assertions and comments of educational reformers, he was correct. He is still correct in 2008. Perhaps through this book the words of veteran and retired social studies educators will finally be heard. Innovators and early adopters who came through the 1960s both need and want to be heard instead of denounced or ignored as misguided or unpatriotic. Reforms were complex and earlier efforts require critical and complete analysis to be built upon rather than watching the next generation waste time reinventing old solutions. This is important because the New Social Studies was a well-funded cooperative endeavor, and today, social studies education is not well funded and—social studies professionals are—widely dispersed in a new academic climate that focuses mostly on the quantity of output. I am glad to join with a group of social studies professionals, some of whom I know well as professional friends and others only from their writings, to revisit and share the lessons of the New Social Studies. It is in this hope that I offer an explanation of what I have learned and the questions I have asked and sought to answer in subsequent years based on my personal 7 year experience teaching the HSGP materials.

During the spring of 1998 Margaret A. Laughlin and I discussed our social studies careers and speculated on the future. We were concerned with the demise of the many centers of social studies education at universities. We concluded that there was a need for social studies educators to record some of the recent history of the profession and decided to survey a large number of national leaders, over 50 years of age, all with a national reputation in social studies. We asked them to comment on what they thought to be the most important trends they had observed during their social studies careers. Two responses tended to dominate the replies. The most identified trend was the impact of multicultural knowledge on the profession, but nearly as many indicated the emphasis of the New Social Studies with its emphasis on inquiry learning and the inclusion of content from social sciences (Haas & Laughlin, 1999). Beyer (1994) identified two movements that followed soon after the New Social Studies that seemed to hinder or weaken the impact of the New Social Studies. One was the inclusion of greater multicultural concerns in the curriculum. Perhaps the reader will agree with me—the inclusion of perspectives from more cultural groups and a focus on inquiry and the social sciences are complementary and not either or choices. Nonetheless, I can see how some educators might believe that the introduction of too many new ideas at the same time might be beyond the resources and time allocated for the social studies curriculum. Of course, employing the tactic of divide and conquer is a strong tactic for advocates of maintaining the status quo, always a large group in education for a variety of reasons.

As a beginning, female teacher in socially turbulent times with large classes of mixed racial and ethnic students with middle and lower socioeconomic parents and mostly male colleagues, I was most concerned with being successful in the classroom on a daily basis. To me success meant having no negative confrontations either among the students or between them and me. I believed the way to accomplish this was to keep students busy during the entire class period with interesting content to be completed within the class period. I knew that a large number of students would refuse to do homework. I needed to pay off my college loan of which half would be forgiven if I taught for 3 years. I had worked hard to get my teaching certification, and I knew I wanted to earn a master's degree in geography. I completed my master's in geographic education during the summer of 1969 and returned that fall, looking forward to a new teaching assignment teaching five classes a day in ninth-grade geography.

ENCOUNTERING THE HSGP MATERIALS

The 1960s Focus on Inquiry

My first encounter with the HSGP was in an advanced social studies methods course I took during the summer of 1969. At the same time, I was also taking a course in the geography department devoted to teaching geography. During her undergraduate years, a student in this g class had taken a geography course with a faculty member at a university who was taking part in the development of the HSGP. She related to us that they used the materials in class as part of the evaluation process. She and her classmates indicated that they had difficulty doing the lessons and informed their professor of that fact and questioned how high school students could be expected to use them successfully. We learned that several of the geography professors at our university had copies of the early versions of materials. We looked at these with interest. The topic of inquiry was important in the advanced social studies methods course and the nationally funded projects were being discussed.

Another classmate related that he had been in a class that piloted some history materials. He said that his class was especially created to pilot the materials and that only the best students in history were admitted. These students thought that the selected teacher was not doing things well and declared they would not continue unless a new teacher were not provided for the second semester. The students won, but as a former teacher, this knowledge contributed to my being somewhat skeptical about such materials. We all recognized that these new materials with their inquiry focus were written predominately for students who planned to go to college.

The course instructor, who had a doctorate and taught in a local public school, assigned group reports on the New Social Studies projects and materials. A fellow student from the geography class and I volunteered to report on the HSGP. Our report provided detailed descriptions of lessons and was unique. The instructor asked us where we found the instructional materials, and we replied in the geography department. Since we thought the analysis of primary sources was a sound procedure, we were surprised to be told by the instructor that the geography department was not exactly a legitimate source of information. Neither of us replied, but we recognized that we were privileged to have access to the primary sources and did not have to rely only on journal references as was the case for other students.

When I returned to the classroom, I relied on my increased knowledge in geography and the available textbook written by my former political geography professor, Dr. Norman J. G. Pounds. I created a number of activities for the students and with the war in Southeast Asia very much in the news. I focused on world regions and used current international events to help me teach the class. I knew that this would be the only course that many students would take where they would have an opportunity to learn about places and nations other than the United States. With my background and personal interests, I believed this global exposure to be very important.

During the school year I received a call from another teacher who told me of the availability of workshops for groups of teachers from a school system on the HSGP during the summer. HSGP materials were to be available from a publisher for the next year. She was organizing a group from our community to apply for a workshop. The group would also be committed to sharing our knowledge and experiences by local and regional presentations. I anxiously agreed to be included in the application. Our application was accepted, and we spent several weeks learning about the materials and their strategies at Western Michigan University. Workshop participants did not have to imagine how students might respond to the HSGP. The workshop not only taught us to use the strategies, but also had us teach actual students. We observed the students during instruction, often recording student responses and timing students behaviors as they performed selected academic tasks. We also heard from students concerning what they liked and what they saw as problems with the lessons.

Obtaining and Maintaining the Materials

Patton (1970) explained the many decisions that confronted the developers of the HSGP and their problems with commercially publishing the materials in the Final Report on the HSGP. I do not recall how I managed to get class sets of several units that first year, but I did. Beside the cost, an important adoption problem was that the materials were not hard cover books and supplemental materials were needed to teach each unit. As I recall, a supportive principal helped me use some creative purchasing to acquire some of the needed supplemental materials through the supply account rather than the textbook account. By keeping the books and re-usable supplies in the hands of the same student each period and only when materials were actually being used, the teaching materials remained in very good condition at the end of the first year—then I sent the books out for hard binding. I followed similar procedures each year and managed to gain all six of the units by the end of the second year. I also purchased those extra materials, such as topographic maps of our local community and of Seattle. I obtained a set of slides of the neighborhoods referred to in New Orleans lesson to help students to better understand the statistics and to update information provided in the readings. I also experimented with the use of the Portsville activity in which students built models of the development of a city using lego blocks on base that was a drawing of a physical landscape similar to that of the location of Seattle as they read accounts of early events in its settlement. Eventually, I created a way to build the city using paper to hold down the costs, while still keeping the activity. My routines for distributing, collecting and checking the learning resources as they were collected, combined with the students' respect for the materials contributed to their longer life.

My Growth as a Teacher

The wisdom I gained through use of the HSGP sometimes strikes me as familiar truisms, ideas that educators, including my students, have heard over and over again. This may explain why we hear reformers today making their case by saying the "same old things." However, there are degrees of agreement; surface agreement tends to be superficial while deep agreement becomes a part of a person's consistent behavior and applies ideas to life. Deep agreement comes about only when the listener has a reason to hear what is being said. It is then that a person receives a combined affective and cognitive impact and becomes the owner of the ideas and is compelled to act and carry out the ideas. In reflecting on my experiential learning from teaching the HSGP, I elaborate on three broad classifications of knowledge. Of necessity are the affective and the cognitive domains both specified as goals in the HSGP project (Helburn, 1998). To those, I add the category knowledge of the cultures of classrooms and schools that were largely unaddressed by printed materials, but are necessities for practicing teachers to consider for adoption and implementation. I experienced each and translated each into my practices, providing wisdom to my professional growth.

KNOWLEDGE RELATED TO THE COGNITIVE DOMAIN

Activities in HSGP were inquiry-oriented. All activities were sequenced through five procedures: teacher posed a generalized question or problem, students were given data, students interacted with the data and/or with other students to explore the problem, teacher posed an interpretive question, and students formed generalizations that illustrated concepts (Patton, 1970). Maps, pictures, and charts provided more of the data than did traditional narrative materials. I quickly found that, although I had to help students use new data gathering and reading skills to gain information or ask questions, students of all abilities were willing to delve into the materials and were pleased to figure out their own answers. Students overwhelmingly told me they enjoyed deciding the location in the simulation for the Metfab company because they got to compare the facts about many cities and make their own choice about which site was the best. Many commented about feeling pride in using unique and new representations of information such as population pyramids, historical newspaper articles, aerial photographs, maps of cultural information, and interesting pictures. Clearly, students exhibited interest and that was cited as a major affective goal for HSGP. I taught in an area where many students came from laboring families and from lower socioeconomic neighborhoods. Colleagues complained about students not being able to read the textbooks, but we did not read long narrative passages and the multiple visual presentations helped to stimulate interest and directed the reading. The students mastered the skills for gaining data from other sources. I personally thought the inquiry model needed to be related to the real world that the students observed and so I would tried to find ways to link the activities to the local or regional situations that dominated our area of the nation or to things that students heard about in the news.

The rationale for our school system having a required geography class for all students was the need to know about the rest of the world, as well as our nation. Patton (1970) charted the distribution of the lesson content by continents to illustrate that information about all continents was presented. South America, Africa, Australia, and Asia were present in about four to seven lessons; North America and Europe dominated five units and a short unit was devoted to the study of Japan. I tried to globalize the curriculum even more. My students expected this because their classmates were learning about other nations and they did not want to be left out. However, they did not want to learn from those fat books or spend a large amount of time coloring maps. The students were happy to try things as long as they thought we were headed toward something meaningful or in the more prominent term of the time "relevant." Depending on school boundaries for the year and the particular class during the day, the makeup of my classes went from a small number of African American students to more than 50%. Some of my students had Middle Eastern heritage and many Eastern European heritage.

President Nixon opened China during this time period and there was war in Southeastern Asia. With a degree in geography, I had encountered many people from Asia and Africa and I thought it important that American students all should be more familiar with a greater portion of the world so I added and expanded lessons to provided information and experiences about Asian and African nations. I saw that the news was often very negative about other nations, and I tried to help students overcome negative stereotypes with accurate knowledge and positive experiences. I continue this today, but gladly find that my university students accept my doing so without my need to justify such inclusions and often express thanks for my increasing their world view.

Before I had the HSGP materials, several of my students indirectly informed me that they were not studying geography because they had not learned about volcanoes! I surveyed student expectations at the beginning of the course and made an effort to include the students' anticipated topics. Most students have some preconceptions. Rarely did you get the trusting student who wrote, "Whatever you think I should learn."

The knowledge base of the New Social Studies was key concepts and generalizations that help students to organize information and remember knowledge about a particular academic discipline. As best as the authors were able, they linked concepts to generalizations, thereby supporting higher levels of learning and breaking the stereotype of geography courses as the memorization of bits and pieces of factual information. The HSGP used a number of key geographic concepts to teach generalizations about the world. If you used all six units, the curriculum would both introduce new concepts and process skills and provide for necessary review and practice of the key ideas and skills. Students were called upon to transfer or expand their use of a theory to other types of geographic content or to the appropriateness of applying generalizations in various cultures and the requirement to qualify or modify generalizations for greater accuracy and utility. The inclusion of simulations with unique perspectives elaborated on participant role cards helped to point out the various possible choices that societies have in making decisions. Clearly, much of the HSGP content was practical and illustrated the complexity within the world and the discipline of geography. With its focus on urban geography the author's recognized the important trend in population redistribution that was missing in traditional instructional materials.

However, the choices made clearly left out some important elements of geography. In hopes of reforming the emphasis on geography in the curriculum, the HSGP through deliberate choice did not include much geographic information evaluated on the existing standardized tests and present in the other textbooks or the accepted geography curriculum of the time. This presented the problem that the course did not meet all of the necessary student, teacher, and general educational cognitive domain expectations. It also failed to devote enough time address the entire world in a way adequate to assist the students in becoming internationally knowledgeable and to support learning in the history courses that dominated the curriculum in higher grades.

I believed that no one would question my use of materials not officially adopted by the school system as long as my students were not perceived by the high school teachers as being less prepared than the students of other teachers. So as I taught I modified the HSGP materials to add what I thought appropriate to try to support the needs of the students in relation to the larger social studies curriculum. The first year, I had to do this because I did not have the entire set of materials. I had taught and prepared some lessons that students had enjoyed and I reused these. I used many of the supplemental lessons provided in the materials because these often added an international dimension or reinforced the theory with new data. Importantly, I had the content background and geographic skills that many teachers did not have to do this. I also added lessons drawn from data from current events or local resources. Our city was a part of the Megalopolis around the Great Lakes and the areas multiple industries and farms could be integrated into unit 2 on manufacturing and agriculture. I encountered many people from Africa and Asia and I devoted my summers to international travel and read much about areas of the world in which I was interested and that were mentioned in the news.

Students enjoyed the cultural geographic lessons in unit 3, but there were some problems. I believed that it was too short. I forcefully made the point at the beginning of the unit that we were not studying cows, but using the cow as an example of all potential resources. Still some teachers mentioned to me that the students wondered why they would need to study cows. Clearly, I needed to do more with this area of geography.

The study of Islam was accepted well with my students because they knew of families and several teachers who were from families from the Middle East. When I saw that the written materials on Islam were not enough, I found a guest speaker who provided knowledge about the religion that helped to clarify its role in the lives of its followers. I had traveled in areas where Islam was practiced and had pictures that illustrated the presence of the religion on the landscape. I also had many pictures that illustrated the presence of Buddhist and the Hindu religions on the landscape. Students, especially the girls, commented on the beauty of the art works. I purchased some special activities on Indian and China because I believed that students needed to spend some time learning about the nature of these nations due to their vast populations and the past civilizations found within their borders. I found that these commercial materials also had some short-comings so I created more lessons and re-ordered the materials in ways that provided for better understanding.

I created the board game *Up Caste, Down Caste: A Hindu Game of Life* Students rated my game as favorable as *The Game of Farming* and the *Portsville* activities, two of the most popular activities in the HSGP. Again, I asked for and received some assistance from the school system whose printer helped me by printing the materials I used for piloting my board game. The game was so well received that I gave several presentations at national conventions and ended up selling the board game through the Social Studies School Services for a number of years.

My interest in travel and photography enabled me to make slide presentations the equal of those of some of my former professors of geography. I also incorporated rental films to support our studies, but held them to about one per month and only those that supported or supplemented what was in the course.

Through these experiences, I became convinced that students can become interested in topics about which they have practically no prior knowledge or interest and that teachers need to make a concentrated effort to measure interest prior to launching into a study. When I first taught the agricultural unit, students had some difficulties grasping the meaning of the lesson on Hunger. I concluded that it was because most of the students did not understand the link between healthful eating, personal food choices, and climatic problems. I devised a short forced choice exercise using pictures of foods followed by pictures of people. The discussion of this experience provided some background and increased student interest in learning the implications of city students learning about farming throughout history and the world. Promoting student interest is an important part of the job a teacher.

Today, I begin a study with an exploratory introduction that has as its stimulus a short examination of something related to the topic or skill being taught. Higher levels of learning are promoted by the transfer of knowledge among disciplines and through real life linkages. Such links are an integral part of the lessons that I still write. I frequently put them into the expansion phase that ends the lesson after the concepts and generalizations important to the lesson have been examined and developed.

In my first experiences with teaching geography, I learned that students did not know the names and locations of nations and important cities or regions of the world. Incorporating a factual recall objective into an inquiry-based curriculum was a challenge. I tried a number of ways to incorporate location learning into the lessons. To draw a map of the world from memory on an 8½ by 11 piece of paper was the first activity and it took several weeks because it incorporated latitude, longitude, and the location of the mountains and volcanoes. Students responded well to this exercise and some surprised me with their excellent drawings. Learning about nations each day and analyzing their location at the beginning of each class followed by tests each 2 weeks had only limited success. Students seemed to enjoy plotting statistical information or cultural traits (major religions added to the lesson on Islam) on a world map several times during the year. But only students with an interest in knowing locations and names of nations in September were the ones likely to learn additional nations while those who did not know such information in September remained ignorant in June.

As I watched students, even in college, take map tests and observed them using personal memorization schemes to recall locations, I became convinced that learning the nations of the world should be done in the elementary grades and reinforced in subsequent grades. Older students many times commented, "If I need to know where a place is, I will use an atlas." Sure! Want to bet how many youthful geeks have an atlas reference on their Ipods? That was just an excuse. Trying to establish that there was a need for such memorized information with students who prefer inquiry and problem-solving learning approaches or who saw little or no value in an education for their future life was largely a lost cause. Many students do not trust the statement that teachers and schools help them because they do not look toward the future with a positive outlook. Developing a mental map as an organization scheme adds understanding to life and scholarship. But even bright students, including secondary social studies majors, do not choose to use a map when it is appropriate.

The developers of the HSGP made the choice to focus on the processes involved in higher levels of learning but my experiences taught me to support the need to incorporate some of the traditional approaches to learning geography as important to include even as you emphasize higher levels of learning. For mastering geography the HSGP taught me to stress the need for place, name, and description activities in the early grades. I encourage educators at all grades to find additional creative approaches to add to the traditional strategies such as those described in Haas and Laughlin (2007) and Thornton (2007).

KNOWLEDGE RELATED TO THE AFFECTIVE DOMAIN

Teachers and Teacher Candidates Need Support

Support goes beyond the knowledge presented at workshops. Teachers need support that both enables and encourages them to function. Carefully prepared and tested materials provide support, but that is not enough. Just as I received help to obtain the HSGP teaching resources, I also did not have to share my room with other teachers or move from room to room to teach because my principal recognized that the use of multiple types of resources presented an additional need. He was willing to allow that exception to school procedures in a time when the student population was high and the norm was to share rooms.

One day another teacher confided to me in the teacher's lounge that she became very frustrated with another faculty member. In a workshop that I presented on the strategies used in the HSGP materials, it seemed to her that the teacher was slowly trying to make an analytical choice in the sample simulation lesson. She said that she just wanted him to make any choice so they could finish. "Didn't he realize that they would never have such nice materials, and it was getting late?" I had thought that by presenting a simulation lesson and having teachers work through it, I was helping fellow teachers become aware of the criteria for effective simulations, and that by encountering a good models teachers would see that they might be able to created their own simulations and inquiry lessons. What this teacher related to me was that she had other pressures that blocked her consideration of the possible transfer of a learning experience. Her comment surprised me, I did not expect to hear this from a teacher who had recently completed her degree and with whom I thought I shared some common experiences and frustrations with teaching and administrative procedures. Older teachers told me that I could do instructional procedures, that they were not capable of doing.

Clearly, there was something wrong with the model of teachers presenting in-service workshops on innovations in those days. Though the style of in-service workshops has changed from one-shot short presentations and from inquiry-based instruction toward general and more communication focused strategies, I still hear evidence of the need for individuals to receive the support that they want as they need it rather than when it is offered or required by the school calendar or administrative decision. The opportunity to attend a workshop is largely a choice of the school administration. The reformers of today, who focus on the content of the curriculum like those of the 1960s, still fail to see that individual teachers put the reforms into effect. What individuals perceive as their own need for support must come in a timely manner to make an impact.

In subsequent years, I learned that, indeed, I seem to have special talents in synthesis of information and translating it into instructional procedures and materials. It is essential to provide the support for groups, as well as for individuals. The New Social Studies did not have the ability to support large numbers of individuals who adopted the materials and thus many tried and then abandoned them. Adopting a new style of behavior is difficult. As senior editor for the elementary section of *Social Education*, I frequently assist individual authors to refine articles to provide support for very busy teachers by providing usable classroom examples. One to one support is essential for all teachers and students, not just to beginning university faculty who are the only social studies professional at a university. Support is essential even to those who have had past successes when they are venturing in a new direction. I am lucky to be in a location where the prevailing attitude is one of support and not rivalry and I believe that it is my obligation to support the efforts of others for the betterment of all. This is a an essential civic value and it is my experience that most social studies educators share this value in common.

I try to provide support to my students' growth as a professional through readings, class activities and summative assignments. Written directions provided with the syllabus for summative assignments help students to organize their busy schedules. Personal conferences are encouraged to help define problems and provide support as students plan and work. I find that a little support or scaffolding encourages student growth. I include several assignments early in the semester that require students to devote time to thinking through and preparing lessons that they will use when they are in the classroom during their internship or student teaching. I do not seek to create clones, but independently functioning teachers. Today, overly-programmed students are inclined to grab a lesson from the Internet or the nearest trade book and rush through teaching one or two lessons as part of a short field placement. Trying to complete and teach an assignment does not provide enough time to work and think through necessary procedures.

If teachers are to be expected to devote considerable time in the classroom teaching powerful and meaningful social studies, they need experience in planning such lessons and observing and evaluating their efforts in carrying through on the lessons with students over a number of days. Daily situations do impact the success of lessons and students' abilities to complete lessons. If teacher candidates just check off a requirement to teach a lesson or two in social studies on a list of qualifications for completing a teacher certification program, they are likely to continue using disconnected occasional lessons or worse, conclude that social studies lessons are not important enough to merit inclusion at all. Problem-solving situations including writing an article, lesson, dissertation or analyzing complex topics all begin with a careful and thorough defining of the problem. To learn this there is a need to slow down and take the time needed to do it correctly. Although modern culture seems to be moving faster and faster, teachers need to find ways to take the time to educate students properly. Research indicates that many elementary teachers are continuing to include social studies out of personal conviction and satisfaction even when administrators suggest devoting time to others subjects (Haas & Laughlin, 1998; Rock et al., 2006). Such teachers trust their own decisions and receive support for their convictions and the efforts of their students. More of such support is needed from those creating and administrating educational policies.

Students Need Support

An important affective idea I learned from students in the workshop at Western Michigan University was that they came to the workshop with certain preconceptions of how they would be viewed by students from the other local schools. The group that was assigned seats the first day made friends with everyone. The students who selected their seating arrangement sat together by school, even if they did not personally know the individual. The students in assigned seats had less fear in taking chances when answering questions, in expressing views, and had less fear of being made fun of should they not be accurate all of the time. This lesson on creating a supportive class atmosphere for individuals was key to gaining maximum learning from inquiry strategies. Students must be supported in taking risks when making predictions, questioning resources and drawing conclusions. I kept that knowledge in mind and worked on building class group dynamics and individual support starting the first day of school. I always assigned students to pairs and small groups to complete short tasks at the beginning of the year. I used self-selected groups later in the year as a "reward" with some activities only after the class proved itself a well-functioning community of learners and remained so when working with good friends. These short assignments were such that students would have success in completing and confidence in the reasonableness or accuracy of their answers. I also made a contract with the students that guaranteed a passing grade to everyone who took part in the class and kept a record in a simple notebook. Those who wanted to get a higher grade performed additional activities that I also kept attainable. I kept accurate records and students received their grade rewards. Rarely, did a student fail. Students made choices about their grades and the time they spent doing homework. I was really surprised when one girl whom I thought to be very self-confident told me with delight in her voice that she earned her first A on her report card in geography class. Students made presentations before the class with confidence and often were better dressed on the days when they made presentations. When challenged about presentations, students pointed out their data sources. They never made negative comments about individual students. There were laughs with students, but never aimed at students. To my relief and pleasure these young teens from very different socioeconomic, racial, and ethnic groups got along well. I learned that if you trust the students and give them the opportunity, the vast majority will try to do what they consider correct and proper. Students will also ask for and benefit from affirmation and clarification. Look for opportunities to provide these genuinely when needed.

Because of curriculum decisions made by material developers, inquiry lessons in many social studies classes do not have consequences that impact the immediate life of students. It becomes the task of the teacher to help students consider potential consequences of choices in personal behavior or governmental policy as a part of a lesson. This is one way they come to see the content as worth learning. Successful teachers do this by assessing students' responses and adding these connections to lessons. The 1960s were a time of social unrest, and I did not have an intercom connection to the office, let alone a cell phone, had I needed help. Interesting materials helped and so did making the objectives clear. When students know what is to be learned and can accept it as worth learning, they are much more likely to apply their energies toward learning rather than toward challenging classmates or the teacher. They build their self-esteem through learning the content rather than through using bullying tactics. Class becomes an appropriate challenge rather than something boring that must be endured.

Principals need to trust their faculty and teachers' actions need to establish and maintain that trust. I learned that I was going to have a new principal and I knew that with his math background, he might be inclined to want very quiet classrooms. Before the school year, I made an appointment and explained that inquiry lessons were active and had very specific and important learning outcomes. Often, he stood outside the door because he heard noise coming from the room. But, there were no harsh or prejudiced words among the students. Sometimes he stepped into the classroom and watched. If students saw him they would explain to him what they were doing. He often said of my teaching, "They sure teach social studies differently from when I was in school." But he was willing to trust. In a rare conference with an assistant principal and a problem student, who several years later was sent to prison, the assistant principal asked this student if he thought that I did not treat him fairly. His reply, "Oh no, she is a nice lady!" That comment was the best compliment I have ever received.

Today, educators and especially methods students, are in stressful situations, trying to earn grades, please multiple instructors, meet very high standards in their placements, and make multiple trips per week many miles on roads that are often icy or narrow. I maintain high standards while trying to support students to take chances by doing active learning lessons and teaching content with which they have little prior background. I try to help teacher candidates balance their time to curb stress. I encourage them to make their own reasonable choices. I encourage my students to give careful consideration to preparing lessons with enough details that will not only help them to teach but also that support a substitute teacher. I stress that doing this is a practical procedure to save planning time in future years. I saw the importance of this when teaching the HSGP materials with its focus on inquiry strategies. It was necessary to provide detailed instructions for substitutes, especially if I were going to conference for several days. Students also need to learn to support their own growth through specific behaviors. I explained to students when I was going to a meeting, what assignment they would be doing, and the types of behaviors that they needed to exhibit while I was gone. The students cooperated with the substitutes and performed interactive student-centered lessons. Some substitutes would not follow the plans and the students expressed pleasure when I returned because they knew that inquiry class activities would also return!

Problems can be overcome by using thoughtful, creative approaches. Just as I would not have had the ability to use the HSGP materials had I not been able to obtain them, I might have had failure had I not planned to confront potential and unexpected student-teacher problems and student interrelationships creatively or if had I not given up time from my summer vacation to attend the workshop at Western Michigan. Trusting students, listening to and giving students a voice in solutions is still considered an unusual tactic for the majority of teachers. Administrative decisions in recent years have tended not to trust teachers. Such lack of trust often passes into classroom procedures resulting in teachers failing to listen to students or providing opportunities for students to have a voice in their class. Students will soon be voters, workers, and possibly, teachers, they have to be supported and trusted for the nation to succeed. There is a limit to the use of cynicism. Just as cynicism is learned so is trust. There is no standard that says to teach trust, but it is an unstated assumption for civic participation.

KNOWLEDGE RELATED TO THE FUNCTION OF SCHOOLS

A major problem with the New Social Studies was that it focused on learning at the high-school level and failed to address the entire curriculum and the need for life-long learning. The developers of the HSGP knew that the higher levels of learning they sought to promote should build on key concepts and skills. The assumption that the school curriculum included, let alone taught, important geographic concepts and skills before high school, was not accurate. Even if the goals of educators were the same, the decisions and choices on what to emphasize was not the same among teachers, schools and communities. While the HSGP developers indicated that they were working on attitudes, the attitudes were largely limited to the importance of geography. Without a concerted effort to help students view their futures in a positive way all reforms will have limited success.

Helburn (1998) in retrospect commented that he knew of teachers who used the HSGP until they retired, while other teachers quickly turned to other things. The difference rested with the teacher and his/her knowledge of the students, school, and the support or pressures they perceived. As I interacted with students, I learned that within all classrooms there was great variety and it had nothing to do with the popular definition of diversity: race, ethnicity, or sex. I learned that with teens it was necessary to involve students in the assessment of their own progress, to recognize students in different ways and to help students recognize their own progress. Creative thinking and reasoning applied to both the class and the individuals within were better approaches than to apply the rules and laws imposed by outsiders whatever the intention.

Support and trust were the keys to my learning and to that of my students. Had I not had support from the principal to obtain the materials and trust that I would know or learn how to use them to improve teaching, had I not supported my students and trusted that students would perform the activities so all in the class could learn, neither I nor the nearly 1,000 students I taught in those years would have learned and grown. I am not the first to reach this conclusion—that is why there are excellent teachers, even many without a single degree from a university. The culture of each school is different and the culture of the times impacts each school year in a slightly different way. Throughout the years when the New Social Studies projects were developed changes were happening and some adjustments were made. However, once published, the materials were locked into a set of assumptions that could only be changed by the teacher.

CONCLUSION

As an educator in a fast changing world with swings in the political climate and changes in schools that are not necessarily rational or adequate, how do you continue to teach from year to year? You recognize certain things, many of which are present in the design of the New Social Studies. Facts change quickly; concepts and generalizations change more slowly. Students pass through developmental phases. Therefore, certain knowledge needs to be taught every year. Dispositions are learned but usually change very slowly. You can cope with some behaviors because they will eventually change and some actions might bring improvement. You support and trust your students, colleagues, and parents and trust yourself to solve problems as they arise in creative ways that incorporate that support and trust for others emotionally and intellectually.

REFERENCES

Beyer, B. K. (1994). Gone but not forgotten—reflections on the new social studies movement. *The Social Studies, 84*(6), 251–255.

Haas, M. E., & Laughlin, M. A. (1998). A contemporary profile of elementary social studies educators: Their beliefs, perceptions, and classroom practices in the 1990s. *The Journal of Social Studies Research, 22*(2), 19–30.

Haas, M. E., & Laughlin, M. A. (1999). *Perspectives of social studies over a quarter of a century: Reflections from veteran social studies leaders.* ERIC Publication ED 432 516.

Haas, M. E., & Laughlin, M. A. (2007). Making and playing small group games: Practicing collaboration while mastering content. *Social Studies and the Young Learner, 19*(4), 1–4.

Helburn, N. (1998). The high school geography project: A retrospective view. *The Social Studies, 89*(5), 212–218.

High School Geography Project. (1970). *Geography in an urban age: Unit 1 geography of cities.* New York: Macmillan.

High School Geography Project. (1970). *Geography in an urban age: Unit 2 manufacturing and agriculture.* New York: Macmillan.

High School Geography Project. (1970). *Geography in an urban age: Unit 3 cultural geography.* New York: Macmillan.

High School Geography Project. (1970). *Geography in an urban age: Unit 4 political geography.* New York: Macmillan.

High School Geography Project. (1970). *Geography in an urban age: Unit 5 habitat and resources.* New York: Macmillan.

High School Geography Project. (1970). *Unit 6 Japan.* New York: Macmillan.

Patton, D. J. (1970). The product. In D. J Patton (Ed.), *Final report on the high school geography project: From geographic discipline to inquiring students* (pp. 12–18). Washington DC: Association of American Geographers.

Rock, T., Heafner, T., O'Connor, K., Passe, J., Oldendorf, S., Good, A., et al. (2006). One state closer to a national crisis: A report on elementary social studies education in north carolina schools. *Theory and Research in Social Education, 34*(4), 455–483.

Thornton, S. J. (2007). Geography in american history courses. *Phi Delta Kappan, 88*(7), 535–538.

CHAPTER 21

INQUIRY TEACHING AND LEARNING

Is There, Was There, a Cutting Edge in Social Studies? Or, My Life As An "Inquiry" Social Studies Teacher

Jack Zevin

The authors take the point of view that in an age of crisis the social studies teacher must locate his authority to teach in those postulates related to inquiry, decision making, and adjudication. (Massialas & Cox, 1966, p. 23)

PROLOGUE

A Word of Caution on Reconstructing History

Reconstructing the past, even my own, which I should know as well as anyone, is fraught with problems and dangers. First of all, as a good social scientist and historian, I want to lay bare my assumptions, one of which is

The New Social Studies: People, Projects, and Perspectives, pp. 451–470
Copyright © 2010 by Information Age Publishing
All rights of reproduction in any form reserved.

that inquiry teaching, and the New Social Studies of which it was an integral part, was a "cutting edge" in the field during its time. In my experience, it was a cutting edge in a way that I think does not exist now in the "reform" minded, No Child Left Behind, NCATE (National Council for the Accreditation of Teacher Education) driven, heavily tested, score conscious period of the 2000s, particularly since we seem to be reliving a return to textbooks, fixed curricula, standardization, and suspicion of teacher professionalism. During the "cutting edge period" of the 60s and 70s, there was a broad based effort to move away from textbooks toward primary sources and hands-on activities that included examination of material culture, experimentation and discovery, much of it in imitation of what was happening in the "hard" sciences, the acknowledged leaders in curriculum reform during most of the 60s and 70s. There was widespread experimentation that encouraged teachers to take risks with their subject matter and pedagogy, often with considerable government support through public and private university and professional programs (Shaver, Davis, & Helburn, 1979).

This is how I would like to have inquiry and the new social studies movement remembered, keeping in mind that "Our tendency to better remember facts that fit certain [unmistakably cultural] mental schemata is quite evident in the highly formulaic plot structures we often use for narrating the past" (Zerubavel, 2003, p. 5). This movement, dubbed the "new" social studies, was a combination of programs, agendas, philosophies, and reformists, but all generally shared a deep desire to change how and what teachers taught (Herbert, & Murphy, 1968). Many within this movement called their philosophy one of "inquiry" following the ideas of John Dewey and others, but "inquiry" included advocates of values education, scientific and critical thinking, creativity—in other words a range of views rebelling against the rather conformist textbook education that characterized the largely staid post-World War II era in the schools.

> Inquiry is the active pursuit of meaning involving thought processes that change experience to bits of knowledge. When we see a strange object, for example, we may be puzzled about what it is, what it is made of, what it is used for, how it came into being, and so forth. To find answers to questions such as these we might examine the object closely, subject it to certain tests, compare it with other, more familiar objects, or ask people about it, and for a time our searching would be aimed at finding out whether any of these theories made sense. Or we might simply cast about for information that would suggest new theories for us to test. All these activities—observing, theorizing, experimenting, theory testing—are part of inquiry. The purpose of the activity is to gather enough information to put together theories that will make new experiences less strange and more meaningful. (Suchman, 1968, p. 1)

Cutting edge is perhaps a sharp way of defining events, but I would say that the period of the "New" Social Studies had several defining characteristics, and a sense of mission, that the present largely lacks.

1. Engagement with theory, with the philosophical and psychological roots of teaching and learning, including widespread attention to the ideas of a dozen or so "thinkers" with whom most social studies and history educators were familiar, and from whom we absorbed and applied key ideas.

2. Concern for the deeper underpinnings of human learning, particularly issues of motivation and interest, and how to adapt curriculum and instruction to take advantage of and to foster student fascination with history and the social sciences.

3. A shared feeling that "the times' they were a-changing," and that there were opportunities to do serious damage to those practices in education that we all grew up with and disliked intensely.

4. A broad-based attempt to deepen social studies education with a heavy infusion of the social sciences, and integrate a wide variety of disciplines with each other and the dominant subject, history.

5. The beginning of general attention to largely forgotten and overlooked student populations, including newcomers, those with health problems and handicaps, and particularly the disadvantaged and those in need of special education (Kozol, 1967).

In my view, inquiry and its ally, the new social studies, resulted from a heady mix of theories and practice, derived from many sources, perhaps most notably the work of Jerome Bruner (1962) whose little book, "Process of Education," was one of the most widely read books on education of the 1960s. An evolving type of gestalt psychology was combined with the philosophy of John Dewey and others to form a potent guide to creating curriculum materials that were evidence-based, inquiry-oriented, and student-centered in powerful contrast to the teacher-centered, factual, textbook-driven instructional system of the 1950s. Sputnik, The Civil Rights Movement, and generous government funding for many National Science Foundations science and social science programs produced an outpouring of new materials and projects designed to enliven courses, particularly in science and math at the start, and spread to history and the social sciences, and much later, the humanities. A central idea was to involve students in the process of investigation and discovery imitating the research procedures and thinking of a scientist, historian, or social scientist (Bruner, 1969).

For me, the current era of education may very well be the third or fourth wave of "reform," now shaped by that first reform effort, that was the "new" social studies, as it developed in the 1960s after Sputnik, the 1957 Russian rocket launch that made Americans feel wonderfully nervous and competitive, suddenly interested in science, mathematics and then, a bit later, social science and history education.

In short, the era of Sputnik, The Civil Rights Movement, The Vietnam War, and President Johnson's "New Society" legislation spurred a re-examination of social, political, and educational practices and unleashed a wave of well-funded, underfunded, and nonfunded educational experimentation in almost all aspects of education that we take for granted today, for example, special education, concerns for diversity, civic education, and attention to public and private values and beliefs (p. 458). Over a decade or so, I was personally involved as an experimenting teacher with at least four of the major projects: The Chicago Anthropology Curriculum Study (ACSP), Sociological Resources for the Social Studies (SRSS), The High School Geography project, and The Human Sciences Program (BSCS).

Many new cutting edge ideas began to seep into the mainstream such as ideas like hands-on activities, investigative research, simulation games, debate on social issues, cooperative and group learning techniques, multitasking, and interdisciplinary frames of reference. The social studies received many of these thanks to the leadership of the sciences but has rarely acknowledged the debt or identified the sources of innovation. Slowly, slowly, textbooks altered their composition to include more and more of the new trends, trying to incorporate and encapsulate all of the above within the traditional twenty pound slick voluminous covers on one weighty book, eventually progressing to packages of multimedia components of which the book was but a centerpiece.

Thus, I begin with a positive feeling in favor of my early "new" social studies experience as truly creative and rigorous, with all but a few efforts after that paling by degrees up to the present. The current period has qualities that disturbingly remind me of 1950s and early 60s conformity in thinking (including primitive teaching machines, now morphed into sophisticated models), and frozen social relations, as well as the 1980s push toward standards and standardization, though without much quality control save for mass testing. And those big, heavy, backbreaking school textbooks are back, somewhat improved (having taken in the reforms of the 60s and 70s), yet still basically catering to those who view knowledge as didactic and cumulative rather than reflective and problematical. There are some bright spots, of course, particularly the return to teaching history as process, not just as content, based on primary and secondary sources that combine to provoke thought about historical habits of mind and persisting social, political, and economic issues (Levstik & Barton, 2001).

My Origins in Theory and Practice: The Matter of Inquiry

As a teaching philosophy the inquiry method laid out a Deweyan argument that student motivation could and should be aroused by offering real problems to work out (Kaplan, 2002). Problem solving proceeded by a process of shared discussion, negotiation, questioning, and analysis. Inquiry demanded a knowledge base, skills of reflection, and a willingness to extend debate from the lowest levels of factual accuracy through reasoned argument to value conflicts and conflict resolution (Dewey, 1901). Deeply embedded in this philosophy was the idea of a kind of Socratic conversation that, unlike Socrates himself (as reported by Plato), seriously invited, allowed, and supported students in thinking aloud about their own ideas and views, independent of the teacher's goals, and most particularly without the necessity for any teacher approved "right" answers at the end of a lesson (Dewey, 1912).

Inquiry was, I now see clearly, a radical view of instruction in that it "de-centered" the teacher, giving the teacher more of a role as guide, coach, and devil's advocate than as a lecturer, walking encyclopedia, or dictator. The burden of solution and debate was placed upon the students' shoulders, provoked and sustained by a complex series of behaviors that depended on questioning, using students' ideas, reward (not much punishment, sorry), and direction (but not to a particular sought-after conclusion). "The authors endorse the position that in a democratically oriented community characterized by cultural pluralism every person should be given a chance to contribute his views on controversial social issues" (Massials & Cox, 1966, p. 174). In effect, inquiry was a process, a theory, and a praxis for guiding student learning in the path of finding, analyzing, shaping, and solving problems using their own and their peers' knowledge and skills (Bruner, 1969). The teacher was supposed to prod and provoke, not supply easy answers to problems, and certainly not shape the particulars of the outcome (Newmann, 1970). This had the advantage of engaging students with ideas and information in ways they perhaps had never experienced, but which empowered them to work it out together, or on their own, using their own ideas and interpretations, but guided by an instructor. Many versions of inquiry had, and still have a variety of labels that are more like brand names than basic product differences. Inquiry, practiced honestly, is still much the same heady elixir of discovery, the quest itself perhaps more important than the actual find (Nosich, 2001).

Sometimes, inquiry was termed problem solving, other times discovery, and frequently viewed as "inductive" reasoning or critical thinking (Hammer, 1997). All of these terms seem to be very much in evidence these days, as well as in their time of origin. One has only to Google the idea, and lo and behold, you find a great deal of current work applying inquiry to science, mathematics, social studies, and many other fields (Chard, 2004). There were disputed areas of definition and styles, but overall, I would argue that all the processes shared a strong set of common characteristics favoring creative solutions, publicly shared reason and debate, and an inclination to examine the ethical and value foundations underpinning contrasting views and interpretations of history and the social sciences (Haas, 1977). The sciences inspired the model for gathering evidence and looking for patterns, but dealt poorly with value issues and controversies, subjectivity and objectivity, which carried over into the social sciences and the social studies, where many did a much better job on ethical questions (Oliver & Shaver, 1967).

As you might expect, in a culture emerging from a happy period of peace and conformity, and moving into an upsetting shift in government policy, race relations, social change, and cultural fermentation, the idea that teachers *should not* control the outcomes of thinking and should purposely back away from giving direct answers was somewhat of a shocker to many pedagogues at the time. Inquiry, however, was a way of fighting the boredom and alienation that many of us grew up within typical social studies and history classrooms where lessons were laid out nicely, logically, chronologically, and authoritatively in a clear linear fashion with little variation or room for disagreement.

As the rhyme goes, "Columbus sailed the ocean blue in 1492" to which an inquiry approach added the line, "but someone was already here!" The 'Big Idea" in inquiry was that everything was on the table for discussion, no matter how challenging, unpopular, upsetting, or unusual, as long as thinking was based on a groundwork of evidence, public reasoning, and an honest expression of values and assumptions.

You must keep in mind that inquiry was and is the descendant of a long line of democratic philosophies in which the training of citizens takes place through public debate and discussion of the issues. Earlier periods of social change also had their exponents of new and provocative ideas, many still read and cherished in education such as Harold Rugg, George S. Counts, and Ralph Tyler (Tyler, 1950). Participants are to be prepared for a give and take of ideas and arguments respectful of differences and different viewpoints. How can children and youth, you might ask, be raised as good citizens if they cannot think for themselves, judge fact from opinion, reasoning from propaganda, and ethics from interests? Inquiry as a teaching philosophy and practice sought to provide a teacher with

the training and skills needed to foster intellectual and moral development without preaching, but through a kind of discovery and investigative
process (Morrissett, 1967). It is the students who must be facilitated to discover answers and questions for themselves, not simply be provided such
by their loving and overly directive teacher.

At its heart, citizenship is born of decision making and debate, reflection and analysis, not by creating dependency (Engle, 1966). This is not
to say, of course, that teachers cannot stake out positions for themselves,
give answers, show students how to conduct research, or organize an argument. These normal acts are still part of everyday teaching. In an inquiry
structure, however, the students must arrive at their own answers and
decisions for their own reasons, not simply conform to the given wisdom
of the day or to a teacher's grasp of what is correct.

> In the past error was tolerated because error would only corroborate an
> already known and consistent body of truth, or because persecution of error
> would simply strengthen its proponents, or because error could never
> defeat invincible truth. But the modern rationale takes the view that all
> beliefs are tentatively true or false and only verifiable through a continuous
> process of inquiry. Therefore, all errors must be tolerated as tentative
> hypotheses in the search for reliable knowledge and valid belief. (Massialas
> & Cox, 1966, p. 295)

Explicitly, Massialas and Cox's idea of toleration means that teachers will
have to stand for a great deal of error in student research and review until
progress is made in arriving at a fairly well validated conclusion, one
based on a good enough sample of data, and strong enough reasons, to
survive contestation and cross-examination. No easy matter in a teaching
world based largely on the command, "Tell, lecture, pontificate: don't
ask!"

Deciding to Teach

As a young man growing up on the South Side of Chicago, I went to a
very ordinary high school where intellectuals went unloved except by a few
caring teachers and counselors. Nearing graduation, my counselor
decided that I should apply to the University of Chicago, a college that in
current parlance, I considered quite a "reach." This great lady insisted my
mother fill out all the papers and off it went to admissions. We had trouble making the application fees although they were small compared to the
present charges.

I was bowled over when accepted with a full scholarship. Off I went,
only to find myself in an atmosphere so intellectual it took my breath

away, causing adjustment problems for a year or 2. Upon graduation, after dabbling in social science, history, biology, and biopsychology, I was unsure of what to with myself, but was attracted by an announcement that fabulous scholarships were available in the School of Education for a master of arts in teaching degree, paid for by the federal government to create scholars and teachers who would help us "beat the Russians." Again I applied, this time entirely under my own volition, and was again accepted into the heady atmosphere of educational arguments, change, 1960s social movements, a newly born sense of race relations, and a newfound caring for the "underpriviledged" in our society (Kozol, 1967). This caring for less advantaged is very much a current issue as well since the overall structure of society doesn't seem to have altered all that much (Kozol, 2007).

It was into this flux that I prepared to be a teacher and met many of the key players in my educational life, including Professor Byron Massialas, one of the leaders of the MAT program at the University of Chicago, and members of the newly funded Anthropology Curriculum Study Project (ACSP, 1965-1970). This was an National Science Foundation (NSF) funded "alphabet soup" project modeled after a science program. It was with Massialas that I was introduced to the "inquiry method" of teaching, bolstered by rich and complex readings from Dewey, Bruner, Bloom, and other key contributors to the field of education.

I was strongly encouraged to begin experimenting with curriculum melding social studies and science, history and literature, even during student teaching, and carried this into my first position in the Chicago public schools. I wrote a book with Massialas on my classroom experiments, many of the lessons based on, or drawn from, ACSP curriculum, new social studies ideas, and NSF project materials (Massials & Zevin, 1967). Thus, the first 3 years of teaching on the South Side were influenced by my university and project training, bolstered by thousands of dollars worth of the most unusual materials I had ever seen. These materials included an entire course on "early man" followed by one on the "agricultural revolution," and "the first cities," which were followed by supplements and contacts with other projects in the NSF network.

Chicago Public Schools

I took the anthropology materials, the spirit of the new social studies, and myself into the high schools of the South Side of Chicago with all their attendant problems and prospects, as unlikely a place to try the great experiment as any you might think of today.

However, the anthropology folks, to their credit, wanted teachers to try the stuff out with ordinary students, not necessarily the elite. Many of my students were not only ordinary, but had problems: reading, social, writing, listening, behavioral, critical thinking, the whole range, but perhaps with different and less euphemistic labels than those currently in vogue.

The wonder is that while I was conscious that the students had many learning and personal problems, I proceeded anyway, with unusual results and feedback. Though many of the anthropology materials could be technical and wordy, scientifically cautious, and discovery-oriented, my students, for the most part, attended to their lessons and rarely cut class as they did for many of my colleagues. I attributed this to the striking and dramatic qualities of the materials, so unlike the "usual" and to my brash adherence to 'inquiry method' come hell or high water. Between me throwing out lots of questions and doing almost constant activities, supported by wild materials like a human Neanderthal skull (dubbed "Yorik"), stone tools, tool-making chimpanzee films by Jane Goodall, and site maps of archeological finds, most students were entranced even if they didn't quite know what was going on. It sure beat memorizing the dynasties of ancient Egypt, labeling places in the ancient world that had funny sounds like Cisalpine Gaul, or naming the rivers and towns in The Fertile Crescent, or intoning the litany of "the three branches of government" and the "causes of the Civil War."

My Perceptions of The New Social Studies

At the time of my induction into the ASCP, I had no particular views on what was or wasn't possible to do with kids. I was possessed of an idealism supplied by the professors and project leaders I worked with who were in wholehearted agreement with Jerome Bruner's incredibly optimistic dictum that "any idea can be taught to anyone in an intellectually honest way" (Bruner, 1962). Once I was on the job, I rapidly came to realize that only a portion of the teachers agreed with the ideas I espoused, and that I was unusual in terms of teaching philosophy. Certainly, in terms of what I was using in my classroom, I was rather "off beat." Many displayed a somber and largely pessimistic mood, what they called "realistic," meaning that they were not all that pleased with the students, the social upheaval, or newfangled pedagogues. It was thus that I was introduced into a field where there was no cutting edge at all, social studies, and for which we were supplying a new and very strong yeast to see what kind of a rise we would get for our effort.

So I think it is a fair question to ask just what was the cutting edge, don't you agree?

The much ballyhooed and admired push for better history teaching, in recent years offering their techniques and methods to school youth is an echo of these earlier attempts to promote the process of inquiry rather than focus simply on product (Fenton, 1967). Reflection trumped mere knowledge, providing students with the data and wherewithal to develop and test their own hypotheses [up to a point] (Fenton, 1966). There was a good deal of debate about structured and unstructured learning, open and closed questioning, and a great deal of debate about scientific method and whether that was objective or included value components (Simon, Howe, & Kirschenbaum, 1972). As these debates got under way and flourished through the 1960s and 70s, the social sciences and history, call it social studies, began to diverge or fragment with distinct philosophical movements developing. My view is that these movements generally split in two directions: one tending toward frank and outspoken discussions of values, issues, and controversies as a core, and the other tending in toward reflective scientific investigation that treated knowledge as evidence open to interpretation (Allen, Fleckenstein, & Lyons, 1968). A few holdouts continued to promote facts, didactic instruction, and narrative history, but this group became a distinct minority among the social studies professoriate. However, even with all this innovation and tumult, teachers on the whole remained devoted to their textbooks, their tests, and their traditional lessons delivered as packaged products in neat lectures and discussions, but which lacked the sense of scientific probabilistic reasoning that characterized so much of the new social studies and the new sciences (Cuban, 1986).

Though most teachers like to stay within their subjects, much of the new social studies crossed the boundaries of one or more disciplines, advocating interdisciplinary studies. Most teachers wanted to engage students' attention and beat the Russians with dazzling displays of knowledge and skill, but were uncomfortable with turning reasoning and conclusion power over to their charges. Most teachers valued evidence and primary sources, experimentation, and discovery, but were not quite sure how to implement these components into a system that demanded coverage and tested facts. The connection between inductive and deductive reasoning was unclear, and the increasing lobby for discussing values and issues made them nervous, with of course the exception of a large minority. Most continued to serve and laud Caesar, only questioning relatively safe social issues, such as class and race, both of which became much more open in the era of the civil rights and antiwar movements.

THE ANTHROPOLOGICAL CURRICULUM STUDY PROJECT
AND OTHER INVENTIONS

Into this heady mix of innovation and traditionalism motivated by often competing, sometimes overlapping philosophies and special interests, with the blessings of professional organizations, in this case the American Anthropological Association School curricula, were debated, designed, funded, and implemented across the nation.

As a young teacher in Chicago's South Side, I was working at a local high school when I was approached with an offer I could not pass up to implement a new curriculum designed to teach about "early man" in a scientific way that gave students the chance to make up their own minds about the meaning of the evidence, with a little help from their friends, and the anthropologists who created the lessons, units, and courses. Of course, I raised my hand, and said, "Yes, indeed, I will try it out for you."

So during my second year as a teacher, I became the most widely recognized weirdo in my school building as I presented lessons on the nature of scientific thinking, human evolution, Neolithic technology and religious beliefs (insofar as we could infer these), the agricultural revolution, the rise of cities, and the development of states and empires.

My course was as different as different could be from the standard of the times which is STILL pretty much standard, that is, early humans, a day or two on prehistoric people, a couple of days on ancient river valley civilizations, maybe several days on the fertile crescent, and ancient Greece and Rome in a week or two. WE dug in, sometimes literally, to the skulls of Australopithecus, Neanderthal, and Cro-Magnon, measuring skull capacities, estimating brain size, examining stone tool casts, comparing manufacturing techniques, making flints ourselves, going out on a dig, etc. If I couldn't find bus money for a field trip, then I buried stuff in the school lawn (over official objections) and took the kids out on a mock dig which did lead to conversations about stratification and identification, comparing flints, potsherds, or whatever else I had to bury, and concluding with talk about the nature of evidence-based inferential thinking.

The vast majority of students may not have understood at first what I was asking or talking about but they loved working with their hands, making their own decisions, and being treated as scientific equals in the voyage of discovery.

Some even began to read their newspapers, senior scholastics, and a few even went out and BOUGHT a Scientific American or two. The curriculum created its own discipline as naughty "in-your-face" students were not permitted to work with delicate or unusual specimens or handle plaster cast skulls. As the year wore on, I became less inhibited, trying out all sorts of group arrangements and cooperative learning ideas, creating my own versions of procedures or readings I thought impractical or difficult. We almost never had a lecture. Always there was stuff to look at, touch, think about, and I was there, prodding with questions, ideas, complaints, issues, rarely supplying answers. Some students became aggravated, others exhausted, but this only seemed to make me more playful, particularly since I was buoyed by thousands and thousands of dollars worth of the most wonderfully wacky curriculum materials, like a site map of an entire cache of tools from Torralba, Spain, my own set of clay tablets with cuneiform writing (thankfully translated), and a copy of Samuel Noah Kramer's book, "The Sumerians," including blanks for practice!

Thus, the first 3 years of teaching on the South Side were influenced by my university and project training, bolstered by thousands of dollars worth of the most unusual materials I had ever seen. These materials included an entire course on "early man" followed by one on the "agricultural revolution," and "the first cities," which were followed by supplements and contacts with other projects in the NSF network.

Favorites and Failures

My affair with the anthropology project went on for 2 years and my course covered human evolution and cultural development from the apes to the earliest known "humans," and on to Greeks and Romans, which is about where I remember stopping. Much has been lost and I left most of my best and least portable materials to my successor, never knowing quite what has ever happened to those lovely things. But many lessons stand out in my mind as great successes and others as failures for a variety of reasons. Anthropologists, like all historians and social scientists, can be verbose and obscure, given to the language of scientific caution and technicality, resulting in long, long readings that my students did not like at all. However, anthropologists also loved "arrays," trays of finds, charts and graphs, pictures and drawings, and models of specimens carefully and exactly molded to duplicate the real things. These visual, tactile, and manipulative lessons almost always met with great enthusiasm and participation.

Two stand out in my mind right now. One was quite a simple set of drawings of hominid skulls, pictures on the front, and descriptions on the back, with a set of activities for the teacher. Most of these activities involved comparison and contrast, such as, measuring the size and shape of skulls, estimating brain size, measuring the size and number and kinds of dentition, jaw size and shape, and overall structure. The gorilla was compared with modern humans, with students receiving tracing paper to outline the gorilla and then overlay that on and outline modern man. I

got to ask questions about size, shape, contour, potential muscle placement, brain size, as the students and I began to verbalize differences and
similarities, leading eventually to an overall set of inferences about people
and our big furry cousins. The students loved this and, as the week went
on, we added other skull drawings for as many specimens as they could
think about between gorillas and modern people with a lot of attention to
Homo erectus and Homo neanderthalensis. We had fun drawing possible
faces, and making wild generalizations. No one was bored.

A second favorite that my wife and I used for many years after to provide a sense of a "dig" was a lesson called "Mystery at Torralba," which
was composed of a series of three "investigations" based on actual site
maps done by archeologists in Spain during a 1962–63 excavation on a
plateau that was apparently once a favorite hunting and killing ground
for very early peoples then labeled "Homo erectus," who seemed able to
make fires. The evidence consisted of a lot of animal bones and human
tools, but no human bodies. Bones and stones were scattered around in
clumps across a wide swath of ground, and students were presented with
several charts, called plates, showing location, variety, and overall distribution of artifacts. One investigation focused on tools and the other
mainly on animal remains. A third attempted to integrate all of the findings and help students reach general conclusions about early people,
their eating habits and technology. Casts of tools accompanied the drawn
images, and despite my skepticism that students would become frustrated
with the "mystery," they did not and dutifully counted and classified frag-
ments. The goal of the mystery was to encourage inferences about our
ancestors based both on what was there and what was missing. One mystery was why there were non-human bones found with the animal remains
and another mystery is why they abandoned their tools. My students saw
other mysteries as well, such as why was there a variety of tools for different purposes, why they had favorite quarry (cows, elephants, horses, and
deer), why they butchered in a place they did not live in, and other minor
issues. Answers as well as questions exceeded expectations in what I saw as
a conceptually sophisticated problem and students enjoyed having a set of
maps and plates of their own to play with individually and later in small
groups, readily sorting data and developing hypotheses which they tested
against each other just in the way the project hoped young citizen social
scientists would carry out. In short we had a model lesson.

Short-Term Impact

For me, the short-term impact was dramatic! I found a method,
materials, and a project that was engaging, interesting, and drew my

students almost effortlessly into discussion and debate. Even the classes dubbed "slower" in those days, generally responded enthusiastically to the inquiry process and were excited by the prospect that they were partners in classroom and field investigations, partners whose views were taken seriously. They were made comfortable, I later concluded, by my "inquiry" manner inviting their ideas, legitimized by verbal encouragement and the recognition and use of their contributions to the classroom discussion. Ideas were the classroom currency that counted, and those of us experimenting with inquiry tried as hard as we could to keep lines of communication open and resist the "teacher disease," that is, providing nicely rounded conclusions.

Lessons were often messy affairs with give and take starting in an orderly manner with hands raised and slowly heating up into a complex argument with multiple speakers, often relieving me of the need to intervene at all. The aim, as I interpreted inquiry was to foster as much quality and quantity in terms of student ideas and participation as possible, and this meant focusing on a problem, aided by thought-provoking questions, while keeping lecture and direction-giving to a minimum. Playing with ideas, play as an activity, was part of the process (Youngquist & Pataray-Ching, 2004).

> It is claimed that the highest state of human autonomy and perfection is achieved when the individual begins to discover for himself regularities or irregularities in his physical and sociopolitical environments. In this sense the process of discovery also serves as a potent motivational device. When the individual is involved in discovery, motivation for learning comes from within, rather than being imposed from without. (Massialas & Cox, 1966, p. 137)

I often recorded student conversations, later used in a book, an 'action' research process that was fairly common within the inquiry movement. After all, we all wanted to know if our method was working and one way of finding out was to record and analyze classroom thinking from the students. The shape, breadth, and depth of a lesson was one way of assessing progress, often measured in terms of Bloom's taxonomies, Newmann's (1988) levels of thoughtfulness, and other criteria (Newmann, 1988).

In the field, insofar as I experienced a wider impact, usually from NCSS and regional conferences, or at Anthropology Curriculum Study meetings, there was a strong tendency to value and encourage much greater student participation, even in classroom governance, than was common before this time. Along with the new emphasis on participation, was a push for higher quality thinking, focused on problems, both intellectual and ethical. Students were asked much more regularly to express and defend their views, preferably supported by good reasons and evidence. There was a growing sense that classrooms should not only permit, but also demand the expression of views, across a broad range of fields, history, economics, anthropology, geography, sociology, and so forth.

The inquiry process, as pedagogy, supported and was supported by curricula that followed a much stronger science and values examination approach than characterized what might be called "traditional" classrooms. Nearly all inquiry teaching that I carried out and that I had the chance to observe in local schools or at conventions and conferences began with primary sources of great variety using all kinds of media: film, song, story, historical documents, art, photographs, maps, and statistics. This was combined with secondary scholarly and textual sources, but what drove the field, what most teachers who professed an inquiry approach loved to play with were primary sources. I accumulated a garage full of sources myself and still treasure new collections of sources, particularly those that fill in a missing area like Islamic translations, or African literature, or ancient Incan poetry and song. These sources were edited and structured for classroom use that promoted inquiry around a problem or big idea of some kind that students and teacher had to "translate," analyze, and summarize before finally coming to tentative conclusions about meaning and message, intent and values orientation.

Long-Term Effects

Despite some general opprobrium concerning the effects, short-term and long-term of the inquiry method and the new social studies on the entire K–college field, I strongly believe that the impact has been more powerful, widespread, and subtle than is generally given credit for by critics and those who witnessed its supposed demise (Gordon, 2004).

The gist of most of the criticism at the time of the great cutting edge of inquiry rested on three pillars of evidence.

The first pillar of criticism raised the issue of difficulty. An inquiry method was seen as relatively difficult to put into practice by most teachers on a daily basis compared with conventional methods like chalk and talk. This was because of its student-centeredness, and its philosophical commitment to the negotiation of knowledge. In effect, nothing was exempted from examination because it demanded a great deal of ad hoc "thinking on your feet." Oh dear! Worry, worry, worry, about the students' coming to the "right" conclusions (Hahn, Marker, Switzer, & Turner, 1977).

The second pillar of criticism raised the issue of complexity and elitism, mostly aimed at the programs and materials invented to promote inquiry. These critics contended that the materials demanded high reading levels, deep insight, and critical thinking that was above the head of the "average" student. Some of this criticism was probably correct, but why should not the higher-level students benefit from a tough program that others might shun? Some of the programs such as the Harvard series of pamphlets on persisting issues designed by Oliver and Shaver were direct, easy to read, brief, and presented in a friendly newspaper format, while at the same time asking some very provocative questions about political, social, and economic issues (Sanders & Tanck, 1970).

The third pillar of criticism raised the issue of relativism, in contrast to the prevailing essentialism that has long characterized American education, arguing that inquiry could destabilize cherished beliefs in citizenship and values (Newmann, 2002). This is a kind of classic argument about 'cloistered virtues' going all the way back to John Milton's day, but always meets a sympathetic audience that does not particularly want the schools to debate accepted norms and virtues. Milton argued then, as others do now, that ideas have to stand up to the competition of the marketplace in a free society or they will breed authoritarianism and control, or worse, a very inquiry type of philosophical commitment to free speech (Selwyn & Maher, 2003).

Classic tensions have always existed in our democracy between free speech and conformity, between free thought and control, with the pendulum of expression and repression swinging with the temper of the times (Greenwood, Mann, & McLaughlin, 1975). For a subject like social studies, with citizenship education at its very core, the problem of fostering free discussion, and looking at primary sources, eyewitness accounts, and making up one's own mind about issues, problems, controversies, and choices, inquiry may be viewed as an important way to deal with claims for truth in a classroom that privileges no one (Patrick, 1969). Of course, if a teacher, school, community, or nation expect and demand only one "right" outcome in any debate or topic, then inquiry becomes disturbing and controversial, though it was born as an idea out of American pragmatism.

It is evident that inquiry and the "new" social studies had a considerable long-term impact on our field and science education if you take the time to look for the evidence of its distribution and retention in our memories and practices (Nosich, 2001). For example, most U.S. and World History texts now include primary sources and provocative questions about these side-by-side with the standard textual narratives and timelines. Some texts are more open-minded than others and present greater quantities of evidence to use, often even providing media and literature as supplements. Throughout the field, the newest research and practice on how students think about and develop a sense of history is mainly concerned with interpretations of primary sources, or primary sources in relation to secondary, with a strong emphasis on student understanding and decision-making In my view, this an inquiry lineage, supported by bibliographies and references that consciously go back to earlier models and sources (Barlowe, 2004).

While many teachers have always lectured, and still do, most know that other methods and styles are available for inclusion in their overall arsenal (Cuban, 1986). Ideas such as simulations, debates, panel discussions, research projects, discussions, are widely employed if not pervasively so (Wallace, 2002). Of course, much depends on the way in which any of these are conducted, whether the students manage their own ideas or the teacher does it for them. Nonetheless, the existence of a great many of these techniques and strategies grew out of examples developed in the 60s and 70s that have become part and parcel of current teaching practices, although not dominant (Bennett, Joyce, & Showers, 1987).

The professoriate, those who are social studies educators at this very point in history, exude a general agreement and tone of approval for teaching primary sources, advocating problem solving, critical thinking, different forms of inquiry, debate and discussion, much more strongly and frequently than those who advocate lecture or chalk and talk (Cuban, 1991). Now you said this earlier so again, consolidate to put it all in one place so it flows. That might mean cutting out some stuff from the earlier portion and leaving it all here under the anthropology project. That is because most of the professoriate today, in my view, are descended from others in the field who were advocates of inquiry, discovery, problem-solving, and alternative educational methods that promote student thinking as much if not more so than student acquisition of knowledge. The political and social "heart" of social studies education, marches to a beat that was formed during the age of the 'new' social studies because that was our "cutting edge," the period in which important ideas and philosophies, methods and strategies, were given voice, debated, and reviewed, forming a powerful influence on the present. Consciousness and memory weaken, however, and in some cases, our culture seeks to create discontinuities that hide or shunt aside important problems and issues that are disturbing to think about, or which were never quite solved to our satisfaction.

However, I think that these issues and problems return and will continue to return, because they have never been solved. It is much better to build links to the traditions of our own past professionalism rather than be condemned to repeat both the mistakes and discoveries anew in this, the Age of Testing, the Age of Standards, and the Age of (Attempted) uniformity.

EPILOGUE

To return to the training and ideas I received during my first encounter with inquiry, I would like to end with a quote I've always liked, to wit: "The climate of the reflective classroom is psychologically open and permissive. All points of view and statements are solicited and accepted as propositions which merit examination" (Massialas & Cox, 1966, p. 112). In other words, pay attention to and respect students' ideas, stimulate their thinking, and be ready for some knock down, drag out, arguments, and be ready to tolerate a lot of views you don't like, OK? Let's *bring a new cutting-edge* to social studies, one that is dynamic and organic, rather modeled after industry.

REFERENCES

The Anthropology Curriculum Study Project. (1965–1970). *Chicago Studies Project, Early Man, The Agricultural Revolution, and other units.* Chicago: American Anthropological Association

Allen, R. F., Fleckenstein, J. V., & Lyons, P. M. (Eds.). (1968). *Inquiry in the social studies.* Washington, DC: National Council for the Social Studies.

Barlowe, A. (2004). *Teaching American history: an inquiry approach.* New York: Teachers College Press.

Bennett, B., Joyce, B., & Showers, B. (1987) Synthesis of research on staff development: A future study and a state-of-the-art analysis. *Educational Leadership, 45,* 77–87.

Bruner, J. (1962). *The process of education.* Cambridge, MA: Harvard University Press

Bruner, J. (1969). *Toward a theory of instruction.* Cambridge, MA: Harvard University Press

Chard, S. (2004). How to develop an inquiry-based project. *The YouthLearn Initiative.* Retrieved June 30, 2004, from http://www.youthlearn.org/learning/activities/howto.asp

Cuban, L. (1986). Persistent instruction: Another look at constancy in the classroom. *Phi Delta Kappan, 68*(1), 7–11.

Cuban, L. (1991). History of teaching in social studies. In J. Shaver (Ed.), *Handbook of research on social studies teaching and learning* (pp. 197–209). New York: Macmillan

Dewey, J. (1901). *How we think.* New York: MacMillan.

Dewey, J. (1912). *Democracy and education.* New York: MacMillan.

Engle, S. (1960, November). Decision-making: The heart of social studies. *Social Education, 24*(7), 301–306.

Fenton, E. (1966). *Teaching the New Social Studies in secondary schools.* New York: Holt, Rinehart, and Winston.

Fenton, E. (1967). *The New Social Studies.* New York: Holt, Rinehart, and Winston.

Fenton, E. (1991). Reflections on the "New Social Studies." *The Social Studies*, *82*(3), 84–91.

Gordon, K. (2004). Practical ways to use inquiry approaches in the classroom. *Primary and Middle Years Educator*, 1.2 (2003): 15–19. *Academic Search Premier*. EBSCOhost. BGSU Firelands College Lib., Huron, OH. Retrieved June 21, 2004, from http://80-search.epnet.com.proxy.ohiolink.edu: 9099/direct.asp?an=1076097 0&db=aph

Greenwood, P. W., D. Mann, & McLaughlin, W. M. (1975). *Federal programs supporting educational change: The process of change* (Vol. III). Santa Monica, CA: The Rand Corporation.

Hahn, C. L., Marker, G. W., Switzer, T. M., & Turner, M. J. (1977). *Three studies on perception and utilization of "New Social Studies," materials*. Boulder, CO: Social Science Education Consortium.

Hammer, D. (1997). Discovery learning and discovery teaching. *Cognition and Instruction, 15*(4), 485–521.

Haas, J. D. (1977). *The era of the new social studies*. Boulder, CO: Social Science Education Consortium.

Heath, R. W. (1964). *New curricula*. New York: Harper & Row

Herbert, L. J., & Murphy, W. (Eds.). (1968). *Structure in the social studies*. Washington, DC: National Council for the Social Studies.

Hunt, H. C. (Ed.). (1962). *High school social studies perspectives*. Boston: Houghton-Mifflin.

Kaplan, J. (2002). John Dewey at the beach. *Kappa Delta Pi Record, 38*(4), 156–159. *ERIC Document Reproduction Service* EJ656611.

Kozol, J. (1967). *Death at an early age*. Boston: Houghton-Mifflin.

Kozol, J. (2007). *Letters to a young teacher*. New York: Crown.

Levstik, L., & Barton, K. (2001). *Doing history: Investigating with children in elementary and middle school* (2nd ed.). New Jersey: Erlbaum.

Massialas, B. G., & Cox, B. (1966). *Inquiry in social studies*. New York: McGraw-Hill.

Massialas, B. G., & Zevin, J. (1967). *Creative encounters in the classroom*. New York: Wiley.

Morrisett, I. (Ed.) (1967). *Concepts and structure in the New Social Science curricula*. New York: Holt, Rinehart, and Winston.

Newmann, F. M. (1970). *Clarifying public controversy: An approach to teaching social studies*. Boston: Little Brown

Newmann, F. M. (1988). Can depth replace coverage in the high school curriculum? *Phi Delta Kappan, 69*(5), 345–348.

Newmann, F. M. (2002). *Authentic pedagogy*.

Nosich, G. (2001). *Learning to think things through: A guide to critical thinking across the curriculum*. New Jersey: Prentice Hall.

Oliver, D., & Shaver, J. (1967). *Teaching public issues in the high school*. Boston: Houghton-Mifflin

Patrick, J. J. (1969). Implications of political socialization research for the reform of civic education. *Social Education, 33*, 15–21.

Rodgers, C. (2002), Defining reflection: Another look at John Dewey and reflective thinking. *Teachers College Record, 104*(4), 842–866. *ERIC Document Reproduction Service* EJ651409.

Sanders, N. M., & Tanck, M. L. (1970). A critical appraisal of twenty-six national social studies projects. *Social Education, 34*(Special Issue).

Selwyn, D., & Maher, J. (2003). *History in the present tense: Engaging students through inquiry and action.* New Hampshire: Heinemann.

Shaver, J. P., Davis, O. L.., Jr., & Helburn, S. W. . (1979). The status of social studies education: Impressions from three NSF studies. *Social Education, 43,* 150–153.

Starnes, B. A. (1999). The Foxfire approach to teaching and learning: John Dewey, experiential learning and the core practices. *Office of Educational Research and Development.* ERIC Document Reproduction Service EDD00036.

Simon, S. B., Howe, L. W., & Kirschenbaum, H. (1972). *Values clarification: A handbook of practical strategies for teachers and students.* New York: Hart

Suchman, J. (1968). *Inquiry development program.* Washington, DC: National Science Foundation

Tower, C. (2004). Questions that matter: Preparing elementary students for the inquiry process. *Reading Teacher, 53*(7) (2000): 550-557. *Academic Search Premier.* EBSCOhost. BGSU Firelands College Lib., Huron, OH. Retrieved June 21 2004, from http://80-search.epnet.com.proxy.ohiolink.edu: 9099/direct.asp?an=2984309 &db=aph

Tyler, R. W. (1950). *Basic principles of curriculum and instruction.* Chicago: University of Chicago Press.

Wallace, B. (2002). Don't work harder! Work smarter! In B. Wallace & R. Bentley (Ed.), *Teaching thinking skills across the middle years: A practical approach for children aged 9–14* (pp. 1–24). London: David Fulton.

Wiggins, G. (1989). The futility of trying to teach everything of importance. *Educational Leadership, 47*(3) 44–59.

Wiley, K. B., & Superka D. P. (1967). *Evaluation studies on "New Social Studies" materials.* Boulder, CO: Social Science Education Consortium.

Youngquist, J., & Pataray-Ching, J. (2004). Revisiting "Play": Analyzing and articulating acts of inquiry. *Early Childhood Education Journal, 31*(3) 171–178.

Zerubavel, E. (2003). *Time maps: Collective memory and the social shape of the past.* Chicago: University of Chicago Press

CHAPTER 22

LEVERAGING TECHNOLOGY FOR STUDENT INQUIRY

Technology in the New Social Studies and Today

Meghan McGlinn Manfra

INTRODUCTION

In 1960, Jerome Bruner warned educators against viewing technology as a panacea for the ills of American education in *The Process of Education*. He wrote, "Unbridled enthusiasm for audio-visual aids or for teaching machines as panaceas overlooks the paramount importance of what one is trying to accomplish" (p. 88). Bruner believed technology would improve education if it was clearly linked to learning objectives and if teachers were adequately trained. He felt that social studies education should emphasize inquiry in an effort to instill in students the structure of the disciplines. Referring to *Man: A Course of Study* (MACOS), a New Social Studies project he developed, Bruner (1965) wrote:

The New Social Studies: People, Projects, and Perspectives, pp. 471–491
Copyright © 2010 by Information Age Publishing

> For it is only in a trivial sense that one gives a course "to get something across," merely to impart information.... Unless the learner also masters himself, disciplines his taste, deepens his view of the world, the "something" that is got across is hardly worth the effort of transmission. (p. 4)

He saw new technologies as an important tool in helping students develop inquiry-related skills. Bruner was one of the more well-known educators associated with the New Social Studies who addressed the integration of technology in the classroom. He was joined by others of his day, including Edwin Fenton, who believed that technology integration, when done well, could help teachers achieve the aims of the New Social Studies curriculum in their classrooms.

Today, educators still believe that harnessing the latest technological innovations for classroom outcomes will improve social studies teaching and learning. While most of these educators do not explicitly refer to Bruner and his colleagues, many of the themes of the New Social Studies appear in their work. In particular, there remains a continued concern to leverage technology to engage students in content instruction, inquiry-based learning, and citizenship education. Teachers continue to be recognized for their roles as curricula gatekeepers in the classroom.

This chapter provides a historic overview of technology integration in the New Social Studies projects of the 1960s and 1970s. In characterizing the materials used in the projects as "instructional technology" I refer to Cuban's (1986) definition: "What I define as useful instructional technology, then, is any device available to teachers for use in instructing students in a more efficient and stimulating manner than the sole use of the teacher's voice" (p. 4). This chapter also traces the implied and explicit contributions of the New Social Studies to current technology integration practices, specifically to highlight the continued emphasis on technology integration for content instruction, inquiry, citizenship education, and the role of the teacher as technological and pedagogical gatekeeper in the social studies. It describes the implications of this trend for the integration of new communication and social networking technologies in the social studies today. Finally a discussion of the limitations and critiques of both eras (of technology integration) is offered as a basis for suggestions regarding future practice.

The "New Social Studies" referred to a period of intense curriculum reform in the 1960s. It originated from criticism of the 1950's life adjustment curricula and an interest in reforming K–12 social studies curriculum (Bestor, 1953; Fenton, 1991; Rossi, 1992). The emergence of the New Social Studies coincided with the start of the Cold War. It was propelled by federal funding and resulted in an emphasis on the disciplines and problem-based learning or inquiry. It also coincided with similar reform efforts in science and math. The launch of the New Social Studies came after the Woods Hole Conference in 1959. According to Rossi:

> At the [Woods Hole] conference, Jerome Bruner supplied the psychological and educational rationale that was to influence the forthcoming social studies projects. He asserted that all disciplines have structures that tie knowledge together. The mastery of these structures involved an attitude of inquiry toward learning that allowed any subject to be effectively taught to a child. (n.p.)

A variety of "projects" emerged from the New Social Studies that shifted the emphasis towards developing a rational understanding of the structures of the disciplines that made up the social studies (Fenton, 1991; Goetz, 1994; Helburn, 1997). According to Beyer (1995), "Students, in effect, did history, did geography, did sociology" (p. 67). Evans (2004) maintained, "The aim of the New Social Studies movement was to 'transform ... students into junior historians and social scientists' " (p. 123). In his "memoir of a practitioner" Goetz recalled the excitement surrounding the New Social Studies and the feeling that it would "revolutionize" the curriculum. The curriculum projects of the New Social Studies emphasized "structure, inductive teaching, the disciplines, sequential learning, new types of materials, new subjects and emphasis on evaluation" (Evans, 2004, p. 127). In the New Social Studies, "structure" referred to the undergirding concepts and method of a discipline or the "body of imposed conceptions which define the investigated subject matter of the disciplines and control its inquiries" (Schwab, 1962, p. 199). Importantly, Bruner (1960) claimed students of any age could be taught social studies subjects in an authentic manner (p. 32). Added to this, Hilda Taba and colleagues introduced the notion of a spiral curriculum in which curriculum was repeated in a cycle of exposure and accommodation to new ideas (e.g., Taba, Durkin, McNaughton, & Fraenkel, 1967). Many of the projects of the New Social Studies, in order to facilitate student understanding of the disciplines, emphasized inquiry and discovery learning (Keller, 1974).

Two "streams" of curricular thought flowed through the New Social Studies (Rossi, 1992). The first stream focused on concepts, generalizations, and modes of inquiry within the disciplines (e.g., Bruner, 1965; Fenton, 1966, 1967). The second evolved as a way to emphasize reflective thinking to analyze social problems and value conflicts (e.g., Oliver & Newman, 1969; Oliver & Shaver, 1966). Technology, especially audiovisual, was used to meet the instructional goals of both "streams" of the New Social Studies.

The Role of Technology in the New Social Studies

The integration of technology in the New Social Studies reflected the general trend of the time period to bring audiovisual equipment and materials into all aspects of schooling (Cuban, 1986). Signaling an explicit interest in using audio-visual materials, two cinematographers were invited to participate in the Woods Hole Conference (Bruner, 1960). According to Fenton (1967), "Instead of relying solely on the printed word, the New Social Studies embrace[d] a systems approach with a heavy audiovisual component" (p. 111).

Due in large part to the space race and the Cold War, consumer access to new media increased throughout the 1960s. Technological competence and scientific knowledge were increasingly viewed as essential for American students. The National Defense Education Act (NDEA) of 1958 and the Ford Foundation's Fund for the Advancement of Education provided monies for the procurement of audiovisual equipment and materials (Bender & Conrad, 1983; Bruner, 1960; Cuban, 1986). According to Bender and Conrad it was common throughout the NDEA period for schools to promote the purchase and use of technology. They wrote, "Many administrators proudly pointed out their sparkling hardware as though it were the improvement of instruction rather than a tool to improve [instruction]" (p. 20). Of course, "technology" in the New Social Studies was not shorthand for "computer and digital technology" as it is today (Ceruzzi, 2005). Rather, audiovisual equipment and materials including film and film strip projectors, slide projectors and slides, opaque projectors, tape recorders and audio recordings, and educational television comprised the new technologies that were integrated into K–12 social studies classrooms.

These new technologies, especially audiovisual materials, were integrated into the New Social Studies projects in an effort to reform social studies teaching and learning. At the same time, audio-visuals were being integrated into the K–12 curriculum through programmed instruction. For instance, B.F. Skinner demonstrated his "teaching machine" at the Woods Hole conference (Bruner, 1960). While Skinner was interested in drill and practice capabilities of new technologies, the authors of the New Social Studies projects referred to technology as a means to promote inquiry-based learning (Bruner, 1960). Often film and other audiovisual materials were listed along-side paper materials such as text books and pamphlets in the curriculum materials of the New Social Studies. Technology was included to help students develop a deeper understanding of the disciplines and their structures, specifically to teach the basic conceptual understandings of the disciplines, the processes or paths of inquiry to uncovering these understandings, and the values relevant to the social studies.

Technology for Basic Conceptual Understanding

Technology was integrated in the New Social Studies to teach students basic concepts of the disciplines. For instance, film strips and sound tracks, according to Fenton (1967) "bombard the senses with data" and "cover a wide range of material in very short order" (p. 72). New media, while exposing students to factual content in new ways, also expanded the curricular choices of teachers. According to Bruner (1960), "Some of them [film strips and audio recordings] are designed to present material to the student of a kind that would not be available to him in his ordinary school experience" (p. 81). For example, Bruner's (1965) "Man: A Course of Study" (MACOS) was a fifth-grade course designed to introduce students to key concepts related to anthropology. Rather than use a traditional textbook, the curriculum relied heavily on film and pamphlets to simulate field experiences (Fenton, 1991; Woolfson, 1974). Similarly, the High School Geography Project included a variety of new technology in its list of resources, including uncaptioned filmstrips, audio recordings, and sound filmstrips (Helburn, 1998). The advent of public television also influenced the types of materials used to teach content knowledge in the K–12 classroom and expanded the curricular options. For example, instructional television contributed to the development of anthropology courses for secondary students (Dynneson, 1981).

Audiovisual equipment and materials were integrated into the curricular projects of the New Social Studies to help students develop content knowledge (Bruner, 1960; Lichtenberg & Fenton, 1969). Technology, in this case, expanded the curriculum options and made content instruction more efficient. Summarizing the New Social Studies view of audio-visual materials, Lichtenberg and Fenton wrote, "If the sole objective is the mastery of a pre-selected body of facts and generalizations, then a film or a sound filmstrip designed for expository teaching may be appropriate" (p. 396). Within the New Social Studies, however, mastery of facts and generalizations was buttressed by inquiry-based learning.

Technology and Inquiry

The New Social Studies projects emphasized an inquiry-oriented approach to teaching the disciplines that enabled students to understand the structure of the disciplines (Fenton, 1966, 1967; Helburn, 1997; Suchman, 1966). According to Fenton (1967), "Unless students also learn the method of inquiry, they cannot continue to learn independently once the classroom door shuts behind them for the last time" (p. 7). The inquiry process included forming hypotheses and applying logic to solve problems. In the New Social Studies, inquiry was viewed as inherently related to the structure of the disciplines that made up the social studies. According to Fenton, "In layman's language structure consists of a method of inquiry made up of two parts: the formation of a hypotheses and the process of proof" (p. 12). Within the New Social Studies audio-visual materials were leveraged to teach students the skills of inquiry. Single concept filmstrips or overhead projectors and transparencies were used to begin inductive lessons (Bruner, 1960; Fenton 1967; Lichtenberg & Fenton, 1969). In one representative example, a filmstrip on slavery was included to engage students in discussion:

> The unit [on slavery] began with the filmstrip on the slave trade but instead of the usual statement by the teacher of "we see here," which is usually followed by an explanation of what is before the students, the teacher asked, "What do you see?" and 'What do you know about slavery from what you see?' A filmstrip originally scheduled for one or two classes was used in four. (Lord, 1969, p. 27)

Learning activities like the one described above were intended to lead to individual student research and further inquiry. Here technology was used to elicit student hypotheses and opinions. This technique was repeated in many of the New Social Studies manuals and projects. According to Bruner (1960):

> In sum, then, there exist devices to aid the teacher in extending the student's range of experience, in helping him to understand the underlying structure of the material he is learning, and in dramatizing the significance of what he is learning. (p. 84)

Audiovisual technology repeatedly was integrated into the New Social Studies in an effort to instill in students a more sophisticated understanding of the disciplines and their structures through inquiry-based learning.

Technology and Values

Not only did audiovisual materials help students learn basic concepts and inquiry skills, but they also promoted the development of values associated with the disciplines. In particular, proponents viewed understanding the disciplines as an important path to citizenship education (Helburn, 1997). Although the New Social Studies has been criticized for failing to address the Civil Rights Movement of the 1960s (Fenton, 1991), several of the projects did encourage reflection on controversial social issues. Engle (1960) was influential in promoting decision making as the "heart of social studies instruction." His influence was apparent in the Harvard Public Issues Project (Oliver & Newmann, 1969)—a New Social

Studies project that focused on citizen development in a democratic society. Consisting of 30 units each including cases studies, the project materials included both texts and audiovisuals. These materials were used to achieve three basic elements of the project:

> The analysis of public controversy in terms of prescriptive, descriptive, and analytic issues; the use of distinct strategies for justification and clarification of one's views on such issues; systematic attention to the discussion process as one deals with a controversial issue. (p. 4)

Film strips were used along with traditional lectures and case texts to promote inductive lessons that led to deep discussion essential for citizenship (p. 7). Teachers were encouraged to tape record class discussions to help assess the level and effectiveness of classroom discussion (p. 12). These tape recordings were played back to promote student-development of discussion skills and teacher reflection on practice.

In summary, in the New Social Studies, technology was integrated into the curriculum projects to enhance the curriculum. New materials, especially audiovisuals, were used to teach content, inquiry, and values, including citizenship. Throughout the projects these materials were interwoven with traditional materials and pedagogies such as lectures, group discussions, and written texts. The materials consistently were viewed as a tool to reform the curriculum, in particular to enhance the curricular options and make instruction more authentic and meaningful.

Teacher Preparation

Given the widespread inclusion of technology in the New Social Studies projects, instruction on the use of audiovisual and other technologies in the classroom became an important aspect of teacher training (e.g., Bruner, 1960; Fenton, 1967; Lichtenberg & Fenton, 1969). In order for the New Social Studies projects to be integrated successfully, it was believed that teachers needed guidance in appropriately selecting and integrating audiovisual materials for instruction (Kentworthy, 1966). For instance Bruner (1960) wrote, "The film or television show as gimmick, the television system without substance or style in its programs, the pictographically vivid portrayal of the trivial—these will help neither the teacher nor the student" (p. 91). Proponents of the New Social Studies viewed technology as pedagogically neutral. So the emphasis of teacher training was on the way in which the technology was used to promote the aims of the New Social Studies. For instance, Lichtenberg and Fenton wrote, "Not that the [technological] material is either inductive or expository; it is neutral. The way in which instructional materials are used to attain particular objectives determines whether they are 'inductive' or 'expository' " (p. 396). New Social Studies curriculum manuals outlined criteria for selecting audiovisual materials and guidelines for using technology to teach conceptual understanding or inquiry. For example, Lichtenberg and Fenton (1969) listed several guidelines for the use of audiovisual materials:

> The particular audio-visual medium chosen should be a function of the objectives. (p. 397)
>
> Audio-visual materials should be designed as part of a systems approach to learning. (p. 398)
>
> The class time devoted to the use of AV materials can vary widely. (p. 398)
>
> Inductive audio-visual materials should not give away the answers. (p. 398)

and

> Teachers need lesson plans to accompany inductive AV materials. (p. 400)

Technology use was also modeled in teacher professional development workshops. Films were used to train teachers to integrate New Social Studies curriculum and materials (Fenton, 1991).

The New Social Studies projects emphasized the role of the teacher as curricular and pedagogical broker in the classroom. Bruner (1960), for instance, acknowledged that "the teacher constitutes the principal aid in the teaching process as it is practiced in our schools" (p. 88) and as such "not only a communicator but a model" (p. 90). Unfortunately, the proponents of the New Social Studies failed to include teachers in the development or dissemination of the projects. This contributed to the inability of the New Social Studies to change the status quo and to promote the integration of technology for inquiry learning in the social studies (Evans, 2004).

Limitations and Lessons to be Learned

Teacher Professional Development

Although proponents of the New Social Studies viewed teachers as curriculum gatekeepers, they did not involve teachers in the development of the projects. Rather an "agriculture model" of "research, development, dissemination, and adoption" (Fenton, 1991) was used to develop and promote the New Social Studies. Perhaps due to this top-down approach, the curriculum reform of the New Social Studies often did not reflect the realities of teaching or inspire a sense of ownership among teachers (Fenton, 1991; Rossi 1992). According to Rossi, "Thus, a serious gap existed between the goals and demands of the New Social Studies and the realities of the beliefs and cultures found among teachers and in schools" (n.p.). The teachers worked in a culture of teaching very different from that of the authors of New Social Studies projects (Fenton, 1991). The New Social Studies failed to close the gap between theory and practice. Looking backward Fenton recognized that the teacher summer institutes (the most relied on method for disseminating the projects) were ineffectual at changing teacher behaviors. Once teachers returned to their classrooms they reverted back to traditional materials and pedagogies (Rossi, 1992). In the context of the New Social Studies, teachers tended to adopt tenets of the projects that matched their beliefs and could be integrated into the existing school structure.

Hindering Factors to Technology Integration

Despite increasing access to new forms of media, teachers tended not to integrate these teaching materials as suggested by the New Social Studies projects. This disuse was blamed in part on the unwieldy nature of these materials for teachers. According to Fenton (1991):

> These new materials organized as an educational system, placed new demands on teachers accustomed to teaching from a text supplemented with film and captioned filmstrips. The materials complicated the teachers' lives. These shortcomings in the materials themselves help to account for the demise of the New Social Studies. (p. 86)

Although the New Social Studies projects included familiar content and learning objectives, teachers often lacked efficacy to integrate audio-visual aids. Instead, these new materials "complicated their lives." Cuban (1986) wrote:

> Invariably, the following reasons turned up on lists of obstacles blocking increased film use in classrooms: Teachers' lack of skills in using the equipment and film; cost of films, equipment, and upkeep; inaccessibility of equipment when it is needed; finding and fitting the right film to the class. (p. 18)

Reluctance on the part of teachers to integrate technology into their teaching was connected to the general failure of the New Social Studies to significantly change social studies pedagogy. As early as 1960, Bruner warned that technology was not a "panacea." Despite these warnings, new teaching materials were oversold and they could not live up to their potential. Beyond the logistical factors that blocked integration, there was also the enormous task of changing school culture (Penna, 1995). The lack of any notable reform due to the New Social Studies was reflected in the reluctance of practitioners to integrate new technologies into the social studies classroom.

Section Summary

The New Social Studies projects of the 1960s and 1970s failed to achieve their aims to fundamentally improve social studies instruction through a focus on the disciplines, inquiry, and citizenship education. According to Fenton (1991), "Expectations [for the New Social Studies], however, outpaced reality by a wide margin" (p. 85). According to Helburn (1997), only a handful of affluent suburban schools adopted the projects in a meaningful way. This was due in part to the exclusion of teachers in the design of the curriculum reform and a lack of teacher efficacy integrating new materials and technologies into their classrooms. As a result, the widespread adoption of teaching strategies proposed by the New Social Studies projects, including the including the integration of technology for student inquiry, failed to materialize.

Many of the themes of the New Social Studies appear in current efforts to reform social studies curriculum through the integration of new technology. These efforts include the integration of Web-based technology and digital materials to spark inquiry and promote civic engagement. Unfortunately, these current efforts seem to be tempered by similar issues faced during the era of the New Social Studies—lack of teacher efficacy and over-reliance on technology as an improvement for teaching. Below, I trace the intersections of *current* technology integration and the New Social Studies. Perhaps by evaluating current reform efforts through the lens of the New Social Studies, social studies educators can develop more robust and potentially effective techniques to reform the field.

Technology Integration Today

Technology, especially Web-based tools and digital technology have been promoted as twenty-first century tools to reform the social studies. This reform leverages technology to shift social studies pedagogy from teacher-centered to student-centered and from behaviorist to constructivist (Rice & Wilson, 1999). It also builds on the work of social studies researchers who de-emphasize student memorization of facts in favor of engaging students in historical inquiry (Barton & Levstik, 2003; Downey & Levstik, 1998; Foster & Padgett, 1999). Students are encouraged to develop the skills of the discipline and "do history." Teachers create learning situations in which students act like mini-historians and engage in primary source work (Donovan & Bransford, 2005; Sexias, 1998; VanSledright, 2002; Wineberg, 2001). Instructional technologies are considered a valuable resources for this work (Barth, 1990; Vockell & Brown, 1992). According to Diem (2000), "The promise of technology is not so much its cutting-edge advances as its innovative and imaginative applications" (p. 494).

In the field of social studies and technology integration there have been some educators who trace a direct connection back to the New Social Studies. Jones and Reeves (2006) for instance described Bruner as "a significant contributor to the field of educational technology" since his theories of spiral curriculum, discovery learning, and representation have "helped structure the way educational technologists of today design instructional systems and conduct research" (p. 60). Similarly, Knight and Knight (1995) and Dowding (1993) viewed Bruner's spiral curriculum as a roadmap for the appropriate use of technology with K–12 audiences. Milson, Gilbert, and Earle (2007) referred to Bruner's (1960) *Process of Education* in their article on Geographic Information Systems (GIS); they linked emerging technology with Bruner's discovery learning. Collectively these authors illustrate that, much like the era of the New Social Studies, social studies curriculum reform today focuses on providing students with authentic learning opportunities through the use of new materials. At the same time, several themes of the New Social Studies are implicitly reflected in the current literature on technology integration related to digital history, inquiry, citizenship education, and teacher professional knowledge.

Digital History

Due in part to the Internet revolution, digitized archival resources are freely available to K–12 audiences. Capturing the viability of technology integration in historical instruction, historian Ed Ayers (1999) remarked, "History may be better suited to digital technology than any other humanistic discipline" (n.p.). Lee (2002a) defined digital history as "the study of the past using a variety of electronically reproduced primary source texts, images, and artifacts as well as the constructed narratives, accounts, or presentations that result from digital inquiry" (p. 504). Just as primary source texts were integrated into New Social Studies projects, digital history is integrated into the today's social studies classrooms to provide students the opportunity to develop discipline-specific skills (Bolick, 2006; Cantu & Warren, 2003; Craver, 1999; Lee, 2002a; McGlinn, 2007). Digitized primary sources provide access to real world situations in the classroom and go well beyond the traditional text-based curriculum. According to Tally (1996), "On-line primary sources promise, most of all, more authentic materials that can enliven history for students and teachers" (n.p.). The advantages of digitized primary sources include their availability, flexibility, and accessibility (Bolick, 2006; Lee, 2002a; Marri, 2005). According to Berson (1996), "By using the computer, students can gain access to expansive knowledge links and broaden their exposure to diverse people and perspectives" (p. 486).

Digital libraries provide relatively unfettered access to digital history resources. Some of the most popular digital libraries include the National Archives [see http://www.archives.gov/] and the Library of Congress' American Memory collection [see http://memory.loc.gov/ammem/index.html]. According to Veccia (2004), by working with digitized primary sources from the American Memory collection "students came to understand that all big stories begin with small bits of evidence, which when strung together and interpreted allow a scholar—or a high school student – to tell a story accurately" (p. 110). These mammoth collections are joined by a host of other collections from regional or special collections around the world. Collectively digital libraries provide access to primary source texts, audio files, films, fine art, and much more. Digital libraries have effectively dissolved the boundaries between university-based scholarship and K–12 audiences (Bull, Bull, & Dawson, 1999). By granting access to resources, formerly only available to scholars, digital archives have fundamentally democratized access to historic information (Bolick, 2006).

Digital resources are not only used in the history classroom. Web-based resources have been effectively used throughout the curriculum to provide students with authentic, discipline-based learning activities (Berson, 1996). In geography education, for instance, Geographic Information Systems (GIS) has been integrated to provide sophisticated access to interactive maps and geographic data online within inductive learning activities (Milson, Gilbert, & Earle, 2007).

Inquiry

Digital history resources are integrated into the social studies curriculum to teach content and engage students in authentic inquiry (Ehman & Glen, 1991). Representative of the close connection between social studies content, technology integration, and inquiry, a variety of Web-based learning activities have been developed to scaffold student inquiry in the social studies. Clarke and Lee (2004) connected digital history resources to the investigation of local history. Bernie Dodge developed WebQuests which are, "used by students to structure the process of inquiry-oriented activity defined by the teacher" (Molebash & Dodge, 2003, p. 158). Completing a WebQuest, students not only learn about social studies content in more detail, but also they develop skills of inquiry in a structured, yet student-centered environment (Milson, 2002). Saye and Brush's (2005) "Persistent Issues in History Network" similarly encourages students to develop the skills of inquiry including analysis and synthesis in an online environment. Just as the New Social Studies projects integrated media to promote inquiry, so too contemporary reform efforts focus on the use of technology to create opportunities for "authentic intellectual work" (Scheurman & Newmann, 1998) in social studies classrooms.

Citizenship Education for Civic Engagement

Another thread of the New Social Studies curriculum – citizenship education through civic engagement—continues to be a priority among social studies educators (e.g., Banks, 2001; Barton & Levstik, 2004; Parker, 1996). According to Barton and Levstik (2004), "Teaching students to reach decisions about social, political, and economic issues—and giving them a chance to do so—is part of a long tradition in the social studies" (p. 30). This tradition traces back to the work of Engle (1960), Newmann (1975), and other proponents of the New Social Studies. Today the National Council for the Social Studies (NCSS, 1994) endorses the integration of citizenship education in the curriculum. Citizenship education is integrated into content instruction and skill development for the "common good."

Just as the New Social Studies projects integrated multi-media to provide authentic curricular experiences related to civic life, today technology integration has been leveraged to encourage civic engagement among social studies students. While the technologies have changed, the premise remains the same—technology can promote the development of values associated with citizenship. For example, Marri (2005) described a U.S. history teacher who incorporated the Internet and multimedia technology to prepare students "for active and effective citizenship through multicultural democratic education" (p. 395). Lee (2002b) encouraged teachers and students to analyze the underlying ideology of current political debates such as globalization through the analysis of related Web sites.

At the same time, due to the ubiquitous nature of computer technology in society, citizenship education includes training students to use computers effectively and ethically. According to Martorella (1997), "Increasingly effective citizenship involves mastery of computer technologies" (p. 513). Civic life is now dominated by a variety of technologies including electronic voting machines, political Web-blogs, MySpace accounts for political candidates, and more. It is widely believed that students must not only be able to navigate these resources, but approach them critically. Perhaps the greatest change in technology since the era of the New Social Studies has been the rapid diffusion of digital communication technologies and Web 2.0 technologies. Students are carving out new social and creative spaces online. This connectivity has shifted notions of citizenship, especially the need to scaffold student use of technology for learning and their interpersonal communication.

Technological Pedagogical Content Knowledge

Contemporary social studies educators recognize the importance of teacher professional development to reform the field. According to Thornton (2001a, 2001b), teachers act as "gatekeepers" in the classroom —determining the content, materials, and pedagogy. In Wineberg's (2001) study of four novice social studies teachers he alluded to the teacher as curricular and pedagogical gatekeeper. He wrote, "Our teachers' disciplinary perspectives also influence their goals for instruction" (p. 151). Technological pedagogical content knowledge (TPACK) (Mishra & Koheler, 2006) extends Shulman's (1987) "pedagogical content knowledge" to add technology as an third factor in successful classroom instruction:

> Quality teaching requires developing a nuanced understanding of the complex relationships between technology, content, and pedagogy, and using this understanding to develop appropriate, context-specific strategies and representations. Productive technology integration in teaching needs to consider all three issues not in isolation, but rather within the complex relationships in the system defined by the three key elements. (p. 1029).

According to the TPACK framework, technology alone does not determine pedagogical decisions. Rather, TPACK suggests the need to evaluate the interplay among all three components (technology, pedagogy, and technology) and how newer technologies often disrupt the status quo, requiring teachers to reconfigure not just their understanding of technology but of all three components (p. 1030).

TPACK is predicated on pre- and in-service teacher education in the use of educational technology. According to Rice and Wilson (1999), "Technology supports a critical function in promoting reforms in [social studies] education. However, its effectiveness in promoting such reforms correlates with a shift in teaching techniques" (p. 28). Just like their colleagues during the era of the New Social Studies, today social studies educators view technology as a *means* to improving education. Reform is contingent on teacher efficacy with technology and the adoption of inquiry-oriented strategies for its integration. According to Diem (2000), "In meeting this moment we know that delivering the technology, the hardware and the software, to teachers is the easy part; it is getting them introduced, comfortable and proficient with it that requires time and effort" (p. 494). As a result TPACK has been integrated in preservice teacher education as a framework to change teacher philosophies and attitudes regarding technology integration.

New Trends in Technology Integration

While several themes remain consistent across time, social studies education has also evolved in new directions due to technology integration. The most obvious difference between technology in the New Social Studies and today is the rapid diffusion of ever-changing technology (Moore, 1965). Ushering in the Information Age, the Digital Age, or the Internet Revolution, technology continually shifts social practices. The proponents of the New Social Studies could not have fathomed the possibilities now afforded by technology to change social studies education.

One example of the new curricular possibilities afforded by technology is the integration of digital documentaries in the social studies classroom. It is believed that more than a half of American teens have created online media including movies, music remixes, and Web-blogs (Lenhart, Rainie, & Lewis, 2001). This prior experience is put to good use in the social studies classroom when students create their own digital documentaries. Going beyond analyzing digitized primary sources, they explore digital libraries and use a variety of digitized primary sources to create their own documentaries. Whereas before students passively watched these movies, now they can create their own interpretations of the past based on historical evidence (Hofer & Owings-Swan, 2005). Creating a digital documentary is a sophisticated demonstration of student understanding.

> To produce the [historical] narrative, the learner must research the topic, actively construct meaning from the media available, craft a written story that conveys that understanding to others, and finally, create a movie that uses the visual media to accompany the narration in a compelling manner. (Ferster, Hammond, & Bull, 2006, p. 148)

Creating digital documentaries requires students not only to present the topic in a compelling manner, but also to understand the content and significance of the historic past. According to McGlinn et al. (2006), "Through the integration of digital history tools and techniques, students can both approximate the work of professional historians (collect data, create history, preserve history) and build historical thinking skills" (p. 4137). By providing a structure within which students can approximate the work of historians, emerging technologies facilitate the completion of aims originally promoted by the New Social Studies.

Hindering Factors

Despite new and exciting curriculum opportunities afforded by new technologies, it is still unclear whether technology integration can effectively reform social studies teaching and learning. Ever since Martorella (1997) asked, "Which way to the sleeping giant" (p. 511), the ability of technology integration to reform the social studies has been questioned.

In general, social studies teachers continue to appear apprehensive about the integration of technology and are slow adopters (Berson, 1996). There is continued evidence of inhibiting factors to teacher integration of technology, including: lack of equipment, unreliable hardware or software, limits on instructional time, standardized curriculum constraints, lack of efficacy, and fear of student exposure to unwanted or unreliable information (e.g., Cantu & Warren, 2003; Cuban, 2001; Friedman, 2004, 2006; McGlinn et al., 2006). Perhaps most important among the list of hindering factors are the time constraints placed on teachers by high-stakes testing and standardized curriculum (Berson, 1996; Friedman, 2006). Current state and national standards push classrooms towards teacher-centered curriculum (van Hover & Yeager, 2004). Technology integration necessitates pedagogical change from teacher-centered to student-centered (Friedman, 2006). Added to the failure of current proponents of technology integration in the social studies to change school policy and pedagogy, there is a chronic lack of research demonstrating the impact of technology on student outcomes (Becker, 1990; Berson, 1996; Diem, 2000). The paucity of research on the impact of technology on student learning leaves advocates with little more than potential literature that runs the risk if over-selling technology (Cuban, 1991).

Moving Forward

For real sustained reform of the social studies curriculum to occur, educators must learn from the experience of the New Social Studies. Emphasis must be placed on providing content that motivates and interests children and engages them in constructing their own learning (Rossi, 1992), including teachers in the development and implementation of curriculum, and acknowledging the realities of schools and classrooms. Educators must not lose sight of the New Social Studies goal of selecting the best materials to meet inquiry-based and discipline-relevant learning objectives. At the same time technology integration that capitalizes on current affordances must occur at the grass roots level. One part of making curriculum relevant to students is closing the gap between inside and outside school behaviors, especially related to communication technologies. At the same time proponents of technology integration in the social studies are wise to follow Bruner's (1960) advice that technology is not a panacea. Rather, it is a tool that can be used to expand the social studies curricula and encourage authentic inquiry. By recognizing both the potentials and limitations of technology and working within the framework of TPACK current social studies reformers will begin to make change in the field. Social studies reformers must also go beyond classroom-based research to focus on the cultural and societal factors that impact schooling. Rather than focusing on specific technological tools, they must move toward researching sound educational practices and their impact on student outcomes; they must gain more knowledge about how the use of technology facilitates student inquiry and effects student achievement.

REFERENCES

Ayers, E. (1999). *The pasts and futures of digital history. Virginia Center for Digital History.* Retrieved January 28, 2007, from http://www.vcdh.virginia.edu/PastsFutures.html

Banks, J. A. (2001). Citizenship education and diversity: Implications for teacher education. *Journal of Teacher Education, 52*(1), 5–16.

Barth, J. L. (1990). *Methods of instruction in social studies education* (3rd ed.) Lanham, MD: University Press of America.

Barton, K. C., & Levstik, L. S. (2003). Why don't history teachers engage students in interpretation? *Social Education 67,* 358–361.

Barton, K. C., & Levstik, L. S. (2004). *Teaching history for the common good.* Mahwah, NJ: Erlbaum.

Becker, H. J. (1990). Computer-based integrated learning systems in the elementary and middle grades: A critical review and synthesis of evaluation reports. *Journal of Educational Computing Research, 8*(1), 1–41.

Bender, L. W., & Conrad, L. P. (1983). Colleges bent on computers benefit from NDEA glitches. *Community College Journal, 53*(8), 20–22.

Bestor, A. E. (1953). *Educational wastelands: The retreat from learning in our public schools.* Urbana: University of Illinois Press.

Berson, M. (1996). Effectiveness of computer technology in the social studies: A review of the literature. *Journal of Research on Computing in Education, 28*(4), 486–500.

Beyer, B. K. (1995). Is the old "New Social Studies" back? *Education Digest, 60*(8), 67–70.

Bolick, C. M. (2006). Digital archives: Democratizing the doing of history. *International Journal of Social Education, 21*(1), 122–134.

Bruner, J. S. (1960). *The process of education.* Cambridge, MA: Harvard University Press.

Bruner, J. S. (1965). *Man: A Course of Study.* Occasional Paper No 3. Cambridge: Social Studies Curriculum Program, Educational Services Incorporated.

Bull, G., Bull, G., & Dawson, K. (1999). The universal solvent. *Learning and Leading with Technology, 27*(2), 36–41.

Cantu, D., & Warren, W. (2003). *Teaching history in the digital classroom.* Armonk, NY: M. E. Sharpe.

Ceruzzi, P. E. (2005). Moore's law and technological determinism: Reflections on the history of technology. *Technology and Culture, 46,* 584–593.

Clarke, W. G., & Lee, J. K. (2004). The promise of digital history in the teaching of local history. *The Clearing House, 78*(2), 84–87.

Craver, K. W. (1999). *Using Internet primary sources to teach critical thinking skills in history*. Westport, CT: Greenwood Press.

Cuban, L. (1986). *Teachers and machines: The classroom use of technology since 1920*. New York: Teachers College Press.

Cuban, L. (2001). *Oversold and underused: Computers in the classroom*. Cambridge, MA: Harvard University Press.

Diem, R. A. (2000). Can it make a difference? Technology and the social studies. *Theory and Research in Social Education, 28*, 493–501.

Donovan, M. S., & Bransford, J. D. (2005). *How students learn: History, mathematics, and science in the classroom*. Washington, DC: National Academies Press.

Dowding, T. J. (1993). The application of a spiral curriculum model to technical training curricula. *Educational Technology, 33*(7), 18–28.

Downey, M. T., & Levstik, L. S. (1998). Teaching and learning history: The research base. *Social Education, 52*(6), 336–342.

Dynneson, T. L. (1981). The status of pre-collegiate anthropology: Progress or peril? *Anthropology and Education Quarterly, 12*(4), 304–309.

Ehman, L. H., & Glen, A. D. (1991). Interactive technology in the social studies. In J. P. Shaver (Ed.), *Handbook of research on social studies teaching and learning* (pp. 513–522). New York: Macmillian.

Engle, S. H. (1960). Decision-making: The heart of social studies instruction. *Social Education, 24*(7), 301–304.

Evans, R. (2004). *The social studies wars*. New York: Teachers College Press.

Fenton, E. (1966). *Teaching the New Social Studies in secondary schools: An inductive approach*. New York: Holt, Rinehart, and Winston.

Fenton, E. (1967). *The New Social Studies*. New York: Holt, Rinehart, & Winston.

Fenton, E. (1991, May/June). Reflections on the "New Social Studies." *The Social Studies, 82*, 84–90.

Ferster, B, Hammond, T., & Bull, G. (2006). Primary Access: Creating digital documentaries in the social studies classroom. *Social Education, 70*(3), 147–150.

Foster, S., & Padgett, J. (1999). Authentic historical inquiry in the social studies classroom. *The Clearing House, 72*(6), 357–363.

Friedman, A. (2004). *Digital primary source use in world history and world geography*. Unpublished dissertation, University of Virginia, Charlottesville.

Friedman, A. (2006). State standards and digital primary sources: A divergence. *Contemporary Issues in Technology and Teacher Education* [Online Serial] 6(3). Retrieved April 4, 2007, from http://www.citejournal.org/articles/v6i2socialstudies1.pdf

Goetz, W. W. (1994). The New Social Studies: The memoir of a practitioner. *The Social Studies, 85*(3), 100–106.

Helburn, N. (1998). The High School Geography Project: A retrospective view. *The Social Studies, 89*(5), 212–218.

Helburn, S. W. (1997). ECON 12 and the New Social Studies: Love's labor lost? *Social Studies, 88*(6), 268–277.

Hofer, M., & Owings-Swan, K. (2005). Digital moviemaking—the harmonization of technology, pedagogy and content. *International Journal of Technology in Teaching and Learning, 1*(2), 102–110.

Keller, C. W. (1974). *Involving students in the New Social Studies*. Boston: Little, Brown.

Kentworthy, L. S. (1966). *Guide to social studies teaching* (2nd ed.). Belmont, CA: Wentworth.

Knight, B. A., & Knight, C. (1995). Cognitive theory and the use of computers in the primary classroom. *British Journal of Educational Technology, 26*(2), 141–148.

Jones, F. S., & Reeves, T. C. (2006). Jerome Bruner: A significant contributor to the field of educational technology. *Educational Technology, 46*(5), 58–60.

Lee, J. K. (2002a). Digital history in the history/social studies classroom. *The History Teacher, 35*(4), 503–517.

Lee, J. K. (2002b). Ideology and the Web. *Social Education, 66*(3), 161–166.

Lenhart, A., Rainie, L., & Lewis, O. (2001). *Teenage life on-line: The rise of the instant message generation and the Internet's impact on friendships and family relationships*. Washington, DC: Pew Internet and American Life Project. Retrieved January 14, 2007 at http://www.pewinternet.org

Lichtenberg, M., & Fenton, E. (1969). Using AV materials inductively in the social studies. In M. Feldman & E. Seifman, (Eds.), *The Social Studies: Structure, models and strategies* (pp. 395–400). Englewood Cliffs, NJ: Prentice Hall. (Reprinted from *Audiovisual Instruction, 2*(5), 330–332.

Lord, D. (1969). Teacher training and the inquiry method: The program at Texas Women's University. *The History Teacher, 2*(2), 24–32.

Marri, A. R. (2005). Educational technology as a tool for multicultural democratic education: The case of one U.S. history teacher in an underresourced high school. *Contemporary Issues in Technology and Teacher Education* [Online serial], *4*(4). Retrieved March 8, 2007, from http://www.citejournal.org/vol4/iss4/socialstudies/article1.cfm

Martorella, P. (1997). Technology and social studies: Which way to the sleeping giant? *Theory and Research in Social Education, 25*(4), 511–514.

McGlinn, M. (2007). Using the "Documenting the American South" Digital Library in the social studies: A case study of the experiences of teachers in the field. *Contemporary Issues in Technology and Teacher Education* [Online serial], *7*(1). Retrieved from http://www.citejournal.org/vol7/iss1/socialstudies/article1.cfm

McGlinn, M., Hammond, T., Friedman, A., Bolick, C., Bull, G., Ferster, B., et al. (2006). Digital history in social studies teacher education: Practices, promises and provisos. In C. Crawford et al. (Eds.), *Proceedings of Society for Information Technology and Teacher Education International Conference 2006* (pp. 4134–4147). Chesapeake, VA: AACE.

Milson, A. J. (2002) The Internet and inquiry learning: Integrating medium and method in a sixth grade social studies classroom. *Theory and Research in Social Education, 30*(3), 330–353.

Milson. A. J., Gilbert, K. M., & Earle, B. D. (2007). Discovering Africa through Internet-based Geographic Information Systems: A Pan-African summit simulation. *Social Education, 71*(3), 140–145.

Mishra, P., & Koehler, M. J. (2006). Technological pedagogical content knowledge: A framework for teacher knowledge. *Teachers College Record, 108*(6), 1017–1054.

Molebash, P., & Dodge, B. (2003). Kickstarting inquiry with WebQuests and Web Inquiry Projects. *Social Education, 67*(3), 158–162.

Moore, G. E. (1965, April). Cramming more components onto integrated circuits. *Electronics, 38*(8), 114–117.

National Council for the Social Studies. (1994). *Expectations of excellence: Curriculum standards for social studies.* Washington, DC: National Council for the Social Studies.

Newmann, F. M. (1975). *Education for citizen action: Challenges for secondary curriculum.* Berkeley, CA: McCutchan.

Oliver, D. W., & Newmann, F. M. (1969). *Guide to teaching the Public Issues Series/Harvard Social Studies Project.* Middleton, CT: Xerox.

Oliver, D. W., & Shaver, J. P. (1966). *Teaching public issues in the high school.* Boston: Houghton Mifflin.

Parker, W. C. (1996). "Advanced" ideas about democracy: Toward a pluralist conception of citizenship education. *Teachers College Record, 98*(1), 104–125

Penna, A. N. (1995). The New Social Studies in perspective: The Carnegie Mellon slow-learner project. *Social Studies, 86*(4), 155–162.

Rice, M. L., & Wilson, E. K. (1999). How technology aids constructivism in the social studies classroom. *Social Studies, 90* (1), 28–33.

Rossi, J. A. (1992). Uniformity, diversity, and the "New Social Studies" [Electronic version]. *Social Studies, 83*(1), 41–46.

Saye, J. W., & Brush, T. (2005). The persistent issues in history network: Using technology to support historic and civic reasoning. *Social Education, 69*(4), 168–171.

Schwab, J. J. (1962, July). The concept of the structure of a discipline. *The Educational Record, 43*, 197–205.

Scheurman, G., & Newmann, F. M. (1998). Authentic intellectual work in the social studies: Putting performance before pedagogy [Electronic version]. *Social Education, 62*(1).

Sexias, P. (1998). Student teachers thinking historically. *Theory and Research in Social Education, 26*(2), 310–341.

Shulman, L. (1987). Knowledge and teaching: Foundations of a new reform. *Harvard Educational Review, 57*(1), 1–22.

Suchman, J. R. (1966). *Analysis of concept learning.* New Yoek: Academic Press.

Taba, H., Durkin, M. C., McNaughton, A. H.,& Fraenkel, J. R. (1967). *Teachers handbook for elementary social studies.* Menlo Park, CA: Addison-Wesley.

Tally, B. (1996). History goes digital: Teaching when the Web is in the classroom. *D-Lib Magazine* [Online serial]. Retrieved April 30, 2007, from http://www.dlib.org/dlib/september96/09tally.html

Thornton, S. J. (2001a). Educating the educators: Rethinking subject matter and methods. *Theory into Practice, 40*(1), 72–79.

Thornton, S. J. (2001b). From content to subject matter. *The Social Studies, 92*(6), 237–242.

van Hover, S., & Yeager, E. A. (2004). Challenges facing beginning history teachers: An exploratory study. *International Journal of Social Education, 19*(1), 8–26.

VanSledright, B. (2002). *In search of America's past: Learning to read history in elementary school.* New York: Teachers College Press.

Veccia, S. H. (2004). *Uncovering our history: Teaching with primary sources.* Chicago: American Library Association.

Vockell, E. L., & Brown, W. (1992). *The computer in the social studies curriculum.* Watsonville, CA: Mitchell McGraw-Hill.

Wineberg, S. (2001). *Historical thinking and other unnatural acts: Charting the future of teaching the past.* Philadelphia: Temple University Press.

Woolfson, P. (1974). The Fight over "MACOS": An ideological conflict in Vermont. *Council on Anthropology and Education Quarterly, 5*(3), 27–30.

ABOUT THE AUTHORS

Beverly Jeanne Armento is research professor emerita from Georgia State University, Atlanta where she taught social studies education, chaired the Middle/Secondary Education and Instructional Technology Department, and served as director of the Center for Business and Economic Education. She studied with Professor Larry Senesh at Purdue University, 1968–1969, as part of the master's program in economic education. Her doctoral work was completed at Indiana University. Professor Armento's major areas of professional research and writing are economic education, diversity issues, and excellence in teaching and learning. Dr. Armento's works include chapters in the *Handbook of Research on Teaching*, the *Handbook of Research on Teaching* and *Learning in Social Studies*, and the *Handbook of Research on Teacher Education*. Beverly continues her work in teacher education at Oglethorpe University, Atlanta.

Jane Bernard-Powers is a professor of education at San Francisco State University where she has taught credential courses and graduate courses in elementary social studies and educational foundations for 20 years. She has a BA from the University of Michigan and an MA and PhD from Stanford University. Gender and social studies have been a central focus of her writing and scholarship, and her interests have included biography and life-interviewing. Her research and publications on female leaders in Social Studies led her to Dr. Fannie Shaftel who was introduced by a mutual friend. Over the course of 4 years, she interviewed Dr. Shaftel in Menlo Park, CA and in Honolulu, Hawaii, discussing her life, her work and the significance of role playing.

Chara Haeussler Bohan is an assistant professor in the School of Education at Georgia State University. Having studied under O. L. Davis, Jr., she earned her doctoral degree at The University of Texas at Austin. She has published articles in *Theory and Research in Social Education* and *Social Studies and the Young Learner* and has authored a book titled, *Go to the Sources: Lucy Maynard Salmon and the Teaching of History* (Peter Lang, 2004) and edited a book titled *Readings in American Educational Thought: From Puritanism to Progressivism* (IAP, 2004).

Gloria Contreras, professor of social science education, teaches at the University of North in the Department of Teacher Education and Administration. She is executive editor of *The Social Studies* and teaches classes in multicultural education, social studies, and curriculum history and philosophy. Her current research is on education reform and decentralization in Mexico.

Michelle D. Cude graduated from the University of Virginia in Social Studies Education after completing her dissertation research abroad in St. Petersburg on the state of civic education teacher training in Russia. Prior to graduate school, she taught U.S. history in Fairfax County for 7 years, preceded by character interpretation and public education at Colonial Williamsburg where she recieved her masters in American Studies at William and Mary. She now happily teaches social studies methods at James Madison University, residing nearby with her two daughters adopted from abroad.

Robert L. Dahlgren is an assistant professor at the State University of New York at Fredonia, where he is the program coordinator for graduate studies in the Department of Curriculum and Instruction. He received a PhD in Social Studies Education at the University of Florida in August 2008. Prior to working in higher education, Dr. Dahlgren taught for many years in high schools in Massachusetts and Florida. Dr. Dahlgren is principally concerned in the issue of academic freedom for secondary social studies teachers and has several research projects in progress, including an edited volume on critical views of service-learning projects.

Ronald W. Evans is a professor of social studies education in the School of Teacher Education at San Diego State University and is a longtime advocate of issues-centered approaches to social studies. He served as a founding member of the Issues-Centered Education Special Interest Group of the National Council for the Social Studies and as the group's first executive secretary. He is the author of *The Social Studies Wars: What Should We Teach the Children?* Also, he served as first editor of the *Hand-*

book on Teaching Social Issues. He has published widely in social studies journals and is currently working on a biographical account of the life and work of Harold Rugg.

Joseph R. Feinberg is an assistant professor of social studies education at Georgia State University. Formerly an assistant professor at UNC Wilmington, he also taught social studies at Campbell High School in Smyrna, Georgia. His research interests include simulation games, civic education and service-learning.

Mary E. Haas is a professor of curriculum and instruction specializing in social studies K–12 at West Virginia University. When teaching in the public schools, she used the new social studies materials prepared for geography and won national recognition for her teaching in the ninth grade with these materials. She holds an EdD from Indiana University and has worked in teacher education at universities in Arkansas, Mississippi, and West Virginia for 30 years. She has taught geography at the university level and currently also holds an adjunct position in the geography department. The lessons that she learned through her experiences in teaching the New Social Studies materials are used in her teaching, supervision, in-service work, and writing to this day.

Carole L. Hahn is the Charles Howard Candler Professor of Educational Studies at Emory University in Atlanta, United States, where she teaches courses in comparative education as well as social studies education. She was the U.S. national research coordinator for the Civic Education Study of the International Association for the Evaluation of Educational Achievement (IEA) and she is an advisory professor at the Hong Kong Institute of Education. She is a past president of the National Council for the Social Studies (NCSS) and recipient of the Jean Dresden Grambs Distinguished Career Research Award from NCSS. She has conducted comparative studies of citizenship education and written about civic education in the United States and comparatively. As a graduate student at Indiana University in the 1970s she worked with the New Social Studies project, *American Political Behavior*.

John D. Hoge is an associate professor in the Department of Elementary and Social Studies Education at the University of Georgia. He teaches graduate and undergraduate courses in the social studies, elementary, and middle school programs and has recently collaborated on studies of the status of social studies instruction in the state of Georgia. His early career was spent at the Social Science Education Consortium, Boulder,

Colorado. He taught at Boise State University, and Indiana University prior to joining the faculty at UGA.

Chrystal S. Johnson received her PhD from the University of Virginia and is an assistant professor of social studies education at Purdue University, West Lafayette, IN. Her research interests include educational methods for promoting powerful social studies, using cultural historical activity theory (CHAT) to understand African American perspectives of care and justice.

Carol Klages received her PhD from the University of Texas at Austin. She is an associate professor of curriculum and instruction with emphasis on social studies and reading education at the University of Houston-Victoria in Victoria, Texas. Her research interests include educational methods for promoting the reading of social studies texts.

Larry L. Kraus wrote his doctoral dissertation on Man: A Course of Study when he was in graduate school at The University of Texas at Austin. He is currently a professor of curriculum and instruction at The University of Texas at Tyler.

Meghan McGlinn Manfra is an assistant professor in College of Education at North Carolina State University. She coordinates the undergraduate and graduate secondary social studies programs and serves as co-editor for the instructional technology section of Social Education. Her current research interests include the integration of digital history to make social studies instruction more authentic and meaningful for students. She may be contacted by e-mail at: Meghan_manfra@ncsu.edu.

Murry Nelson is professor emeritus of education and American studies at Penn State University. He was the Laszlo Orszag Distinguished Fulbright Chair in American Studies at the University of Debrecen (Hungary) in 2007–08. He held previous Fulbright Lectureships in Iceland (1983) and Norway (1990–91). His most recent books are *The National Basketball League: A History* (Spring, 2009), *Encyclopedia of American Sports: From Foot Races to Extreme Sports* (2009), *Shaquille O'Neal: A Biography* (2007).

Mark A. Previte is an assistant professor of secondary education at the University of Pittsburgh at Johnstown. His research interests include issues-centered education, teacher supervision and the historical foundations of social studies. He is program chair of the NCSS Issues Centered Education Community and president-elect of the Pennsylvania Council for the Social Studies.

Keith Reynolds teaches American History at North High School in St. Paul, Minnesota, where he coordinates the Advanced Placement program in American History. He is distinguished for designing authentic disciplinary teaching activities, some of which he has published.

Karen L. Riley is a distinguished research professor and distinguished teaching professor at Auburn University, Montgomery, Alabama. Her research interests include the history of education, the politics of education, and curriculum history. She is also a consultant to the movie industry on the topic of the Holocaust, and the author of *Schools Behind Barbed Wire: The Untold Story of Wartime Internment and the Children of Arrested Enemy Aliens*.

David Warren Saxe is a professor at Penn State University where he specializes in heritage education and historical interpretation. Among his ongoing projects are work on German Heritage Museums (how Germans remember the National Socialist era); the Holocaust on the Eastern Front (Hell Unleashed: February to May 1945); and interpreting the French and Indian War at the Arboretum at Penn State (Staging Ground of the American Nation). He is the author of the traditional American history volumes, *Land and Liberty*.

Geoffrey Scheurman is professor of teacher education at the University of Wisconsin—River Falls, where he teaches techniques for teaching social studies, educational psychology, and historical and philosophical foundations. He spent a dozen years in high school social studies and still returns to the classroom on a regular basis. His areas of expertise include constructivism and authentic pedagogy, critical thinking, intellectual development and intrinsic motivation.

Barbara Slater Stern is a professor in the Department of Middle, Secondary, and Mathematics Education at James Madison University. She teaches curriculum theory; methods of teaching middle and secondary social studies; and internship seminar in the MAT and MEd programs. Her research interests include curriculum, the history of teaching social studies/history, and integrating technology into social studies. She is the co-editor of *Contemporary Readings in Curriculum*; the author of *Social Studies: Standards, Meaning, and Understanding* and the editor of *Curriculum and Teaching Dialogue*, the journal of the American Association of Teaching and Curriculum. In addition, she serves on the editorial review board for the Kappa Delta Pi *Forum*, the *Journal of Social Studies Research,* and for SAGE publications.

Joseph P. Stoltman is professor of geography and science education at Western Michigan University, Kalamazoo, MI. His professional writing is in geography education and the social studies curriculum. His research is on spatial thinking and the diffusion of curriculum innovations in education.

Elizabeth Yeager Washington is professor of social studies education at the University of Florida and former editor of *Theory and Research in Social Education*. She is also a senior fellow with the Florida Joint Center for Citizenship. She specializes in research on the teaching and learning of history and on democratic citizenship education.

Jack Zevin is professor of social studies education at Queens College in New York. A former secondary school teacher in Chicago, he has championed the cause of inquiry and discovery teaching methods and has worked extensively with preservice and in-service teachers on curriculum projects, preparation programs, and research studies. He is the author of a recent methods book, *Social Studies for the 21st Century*.

LaVergne, TN USA
28 July 2010
191105LV00002B/23/P